Notes from
the Minefield

Notes from the Minefield

United States Intervention in Lebanon and the Middle East, 1945–1958

Irene L. Gendzier

Westview Press
A Member of the Perseus Books Group

Copyright © 1999 by Westview Press, A Member of the Perseus Books Group

Published in 1999 in the United States of America by Westview Press, 5500 Central Avenue, Boulder, Colorado 80301-2877, and in the United Kingdom by Westview Press, 12 Hid's Copse Road, Cumnor Hill, Oxford OX2 9JJ

Library of Congress Cataloging-in-Publication Data
Gendzier, Irene L.
  Notes from the minefield : United States intervention in Lebanon
and the Middle East, 1945–1958 / Irene Gendzier.
      p.   cm.
  Includes bibliographical references (p.   ) and index.
  ISBN 0-231-10474-X (hc.) — ISBN 0-8133-6689-5 (pb.)
    1. Middle East—Foreign relations—United States.   2. United
States—Foreign relations—Middle East.   3. United States—Foriegn
relations—1953–1961.   I. Title.
DS63.2.U5G43   1999
327.73056,dc20   96-35037
                                                                CIP

The paper used in this publication meets the requirements of the American National Standard for Permanence of Paper for Printed Library Materials Z39.48-1984.

10   9   8   7   6   5   4   3   2   1

For Assaf J. Kfoury

Contents

List of Maps and Illustrations

Maps

Following page 263

Illustrations

Following page 226

Preface

Military intervention by invitation was the preferred formula adopted by the Eisenhower administration when it intervened in Lebanon's first civil war in 1958. U.S. action passed into the annals of U.S. foreign policy as a triumph of military diplomacy, a high point in the largely untroubled relationship of the United States with one of the most pro-Western regimes in the Middle East. The disingenuous formula has long served to trivialize the nature of Lebanese politics and U.S. policy in Lebanon and the Middle East.

The pre-1975 Lebanese state, a pro-Western center of regional and international trade and finance was advertised as a "confessional democracy," a term that continues to appear as the description of the Lebanon that was. The image served primarily those in power. It offered no credible guide to the understanding of Lebanese politics or its particular mix of religion and politics. The same can be said with respect to the reified fantasy concerning U.S.-Lebanese relations. U.S. sources confirm a different history, one in which U.S. policy systematically reinforced the Lebanese system that exploded in 1958, and again with unparalleled ferocity in 1975. And as the same sources make amply clear, intervention went beyond military form. It was an integral part of U.S. policy. The penetration of the Lebanese political system was the product of a calculated and exploitative relationship between Washington and Beirut in which the subordination and collaboration of the Lebanese ruling class were not in doubt. Lebanon is not a unique case in this regard. The evolution of U.S. policy in Beirut was part of a broader expansion of U.S. economic, political, and strategic interests in the Middle East, in which intervention reflected the unswerving pursuit of interests as well as the imbalance of power that characterized U.S. relations with local regimes.

The present study was conceived during the later phase of Lebanon's second and far more protracted civil war, between 1975 and 1990, which was accelerated and deepened by Israel's invasion of south Lebanon in 1978 and its U.S.-backed invasion of Lebanon in 1982. The search for origins led back to an earlier intervention and civil war, however—that of 1958—which in turn provoked a more systematic inquiry into U.S. relations with Lebanon. In the process, it became apparent that to understand U.S. policy and the evolution of the Washington-Beirut connection, it was imperative to go to the root of postwar U.S. policy in the eastern Mediterranean and Middle East, in which oil and politics were key factors.

The results demythologize the nature of U.S. policy and expose the ideological caricature of Lebanese politics that has dominated accounts of this period. What emerges from U.S. sources is evidence of the pursuit of U.S. interests in a Lebanon dominated by a conservative ruling class, committed to its profitable survival, in a terrain marked by struggles over access and power. The secular politics of profit and power exploited by U.S. interests explains the explosion of the Lebanese political minefield in 1958. It is neither confessionalism nor the politics of extremists versus moderates that makes sense of that development.

There is nothing exceptional, then, either in the nature of U.S. policies or in Lebanese politics exposed. What is historically significant is the nature and impact of American interests on a state and a region whose development became and remains a matter of integral concern to American policy.

The text that follows is organized into five major parts. The first two situate the origins of U.S. policy in Lebanon in post–World War II U.S. policy in the eastern Mediterranean and Middle East (part I), while identifying the earliest expression of U.S. economic interests in Beirut in terms of postwar U.S. policies on oil and aviation (part II). The next develops the expansion of such interests through the uneven relationship between Washington and a dependent Lebanon in the face of mounting regional crises (part III). With part IV, the increasing political and military intervention by the United States in Lebanese politics is explored in the context of civil war. Part V elaborates the determining role of such military intervention prior to July 14 and the extent of U.S. political intervention in the postwar settlement.

A word on transliteration is in order. A simplified version of the code offered in the *International Journal of Middle East Studies* has been used. To avoid confusion in the spelling of proper names, brackets are used around names in quoted material that have been changed according to this code. Inconsistencies remain, however, as readers familiar with Arabic sources and divergent patterns of transliteration will readily recognize.

Acknowledgments

In many respects, this work represents a collective effort. It could not have been written without the immeasurable contributions of innumerable friends, colleagues, former officials, and those involved in this history, as well as those encountered in the process of deciphering it. Our common conviction that it mattered was as important as the willingness to share information, to read endless drafts, and to engage in countless discussions that have continued across continents. Those identified below know how grateful I am, how little these words convey of their role in this project, and how deeply felt is my appreciation and admiration for their own struggles to make sense of the world. It should be said at the outset that none of them is responsible for the interpretation that follows, or the errors that may be contained in it.

Carolyn Gates, Fawaz Traboulsi, and Assaf J. Kfoury played a special role in the evolution of this work; without them this project would not have been possible. The late Albert Hourani was present at its creation and earliest formulations. Among other guides to Lebanese politics of the period were Nubar Hovsepian, Clovis Maksoud, Nawaf Salam, Hisham Sharabi, and Walid Khalidi.

Bruce Cumings and Noam Chomsky were invaluable readers and critics. They, as well as Edward Said, offered assistance as well as moral support at strategic moments, of which there were many. Among those who shared their own insights of the period were Stephen Ambrose, Hanna Batatu, Cyrus Bina, Michael Frye, Thomas Ferguson, Fawaz Gerges, David Painter, and Richard Falk. Paul Jabber made some of his research materials available to me. Douglas Yates and Samira Atallah, while graduate students in political science at Boston University, provided assistance, as did Alexander A. Gendzier, while in legal studies at New York University.

Former U.S. officials who were interviewed include those whose generosity extended well beyond the discussion of their own roles, such as Samuel O. Ruff, Harrison Symmes, and Hermann Eilts. William Chandler, the former president of TAPLINE, who entered this project when it was in its final stages, is in the same category.

Halim Barakat first invited me to write on U.S. policy for a conference on Lebanon that he organized at Georgetown University. Nadim Shihadi, director of the Centre for Lebanese Studies at Oxford, made its documentary resources on U.S. policy, collected under the direction of Carolyn Gates, available, while Fida Nasrallah and Ingrid Hobby generously provided assistance from near and far.

Wm. Roger Louis, Albert Hourani, and I organized a conference on Lebanon in the 1950s at the University of Texas at Austin in 1992, which provided the setting for productive exchanges with former ambassadors Nadim Dimechkié and Richard Parker, as well as Kamal Salibi, Carolyn Gates, Fawaz Gerges, and David Lesch, among others.

Over the past few years different aspects of the present study have been presented at seminars in the Departments of History and Political Science of Boston University, at the Center for Contemporary Arab Studies at Georgetown University, and at the Middle East Center at Harvard University, the Middle East Center at Columbia University, the University of Texas at Austin, the British Middle East Study Group, the Centre for Lebanese Studies and St. Anthony's College in Oxford, the Middle East Center of Princeton University, the Middle East Center and the Department of History of the University of Chicago, the Society of the Historians of American Foreign Relations, and the Emile Bustani seminar at MIT.

The American Philosophical Society provided a travel grant in 1990, and the Centre for Lebanese Studies at Oxford offered support during my brief residence in the same year. The Department of Political Science of Boston University extended support for research-related travel.

The following individuals and agencies provided assistance in the collection and preparation of the maps and photographs that appear in this volume. In addition to William Chandler, who made his personal collection available to me, I am grateful to Miklos Pinther, Chief Cartographer Section, LPD, Department of Public Information, United Nations; to the

Cartographic Division of Harvard Library and the photographic services of Stephen Sylvester of Harvard University; and to Marcia Lein Schiff of AP/World Wide Photos.

Finally, I remain indebted to Columbia University Press: to editor Kate Wittenberg for her commitment; to the expert editorial hand of Ron Harris and the independent role of editor Jan McInroy; and to others at the Press, whose support was invaluable.

PART I

The Setting of U.S. Policy

1

The Dynamic of Collaborative Intervention

The U.S.-Lebanon Connection

In July 1958, close to 15,000 marines landed in Beirut, while some 11,000 air sorties were flown over Lebanon. Two months after civil war broke out in Lebanon, U.S. forces intervened at the urgent invitation of President Sham'un of Lebanon. Less than twenty-four hours earlier, a military coup in Baghdad had brutally terminated the reign of King Faysal and the pro-British regime of Nuri Sa'id. The proximity of the two events, in Beirut and Baghdad, and their allegedly causal connection, were what remained in the collective memory, to judge by conventional accounts of U.S. action.[1] But the official record suggests a history that differs substantially. It is one that reveals the previously veiled contours of U.S.-Lebanese relations, their domestic origins, and regional significance in the larger construct of U.S. Mediterranean and Middle East policy. It is in this context that the U.S.-Lebanese connection has to be situated, one in which the tensions between internal and external politics defined the framework of U.S. policies, as these policies evolved in Beirut between 1945 and 1958. Against this background, the purpose, nature, and consequences of U.S. military intervention have to be reconsidered, insofar as they make sense of U.S. policy and Lebanese politics. Why, finally, did the Eisenhower administration intervene in Lebanon? What assets was it protecting? What Lebanese interests did it serve? What regional forces endorsed U.S. policy? And what was the political outcome of Lebanon's first civil war, in the political settlement of which the United States was intimately involved?

The above questions are key to decoding the mythified image of U.S.-Lebanese relations, as well as the trivialized souvenir of U.S. military intervention in 1958. Nearly four decades after the events of 1958, the significance of the postwar U.S.-Lebanon connection remains vastly understated, if not ignored. Its place in the analysis of post–World War II U.S. policy is similarly unexamined, in spite of its relevance to the role of the eastern Mediterranean and the Middle East in American postwar planning. Yet the available documentary evidence of U.S. sources suggests both the value placed on the Beirut connection and its long-range impact on the formative phase of Lebanese political development, a facet of U.S. policy far less familiar to Americans than is the recent troubled history of this state.

When Lebanon's far more virulent second civil war broke out nearly two decades after the first, it was the epicenter of a region whose leaders were alarmed at the prospect of victory for the Lebanese National Movement and its allies. They understood that this was a challenge to the existing disorder and its system of privileges for beneficiaries of the status quo. In the very different domestic and regional circumstances of the 1950s, Lebanon had already become a mirror of the political currents dominating the Arab world. And the intense regional interest aroused by the outcome of its political struggles was indicative of the obstacles that it would face—then and later—in the conduct of its internal affairs. Lebanon's first civil war involved some of the same issues and was a response to some of the same grievances. It involved the same cohort of political figures, even though the opposition challenging the president in 1958 was led by a largely conservative coalition of political leaders bent on the restoration of their own power rather than its dissemination. Outside of Beirut, some of the same regional actors pressed for U.S. intervention to contain the Lebanese regime. And in 1958, as later, the Lebanese regime was the beneficiary of U.S. support, without which it would most likely not have survived.

However idiosyncratic U.S.-Lebanese relations were in 1958, then, as later, they were inextricable from broader U.S. interests and policies in the Middle East. Moreover, in the context of U.S. foreign policy in the Eisenhower administration, U.S.-Lebanese relations did not constitute an exceptional case. The assessment of power and influence, and the identification of compatible interests, particularly among business elites, were not features exclusive to Lebanon. Nor was there anything unusual about the gap between U.S. officials in the field and their superiors in Washington—or the ease with which the former evaluated the abuses of power and the latter subordinated such considerations to their reliance on the class in power. The same administration responsible for intervening in Beirut in 1958 authorized interventions in Burma, Cambodia, the Congo (Zaire), Guatemala, Indonesia, Iran, Laos, the Philippines, and Vietnam.[2] And, as in the case of Beirut, such interventions assumed the collaboration of compatible elements whose identity and function were defined in accord with the particularities of individual regimes. In such instances, an "entente cordiale" developed among networks of protective and profitable relations, becoming a feature of U.S. foreign policy in the postcolonial era. The results enhanced the power of local elites, often backed by U.S.-supported military and security arrangements, which amplified their ability to control domestic politics. The cost, in terms of social and political development, is difficult to calculate and has seldom been considered a valid subject of foreign policy analysis.[3] Routine accounts of postwar development throughout the Middle East, Africa, Latin America, and Southeast Asia, in which political dissent and revolt against repressive regimes have been commonplace, often label such expressions of opposition as evidence of political incompetence and of the failure to meet the elementary standards of civic culture.[4]

In the well-known instance of Anglo-American intervention in Iran, the objective was to bring down the prime minister who had endorsed the 1951 nationalization of the Anglo-Iranian Oil Company. As recent research has shown, Operation AJAX was delayed to coincide with the advent of the Eisenhower administration, which was expected to be a more reliable partner in this project than its predecessor.[5] With Mossadeq out of the way, Shah Pahlevi returned with U.S. military and security backing until the seizure of state power by the Ayatollah Khomeini's forces in 1979. In Guatemala it was President Arbenz who was overthrown in 1954, in response to reformist policies considered unacceptable because they posed a challenge to local elites and U.S. agribusiness.[6] Castillo Armas, who replaced Arbenz, was assured of U.S. military and intelligence backing, with domestic consequences in evidence four decades later. In 1959, the Eisenhower administration supported the secessionist Katanga province in the Congo crisis (Zaire) (1959–1961), which culminated in the assassination of Congolese prime minister Patrice Lumumba. The events set the stage for the repressive practices of the Mobutu regime. According to the most authoritative work on the subject, "the Eisenhower administration supported Katanga because it had a financial interest in doing so."[7]

The events in Iran had a decisive echo in Lebanon, the experience of Guatemala was not lost on Beirut, while the Congo was linked by the unfortunate experience of the United Nations in both cases. The circumstances surrounding the Anglo-American response to Iranian oil nationalization inspired political intervention by U.S. oil interests in Lebanon in the fall of 1952. The Iranian case, however, had a more general impact in Beirut and the Middle East, as U.S. officials hoped it would. Guatemala and Lebanon had little in common. Yet the nature of the Eisenhower administration's political preferences, its identification with local business interests, and rationalization of policy in anticommunist terms, and the reliance on covert policies, had their analogs in Lebanon as well as in the Middle East. In the Congo, UN officer Rajeshwar Dayal, who had previously been in Beirut as head of the United Nations Observation Group in Lebanon (UNOGIL), encountered similar frustrations in carrying out his assignment in utterly different circumstances. Chief among them was U.S. policy.

Even though the formal entry of U.S. forces into Beirut differed dramatically from that in the above cases, the underlying conditions of policy raise similar questions. Admittedly, U.S. forces intervened in Lebanon at the express invitation of President Sham'un, hardly an externally manipulated coup. But appearances are deceptive. They give no indication of the existing relations between Washington and Beirut that explain the conditions of intervention. Nor do they provide a clue as to the extraordinary situations in which Secretary of State John Foster Dulles of the United States prompted President Sham'un on how to request U.S. intervention[8] or to the equally striking phenomenon in which incremental doses of the military assistance allowed the Lebanese regime to survive long after it had lost its domestic base and before the dramatic events in Iraq on July 14. Above all, the formal description of U.S. intervention is entirely inadequate to explain U.S. policy. However dramatic it was, U.S. intervention did not so much alter the nature of U.S. policy as perpetuate it under changed political circumstances. Its long-range significance in terms of the U.S.-Lebanese connection and its meaning for U.S. policy in the Middle East, however, compel a fuller investigation.

The origins of such a policy predate the crises of 1958 and belong to a formative period of U.S. policy and Lebanese state formation. It was

World War II that reinforced the value of Britain's role in the Middle East, while underscoring the invaluable prize that the region offered—its petroleum resources. Lebanon had no oil, but by 1946 it was one of the transit states through which pipelines passed to the Mediterranean. In the same year, U.S. airlines were negotiating bilateral concessions in Beirut as well. With a role in no sense comparable to that of Turkey, Iran, or Saudi Arabia, Lebanon nonetheless had a place in the hierarchy of U.S. policy. It fit the commitment of U.S. military and civilian planners to assure access to petroleum resources, the construction of bases, the acquisition of air transit rights, and the more general consensus on commercial expansion in the region. Such policies directly competed with those of the dominant Western power in the region, Great Britain, the special ally with whom the United States would cooperate, collide, and bitterly compete even as the two publicly celebrated their mutual interests in the area. The familiar crises associated with Turkey and Iran in the mid-1940s and the far less frequently mentioned crisis over interests in Saudi Arabia in the same period illustrate the stakes for the parties involved. The exclusion of the Soviet Union from "Eurasia" was an axiom of Anglo-American policy in the eastern Mediterranean and the Middle East. Although the USSR was a significant actor in the crises over Turkey and Iran, U.S. and Anglo-American interests were not merely reactive to assessments of Soviet intentions or actions in, respectively, Ankara and Teheran.[9] And in Saudi Arabia, it was the bitterness of Anglo-American competition that dominated, as U.S. officials sought to define their military presence in Dhahran at the expense of British influence.

Without oil or strategic depth, Lebanon proved to be a hospitable and invaluable terrain in this context. Its integration into the regional oil economy dominated by the U.S. international petroleum cartel identified it as a strategically important state. The events of the late 1940s in the region served to confirm its value, as U.S. officials and influential Lebanese personalities recognized. The regime of Besharah al-Khuri was the first following Lebanese independence from French mandatory control. Influential elements of the Lebanese commercial and financial bourgeoisie with close access to presidential power were highly sensitive to the advantages of continuing French monetary and banking controls, expanding regional trade relations, participating in the expansion of the oil economy, as well as developing connections with Washington and U.S. commercial and economic interests. U.S. international oil companies and U.S.-supported aviation interests were the founding elements of U.S. policy in the mid-1940s.

The members of the Lebanese ruling class who paved the way for U.S. companies belonged to a remarkably coherent elite. For the most part, its powerful members were part of the French financial orbit that remained influential in Beirut. Nonetheless, it was out of this milieu that openings to the United States appeared, whether in the form of oil or aviation, or banking, or the multitude of corporate enterprises that found willing agents in Beirut. In the mid-1940s, Trans-Arabian Pipeline (TAPLINE) succeeded in obtaining a concession to construct pipelines leading from Saudi Arabia through Lebanon to its southern port at Sidon. The concession transformed the relations of Lebanon and Washington far more profoundly, perhaps, than its Lebanese supporters imagined at the time.

From the point of view of U.S. oil company executives and the State Department that protected their interests, the advantages of collaborating with Lebanon's mercantile and financial bourgeoisie were evident. Here was a class whose members enjoyed enormous influence over the direction of state and regional policies that were compatible with those of Washington. Domestically, the class in question was averse to democratic, reformist, socialist, populist, and nationalist movements. The Lebanese business elite, in short, posed no problems for U.S. corporate or political leaders. Yet the fragility of the nation's political consensus did not escape notice in Washington, nor did the corrupt practices of its ruling class. On the contrary, U.S. officials in Beirut and the State Department openly discussed the risks of an excessive individualism and the system that supported it. But such criticisms were gratuitous, since the basis of U.S. support in Lebanon rested on precisely this class and system. Collaborative intervention involved an entente cordiale with its members, but that did not preclude disputes over power and profit. Thus, conflicts over concessionary benefits and the negotiation of trade agreements resulted in confrontations between even the most pro-American of Lebanese officials and the State Department. The inability to challenge such arrangements effectively was evidence of Lebanon's subordination. It was manifest in the regime of Lebanon's most pro-American president, Sham'un, who balked at the extent of American penetration of a state that was virtually open to U.S. inspection at will.[10] The hesitation of the Sham'un cabinet and its subsequent approval of a U.S. military mapping mission of Lebanon in 1954 were symptomatic of a dependent regime whose leader had volunteered the state's assets as the price of a promising and increasingly essential support. Against this background, U.S. policies in Lebanon cannot be interpreted as favoring Lebanese Christians or approving the confessional system as a political instrument, save insofar as these preserved the ruling class and system on which U.S. policy rested. In a period of increasing U.S. regional involvement, which included covert policies in Syria and the crises at Suez and Sinai in 1956, the importance of maintaining a favorable balance in Beirut was obvious.

By 1958, the political landscape in Beirut had become considerably more problematic, partially in response to Sham'un's accession to the Eisenhower Doctrine. In spite of U.S. funding of Lebanon's 1957 parliamentary elections, Sham'un's domestic base consistently weakened, leading to U.S. assistance, which continued through 1958. With the mobilization of opposition forces and the outbreak of civil war in the spring of 1958, Washington monitored developments in the country to determine whether and when they constituted a threat sufficient to justify full-scale military intervention. Under pressure of U.S. allies who advocated such action, Eisenhower and Dulles moved, albeit in response to internal developments—specifically the fear of an opposition-led political victory. By 1958 the pro-American Lebanese ruling class was arrayed against President Sham'un and his defenders. Portrayed in conventional accounts as pro-Nasserist anti-American "rebels," they were neither anti-American nor rebels. They were, however, hostile to Sham'unist domestic policies that excluded them from politics, as, for example, after the 1957 parliamentary elections. And they were opposed to Sham'un's unconditional support for U.S. regional policies, which they similarly regarded as detrimental to their interests.

In Washington, the pressures of Lebanese politics from the winter of 1958 through the crises of civil war revealed the multiple facets of policymaking that shaped the nature of the U.S. presence in Beirut. Eisenhower's prerogative in the making of foreign policy, and the indispensable role of his first lieutenant, Secretary of State Dulles, were unquestioned. Yet both men remained distant from the events in which they involved U.S. forces in 1958, and they systematically ignored the recommendations of U.S. officials—such as the U.S. ambassador, who opposed military intervention. Then, as earlier, the making of policy was a matter of direct concern not only to Defense officials with an eye to protecting the transit functions of Lebanon and its overall political role but also to officials bent on protecting Beirut's intelligence role in the region and U.S. international oil companies committed to protecting their profits. The latter involved calculations with respect to concessionary arrangements, as well as the internal competition between companies involved in the local Lebanese market.

By contrast, there were the formal connections linking the Embassy in the field to the State Department. These operated through a bureaucratic chain of command that determined the fate of the innumerable cables and dispatches sent to the State Department. And there was the informal sector, in which a highly personalized politics transcended bureaucratic lines, as in intelligence operations. Thus, CIA agent Wilbur Eveland had access to both CIA director Allen Dulles and his brother, the secretary of state. And Eveland was able to introduce his favorite Lebanese ally, Charles Malik, into highly influential National Security Council (NSC) circles. Malik's relationship with John Foster Dulles belongs in the same category: a personal, ideological, and theological rapport with political ramifications, given that Malik was a frequent interlocutor for the State Department and for Dulles. Along with a very few other Lebanese with access to influential circles in Washington and New York, these figures shaped Washington's thinking on Lebanon and the region in a manner compatible with U.S. interests. The other Lebanon, which represented the vast majority of the population of the country, had no such spokespeople in the same circles. Aside from Eveland, former CIA agent Miles Copeland acted as intermediary for certain U.S. oil and related interests in Beirut, as well as for Lebanese entrepreneurs eager to persuade Washington of the risks of a Sham'unist deadlock in 1958.[11] Copeland operated through the U.S. ambassador in Cairo but failed to move Secretary of State Dulles.[12]

Between the public and private corridors of policymaking in Washington, relations were of another order. Toward the Senate Foreign Relations Committee considering U.S. policy in Lebanon and the Middle East in the summer of 1958, the dominant attitude of U.S. administration officials was one of contempt. To those senators who challenged the language and the policies, answers were sorely inadequate. The demand to know the policies pursued in the name of the United States elicited a filtered and opaque response that effectively eliminated the bulk of what U.S. sources disclose, whether in terms of U.S. policies in Beirut or Anglo-American planning to protect Western oil interests. In July 1958 these issues were of greatest importance.

The choice facing the Eisenhower administration in Beirut prior to July 14 was not about the immediate collapse of the Lebanese state; it was about the erosion of the regime's power. Conventional accounts focus on the importance of presidential politics in Beirut, but here, as elsewhere, the presidential campaign, its funding, its constituencies, its political agenda involved far more than the choice of an individual. So in Beirut, it was not merely the future of Sham'un but the role that he had played. In the aftermath of civil war, his successor was approved by Washington on the basis of his reliability. The process, and its accompanying cabinet formation, occurred while U.S. forces occupied Beirut. In Jordan, meanwhile, Britain protected the monarch, while in Washington and London, Anglo-American officials secured their oil interest in the Arab East.

The Myth of Surrogate Intervention

On July 14, 1958, the pro-Western regime in Iraq was overthrown by military officers who assumed power with an ambitious agenda. Their identity, political orientation, regional and international connections were the subject of immediate speculation in Washington and London, as well as in the capitals of the Middle East. Did the military coup in Baghdad on July 14 influence the U.S. decision to intervene militarily in Beirut? And if so, was U.S. intervention indirectly designed to impress Iraqi officers with the weight of U.S. military armor? The question has long vexed interpretations of U.S. action in Beirut, deflecting attention from the significance of U.S. intervention in Lebanon's civil war. Did the United States intervene in Beirut while aiming for Baghdad with the knowledge that intervention in Lebanon represented far fewer military and political risks than did Iraq? The assessment of comparative risks is legitimate but insufficient to make sense of the unfolding developments in Washington and Beirut in the preceding months, a period when the objectives and implementation of U.S. policy were well in place. By July 14, the United States had already become a powerful partisan in Lebanon's civil war, even though disenchanted with the leader to whose desperate call it responded with alacrity on the day of the military coup in Baghdad.

To distinguish the separate developments that unraveled in Beirut and Baghdad is not to deny the importance of the fall of the Nuri Sa'id regime. From a political perspective, the successful military coup identified Baghdad as the third of the historic challenges to Western hegemonic control over Middle East oil to occur in the decade of the 1950s. Its impact thundered across the Middle East, jolting the seats of pro-Western regimes, much as it dislocated Western leaders unprepared to face another Suez. Lebanon's civil war involved no comparable challenge to TAPLINE's place. The conservative nature of the opposition leadership virtually guaranteed that any radical initiative would be locally suppressed. Yet in spite of these evident incompatibilities between the Beirut high-table politics of civil war and those of neighboring regimes undone by politically ambitious military officers, Lebanon's civil war was perceived by internal, regional, and international forces as an unacceptable challenge to the domestic and regional order whose potential disruption was suddenly accelerated by the events of July 14.

That Prime Minister Macmillan of Britain and President Eisenhower disagreed on how to respond to those events does not alter their mutual recognition of the significance of the new regional context of the Lebanese crisis. The difference in their responses was partially a function of the evaluations of their respective interests in Lebanon, Iraq, and the region. For Britain, the primacy of its interests in Iraq was not questioned. But for Eisenhower and Dulles, U.S. interests in Lebanon were by no means to be subordinated to Macmillan's proposals for a joint response to the Iraqi coup. Macmillan and Eisenhower resolved their differences with the reassertion of Anglo-American control over the critical centers of petroleum production and a division of labor with respect to Beirut and Jordan. For Macmillan, Lebanon was now only part of a "much larger operation because we shall be driven to take the thing as a whole."[13] U.S. intervention in Lebanon, Macmillan feared, might well set off the Middle East powder keg, since "the oil will be in jeopardy," he explained. Far from supporting U.S. intervention in Lebanon as a response to the military coup in Baghdad, Macmillan was apprehensive lest U.S. intervention in Beirut act to deflect American energies from a more comprehensive rollback campaign and/or contribute to the explosive situation in the region. Eisenhower's rejection of the proposed campaign reflected the skepticism and open opposition to Anglo-American military collaboration by Defense and State Department officials. As to Lebanon, Eisenhower and Dulles had no reason to abandon U.S. interests, the "assets" to which Dulles referred.[14]

The coup in Baghdad, then, led to the finalization of the decision to separate Anglo-American interventions in Jordan and Lebanon, while consolidating cooperation farther east. As Eisenhower informed Macmillan on July 18, it was essential not only to "bolster up both the loyalties and the military and economic strength of Lebanon and Jordan," but also to, "and this seems to me ever more important, see that the Persian Gulf area stays within the Western orbit."[15] While the British investigated the conditions of intervention in Kuwait, promising "ruthlessly to intervene" if necessary, Secretary Dulles concurred that similar conditions might arise in Saudi Arabia.[16] And according to contemporary British sources, the United States not only agreed that the British would "hold Bahrain and Qatar, come what may. They agree[d] that at all costs these oilfields must be kept in Western hands."[17]

In Lebanon the events of July 14 intervened to precipitate a policy that had long been in place, as the U.S. response to civil war materialized days after its outbreak. On May 13, Secretary Dulles instructed Sham'un on how to request intervention, while claiming that the United States was opposed to it. By the end of June, when the U.S. military estimated that the regime controlled no more than 30 percent of Lebanese soil, its provision of military assistance to Sham'un played a determining role. In the first week of July, the Embassy was conducting surveys throughout the different political constituencies to assess conditions on the ground and popular sentiment toward the United States. It did so with the full knowledge of the pressure being applied on Washington by Israel and Iran to back Sham'un. Dulles's policy of steady, incremental assistance to the regime undermined any warnings to the Lebanese president as to U.S. skepticism about full-scale military intervention. Dulles, with British support, though privately embarrassed by the inability of the United Nations team (UNOGIL) to find evidence corroborating Sham'un's charges of massive intervention of foreign forces in Lebanon, elected to ignore its political significance and to continue to back Sham'un and his regime. The paramount consideration in Washington by the end of June was the containment of political victory by opposition forces and the avoidance of a military coup.

To this end, the United States exploited the internecine conflicts within the opposition leadership and cultivated the more "moderate" and heavily pro-American Third Force. In turn, Dulles pursued a politics of opportunism that involved reassuring Sham'un of U.S. support while remaining indifferent to his rejectionist domestic politics that blocked any effective compromise. Throughout the successive phases of the Lebanese crisis, Dulles simultaneously chastised Sham'un as to the risks of intervention while at the same time approving the provision of military assistance to the Lebanese gendarmerie and advising Sham'un on how to deal with the international community, including the strategy to be followed at the United Nations. In time, an administration cautious about the prospect of military intervention increasingly came to view it as a likely option in the face of the changes occurring on the ground. These made ever more clear the possibilities of an opposition victory that included the socialist leader whose views were regarded in Washington as anathema to U.S. interests, whether in oil, business, or politics— namely, Kamal Junblat.

Whatever his faults, President Sham'un read Washington's actions correctly. He had sufficient experience to be confident in the utter indifference of Secretary Dulles and Eisenhower to the imperatives of domestic reform, since its advocates would be viewed as politically suspect. Thus, although Sham'un was fully aware of U.S. reluctance to intervene militarily, he had no reason to heed warnings that accompanied support. By regionalizing the civil war he played Dulles's anti-neutralist card, backed by Israel and Iran, as well as Jordan and Iraq, all of whom feared the possibilities of a rapprochement between the United States and the United Arab Republic (UAR). Dulles's credibility problem had less to do with credibility than with the pressures of regional allies who considered their vulnerability an American responsibility.

In Washington, U.S. involvement in Lebanon and the Middle East unfolded in a very different ambience. Members of the Senate Foreign Relations Committee concluded that the American people had been misled in the Lebanese crisis.[18] There was no incontrovertible evidence of Soviet or Egyptian involvement in Baghdad, no proof that what occurred in Iraq directly affected the situation in Beirut, and no evidence of the massive interference by UAR forces in Lebanon, claimed by the Sham'un regime and by British and U.S. officials, who knew otherwise. If Lebanese politics was as ludicrous as the description offered by U.S. administration officials before the Senate committee, then, as its members opined, U.S. forces should have kept out. Otherwise, the Lebanese should have been allowed their civil war and granted the rights of self-determination. And as for Kuwait, as Senator Fulbright argued, the Anglo-American condominium was or should be obsolete, its justification valid only in the highest academic circles.

Neither the disclosures of Anglo-American planning regarding their respective oil interests nor revelations of U.S. political and military intervention in Beirut before, during, and after the civil war were for public consumption. Evidence of the nature of the political conflict in Beirut, as well as evidence of widespread disapproval of U.S. policy, including among NATO allies, was minimized if not masked before a vision of Lebanese society and the achievements of U.S. policy that rapidly became standard fare. In the absence of historical memory and a persistent questioning of U.S. Middle East policy, Lebanon faded into the canonical image of a confessional society that seldom revealed its live connections with struggles over power. The political minefield, which U.S. officials in Beirut had so lucidly described in their communiqués to Washington, was secured by U.S. policies.

Confessionalism as Ideology

Among the major instruments that contributed to the mystification of Lebanon and, by extension, U.S. policy in Beirut was the role of confessionalism. Its ideological function in obscuring the nature of Lebanese political conflicts was fully appreciated by U.S. officials in Beirut who recognized the advantages of confessionalism in terms of U.S. policies. In Lebanon itself, the political impact of confessionalism was never in doubt.

In place before French mandatory rule, confessionalism was reinforced in the 1926 Lebanese constitution. When Lebanon became independent in 1943, the National Pact furthered the practice of shaping the electoral system of proportional representation according to a sectarian basis and of making ministerial and politically sensitive appointments along similar lines. In this scheme of things, Lebanon's president was to be Maronite Christian, its prime minister Sunni Muslim, the speaker of its Chamber Shi'ite Muslim, and his assistant deputy Greek Orthodox. Deputies to the parliament were elected on the basis of a 6:5 ratio of Christian to Muslim Lebanese.[19]

The modern history of the state affords ample evidence of the social and political forces at work in promoting and resisting this arrangement. Partisans of the system justified its existence in terms that masked past as well as present signs of political self-interest and conflicts over power. Apologetic interpretations of confessionalism promoted an approach that may be described as the "Lebanese syndrome," which has been applied to other areas of North Africa and the Middle East in which the relationship of religion to politics is often similarly misconstrued.[20] In Beirut, as in Washington, the syndrome served its purpose, which was to subordinate the disorderly history of political struggles in a reified vision of a harmonious community of confessions gone awry as a result of outside interference. The latter referred to the UAR and, indirectly and more ominously, to the Soviet Union. In this optic, the linkage of confessionalism and cold war ideology is evident. "The Lebanese syndrome" was accepted and disseminated in U.S. official sources, as well as academic and journalistic circles, as the debate on the meaning of Lebanon's second civil war so vividly demonstrated.

In the winter of 1958, the National Security Council advised officials discussing Lebanon to emphasize the harmony of different religions constituencies as a leitmotif in depicting the uniqueness of Lebanon in the Middle East. The NSC thus recommended that in discussing Lebanon, U.S. officials "stress within and outside Lebanon the theme of Lebanon as a highly successful experiment in which many peoples of diverse religion and culture work together amicably and effectively for the advancement of their country."[21]

The assignment was in total contradiction to the experience of U.S. officials in Beirut, who not only sent evidence to the contrary but were instrumental in funding parliamentary elections to assure the "amicable" results intended. Years earlier, in the winter of 1952, a very different U.S. assessment of the place of religion in Lebanese politics and society was issued. As the U.S. officer who authored the report concluded, "While other aspects of Lebanese politics have religious overtones, the political attitude of the commercial class is primarily secular. Maronites, Greek Orthodox believers, Sunni Moslems, Shia Moslems and Druzes, resolve their differences and combine harmoniously for profitable transactions."[22]

What was the purpose of stressing the "harmonious" view of Lebanon, given its absence in 1958? And why stress the cooperation of religious communities, as though these were the effective sociopolitical units whose functioning explained Lebanese society? The contrast with the 1952 account of the Lebanese bourgeoisie was striking in this respect. For not only did it demonstrate the separation of ruling class operations from religious or confessional considerations, it altogether denied their relevance. There was no change on this score between 1952 and 1958. What transpired in the interval, however, was a reaffirmation of the importance of the confessional system in maintaining the status quo in Beirut. The NSC's recommendation of 1958, then, was a de facto reaffirmation of the political role of confessionalism in Lebanese politics and its endorsement in Washington. Both emerged as an integral part of the apologetic account of U.S. policy in 1958. Confessionalism, detached from the historic or political context, then, became a fixed image in the popular view of Lebanon, and in the rationalization of U.S. policy.

Yet by 1958 there was no doubt in U.S. official circles as to the nature of the Lebanese regime or of the social and political bases of civil war. Confessional differences were not the central issue, as U.S. officials in Beirut recognized and as the future president of Lebanon, General Fu'ad Shihab, insisted in his exchanges with the U.S. ambassador in 1958, in spite of the fact that he knew that the opposition to the regime was largely, though not exclusively, Muslim in composition. The reasons for this opposition, however, had little to do with religion. Lebanese Christians opposed to the regime took their stand on political issues, as did the regime's regional allies. While the regimes of Jordan, Turkey, Iraq, and Iran gave Sham'un unconditional support, it was not in function of his Maronite identity or as a sign of their support for the Christian constituency that endorsed him. For the Israeli Labor party, on the other hand, there was a legacy of Zionist-Maronite relations that predated the emergence of Israel in 1948 and that continued to appeal to those prepared to exploit the advantages of a Maronite-dominated Lebanon in alliance with Israel.[23] In this light, Lebanese critics of confessionalism who favored the secularization of politics and its reform were highly unwelcome. Yet to oppose them as advocates of the rationalization and reform of Lebanese politics was far less acceptable in Israel and the United States than denouncing them as critics of an allegedly authentic confessionalism protective of Lebanon's exceptionalism and its pro-Western outlook.

In Washington, such calculations were safely obscured from public view. However, U.S. officials serving in Beirut in the first decade of Lebanon's independence were not reticent to describe the uses of confessionalism or its distorting effects on the political system, and particularly on political representation. The same officials were also lucid in their analyses of the connections among the politics of confession, social privilege, and political power.[24] Nor did they fail to see how debates on confessionalism were used for self-serving purposes, even by those who claimed to favor the deconfessionalization of Lebanese politics. The identification of U.S. interests with those of the Lebanese ruling class blunted the critical voices of U.S. officers in favor of a more opportunistic assessment of the same system.

Seldom were such internal criticisms reflected in the interpretations of U.S. intervention that appeared after 1958. These varied, although some of the earliest commentaries included sharply critical accounts at odds with the mainstream apologies. In the latter, the cold war was offered as the rationale for U.S. intervention, and the impact of U.S. policy in Lebanon was a secondary affair. Among critics, I. F. Stone exposed the absence of congressional consultation, comparing Beirut to "a banana republic on our doorstep," and lamented the fact that "the most lethal weapon [is] still the machine gun."[25] Legal scholars questioned the premises of U.S. policy.[26] Former officers of the State Department produced skeptical analyses of policy rationalizations, and CIA agents such as Wilbur Eveland amassed a searing exposé of U.S. practice, notwithstanding his support for Sham'un and Malik.[27] Iconoclastic accounts were not the norm, particularly among those persuaded of the role of the United States and Britain in holding the line of the "Free World" against "Soviet missile and 'volunteer' threats," allegedly represented by the UAR, Iraq, and Lebanese "rebels."[28] There were other denunciations of the "Pan-Arab frenzy" confronting the United States, with Lebanon as its latest victim.[29] From this perspective the "startling celerity" of the president and his commitment to "protect American lives and preserve world peace by forestalling aggression" were laudatory.[30]

More detached were those specialists of decision making,[31] and more critical were those with access to U.S. sources of Eisenhower administration foreign policy, in which the Lebanese exercise figured.[32] Such works broke the pattern of conventional interpretations, without necessarily extending their analyses to U.S.–Middle East policy. In addition, the proliferation of specialized works on Lebanon and the Middle East further contributed to such analyses, albeit without a consensus on U.S. policy or Lebanese politics.

Academic analysts of the state who were less interested in the 1958 civil war than in Lebanon's political system nonetheless often reproduced conventional views of its operations. Among students of the state, confessionalism was examined as a defiant and/or resilient example of the premodern phase of Lebanese politics. It was associated with sectarian political arrangements, considered as proof of Lebanon's weak state, and identified with the bargaining process between communal groups.[33] Others saw it as a protective cover for minorities in an age of aggravated nationalism,[34] as an ineluctable part of Lebanese clientalism,[35] and as an expression of Lebanese authenticity that blocked secular and democratic transformation. In a more recent case, Lebanon emerged as a form of "consociational oligarchy" that collapsed in the face of a Muslim majority.[36]

Those who challenged such accounts were aware of the nation's historical fallibility and its political consequences. The eminent historian of the Arab world and Lebanon Albert Hourani reminded readers that "the most important event in Lebanese history after 1920 was the transformation of an agrarian republic into an extended city-state, a metropolis with its hinterland." That transformation, according to Hourani, influenced the relations of confessional and political constituencies in Lebanon in the interwar and postwar years.[37] Supplementing and extending Hourani's interpretation are works that continue the inquiry into the social and political origins of the Lebanese state, without reducing politics to confession.[38]

When Lebanon's second civil war broke out in 1975, apologists for the regime and the status quo continued to obscure the nature of the political conflict through confessionalist interpretations.[39] The results then, as earlier, promoted a view of Lebanon as a tribal enclave in which a "moderate" minority of Christians was surrounded by political extremists of a common confessional and ideological stripe. Issues of power were routinely demoted to second place.

There is no simple correlation between the first and second of Lebanon's civil wars, particularly as the latter extended from 1975 through 1990. Nor is it possible to make comparisons without taking into consideration the demographic transformation of the state, the wartime casualties, and the international conjuncture. Out of a population of fewer than three million during the period 1975–1990, the numbers of dead and wounded were placed at approximately 120,000 and 300,000, respectively.[40]

The context in which Lebanon's second civil war took place was altered by a succession of related events whose origins were clear in 1958, but the dimensions of their consequences were not then conceivable. The impact of the 1967 Israeli-Arab war and the defeat of Nasserism, the reemergence of the Palestinian movement, and the resurgent power of Arab conservative forces that polarized the region with U.S. support affected Lebanese politics. Beirut was not spared the transforming effect of these developments, even as members of its remarkably resilient political elite who had been active in 1958 continued their political struggles, in coalitions that sometimes differed. But the skewed system of political offices and privileges and the aggravation of social disparities, vastly intensified in the intervening years, echoed earlier conditions that had never been satisfactorily addressed.

Unlike 1958, however, the protracted struggles between 1975 and 1990, including the Israeli invasion of southern Lebanon in 1978 and the vastly expanded invasion that extended to Beirut in 1982, were widely covered in Europe and the United States.[41] The impact of internationally televised coverage alone exposed the myths surrounding the war, including those bearing on Israel's role in Lebanon. Lebanon emerged in a different light as well, one in which the apologies of confessionalist interpretations became irrelevant before the realities of human suffering and continued political struggle. American audiences responded, particularly in the aftermath of the killing of 243 U.S. marines and other Americans in the fall of 1983 in Beirut. By contrast, there had been 8 American casualties in 1958, with all but one killed by accident.[42] The Reagan administration's principal concern, however, was to table the Lebanese crisis and remove it from public debate, along with the question of U.S. support for Israel and its Palestinian and Lebanese agendas.

Admittedly, public contestation of U.S. policy in Lebanon was intense but brief. For the administration, the closure of debate posed fewer risks than did an informed and demanding public. To most Americans, it is safe to say, U.S. involvement in Lebanon appeared to be without historic precedent. It seemed a response to the catastrophic developments that befell a republic of moderation devoured by its internal enemies and their regional allies. That there were nearly three decades of U.S. involvement in Beirut and that an American president had previously given his approval to political as well as military intervention in Lebanon were not in the public memory. In sum, the record of American policy and the nature of the U.S.-Lebanese connection were largely obscured, distorting the vision of past as well as present actions by the United States in Beirut. The result promoted a sense of utter detachment, if not indifference, on the part of the public. With the availability of U.S. sources for the short history of U.S.-Lebanese relations between 1945 and 1958, neither response is justified. It remains for us to confront the record and to consider its consequences, in terms of both Lebanese politics and U.S. responsibility.

2

U.S. Postwar Policy and the Middle East

Opening Doors in the Middle East

The United States emerged from World War II with unprecedented economic power and the conviction that its global leadership would serve to restore the shattered international order. Such ambition assumed the structuring of an international liberal economic order that would stem the excesses of economic nationalism, while arresting political radicalism in Europe, occupied Germany, and Japan.[1] Allied to this design was another, which involved the projection of U.S. power through the acquisition of bases, transit and landing rights, stretching from the Atlantic to the Mediterranean and the Pacific. Support for the domestic and foreign policy aspects of this postwar vision came from the internationally oriented U.S. corporate elite whose influence and political allegiance transcended partisan lines.[2] Its members understood, as did the military and civilian leaders of the Roosevelt and Truman administrations, that petroleum resources were a prerequisite to such postwar reconstruction and that the unparalleled petroleum resources of the Middle East constituted the chosen means to its implementation. The resulting enhancement of the economic and strategic value of the Mediterranean and the Middle East shaped U.S. policy, in consequence. Given the dominant role of France in North Africa and the legacy of its Syrian and Lebanese mandates in the Middle East, as well as the far more formidable presence of

Britain in the eastern Mediterranean and the Middle East, U.S. foreign policy in the postwar period virtually guaranteed a competitive relationship with its chief European allies.

The triad of policies that distinguished the postwar American epoch—the Marshall Plan, the Truman Doctrine, and NSC 68—addressed the interrelated objectives of U.S. policy. The U.S. commitment to the restructuring of the European economy identified with the Marshall Plan involved an unprecedented level of economic and political intervention in postwar Europe.[3] With the Truman Doctrine, the roughly $400 million earmarked for Greece and Turkey committed the United States to replacing Britain's role in the eastern Mediterranean and subsidizing it in the Middle East.[4] In Asia, U.S. policy involved maintaining access to raw materials and promoting the development of its industrial core, while overseeing its political course. With the passage of NSC 68, justified in terms of Soviet aggressive intentions, the militarization of U.S. foreign policy was accelerated. Drafted by Paul Nitze, George Kennan's successor as director of the Policy Planning Staff, and an informal committee of the State and Defense Departments, U.S. military spending increased from approximately $13.5 billion to $50 billion.[5] In the process, the U.S. military claimed responsibility for the defense of Canada, Alaska, the western Pacific, and Africa, as well as the Near and Middle East.[6]

The petroleum resources of the Middle East were instrumental in the implementation of such policies. In 1947, ARAMCO, whose merger became effective on the same day as the passage of the Truman Doctrine, provided roughly 50 percent of Western European oil needs, while between 1948 and 1951, 56 percent of the oil provided to Europe by ARAMCO companies was subsidized by the ECA (Economic Cooperation Administration) and the MSA (Mutual Security Agency).[7] The years 1946–1950 witnessed an increase of 143 percent in U.S. foreign investment in the petroleum sector.[8] And in the period 1945–1950, ARAMCO's production rose at phenomenal rates. In 1944, ARAMCO crude oil production was on the order of 21,296 barrels daily, while in 1950 it reached 546,703 barrels daily.[9]

Much as U.S.-Soviet relations dominated the thinking of U.S. administrations, the immediate postwar years revealed that Defense Department officials were not of one mind as to Soviet intentions or capacities. In 1945, the Defense Department's Joint Logistic Plans Committee as well as U.S. Military Intelligence estimated that the Soviet Union would require approximately fifteen years to overcome wartime losses in manpower and industry, ten years to redress the shortage of technicians, five to ten years to develop a strategic air force, fifteen to twenty-five years to construct a modern navy, ten years to refurbish military transport, ten years (or less) to quell resistance in occupied areas, fifteen to twenty years to establish a military infrastructure in the Far East, three to ten years to acquire the atomic bomb, and an unspecified number of years to remove the vulnerability of the Soviet rail-net and petroleum industry to long-range bombing.[10]

Those who, along with Intelligence and State Department analysts, were less persuaded of Soviet intransigence than of its industrial weakness and concern with security nonetheless agreed in principle on the necessity of excluding the Soviet Union from the so-called Eurasian land mass. To this ban was added a categoric suspicion of the objectives of indigenous nationalist and populist as well as communist parties or movements, on the presumption that they constituted a potential threat to U.S. and Western interests. The ban was applied to the Middle East.

The logistical planning for an extensive system of U.S. bases began in 1943–1944, before the end of the war. At the time, the State Department supported the Joint Chiefs of Staff proposal for a network of bases in the Atlantic and Pacific zones, as well as over polar air routes. In October 1945, Secretary of the Navy Forrestal and Secretary of War Patterson, with Admiral Leahy of the Joint Chiefs of Staff and Secretary of State Byrnes, endorsed such a project as enhancing U.S. offensive strategy. In addition, contingency plans formulated by the Joint Chiefs of Staff in the winter of 1945, such as "PINCHER," assumed the preeminent role of the navy as "the service most concerned with logistics for a long war, and therefore the one most concerned about defense of the Persian Gulf area."[11] In practice, Forrestal became an adamant proponent of policies designed to assure the U.S. access to Middle East petroleum and to maintain control over its conduit through the Mediterranean. He regarded Saudi Arabia, "one of the great puddles left in the world," as an indispensable resource in the service of U.S. policy.[12] Patterson, on the other hand, gave instructions to General H. W. Aurand in 1945 to "make preparations for permanent rights at seven airfields in North Africa and Saudi Arabia."[13] At the same time, Assistant Secretary of War John McCloy urged the State Department to rely on a "strong United States air transport system, international in scope and readily adapted to military use," which in his view was "vital to our power and future national security."[14] The recommendation coincided with the expanded activities of the major U.S. carriers, Trans World Airlines (TWA) and Pan American Airways (PAA), and entailed conflict with European allies reluctant to cede their spheres of influence to the United States, whether on the ground or in the skies.

The above policies, which signaled the expansion of the U.S. base system, coincided with the contraction of wartime military forces, which were reduced from 12 million in 1945 to 1.6 million by 1947, while Defense spending declined from $81.6 billion in 1945 to $13.1 billion.[15] Such moves assumed no lessening of U.S. commitment to the Mediterranean or the Middle East, as the course of the debate on the Palestine conflict and the passage of the Truman Doctrine demonstrated. Indeed, by 1947, the importance of the eastern Mediterranean and the Middle East to U.S. policy was beyond argument. Economic and strategic interests dominated calculations of U.S. policy, whether in Turkey, Iran, Saudi Arabia, Palestine, or Lebanon. How such interests were to be secured was the question. Britain's role, as the discussion that follows indicates, was far more problematic in terms of U.S. policy than conventional interpretations of the "special relationship" suggest. Where both powers were in solidarity, however, was in their commitment to the exclusion of the USSR from the eastern Mediterranean as well as the Middle East.

The Roosevelt administration regarded Anglo-American cooperation as a sine qua non of the postwar order. But what kind of cooperation was assumed? Britain emerged from the war with a debt of £3 billion, partially covered by the £3.75 billion that the United States lent Britain after the termination of Lend Lease in 1945.[16] Under the circumstances, British economic interests in the Middle East were all the more important to London, which did not inhibit U.S. international oil companies from expanding their operations or the State Department from protecting them. Roosevelt, moreover, as did Truman after him, continued to extol Anglo-American cooperation as indispensable. There was less hypocrisy than calculation in the position, particularly in the light of Britain's political and military presence in the region and the reluctance of the U.S. military to commit troops to the area.

From Egypt and the Sudan to Palestine, Transjordan, Iraq, Kuwait, the Gulf, and Iran, British political, economic, and military power was paramount. Iran and Egypt were the two principal British enclaves. In the former, Anglo-Iranian Oil Company (AIOC) installations in Abadan included oil fields and refinery and adjunct facilities that capped British economic interests in the region. As State Department officials conceded in the course of the Anglo-American Pentagon talks on the Middle East, it was "difficult to believe that any British Government would willingly leave its interests there (or in the nearby oil producing areas on the Persian Gulf) unprotected."[17] If Abadan was Britain's largest oil installation, before 1947 the 200,000 British troops in Egypt represented its most extensive concentration of military force outside of India.[18] In addition, Britain had military installations in Palestine, Iraq, Transjordan, Sudan, Bahrain, Aden, and Cyrenaica. And in Saudi Arabia, which international U.S. oil companies came to regard with a distinctly proprietary air, British influence was dominant. Aside from petroleum, British interests in "banking, insurance, aviation, shipping, construction, and mining" could hardly be neglected.[19]

Notwithstanding the weight of the British presence, postwar U.S. foreign economic policy provided the impetus and the rationalization for the penetration of the region. The United States was not to be inhibited by the extensive perimeter of British power or by the ensuing antagonism that characterized Anglo-American relations in the Middle East. The commitment to expand foreign trade and investment, justified in terms of peace and prosperity, was fueled by past memories of the Depression and present pressures to find markets and resources. The resulting drive constituted a formidable engine of policy harnessed by a power of unprecedented proportions. In 1945 the State Department's Coordinating Committee argued that "in general, we should seek economic liberty without inequality, in all matters of trade, transit and other economic activities in accordance with the broad objectives of our commercial policy as expressed in Article VII of our mutual aid agreement and in the Joint Declaration of 1941."[20] The point was repeatedly emphasized, as the State Department underscored the fact that the U.S. "will have to rely heavily upon an actively implemented economic policy . . . if our efforts are to have real force and effect."[21] The Open Door was applied in trade, exports, monetary policy, and the expansion of U.S. oil and aviation interests in the Middle East, to the consternation of British allies who looked upon the conduct and content of U.S. policy in the region with unsentimental sobriety. The results locked the eastern Mediterranean and Middle East into U.S. foreign economic policy, if only because the region was both an indispensable source and a passageway. The importance of these economic and strategic zones guaranteed Anglo-

American cooperation and bitter competition simultaneously. In the later 1940s, 73 percent of U.S. imports were raw materials, and 55 percent of these issued from areas under British control and passed through the Mediterranean on their westward course.[22]

Three crises in this period illustrated the causes and complexities of Anglo-American tensions in the eastern Mediterranean and the Middle East. Of these, two are well known, while the third has been segregated as a case of interest to specialists in the Middle East only. In fact, the crises surrounding Iran, Turkey, and Saudi Arabia have much in common, in spite of their differences. Their brief appraisal underscores the issues at stake for the closest of Western allies and the implications for the regimes in the states directly concerned.

The Saudi case erupted in mid-1944 over plans for the construction of a U.S. airfield at Dhahran. To the resident British minister the expansion of the existing wartime airfield stood to enhance American power at the expense of British influence. "This is not Panama or San Salvador," the British minister in Saudi Arabia declared in 1945, referring to U.S. policy.[23] The U.S. position was formally justified in terms of an open skies policy, which was officially launched at the 1944 International Civil Aviation Conference. Two years later the U.S. withdrew from the Air Transport Agreement in light of its evident failure to attract support. Nevertheless, on the earlier occasion, U.S. representatives argued in favor of an injunction against "the establishment of 'closed air' blocs between any group of nations or against any one nation."[24] In May 1945, John Loftus, acting chief of the Petroleum Division of the State Department, informed John Linebaugh of the Division of British Commonwealth Affairs, that the United States wanted "a cessation of British political interventionism in the process of obtaining petroleum concessions in areas directly or indirectly dependent upon British sovereignty." Forty-one U.S. officials, arguing in terms of Open Door principles, were not about to countenance its closure.[25]

In July 1945, TWA proposed—and in January 1946 the Saudis accepted—cooperation with the Saudis in development of both an airline and an airport at Dhahran. Within a year, the State Department confirmed the now uncontested presence of some seventy-five U.S. military personnel in Dhahran, "maintaining and operating the airport and carrying on a program to teach the Saudi Arabians to take over this field," a project that was expected to last some years "because of the backwardness of the Saudi Arabians in such matters."[26] American rejection of British requests for the servicing of British Overseas Airways Corporation (BOAC) planes at the airfield along with those of French and Dutch carriers was explained as extraneous to U.S. military concerns. It was subject to other interpretations.

In the Iranian case of 1946, oil and politics combined to undermine Anglo-American and Soviet wartime collaboration. International attention in the West focused on the question of Soviet troop withdrawal, which along with that of Britain, was discussed at the Teheran, Yalta, and Potsdam conferences of 1943–1945. The presence of foreign troops was a result of the Allied invasion in 1941, to which the United States had contributed some 30,000 troops. By war's end, the question of troop withdrawal had been effectively superimposed on the contentious matter of oil concessions. The volatile combination of oil, politics, and the military, in which the Iranian regime faced Britain, the USSR, and the United States, virtually guaranteed deadlock. With the British in total control at Abadan, the prospect of U.S. international companies' obtaining oil concessions from the Iranian regime was considered distasteful by the British, while similar Soviet objectives were collectively viewed by both Britain and the United States as disastrous.[27]

To complicate matters, there was the prehistory of British and American influence in Teheran. Britain controlled the considerable enclave at Abadan, with the world's largest oil refinery. But the United States had its informal army of experts in Teheran, who were now infringed upon by the advent of Soviet officials who had close relations with the Tudeh, the Iranian Communist party. To this scenario must be added the existence of insurgent movements against the regime in Teheran, to which Soviet policy contributed. The ability of the Soviet Union to prevent Teheran from sending troops to the northern provinces where uprisings occurred in 1945 was interpreted by U.S. and British officials as proof of the subversive power wielded by the Soviets. Azerbaijani separatists were helped in their attempt to establish an autonomous government by the intervention of the USSR. The momentum worked in favor of other such movements in Kurdistan and the Caspian. The question came before the newly established United Nations in 1946, as the Iranian prime minister prepared his brief with U.S. backing. In Teheran, meanwhile, U.S. officials sought to disengage the Iranian regime from its accord with the USSR on oil concessions, which had constituted the basis of an Iran-Soviet agreement on troop withdrawal.[28] With its contingent of advisers counseling police, military, and politicians, in addition to U.S. oil consultants mediating differences between British-owned Shell and AIOC and U.S. oil interests, U.S. ambassador Morris maintained that the Soviet Union would have no difficulty in concluding that the United States was seeking to secure its position in Iran.[29] From Moscow, George Kennan, then U.S. chargé d'affaires, confirmed Soviet frustrations on the subject.[30] In Washington, however, the crisis persuaded White House adviser Clark Clifford as well as the Joint Chiefs of Staff that it was in the strategic interest of the United States to exclude the Soviets from the petroleum resources of Iraq, Iran, and the Middle East, a position reinforced in the 1947 Anglo-American Pentagon talks on the Middle East.[31]

Recent reconsideration of the nature of the postwar crisis in Turkey provides further insight into the place of oil in postwar U.S. foreign economic and strategic policies in the eastern Mediterranean. Contrary to the conventional view that has long dominated interpretations of the Turkish crisis of this period, its origins cannot be solely attributed to the aggressive intentions of the USSR vis-à-vis the Turkish regime. U.S. policy in Turkey recognized the legitimacy of Soviet interests and feared their realization, which in turn led to the decision to empower the Turkish military. Oil was not an indifferent matter in such considerations. In 1946, according to Melvyn Leffler's study, U.S. military and British intelligence estimated that the objectives of Soviet intentions in the region were its industrial bases and oil fields. The areas of the "Caucasian and Ploesti oil fields and the Ukraine and Ural industrial centers" were recognized as regions of legitimate Soviet interest. They were also identified by the U.S. Joint Planning Staff in 1945–1946 as the very areas to be targeted in the event of war.[32] Although U.S. officials of the Defense Department discounted the likelihood of direct Soviet military action in Turkey, they feared the ratification of Soviet base acquisition in the Turkish Straits. Such a move was viewed as facilitating Soviet eastward expansion, which was unacceptable given British oil interests and communications systems in the Middle East. To Acting Secretary of State Acheson and Secretary of the Navy Forrestal, modernizing the Turkish military force and expanding its airfields was a means of increasing Turkey's offensive capacity in relation to "vital Soviet petroleum resources in Rumania and in the Caucasus," while making its airfields readily accessible to the U.S. Air Force in the event of confrontation with the Soviets.[33] The Greek-Turkish Aid Bill of the Truman Doctrine provided approximately $100 million of military and naval matériel to

Turkey, out of the total $400 million allocated for Greece and Turkey together. When Anglo-American delegates conferred on their Middle East policies throughout the fall of 1947, their depiction of the situation in the eastern Mediterranean was utterly unlike what Congress had been told by the administration. It was not alarm but reassurance that the Turkish regime was offered. Ankara was assured that the United States did not regard the USSR as belligerent, that "we do not consider war imminent and do not believe that the reduction in Turkish forces would materially affect the Soviet course of action towards Turkey."[34] The Turkish regime was, however, advised to avoid giving the impression that its foreign policy had in any way changed.

In short, U.S. policy in Iran and Turkey reinforced the U.S. position in what Dulles would later refer to as the states of the "Northern Tier." Its objectives involved protecting access to Middle East oil while positioning U.S. and Allied forces in relation to Soviet strategic centers.

Oil Politics and Policy

The above cases, abridged as they are, suffice to indicate that oil was a key factor in British-U.S.-Soviet relations in the region that was recognized as the new "center of gravity of world oil production."[35] The urgency with which U.S. officials in the Departments of State, War, the Navy, and the Interior regarded the acquisition and protection of Middle East petroleum reserves underscores the position implicit in the above cases. That position had evolved in accord with the changing assessment of domestic reserves and the extent to which these would be depleted. In 1941, U.S. oil production represented "63 percent of the world crude output."[36] When the United States entered the war, it had "a surplus production capacity of over one million barrels a day, representing almost 30 percent of total U.S. production in 1941."[37] The generous margin allowed the United States to fuel both its own war effort and that of its allies. But this situation rapidly changed, as actual and anticipated consumption increased at heady rates of growth. In this context, the reserves in the Middle East offered an alternative, to which the Roosevelt administration responded with alacrity. As early as 1941, the California Standard Oil Company, which operated as corporate-diplomatic agent for the United States, requested that Roosevelt contribute to resolving the financial dilemma facing the Saudi king, with an obvious eye to reaping the advantages. These proved to be indirect, as

Roosevelt arranged for Britain to act as the conduit for U.S. funds. In 1943, however, Roosevelt agreed to the request of the Department of State's Near East Division that Saudi Arabia be granted Lend Lease assistance.[38] The tactical decision involved the recognition of the role of King 'Abd al-'Aziz al Faisal al Sa'ud, more frequently referred to as King Ibn Sa'ud.

In June 1943, at a White House meeting under the direction of James Byrnes, director of the Office of War Mobilization, in which the Secretaries of War, the Navy, and the Interior, among others, participated, it was agreed that the United States should obtain Middle East petroleum reserves at the earliest possible time. To this end, the Petroleum Reserves Corporation (PRC) was to be established, with the directive that it promptly move to look into "the acquisition of an interest in the highly important Saudi Arabian fields."[39] The members of the PRC board of directors included the Secretaries of State, War, the Navy, and the Interior, which reaffirmed the role of said agencies in U.S. petroleum policy and, by extension, involved their continuing concern with U.S. interests in the Middle East.

Efforts by the PRC to obtain all or part of the shares of U.S. international oil companies' concessions failed, as did parallel efforts to obtain control over the projected pipeline.[40] Was such opposition a function of traditional opposition to U.S. government involvement in business, the opposition of U.S. domestic producers, or the fears of U.S. international companies concerned with the potential loss of profits? While the first reason was offered by U.S. companies operating in the Middle East, the U.S. domestic companies were adamant about keeping the government out of the industry. Oil geologist Everett De Golyer, who had been sent by the PRC to investigate the petroleum resources of the Arab East, was strongly in favor of an American role, persuaded "that the traditional free enterprise in foreign countries did not apply in the case of oil."[41] In practice, the rejection of a controlling role for the U.S. government in private U.S. oil interests was offset by the latter's acceptance of Washington's role in providing assistance to Ibn Sa'ud and in offering them permanent protection.

In 1945, Loy Henderson, director of the State Department's Office of Near Eastern and African Affairs, who obtained his professional training in Riga along with George Kennan, and Gordon Merriam, director of its Near East Division, urged President Truman to make certain that Saudi oil would remain in American hands:

In Saudi Arabia, where the oil resources constitute a stupendous source of strategic power, and one of the greatest material prizes in world history, a concession covering this oil is nominally in American control. It will undoubtedly be lost to the United States unless this Government is able to demonstrate in a practical way its recognition of this concession as of national interest by acceding to the reasonable requests of King Ibn Sa'ud that he be assisted temporarily in his economic and financial difficulties until the exploitation of the concession, on a practical commercial basis, begins to bring substantial royalties to Saudi Arabia.[42]

When U.S. international oil companies in the Middle East (Standard Oil Company of New Jersey and Socony-Vacuum) succeeded in making the arrangements permitting them to join Texas and Standard Oil of California in what became ARAMCO, the geopolitics of oil and U.S. Middle East policy were joined. The 1947 agreements signaled a historic moment that a knowledgeable insider claimed compelled public attention.[43] The claim was vastly exaggerated outside of the business community. It is open to question as to what part of the public was aware of the U.S. Senate hearings before the Special Committee Investigating Petroleum Resources (1946), let alone the report, *The International Petroleum Cartel*, which was the subject of the federal antitrust suit in 1952. With ARAMCO in place, TAPLINE, the pipeline project that was to carry Saudi oil to the Mediterranean became possible. The inaugural of its operation in 1950 heralded a financial as well as political turning point. ARAMCO profits soared. Its workings were henceforth to be protected by the State Department's overall commitment to assure an "international environment in which private companies could operate with security and profit."[44]

The date on which the consolidation of the four companies of ARAMCO occurred coincided with the announcement of the Truman Doctrine. The two events were organically connected, as the integration of the "four giants of the American oil industry in the riches of Saudi Arabia now assured a substantial American presence and interest in a vast area, stretching from the Mediterranean to the Persian Gulf."[45] While this was not the language in which the Truman Doctrine was presented to the American public, it corresponded to the understanding of those directly involved in the crafting of the doctrine. Joseph Jones's well-known capsule eulogy, *The Fifteen Weeks*, which emphasized the doctrine's anticommunist character, nonetheless left no doubt as to the connections between the Truman Doctrine and U.S. petroleum interests that the so-called Greece-Turkey-Iran barrier was designed to protect.[46]

The doctrine in question simultaneously protected and undermined Britain's position in the area. The question of Britain's economic weakness and consequent subordination to U.S. policy was discreetly left unstated in the major review of Mediterranean and Middle Eastern politics that was undertaken by representatives of both governments some months later. The Anglo-American Pentagon talks constituted the first comprehensive review of Anglo-American interests in the area since the 1944 assessment of U.S. petroleum policy. The underlying premise of the 1947 talks was that the eastern Mediterranean and the Middle East were vital to the security of Britain and the United States and that the USSR was to be excluded from these regions. The Soviet leadership was, incidentally, also to remain uninformed with regard to the content of the talks, as Secretary of State George Marshall and Foreign Minister Ernest Bevin agreed.[47] Those present on the occasion of the reaffirmation of the Anglo-American position included officials of the Departments of State and Defense, Policy Planning Staff, including Under Secretary of State Robert A. Lovett, Loy Henderson, George Kennan, Raymond Hare, Lieutenant General Lauris Norstadt, Vice Admiral Sherman, and Major General Gruenther with, on the British side, Lord Inverchapel, British Ambassador in Washington, Assistant Under Secretary of State, Foreign Office Michael Wright, Minister to Washington John Balfour, Admiral Sir Henry Moore, Air Chief Marshall Sir Guy Garrod, General Sir William Morgan, and members of the British Joint Staff Mission in Washington, along with Lieutenant General Sir Leslie Hollis, Chief of Staff to the Minister of Defense and Air Vice Marshal R. M. Foster, Assistant Chief of the Air Staff.

The Pentagon talks opened with a review of imperial interests and how best to assure their continuity under the altered circumstances of the postwar period. The latter referred both to Britain's depressed economy and to Foreign Minister Bevin's conviction that it was incumbent on Britain to transform its colonies into partnerships. The ideology of development was common to U.S. foreign economic policy as well, and in both cases it remained more of a mask than a practice. In both instances, it was premised on the commitment to avoid radicalization of the region by supporting conservative elites and thereby undercutting the risks of Soviet influence. Even though the Pentagon talks affirmed that "Communism was not widespread in the Middle East and that the Moslem religion was not favorable to it," according to the summation of the British position, measures were to be taken to assure its continued exclusion (p. 610). Moreover, one of the designated areas of concern with respect to radicalization was trade union activity, identified with Lebanon in the Anglo-American talks, to the consternation of those concerned with pipelines. Given the overall risks, then, the conclusion was that it was desirable to "break down the myth of Soviet perfection" by encouraging U.S. and British controlled media in the area to take appropriate positions (p. 611).

Encompassing a region that stretched from North and East Africa to the Arab East and Afghanistan, such talks focused on military and political priorities. Conditions were reassessed in Greece, Turkey, Iran, Afghanistan, Palestine, and French North Africa, as well as in British-controlled areas in the Gulf, Iraq, and Egypt. In their September 9 session, Foreign Minister Bevin, U.S. Ambassador to Britain Lewis Douglas, and State Department Near Eastern and African Affairs director Loy Henderson exchanged views on Palestine, Transjordan, Egypt, Cyrenaica, Iraq, and Iran. Bevin revealed his conception of the unchastened elasticity of empire as he reviewed the imperatives of holding on to Suez, reminding his colleagues that Egypt meant the Sudan. Given the difficulties that Britain faced in its negotiations with nationalists in both places, Cyrenaica emerged as a possible alternative and supplement to the British position (p. 500). U.S. officials agreed without hesitation that the former Italian colonies be reallocated, with Somalia and Libya under international trusteeship and Eritrea "ceded in full sovereignty to Ethiopia, except for the area in the northwestern part of Eritrea inhabited by Moslem-Sudanese, which should be incorporated into the Anglo-Egyptian Sudan" (p. 544). Apparently the impact of such manipulations on both the Eritrean and the Sudanese societies and other respective struggles was of minor consequence. In Transjordan, Britain wanted its bases strengthened, and further east, Bevin explained, "we would like to create in Kuwait one of our strongest military bases of the Near East" (p. 501). But U.S. interests were not to be ignored there, as they were "predominant in Saudi Arabia and Bahrein, and rapidly growing in importance in Kuwait," which rendered British policies in Kuwait, South Arabia, and the Gulf a matter of concern (p. 535). In spite of such reservations, Anglo-American agreement on the importance of endorsing Britain's military presence in the area extended along the "Central African Road," which meant establishing "communication links across

Central Africa from Nigeria on the West Coast to Kenya on the East Coast," and with the approval of the French, "crossing French controlled African territories in the process" (p. 528).

In the meetings that ensued through the fall of 1947, Britain's dire economic situation was left unstated, as was its political predicament throughout the region. On the other hand, there was no reluctance to clearly define the basis of U.S. economic policy and its rationalization in areas that directly impinged on British interests and spheres of influence:

> If they indicate fear that our present economic strength relative to their own will enable our private interests to "capture the markets" to British disadvantage, and establish a preferred position through preclusive or monopolistic arrangements, we might point out: that adherence to the general principles of equality of access and maximum freedom of competition will serve as a protection to British as well as American and other commercial interests; and that as a matter of fact the extent to which American business can "invade the markets" of the Middle East is limited by the shortage of dollars and the causes of that shortage.   (p. 520)

There was little consolation in the conclusion of the American delegation that U.S. business activity in the region was limited by the dollar shortage, particularly since the proposed solution included expanding U.S. oil interests. The argument of the U.S. delegates was that "pipeline and refinery activities in the Levant might help in relieving the dollar situation and should give some employment to skilled and semi-skilled labour thrown out of employment by the departure of the Allied forces" (p. 619).

1947–1952: The Local as Regional and International

In the course of the next four years, between 1947 and 1952, it was not U.S. objectives but U.S. strategy that changed in the Mediterranean and the Middle East. Under pressure from regional developments that collectively signified the further weakening of Britain's position, Washington remained publicly in solidarity and privately at greater odds with its ally. Yet with the acceleration of international crises, interpreted in Washington as signaling Soviet advances, there was an ideological and politico-military mobilization within, in the form of the passage of NSC 68. And there was a reassessment of the situation in the field, including that in the eastern Mediterranean and Middle East, with an eye to enhancing the

U.S. position. The crises prompting such reassessments included that in Berlin in 1948, Soviet intervention in Eastern Europe, the Soviet explosion of a nuclear bomb, the defeat of Chinese Nationalists, and war in Korea. The effect in terms of the State Department's position in the Middle East was to resensitize its officers to the incalculable strategic value of the region—which, in turn, led to a reassertion of Anglo-American support that masked a more critical appraisal of British policy and the risks of being identified with it.

On the regional level, there was disagreement over the struggle in Palestine, and criticism of British policy vis-à-vis Egyptian nationalists in the crisis over Britain's military presence at Suez. In Saudi Arabia, to Britain's extreme disapproval, Washington endorsed the arrangement between ARAMCO and Saudi Arabia in the 50/50 accord that had reverberations throughout the region. In Iran, the British faced a nationalist regime demanding more favorable concessionary arrangements in AIOC that British oil interests regarded as anathema. Not only did the State Department disagree with British rejectionism, but U.S. international oil interests were among the beneficiaries of the concessionary arrangements that followed nationalization. What reticence there was in undermining Prime Minister Mossadeq of Iran in 1951 vanished by 1953, when Eisenhower was in the White House and John Foster Dulles was at the helm in the Department of State. Anglo-American cooperation on that occasion assumed the form of covert action that brought down the Iranian prime minister and reinstated a U.S.-backed shah.

In 1951–1952, Washington supported British efforts to create a Cairo-based defense arrangement in the form of the Middle East Command (MEC), which upon its failure was followed by the Middle East Defense Organization (MEDO). These instances of collaboration were not deceptive, but they reflected Washington's conviction that the time had come to assume a more active presence in the region. With the failure of MEC and MEDO, about which the U.S. military were not overly enthusiastic, a far more significant arrangement was arrived at in terms of enhancing U.S. power in the region, namely, the admission of Turkey into NATO. Five years after the Truman Doctrine, Turkey's role as bridgehead between Europe and the Mediterranean and the Middle East was reaffirmed by its integration into the U.S.-dominated NATO, a fitting sequel to the Truman Doctrine.

Independently of the inherent importance of the above developments, the situations in Palestine, Iran, Cairo, and Saudi Arabia proved to be particularly significant in shaping the attitude of the U.S. State Department toward its interests in the eastern Mediterranean and the Middle East, including Lebanon. The experience of nationalization in Iran was read as a direct threat to Western oil interests, although there were differences in how to respond to it. The failure of MEC and MEDO was a reminder of the arrogance of British power, whose obsolete expression was inevitably rejected by Egyptian nationalists. The same experience persuaded the State and Defense Departments under both Truman and Eisenhower of a foreign policy "truism" in this region—namely, that the defense of the region should not be left to its leaders, let alone its people. They were evidently incapable of grasping the seriousness of Western intentions, i.e., in preparing the region for defense against potential Soviet advances, which appeared to Egyptians and others as highly implausible. The struggle in Palestine alerted the State and Defense Departments to the risks of unresolved conflict, but it also revealed the distinct advantages of Israeli military capacity. Saudi Arabia represented another form of conflict, in which demands for increased shares of profit led to favorable negotiation involving the Saudis, ARAMCO, and the U.S. government—including the Treasury—in a historic resolution of consequence to the U.S.-Saudi relationship.

In the case of Palestine, the State Department viewed the Palestine conflict, when the British placed it before the United Nations in 1947, as hazardous to U.S. petroleum interests, a position supported by Secretary of State George Marshall as well as Defense officials Robert Lovett and James Forrestal, who covered the military aspect of the conflict. Their common fear was that the struggle in Palestine would jeopardize U.S. oil interests and that the USSR might exploit Zionist objectives and the destabilization of the region. The U.S. military maintained a consistent position in opposition to direct military involvement of U.S. (or Soviet or Soviet-supported) forces in Palestine.[48] The State Department, meanwhile, opposed partition in favor of trusteeship, only to renege on its position on both in favor of statehood in 1948. Differences between Defense, State, and the White House on Palestine were legion, and those separating the White House from Whitehall no less profound. In 1948, the U.S. and the Soviet Union recognized Israel, while in London there was talk of another Spanish civil war.

In 1948 U.S. military planners had other considerations in mind. The Joint Chiefs of Staff and the NSC (NSC 26) concluded that Saudi oil facilities should be made unavailable to the USSR in the event of war. "It called for advance preparations to destroy all above-ground facilities within a matter of hours, and to plug all wells with concrete blocks 1,000 feet down, which would take an estimated thirty days. The latter was designed to make the wells unusable without the waste of reserves caused by fire or dynamite."[49] According to Irvine Anderson's study of ARAMCO, the plan was not discussed with the Saudis or approved in Washington, and its "final disposition" remained unclear. William Chandler of TAPLINE, who was in the area at the time, reports otherwise, noting that the plan in question involved no plugging of oil wells but rather the destruction of certain key elements in aboveground facilities. The "denial program" was operative for some two to three years, according to Chandler. It had the approval at the highest levels of the State and Defense Departments and was directed at blocking the Soviet Union.[50]

U.S. officials in the Middle East between 1947 and 1949 were pessimistic with respect to the prospects of a political solution to the crisis over Palestine. Such pessimism did not preclude a positive assessment of Israel's military performance in 1948, notably among U.S. officials concerned with intelligence and defense matters, who found the results compelling.[51] There were no illusions among U.S. officials involved, however, concerning the costs on the ground. Between 1947 and 1949, Israeli-controlled territory expanded from an area of some 5,600 square miles to 7,750 square miles, as Israeli actions on the ground led to the flight of some 700,000 Palestinians who "fled or were expelled from Israeli-controlled territory," according to U.S. sources.[52] In June 1948, the Israeli Defense Forces (IDF) Intelligence Branch concluded with respect to the causes of the Palestinian exodus that 55 percent was attributable primarily to Jewish military operations (Haganah/Israel Defense Forces), 15 percent to Jewish terrorist organizations (Irgun and Stern gang), and the other 30 percent a function of psychological warfare, fear, and demoralization of the Palestinian community.[53] Fears of Israeli extremism and expansionism, as well as the conviction that Israeli military preparedness did not justify U.S. aid, did not block a $100 million package of U.S. economic aid to Israel in 1948.[54]

At the UN, Dean Rusk and his special assistant on Palestine, Robert McClintock, who later became U.S. ambassador to Beirut, were in search of "pragmatic" Arab leaders prepared to adopt policies compatible with those of the United States. Among the candidates was the Jordanian king, a choice that consolidated the accord reached between the Jewish Agency in Palestine and Abdallah in Transjordan prior to May 1948.

McClintock, among other U.S. officials, was increasingly apprehensive lest Israeli intransigence on Palestinian repatriation, the risks of right wing terrorism, and the pursuit of undefined borders yield only further conflict. In the summer of 1948, McClintock favored international-UN guarantees in addition to Israel-Arab treaty accords on the definition of boundaries. "This would be of particular advantage to the Arabs," he asserted, "as 'freezing' the boundaries of Israel and thus affording protection to the Arab states against the wider pretensions of the Jewish revisionists and such fanatics as those of the Irgun who have pretensions to the conquest of Transjordan."[55] The possibility of Israel's occupying the West Bank in the event of the destabilization of Jordan remained a feature of Israel's Arab policy that was of considerable concern to U.S. policymakers in the coming years. The Tripartite Pact of 1950, in which the three major Western powers—Great Britain, France, and the United States—legitimated the Jordanian annexation of Palestinian territory, was publicly rationalized as an effort to stem the arms race in the region.[56] It was the events of 1957–1958 that signaled a rapprochement between Washington and Tel Aviv, the long-term significance of which emerged in the subsequent roles of Israel and Saudi Arabia as the twin axes of U.S. and Anglo-American Middle East policy, supported by Iran, Turkey, and Iraq, as well as by the pro-Western Arab states of the Arab interior, Jordan and Lebanon.

In the intervening period—1950—a major development involving U.S.-ARAMCO-Saudi relations reflected the deepening ties between U.S. public- and private-sector interests that affected the oil-producing state. The so-called 50/50 agreement between ARAMCO and Saudi Arabia was inherently important in terms of its financial impact on the U.S. petroleum cartel, but its timing in terms of parallel regional and international developments made it additionally significant. The Korean War provoked a reevaluation of the status of U.S. Middle East oil interests and accompanying political relations, rendered all the more important in the light of the Chinese Nationalist defeat in 1949, and the growing strength of Japan's regional economic role. Saudi irritation with U.S. policy in Palestine was another problem, one that officials of the U.S. international oil companies understood would not stand in the way of amicable business relations. Those relations, however, were strained by the Anglo-American dollar-sterling crisis, which supported the Saudi demands for more profitable oil pricing arrangements.

Translated into policy at a higher level, the deal negotiated by ARAMCO was agreed to by the State Department. Among those involved were Assistant Secretary of State for Near Eastern and African Affairs George McGhee, and political advisers, including John J. McCloy, whose law firm had experience with "tax exemption and anti-trust waivers through which major U.S. oil companies prospered, nearly tax-free abroad."[57] ARAMCO agreed to the payment of a Saudi income tax, " 'it being understood' that in no case would the taxes exceed fifty percent of ARAMCO's net income after deduction of operating expenses and foreign taxes."[58] The Treasury Department, in turn, agreed to ARAMCO's subtracting its Saudi taxes from those it owed the United States. This arrangement, in sum, allowed ARAMCO to subtract the results of its profit sharing with the Saudis from its U.S. corporate taxes. The accord appealed to other oil producers and transit states in the Middle East, who proceeded to make comparable demands. Among those who remained ignorant of such arrangements as well as its deeper politico-economic significance, were U.S. taxpayers and Saudi subjects.

Britain regarded the above arrangements as particularly disturbing in the context of its own frustrated negotiations in Iran, where Mossadeq was pressuring the British to renegotiate more favorable terms in AIOC. At the time, in 1951, "AIOC produced 51 percent of the Middle East's oil, three-quarters of it from Iran and the rest from its share of production in Iraq, Kuwait, and Qatar. Of the remaining 49 percent, 44.5 percent was produced by American companies and the rest by Dutch and French companies."[59] Britain's margin of petroleum power was being steadily eroded by U.S.-protected international companies in the region. Churchill, mindful of British support for the United States in Korea, appears to have assumed that the anticipated quid pro quo in the form of U.S. support for Britain's position in the AIOC controversy would be forthcoming.[60] Not only was no such backing to materialize but the results backfired in terms of British expectations. Mossadeq found the highest echelons of the State Department receptive, though insistent that he compromise with Britain. The decision to nationalize AIOC in 1951 sent political tremors through the Middle East. For two years, Iran faced British-led efforts to undercut its oil policies, while American oil interests increased their share in the AIOC consortium that emerged after nationalization to 40 percent. Two years later, the Anglo-American covert effort to break Mossadeq succeeded in the Anglo-American coup that returned the Shah to power. Among the Shah's recommendations to Eisenhower and Dulles was that the United States promote the Saudis as a counterweight to Nasser, a recommendation recalled on July 1,

1958, when the Shah was in Washington to consult on developments in the region.[61]

The political marriage of the United States and the petro-princes of Saudi Arabia and the Gulf represented the cartelian logic of U.S. Middle East policy in the decade of the 1950s. In 1952, however, it appeared to be threatened by the U.S. government's federal antitrust suit against the international petroleum cartel. In 1952, the attorney general of the Truman administration informed the Federal Trade Commission, the Secretaries of State, Defense, the Interior, and Commerce that the international oil cartel was to be investigated at the highest levels. The report on which the federal case rested, *The International Petroleum Cartel*, was issued as a Staff Report to the Federal Trade Commission and submitted to the Subcommittee on Monopoly of the Select Committee on Small Business of the U.S. Senate in the summer of 1952.[62] The FTC report offered an undiluted account of the international cartel and its control over the production, refining, transportation, and marketing of petroleum. More than 50 percent of tanker traffic was in its hands, and outside of the United States, all existing and projected pipelines were in the control of the same "seven sisters" that made up the cartel. Of the seven, five were American. Four constituted the ARAMCO group— Standard Oil of California (Chevron), Texaco, Standard Oil of New Jersey (Exxon), and Socony-Vacuum (Mobil). The fifth U.S. company was Gulf. In addition, there were Royal Dutch/Shell, and British Petroleum (which was the designation by which Anglo-Iranian "rechristened" itself after 1954), which with Gulf were involved in Kuwait.[63] The report estimated that "outside the United States, Mexico and Russia, these seven companies, in 1949, controlled about 92 percent of the estimated crude reserves."[64] Control was maximized through joint ownership of subsidiaries and by means of interlocking directorates, leading to the baldly stated conclusion that "control of the oil from the well to the ultimate consumer is retained in one corporate family or group of families."

> Four of them own over 70 percent of the shares of Iraq Petroleum Co., Ltd., which, in turn, controls all the oil of Iraq, Qatar, the Trucial coast, and other less important areas in the Middle East; four of them own all the shares of Arabian American Oil Co., which controls all the oil in Saudi Arabia, and two of these four own the Bahrein Petroleum Co., Ltd., which, in turn, controls the oil resources of Bahrein Island; one has exclusive control of all the oil in Iran, and in partnership with

another of the seven companies, controls all the oil in Kuwait; three of the seven, in partnership and in separate operations, control most of the oil resources of Venezuela and other Latin-American countries, except those with state monopolies; five of them, operating as three corporate entities, control most of the oil resources of the Netherlands East Indies.[65]

It is interesting to note that ARAMCO had obtained immunity in the ongoing federal antitrust suit during the Iranian crisis, a measure whose meaning with respect to the importance attributed to the U.S. cartel, is evident. With the Iranian crisis "resolved," the implementation of the federal antitrust suit generated a deep and wide swath of anxiety at nearly all levels of the U.S. government, as well as in London, although British companies were excluded. While the status of the criminal suit was eventually changed to that of a civil suit, U.S. officials in the Departments of State, Defense, Intelligence, the Interior, and Commerce clearly regarded the federal suit, and not the petroleum cartel, as the primary threat to U.S. security. After Eisenhower took office, Secretary of State Dulles was informed by Special Assistant to the President Robert Cutler: "It will be assumed that the enforcement of the Antitrust laws of the United States against the Western oil companies operating in the Near East may be deemed secondary to the national security interest."[66]

In five brief and extraordinary years, from the passage of the Truman Doctrine to the federal antitrust suit against the international petroleum cartel, the principal anchors of postwar U.S. foreign policy in the eastern Mediterranean and the Middle East had been securely put in place. They included the special relationships with the subsidized Saudi regime and the protected Iranian monarchy, as well as the role assigned to Turkey, which was legitimated in NATO.[67] In this structure, superimposed upon a network of relations that included America's special ally in Europe, and its permanently defined nemesis in the USSR, the reflections of an oilman on the preponderance of U.S. power in the postwar era merit consideration. In the words of the treasurer of Standard Oil Company of New Jersey, "As the largest producer, the largest source of capital, and the biggest contributor to the global mechanism, we [as a nation] must set the pace and assume the responsibility of the majority stockholder in this corporation known as the world."[68]

This, in brief, was the setting of postwar U.S. Middle East policy, in which economic and strategic considerations were integrally related, movements for social and political reform were suspect and consistently subordinated, and cooperation and competition with Great Britain were based on political calculations. It was in this context, moreover, that U.S. policy in Lebanon was situated. The importance of this former French mandate rested on its congruence with U.S. interests. The Mediterranean state offered an invaluable physical location and a commendable geopolitical situation, a state with a good port, air bases, and communication system, and a regime that welcomed the oil pipeline that linked U.S. oil interests in Saudi Arabia with Sidon, Lebanon's port on the Mediterranean. Therein lay the foundation of U.S. interests in Lebanon, the "assets" of U.S. policy in Beirut.

3

Learning Lebanon: A Primer

Ideological slogans apart, Lebanon is the only true citadel of private enterprise which remains in the Arab world.
Galal Amin, *The Modernization of Poverty* (1980)

Beirut: Aspects of Economic Growth

The American attraction to Beirut in the mid-1940s was a function of several overlapping factors: the potential it represented for the expansion of U.S. corporate interests in oil and aviation, which were essential instruments in postwar U.S. economic policy; Beirut's location outside the bloc of British-controlled mandates, protectorates, and spheres of influence; and the capitalist and pro-Western orientation of a regime that was effectively tied to French influence. In the broad political panorama of the Middle East, the state of 1.1 million inhabitants would appear to have been an odd partner to court. But State Department officials and their Middle East hands had a keen sense of the possibilities of the Beirut enclave, the corporate entity on the eastern Mediterranean whose importance for U.S. oil coming from Saudi Arabia was among its chief attractions, along with its virtually guaranteed passivity on the Palestinian question.

Lebanon was granted independence in 1943, although French forces withdrew only in 1946 as a result of Anglo-American and nationalist pressure. The historic link with Syria, which survived French mandatory policies, was severed only in 1950 with the dissolution of customs accords in that year, a break anticipated with considerable apprehension in Beirut. In sum, Beirut was a state in formation, almost. The poverty of its state institutions was regarded as a characteristic deficiency of the regime by later academic analysts. To its ruling elite, however, the same conditions were appreciated as a prerequisite for their own profitable development. In Washington, the disparity between Lebanon's stymied political institutions and its economic achievements was assessed with a cautious interest that changed to approval, in accord with the penetration of the two dominant American corporate interests in Lebanon, oil and aviation. Furthermore, on indices of per capita income, mortality, and birth rates, as well as literacy, urbanization, and manufacturing, the Lebanese record was favorable. It had the characteristics later attributed to modernization. And in comparison with other Arab states, in which per capita income was on the order of $100 annually, and in some instances below $50, Lebanon's per capita income was about $140 in 1949.[1]

Lebanon's economic situation in the postwar years was not only favorable, it was unique. Allied expenditures in wartime contributed to it. According to Charles Issawi, Syria and Lebanon accumulated a surplus in their accounts of some 607 million Lebanese-Syrian pounds between 1939 and 1945.[2] In addition, regional developments appeared to conspire in Lebanon's favor. The Palestine conflict, as well as transitions in neighboring states that ranged from an increased role of the state to attempts at revolution, resulted in capital flight that found its way to Beirut. Not only did the financial markets of Tel Aviv become secondary to those of Beirut, but the Beirut port profited from the boycott of Haifa that followed upon Israel's emergence as a state.

Beirut's commercial success and entrepôt role was, however, not only a postwar phenomenon. Its transit function was well established before World War II, as was the organic integration of Lebanon's silk industry with that of France.[3] World War I ended that phase of Lebanon's economic development, as the destruction of mulberry trees for use as timber and the unmatched competition with synthetic fabrics weakened this and other industries. After 1945, the influence of France remained potent even as the French mandate was dismantled. French concessions and financial control represented an effective and long-lasting penetration of the Lebanese economy that undermined the state's independence.

In spite of such limitations the postwar years witnessed an extraordinary surge in Lebanon's financial status. Between 1945 and 1954 the number of banks had increased from seven to twenty-one, and capital flows into such institutions rose in the later years of the Besharah al-Khuri regime from LL15 million (Lebanese pounds) in 1951 to LL44 million in 1952.[4] Among other factors favorably affecting the Lebanese economy was the staggering growth of U.S. international oil companies in Saudi Arabia, which made Lebanon's transit role significant when pipelines became operative in 1950. In 1947 and 1952, crude oil made up some 96 percent and 97 percent, respectively, of the tonnage and 23 percent and 45 percent of the value of goods in transit through Lebanon.[5] The transformation of the Saudi, Kuwaiti, and Gulf oil economies had a direct impact on Lebanon, where the sectors of shipping, aviation, and banking were affected. Gold traffic in 1951 "accounted for a little more than 90 percent of the gold officially shipped into Beirut."[6] In the seven-year period between 1946 and 1952, "transited gold comprised about 75 percent of total gold operations."

Lebanon's Middle East Airlines (MEA), which developed the Kuwait-Beirut connection, was among the chief agents and beneficiaries of such developments. In addition, Lebanon's minuscule fleet of some fifty vessels plied an increasing trade, while local warehouse space in Beirut expanded to absorb the growing volume of incoming goods.[7] Smuggling, including narcotics and currency exchange, was a source of profit as well, amounting to some LL60 million pounds generated by the irregular activities of Lebanon's shipping fleet, according to contemporary U.S. Legation officers. The cumulative result of these developments was reflected in the growth of Lebanon's preeminent first city. The enclave that was Beirut flourished.[8]

Two features of the Lebanese ruling class responsible for guiding the country's postwar economy are of particular importance in the present context—its vision of the nature of desirable economic growth and its connection to French capital. Both were relevant to U.S. interests in Beirut. The first had an appeal for reasons previously cited; the second was a matter of grave concern, since it blocked the entry of American capital and acted as a constraint on U.S. policy. The members of the Lebanese mercantile and financial bourgeoisie, who shaped the economic direction of the postwar state, were committed to the expansion of Lebanon as a thriving service economy. They justified their antagonism toward a greater emphasis on industrialization in terms of a disadvantageous division of international labor, as well as an effort to exclude the debilitating social and political costs of industrialization. Lebanon, they insisted, was historically suited to specialize in trade, finance, and transportation. It was therefore destined to find its profit and salvation in a mode of economic growth that would be bound by regional and international, not domestic, factors. By 1952 the service sector in fact contributed "about 57% to NNP as compared to 19% in agriculture and 14% in industry."[9]

The same circle of core merchants, bankers, and financiers with access to the all-powerful president, figures who were key to Lebanon's economic policies, operated within a French financial orbit. The practice was not without its highly placed critics, who incidentally proved to be sympathetic to developing an American connection to offset French influence. In the beginning of Besharah al-Khuri's regime, however, this was a minority position, to the chagrin of American observers. Nonetheless, the demand to limit French concessions, control over public utilities, and domination of Lebanon's monetary system had an appeal to a growing number of domestic critics who looked upon the continuing proposals for French-directed projects in Lebanon with skepticism. The combine known as SERIAC (Société d'Etudes et de Réalization Industrielles, Agricoles, et Commerciales) was illustrative of French plans that stood to increase the French role in Lebanon's economic development. That role was evident in the operations of the Banque de Syrie et du Liban (BSL), which functioned as the country's primary bank of issue. Its director, René Busson, was considered among the most powerful figures in Lebanon before 1951, the year of his downfall.[10] The BSL controlled access to capital and currency for all manner of local and foreign development projects, dispensing favors and itself favored by virtue of its contacts with the presidential circle.

By comparison, British efforts to penetrate the Lebanese market were limited, though not inconsequential. British consultants working with Alexander A. Gibb and Partners advised Lebanese businessmen on the construction of Lebanon's telephone lines and hydroelectric power system, while British oil interests in IPC watched over pipelines that linked Iraqi oil fields through northern Lebanon. Britain's influence, relative to that of France, was minor. Its strength lay far more in its regional situation, where the sterling-based economy redounded to the disadvantage of Lebanese entrepreneurs, who were increasingly frustrated by the limitations of French financial controls. Such considerations were evident in the controversy surrounding the decision to accept the Franco-Lebanese monetary accords in 1950, as opposed to severing such ties. Those who favored maintaining the French financial connection included Maronite separatists as well as powerful merchants eager to protect themselves against Syria, whose protectionist measures they regarded as unacceptable.

Knowledgeable insiders assert that there was little debate at this stage on the nature of Lebanon's economic development.[11] Dissenting views were not uncommon, they were merely bypassed by those in positions to influence the direction of the economy. But young reformers, including those in government positions, were not averse to expressing their views in a highly politicized milieu in which the excesses of Lebanon's possessive individualism were regularly criticized, as was the lopsided nature of its trade-oriented, finance-centered economy, with its open door policy toward foreign investment. In the mid- to late 1940s, the Ministry of National Economy housed such critics. They included its Minister Kamal Junblat and Assistant Director Na'im Amyuni, both of whom argued against the nearly exclusive emphasis on developing Lebanon's service economy. They were among those who questioned a policy that favored Beirut while neglecting rural areas and contested the benefits of a policy open to foreign concessions while calling for further investment in and development of the agricultural, industrial, and manufacturing sectors. Junblat was also among those favoring land reform, which he implemented in his own estates. As late as 1960, more than 50 percent of cultivated land remained in the hands of no more than 5 percent of Lebanese landowners, making Junblat's position all the more unusual.[12]

In the summer of 1946, when unemployment and labor protest were high, Amyuni argued that the Lebanese could not survive current policies. His estimates of those currently employed in productive labor left him with little optimism regarding continued trends in the economy. Amyuni concluded that "about one-tenth of the population is contributing to create material wealth and providing means of existence for the rest of the community, whose greater sections engage in administrative or speculative work or remain idle."[13] The results risked the erosion of rural development and the immiserization of the urban labor force, while raising false expectations. What Amyuni termed "auxiliary sources of income," which included "bases for foreign enterprises, such as the leasing of airports, free trade zones, pipelines, refineries, etc.," could not be expected to improve the overall situation.[14]

Tripoli provided a shattering example of what was to be expected. Since 1920, according to Amyuni, Lebanon's second-largest city and once its "prosperous trade port, has been living in the hope of Iraq oil." When the dream materialized, it turned out to be an illusion on which many had depended. Amyuni's exposé of the limits of oil-related development was significant in terms of concurrent planning for TAPLINE, the ARAMCO pipeline project that was signed into existence in Lebanon in 1946. Referring to the IPC pipeline, Amyuni explained its limits as follows:

> The pipeline was laid and a small refinery built in the vicinity of the Tripoli Terminal Station. Today two million tons of oil flow every year through Tripoli, but what does the huge installation represent in the economy of the town? Few perhaps know that a single cotton spinning and weaving plant in Tripoli itself employs four times as much labour as the whole Iraq Petroleum terminal and refinery together.[15]

Others at different times expressed criticism of the regime for its indifference to developing the rural sector, a cry that outlasted this and succeeding regimes. While cultivated and irrigated areas expanded at the rate of 3 percent annually after 1948,[16] "in 1946, Beirut Deputy Abdallah al-Yafi excoriated the 1944–1946 governments for not developing a national agricultural policy," a complaint voiced by others as well.[17] Two years later, development plans designed to respond to some of these criticisms were jarred by systemic constraints involving inaccessibility of credit, absence of technological improvements, and in rural areas, discrepancies in land ownership. The problem of credit and the deficits of labor affected other sectors as well. Industry suffered from a shortage of capital that found its way to commercial and financial interests in search of short-term loans, as well to construction.[18] By 1948, the share of industry in total national "production" was nonetheless more than 40 percent, and its contribution to employment was on the order of 25,000–50,000 workers.[19] Estimates for 1946–1952 indicate that investment in industry was partial to "food, textiles, and non-metallic minerals (cement) [which] represented 62–66 percent of the eight major industries."[20] The absence of government protection undermined efforts to stimulate local industry, but some important sectors expanded in spite of such limitations, as in the modernized textile sector.

Perhaps the single most revealing indicator of the attitude of the regime toward national development was the taxation system. Its nature reflected the stark indifference of the government toward the public sector. The purpose of revenue collection appeared to have more to do with supporting the regime than allocating resources to the state.[21] The bulk of revenue collected as indirect taxes came from customs duties, which constituted a lucrative source of wealth for the merchant class. Taxes on income and property constituted less than 18 percent of the total. Most of the resulting expenditures were reserved for development of the country's infrastructure—its roads, ports, telephone and communication systems—which consumed approximately 60 percent of such allowances, while agricultural development projects in the same years, 1945–1954, received about 10 percent. The disparity led to consistent criticism of the socially indifferent elite that justified its policies in the name of a sacrosanct individualist ethic. It was one that Lebanon would one day no longer be able to afford, as a keen observer of the Lebanese state and society later noted.[22]

The Organization of the "Weak State"

American officials in Beirut in the days of the Besharah al-Khuri regime regarded the dominant elements of the ruling class as supine followers of the French, whose legacy was a high level of bureaucratic incompetence. What such officials soon realized, however, was that the victims were also beneficiaries. Incompetence may have been rife, but those with influence were highly sophisticated in making the system work to their advantage. Among them were those in the circles of privilege and power around the president. They understood that the "soft state" environment in which Lebanon's liberal economy developed was integral to the survival of their own power.[23] This was not a rationalization of corruption, but rather the expression of a supremely self-confident ruling class acting out of rational calculations of self-interest. In spite of this, some in the political elite, such as Michel Chiha, the ideological architect of modern Lebanon, saw fit to decry the excesses of individualism and the absence of civic consciousness.[24] No connection was made, however, between these vices of Lebanese society, as Chiha viewed them, and the dominant ethos of the system that guided the ruling class and influenced the course of the state.

In 1943 Chiha was one of the cofounders of the Société Libanaise d'Economie Politique, a contemporary Lebanese "think tank" of the elite, in which Gabriel Menassa, Henri Far'oun, and Alfred Kittaneh, Lebanon's preeminent bankers and financiers, participated. Advocates of a liberal economy that they controlled, they viewed the national pursuit of commerce and finance as a rational response to Lebanon's resource limitations. Lebanese liberalism, in this interpretation, did not support the Western "craze for making laws and imposing taxes" that Chiha warned against. The legislative experience of England and the Scandinavian countries, transplanted to the Lebanese environment, would bankrupt the country, according to Chiha, provoke emigration, and put the rich in power.[25] In the vision that Chiha espoused and that inspired the milieu of which he was a part, however, there was to be no place for the "rule of the demos," as Malcolm Kerr recognized.[26]

The Lebanese experience under French mandatory rule (1920–1943) hardly provided an alternative model. A political entity of some 1.1 million inhabitants and seventeen religious sects at the time of its independence, the country was adversely affected by the absence of a national consensus, as much as its political development was stunted by French rule. Indeed, French policy deepened existing divisions. Mandatory authorities relied on their connections with Lebanon's merchant class and its Christian Maronite hierarchy. With independence, the vision of a "Greater Lebanon," an idea that had taken root in the mandate period, was translated into practice. The result extended the coalition forged between the dominant Christian elite and its urban Sunni cohorts, whose common interests were central to the project of those in command of the Lebanese state. Promoted in the 1926 constitution and later reaffirmed in the 1943 National Pact, this coalition united "the mountain of refuge and Lebanon the meeting place," as Albert Hourani referred to Michel Chiha's vision of Lebanon.[27] Translated into political practice, the interests of the coalition were sustained and reproduced through the country's confessional system, whose own roots antedated such arrangements.

According to a 1932 census, cited repeatedly over the coming years irrespective of demographic changes, there was a 6:5 ratio between Lebanese Christians and Muslims. It was estimated at the time that "Maronites then constituted thirty percent of the population, Sunnis twenty percent, Shi'a eighteen percent, Greek Orthodox ten percent, Greek Catholics six percent, Druze six percent, Armenian Orthodox five percent, with the remaining five percent being Armenian Catholics, Protestants, Jacobites, Syrian Catholics, Syrian Orthodox, Nestorians, Latins, Jews, and others."[28] The single most powerful political office, that of the presidency, remained in Maronite hands, and the prime ministership was habitually assigned to a prominent Sunni Muslim, while the speaker of the parliament was Shi'i.

The practice of apportioning offices continued throughout the bureaucracy, thus reinforcing patterns of privilege. At the same time, the reconciliation of a "Syrian unionism and Lebanese particularism" had become evident to the Sunni Lebanese bourgeoisie.[29] By then, the advantages of a "Greater Lebanon," with its collaboration in favor of common interests that transcended sectarian lines, was irresistible to all except the Maronite clergy and its supporters, who remained opposed to any such collaboration. For the Sunni bourgeoisie, however, the advantages of participating in Lebanon's Western-oriented economy were becoming ever more apparent.[30]

War complicated these developments. In the struggle between Vichy and Gaullist authorities, recognition of Syrian and Lebanese independence was consistently postponed, until the accelerated collaboration between British and Free French forces altered the power balance in the region. With the 1941 invasion of Lebanon, the Vichy regime agreed to an armistice that was the prelude to the declaration of Lebanese independence on November 26, 1941. The policies of De Gaulle in Lebanon, a matter of suspicion in London and Washington, proved to be detrimental to its implementation. Gaullist policies involved plans to remain in the eastern Mediterranean, an arrangement that assumed a tacit British accord.[31] When, on September 21, 1943, Besharah al-Khuri became president and Riad al-Sulh, prime minister, with a cabinet that included such men as Kamil Sham'un, 'Adel 'Usayran, Salim Taqla, Habib Abu Shahla, and Majid Arslan, French forces were still in Lebanon, and the worst of postwar crises had yet to come.

The reassertion of French authority in 1945 created havoc in Beirut, as it did in Damascus, solidifying Anglo-American pressures against the French in the process. France was unprepared to withdraw its forces or to concede that their presence invalidated the commitment to recognize the sovereignty of the new states. In 1946, after the humiliation of French policy in the former mandatory states, Lebanon and Syria took their case to the newly formed United Nations. By the end of the year, the withdrawal of French forces was complete, although French political and financial influence remained.

It was in the midst of the protracted conflict with France that the design of the National Pact was completed. Its significance requires further elaboration. Against a background that rendered the realities of political independence moot, Lebanon's elite contemplated the construction of the state in which religious (confessional) interests would be recognized no less than the political. Chiha was pessimistic about the marriage of confessional and political representation, which he recalled had led to failure and even the need for European intervention.[32] The figure whose legendary importance in shaping Lebanon's political order was widely recognized argued that

Lebanon's unique experience rendered Europe's democratic abstractions inappropriate.[33] In the fall of 1943, President Khuri and Prime Minister Sulh crafted an accord whose historic impact on Lebanon is difficult to exaggerate. The National Pact emerged out of a series of statements made by both officials that found wide support in ruling circles. While the 1926 constitution assigned extraordinary power to a Maronite president, the National Pact was an endorsement of Lebanist-centered, as opposed to French-centered or pro-Syrian, politics. It committed the leadership to avoid entangling alliances with foreign powers—a reference to France and Syria, though later extended by critics of its abuse to the United States. Neutralism was to be Lebanon's hallmark, in principle only. Domestically, the National Pact was interpreted by the prime minister as a denunciation of sectarianism and its divisiveness.[34] Besharah al-Khuri later recalled the objectives of the pact in other terms.

1. Complete and full independence from the Western states, all Western states.
2. Complete and full independence from the Eastern (Arab) states, all Eastern states.
3. No mandate, no protectorate, no concessions, and no privileged position for any state.
4. Cooperation with the sisterly Arab states to the greatest extent.
5. Friendship with all foreign states that recognize and respect Lebanon's full independence.[35]

Between the principle and the practice, the gap was immense. French influence continued throughout the Besharah al-Khuri regime, and on the economic level alone it involved presidential intimates among its agents and beneficiaries. More generally, however, controversy over the precise intentions and interpretations of the National Pact was never-ending. Was it an innovation, or a restoration? Was the objective to rein-vigorate an earlier pattern of sectarian collaboration and to contain the possibilities of fundamental change?[36] Some claimed that the National Pact represented a viable if imperfect compromise that was a prerequisite to political stability.[37] To others it represented failure to forge a national consciousness as opposed to legitimating multiple parochial identities.[38] Interpretation was embedded in practice, and the practice of Lebanon's first independent regime was revealed in the workings of an elite that left little doubt that the National Pact provided the most effective rationalization of the existing division of power and deserved to be protected.

What follows is a nominal description of the governing apparatus of modern Lebanon as it emerged in the postindependence period. In a highly abridged manner, it indicates the central axis around which power was concentrated and disseminated. And it highlights the limited functions of an unrepresentative political system whose reproduction guaranteed the status quo, even as it was regularly punctured by the mobilization of political forces outside of its formal structures. The new republic was Janus-faced, with a modern exterior and a "traditional" interior that far more accurately represented the organization of the clientage system that operated through its carefully tended interstices. As abortive and abhorrent as the institutions of state were to its critics, they cannot be ignored by those committed to delineating the bases of power in the Khuri and Sham'un regimes, as the relations of class and state were defined and refined.

At the apex of the system was the president, whose wealth and power were immeasurably increased by the transfer of French-controlled customs, taxes, and other benefits of state power. Elected by the Chamber of Deputies for a six-year term, the president appointed the prime minister, and with his cooperation as well as that of the speaker of the Chamber, a cabinet. The power of the presidential office was evident, as was the control of the patronage system it allowed the incumbent.[39] The Chamber's role in selecting the president, on the other hand, made this the body's most influential single act. This function was rarely overlooked by U.S. officials, who clandestinely funded the parliamentary elections of 1957 to achieve favorable results.

The Lebanese Chamber was a unicameral assembly whose numbers were elastic. Its members, serving a four-year term, elected a Shi'i speaker, a Greek Orthodox vice president, and two secretaries, one Sunni, the other Maronite. Its composition is a matter of interest. "During a period of 21 years (1943–1964) between 42 and 54 percent of the deputies in the Lebanese parliament were designated 'propertied,' having no particular profession, and living off their land and/or other property."[40] The rest were professionals who may have been propertied as well.

Close to the president in terms of institutional power was the prime minister, who, in Besharah al-Khuri's regime, was most often Riad al-Sulh, a Sunni za'im, a political leader of notable origin who remained at the president's side through most of his life. Khuri had fifteen cabinets and nine prime ministers.[41] The Sunni Muslim notable whose political experience rendered him an invaluable partner was prime minister on nine different occasions.

With the president, the prime minister was responsible for selecting a cabinet whose overall composition and number were subject to political calculations. Besharah al-Khuri's first cabinet consisted of the following ministries: Foreign Affairs, Defense, Education, Public Works, National Economy, Finance, Agriculture, Health and Social Assistance, Justice, Posts and Telegraphs, Information, and Interior. To this executive structure must be added the elaborate organization of local government with its five administrative units (*muhafazat*) that corresponded to the major electoral districts of the state, whose leaders were presidential appointees. Below them was the network of subordinate provincial and village units.

Elections were limited to males in a list system based on confessional identification. Ideological parties were excluded. Their members appeared on ballots under their confessional identities. The arrangement guaranteed the perpetuity of the existing system and its loose traditional party coalitions. It was also guaranteed to perpetuate the frustrations of those who felt themselves politically alienated and excluded from such a "legal" system. Contrary to the political culture of imperialism and academia in which vast areas no longer under foreign domination were described as power vacuums, no such vacuum existed at the base in the Middle East. Politics was everywhere, including in the Lebanese system, with its idiosyncratic traits.

The status quo, characteristically the objective of those in power, was maintained at great effort and with external support. In the Beirut of the 1940s and early 1950s, politicization and political mobilization were rampant, in spite of the limitations of the political system with its exclusionary confessional prerequisites. Sectarian movements and parties, along with those of a paramilitary character, confronted those of a pan-Arabist and decidedly secular cast. The Kata'eb and the Najjadah, the Arab Nationalist Movement, the Syrian Social Nationalist Party (known under its French acronym, PPS, as well as its English acronym, SSNP), the Communist Party (functioning with its Syrian counterpart until 1944), the Progressive Socialist Party (PSP), and ideologically distinct Armenian-based parties of Tashnaks and Hunchaks were among the dominant groupings. Their very existence exercised an undeniable pressure on the system, which they simultaneously penetrated and opposed.

The "weak state," it emerged, represented the interests of those with political and economic influence who were committed to minimalist government. "Weakness," in this instance, was a deliberate function of power, not its absence.

In Practice

The cliché of Lebanese politics, that those who ruled did not govern, was an exaggeration with a substantial kernel of truth in the Besharah al-Khuri regime, even though it would be an error to view class and state in Lebanon as identical. The concentration of power in the hands of the chief executive was paramount. It was, however, given definitive shape by the mercantile and financial bourgeoisie, and supported by Lebanon's feudal landlords, who had, in fact, become capitalist landlords of vast estates—some of which had armies that rivaled those of the state.

The principal figures in the former category were Lebanese bankers and financiers, an assortment of men that U.S. Legation officer Samuel O. Ruff described in 1952 as moving in concentric circles of power around the president. For these mostly, though not exclusively, non-Maronite Christians at the inner core of this circle, political office was not a pre-requisite for political influence. Men such as the Greek Catholic Michel Chiha and Henri Far'oun were related to the president through marriage. There were others, including Husayn 'Uwayni, Alfred Kittaneh, and René Busson, who represented, respectively, the Sunni financiers responsible for Beirut's monetary policies, the dynasty of merchants and capitalists that included expatriates in the United States, and the éminence grise that acted as a conduit of French financial influence that affected practically everyone in the Besharah al-Khuri circle.

Tied primarily to French capital, they were committed to a liberal economy, but they were by no means indifferent to maintaining control over its course. Disdainful of democracy, hostile to populism, they were the natural antagonists of nationalist as well as pan-Arab or pan-Islamic movements. This, in spite of their role as committed advocates of Lebanese statehood. Cosmopolitan and secular, they remained wedded to the confessional system as a guarantor of the status quo. Lebanese Christians in the main, they were not primarily Maronite, and they included key players who were members of the Sunni bourgeoisie, such as Husayn 'Uwayni and Sa'eb Salam, although the latter was not identified primarily with French capital. Operating within a pro-French orbit and fully integrated into the French-dominated monetary system in Beirut, elements of this circle were sympathetic to closer connections with U.S. interests.

Unlike this urban-centered bourgeoisie, the chief executive also relied on more traditional rural networks, to which some of the above were linked. The broad-based and highly personalized coalition on which Besharah al-Khuri relied was a prerequisite to the stability of the regime. The construction of this network of rural and urban leaders with strong regional bases guaranteed needed support for Khuri and provided the respective regions of the country with the necessary services and privileges that the state did not provide.[42]

Maintaining the integrity of such networks in the face of political defection was no small achievement. Khuri relied on power blocs that covered the country and that included major Sunni landed families such as the Karame, Muqaddam, and Jisr; the al-'Ali and 'Abbud; the Maronite Hamid Franjiyyah; the Shi'i landlords, Sabri Hamadeh and Ahmad al-As'ad; the Druze, Majid Arslan and Kamal Junblat, until the latter proved too critical of presidential power and politics.[43] This listing of prominent figures reveals little of the maneuvering and internecine struggles that were a mainstay of local and national politics.

Traditional as such arrangements were, they operated in a system that was by no means impervious to change. Nor were the beneficiaries of such clientelist relations isolated from other currents affecting Lebanese society. Beirut, which clearly played a dominant role in the state and economy, was the center of the trade union movement, the heart of its politicized intellectuals, and the arena of mobilization around the Palestinian issue. It was also where the corruption of the regime was flagrantly exposed and those deemed responsible were challenged. In sum, Beirut was the scene of contemporary political struggles in what Malcolm Kerr later described as a "parochial and archaic-premodern" political order.[44]

In spite of the commitment of the Lebanese bourgeoisie to inhibit the emergence of an industrialized proletariat, which Chiha urged, the expansion of the Lebanese economy contributed to the growth of the trade union movement in the mid-1940s. Its members drew their strength from trade unions that included an eclectic constituency of white-collar, blue-collar, and service-sector employees who reflected Lebanon's service-centered economy. There were those who worked in banks, petroleum companies, hotels, restaurants and cafes, along with railroad workers, stevedores working in ports, machinists, mechanics, mattress makers, tailors, tanners, and private chauffeurs, hairdressers, secretaries, and typographers.[45]

In 1946 widespread strikes and rising unemployment led to support for the passage of a progressive labor code, in which the communist trade union leader Mustafa al-'Arees played a prominent role. 'Arees, as later discussion will show, was the nemesis of U.S. and Lebanese officials committed to curbing his influence. The Ministry of the Interior was actively engaged in this project, as were other influential Lebanese working with anticommunist political mercenaries hired for the cause. The U.S. Legation took an interest in these proceedings, as in the struggle to obtain a meaningful labor code, which the chief of the U.S. Legation considered an undesirable prospect that would discourage U.S. business interest in Lebanon. Those in the oil business managed to get the regime to guarantee that they would not be affected by any attempts at unionizing their workers. They succeeded.

There were other signs of discontent from within the ranks of the political class, which was frustrated by nepotism and the increasingly oppressive political atmosphere. The judicial system was accused of corruption. There was press censorship. There were scandals that touched the president's family, with revelations concerning favoritism and lucrative contracts, and price-fixing. Tales of corruption exposed conditions that adversely affected the petty bourgeoisie, which was no match for Lebanon's power elite. The controls that the latter exercised over the economy, as U.S. officials readily conceded in the mid-1940s, were profitably self-serving. They had little to do, however, with the advertised endorsement of the free enterprise system by members of the same class. It was as a form of self-protection that the opposition to the Besharah al-Khuri regime gradually coalesced, although it did not long survive as a coalition. There were a former president, Sunni notables, reformist politicians such as the Druze leader Junblat, and the lawyer-diplomat Kamil Sham'un, and Kata'eb (Phalangist) leader Pierre Jemayyel.

The 1947 elections proved to be a turning point in the annals of political scandals surrounding elections. They were also a turning point for those in opposition. Yet it would be an error to read this period, or indeed the fraudulent elections, as signaling the demise of Khurist power. That power increased in spite of the *Black Book* that was issued by opposition forces. The efforts to fix the elections in order to legitimate the president's succession notwithstanding, Besharah al-Khuri was still a political figure with whom to contend. Nevertheless, the effort to arrange his succession was clearly illegal and required a constitutional amendment, as Kamil Sham'un was reminded in 1958, when he was in the same situation. In Besharah al-Khuri's case, there was a broader base among traditional allies, including the ministers of Public Works (Ahmad al-As'ad) and Defense (Majid Arslan), and the president of the Chamber (Sabri Hamadeh), in addition to the financial bourgeoisie represented by Finance Minister Husayn 'Uwayni.

Regional developments contributed significantly to these domestic trials. The Palestine conflict was a litmus test in Lebanese politics, exposing diverse positions and pressures. The Lebanese south was occupied by Israeli forces, in no hurry to evacuate, irrespective of UN pressure—which contributed to political damage in the capital and to economic damage for those resident in the affected areas. The regime's press censorship was an attempt to contain the repercussions of the regime's impotence. But this did not prevent it from bringing charges against the Israeli military occupation before U.S. and UN officials. Ralph Bunche's deputy in the armistice negotiations, Henri Vigier, wired Bunche with the warning that Israelis were reluctant "to evacuate Lebanese territory while Syrians remain on Lebanese front. Also object to an international frontier armistice commission, stating that the frontier will require rectification for security reasons."[46] Beirut was unprepared to contemplate territorial concessions. In Tel Aviv, meanwhile, Prime Minister Ben-Gurion of Israel and Defense and Foreign Ministry officials were in disagreement on whether or not to link Israeli-Lebanese and Israeli-Syrian negotiations. Ben-Gurion eventually moved to endorse separate negotiations. Those anticipated with Lebanon, the Israelis assumed, would facilitate negotiations with Syria, the Israeli seizure of Eilat, and a possible move into the West Bank.[47]

The Lebanese regime's predicament was tangible. It had no military force to rely on, aside from a volunteer army of some 3,600 men and a gendarmerie of some 2,500. Further, it viewed the prospect of assimilating the 140,000 Palestinian refugees as an unwelcome burden. Its poorest members were spread through some seventeen refugee camps, for which UNRWA provided assistance for resettlement.[48] Palestinian refugees became a source of cheap labor in the capital. But in the south, the closure of Lebanon's southern frontier and the forcible reorientation of its markets destabilized the impoverished southern economy.

To this must be added the considerably different situation of the Lebanese bourgeoisie who profited from the sale of their lands in Palestine and who were in a position to exploit the benefits of the Arab boycott of Israel. Compromised at one level, they emerged as beneficiaries of an Arab mobilization against Israel at another. It was this influential core that U.S. officials recognized as prepared to forgo resistance to U.S. policy in Palestine. Nonetheless, even Lebanon's most ardently pro-Western minister, Charles Malik, was persuaded of the urgency of obtaining a U.S. commitment to a political settlement of the Palestine conflict, which he and others failed to do. In Washington, however, Lebanon had little leverage in this regard. U.S. State Department officials and Legation officers regarded the Lebanese leadership as both opportunistic and passive.

During the French mandate, the Jewish Agency's political division in Palestine developed contacts with such Lebanese Maronites as Patriarch 'Arida, Archbishop Mubarak, Abdallah al-Khuri, and President Eddeh, with an eye toward forging a Zionist-Maronite alliance. Such an option receded among the influential members of the Christian bourgeoisie close to President Besharah al-Khuri, whose endorsement of the 1943 National Pact signaled a commitment to the integrity, as opposed to the partition, of Lebanon.[49] For Maronite clergy and Kata'eb politicians who were supporters of a Maronitist separatism, the motivation behind the contacts with the Jewish Agency remained. Among its manifestations was the May 30, 1946, "Treaty Between the Jewish Agency for Palestine and the Maronite Church," signed by Patriarch Antoine Pierre 'Arida and Bernard Joseph of the Jewish Agency.[50] For the regime, the accord was an embarrassment. For the church, on the other hand, Khuri's efforts to distance himself from the church and its claims to political influence were no less an indictment. In practice, however, the persistence of a separatist strain among Maronites who could not fathom a Lebanese-Christian and Muslim republic fueled other efforts at consolidating an Israeli connection. According to Israeli sources, former president Eddeh consulted with Israeli Foreign Ministry officials in early July 1948 on the "possibility of a Christian revolt in Beirut should the Israeli Defense Forces (IDF) invade southern Lebanon."[51] Following Israel's emergence as an independent state, contacts persisted in Europe as well as the United States, where collaboration between Israeli officials and Lebanese Maronites extended to public relations efforts on behalf of the latter. And in 1954, in the regime of Besharah al-Khuri's successor, Israeli leaders deliberated on the possibilities that political and confessional tensions offered for the creation of an Israeli-supported Maronite state.[52]

Familiar with Lebanese positions on the Israeli-Palestinian-Arab conflict, Israeli representatives to the 1949 Israeli-Arab armistice talks anticipated a positive response from Beirut. Israeli sources claimed that the Lebanese delegation did not disappoint them in this respect. Besharah al-Khuri's "readiness to mediate between Israel and the Arabs if Israel would commit itself to political and economic integration in the region," as reported in Israeli sources, was a function of sober calculations.[53] The options available to the Lebanese regime were slim, given the preponderance of Israeli military power relative to that of Lebanon and the continued occupation of the Lebanese south.

It was not only in relation to Israel that the Khuri regime faced difficulties. There were also noteworthy developments in Syria, where the first military coup brought Colonel Husni Za'im to power long enough to sign an armistice agreement with Israel and to finalize concessionary agreements with TAPLINE. In Beirut, 1949 proved ominous for other reasons. The regime was accused of involvement in the execution of the founder of the PPS, Antun Sa'adeh, on Lebanese soil. Even those who dissented from Sa'adeh's views and those of the PPS were inflamed by these events.[54] Sa'adeh was a major political figure in postwar Arab politics whose influence is difficult to exaggerate, and his execution raised questions of Syro-Lebanese complicity as well as of the covert actions of the Lebanese state. Two years later, the Lebanese prime minister, Riad al-Sulh, was assassinated in Amman, in what some assumed to be a retaliatory move.

By then, Lebanese domestic and foreign policies were being actively challenged, the former by internal critics of the regime and the latter by U.S. State Department officials now keen on having a more overt commitment of Lebanese support for U.S. policies. Regional developments encouraged such a move, as did those further afield, such as the defeat of American-supported Chinese Nationalist forces and war in Korea. The unmistakable signs of nationalist protests in the Middle East rendered Lebanon all the more attractive to Washington, where its antistatist regime was appreciated. There was no imminent danger of a Mossadeq-type nationalization, even though U.S. oil executives had other thoughts on the question. Still, Beirut was neither Teheran nor Cairo. And Palestine was viewed as a relatively safe issue among the influential members of the Lebanese elite. In the light of such considerations, the U.S. State Department took a more aggressive position toward the Lebanese regime, one that favored a political rapprochement that Besharah al-Khuri had until then resisted.

While the nature of U.S.-Lebanese relations is unraveled in the pages that follow, the timing of the State Department's moves in terms of

Lebanese domestic politics is worth noting. Besharah al-Khuri was under increasing domestic pressure. His reliable allies appeared to be secure, yet opposition from a variety of sources indicated more vulnerability than his regime could tolerate. In addition, the Sunni elite was not mollified by the role that Riad al-Sulh had so consistently and effectively played. Nor was the Kata'eb leader, Pierre Jemayyel, inclined to be sympathetic, as he argued in favor of the nationalization of "the exploiting companies and the imposition of heavy taxes on larger fortunes," a direct attack on the policies of the regime.[55] In the 1951 parliamentary elections, Khuri did poorly. "Out of nine seats the Destour list [supportive of the president] won only four, and the opposing list headed by Kamal [Junblat] polled 49.6 percent of the vote, winning the remaining five seats."[56]

Junblat's success was significant in the light of the coalition of opposing forces mobilized against Khuri in the FPS (Front Patriotique Socialiste [Patriotic Socialist Front]). In addition to the Kata'eb's position, Junblat's platform influenced the FPS program. Its scope was comprehensive. It envisioned plans for educational, political, and economic reforms. Advocating free and obligatory education on the primary level, it supported unemployment insurance and social security, along with the transformation of concessionary companies into cooperatives. Among the program's signatories were prominent political figures in addition to Junblat, such as Kamil Sham'un, Ghassan Tuwayni, Abdallah Haj, and Emile Bustani.

Within a matter of months, the Khuri regime was replaced by that of Kamil Sham'un, and the FPS program was set aside no less ceremoniously than its principal author. The new regime realigned domestic forces without altering the foundations of the system it had so strenuously criticized, while the American connection became the unquestioned axis of its foreign policy. It remains now to consider the evolution of the American connection in Beirut's first postindependence regime and to situate its significance in this array of competing political forces.

PART II

Formative Years in the Evolution of U.S. Policy: 1944–1952

4

Alternating Currents of Criticism and Conformity

Although the commercial class in Lebanon is not primarily interested in politics, it succeeds in maintaining and exercising political control in all government activities which can be of value to it in commercial transactions. Even the government's compromises in the field of Arab League politics are only top level expressions of the bargaining of this class.
January 21, 1952, "The Political Control Exercised by the Commercial Class in Lebanon," Foreign Service Dispatch*

Habits of Dependence

Early Signs

Less than a year after the United States recognized the Syrian and Lebanese republics, George Wadsworth sent Loy Henderson, director of the State Department's Near East and African Affairs Division, an optimistic assessment of Lebanon's potential for the United States:

> You know my "vision" that this little country can, as living standards rise in Arab lands, become not simply the Adirondacks of the Near East but also, as American cultural and material investment increases, as it seems bound to do, a vital focus of American influence based on mutual interest rather than special privilege.
>
> If we are to play a major role in world politics it would seem to follow that we must do so regionally and not primarily by long-range propaganda from Washington. And in this region of the Arab Near

East, Lebanon-Syria would seem to be the most inviting spot to cut our teeth.[1]

Henderson did not need to be convinced that the United States would play a "major role in world politics" or that the Middle East was one of the areas essential to such a role. And Wadsworth, American minister to Lebanon and Syria, similarly had no doubts that American "cultural and material investment" included Lebanon's function as a possible transit state for ARAMCO's pipeline project, TAPLINE. Between them, Henderson and Wadsworth were hardly novices in American forays into the Middle East. The former had been appointed director of NEA in April 1945, with Gordon Merriam head of the NEA division as of January. Merriam described his tenure as one in which Palestine, Greece, and Turkey, not Lebanon, were the main objects of concern.[2] But for U.S. international oil companies in the Middle East, as well as major air carriers such as Pan American Airlines, Beirut was hardly negligible. Lebanon and Syria were on ARAMCO's list as possible alternatives to Palestine for the construction of its pipeline project, and in 1944 an ARAMCO attorney, William J. Lenahan, was in the area on precisely such business. This represented no contradiction insofar as Merriam's views were concerned; it merely identified ARAMCO and TAPLINE's role in the making of U.S. policy in a more precise way.

In the span of eight years, from 1944 to 1952, U.S. policy in Lebanon evolved in accord with the expansion of American hegemony in the Middle East. The postage stamp state, as unsteady as it was well defined, became a recognized asset in the construct of U.S. Middle East policy. PACLIFT, an acronym I coined to abridge the principal elements of U.S. policy in these years, stands for petroleum, aviation, commerce, labor, intelligence, and FT, which is an abridgement of the Friendship, Commerce, and Navigation Treaty (FCN). Emphasis on economic aspects of policy gave way in the 1949–1951 period to a greater appreciation of the state's potential in terms of bases and communication lines. Prior to that, however, economic policies assumed a collaboration with influential elements of the ruling class and state. These were reflected in containment policies applied to labor and politics. In short, there was no question of the priority of U.S. interests in Beirut in the mid-1940s, but such priorities were not narrowly interpreted.

PACLIFT and the design of a political strategy in Lebanon are discussed in the following chapters. The material that follows explores the opening phase of U.S. policy, in which the critique of French colonialism and Lebanese dependence identified American officials in Beirut as sympathetic to Lebanese reformers and critics of corruption. More simply, U.S. officials were in tune with the State Department's anti-French outlook, which was shared by the British. The position, although consistently expressed in both the Legation, later the Embassy, and the State Department, was nonetheless rapidly and efficiently overruled by other calculations allied to U.S. interests in Lebanon.

Before Lebanon became the center of tourism and U.S. material investment, in Wadsworth's terms, however, it had to resolve its considerable problems in relation to continued French control. In 1944–1946, the American presence was marginal, even if the ambitions of its local officers were not. Along with Syria, the two former mandates remained subservient to France, a predicament affected by the wartime intra-French conflict between the Vichy and Gaullist governments, as well as by Lebano-Syrian nationalists, and Anglo-American officials.[3] Britain, fully cognizant of the implications of French withdrawal for its own contested power in the Middle East, adopted a self-serving position that simultaneously endorsed the implementation of independence on the ground while alternately supporting and retreating from demands for total French withdrawal. As R. M. A. Hankey, British acting head of the Eastern Department in 1945, confirmed, he "did not want the French to be entirely kicked out of the Levant because the British themselves required bases in Syria. If the British moved in as the French moved out, how could the British sincerely maintain that they had no imperialistic aims?"[4]

In both Lebanon and Syria, the war years were marked by conflicts between Vichy-supported forces and those of Anglo-Gaullist backing. In that struggle, retaining control over Syria as over other parts of the French empire was an extension of the conflict that neither power was prepared to abandon. The escalation of the conflict came with French efforts to restore a French presence in Syria and Lebanon, thereby simultaneously warning Anglo-American forces and undermining Syro-Lebanese claimants to independence.[5] By the spring of 1946, the French as well as the British withdrew their forces in the face of widespread local opposition, Syro-Lebanese grievances before the United Nations, and British intervention that was seconded by American support.

In Washington, the U.S. State Department was not indifferent to unfolding events, but criticism of French colonialism aside, there were considerable differences within the State Department and the Division of

Near Eastern and African Affairs as to the viability of Lebanon. This extended to the question of the desirability of having two separate states replace the French mandates. State Department subcommittees dealing with territorial, political, and other dimensions of postwar policy devised plausible scenarios for U.S. policymakers. Philip W. Ireland, William Yale, Wilbur White, Jr., Christina Grant, and Halford Hoskins were among those that provided information for policy, including the future of the Lebanese Maronites.[6] George Wadsworth, then diplomatic agent and consul general, favored the separate independence of the two states in recognition of popular sentiment and his estimate of U.S. interest. It was in the midst of the crises of the mid-1940s that the State Department agreed to the formal recognition of Syrian and Lebanese independence. The date was September 1944. The move reflected Wadsworth's and Henderson's disparaging views of colonial policy and their commitment to a U.S.-supported Lebanese and Syrian independence.[7]

At the time when the U.S. Legation presence was formalized, Washington did not yet have prominent stakes in Beirut, but it was known through its extensive educational activities in Lebanon. Such involvement included seventy-one schools and 11,000 students, in addition to the 2,000 enrolled at the prestigious American University of Beirut, where George Wadsworth had taught in earlier years.[8] By comparison, the scale of the Legation was modest. A single minister was appointed to represent Lebanon and Syria, although there were two separate Legations. George Wadsworth, the key figure at this juncture, made his headquarters in Beirut. There he was assisted by a staff of six officers, who rotated assignments, and an assortment of military, naval, intelligence, labor, and petroleum attachés, indicative of the scope of U.S. activity. Not a formal part of the entourage, ARAMCO and TAPLINE executives were nonetheless at home in this environment, enjoying close relations with the U.S. minister as well as with Lebanese figures interested in petroleum-related matters. As U.S. commercial attaché John Bruins candidly informed Prime Minister Abdallah Yafi in 1953, his function was not to subvert U.S. commercial interests but to protect them.[9] The remark was, of course, in keeping with the functions of the office, but in the Lebanese case it had special meaning. U.S. diplomacy in Lebanon was inseparable from the interests of TAPLINE and ARAMCO.

Three ministers represented the United States in Lebanon's first presidential regime. They were George Wadsworth, Lowell C. Pinkerton, and

Harold Minor. Among them, they spanned the critical era of U.S. policy formulation.

George Wadsworth was diplomatic agent and consul general in Lebanon and Syria between 1942 and 1944, becoming envoy extraordinary and minister plenipotentiary in 1944–1947 and later serving in Iraq, Turkey, Saudi Arabia, and Yemen. Close to ARAMCO-TAPLINE, Wadsworth had an eye for the interests of the American and Lebanese business class, and it was from this perspective that he surveyed the discontent of Lebanese labor, concerned with its destabilizing potential in Lebanon and its negative effect on U.S. corporate interests considering moves to Beirut.

Lowell C. Pinkerton (served 1947–1951) was in Beirut when radical innovations occurred in U.S. oil company relations with major producers that affected U.S. and Anglo-American relations in the entire region. He witnessed the repercussions in Beirut of the famous ARAMCO-Saudi 50/50 deal, as well as the impact of the nationalization crisis in Teheran. But Pinkerton was also sensitive to Lebanese responses to the Palestine conflict, which he knew from firsthand experience in Jerusalem. It was Pinkerton who was in charge as the State Department assumed a more aggressive stance, decrying signs of neutralism and attempting to mobilize friendly regimes.

Harold Minor (served 1951–1953), who eventually became assistant to the vice president of ARAMCO, was minister and then the first U.S. ambasssador to Lebanon, as the Legation was given Embassy status in 1952.[10] Minor was in charge at the time of the presidential transition from Khuri to Sham'un, a period that inaugurated a new phase of Lebanese politics under the aegis of a pronounced pro-American leadership.

In 1946 Secretary of State Byrnes urged George Wadsworth to be forthcoming with recommendations and comments on State Department proposals concerning Lebanon. Byrnes explained that this would be invaluable for an overburdened and understaffed bureaucracy and that it was "part of the plan to prepare regularly, possibly quarterly, a concise document for each country which will summarize current U.S. foreign policy toward that country and the principal items of information concerning it."[11] What Byrnes and his successors in the State Department received in return were Wadsworth's missives with their warnings of the evils of French colonialism and the foibles of the Lebanese elite. Wadsworth's position was that of the State Department, reflecting its posture toward the Gaullist regime.

British officials assessed internal divisions in Beirut in much the same way as did their American colleagues. British Minister Terence Shone maintained that the outlook for democracy in Lebanon was not bright. "Chamber debates, and politics in general, are squabbles between cliques. Centuries of domination or protection, and a common consciousness of minority status, have deprived all but a few Lebanese of any civic spirit or true nationalist feeling."[12] Shone went so far as to argue, as did earlier American consuls, that the Lebanese "requires to be ruled"—although he did not indicate by whom.

Prior to Lebanese independence, U.S. officials in Beirut had expressed considerable doubt about the Lebanese capacity for independence. The theme was reiterated in a variety of communiqués that became more emphatic in the first year after independence, when they were allied to vehement denunciations of French colonial rule. Theodore Marriner, consul general in 1936, found the Lebanese of "sober judgment" afraid of independence as well as republicanism, favoring the continued presence of France as "a guarantee of their independence and of the protection of the Christian communities."[13] There were those inclined toward a monarchical system, provided that the proper prince be found. Lebanon as a future colony of France was a desirable objective in such company. In 1942, Consul General William Gwynn lamented the absence of a sense of civic responsibility necessary "to create a national sentiment freed from all confessional ideas." He was not convinced that Lebanon was a nation, as opposed to a religiously based community. "To think of the Lebanon as a small nation, as Switzerland or Denmark, for example, are small nations, is to commit a fundamental error which must necessarily lead to others. The national sentiment is lacking."[14]

U.S. military attaché Virgil Jackson continued in the same vein in January 1945. Jackson viewed Lebanese politics as a sinister combination of dependency and incompetence. The euphoria of independence had dissipated, leaving in its wake a pro-French privileged class that was satisfied to operate as French agents. French policy options for Lebanon, Jackson opined, would most likely ruin the country by deepening existing cleavages. "Outside of sectarian arguments, main charges against the Government are inefficiency, corruption, dictatorship and nepotism," Jackson maintained.[15] French mandatory rule was condemned for its depoliticization of the Lebanese elite, who were held to be unfit to take responsibility. French influence in the areas of culture and education was, for Jackson, a sign of failure.

Wadsworth himself held the French responsible for the political deficiencies of the new regime. He commissioned a study of French claims to
Syria and Lebanon, arguing that they were merely rationalizations of
power. The kind of history that justified French policies, Wadsworth
declared, was that which "was the servant both of imperialism and of
nationalism and which, rediscovered, rearranged, and re-created the
facts of history to serve the uses of those statesmen and politicians who
rely on a belief in Great Traditions."[16] The message reached Washington,
where Truman contemplated further evidence of French colonial misrule,
as Loy Henderson and Gordon Merriam kept him apprised of the failures of Britain as well as France to deal with the poverty of the region.
Wadsworth reinforced this view in 1946, as he argued that French rule
had been

> a preparation for the perpetuation of French influence along lines sim-
> ilar to that followed in French colonies. The Lebanese who were
> trained in governmental position were either relegated to minor roles
> in the administrative cadre, where responsibility did not enter into the
> picture, or established as puppets in the pseudo-independent picture
> which the French endeavored to maintain in the eyes of the world.[17]

Pinkerton, no less anti-French in outlook, was persuaded that the
object of French policy was to remain in control and to check any possibilities of a British challenge. This was done through the effective political role of the Maronite clergy, Pinkerton affirmed, uninhibited in identifying the origins of its wealth and influence.[18]

After Independence

The critical edge of U.S. Legation commentaries was to change after
independence. French influence continued to be a source of irritation in
Washington, as it was among certain elements in the Lebanese bourgeoisie unconnected to French capital. Similarly, the corruption of "soft
state" rule in Lebanon continued to generate a critical undertow among
U.S. officials in Beirut and Washington. But the shift in emphasis from
the singular focus on the unrepresentative character of Lebanon's political institutions and the privileged quarry of its ruling class was altered in
light of the definition of U.S. interests. The critical refrain did not disappear, but it was overruled. Hence, the evident sympathy for political and
economic reform in Lebanon, which placed the Legation in a position of

supporting Lebanon's dissenting politicians, was checked by the recognition that reform constituted a risk to the ruling class on which the U.S. depended. The immediate subjects at issue, such as confessionalism and the urgency of reform, reflected the change. The meaning and scope of deconfessionalizing Lebanese politics was a perennial subject of controversy in Beirut after independence. Opponents of the intermarriage of confessionalism and politics struck at the heart of the institutionalized privilege of the Christian elite, which explained the regime's resistance.

When Sabri Hamadeh proposed the abolition of confessionalism, it was seen as a ploy by one of Lebanon's most powerful landed Shi'i politicians, who was not so much interested in the secularization of politics as in political retribution. Still, his proposal was taken seriously enough to be reported to the State Department. According to Hamadeh's plan, "considerations of confession shall be abolished from rules, decrees and laws in force concerning elections of moukhtars, municipalities, administrative councils, the Chamber of Deputies and in the distribution of administrative posts. The notation-sect shall be replaced on cards of identity by the notation-nationality: Lebanese."[19] U.S. officers described the project as "revolutionary" and predicted that it would be subjected to great scrutiny by those who stood to lose in the process. The plan was blocked. Some months later, Pinkerton reported on the project, pointing out that the plan was backed by one of the country's more reactionary politicians, albeit a man with enough power to challenge the state. He allegedly had a personal army of some 50,000 villagers that could be mobilized at will.[20] Hamadeh's proposal failed, predictably evoking the routine rejoinder of the Kata'eb that took the form of threatening to move parliament to permit Lebanese emigré representation. Since that emigration was largely Christian, the results would effectively block what Hamadeh sought to achieve.

Such polemics aside, the U.S. Legation clearly supported the idea of electoral reform. At the time of the 1947 parliamentary election, it joined other Lebanese scandalized by the level of corruption. Arguing that the existing system and its false representatives could not survive a popular vote, Legation officers insisted that their election merely sanctified the continuing role of those with power. "By the same token, many outstanding individuals are unable to run on any ticket. With certain rare exceptions, therefore, the same faces will appear in the next Parliament unless the present Chamber has the courage to pass a new law."[21] In mid-April, Pinkerton returned to the aggravated question of confessionalism as one that was fundamental to any significant electoral reform project. In sympathy with political reformers on this issue, the Legation insisted that

> at the basis of all electoral reform, unquestionably, is the desire of most of the electorate to be rid of the bane of confessionalism, that is, of vote according to religion. Jumblatt [Junblat], like many others, desires that the country renounce the apportionment of seats according to faith. While many politicians do not profess so publicly, it is known that they would like to see no more of a division than, say, that between Moslems and Christians, which is approximately equal at the moment.[22]

Was change possible? Legation official Bertel Kuniholm was not an idealist. The electoral system would have to be revised first, he wrote in a statement signed by the resident minister. Otherwise "the same individuals, or their henchmen, will take their places in the Chamber, most of them bound by no electoral promises which need disturb their sleep" (ibid.). In the absence of such systemic changes, Lebanon would have to rely on its younger reformers, "zealots like Jumblatt, Chamoun [Sham'un], and Gemayel [Jemayyel], who alone seem to have a crusader's zeal for the welfare of Lebanon and whose strength is rapidly increasing" (ibid.). All three of these "zealots" were already well-known political figures, familiar to the Legation officials who tended to look on reformers such as Junblat sympathetically, as he struggled with other like-minded colleagues to no avail.

In 1947, U.S. officials tracked the results of an election that came to be identified with scandalous corruption, at the home of the ex-president of the Chamber, Habib Abu Shahla, formerly a critic of TAPLINE and now its attorney. They listened as the director of military intelligence explained how the army and gendarmerie intervened in the elections and how the president had directed Commander in Chief Fu'ad Shihab "to use force to keep opposition supporters from reaching the polling booths. The Beirut Chief of Police expounded on his activities during the elections, disclosing how he had been obliged to use strong-arm methods to insure the victory of the principal metropolitan lists."[23] About twenty new deputies were chosen, and another nine or ten were expected to win in runoff elections. According to the same U.S. sources, these "hardly represent an infusion of new blood, for they have attained their glory only through the purchase of their places on the lists of the stronger political personalities, to whom they are now bound" (ibid.). What had occurred, then, was really "no election at all, since the electorate was simply called upon to pass judgment on lists of candidates which stood, for all practical purposes, without effective opposition." Legation officers noted Junblat as among those who had earlier resigned in protest, describing him as "undoubtedly the ablest young statesman in this country today, [who] had already resigned prior to the polling, since [he felt] that the Government could not guarantee fair elections" (ibid.).

Corruption, manipulation, gerrymandering were only some of the criticisms made of the farcical election.

> The new members of the House, frankly, were nominated and not elected. Many of them represent neither the Lebanese people nor the prevailing political currents of the nation. Even geography was flouted and deputies were elected, by pre-arrangement, from districts where they have no roots whatsoever. There is no effective opposition; whatever there is of protest and censure will have to come henceforth from outside of Parliament. Under the existing electoral law, there was probably little else to be expected than the imposition of single lists. What was not expected, however, was so obvious and brutal an interference on the part of the group in power. So, until Parliament can be prevailed upon to change the electoral law and the machinery of elections, there will be no forum for the Lebanese people to express its opinion.   (Ibid.)

The *Black Book of the Lebanese Elections*, issued on May 25, 1947, told all with respect to scandals and their authors. It was the manifesto of the politically aggrieved who were joined in the growing anti-Khurist coalition. The same text appeared in the mail of the State Department on the eve of the 1951 parliamentary election, sent by a Lebanese-American Maronite clergyman hoping thereby to obtain support for disenchanted Maronite constituencies in the United States and Lebanon.[24]

By the end of summer 1947, Legation reports were little short of disdainful and pessimistic on political prospects in Lebanon. Not violence but good government was the antidote that Lebanon desperately needed—so Legation officers convincingly argued.

> There is no antidote but good government and political freedom which could satisfy public opinion today provided a vociferous opposition can be said to represent public opinion, nothing, short of a miracle, can throw the present Government out of power. Only a revolution involving the use of force, and embracing the Army and Gendarmerie, could possibly change the situation.[25]

Such expressions were doubtless genuine, but they were irrelevant in the light of the policy articulated by the Legation. The legacy of critical reports did not end at this point. On the contrary, such reports represent a continuing strain in U.S. Legation-Embassy and State Department reporting on Lebanon. But the reports were overruled. In 1947, the same year in which the above statement was issued, the pendulum had swung in the opposite direction as Legation officials came to appreciate the reasons for supporting confessionalism. These were not confessional in origin but political. The power elite was largely Christian. To unseat its representatives was tantamount to upsetting the balance whose benefits U.S. officials in Beirut understood. The business elite with which it was engaged was not exclusively Christian, but the operative principle was the same. To alter the balance of power by severing the link of confession and politics, which meant fundamental reform in the electoral and political systems, risked undermining the existing political class. This, and not the possibility of a "rising tide of Islam" that would envelop Lebanon, as Legation officer Kuniholm argued, was the central concern.[26] Anxieties about Islam provided a suitable rationalization, one that was to be used for future public consumption.

Labor relations in Beirut, which were closely observed by U.S. officials in accord with U.S. and Anglo-American interests in containing radical trade union movements, as the Anglo-American Pentagon talks of 1947 confirmed, illustrate the logic of U.S. policy. It was hardly the search for good government or political freedom that was disclosed in the cynical appreciation of Lebanese labor policy. U.S. Legation officers understood how Lebanese officials controlled the trade union movement in 1946, if not earlier. However, 1946 was a particularly critical year for the labor movement in Lebanon, as its leaders pressed the regime to adopt a labor code that, to judge by U.S. observations on the subject, was more than justified by existing conditions. But this was also the year in which the Legation submitted a report indicating how the Ministry of the Interior controlled the labor movement, a process whose objective was not to promote good labor relations, let alone good labor conditions, but simply to promote a politically reliable and compliant movement.

It was the Ministry of the Interior that screened applications requesting certification, which provided it with the power to block those it wished to exclude. Under existing arrangements, anticommunist ideologues in the Kata'eb, along with other political operatives, volunteered their services as informants and strong-arm assistants to assure implementation of government regulations. The role of the Kata'eb in such activities doubtless impressed those U.S. officials bent on assuring an anticommunist thrust in Lebanese politics, irrespective of what Legation officers described on other occasions as the party's fascist and separatist orientation.

What is one to conclude with respect to U.S. attitudes toward Lebanese politics at this period? The answer is to be found in the uneven weight attached to the alternating currents of criticism and conformity that punctuated U.S. reports on Lebanon. Those that were critical shed light on Lebanese conditions but not on U.S. policy, which unquestionably tilted in favor of conformism and the status quo. The alternating currents remained a feature of the inside talk of U.S. officials and was consistently at odds with U.S. policy. In 1948, the State Department's State-War-Navy Coordinating Committee judged Lebanon to be a valuable asset.[27]

Economic Indulgence

The contradictory impulses at the political level were no less apparent on the economic plane, where they issued into a common fate. Thus sharply critical assessments of the limits of Lebanon's excessive individualism gave way to an appreciation of the indices of economic growth and their compatibility with postwar U.S. economic interests.

> The private enterprise and property system has been badly abused through a general lack of social progressiveness on the part of the moneyed interests with which the government is identified. Trade and communication with the west has been beneficial, but undue devotion to mercantile and brokerage pursuits has created a one-sided entrepôt economy favoring the merchant class to the neglect of internal agricultural and industrial developments which could, if properly conceived and carried out, bring benefits to labor and farm groups.[28]

It was, however, the lopsided emphasis on trade and communication in the Lebanese entrepôt economy that enriched its ruling class, and appealed to U.S. commercial and corporate interests, including those involved in oil and aviation. Such attraction made the potential instability of harsh economic conditions for Lebanese workers a matter of concern. State Department reports in February 1951 that were based on U.S. military sources in Beirut indicated that wages of unskilled workers were

$0.56 for eight to ten hours of work.[29] In the previous month, the State Department urged that "wherever practicable we should encourage liberal reforms and if necessary direct any technical or financial aid we extend in a manner calculated to give the greatest support to those elements in the Lebanese Government willing and able to introduce progressive measures as opposed to those seeking their own aggrandizement or enrichment."[30] To those who had doubted the commitment to progressive change, the statement affirmed the need for a greater American commitment to economic equality, and identified particularly vulnerable sectors needing reform—taxation, welfare, farm labor, and white-collar and industrial policy.

In December 1945, Clayton Lane, the American commercial attaché who later attacked Lebanese officials for their laxity on communism, was imbued with a reformist zeal. The object of his disclosures was the unethical practices of the Khuri regime. His exposé provided a list of those individuals and firms identified as suspects. They represented the elite members of the Lebanese commercial class, and soon-to-be-favored U.S. commercial and political allies. In the winter of 1945, Lane met with Prime Minister Sami Bey Sulh of Lebanon to discuss Lebanese requests for U.S. economic assistance. The exchange was prefaced by Sami Bey's grievances about the state of the Lebanese economy, which Lane duly absorbed. On purely economic matters, the U.S. attaché pointedly added a list of projects of particular interest to the United States, such as the expansion of Beirut's international airport, which was a prerequisite for U.S. carriers' landing in Beirut. But in his report to the State Department, Lane had a good deal more to say, much of it uncomplimentary with respect to Suhl, whom he accused of deception.[31] Also minister of national economy, the prime minister was directly responsible for the Lebanese Supply Department, which charged exorbitant customs duties on major products. There was a 30 percent tax on imported goods "collected in kind" and then "put at the disposal of the Supply Department, now a part of the Ministry of National Economy of which Sami Bey Sulh is the responsible head" (ibid.). Lane reported that the "Department's warehouses were recently sealed to make an inventory of the stocks, particularly of bread cereals. Black market sales of bread cereals are large and there has been no distribution of these commodities by the Supply Department for several weeks. Stocks of textile goods and 350 tons of peanut oil are reliably said to have disappeared from the Supply Department stores" (ibid.).

Clayton Lane provided Washington with a list of those individuals and firms that benefited from such arrangements. They were a veritable who's who of influential Lebanese, including the president's son, Khalil, and brother, Fu'ad Khuri, head of the Etablissements Derviche Y. Haddad, and one of the principal importers of iron and steel, owner of a factory that produced cement, tile, and concrete, and a board member and stockholder of a glassmaking and cement factory.

There were other importers of iron and steel, such as the Sahnawi family, former ministers of finance and parliamentary deputies in Damascus. There was the firm exporting raw silk, Fils de S. Kattar, which included the president of the Lebanese Industrial Chamber, who was also a board member of the influential Banque Misr-Syrie-Liban. The Kittaneh were here as well, among major importers of U.S. automotive products along with pharmaceutical drugs, dyes, and other items to Lebanon, Syria, Iraq, Iran, and Saudi Arabia. "Reported to have influence through the relationship with the President of the Republic (the eldest brother, Francis, who has been in the United States for several years and established there, is married to the niece of the Lebanese President's wife" (ibid.).

In 1945–1946 Lane and others in the Legation were openly sympathetic to reformist politicians keen on economic reform and development policies.[32] They reported to Washington on those who recognized the need for diversification of the economy, such as the assistant director of the Lebanese Ministry of National Economy, Na'im Amyuni, who emphasized that "prosperity cannot come through trade alone; indiscriminate imports are damaging, they cannot be continued and nobody is prepared to help Lebanon sustain them" (ibid.). When Kamal Junblat resigned from the Ministry of National Economy, Pinkerton cabled Washington with the news that his resignation would constitute a major loss, since he had

> a constructive economic program, energy, social imagination, courage and forthrightness [that] had in only six months of office made him most widely respected and admired personality in Lebanon, though youngest Minister and without previous experience in office. His political and personal integrity made him impatient, perhaps excessively, of inertia and obstruction of his older and less progressive colleagues.[33]

Pinkerton similarly considered the loss of such critics as regrettable, particularly since they were prone to be pro-American.

In 1946 George Wadsworth warned the State Department not to ignore Lebanon's precarious economy since it would lead to domestic instability and nullify conditions necessary for American business. He provided the evidence to make his case, but he remained staunchly opposed to labor legislation that would adversely affect Lebanese entrepreneurs. Over the ten-year period 1936 to 1946, wages lagged far behind the cost of living and labor unrest was pervasive. Perhaps Lebanon was in a better situation than postwar Europe or Asia, Wadsworth conceded, but he reported on the "bare subsistence many workers on very high-priced bread, which is basic fare of working classes, and growing unemployment are causing increased insistence on government actions. Response to Communist leadership if not to doctrine is apparently increasing."[34]

But it was also Wadsworth who cautioned against supporting the passage of labor legislation that might be adverse for business. "While much improvement real wages and workers standard of living is warranted on social grounds and by political expediency, labor bill proposals unless much amended would materially increase production costs, obstruct export recovery, and check production and restoration economic balance." Such a balance, he pointed out, was basically unattainable unless workers agreed to lower living standards. Hence, he recommended a cut in basic subsidies. Yet Wadsworth recognized that the "drift is toward serious labor troubles," a situation that would promote political instability, thereby "increasing influence of communists; and more obstacles to establishment of American assembly plants and other enterprises seeking low production costs and stability." Under the circumstances, Wadsworth requested that the U.S. Department of Commerce inform the interested parties—General Motors and Libby, McNeil and Libby, among others—that the climate was adverse for U.S. manufacturing and industrial interests.

In 1948, the State Department's State-War-Navy-Coordinating Committee offered its own evaluation of Lebanese independence in the light of continued French financial influence. "The indirect but effective control of the French over the Lebanese monetary system, the scarcity of hard currencies, the operation of concessionary companies, as well as the continuation of the wartime inflated economy, are problems which would present a severe challenge to any government, however stable."[35]

Who Rules? The Anatomy of Power and Wealth

In the summer of 1947 the State Department received euphoric cables from Beirut about the outlook of the Lebanese mercantile bourgeoisie, emphasizing its devotion to capitalism and the United States. The chief of the Legation, Lowell C. Pinkerton, and his officers monitored economic trends in Beirut, noting the resilience and political influence of these committed capitalists. Informal contacts between Legation officers and members of the Lebanese elite provided regular occasions that served to educate U.S. officials as to the general orientation, ideological outlook, and economic views of those involved. Such visits, moreover, inevitably served to make the connections necessary for effective political reporting.[36] Before U.S. Treasury Department representative Judd Polk's visit to Beirut in 1947, then, the Legation was well informed about the character of the Beirut economic enclave. Polk himself appears to have been pleased with the discovery that Beirut's cosmopolitan, commercial bourgeoisie spoke a common language.[37]

In the context of the evolving analysis of Lebanon's political economy by members of the Legation, the timing of this visit and the more general reappraisal of the Lebanese bourgeoisie are significant. Developments in Washington, from the Truman Doctrine to the Marshall Plan and the National Security Act, doubtless contributed to the positive reappraisal of some of the most influential members of the Lebanese bourgeoisie, hitherto criticized in Legation reports for their corrupt practices and social indifference. There were other intervening developments, such as those bearing on TAPLINE, whose importance cannot be ignored. Offsetting the effects of the critical assessments of the Lebanese system were other appraisals that revealed an intimate familiarity with the operations and achievements of the Lebanese ruling class. It was not its penchant for economic or political reform that emerged from such compilations, but the sources of its power and wealth. Among the most succinct statements to be produced on the subject by Legation officers was the report titled "The Political Control Exercised by the Commercial Class in Lebanon," written by economic officer Samuel O. Ruff.[38] It appeared in January 1952, on the eve of Kamil Sham'un's accession to the presidency and at the opening of a new phase in Lebanon-U.S. relations. Ruff provided an appropriate summation of the economic "miracle" of Lebanon's first independent regime, including the role of French capital and its penetrating influence on the political economy of Besharah al-Khuri's ruling

class. The crisis of Khurist economic policy was marked by the demise of
the French connection, a cause of evident celebration in U.S. circles in
Beirut. Singularly free of moralistic pronouncements, though armed with
a deadpan iconoclasm, Ruff provided the rudiments of a portrait of the
Lebanese ruling class that remains invaluable in interpreting U.S. policies.

Relying on statistics assembled when the Syro-Lebanese customs
union was still in operation, i.e., prior to 1950, Ruff argued that Lebanese
commerce had grown at least 60 percent in volume between 1938 and
1941. Examining figures since 1946, and excluding transit oil figures, the
commercial sector, which was valued at LL86,687,000 in 1946, was
assessed at LL366,495,000 in 1950. In 1951, the first year following the
dissolution of the Syro-Lebanese customs union, Lebanese commercial
activity measured in terms of volume was 90 percent of what it had been
in the previous year. "Since these statistics include no record of the large
smuggling traffic, they are further limited for our purpose," Legation officer Ruff added. But, limits aside, he concluded that "the increase in transit trade is well over 200 percent," the result of factors that included the
benefits derived from the Arab boycott of Israel, as well as the expansion
of the oil economies of the Gulf, i.e., Saudi Arabia, Kuwait, and Bahrein
(p. 111). Lebanon's situation between Israel and the Gulf was not lost on
the State Department, as its political implications were no less important
than their economic impact. What accounted for Lebanon's growth?
Who was responsible for its economic policies? Samuel Ruff estimated
that the keys to its success rested on three assets: capital accumulation,
monetary policies, and tourism.

> These assets have added wealth and esprit to the commercial commu-
> nity. The leaders have strong convictions with regard to commercial
> policy and now exercise a degree of political control which has mani-
> fested itself in a series of free trade facilities. They include all policies
> that enhance Beirut as a commercial capital in the Near East; a free
> trade policy, a free money market, a policy of low import duties, a
> sound money policy, and a regional tourist policy designed to extend
> Lebanese markets in the Middle East.   (p. 112)

Free trade and free enterprise in the vocabulary of Lebanon's financial
and commerical bourgeoisie, as Samuel Ruff explained, entailed a
shrewd control of domestic markets and an uncanny ability to exploit
wartime profiteering, warehouse stocking with its hoarding of scarce
commodities, monopolistic practices, and smuggling, among other

things. Nor was tourism quite as straightforward an operation as it first appeared to be. Though some 25,000 annual visitors were reported from the Arab League states alone, Ruff noted that they came "because of the attractive schedule of transportation payments which has been worked out by the Lebanese Government. Lebanese importers escort these visitors to the Free Port and show them stocks on hand which can be brought at low competitive prices" (p. 111).

Three individuals were considered key to the success of Lebanon's economic policies: Michel Chiha, Husayn 'Uwayni, and René Busson. The first, already identified as one of the architects of the modern state, was committed to Lebanon's pursuit of a trade-centered liberal economy. Rationalizing such in terms of Lebanon's historic role as regional entrepôt, the current international division of labor, and the absence of resources, Chiha and others were also concerned to avoid the social ills of industrialized societies.

> Commercial figures know that they cannot compete with the manufactures of Great Britain, France, and the United States. Industrial expansion that yielded profits in war years is a serious embarrassment now when the Lebanese cannot find markets for high priced industrial surpluses. They do not want to see the creation of an industrial class, with its problems of employment and unemployment. They consider industrialization a breeding ground for many problems including communism.   (p. 126)

But even within the elite, there was a minority view that dissented, strongly endorsing an increase in local manufacturing and industry as fully within the nation's capacity.

Husayn 'Uwayni was credited with initiating the free trade and monetary policies that found support in presidential circles. Samuel Ruff regarded 'Uwayni's initiatives as being responsible for Lebanon's unique status in the region. With a steady supply of dollars, sterling, francs, and gold, Beirut's financial elite were able to maneuver with extraordinary agility, dramatically increasing the currency in circulation. Illegal wartime transactions, including gold smuggling, confirmed this. The lesson that the influential men of Lebanese business and politics drew from such experience was that they needed "complete freedom for the rapidity of decision and boldness of enterprise that yields profit. They must have freedom to deal with the West since the West is their source of manufactured goods" (p. 126).

As minister of finance in 1948, Husayn 'Uwayni was well placed to implement such policies, operating within the presidential orbit, where he was linked to French capital and Saudi interests. He had worked for Ibn Sa'ud for some twenty years, according to Samuel Ruff, arranging the exchange of dollars for gold on behalf of the Saudi royal house, through his role as director of the Banque Indochine in Jidda. In addition to the contacts that 'Uwayni had with TAPLINE, he was viewed by the delegation as a potential supporter of U.S. development proposals in Lebanon, such as the Litany River project. In short, in spite of his role within the presidential orbit with its French connections, he was regarded as open to U.S. interests. In January 1952, Ruff concluded that "he actually represents the type of Lebanese leader who is assuming greater importance with the decline of the French" (p. 113). In 1958, he was one of four ministers to emerge in Fu'ad Shihab's post–civil war cabinet, in whose formation U.S. officials played a significant role.

Competing in terms of his impact on postwar Lebanon's economic growth was René Busson, the single most powerful figure in the presidential circle and the key to French economic influence in Beirut. Before Busson's demise, Ruff judged him to be the "strongest financial figure in Lebanon occupying a position of influence even greater than that of any of the seven men in the Presidential circle" (p. 130). René Busson was, in fact, at the center of interlocking interests that guaranteed French capital unparalleled access for Lebanese and extra-Lebanese activities. As director of the Banque de Syrie et du Liban (BSL), which functioned as Lebanon's bank of issue, Busson was uniquely situated to influence development projects in both Lebanon and Syria. In Beirut, the BSL was involved in lucrative development projects, such as the construction of Beirut airport, numerous public buildings, and insurance companies. Busson was additionally involved in SERIAC (Société d'Etudes et de Réalisations Industrielles, Agricoles, et Commerciales), an organization that caused much consternation among British and American diplomats.

(Incidentally, the attorney for SERIAC, former cabinet minister Hamid Franjiyyah, and Fu'ad Khuri, brother of the president, were accused of vastly overcharging for materials used in this and other construction projects. The charge made them vulnerable to criticisms of high-level corruption, from which the president himself was not excluded.) Busson, meanwhile, was also active in establishing one of the major insurance companies operating in the country, Ittihad al-Watani.

The banker, financier, and entrepreneur was adept at bringing in French concessions, thus guaranteeing sizable profits. 'Uwayni was in a position to benefit from these arrangements as director of the Saudi-based bank connected with the BSL and as a result of his connections with Busson's financed insurance complex.

In his graphic reconstruction, Ruff conceived of Lebanon's economy in terms of three concentric circles, with President Khuri at the center. Those in the first circle, which was the most powerful, were distinguished by three interlocking conditions: their wealth, their affiliation with French capital, and their access to the president. Family ties were a key.

> Marriage or blood relationships with the President is a factor of spe- cial importance in the composition of the group since five of the seven members are thus related to the President. Fouad Khoury is the President's brother; Khalil el-Khoury is his son. Jean Fattal and Francis Kettaneh are each married to nieces of the President's wife, who is a Chiha. Henri Pharaon [Far'oun] is a partner of Michel Chiha, brother of the President's wife, and Michel Chiha married Henri Pharaon's sister.   (p. 127)

Those included in the first circle were 'Uwayni, then Fu'ad and Khalil Khuri, respectively brother and son of the president; Henri Far'oun, brother-in-law of the president and Chiha's partner in the Bank of Far'oun and Chiha; Michel Doumit; Jean Fattal; Alfred Kittaneh and family. Men of exceptional personal wealth, connected through family ties to the president's family, they were linked to French capital through Busson's banking establishment and insurance networks. Their place in this inner sphere gave them an advantage with respect to exceptional favors in their business ventures, speculations, investments, and con- tracts. Collectively, though not exclusively, the members of the first cir- cle represented the core of the Lebanese financial class that constituted one of the prime pillars of presidential power.

The president's son and brother held privileged places in this circle, son Khalil Khuri through his role with French concessionary companies that retained him—at exorbitant fees—as their attorney. The fact that such companies paid no taxes, as opposed to their Lebanese counter- parts, was a matter of public indignation. And the fact that the Litany River project, which was part of U.S. Point IV in Lebanon, proposed to make electric power available at much cheaper rates did little to endear Khuri to the United States.

Fu'ad Khuri was equally well situated to enrich himself on contracts for major construction projects, such as those involved in the international airport and the new Posts and Telegraph Building. Furthermore, he was in a position to assign lucrative projects to those who were also identified with French commercial interests, as in the case of the SERIAC project.

Among others of prominence in this first circle was Henri Far'oun, a man of inherited wealth with considerable real estate holdings in Beirut whose financial reputation rested on his role as banker and partner of Michel Chiha, one of the architects of the Lebanese state and a brother of the president's wife. Deeply rooted in the inner circles of the Khuri presidential milieu, which defined Far'oun as a high-ranking member of French financial orbit, he was known to U.S. officers in the Legation as particularly well disposed toward the United States.

With comparable connections on this top level, Michel Doumit was also part of the French group identified with the Banque Indochine, involved in real estate and one of the contractors associated with the Beirut International Airport, a project in which U.S. officials were keenly interested, as its expansion was a prerequisite for the landing of U.S. carriers committed to developing Lebanese air routes. There was an additional connection that linked Doumit to U.S. interests, notably his political relationship with Habib Abu Shahla, the attorney who was invaluable for TAPLINE in Lebanon.

In addition, among these elite was Jean Fattal, who was in control of the largest pharmaceutical import firm in the region, "credited with having created the typhoid epidemic hoax in Syria in 1950 which led to the sale of large quantities of typhus antitoxin" (p. 115).

The Kittaneh family, regarded as among the wealthiest in the country, was related through marriage to President Khuri. Linked with Busson's financial and insurance establishment, the firm, known as F. A. Kittaneh, was associated with French concessions as well as American firms. Francis, the oldest member of the family, was a U.S. citizen. In Beirut, there were other siblings who were partners and managers and a sister and brother-in-law who functioned as "silent partners."[39] As the agent for more than fifty U.S. companies throughout the Middle East, the company had headquarters in Beirut, with branches in Damascus, Aleppo, Baghdad, Teheran, Cairo, Jerusalem, and Jidda. It exported wool, tobacco, and olive oil and imported "motor vehicles, automobile spare parts and accessories, tires, electrical appliances and equipment, iron and steel, industrial machinery, pharmaceuticals, heavy chemicals, and dyestuffs." In addition, the Kittanehs owned the Egyptian-based Chemifa-Cicurel and Company and held controlling shares in other companies in Palestine and Baghdad.

Francis Kittaneh, along with Charles Malik, was active in pressing for closer Lebanon-U.S. political ties in Washington in the late 1940s, a subject discussed in the chapters that follow. Francis Kittaneh's connections with U.S. corporate and financial institutions gave him an entrée to the corridors of political power in Washington and New York, where he was among the few Lebanese, with Charles Malik (whose mentor was Michel Chiha), to address the Council on Foreign Relations, the meeting place of U.S. corporate and political leaders.

The second major circle of Lebanon's commercial and financial class included those with significant ties to French capital, though less closely affiliated with President Khuri. Like their peers in the first group, their commercial operations were not confined to Lebanon. George Karam was the largest wood and lumber importer, obtaining his products from the United States, Sweden, and primarily Romania. Michel Sahnawi et Fils, invested in Air Liban as well as other French firms, was the premier importer of steel from Belgium, Luxembourg, France, and the United States during World War II. The firm profited from its iron and steel purchases made at the time of the Korean War. The Legation report asserted that Sahnawi's stocks, "maintained at a constant level, are a tremendous asset to the Near East now that steel is in short supply throughout the world."[40]

Michel Kattar and his brothers, associated with Air Liban and stockholders in the Union Nationale, were identified with the sale of silk reelers and the manufacture of woolen cloth. Gabriel Trad, and Robert and Pierre Sabbagh, represented significant banking interests. The Trad and Company bank, of Ottoman origin, had been integrated with the Crédit Lyonnais, which it had previously represented, while the Sabbaghs rolled the old Banque Sabbagh into the powerful exchange bank, Banque Indochine. One of the Sabbagh brothers was 85 percent owner of the water concession, Compagnie des Eaux de Beyrouth, which produced an annual income sufficient to manage both the Banque Indochine and the Banque Commercial Italia.

Joseph Khadige, a prime informant on French financial connections in Lebanon, according to Ruff, was an importer of French commodities and luxury items who operated in Paris and Lyon, and was president of the Merchants' Association in Beirut. Joseph and Nicola Salem had worked in construction with TAPLINE and were owners of the Coca-Cola plant in Lebanon. Joseph was part of the Busson insurance group and a board member of the Compagnie des Eaux as well as the Banque de Syrie et du Liban.

The third circle included major figures in the manufacturing, agricultural, industrial, and real estate sectors. It included the Essayli, of textile fame, and the 'Arida family, in textiles and real estate. In this instance, in spite of marital connections with the presidential family (George 'Arida's daughter was married to the son of Besharah al-Khuri), they were not part of the inner circle, perhaps because George 'Arida "spent LL3,000,000 purchasing Hitler's yacht" (p. 120). Patriarch 'Arida, who was for a considerable period in charge of the Maronite Church's funds, was invested in real estate in Beirut as well as Sydney, Australia, a stockholder in the French power concession in Tripoli, and sponsor of the Chekka Cement Plant, in which the president's brother Fu'ad played a dominant role.

Sa'eb Salam, a major political as well as economic force who additionally represented the interests of the Sunni bourgeoisie, rose to become prime minister. Known as a supporter of industrialization, which put him at odds with the financial and mercantile class who opposed such initiatives, Salam was not identified with French capital.

Associated with a variety of enterprises, including a "vegetable oil hydrogenation plant," and real estate ventures that capitalized on the Beirut International airport project, Salam played a part in the creation of Middle East Airlines (MEA) that contributed significantly to the enhancement of his power, as well as that of the Lebanese bourgeoisie. MEA's role in linking Beirut and the Gulf effectively expanded the economic reach of the new petro-princes in Beirut, much as it consolidated the relationship of Beirut to the Eastern Arab oil producers. The connection attracted attention in Washington. Pan American Airways, which became MEA's U.S. affiliate, and U.S. oil interests rapidly recognized its potential. Salam reportedly visited the United States in 1952 to consult with the Chase National Bank, the second-highest-ranking bank in the United States, to encourage it to open a Beirut office. Chase was subsequently the first U.S. bank to enter the Beirut field.

Others in the third circle included such figures as Emile Bustani, Assad Jabre, Elie Abu Jawdeh, Ahmad Da'ouk, H. G. Tufenkdjian, and the Sursuk. Of these, Bustani, though associated with the IPC and British interests, had connections with TAPLINE and was well known in U.S.

Legation circles. Tufenkdjian was the U.S. Oldsmobile agent in Lebanon. Abu Jawdeh was also connected with TAPLINE, and Da'ouk held political office and appointments, the first as deputy to the Lebanese parliament and the second as ambassador to France. The Sursuks, major landowners in Palestine who had sold thousands of acres to the Zionist movement prior to 1948, were invested in Beirut "real estate, apartment houses, the race track, etc." Samuel Ruff estimated that their social standing had not diminished in spite of their relative economic decline. Moreover, their political connections were sufficiently intact to allow Alexander Sursuk to obtain a position on the electoral list.

Lebanon's commercial class was not limited to the above. It included approximately 150 to 200 individuals whose wealth ranged from LL500,000 to LL1,000,000. Those at the core who were closest to the president, however, represented the highest concentrations of wealth and capital, amounting in 1948 to 40 percent of the national budget.[41]

However incomplete, the value of Ruff's unsentimental portrait lies in its content and authorship. The capsule analysis of the distinguishing features and personalities of the Lebanese economy in the formative period of the state, as assessed by a well-informed U.S. Legation officer, is suggestive on two interrelated levels. First, it clarifies relations of class and power in the Besharah al-Khuri regime in the period of continuing French financial influence; second, it explains the function of confessionalism. The latter emerged as a safeguard of multiconfessional ruling-class interests. As Ruff observed, "While other aspects of Lebanese politics have religious overtones, the political attitude of the commercial class is primarily secular. Maronites, Greek Orthodox believers, Sunni Moslems, Shia Moslems and Druzes, resolve their differences and combine harmoniously for profitable transactions."[42]

What emerged from Samuel Ruff's analysis was both a portrait of the Lebanese ruling class and a map of the class base on which U.S. policy relied. The two coincided. By the late 1940s, the attractions of a largely secularized and competitive mercantile and financial bourgeoisie with unlimited access to state power and a growing interest in U.S. capital were irresistible. In this context, the opposition to continuing French financial control was a welcome phenomenon to Washington, particularly since it was untainted by nationalist zeal and hostility to foreign capital investment.[43] The ensuing marriage of convenience guaranteed that the accompanying characteristics of the class and system on which it relied, including existing confessional arrangements and the eminently porous "weak state," would not be a matter of undue concern to U.S. interests or policymakers. The evolution of U.S. policy does not belie this conclusion.

By the end of 1951, as the decline of French economic influence became evident, U.S. officials saw an opportunity for the United States. As the U.S. chargé d'affaires recommended to Washington, the United States should offer Lebanon's minister of finance, Philippe Taqla, U.S. fiscal experts and assistance under the mutual security program. The Legation requested the State Department's reaction to such a proposal.

> Leg requests Dept's reaction as to whether it desires to promote Amer interests in this manner and if so, to what extent we are prepared to take advantage of this turn of events. Since Leb wld doubtless be slow to request our aid, best means of approach, if Dept so authorizes wld be to sound out Takla informally. During his recent term as FonMin he was quite friendly to US and, as Dept is aware, is protege of Pres of Leb.[44]

Dean Acheson adopted a somewhat cautious position. There was, after all, the unfinished matter of the Friendship, Commerce, and Navigation Treaty, which was a major irritant to Washington and, for opposite reasons, to Lebanese officials. But in the face of favorable internal and pressing external developments, such obstacles did not prove insurmountable.

5

The Foundations of U.S. Policy, PACLIFT: Petroleum, Aviation, Commerce, Labor, Intelligence, and the Friendship Treaty

Notify After Burning: Petroleum, Pipelines, and Refineries

When Secretary of State Acheson recommended caution in responding to the demise of René Busson and its implications for Lebanon's political and economic orientation, he did so with a purpose. There was no benefit to be gained from antagonizing the French at this juncture, nor was there anything to be gained by appearing to the Syrians or Lebanese to be overeager to replace French influence in the Levant. Moreover, by 1951 American economic interests were well established in Lebanon. The key features, oil and aviation interests, were clearly defined and unconditionally accepted by the Lebanese regime. In the same year the Korean War persuaded U.S. international oil companies of the urgency of maintaining access and control over Middle Eastern petroleum resources. Under the direction of Under Secretary of State George McGhee, who was among its oil experts, the United States pressured the Khuri regime to adopt a more forthcoming posture vis-à-vis U.S. foreign policy. U.S. policy at the last stage of the Besharah al-Khuri regime can be interpreted in the light of these developments. But the reality of U.S.-Lebanese commercial relations, referring to oil and aviation, was not contested in the Khuri regime or in that of its successor.

By 1951, Lebanon had become an "asset" in U.S. Middle East policy by virtue of its transit role for TAPLINE-ARAMCO. MEDRECO, the

Mediterranean Refining Company (owned by the California Texas Corporation, a subsidiary of the Texas Company and Standard Oil of California, which were joined in CALTEX), promised to construct a refinery at Sidon for ARAMCO oil coming from Saudi Arabia. The impact of TAPLINE, its lucrative tanker traffic and multiplier effects in the Lebanese economy, and the related role of Lebanon's Middle East Airlines in expanding Lebano-Gulf commercial and tourist relations, influenced the course of Lebanon's postwar economy, its domestic politics, and foreign relations—including those with the United States. In the Besharah al-Khuri period, these relations were primarily, but not exclusively, economic in character.

According to the 1952 annual petroleum report issued by the Legation, "Lebanon's principal petroleum activity is to serve as a transit and export point for Saudi Arabian and Iraq crude oil."[1] Through Lebanon passed 78 percent of Saudi and Iraqi crude, on its way to Western Europe, and approximately 22 percent going to the United States and Canada. Lebanon was part of the transport revolution that cut the cost of tanker transport by 50 to 75 percent while increasing the political rent value of its territory, along with that of the region. Lebanon's relations with U.S. oil interests and with Saudi Arabia and the Gulf were further underscored by the role of MEA and its U.S. affiliate, Pan American Airways.

Without the regime's acquiescence in accepting the concessions offered by TAPLINE and MEDRECO, the TAPLINE terminal at Sidon would have been inaccessible, its American and U.S.-connected tankers would have had to operate under far less favorable circumstances, and U.S. aviation traffic between Lebanon and the Gulf would have been hindered. Lebanon's role was undeniably significant, but its capacity to influence its share of profits was marginal.

Negotiations over TAPLINE were simultaneously local and regional affairs. They afforded U.S. international oil companies, as well as the State Department that protected them, an entry into politics on both levels. While Lebanon's transit function undeniably gave it leverage, the advantages of that leverage readily gave way before the reality of cartel policies and Lebanon's de facto integration into the structure of U.S.-dominated regional oil politics.

Such conclusions in no way undermine the proposition that Lebanon's political economy was transformed in the process. That Lebanon's service economy profited by its incorporation into the regional oil economy controlled by U.S. companies and protected by the U.S. government is beyond debate. The connection integrated Lebanon into the network of U.S. Middle East interests that linked Washington to Dhahran and the Gulf. For the Lebanese bourgeoisie who benefited from these arrangements and their extension to the parallel areas of aviation and commerce, the profits were considerable. The broader political consequences of this relationship, however, involved the subordination of the Lebanese political economy to the allied strategies of U.S. oil and diplomacy in the Middle East.

The foundations of U.S.-Lebanese relations in Lebanon's first regime after independence rested on PACLIFT, an acronym for petroleum, aviation, commerce, labor, intelligence, and the Friendship Treaty (full name: Friendship, Commerce, and Navigation Treaty—FCN). Petroleum held first place. U.S. international oil companies were in the Middle East prospecting for options for pipeline locations even before the availability of steel to construct them was assured. Palestine, Transjordan, Lebanon, and Syria were among the states considered. In 1946, John Loftus, head of the State Department's Petroleum Division, urged caution with respect to transit concessions and fees, warning of the importance of recognizing the political sensibilities of those concerned. On July 30, George Wadsworth cabled Secretary of State James Byrnes with news that the ARAMCO representative, William Lenahan, had arrived in Beirut with the purpose of negotiating concessions with the Lebanese and Syrian regimes. As head of the American Legation, Wadsworth was handling the formalities and introductions.

The key issue was compensation. Wadsworth was biased in favor of having the pipeline pass through Lebanon, a decision that was in the hands of the U.S. international oil companies themselves. In conveying his views on the question, Wadsworth indirectly affirmed the "presumption that Lebanon is least likely of Arab states to manifest xenophobic tendencies in treatment of foreign capital investment."[2] Within less than a month, the concession for TAPLINE had been approved, as had bilateral air accords between the United States and Lebanon.

Such were some of the subjects itemized in the Legation's response to Byrnes in the summer of 1946. At the time, Under Secretary Dean Acheson requested the Legation's assessment of the status of U.S. interests as embodied in PACLIFT. In the process, Acheson took the opportunity to complement the chargé d'affaires in Beirut, Bertel Eric Kuniholm, for his valuable reports, indicating that they were important in policy formation. Acheson obviously wanted a regular exchange with U.S. officers in the field, as well as complete discretion, explaining "in this connection, please burn immediately the March 1 issues of the Statements on Syria and Lebanon and notify us, in transmitting your comment, that this has been done."[3]

The Legation's response followed the itemization of the State Department's subject matter along the following lines: (a) commerce, tariff, monetary, investment, and development policies; (b) petroleum; (c) aviation; (d) intelligence; and (e) assessment of local attitudes toward the USSR.

The first set (a) concerned Lebano-Syrian economic relations and the continuing influence of France; the second (b and c) addressed U.S. economic interests; the third (d and e) invoked changes in intelligence planning for the region and queried Lebanese attitudes toward the USSR. The most opaque element remained intelligence, although the move of the Office of Strategic Services (predecessor of the CIA) from Cairo to Beirut was instructive in itself. And Intelligence agents such as Miles Copeland, Wilbur Eveland, and Archie Roosevelt provide considerable data on this and later periods. Lebanese attitudes toward the USSR were not regarded by the Legation as a major problem.

The Lebanese bourgeoisie was described as cynical, opportunistic, and naive in its attitude toward the Soviets. Its major achievements were associated with TAPLINE and aviation. And as the cable from the State Department requested, information on concessions was duly provided. Hence, it was noted that on August 10, TAPLINE was granted "the right to run a pipeline through Lebanese territory and to construct a refinery and port facilities," and on the following day, bilateral air accords between Lebanon and the United States were signed.

Along with other transit states, Syria and Jordan, Lebanon's negotiating posture vis-à-vis the oil cartel was influenced by its earlier mandate experiences. In 1931, IPC had sought to construct a pipeline from its Iraqi fields to the Mediterranean, with Tripoli and Haifa playing major roles. Oil installations and pipelines were hostage to wartime developments, as IPC was affected first by Vichy control and then by the assumption of local power by the Gaullist regime.[4] IPC was owned by British Petroleum, Royal Dutch–Shell Group, Compagnie Française des Pétroles, and the Near East Development Corporation, which was Standard Oil Company of New Jersey, Socony Mobil Oil Company, and C. Gulbenkian. At the end of 1944, William J. Lenahan, chief negotiator for TAPLINE, was in touch with the British on the subject of transit rights through Palestine and Transjordan. Lenahan's area of responsibility included Lebanon, which eventually replaced Palestine as the preferred pipeline outlet, in deference to the volatility of the Palestine conflict. Egypt had been another option, as William Chandler, president and CEO of TAPLINE between 1963 and mid-1972, indicates in the following account of his role in TAPLINE's formative period:

> In April 1946 I was dispatched to the Middle East to participate with engineering representatives of Texaco, Socal (Standard Oil Company of California), and ARAMCO in reconnaissance of possible pipeline routes from the ARAMCO oil fields to a terminal in Egypt. This we did in about three weeks concluding that the prospects were unfavorable.
>
> Following which, in May 1946 I proceeded alone on both an air and ground reconnaissance of pipeline routes from Saudi Arabia to Palestine, Lebanon, and Syria, using a DC-3 from Ethiopian Airways (TWA) based in Jerusalem, and doing a lot of automobile travel as far east as the Transjordan lava beds. My report of this venture resulted in the decision of the shareholder companies to bring the line to a terminal south of Sidon, Lebanon.
>
> The balance of 1946 and early 1947 was spent in organizing personnel and equipment for route surveys and preparations for construction.[5]

That continued under Chandler's direction, as chief engineer and later as general superintendent and assistant general manager for the Saudi part of TAPLINE.

The choice of Sidon had a number of advantages in addition to its primary one for TAPLINE, namely, its Mediterranean location. Lebanon's compatible political environment, which was open to foreign investment, was chief among them. The construction of Lebanon's pipeline had the added merit, moreover, of undermining the British sterling bloc—hardly a minor consideration in the light of U.S. efforts to open the doors of the eastern Mediterranean to its products. In explaining his position to Loy Henderson, Wadsworth extolled the virtues of "the Adirondacks of the Near East," where the combination of pipelines, commercial interest, prestigious American cultural institutions, and the potential influx of tourism augured well for American policy.[6] Henderson, in turn, deferred to U.S. oil company executives, who were mired in negotiations between the British and King Abdallah. In April 1945, Socony-Vacuum and Standard Oil of New Jersey submitted their applications for the construction of refineries in Tripoli to Beirut. On August 8, 1946, TAPLINE executives moved to finalize discussions in Lebanon before attempting to resolve those in Damascus. The Lebanese phase of negotiations had resulted in agreement on a transit tax whose amount was determined by "the quantity of oil crossing Lebanon, with a minimum annual payment of 20,000 pounds sterling . . . this was equal to about $180,000."[7] The August 10 accord involved the commitment to proceed with the refinery at Sidon that MEDRECO had agreed to construct when it first opened negotiations in 1945. In the fall of 1952, shortly after Kamil Sham'un became president, U.S. international oil company executives exploited the as-yet-incomplete project to obtain Sham'un's commitment to keep Kamal Junblat out of the cabinet.

In the fall of 1947, some months after the historic merger of ARAMCO and the announcement of the Truman Doctrine, the question of pipeline construction was still being debated in Washington, as the State Department threw its weight behind the plan. For the U.S. international oil companies, pipelines held out the prospects of a more economic and lucrative arrangement. Formally, TAPLINE and ARAMCO maintained separate identities, but their connection was evident in the interlocking directorates that linked them at the top.

> TAPLINE was responsible for the entire construction project from the ARAMCO oil fields in Abqaiq to Sidon. However, at about the time the project was completed the shareholder companies decided to have the easterly portion of the line from Abqaiq to Qaisumah, a distance of about 315 miles, sold by TAPLINE to ARAMCO, since this portion was expected to serve as a part of the ARAMCO gathering system. This left TAPLINE with about 754 miles from Qaisumah to Sidon, for a total length of 1,069 miles.[8]

TAPLINE was also responsible for conducting surveys in Lebanon, Jordan, and Syria. The contractor, Lockwood, Kessler, and Bartlett, according to Chandler, handled the Saudi surveying. Similarly, different contractors were responsible for pipeline construction: the Bechtel Corporation in Saudi Arabia, and Williams Brothers of Tulsa, Oklahoma, for the transit states of Jordan, Lebanon, and Syria. Williams Brothers was responsible for the Sidon pipeline and terminal. Graver built the storage tanks and station at Turaif in Saudi Arabia, roughly fifty miles from the Jordanian border, while the rest was built by Chicago Bridge and Iron, tank builders.

Unlike their experience in Damascus, TAPLINE officials met with no difficulties in finalizing negotiations for the passage of TAPLINE in Lebanon with Lebanese authorities. Nor, it should be added, did TAPLINE encounter anything but friendly relations with the U.S. Legation that became an Embassy in 1952.

The petroleum attaché reflected the close working relations maintained by TAPLINE and the Legation, just as his reports identified the Legation with TAPLINE's negotiating positions vis-à-vis the Lebanese regime. TAPLINE relied on such figures as the Palestinian attorney, Henry Cattan, to aid William Lenahan in negotiations with Jordanian and Palestinian officials, while in Lebanon, Syria, and Saudi Arabia, Cattan played an advisory role vis-à-vis TAPLINE. In Lebanon, the local attorneys on whom TAPLINE relied were Fu'ad Kawar and Albert Laham.

The principal Lebanese political figure who remained a reliable—indeed, according to U.S. contemporaries, indispensable—hand in mediating petroleum affairs between TAPLINE and the Lebanese regime was Habib Abu Shahla. Abu Shahla, a key figure in the politics of the Besharah al-Khuri regime, was secretary of the eleven-person Committee on Foreign Affairs of the Lebanese Chamber.[9]

The absence of regulations or formal structures facilitated handling negotiations in what remained a highly personalized politics. In 1955, a manual described Lebanese administration that identified the "Liquid Fuel Office" of the Ministry of National Economy as handling domestic transactions related to petroleum. But during the period when concessions were initially negotiated, U.S. Legation officers reported no interference from any such institutions, additionally affirming that "in no instance does it appear that the government has shown any indication of discrimination against American interests."[10] That position was generally confirmed by other Americans with Lebanese experience, including David Dodge, who later was in charge of TAPLINE's relations with Lebanon, Syria, and Jordan. Dodge also confirmed the continuing attention paid to TAPLINE affairs by the highest Lebanese officials, including Kamil Sham'un after he became president. The sole area where differences arose within these ranks was the matter of profit—that is to say, the Lebanese, representing a transit state, demanded higher shares of the concession.

From the Legation's perspective, the prospects of TAPLINE were favorable. TAPLINE, in turn, promoted good relations by accommodating the Lebanese government's wishes with respect to company employment. The labor question, however, as suggested earlier, was problematic from the outset. The regime claimed that TAPLINE held out the promise of massive employment, when in fact the number of those affected was limited. Lenahan was concerned that there might be a labor shortage, a very different outlook.

In practice, neither TAPLINE nor the IPC met Lebanon's labor requirements. In 1953, the U.S. Embassy's petroleum attaché calculated that there were about 3,100 people working for IPC, 950 for TAPLINE, and 750 for local marketing firms, including 300 for Socony-Vacuum, in positions described by the same source as among "the highest paid group of labor employees in Lebanon." How high was the highest? In the case of the Bahrein Petroleum Company, owned by Socal and Texaco, there were those who recalled a far less generous arrangement.[11]

As to the revenue yielded by TAPLINE in Beirut, precise figures were not available when the Legation composed its report. Nonetheless, there were sufficient data to suggest that imports in petroleum products, such as kerosene, gasoline, lubricating oils, fuel, and other oils, had increased in volume and value. Public revenue for 1949 was reported to be approximately LL75 million, with payments by oil companies of LL400,000 and indirect taxes of LL11 million.[12]

The situation in Damascus was dramatically different. Given the economic ties between Syria and Lebanon, and the dependence of Lebanon's pipeline on Syrian approval, the resistance of the Syrian regime to TAPLINE's concessionary offer became a major problem in Beirut. Syria signed an accord with TAPLINE on September 1, 1947, but parliamentary ratification was delayed for political and economic reasons. The regime was critical of U.S. policy in Palestine, and it wanted more favorable commercial terms from TAPLINE. But then U.S. oil executives were unwilling to bend on matters of profit, preferring instead to pressure President Quwwatly of Syria and Prime Minister Mardam indirectly through Saudi Arabia and Lebanon, as well as directly through TAPLINE's officers.

When in 1948 it appeared that the Syrian negotiations might fail, preparations for construction in Syria, Lebanon, and Jordan ceased, only to continue exclusively in Saudi Arabia to assure the ARAMCO operation. In practice, the March 1949 military coup in Damascus solved the problem. Within two months, in the presence of William Owen, attorney with TAPLINE and ARAMCO and later TAPLINE's general counsel, and William A. Campbell of TAPLINE, the concession was approved, leading to the completion of construction at the Sidon end.[13]

Recent investigation of the circumstances surrounding the first military coup in Syrian postwar history indicates that CIA agents Miles Copeland and Stephen Meade, who acted as U.S. military attaché in Damascus, were directly involved in the coup in which Syrian colonel Husni Za'im seized power. According to then former CIA agent Wilbur Eveland, the coup was carried out in order to obtain Syrian ratification of TAPLINE.[14] Douglas Little writes that "Meade and Zaim completed planning for the coup in early 1949. On March 14, Zaim 'requested U.S. agents [to] provoke and abet internal disturbances which [are] essential for coup d'état' or that U.S. funds be given him [for] this purpose as soon as possible."[15] Assistant Secretary of State McGhee, according to the same source, put in an appearance in Damascus at a critical moment in the course of these events, "possibly to authorize U.S. support for Zaim" in addition to discussing settlement of Palestinian refugees in Syria.

On March 30, the coup took place, followed by the arrest of the Syrian president and the prime minister and the suspension of the constitution. In less than a month, the new Syrian regime was involved in negotiations with Israel, planning for the resettlement of Palestinian refugees and, in mid-May, approving the TAPLINE concession.

With the end of the phase of Syrian resistance, TAPLINE and ARAMCO celebrated a banner year: 1950 was the year of the historic 50/50 profit-sharing agreement in Saudi Arabia, which was cause for grief in London and for increased demands for profit sharing in Beirut. But 1950 was also the year that oil flowed to the waiting tankers off the coast at Sidon on their way to Europe and North America. When completed, the pipeline allowed ARAMCO to avoid the sea route through the Gulf and the Suez Canal, a distance equivalent to some "7,200 miles of sea journey." The annual traffic "was the equivalent of sixty tankers in continuous operation from the Persian Gulf, via the Suez Canal, to the Mediterranean."[16] In addition to the 1,069 miles of the Sidon-Saudi pipeline, TAPLINE built a communication system that linked Sidon as well as Beirut with Saudi Arabia.

Turning to refineries, the military coup in Damascus eased the situation of IPC. Making plans to construct additional pumping stations that increased Kirkurk-Tripoli capacities, IPC had the only effective refineries operating in Lebanon in 1952. In 1945 MEDRECO had been formed "to assume a refinery convention originally held by Socony-Vacuum."[17] The agreement was ratified, altered, extended through 1950, and then again subject to approval and ratification. Once approved, MEDRECO committed itself to the construction and operation of its refinery within the next five years. Thus, "on March 1, 1951, Messrs. R. J. Follis and A. C. Long representing the interest of the Standard Oil Company of California and the Texas Company respectively, submitted an aide-mémoire to the Lebanese Government agreeing to construct a topping plant at Sidon for the production of diesel oil only" (ibid.). Discussions were also under way for refinery construction in Syria and Jordan.

While MEDRECO was solely involved in the Sidon refinery project, CALTEX, the California Texas Corporation that owned MEDRECO, joined other companies of U.S. and French origin, along with smaller Lebanese companies, in the marketing of oil for domestic Lebanese consumption. The principal foreign companies involved were Socony-Vacuum (Mobil), Esso, and Shell, which "marketed 78 percent and 85 percent [for Lebanon and Syria, respectively], national marketers accounting for 22 percent and 15 percent."[18] Of U.S. companies, the dominant one was Socony-Vaccum, followed by Shell and Esso Standard, and the French Compagnie Commerciale des Combustibles (CFP). The intensity of competition and price manipulation was the subject of persistent complaint on the part of the Lebanese companies, particularly when they found themselves undercut by yet another of the international U.S. majors, Standard Oil of New Jersey, which expanded its role in the region. Domestic pressure for a reduction of prices escalated in direct proportion to the increased demand. In 1950, then, Lebanese marketing companies found themselves with sales 13 percent greater than they had been in 1949. Within another two years, local demand for motor gasoline, kerosene, diesel and fuel oils, along with lubricating oils and aviation gasoline, increased again.

In 1952, U.S. petroleum attaché Ortiz reported that Lebanon's domestic demand for petroleum products reached 6,130 barrels a day. "Considering the fact that the foreign marketers [Socony-Esso-Shell] supplied all the imports, to meet the national marketers share of the Lebanese market required delivery to them of around 30 percent of the Tripoli refinery production."[19] At the time, the MEDRECO plant was still under construction. Given the cost of Lebanon's imports, estimated in foreign exchange by Ortiz to be approximately $3.5 million, pressure to lower prices and to renegotiate agreements was a constant factor through the Khuri as well as Sham'un regimes. Lebanese officials complained of the high prices they were charged by the foreign oil companies, which responded with countercharges of constraints imposed by crude oil production costs, unfair prices set by the Tripoli refinery that had precedence, and the taxes imposed by the Lebanese government.

In 1951 negotiations with TAPLINE and IPC led to agreements to increase payments to the transit states, with Lebanon promised about $1.4 million by TAPLINE and IPC £450,000 annually. In the following year, TAPLINE agreed to increase payments for petroleum products consumed within the country. It provided an annual payment to cover highway and communication facilities, including an annual "security fee" of $600,000 paid to all three transit states, in addition to services in Sidon and Beirut.[20] The sums were modest given the profit margins involved, since by 1952 the anticipated increases from IPC and TAPLINE were expected to quadruple. "IPC agreed both to raise royalties from $680,000 to $2 million per year and to expand the output of Tripoli refinery to help satisfy Lebanon's oil needs. TAPLINE accepted to raise its total payments to Lebanon from about LL1.5 million to LL4.5 million per year. These increases were expected almost to quadruple the government's annual receipts from the two oil companies."[21]

Estimated payment for services growing out of the two companies' activities, according to the same source, was on the order of LL28 million. Between 1956 and 1963 TAPLINE's president, John Noble, sought to introduce a "tariff/tax plan," according to which TAPLINE would set a "tariff for the handling of ARAMCO crude, tied to the difference between Mediterranean and Persian Gulf posted prices, and after subtracting operating costs and depreciation would share the profit on a 50/50 basis with all the transit countries, including Saudi Arabia."[22] The plan failed as a result of disputes over comparative mileage, which the Saudis used to their advantage, even though they were already beneficiaries of the 50/50 agreement as well as other arrangements with TAPLINE for services, which gave them a considerable advantage.

What did this mean for Lebanon? In 1947, crude oil constituted close to 100 percent of transit goods by weight, although only 23 percent of its value. In the same year, IPC transit fees paid to Lebanon were on the order of LL45,000 per year. For 1949, LL400,000 was direct payment by oil companies and LL11 million represented indirect taxes.[23] In 1950, oil company payments "represented only O.4 percent of government revenue," then approximately LL83.3 million.[24] Estimates of overall oil company–pipeline payments to Lebanon in the 1950–1961 period increased from $0.1 million to annual payments of $4.1 million. The foreign exchange derived from oil for one year alone, 1951, was roughly $11 million (pp. 139, 147). Such figures shrink in the context of oil company profits that reached some $12.8 billion between 1948 and 1960, of which $9.4 billion represented payments to local governments.[25] Controversy over Lebanon's meager financial rewards was met by counterclaims that Lebanon provided but scant territory through which TAPLINE passed. The failure to reward Lebanon's location value was not an oversight but a measure to maintain profits by forestalling other precedents, such as claims arising from the use of essential facilities such as ports, for example, for which no claim was made.

Aviation

Aviation was second to U.S. interest in TAPLINE, in Beirut. And like TAPLINE, with its interlocking relations with ARAMCO that were well represented in the U.S. private and public sectors, the giant carriers of postwar aviation, TWA and PAA, similarly represented significant corporate and public interests. In the Middle East, moreover, they overlapped with the activities of the U.S. international oil companies. In Lebanon, the key actors in this story were Middle East Airlines, the premier Lebanese airline, and PAA, Pan American Airways, one of the two major U.S. carriers. And as in the case of TAPLINE, where pipelines marked connections of commercial and political importance, so in the case of MEA and PAA, the pathways over Beirut and Saudi Arabia and the Gulf defined connections of inestimable commercial as well as political importance for Beirut, and the United States. The route between Beirut and the Gulf, dominated by MEA, contributed significantly to Lebanon's economic growth as well as to the political influence of its principal participants. There were other parallels between TAPLINE and aviation, including the permissive attitude of the Lebanese regime, which operated in this area, as in the case of TAPLINE, without formal state intervention. And as Samuel O. Ruff's 1952 report indicated, major figures in the Lebanese commercial and financial bourgeoisie were engaged in the sector of aviation, involving not only MEA but Air Liban and smaller enterprises as well.

Regional and international problems nevertheless arose in the negotiation of airline agreements. European states with stakes in air transport in the region were suspicious of the entry of U.S. airliners, whatever the rationalization of such policies. On the other hand, the Arab League was unprepared to cede rights claimed by its member states that were committed to developing their own aviation industry. Further, it opposed the extension of privileges to non-Arab carriers, the object of Anglo-French as well as American pressures.

The brief history of U.S.-Lebanese relations in aviation can be situated in this context. To a large extent, State Department support of U.S. bilateral air accords in Lebanon is a part of the larger story that includes the Anglo-American dispute for base rights in Saudi Arabia. It was 1944 when U.S. plans were aired at the International Civil Aviation Conference in the United States, the same occasion on which U.S. participants justified their positions in the name of an "Open Door" policy in the skies. What U.S. officials spoke of as the "Fifth Freedom" British officials interpreted as American license to expand at British expense. The situation in Beirut unfolded against this background.

Ralph Curren, civil air attaché in Cairo, Syria, Saudi Arabia, Ethiopia, Iraq, and Iran, as well as Beirut, found the Lebanese regime particularly amenable to his suggestions. They included the expansion of the Beirut airport, a project that, as previous discussion has shown, was discussed by Bruins, the U.S. commercial attaché in Beirut in 1945. Besharah al-Khuri allocated some LL4 million for the plan, anticipating the advent of U.S. air traffic. The director of Lebanese Civil Aviation, the accommodating Sami Shuqayr, was appreciated by Legation officers for his willingness to intercede on behalf of the United States. This worked to the benefit of Washington in the parallel conflicts with other European capitals, such as Amsterdam, London, and Paris. In the end, the Arab League approved the U.S. position. By August 1946, the first step in U.S.-Lebanese and U.S.-Syrian air diplomacy was cleared with the signing of the air transport agreements. Under Secretary of State Acheson authorized Wadsworth to sign these bilateral air accords two days after the concession with TAPLINE was signed in Beirut.

In the fall of 1947, the State Department viewed U.S. aviation policy in the Middle East as unproblematic, attributing what difficulties there were to Arab reaction to U.S. policy on Palestine.[26] The interpretation was partial and self-serving. U.S. policy toward Palestine was cause for grievances throughout the region, but there were other reasons for antagonism, such as infringements on sovereign rights and, in the case of Western powers, competition in high-stakes areas. British and French claims were not easily set aside. Both governments viewed the expansion of American aviation as an infringement of their rights in territory where they had priority. For Britain the major concern was to maintain control over the Beirut-Kuwait route, while for Paris the objective was to keep the West and North African routes closed to American carriers. In spite of these constraints, American aviation emerged in a commanding position as the two giant American commercial carriers, TWA and PAA, succeeded in penetrating the major Middle Eastern and North African access routes. Trans World Airlines gained control of the Cairo and Tel Aviv, Basra and Dhahran lines, as well as entry to Algiers, Tunis, and Tripoli, in addition to obtaining internal routes that permitted linkages to Beirut and Teheran. In Saudi Arabia, TWA was in charge of the Royal Saudi airline, a role it performed in Ethiopia as well.

PAA became the first major carrier to use Beirut's international airport, with a regular program of six weekly flights to Beirut from New York, including Panair flights to Brazil.[27] Its director, as of 1949, was former secretary of state George C. Marshall. In the same year that PAA purchased a 36 percent share of Middle East Airlines, it obtained three seats on its seven-person administrative council.[28] Buying shares of MEA, which was comparable to Air France's purchase of 30 percent of Air Liban, was commercially as well as politically profitable. Above and beyond the leasing of equipment and personnel to indigenous airlines, the limits set by international aviation accords, the arrangement promoted the expansion of the American carrier in a coveted region while deepening its ties with influential Lebanese figures who were well situated to exploit the growth of Lebanese aviation.

In 1945 MEA began operating in the Middle East, flying from Beirut to Syria, Egypt, Palestine, Iraq, and Transjordan. The carrier that became the preeminent Lebanese and Middle East airline was founded by Sa'eb Salam, along with his brother and partners, Fawzi al-Huss and Najib Alamuddin. Alamuddin represented a considerable number of U.S. firms in Beirut, among them ITT and its subsidiaries, some of which were involved in the construction of the Beirut airport. The Salams eventually emerged as principal figures in the operation of MEA, however, with Sa'eb Salam in charge. In conjunction with his political role as one of the most influential of Sunni urban leaders, and as an industrialist and a member of the inner core of the presidential circle, Salam held significant importance. In 1951 the Legation report on aviation noted that MEA's "political support in Lebanon is very strong because Saab Bey Salaam, a leading Moslem political figure, is its

President. Mr. Salaam is not only a member of Parliament, but also a potential Prime Minister."[29]

In recognizing the import of the Salam role in MEA, the Legation did not overlook other Lebanese business and political connections with regional and international aviation interests. Husayn 'Uwayni, associated with Air Liban, had Saudi connections through his financial activities. The president of Air Liban, Basil Megherdish, was a banker well connected with Air France; Michel Kattar was administrator of the Syro-Lebanese bank and a leading figure in numerous commercial and industrial associations; Antoine Sahnawi, founder of the Banque Belgo-Libanaise, was with his brother, Michel, agent for various Belgian and Luxembourgian companies, stockholders in various French companies, and premier steel importers.

In addition to MEA and Air Liban, there were a number of secondary lines connected primarily with American and British oil interests that deserve mention. Here again, such lines relied on local agents, invariably the interested members of the Lebanese bourgeoisie. Some of the functions of these secondary lines were not immediately discernible, as the commercial cover masked covert operations. There was the Contracting and Trading Company, whose director and senior partner of a controlling trio, Emile Bustani, worked for IPC as well as TAPLINE. There was the U.S. Charter service, Trans Ocean Airlines (TOA), under the direction of John Russell and his Lebanese associate Carlos 'Arida, scion of Yusef 'Arida, one of three brothers who had made a fortune in textile manufacturing during World War II.

Trans Ocean was "a CIA-subsidized airline-service company," as was Air Jordan, "to which the CIA provided support."[30] TOA was readily extended official approval by the director of Civil Aviation, who permitted it to launch its charter services out of Beirut. It was identified as well with Air Jordan and with Air Djibouti. TOA's importance, however, rested on its connection with the Gulf, to which it ferried fruits and vegetables to U.S. oil companies when it was not busy with its "aircraft and engine overhaul company, ground and flight training schools, crop dusting and spraying, and an export-import business."[31] In addition, mention should be made of Trans Mediterranean Airlines, under the direction of Munir Abu Haidar, that subsequently played an important role as a major freight carrier in the area.

From the perspective of the British in Beirut and Saudi Arabia, U.S. aviation policy was as aggressive as its petroleum politics was. Both were a challenge to British interests, and both generated opposition from London and the field. This was particularly the case in the Gulf, an area that the British regarded as far too important to be open to U.S. competition. MEA played a significant role in this struggle, as its support by PAA immediately identified it with U.S. interests, although its routes to Kuwait and the Gulf had been initiated in 1949, before PAA purchased shares in MEA. Nevertheless, MEA's route was interpreted by London as a challenge to the British monopoly in coveted areas, which it was unable to block any more than it could halt the role of Air Liban. Both proved to be major beneficiaries of this route. MEA became the carrier responsible for conveying some 600,000 kilograms of foodstuffs, machinery, and gold, about 70 tons' worth—critical to Beirut's money markets—to Kuwait. Sa'eb Salam was credited with cultivating relations with Kuwait that led to an increase in tourist traffic in the opposite direction.

In 1950, however, competition between the United States and Great Britain over air access to Kuwait involved the local Lebanese airlines in a larger struggle. The British promoted a Cyprus Airways accord connecting Beirut and Kuwait, according to which their political agent was assigned to pressure the Kuwaiti sheikh not to grant landing rights to Lebanese carriers. MEA's Sa'eb Salam, not to be outdone, challenged British influence through his own connections with the sheikh of Kuwait. The next step was the British-Kuwaiti call for reciprocity in Beirut as compensation for Lebanese carriers' access to Kuwait.

The air wars were concluded in August 1951, in an agreement that granted the British argonaut, Cyprus Airways, Air Liban, and MEA access to the disputed terrain. Competition moved to the level of cost. Here again, MEA proved adept as it remained outside of the international air traffic association, thereby positioning itself to offer lower rates and thus to maintain its advantage. When, in addition, MEA flights to Bahrein and Jidda were increased in 1951–1952, intra-Lebanese as well as Anglo-American competition grew more acrimonious.

In 1951, the U.S. Legation concluded that Lebanese aviation "provided an access to the strong new market in Kuwait for Lebanese foodstuffs, manufactures, and transit goods. Kuwait oil royalties were the most important new purchasing power in the region."[32] MEA was the airline most closely associated with the expansion of the Beirut-Kuwait connection. As a result, it was well placed to benefit from the expansion of Kuwaiti oil production, which increased from "17 million tons in 1950 to 46.9 million in 1954."[33] Kuwait thus became "the largest producer in the Gulf, only being outstripped by Saudi Arabia in 1966," according to the same source. Trade with Beirut increased, along with financial investment, as Kuwait additionally benefited from such regional crises as the nationalization of Iranian oil in 1951. Beirut was the indirect beneficiary of such developments, as well as those consuming Egypt, where riots in January 1952 persuaded the British carrier BOAC to reroute some of its flights from London to Johannesburg through Beirut.

Within a year of its opening, Beirut International Airport had serviced 3,211 carriers with an incoming traffic of 30,202 passengers and an outgoing traffic of some 33,024, in an airport that was still under construction.[34] New towers, terminals, the installation of transmitters and other necessary equipment were expected to be in place by the year's end. In spite of this, the new airport was already in use, not only by the major international carriers PAA, BOAC, Air France, KLM, and SAS but also by local Lebanese airlines, whose gross profits, according to the U.S. Legation report of civil aviation for 1951, were estimated to be LL2 million. Of this, MEA reaped nearly half, or LL900,000, for gross profits and LL500,000 net. The economic benefits accruing to the state from the activity of Lebanese aviation were further boosted by the increase in tourism, as 24,000 Arab League visitors contributed LL30 million to the Lebanese economy (ibid.).

As MEA profited, so did Pan American Airways. In addition to its investment in the Lebanese airline, PAA was responsible for advice and technical assistance, including the purchase of new aircraft and equipment. U.S. Legation officer Samuel O. Ruff regarded this as being of capital importance for the role of the United States in Lebanon, "since MEA is the most successful local line in the region, and is very important to the Lebanese economy . . . this procurement problem becomes the number one problem in Lebanese aviation" (ibid.). Ruff's opinion was that the priority in U.S. "assistance in arranging the procurement of these planes would be of more value in the development of Lebanese transport than in any other project which the Legation can call to mind in the transport field." Procurement involved U.S. planes and equipment. Norman Blake, who was a board member of MEA and director of PAA's Middle East and India office, was in charge of reequipment and fully aware of the profits involved. He was persuaded of the importance to PAA of persuading MEA to "plow part of the line's phenomenal profits back into line in the form of new aircraft to replace the six Dakotas which carry the traffic at present" (ibid.). When Sa'eb Salam, who had planned a trip to the United States for the express purpose of purchasing Consolidated Convairs, decided to postpone his trip, it was for political reasons. Salam was to become prime minister in the last phase of the Khuri regime.

U.S. Commercial Interests and the FCN Treaty

Petroleum dominated U.S. commercial interests in the Middle East in the postwar years. In 1950 U.S. investment of $700 million in the petroleum sector far outweighed investment—$50 million—in nonpetroleum products.[35] In 1947, State Department officers had confirmed that the Middle East was "the source of some fairly important specialty requirements for U.S. import trade such as dates, figs, coffee (specialty grades), long-staple cotton and oriental rugs," which it regarded as a potential source of dollar exchange.[36] The Middle East contributed to the postwar stockpiling program, with Turkey providing chromite; North Africa, lead and zinc; and other areas, copper, manganese, and molybdenum.[37] Insofar as Lebanon was concerned, trade was modest. Yet as the following discussion suggests, there was far greater interest among U.S. firms in exploring Lebanon and Middle Eastern markets than may have been assumed. Further, in some well-developed sectors—shipping, for example—the connection with U.S. oil interests proved a boon to trade.

As early as 1945–1946, which was when Minister George Wadsworth of the U.S. Legation expressed concern that Lebanon's economic condition made it undesirable for U.S. firms to come to Beirut, U.S. officials in Lebanon supported a related effort—namely, the establishment of the Near East Company (NEC), which was to "associate Lebanese, American and Syrian capital to develop the region's natural resources and to invest in various industrial, agricultural, service and financial enterprises."[38] NEC was interested in expanding U.S. banking facilities in Lebanon, as were other Lebanese commercial, industrial, and financial figures. Mattison estimates that two years later, U.S. exports to Lebanon were approximately $25.0 million (1951) and $25.8 million in 1952. Imports from Lebanon, according to the same source, were on the order of $3.15 million in 1951 and $10.36 million in 1952. Gates estimates that in 1951, "the United States was Lebanon's second largest supplier (after Syria), and its most important client. Lebanon exported a little over 40 percent of the value of goods it purchased from the U.S," a percentage figure that must be increased to take account of the fact that about 20 percent of Lebanon's imports from the United States, by value, were gold, whose market price was calculated in dollars.[39]

The nature of the large, internationally oriented American firms interested in exploring possibilities in Lebanon and the Middle East had become evident some years earlier. In 1949. the U.S. naval attaché's report identified the role of the Kittaneh family in this connection. Francis Kittaneh, resident in the United States, represented the following major American corporations: Chrysler Corporation; Fairbanks-Morse and Company; Willard Storage Battery Company; Champion Spark Plug Company; Winthrop Products, Incorporated; Anaconda Wire and Cable Company; General Electric Medical Products Company; International General Electric Company, Incorporated; Berkshire Knitting Mills; U.S. Steel Export Company; S. S. White Dental; International Business Machines Corporation; Master Surgical Instrument Company; Kinetic Chemicals, Incorporated; Hemington Arms Company; and Peters Cartrige Division.[40] Kittaneh's participation in the New York–based Council on Foreign Relations, under the direction of Allen Dulles in 1947–1951, was an expression of his identification with U.S. corporate interests involved in Lebanon and elsewhere in the Middle East and in developing countries.[41]

By 1952 major pharmaceutical, telecommunication, automotive, construction, manufacturing, and shipping firms that were integrated into the interlocking corporate structures of oil and aviation were represented in Beirut. In the absence of figures to confirm the size and impact of their operations, identifying the names of the American firms provides evidence of the international orientation of prominent corporations in the process of extending their operations to the Middle East.[42]

Pharmaceutical companies included Dow Chemical, represented through the American Near East Distributing Company, and E. I. Dupont de Nemours and Company, whose Middle East agents included F. A. Kittaneh. There were also E. R. Squibb and Sons Overseas Operations, along with Upjohn Company, whose Middle East agents were Khalil Fattal and Sons, Beirut. Among telecommunication giants, International Telephone and Telegraph Corporation had its Middle East subsidiaries with Najib Alamuddin, earlier identified in connection with MEA, as the agent for International Standard Electric Corporation, which in turn had its own subsidiaries. Alamuddin was also president of Near East Resources, which was a subsidiary of International Telephone and Telegraph. And in addition, Alamuddin was the exclusive representative for a host of other ITT subsidiaries, such as International Standard Corporation and its subsidiaries, including Bell Telephone Manufacturing Company of Antwerp, Belgium; Standard Telephones and Cables, Limited, London; American Cable and Radio Corporation; and its subsidiary, Mackay Radio and Telegraph Company. Through the latter, "ITT operates the largest American-owned international telegraph service covering the Middle East by radio-telegraph and cable services, through Tangier, Cairo, Addis Ababa, Jidda, Damascus, New Delhi, and Karachi."[43]

Of particular interest in relation to Beirut was the role of International Standard Electric Corporation, which "supplied and installed aerial navigation and runway lighting equipment for the International Airport at Beirut, Lebanon" (p. 37). Lucrative contracts for the project were at the center of scandals involving major Lebanese figures, including those close to President Khuri. Agricultural, construction, and manufacturing equipment, some of which was involved in Point IV projects, was represented in Beirut and the rest of the Middle East. Allis Chalmers, Hyster, International Harvester, and Caterpillar Tractor were international companies with their Beirut agents. Francis Kittaneh was agent in Beirut and Damascus for Allis Chalmers Manufacturing Company and Joy Manufacturing Company for Beirut and Damascus.[44] J. I. Case had Mamarbashi Frères as its Middle East agents; Caterpillar Tractor was represented by M. Ezzat Jallad and Fils, which was also the agent for its allied firm, Hyster; International Harvester Export Company, with numerous Middle East distributors in Beirut; Minneapolis-Moline, represented by Ibrahim J. Sa'd and Fils; and Oliver similarly had Beirut distributors. There were U.S. companies with Lebanese-based affiliates, such as American Near East Distributing, Arling Corporation, the Middle East agent for Allied Chalmers Company, and other firms of more modest size that handled paints, chemicals, tools, cash registers, pens and typewriters, sewing machines, films, and U.S.-based foreign insurance companies.

While the above list identifies those American firms interested in Lebanese–Middle Eastern markets and those Lebanese entrepreneurs who were well positioned to introduce them into Beiruti and regional markets, shipping companies were more closely connected to Lebanon's transit function and more generally linked to U.S. petroleum operations. Shipping companies with a Beirut or Sidon base were organically linked to regional as well as local U.S. oil interests, often interlaced in networks of partnership and collaboration. There were import-export firms, such as the American Eastern Corporation (AEC), founded by Marcel Wagner in the 1920s "for the purpose of introducing American products and technical know-how into the Near and Middle East."[45] The AEC, involved in various development projects, represented European as well as U.S. shipping lines. Its Beirut subsidiary, American Lebanese Shipping Company, often referred to by the initials S.A.L., was based in Beirut and Sidon, the site of TAPLINE's terminal. It was affiliated with the Egyptian-based American Eastern Trading and Shipping Company (SAE), which had been incorporated as an Egyptian firm to assume Marcel Wagner's activities in the 1940s (ibid.).

In 1950, U.S. Legation reports on merchant shipping in Lebanon identified American Eastern Trading and Shipping as an Egyptian firm, describing its function as representative for 60 to 70 percent of tanker firms working out of Sidon.[46] These included: Esso Shipping Company, Esso Transportation, Flotta Lauro, Imperial Oil Shipping, Hillcone Steamship, Keystone Shipping, Mosvolv Shipping, Overseas Tankship Corporation, Trinidad Corporation, and U.S. Petroleum Carriers, Incorporated. Finally, in addition to the above, a number of U.S. passenger and cargo ships called at Beirut—such as the Concordia Lines, eleven ships of the Isthmian Steamship Lines, and four of the American Export Lines.

The Lebanese Industrial and Commercial Company of Beirut, the local affiliate of American Levant Shipping and Distributing, identified as "a Coca Cola bottling plant" in a review of U.S. business interests in the Middle East, did more than bottle the soft drink.[47] Its parent company was the Lebanese and Syrian agent for roughly forty U.S. shipping, agriculture, automotive, and commercial firms and also the "clearing agent to Lebanon and Syria for Trans-Arabian Pipe Line Company and Syrian army" (ibid.). It was, in addition, the agent for the following: Lykes Bros. Steamship Company, Incorporated; Prudential Steamship Corporation; Pacific Mediterranean Line; California Transport Corporation; California Tanker Company; and Mississippi Shipping Company, Incorporated. Not surprisingly, U.S. officials in Beirut regarded American-Levant Shipping and Distributing Company with particular interest and arranged to keep it within the corporate family of oil, aviation, and shipping. In 1947, the commercial attaché of the U.S. Legation recommended to the State Department that the TAPLINE officer who had been its representative in U.S. deliberations on the pipeline terminus, William Campbell, be retained as consultant to the chief executive of TAPLINE. Campbell, it turned out, had been president of American-Levant Shipping and Distributing at Beirut, and he, in turn, recommended that the Damascus representative of Pan American be brought in to replace him as president of the company.[48]

To reflect on the above activity suggests that U.S. interest in commercial relations with Lebanon was far from being as innocuous as conventional accounts suggest. Such interest, however, did not bar discord on the formal aspects of U.S.-Lebanese trade relations. This was epitomized in the continuing disagreements on the Friendship, Commerce, and Navigation Treaty (FCN), which lasted throughout the Khuri regime. At the same time that the State Department authorized recognition of the Lebanese republic, it offered the Lebanese regime the opportunity to sign the FCN Treaty, a standard formula of American postwar trade arrangements that the Lebanese resisted signing. Evidence of U.S. commercial interest and eventual political pressure notwithstanding, the Besharah al-Khuri regime and its most eminent pro-American minister, Charles Malik, refused to accede to an accord that undermined Lebanon's commercial relations. Confrontations on this score were amplified in deliberations on related questions, such as the desire of Lebanon and other Middle Eastern and Latin American states in the UN's Economic and Social Council to determine their own agenda of economic reconstruction.

In the fall of 1947, delegates from the Middle East and Latin America had supported the creation of separate economic commissions to deal with the conditions specific to their regions. Malik was an advocate of such initiatives, countering U.S. opposition with the reminder that such forms of economic regionalism were but a mild response to "economic penetration by extraregional elements and forces."[49] In the course of the next two years, other Lebanese voices, such as those of George Hakim and Albert Badre, argued in favor of a greater UN role in regional economic development. This was not what the State Department had in mind when it proposed that Lebanon ratify the FCN Treaty and accept Point IV technical assistance.

First broached by the State Department in 1944–1945, the FCN Treaty was regarded as a corollary to U.S. recognition of Lebanese sovereignty. The U.S. minister, Wadsworth, informed the State Department that the Lebanese regime was interested, and Malik appeared particularly eager for Lebanon to sign such a treaty with the United States. He was not prepared, however, to relinquish Lebanon's beneficial trade relations in favor of the United States. Lebano-Syrian trade with the Middle East was a vital element of Lebanese commercial relations at the time of its independence. In 1943, Lebano-Syrian imports from the Middle East region constituted 89.7 percent of overall trade, while its exports to the same area were approximately 96.5 percent.[50] In early August 1946, before the signing of the TAPLINE accord, Acheson directed the U.S. Legation to emphasize that the FCN Treaty was standard in U.S. foreign relations and that its principal purpose was the elimination of discriminatory practices between states. Malik requested information, while suggesting that these discussions be withheld from the British and French, a proposal that was ignored. Information did not resolve the problem, as Malik was reticent to abandon the commercial advantages that Lebanon enjoyed in the region, while seeking to avoid antagonizing regional political interests. He argued, to no avail, that the FCN Treaty would be ruinous for Lebanon, only to be informed that anything resembling protectionism was unacceptable to the Truman administration. Aside from the past role of protectionism in U.S. economic history, the present administration was less consistent in its opposition than such a position suggests. But unlike states where import substitution contributed to the creation of favorable conditions for U.S. firms, Lebanon offered no such indirect opportunities.[51]

As Acheson admitted to Wadsworth, the FCN Treaty demanded uncommon rights for novel forms of economic organization:

> The rights and privileges for corporations and associations, as proposed in the draft, are broader than those which have heretofore been specified in commercial treaties of the United States. This is considered to be a timely step in view of the importance of such entities in present-day economic organization, and the desirability of promoting business activity in corporate as well as other forms.[52]

The language pointed to TAPLINE and ARAMCO, as the FCN Treaty envisioned concessions to corporate firms such as multinationals enjoying privileges with restricted obligations in the host countries in which they operated. Malik continued to object, but Washington persisted, recalling its earlier commitments in the Franco-American convention of 1924, and its interpretation of the 1944 U.S.-Lebanese agreement that promised mutual consultation within a two-year period. The time had come, but the times had also changed. So charged had the political atmosphere become as a result of the Palestine war that Malik found himself unable to pursue negotiations.

When they resumed in 1949, it was with a different angle. Lebanon was willing to engage, but at a price. George Hakim, then counselor of the Lebanese Legation in Washington, was with Malik when they discussed the FCN Treaty with State Department officials, including George McGhee. Resuming discussions that had been forcibly abridged because of U.S. policy in Palestine, Malik observed that Lebanon was prepared to accede to a treaty whose advantages would obviously go to the U.S.:

> We recognize that compared to the magnitude of the American economy, the benefits which American enterprise would derive from this treaty would be quite modest, owing to the small size of our country and the limited possibilities of our economy. Yet, despite this fact, it is still true that compared to what we derive from this treaty, these benefits are not only in themselves considerable but also form part of the objectives of United States global policy in this field.[53]

What Lebanon desired in exchange was integration into U.S. Middle East policy, which meant U.S. protection. Returning to the theme of Lebanon's loss, Malik underscored the realities of Lebanon's inferior position, acknowledging that American institutions, including U.S. financial and commercial interests as well as educational establishments, would be the major beneficiaries. The situation was painful, he acknowledged, to those Lebanese who recalled their past history, when the balance of power was in Lebanon's favor. But, as Malik recognized, there were benefits that could not be ignored. Thus, "it is still true that compared to what we derive from this treaty, these benefits are not only in themselves considerable but also form part of the objectives of United States global policy in this field." The political rapprochement that Malik and other pro-American elements of the ruling class endorsed soon came to pass. But the FCN Treaty remained moribund and Lebanon's incentives, in terms of maintaining its favorable regional trade balance, persisted.[54]

The configuration of internal, regional, and international factors was, nonetheless, to the advantage of the U.S. State Department. The principal instrument that remained in the hands of recalcitrant Lebanese officials was that of delaying the conclusion of negotiations. In the summer of 1951, when political tides were changing Lebanese politics, U.S. commercial attaché Bruins concluded that the time for ratification of the treaty was imminent. Accordingly, he sought and obtained official approval from the State Department to enact such formalities as might be necessary in the absence of Minister Wadsworth. Bruins's judgment was premature. Not only did the treaty remain unsigned but other signs of resistance by the regime emerged, such as Lebanon's refusal to approve a Voice of America relay base. When confronted with these rejections, the perpetual minister to American interests, Charles Malik, explained that the State Department would be obliged to wait. The next president and his cabinet would be in a stronger position to accede to U.S. requests.

6
Altered Circumstances and the Design of U.S. Political Strategy

The war has emphasized the strategic importance of the country, with its important port, air bases, railway, and oil pipeline terminal. The commercial and military value of Near Eastern oil reserves, the deterioration of Britain's strength, the emergent interest of the Soviet Union in the Near East, emphasize the importance to the U.S. of a politically stable and economically prosperous Lebanon.
SWNCC Country Study on Long-Range Assistance to Lebanon, June 8, 1948

The "Labor Game"

The above statement, issued in 1948, left no doubt as to the basis of U.S. interests in Lebanon. During the period between 1948 and the end of Besharah al-Khuri's tenure, however, a shift occurred in U.S. policy toward Lebanon that involved a greater emphasis on a political rapprochement and a greater impatience with the frustrations of Lebanese politics.[1] The State Department had grown irritated with the president's neutralism, a position that manifested itself in criticisms of the regime's attitude toward Point IV as well as the Palestine question.

The argument developed in the following pages takes as its premise that a political rapprochement between the United States and Lebanon was blocked neither by the regime's attitude toward Point IV nor by the Palestine question. It was consistently promoted by key Lebanese figures who were unable to persuade the State Department of their views prior to the early 1950s. After that, with critical regional and international developments, and significant changes in Lebanese domestic politics, the situation changed and the pro-American elements of the Lebanese bourgeoisie and political elite scored their victory.

The struggle over Palestine that culminated in the emergence of the Israeli state, with its immediate implications for surrounding regimes, the defeat of the U.S.-backed Chinese Nationalist forces, the outbreak of war in Korea, the passage of NSC 68 with its militarization of U.S. foreign policy and, later, the nationalization of the Anglo-Iranian Oil Company in Teheran combined to persuade State Department officials that it was urgent to consolidate U.S. positions in the oil-rich Middle East. One manifestation of this was the pressure on the Lebanese regime, which posed no threat to U.S. policy. Yet there was no denying the shift in Washington's political attitude.

Whatever the Khuri regime's aversion to political collaboration with Washington may have been, realistically one would have to concede that it was practically offset by the compatible agreements over TAPLINE and the negotiation of air accords and by the evidence of U.S. commercial interest in Lebanon. None of the above would have been feasible in a politically hostile environment. For certain Lebanese political figures, however, this was clearly not enough. Contrary to the leadership of the regime, a pro-American minority element sought to advance the possibilities of a Lebanon-U.S. alliance, rapprochement, or accord. Though the formality was important, the substance was even more so. Arguing in terms of Lebanon's potential as an intermediary for U.S. interests in the region, and as advocates from a state whose cultural and political orientation was Western, these partisans were persistent and unsuccessful. Doubts as to the political viability of the state contributed to the State Department's position, but in addition, there was neither precedent nor perceived need for such a move.

When the discontents with the regime multiplied and the resentment of French financial policies matured, there was an opening for Washington, as the Legation recognized. The ability to exploit it assumed networks of political and other relations that were already in place. Lebanese labor policy with its manipulation of trade unions, the role of the Palestine question, and the controversy over Point IV are useful introductions to the important transition period in Lebanon-U.S. relations that marked the end of the Besharah al-Khuri regime.

The "labor game" was no game. The description comes from the U.S. Legation officer who, in 1946, reported on labor practices of the Lebanese

Ministry of the Interior. Those exposed in the report as political manipulators emerged as the allies of U.S. policy in Lebanon. Their corrupt practices notwithstanding, the results they obtained were highly regarded.

The Truman administration pursued an active international labor policy in collaboration with Britain immediately after the war. Containment of radical trade unionism was an objective in Europe and Asia as much as in the Middle East, where politically active trade unions were commonplace.[2] Among those who supported such positions were U.S. oil officials in Beirut, who feared both the organization of labor and labor's Communist members. TAPLINE and IPC made their positions clear. The regime in Beirut accepted them. It was willing to shield oil companies from the 1946 Labor Code. TAPLINE and IPC were assured that strikes would be avoided at all costs. When TAPLINE was threatened by the unionization of its workers, it moved to rely on short-time assignments to eliminate full-time workers who were eligible to become union members. The task of working out satisfactory arrangements fell to Munir Bayyud, who was responsible for IPC's policy in Tripoli. The appointment had an ironic twist to it, since Bayyud had previously been transferred out of this position on orders of President Khuri's son, who had disapproved of what he considered to be Bayyud's leniency toward Palestinian workers. The information about the appointment was conveyed to the Legation by Sheikh Khalil al-Khuri.[3]

There was more to Lebanese labor politics and to U.S. involvement. In spite of the limits of Lebanon's service economy, the trade union movement in Beirut was growing. Taking in taxi drivers, municipal employees, textile and tobacco workers, construction and port workers, as well as oil company employees, trade union activity gained momentum throughout the 1940s. In 1946, strikes and local actions were commonplace, as labor leaders pressed the government to adopt a comprehensive and progressive labor code. In May of the same year, Under Secretary of State Acheson asked the U.S. Legation in Beirut to keep him informed on unions, their leaders and membership, and their antistrike legislation.[4]

The data that Acheson received included information on the methods adopted by the Lebanese government to undermine Communist unions. The sources cited were directly involved in the activities of which they spoke. On the basis of such information, the Legation explained how the Ministry of the Interior and the Office of Social Affairs (OSA) collaborated with the Lebanese Sûreté in undermining unions they designated as suspect. Mustapha al-'Arees, Communist head of the Lebanese labor syndicate, La Fédération des Syndicats des Ouvriers et des Employées du Liban, was the most widely supported and the most assiduously pursued labor leader in Lebanon. A dominant figure in Lebanese trade unionism, he was the prime target of such investigative activity, and his unions became the favored recruiting ground for government informants. Relying on such informants, prominent political figures who were committed to dismantling the existing trade union movement, and particularly its radical leadership, used anti-communist recruits in labor fronts who were introduced into labor "leagues" organized under their direction. Their financial and political support outside of formal political structures freed the state of responsibility for such intervention. The device was transparent.

In 1946 the minister of the interior, Sa'eb Salam, effectively defused plans for a general strike in protest of the government's failure to support the proposed 1946 Labor Code. The action generated discord within the 'Arees Union, including the defection of one of its former members, who went to work for Salam instead, providing information to the political bureau of the Lebanese Sûreté, "charged with political espionage."[5] Wehbe al-Masri was paid for his services. Salam, in turn, provided assistance and funding to further divide the Ittihad. Four unions were reported to have "seceded" from its ranks in the process. They were reorganized as the League of Laborers' and Employees' Syndicates (Jamiat Naqabat al-'Ummal w'al-Mustakhdamin) and operated with a press run by the anti-communist PPS under the editorship of Fayyez Sayyegh, who was then replacing Charles Malik as professor of philosophy at the American University of Beirut.

In explaining the operations of this system to the State Department, the Legation emphasized that "to understand the labor game that is being played," it was necessary to know something of the man who was responsible for the regime's labor legislation. Joseph Donato, who was in charge of the Office of Social Affairs, had previously been trained "in investigative procedure" by a French Jesuit priest who had been chief of French intelligence in Turkey. Donato had worked in Beirut before independence, at which time the priest, Le Père Genissel, recommended him to the president of the republic as one competent to establish an Office of Social Affairs that would investigate labor practices and legislation. But the OSA had other functions. It was responsible for deciding which labor union applicants to accredit. The grounds on which accreditation were withheld included those of a political nature. Applications for accreditation went first to the Ministry of the Interior, then to the Lebanese Sûreté. If review indicated evidence of criminal record, undesirable political connections, and subversive activity, the OSA withheld licensing. U.S. Legation officials concluded that as a result, "it would be possible to deal the communists a severe blow." The Legation summarized the situation in its report "The Anti-Communist Labor Movement in Lebanon," sent to the Department of State in 1947, as follows:

> Today, although Aris' ['Arees] Ittihad is still the best organized and best disciplined federation, the Labor Front—Jabhat al-Amal—which operates under the patronage of Lebanon's wealthy Foreign Minister, Henri Bey Pharaon [Far'oun], is larger, and a third federation, the League of Laborer's and Employees' Syndicates–Jamiat Naqabat al-'Ummal w'al-Mustakhdamin—which is being promoted by the ex-Minister of the Interior, Saib Bey Salam, hopes to give the communists serious competition. In addition to these factors, the Government's Office of Social Affairs which is empowered by law to administer the provisions of the new Labor Code with respect to unions is under the influence of anti-communist deputies and has the admitted policy of diluting the communist position.

The author of the report concluded that if things continued in the same manner, there was no "serious alarm" insofar as communism and the labor movement in Lebanon were concerned. Danger lurked elsewhere.

> The greatest danger, however, is to be found in the ranks of those very men who today are contributing most to frustrate communist efforts. Some of these individuals who occupy positions of public trust and fill the seats of greatest honor, are so inclined to put private advantage before public duty and to use their office in such a scandalous fashion, that even sober citizens may feel impelled to turn to communism as the only remedy.

The reservation had no effect on U.S. policy in Lebanon. Al-'Arees's involvement in international labor continued to be closely monitored and his movements reported to the State Department. In early 1947 the Beirut Legation informed Washington that al-'Arees was appointed head of a delegation of the International Federation of Trade Unions, on the way to Teheran.[6] The Lebanese and Syrian Communist parties were reported to have been invited by the secretary general of the British Communist Party to participate in London meetings organized in connection with its Nineteenth Congress, along with other Commonwealth

Communist parties. These developments preceded the mobilization of Anglo-American efforts to check the participation of Communist and Soviet members in the international trade union movement. The International Confederation of Free Trade Unions (ICFTU), organized in 1949 in opposition to the World Federation of Trade Unions (WFTU), was designed to weaken the WFTU with its social democratic orientation, its Communist membership, and Soviet participation.[7] Lebanon had been a participant in the WFTU's Fourth World Congress, sending a delegation of six members, the third largest delegation after those of Syria and the Sudan.[8]

The question of labor had been discussed in Anglo-American deliberations on the Middle East in the fall of 1947. At the time, the State Department recommended that "particular emphasis should be laid on the possibility of establishing closer and more effective contact with organized labor in the countries of the Middle East through the appointment of experienced labor attachés, having especial regard for the selection of the right kind of American and British representatives to undertake this important work."[9] The "right kind" of official was one with the capacity to turn radical local unions around. In 1951, when Harold Minor was minister, he was persuaded that "the leadership within the [Lebanese] unions proper, however, is educated and intelligent, and with the proper guidance the principal unions at least could be developed into strong and more truly free trade unions. I believe that they would then be one of the main bulwarks against communism here."[10]

The Legation had the services of two part-time officers—labor attaché Paul S. Lunt, stationed between Cairo and Beirut, and labor reporting officer Wilbur C. Hogue, reputed to be connected with U.S. intelligence. Lunt was in Cairo at a meeting of the Socony-Vacuum Employees Union, organized on February 12 by the U.S.-backed Committee on Egyptian Labor Affairs. The timing of the session was significant. It came several weeks after the political turmoil of January in Cairo, whose occurrence was interpreted in a manner designed to implicate Egyptian radicals in an event widely attributed to right wing and Islamist forces. The U.S. Embassy and the Egyptian government agreed that the time was ripe to identify non-Communist unions and separate them from those of radical character, thus breaking the trade union coalition.[11] Egyptian events resonated in Beirut, where three months later the Legation was awaiting a well-trained labor "expert" with a "background in the social sciences as well as labor experience so that he will be able to make objective evaluations of political-labor problems unique to this country" and be prepared to address issues of industrial safety, agricultural employment, and industrial apprenticeship.[12] Prerequisites for the position included the ability to penetrate Arab psychology, the apparent route into Lebanese politics, according to U.S. sources. These further recommended that the task required "the objective techniques most frequently found in trained sociologists."

Anti-communist labor activity coincided with a more generalized organization of anti-communist forces in Lebanon. Legation officer John Bruins, for example, confronted Prime Minister Abdallah Yafi in the summer of 1951 in an exchange that pitted the expression of American liberalism against Lebanese conservativism. The exercise was revealing but also entirely gratuitous. Bruins tackled Yafi for his unwillingness to resolve Lebanon's poverty, unemployment, and inequity. Yafi's response was the countercharge that Bruins ignored Lebanese social and cultural values, which effectively protected those in need.[13] The problem was one of alienated urban intellectuals, according to Yafi. Bruins, in turn, argued that the Middle East presented an ideal terrain for Communist expansion and that more social planning was imperative. Yafi then reminded his guest that "Lebanon is the Arab country with the most western interests and contacts and with our aid wants to be a leader and model among Arab states toward progress and alignment with the West, without losing its own national characteristics" (ibid.). In the end, a frustrated Bruins retreated to the position that Lebanese political culture was responsible for the nation's condition. But contrary to his advocacy of reform, the preferred technique for containing radicalism in Washington was political containment and internal security, along with collaboration with those whose policies were otherwise viewed as less than admirable.

What the Yafi-Bruins exchange omitted to discuss on this occasion was the areas of cooperation between the United States and Lebanon in their common anti-Communist campaign. In Beirut, the U.S. Legation, in cooperation with British, French, and Turkish missions, organized a campaign to "assist the Lebanese Government in combatting Communism."[14] Bruins himself summarized the policies implemented as a result of "a series of conversations by several of the Chiefs of Mission individually with Lebanese officials, including the President, in which it was indicated that the Lebanese authorities would welcome such suggestions from us, particularly since the Communist Party has long been outlawed in Lebanon." The committee of four met, devised the project, and proposed it to the president, prime minister, foreign minister, and the Chef de Sûreté. No written documents were to be exchanged, and maximum cover was afforded to avoid the risk of disclosure. Among the most carefully guarded information were lists of those liable for arrest. "On that point it was agreed that in dealing with the Sûreté we might informally mention individuals or printing establishments against which repressive measures might be appropriate."

  The project opened with a statement on the illegal status of the Lebanese Communist Party and the reminder that its activity was on the increase in a country "wide open to Communist propaganda, both from abroad and also home-produced." The illegality of the party was hardly the issue. U.S. interest in the PPS, also an illegal party in Beirut and Damascus, was not inhibited by such considerations. U.S. officers in Damascus were straightforward in their identification of PPS support for key U.S. policies, such as the Middle East Command, the Mutual Security Program, and Point IV, which made it "an extremely important and valuable Syrian political group from the standpoint of immediate U.S. policy interests."[15] In Beirut, the campaign focused on identifying Communist Party activists and "agents" and assessing their impact on the media and the public. Strict measures were proposed, including arrests, seizure of printing presses, and prohibition of importation of material regarded as subversive. If necessary, "close cooperation with the Syrian Sûreté may also be required," it continued, although other measures were considered. If necessary, the Legation volunteered to supply information on the following categories:

  a. A list of Lebanese Nationalist organizations that have been, or are being, penetrated by the Communists.
  b. A list of leading Communists.
  c. A list of pro-Communist papers produced in Beirut and Tripoli.
  d. Specimens of Communist pamphlets printed in Lebanon, and also Communist papers, instructions, and pamphlets printed abroad and on sale here.
  e. Master documents showing the tactics and operations of the Communist party in other countries.
  f. A list of Communist Congresses to be held in other countries and for which passport facilities might be refused.
  g. Later, material for an official anticommunist propaganda campaign.

Several months later, on June 17, the Legation sent word to the Department of State that Harold Minor had succeeded in having Communists excluded from the Opposition, in direct response to his pressures.[16] This was followed by another measure regarded as "perhaps the most constructive act of the government this summer." Henri Far'oun and General Shihab had managed to establish an internal security department with powers "to investigate and control all internal disturbances."[17] Far'oun was known to be a reliable anti-communist ideologue, as his actions against the trade union movement showed. He was also an unabashed exponent of closer U.S.-Lebanese relations and a man of means and status in Lebanese society. As for General Shihab, the man who was to become Lebanon's third president was castigated by Eisenhower and John Foster Dulles for his reluctance to politicize the minuscule Lebanese army in 1958. To those who were well informed, Shihab's impeccable past—insofar as the United States was concerned—was not to be forgotten.

Fickle Contingencies

There were other advocates of a muscular anticommunism in Lebanon, among whom Charles Malik must be counted. But Malik's role in U.S.-Lebanese relations was far more comprehensive. Not only was he an exponent of a Lebanese-U.S. political rapprochement, he was considered by the State Department to be a credible spokesperson on the Palestine question. While the Khuri regime's position cannot be reduced to that articulated by Malik, there is little doubt that Malik proved to be a significant intermediary on the subject.

Malik's reputation as Lebanese diplomat in the United States rests largely on his relationship with John Foster Dulles, Eisenhower's secretary of state. Yet on the basis of U.S. sources it becomes clear that Malik had made his mark earlier and that George McGhee relied on him as a valuable interlocutor, not only for Lebanon but also for the Middle East. Much concerning Malik's role remains undisclosed, but there is sufficient evidence in U.S. sources to identify him as one of the key Lebanese figures who had unimpeded access to the State Department. Indeed, it was Malik who repeatedly argued his government's position on the Palestine question with U.S. officials, ultimately conceding that whatever objections it had would not hinder Lebanese-U.S. relations. And it was Malik who argued on behalf of Lebanon's role as international and regional intermediary. For the State Department in the Truman administration, Malik was the preferred interpreter of Arab politics, a choice that prejudiced the results in a manner that conformed entirely to Washington's views and interests.

On Palestine, Malik was adamant and eloquent, a man who confronted political realities on the ground at the same time that he cautioned his listeners not to submit to the arrogance of power in remaining indifferent to what was unfolding. In this mission he utterly failed in his confrontations with U.S. officials. But then the constituency that he represented was more than prepared for concessions.

Along with the Lebanese regime's distinct distaste for Point IV, Beirut's position on Palestine was frequently invoked as the litmus test of U.S.-Lebanese relations. The claim was belied by events, even though there is little reason to doubt that the U.S. Legation in Beirut and the State Department were alarmed and disconcerted by the expression of anti-Zionist and anti-U.S. sentiments, both in parliament and outside of it.

When U.S. officers in the Legation, from Wadsworth to Pinkerton to Minor, insisted that Lebanon's cooperation with Washington on Palestine was a prerequisite to U.S.-Lebanese political relations, the claim was to be taken seriously. But exceptions notwithstanding, the passivity of the Lebanese ruling class on Palestine was one on which U.S. officials relied.[18] Less than a month after the declaration of Israel's independence, the SWNCC Country Study on Long-Range Assistance to Lebanon confirmed the proposition that "it is in the national interest of the U.S. to maintain and develop its friendly relations with Lebanon."[19]

Among the reasons offered were those bearing on the country's strategic importance, which "the war" was reported to have emphasized. The conclusions applied to both World War II and the Israeli-Palestinian-Arab conflict, since the importance of the eastern Mediterranean and Middle East oil was underscored by the first as well as the second. Hence, in spite of the charged political atmosphere in which the conditions of Israel's independence were debated, U.S. officials counted on their knowledge of the compromised position of the Lebanese bourgeoisie in Palestine, and they were well placed to weigh the meaning of official declarations on the subject. The status of Palestinian refugees, the role of the United Nations Relief and Work Agency (UNRWA), and Lebanon's cooperation in the Mixed Armistice Commission were pressure points, not turning points, in U.S.-Lebanese relations. And the aggravations to U.S. visitors caused by the anti-American criticisms in the media and in the Lebanese Chamber, no less seriously taken, remained disturbances that the Legation was confident that the regime could handle.

Throughout 1948–1949, U.S. officials in Lebanon, such as Lowell Pinkerton, who had been in Jerusalem, remained receptive to Palestinian refugees and their plight. But Pinkerton was unable to influence policy in Washington and no less sanguine about the situation in Beirut. As Legation chief, he agreed to convey the grievances of a group of Palestinian representatives of the Jaffa and District Inhabitants Council, who spoke on behalf of residents of Jaffa, Ramlah, Lydda, and other Arab villages of their district before the Palestinian Conciliation Commission and U.S. Secretary of State Acheson. Although armed with evidence of Israeli violations of commitments made to the residents of the aggrieved areas, Pinkerton achieved little by way of redress.[20]

At the same time that this exchange was taking place, the State Department was listening to Charles Malik, who admitted to U.S. officials that the Khuri regime in Beirut had decided not to allow the Palestine question to interfere with U.S.-Lebanese relations. It was Pinkerton who cabled Acheson in January 1949 that the Lebanese foreign minister had informed him that "Lebanon is now prepared to put Palestine episode to one side and consider its foreign policy on basis of friendship with Western powers in possible future global war."[21] Lebanon had rejected its "isolationist" position, and so had Syria, U.S. officials were informed. Indeed, Beirut might be willing to make its ports and military airfield at Rayak available to the United States as evidence of its commitment. Given Beirut's compliance on the subject of Palestine, repeatedly emphasized during this period, the Palestine question was effectively neutralized in Lebanese-U.S. relations (ibid.). The conclusion was expressed in a 1951 State Department position paper on Lebanon declaring that "the major elements of our strength in Lebanon have not been fundamentally impaired despite the Lebanese dislike of our Palestine policy."[22]

One paper hardly defines a policy in perpetuity, but over the course of the next few years there was no reason to assume that the political elite in power in Lebanon had changed their position, particularly those considered to be friends of the United States. This in no way eliminated the Palestine question from U.S.-Lebanese relations, as tensions remained and intensified, magnified by U.S. policy, Lebanese domestic conflicts, and the utter failure to achieve a political solution of the Israeli-Palestinian struggle. But in the transition from the Khuri to the Sham'un regime, the question was contained insofar as U.S.-Lebanese relations were concerned.

The controversy generated by Point IV in Beirut was affected by the Palestine question. Lebanese critics thought that it was intended as a

means of compensating Lebanon for its compliant position on the conflict. In addition, they viewed the program as a sign of American expansion in the area. Lebanon was the first country in the Middle East in
which the Truman administration decided to implement such a program.
Its response was therefore regarded by the administration in Washington
as particularly significant. The test backfired. In spite of their initial caution with respect to the program, Legation officers maintained a correct
posture, explaining Point IV as part of an extended containment program to curb communist inroads, a program that, they alleged, only the
United States was in a position to carry out. As the multiple projects recommended were inaugurated, technical assistance was endorsed as a generous American response to Lebanese needs.[23] Its scope was indeed comprehensive, extending to programs in agriculture, public health, housing,
transport, fisheries, tourism, irrigation, potable water, and others. The
major effort was to be the Litany River project, at a cost of $365,000—
with the Lebanese government providing $90,000. It was estimated that
the Litany scheme, involving dams, hydroelectric plants, and irrigation
systems, "would serve as a tangible example to all Near Eastern peoples
of the possible help to be derived from such a TVA type project in the
way of agricultural expansion, electrification, development of light
industries, and rural reconstruction" (ibid.).

Doubts as to the feasibility of such projects were rampant among U.S.
officials, however. Pinkerton thought that "only a few Lebanese are
interested in anything but their own well-being and that of their family
or clan" (ibid.). But the political atmosphere was also charged as a result
of the Palestine question; hence, to support Point IV was viewed by
Lebanese officials as an unwanted risk. The officer in charge of Point IV
in Beirut, Afif Tannous, was pessimistic for other reasons. Lebanese society was embroiled in a "vicious circle with economic, social and political
implications," reflected "in promising but undeveloped resources, mea-
ger revenues, poorly-paid officials, inadequate governmental services,
low levels of living among the majority, exploitive enterprises, nepotism,
concentration of power and wealth in the hands of the few, and mounting unemployment."[24] Point IV was hardly the cure for conditions where
"discontent, resentment and bitterness are abundantly evident. . . . Beirut
is fast becoming town of milling crowds and slums, boulevards and modern buildings, notwithstanding. . . . Communism is increasingly appealing to large segments in rural and urban areas including educated elements who are unemployed and frustrated." Harold Minor, who became

U.S. minister in 1951, shared the same outlook, persuaded that the Lebanese tended to think of the program as designed to enrich the wealthy, while Lebanese officials remained indifferent since they saw no potential for such enrichment.[25]

Minor was among those who not only met regularly with Khuri but considered his regime's support for Point IV a matter of importance. Yet at the same time Minor was fully aware of the precarious status of Khuri's position. According to reports from the field, Minor was full of advice as to how Khuri should proceed—and equally skeptical that he would or could do so. In August 1952, Minor learned that Khuri was planning to take at least one welcome step that would appease his critics: the president was sending his "bad boy son, Khalil, out of the country for an extended trip."[26] On more substantive proposals for reform, the two continued to talk, although as Minor avowed, he was distressed to learn that Khuri had no plans to promote taxation or land reform laws. Communication problems interfered, some of a linguistic nature, others frankly political. Legation chief Minor admitted that his knowledge of French, the language in which President Khuri communicated with him, was often inadequate to permit him to grasp the details of an exchange.

But Minor felt that his recommendations were not being heard for reasons other than the language barrier. To judge by his suggestions, Minor advocated a more responsive and responsible government. He thought Khuri would be well advised to address "legitimate desires of the masses of the people for better govt and for recognition of their basic rights" (ibid.). Khuri was reported to have been moved, but Minor doubted that he was in a position to act: "I don't know whether he will carry through, but I am convinced this is the way to tackle the problem, i.e., to encourage legally constituted govts to carry out broad social and economic reforms, thus mtg legitimate desires of the masses of the people for better govt and for recognition of their basic rights" (ibid.).

Minor's position, straightforward as it appears, is disingenuous. Discontent with the Khuri regime was rife among U.S. officials, in spite of the president's delayed acquiescence to U.S. pressures, as the following discussion of the "end of neutralism" indicates. On the other hand, the Legation was in close touch with opposition leaders who regularly conveyed their progress as well as their own agenda.

One year earlier, in the fall of 1951, the Lebanese Chamber had ratified Point IV, and Lebanon was thereby included in the U.S. Mutual Security Program. The move was interpreted by domestic critics as proof of the Khuri regime's abandonment of its neutralist stance and/or proof of U.S. efforts to compensate it for its position on the Palestine question. Bruins cabled as an example of "the polit opposition to ratification of Point IV," the reasons offered by "a leading Greek-Orthodox editor Twaini, member of Chamber of Deputies and member of Greek [sic] National Socialist Front," whose views were reported as those of his "polit group."[27] Their content was summarized as follows:

1. What are hidden motives behind Point IV?
2. If purpose is to combat Communism, does govt regard such purpose in accordance with its foreign policy and with its right to self-determination?
3. Would not agreement put us in Amer sphere of influence and tie us to the U.S. to extent that govt policy of neutrality wld be impossible? Does govt regard itself as hving abandoned neutrality already?
4. What benefits wld Lebanon derive which it wld not (rpt not) obtain without the agreement?
5. Wld agreement mean entree for Amer Capital, which means undesirable control of Leb economy?
6. Can Leb budget stand the expense, or are loans contemplated?
7. Does our govt have overall econ plan and policy within framework these Point IV projects wld come?

As Bruins explained, "the above stems from sources usually well-informed and friendly" and could not be classified with the larger body of criticism that he labeled as "irresponsible." Among the responsible critics of Point IV, it turned out, were some who subsequently requested assistance from the Legation in what the State Department's David Bruce described as a "projected coup." That belongs to the discussion of the "end of neutralism," which was, in effect, the end of the Khuri regime. Insofar as the place of Point IV in U.S.-Lebanese relations is concerned, the program's acceptance did not improve the attitude of the Legation toward the regime. Whether it was a factor in overt or covert aspects of domestic politics at this stage, and whether the United States had anything to do with either one, remain unclear.

The End of Neutralism

In the State Department's lexicon, even in the days before John Foster Dulles's role as the iron secretary of state, neutralism aroused unpleasant vibrations. Besharah al-Khuri was tarred with the charge of neutralism. Charles Malik had listened to the vilification of his government as neutralist. What did neutralism mean in the context of Lebanon's openness to U.S. economic interests, to the welcome it gave TAPLINE, and to U.S. aviation interests? Neutralism was interpreted as an insufficiently pro-American foreign policy. Until the 1950–1951 period, however, there was little interest in moving the Khuri regime in this direction, and Lebanese requests for military assistance were similarly rebuffed by the Defense Department.

In the immediate postwar years, the Defense Department was hostile to the idea of committing U.S. forces or providing military assistance to the Middle East, barring Turkey and, in a limited respect, Saudi Arabia. The State Department, in turn, rejected invitations to become cosignatory of a treaty guaranteeing Lebanese sovereignty. The position of both departments eventually changed. In 1948 a credit line for the purchase of surplus was offered for the sum of some $5 million.[28] Lebanon was receiving air force training and equipment from the British and had signed a contract with the Hunting Aircraft Corporation for training and the purchase of "5 Proctor model 5 aircraft, furnishing 4 British pilot instructors, spare parts and accessories, ground installations and training first year. 12 Lebanese pilots, 8 crews and ground staff and navigators."[29] The Defense Department was nonetheless asked by the Department of State to approve the Lebanese request for expert assistance in armored vehicle maintenance, for which Beirut was willing to assume financial responsibility. The gesture, made in 1950, had more political than military significance. The assistance was extended in January 1951, when the State Department approved the military training in the United States of limited numbers of Lebanese, as well as the request for purchase of light weapons "from commercial sources in the U.S. in such quantities as are reasonable for purposes of internal security and self-defense."[30] Included in the U.S. Mutual Security Program, Lebanon could formally request economic as well as military assistance from the Defense Department.

Such moves did not begin to address the demands that Charles Malik considered to be a legitimate aspect of Lebanese-U.S. relations, nor did they speak to the concerns that Francis Kittaneh brought to the attention of the State Department. For both men, the ideological compatibility between Lebanon and the United States and the potential role of Lebanon as intermediary between the West and the Middle East were sufficient to justify the political rapprochement that both strongly favored.

The militant advocacy and access that both had to Washington's corridors of power raises other questions: For whom did they speak? Were
they official (Malik) or unofficial (Kittaneh) spokesmen for the Lebanese
regime that did not formally espouse the position with which they identified themselves? Did they operate as high-level rogue diplomats, as
some former U.S. State Department officials later informally suggested?[31] Were they responsible for preparing fertile ground for future
Lebanese-U.S. relations? Did they reflect internal political breaks not yet
apparent at the overt political level in Beirut?

In 1949 Charles Malik, then in Washington on FCN Treaty matters,
met with Secretary of State Dean Acheson and Assistant Secretary of
State George McGhee. He advanced the position that in exchange for
signing the treaty, the United States recognize Lebanon's exceptional cultural and political status. Lebanon, Malik insisted, needed financial assistance and protection from Israel as well as Arab states and Islamist movements.[32] Malik claimed that other Arab leaders shared his views and
thought some form of Western collective security arrangement was desirable. While emphasizing the primordial role of the United States, Malik
proposed a tripartite agreement for the resolution of outstanding conflicts and the provision of assistance. Appealing for protection of
Lebanon in its capacity as a Christian state allied with the West in culture and religion, Malik insinuated that if the United States did not
respond, Lebanon would look to its European allies for help. Acheson's
reaction was negative. Neither precedent nor political interest gave him
pause to reconsider his views. In the State Department's vision, European
concerns and security arrangements, such as NATO, had priority. Malik
was redirected toward the department's NEA division, as well as to the
International Bank for Reconstruction and Development.

Francis Kittaneh, who had addressed the Council on Foreign
Relations in December 1948 on the advisability of the United States'
assuming Britain's role in the Middle East, was in Washington in May
1950.[33] Meeting with L. Satterthwaite and H. Clark of the State
Department, after a visit to the Middle East that included Yemen, he had
an offer to make.

> Mr. Kettaneh said that while he was in Lebanon government officials
> there spoke of their desire for American economic assistance and will-
> ingness to align Lebanon with the United States for defense purposes.
> He mentioned that should Lebanon sever its ties with Syria or vice
> versa, as seemed possible, Lebanon would probably lose considerable

foreign exchange which now accrues to it through the division between Syria and Lebanon of customs duties. A deficit of perhaps $5,000,000 might result annually in Lebanon's balance of payments for several years. Should the United States be prepared to make up the deficit in one form or another, Lebanon would be willing to make military and naval bases available to the United States.[34]

Clark replied that the subject had already been under discussion and that the Lebanese Ministry of Foreign Affairs had been contacted with regard to this offer.

In June 1949, Malik appeared once again at the Department of State to discuss the FCN Treaty, meeting McGhee and Satterthwaite in the presence of the Lebanese counselor in Washington, George Hakim. This time, elaborating on the circumstances of the FCN Treaty, Malik returned to the idea of a political quid pro quo with the United States. He proposed that Lebanon was ideally situated to act as the intermediary for the West in the Middle East. "We believe American long-range interest should not be limited to what Lebanon is in itself but should go beyond that to what Lebanon is and can be in its relations with its sister Arab countries of the Middle East."[35]

> While thoroughly grounded in Arab existence, Lebanon fundamentally faces West. Consequently it is ideally suited to perform a mediating function. In language, customs, social and political relations, and historical destiny, Lebanon is one with the Arab world; and yet it is profoundly responsive to Western values as no other part of Asia, or even Eastern Europe, is. When therefore Lebanon plays a modest role in the development of the Arab world, it does so as an integral part of and partner with that world, wholly identifying its own fate with it, and not as an alien force imposing its will from outside and really uninterested in the fate of the vast Arab hinterland.

State Department officials responded with caution. They recognized Lebanon's status as "a special friend of the United States and a medium through which American ideas and policies could be transmitted and interpreted to the rest of the Arab world." But in February 1950 it was evident that those officials dealing with Near Eastern affairs were unprepared to endorse guarantees of Lebanese sovereignty, borders, or even a "public declaration of its support for Lebanon's territorial integrity and independence."[36] Territorial guarantees, they thought, were contingent on Lebanon's reaching an agreement with Israel, and the same applied to other states. When, in the fall of 1949, Malik insisted that Lebanon was endangered from within the Arab world itself, he met with no more support in spite of his complaint of American indifference to "the only predominantly Christian country in Asia" at a time when the United States supported a Jewish state in the region (ibid.). The NEA division officers with whom Malik spoke redirected Lebanon to France. Their vision of Lebanon was entirely removed from that of Malik.

> Most Moslems, except a few overlords who have vested interests in the corruption of the present Lebanese Government, would feel no patriotic pangs of discontent if a unified Syria and Iraq, or Syria alone, were to reclaim the "lost" (i.e., detached from Syria and added to Lebanon by the French) predominantly Moslem provinces of Tripoli, Bekaa, and Sidon, the areas, it is noted, of greatest development potential.   (Ibid.)

Only in the Mount Lebanon area, these officials believed, would Malik's views find support. Even among Christian and Druze leaders, such as Sham'un and Junblat, there were disaffected supporters of Arab unity who were alienated by the corruption of the regime. The severance of the Syro-Lebanese Customs Union might adversely affect the Lebanese economy, but this possibility was not viewed as a threat. On the contrary, Department of State officials speculated on the feasibility of creating Lebanon (Beirut) as a regional free trade zone, thus underscoring Beirut's role as an economic enclave.

The Korean War prompted the State Department to review its Middle East petroleum resources and George McGhee to review their protection. In August 1950, McGhee pressed Malik, by then a familiar and trusted informant and interlocutor, on the public mood in the Arab world, on the impact of the Korean War, on the probability of regional solidarity with the United States, and on the risks of Communist and Soviet advances within the area. Malik's presentation impressed McGhee. He was to repeat some of its principal themes in preparatory meetings for the winter 1951 Istanbul conference of American officers in the Middle East. As for Malik, in the summer of 1950 he maintained that faced with an international crisis, "the Christian population would definitely be on the side of the West and the Moslems would not be on the side of Russia although they would be 'open to suggestion' from the Arab hinterland."[37] Malik calculated that about 70 percent of the population would "miss the West," which would "include all of the Westernized, commercial, and landlord classes. The remaining 30% of the people would be apathetic—

never having seen anything better for thousands of years they would not miss what they never had."

McGhee prodded Malik as to where the Egyptian and Saudi monarchs would stand, to which Malik replied that unless they were attacked, they would most likely take no "positive action." Pinkerton added his thoughts on the question, sending the State Department news of the favorable response of Arabs and Israelis to what he interpreted as U.S. decisiveness in Korea.

In Washington, McGhee drew his own conclusions, insisting on the need to reassure pro-Western regimes in the region of U.S. support, lest they be inclined to look elsewhere. The rationale for the endorsement of military assistance offered by McGhee to Major General James Burns of the Defense Department rested on the benefits that would accrue to the United States—including greater internal stability in the region, the continuity of pro-Western regimes, and the increased "opportunities provided for expanded military intelligence coverage."[38]

In January 1951, the State Department's Policy Statement on Lebanon confirmed the U.S. commitment to the maintenance of the Beirut regime and the development of its transit outlets and aviation facilities, as well as expanded trade and communications. U.S. objectives included supporting:

> sound political and economic foundations for Lebanese cooperation with the U.S. and the west in order to prevent the USSR from gaining control by force or subversion of Lebanon's important strategic assets, particularly its harbors on the eastern Mediterranean, its developing aviation facilities and its established and projected transit, outlet and refining facilities for oil transmitted by pipeline from Saudi Arabia and Iraq.[39]

The policy statement confirmed earlier authorizations of military purchases, training of Lebanese personnel, and Lebanon's integration into planning for area defense, along with "other like-minded democracies." U.S. officials were apparently now interested in previous offers, especially "the possibility that Lebanon would agree to renew former offers of naval and air facilities to Western forces in exchange for an appropriate quid pro quo." It was hoped that Beirut and other Arab capitals would agree to support the Middle East Command. Nothing of the kind occurred, as the Beirut regime responded to the Egyptian rejection of the MEC by following suit.

Such positions, no matter how irritating to Anglo-American supporters of the military arrangements embodied in the Middle East Command,
did not damage Beirut's standing with Washington. McGhee, who briefly
visited Beirut in February 1951, after the U.S. Ministers Conference in
Istanbul, described the Lebanese president as utterly reliable, "firmly
pro-Western. He was concerned about possible Communist and radical
Palestinian influence among the refugees in Lebanon, he represented the
old regime and posed no problem to us."[40] Was this expression a reflection of President Khuri's genuine political concerns or a shrewd anticipation of what U.S. officials wanted to hear? The effect was perhaps the
same in terms of the listeners.

The exchange between McGhee and Khuri and officials was followed
some months later by what local U.S. officials regarded as a welcome
event. Five months later, to be precise, John Bruins, the experienced
Legation commercial attaché, was informed by Charles Malik that an
unprecedented all-day meeting on Lebanese-U.S. relations had been held
at the summer residence of the president, with the entire cabinet in atten-
dance. He considered the news to be positive.[41]

Clearly, something in the political climate had changed. As a result of
what internal political struggles? Malik's enthusiastic assurance to Bruins
was indicative of his own sentiments as well as his own "victory." It was
clearly not his alone, however, as the discontent with President Khuri
brought together a coalition that included other friends of the United
States. Surrounded by an increasingly vocal opposition that waxed indignant about corruption, nepotism, and high-level scandals, Besharah al-
Khuri found that his position had become difficult.

Those opposed to his policies now included politicians, lawyers, and
journalists, organized around the program of the National Socialist
Front, such as Kamal Junblat, Pierre Eddeh, Kamil Sham'un, Emile
Bustani, Ghassan Tuwayni, Dikran Tosbath, Anwar Khatib, and
Abdallah Haj.[42] They constituted a professional cohort with a distinctly
different base than the traditional politicians who were not displaced.
Within the ranks of the opposition, however, it was the younger group of
reformers who promised action. Kamal Junblat, a man of "commanding
individual strength," was a prominent figure in the group, a factor that
apparently antagonized others in the same entourage, as subsequent
developments demonstrated.[43] Kamil Sham'un, who emerged as the
nation's second president, was the politician who kept the Legation
informed as to the prospects and progress of the coalition. He predicted

that at least one third of the program proposed by the opposition coalition would be backed by the Chamber.[44]

If the political dynamics within the Lebanese ruling class were shifting, the results were tangible in Washington, where Malik assumed an even more assertive stance with respect to Lebanese-U.S. relations. In Washington at the end of August 1951, Malik met with McGhee and Lewis Jones, director of the Near East Division. Malik proposed a Mediterranean Pact, to which the United States, the United Kingdom, and France, along with Spain and the countries of the eastern Mediterranean, would adhere. Syria would approve, Malik thought, and Iraq and Saudi Arabia would be invited, as would Israel, by "special arrangement."[45] State Department officials reminded Malik of the Anglo-American Middle East Command (MEC) that was frustrated by Egyptian rejection. Jones, in turn, reminded Malik of the importance of Israel's regional role along with its pro-Western orientation and its communication facilities. Neither Malik nor Hakim, the Lebanese counselor in Washington, objected, according to U.S. records.

Insofar as the Middle East Command was concerned, Malik and his American hosts knew how problematic it had been from the outset. Introduced as an adjunct to Western defense arrangements in the Middle East and Western Europe, the MEC aroused suspicion in Egypt, where it was accurately viewed as an arrangement to protect Western-controlled interests. That British officials were unwilling to accept Egyptian nationalists' rejection of their proposal was not difficult to understand. Extremism was not the explanation, but Egyptian rejection set the stage for a similarly cautious and negative outlook in other Middle Eastern capitals. The failure of the MEC was followed by another attempt to organize a Middle East Defense Organization (MEDO), which met a similar fate. What it led to, however, was a reconsideration not of the policies intended but of the strategy necessary to achieve them.

In Beirut, Harold Minor continued to pressure President Khuri on the subject. Taking up the issues of the MEC and Point IV, Minor warned that "a policy of neutrality or non-coop cld bring disaster, while one of coop with Western powers in MEC and Point Four cld on contrary be salvation of NE. Pres agreed with this statement and said Leb leaders have every intention of following Western powers."[46]

Minor did not stop at this, however, accusing Lebanon of going the way of Iran, referring to what U.S. officials feared, namely, the nationalization of Western oil companies. Minor omitted to mention how U.S.

international oil companies benefited from the Iranian nationalization, a detail he may not have been aware of at the time, although his interest in ARAMCO must have been considerable, since he later joined the U.S. international company. Minor must have known, in any case, that his analogy with Teheran was inappropriate, not to say ludicrous. To the charge that Lebanon was going the way of Mossadeq, Besharah al-Khuri responded with vehement denial "that Lebanon 'has drunk of Iranian wine,' " while asking Minor to obtain more U.S. investments in Lebanon.

For a man accused of flirting with nationalization, the rejoinder was striking. Minor nevertheless persisted, insisting that such an outcome was unlikely, as "companies were genuinely concerned at drift of events and wld require assurances from Leb Govt." Minor, the U.S. Legation chief who gave the Lebanese president advice on good government and who was committed to a policy of noninterference in the affairs of sovereign nations, informed the State Department that he thought a properly tough policy was in order, that a "policy of 'friendly firmness' toward Lebanon is required at this time."

One week later, Francis Kittaneh was in New York discussing the Iranian crisis at the Council on Foreign Relations and alarming its corporate members with news that the Iranian prime minister was on his way to Cairo to discuss the creation of a bloc including Egypt, Pakistan, and Iran.[47] The man who acted as liaison for U.S. businesses in the Middle East was a credible witness, and his message was precisely that brought to Washington by Malik and to the offices of the U.S. minister in Beirut. Any change in the regional status quo, as Malik had insisted to Acheson some months earlier, was intolerable. Henri Far'oun took up the question with the U.S. minister in Beirut the following spring, when he further insisted on a Lebanese-U.S. alliance as part of an overall anti-Communist strategy in which a Lebanon defined in terms of its Mediterranean roots would be supported in its efforts to contain Arab-Islamic political moves, whatever their provenance.[48] Here, then, were Lebanese advocates of the military pacts with the West, which doubtless further explained their open-ended access to Washington.

At a different level, a study that was issued in the fall of 1951 and that coincided with the turning and/or conflict within the cabinet assumed particular interest at this juncture. The reference is to the study of Lebanon's minorities that was carried out by the Legation in Beirut. In spite of its failure to distinguish the various constituencies among Lebanese Christians and to single out only Maronites, the report issued findings that, while hardly novel, were politically useful. The writers compiled evidence demonstrating that a preponderance of high officials and influential personalities were Christian and pro-Western. The connection was of the essence. "It thus appears that the President of the Republic, the members of his family, many Cabinet members, important deputies, leading businessmen, large landowners, and many figures in high society are Maronites. As such their thinking is Christian and pro-Western."[49]

The conclusion was self-evident. The incumbent president might have his faults, but he belonged to a confessional group with which U.S. ties ought to be cultivated. As Legation officials explained, "Under these circumstances it would seem that existing contacts with the Maronite churchmen and laymen should be strengthened, and new contacts made in order that the U.S. may be in a position to make the best possible use of this strong pro-Western and potentially pro-American element in the Lebanon." While the president fit the requisite confessional category, he was otherwise an odd man out, as he was bitterly criticized by the Maronite clergy for being too independent, which corresponded to Washington's appraisal.

In late August 1952 the State Department upgraded the U.S. Legations in Jordan, Syria, and Lebanon to Embassy status. The mark of recognition coincided with an important transition period. Precisely how involved the United States was in such a transition remains unclear. Yet in early August, Acting Secretary of State David Bruce cabled the Legation in Lebanon with a cryptic response to what appeared to be an invitation to a coup in Beirut. Bruce firmly endorsed the Embassy's rejection of such an offer. His telegram is doubly instructive for its summary of the official U.S. position.

> Dept fully approves emphatic position you took with Tamer and Tweini re U.S. support projected coup as well as position given last para Leftel 192 July 30. Obviously U.S. cannot in any way abet such plans, despite repugnant practices Khouri regime and need for breath of fresh polit air in Leb. Moreover, highly doubtful that U.S. objectives and Leb welfare cld profit by change govt thru violence, particularly in view deep ideological and personal cleavages among leb conspirators.[50]

Bruce recommended that the Legation persuade Khuri of the urgency of reform so as to avoid a replay of Egyptian events and the mobilization of domestic discontent. "Leb Commies await this development." At about the same time, the first secretary of the U.S. Embassy in London cabled the Department of State with news of a meeting with Lebanon's foreign minister, Charles Hilu, who confirmed that "Lebanon's international position is fundamentally oriented toward the United States and the West."[51] Hilu's worries regarding Israel and its open-ended immigration policy were met with the U.S. official's assurances of U.S. commitment and an indication "that any attempt to suppress the Lebanon by force would be regarded by the United States as a very serious matter." Even with this turning of the tide, Harold Minor, given to reflection on the vagaries of U.S. diplomacy, was not beyond regrets:

> I sometimes worry for fear we are repeating the mistakes of history in supporting corrupt regimes and the status quo. This is always a risk but it can be overcome by letting it be known constantly and positively where we stand and for what we stand. It requires a capable tightrope walker these days to maintain the proper balance, on the one hand of supporting legally-constituted govts, and on the other of not (rpt not) discouraging progressive forces.[52]

Unsentimental analysts of Lebanon in the National Security Council had earlier come to believe that regime politics in states such as Lebanon and Iraq generated wide-scale discontent and that "the governments have been successful in preventing effective organized opposition through bribery, political patronage, and other political maneuvers including outright suppression at times."[53]

In Beirut, meanwhile, electioneering brought politicians to the Legation to discuss possible successors to President Khuri. "They note that Brit are more or less openly backing Camille Chamoun and that French are believed to be supporting Hamid Frangie [Franjiyyah]."[54] The Legation deemed that all candidates were "without exception friendly to America." Although the Legation and the State Department insisted on American neutrality, its meaning was highly contextual. There was, in fact, an American favorite, and he was not receiving much attention. Hence, as "our only personal preference Dr Malik is receiving scarcely any attention we believe we shld officially and unofficially show no favoritism lest by doing so we alienate affections of Pres eventually elected." Indeed, the Legation staff received instruction as to how to respond to requests for evaluations of various political personalities:

> (1) day of imperialism is over; we respect Lebanon's independence and her right select pres in accordance her own constitutional processes;

(2) we hope for a Pres who has universal respect entire citizenry, who will decidedly steer Lebanon on course of progress its people so obviously desire; and (3) we have not and will not support any individual and do not believe any foreign power is or shld be giving active support to any candidate.

A politically astute statement, it offered no guide to U.S. policy.

PART III

The Eisenhower Administration and the Sham'un Regime: A Policy of Information and Consent

7

Pressure Points and Priorities

Transitions in Beirut and Washington

Kamil Sham'un became Lebanon's second president in September 1952. The leader of a reformist coalition, he was known as a champion of the Palestinian cause, a sympathizer of the Egyptian revolution, a critic of domestic corruption, and a man close to British circles. His American supporters were unfazed, neither awed nor indifferent. Two years earlier his political destiny had seemed routine for a Maronite lawyer and former minister, neither eloquent nor charismatic but effective in obtaining British support, without which his career would not have succeeded.[1] By the time Sham'un delivered his inaugural address, he was viewed by the American Embassy as a man with multiple friendships—toward the British, the French, and the Americans.[2] New political obligations were expected to alter Sham'un's attachments.

1. Whether true or not almost every one in Leb believes Chamoun [Sham'un] has Brit sponsorship. As result Brit interests may prosper. On other hand, Chamoun may be forced to react by leaning over backward to avoid stigma of connection with Brit whose interests cld actually be harmed. In any case, many observers believe he will pull Leb from pro-French cultural orbit.
2. In long run, Amer influence will probably be stronger not only with Chamoun but all Lebanese politicians by reason of our much talked

about neutrality during election campaign. Chamoun is definitely our friend and when elected was preparing for Point IV leader-grant visit to US.[3]

From the vantage point of the Embassy, Sham'un was expected to be a reformist president, most likely meeting resistance by "polit barons, who still hold Parl seats and who voted Chamoun to presidency." The same was expected with respect to what was described as his nonsectarian attitude, which would antagonize Lebanese Christians. The Embassy's prognosis was partially correct. Sham'un met resistance in his reforms, but he did not long remain an advocate of "nonsectarianism," for which he was indeed roundly criticized as worse than his predecessor. The one certain presumption was of his positive attitude toward the United States, of which Eisenhower was informed in January 1953.[4]

Four U.S. ambassadors oversaw the economically profitable and politically troubled years of the Sham'un regime between 1952 and 1958. Harold Minor was in charge at the time of the transition process between the Besharah al-Khuri and the Sham'un regimes. If he had certain expectations with respect to Lebanese–U.S. relations, he was more than gratified by the results.

In 1953–1954, Minor was followed by Raymond Hare, who had previously been ambassador to Saudi Arabia and minister to Yemen. Hare's anti-Communist proclivities elicited the support of certain elements of Lebanon's conservative bourgeoisie, with whom he collaborated. In 1955, Donald Heath, in turn, replaced Hare, remaining in Beirut as U.S. ambassador during a period of severe domestic conflicts, aggravated by the Suez and Sinai crises. Heath supported U.S. covert funding of the 1957 parliamentary elections, the success of which contributed to his successor's troubles. Robert McClintock took over as ambassador in January 1958, assuming his position several months before the outbreak of civil war in May, which proved to be the prelude to full-scale U.S. military intervention—as opposed to the incremental assistance that had kept Sham'un alive earlier.

In Washington, in 1953, Eisenhower had just taken office and was given a summary of the status of U.S. policy and Middle East politics. Lebanon passed all tests of friendship and loyalty, yet there were difficult areas that remained, as with respect to MEDO (Middle East Defense Organization), relations with Israel, Point IV, TAPLINE (euphemistically referred to as "private interests"), and Lebanon's insistence on military and economic aid.[5]

There was another area that had been problematic, but it was cleared up before Eisenhower took office. Within a month of his presidency, Sham'un capitulated to U.S. oil company executives bent on obtaining guarantees of the exclusion of Kamal Junblat from the cabinet. At the same time, the Lebanese president let the United States know that he was a reliable partner in the Middle East. If war came with the Soviet Union, Sham'un announced, "Leb is 100 percent on side of West. Our harbors wd be open to your ships, our airfields to your planes, whether or not (rpt not) we have any kind of treaty or agreement in writing."[6]

Sham'un did not await war with the Soviet Union, but neither did he put all of his hopes on Washington. Only days earlier, Sham'un had made the same offer to the British Embassy. On September 30, Ambassador Chapman-Andrew informed Foreign Secretary Anthony Eden that Sham'un had declared that as long as he was president, "the Lebanon would be completely at the disposal of her Majesty's Government in the event of world war. This, he said, would apply whether we have a written agreement or not." Sham'un made clear that he wished Lebanon's army to be "equipped, trained and ready to play their full part in the event of war, and for this purpose he wished to rely on Great Britain and on us alone."[7]

Sham'un could hardly have been faulted for taking out such political insurance, particularly in the light of American recalcitrance with respect to military assistance. In early January he was reported to have approved a dozen more Point IV projects that effectively broke the impasse on that program. As far as TAPLINE was concerned, the agreement signed in May 1952 was under consideration, awaiting parallel Syrian accords. With respect to military assistance, a joint recommendation from the State Department and the Defense Department was sent to the director of the Mutual Security Program asking that Lebanon receive "cash-reimbursable military aid." The vital signs in the relationship were positive, even if Lebanon was known to harbor hopes, as did other Arab regimes, that it would be the recipient of a "New Deal" from the Eisenhower administration.

What the Lebanese president received was less a new deal than a raw dose of the politics of power. The images of the Eisenhower-Sham'un relationship, and more particularly that of John Foster Dulles and Charles Malik as the pinnacle of U.S.-Lebanese relations, deserve a more qualified appraisal. The Lebanese regime complied with U.S. policy in the areas of pipeline concessions, refineries, regional politics, and domestic military intelligence. But even among such "friends," resistance in areas deemed of prime importance to Washington elicited sharp rebuttals. Thus, the persistent demands by Lebanese officials for increased royalties from TAPLINE generated verbal abuse, let alone the response to criticism of U.S. policy on the Israeli-Arab question.

Sham'un's relationship with the Eisenhower administration rested on his unconditional compliance with U.S. regional policy, which directly contributed to the erosion of his domestic support. Influential members of the Lebanese bourgeoisie were by no means unified in their support of Sham'un on this score, fearing that his pro-American policies would isolate Lebanon in the Arab sphere. The crisis over Suez proved to be a turning point in this context, one further aggravated by Sham'un's eager acceptance of the so-called Eisenhower Doctrine.

The long-range implications of this internal division in the ranks of the elite were not immediately apparent in Washington, but they shaped the content of U.S. policy in the aftermath of U.S. intervention in Lebanon's first civil war, in 1958. By the summer of that year, Sham'un was a minority president, with much of the country out of his control. With more legitimacy in Washington than in Beirut, he was understandably embittered when he learned that the American administration that had earlier helped him to survive was now no longer in need of his services. What Sham'un's supporters regarded as betrayal on the part of the United States was, in fact, a misreading of U.S. policies and the calculations on which they were based.

In the fall of 1952 Truman remained at the helm, as the presidential election campaign was under way. In the months separating the Truman administration and the incoming Eisenhower administration, the U.S. government faced two related and intractable political problems concerning the Middle East, neither of which was resolved by the end of Truman's term. The first was the continuing inquiry into the international petroleum cartel, which Truman had authorized the attorney general to pursue in July; the second was the continuing Anglo-Iranian crisis over the Iranian nationalization of the Anglo-Iranian Oil Company.

In the first case, State, Defense, Interior, and Intelligence officials were aghast at the potential political repercussions of a "Grand Jury investigation into possible violations of the Anti-Trust statutes on the part of five major American companies and the Anglo-Iranian Oil Company, and the Shell combination."[8] In December 1952, in a statement crafted by Robert Eakens, the chief of the Petroleum Policy Staff, Acting

Secretary of State David Bruce did not fail to chide an "ostentatiously successful oil industry unavoidably destined to be a primary target for Arab anger and frustration with their lot and with West. Vengeance for Western support of Israel inevitably will be taken out on oil vital to West."[9] Bruce was responding to problems involved in renegotiation of TAPLINE concessions, specifically the question of transit fees. The State Department, he informed U.S. ambassadors in the Middle East, would take no position on the matter. But Bruce criticized ARAMCO for its willingness to risk national—as opposed to commercial—interests. Bruce knew of what he spoke. The cartel report provided detailed evidence of the profit made by ARAMCO-TAPLINE, which went to its shareholders, not to consumers or to the governments of transit states. The subject was at the heart of the cartel investigation, which determined that three of the ARAMCO companies—Caltex, Gulf, and Esso—

> started with the $1.75 Persian Gulf price, f.o.b. Ras Tanura, and in effect added, at their own intra-company rates, the tanker charges from Ras Tanura to the eastern Mediterranean, including the Suez Canal toll charges. This had the effect of charging European importers the same delivered price for Mediterranean as they formerly paid for crude hauled all the way around the Arabian Peninsula—thereby making the pipeline transportation charge equivalent to that of a 10-day tanker haul.[10]

In the second case, British efforts to stifle Iran's capacity to operate its oil industry after Iranian prime minister Mossadeq's nationalization of AIOC in 1951 led Anthony Eden and Winston Churchill to seek active U.S. collaboration. Yet Truman, Acheson, and McGhee were prepared to negotiate with Mossadeq; and along with the Policy Planning Staff's Paul Nitze and State's Near East Affairs director Loy Henderson, they were persuaded that Mossadeq represented Iran's best opportunity for a reformist anti-communist regime.

In November 1952, Kermit Roosevelt, Intelligence operative in the Middle East, rejected British overtures to collaborate in a coup against Mossadeq, "indicating that he had no authorization to discuss U.S. support for such an effort."[11] Roosevelt informed Allen Dulles, deputy director of the CIA, of the exchange, after Eisenhower's election. Dulles's response was to wait until the new administration was in office and he had become head of the CIA and John Foster Dulles secretary of state (ibid. 294). Roosevelt was further advised to keep Truman and Acheson uninformed. Within a matter of months, British efforts were rewarded as anticipated. The Eisenhower administration was, in fact, more pro-business and pro–oil company than its predecessor, as Foreign Secretary Eden had assumed would be the case (ibid. 277).

Eisenhower had no sooner taken office than he was faced with National Security Council Report NSC 138/1, January 6, 1953, "Security and International Issues Arising from the Current Situation in Petroleum."[12] The prognosis could not have been worse. The "problem," as NSC 138/1 described it, was that "the Justice Department has begun a judicial process which can be expected to lead to the indictment and trial of the principal international American oil companies on charges of criminal violations of American law in their foreign operations" (ibid. 637). The statement of this outrageous possibility was followed by repeated summaries of the importance of oil, "vital to the United States and the rest of the free world both in peace and war." And this, in turn, led to unambiguous emphasis on the role of the Middle East, as the area of the "greatest known petroleum reserves" (ibid. 639). In this there was nothing novel. What was striking was the straightforward confirmation of the organic relationship between U.S. foreign economic and political policy in the Middle East and the role of U.S. international oil companies.

> The operations of American oil companies abroad have profound effects on the conduct of American foreign relations. In the first place, oil is the principal source of wealth and income in the Middle Eastern countries in which the deposits exist; their economic and political existence depends upon the rate and terms on which oil is produced. American oil operations are, for all practical purposes, instruments of our foreign policy toward these countries. These oil producing countries are on or near the borders of the Soviet Union. For this reason and because of certain local conditions the Middle East comprises one of the most explosive areas of the world. The oil companies are in a position of great influence upon our relations with the peoples and governments of these countries. What they do and how they do it determines the strength of our ties with the Middle Eastern countries and our ability to resist Soviet expansion and influences in the area.
>
> (Ibid. 641)

In the light of such maxims, and the further evidence of the impact of the cartel investigation in the Middle East, it was little wonder that the

NSC urged that the grand jury proceedings be dismissed. In their place, the NSC recommended that a commission including the secretaries of the departments of State, Defense, Interior, and Commerce review the issues in the case and prepare a classified report for the president with their conclusions. Months before the Anglo-American coup in Iran, the authors of NSC 138/1, in characteristically antiseptic language, indicated that the "motives of any foreign enterprise are still suspect," in the Middle East, although oil companies were "doing much to allay this suspicion." As to local factors explaining anti-Americanism and anti-Westernism, these so-called "basic factors . . . are complicated by the feudal or semi-feudal structure of Arab society, in which certain groups may seek to avert or resolve existing frictions by resort to anti-Westernism" (ibid. 644).

In Lebanon and elsewhere in the Middle East, however, those committed to undoing such feudal and semifeudal structures were the least likely to obtain U.S. support. Kamal Junblat's efforts earned him the suspicion of U.S. international oil companies supported by the State Department. In Iran, Mossadeq's vast popularity and his anti-Communist reformist inclinations had earned him the qualified support of the Truman administration. But Eisenhower approved Operation AJAX, the Iranian coup that involved the bribery and manipulation of Iranian domestic politics at a cost of $7 million, with an unknown sum to be spent on future public relations efforts to complete the demonization of Mossadeq and the legitimation of the Shah. Among the practical results of the coup was an American "consortium," made up of U.S. oil companies, then under investigation in the U.S. antitrust suit, that were its direct beneficiaries. Not only was immunity granted by Attorney General Herbert Brownell and the intervention of Eisenhower and the NSC but Standard Oil of New Jersey, Standard Oil of California, Socony-Vacuum, Texaco, and Gulf, each obtained an 8 percent share in a consortium in which AIOC held 40 percent, Shell 14 percent, and CFP 6 percent shares, respectively.

Among the factors that explain the ambience that favored such policies was Eisenhower's support structure, with its effective integration of corporate and political interests. Such connections were by no means unprecedented in American political experience.[13] The integration of the corporate elite into the highest levels of policymaking was a factor in the Truman era, as the corporate connections of major appointments to the departments of State, Defense, and the Treasury indicated. In Eisenhower's administration, the influential Business Advisory Council (BAC), whose origins were in the New Deal, had on its board representatives of Standard Oil of California and Standard of New Jersey. In 1953 its vice-chairman, Eugene Holman, was the president of Standard Oil of New Jersey. Seven of the NSC consultants in 1953 included heads of Standard Oil (New Jersey), Monsanto Chemical, Pacific Gas and Electric, connected with Standard Oil of California, and headed by James B. Black, a director of Shell.[14] The Operations Coordinating Board (OCB), which monitored NSC policies through interagency groups and the use of covert funds, represented some of the same interests. In 1953, when Wilbur Eveland joined the OCB, Herbert Hoover Jr., Robert Anderson, Allen Dulles, and Nelson Rockefeller were serving on it.

John Foster Dulles, Eisenhower's preeminent secretary of state, had been a senior member of Sullivan and Cromwell, the prestigious law firm to which CIA director Allen Dulles also belonged. Among its major clients was Standard Oil of New Jersey. Before his appointment as secretary of state, John Foster Dulles had served as chairman of the board of both the Carnegie Endowment for International Peace and the Rockefeller Foundation (3.5 percent stockholder in Standard Oil of New Jersey). Herbert Hoover Jr., an oil specialist who had been a consultant in Venezuela and Iran, became under secretary of state and was sent to Iran by Dulles in 1953 after the Anglo-American coup to negotiate the new deal for U.S. companies in AIOC. Robert Anderson was secretary of the navy (1953–1954), deputy secretary of defense (1954–1955), then appointed secretary of the treasury (1957). With a background in oil and finance, Anderson had been counsel and manager of the W. T. Waggoner estate of Texas, president of the Mid-Continent Oil and Gas Association, member of the BAC (1956–1960), trustee of the Committee on Economic Development (CED) (1956–1957), and in addition to holding other corporate positions was "member of the board of the Rockefeller-dominated American Overseas Investing Co., the big Hanover Bank of New York, and the Missouri-Pacific Railroad."[15] He had also been a member of the National Petroleum Council and director of the American Petroleum Institute. Allen Dulles, before his appointment to head the CIA, had in addition to his legal practice served in the Council on Foreign Relations. Among Eisenhower's advisers, John J. McCloy in 1953 was chairman of the board of the Council on Foreign Relations, the head of Chase Manhattan Bank, and a trustee of the Rockefeller Foundation, and he "represented the Rockefeller brothers' legal interests, including those relating to their holdings in companies making up Aramco."[16]

Eisenhower and Dulles: Changing the Guard in the Middle East, 1953–1957

The administration of the two-term president whose wartime reputation gave him a nearly infallible public image pursued a steady course of expanding U.S. economic interests while consolidating its political influence. In Europe the much-disputed policy of German integration into NATO eventually gave way before American pressure that was accompanied by the subsidization of European rearmament. But as the authors of a recent work on Indonesia claim, the brunt of American covert policies fell on the third world. "Probably at no time since World War II has violence—especially on a militarized level—in the execution of covert American foreign policy been so widespread as during the Eisenhower administration," according to Audrey and George McT. Kahin.[17] The Latin American (Guatemala) and Middle Eastern (Iran) cases were by no means isolated instances of U.S. intervention, for U.S. covert policies were also carried out in the Philippines, Burma, Cambodia, Indonesia, Laos, and Vietnam.

In Latin America and the Middle East, covert interventions were justified under the aegis of blocking the subversive aspirations of legally elected presidents and prime ministers whose nationalizations and reformist policies were viewed as threats to U.S. interests. In 1953, AJAX, the Anglo-American coup in Iran, installed the Iranian shah with military and intelligence support from the United States and Israel's MOSSAD, while in Guatemala, "Operation Success" led to the installation of a military regime whose violence was unsurpassed in Central America.[18]

In 1955, as policymakers deliberated on how to respond to the crises in Quemoy and Matsu, news of Soviet bloc arms sales to Egypt prompted a politico-economic alert throughout the region. Its effects directly impinged on U.S. policy in Lebanon, while CIA and MOSSAD officials considered possible Israeli responses to contain the regional ramifications of such developments.

The Anglo-French-Israeli invasion of Egypt in 1956 must be situated against this background, as well as the Soviet interventions in Eastern Europe, which with the central role of the July 25, 1956, nationalization of the Suez Canal Company by Egyptian president Nasser, rank among the epic events of the decade in the Middle East. French expectations of defeating Nasser as a prelude to crushing the Algerian struggle for independence failed, as did the British and Israeli efforts to eliminate Nasser and Nasserism in the Middle East. As in the case of the 1951 conflict with AIOC, the Anglo-Iranian Oil Company, whose nationalization exposed the cracks in Anglo-American solidarity, so the 1956 crisis over Suez and the Sinai invasion that followed exposed the administration's willingness to apply political as well as economic pressure on London. The results constituted a diplomatic success for the United States in the Middle East and a consolidation of U.S. economic and political interests in the region that the events of 1958 reinforced. In the interval, the Middle East Resolution, more commonly known as the Eisenhower Doctrine, promised U.S. assistance to local regimes threatened by international communism, a commitment implemented in spite of the absence of any such regimes in the region.

Framing the above developments were the Army-McCarthy hearings in Washington in 1954 and the conflict over school desegregation in Little Rock, Arkansas, in 1957, which gave global exposure to the virulent nature of domestic anti-communism and the persistence of American racism. In Europe, the French confronted one of their worst postwar crises as the defeat of the French military in Dien Bien Phu escalated the brutalization of the Algerian struggle by French forces. It was in the same year that the military coup in Iraq eliminated the pro-British regime and spurred Prime Minister Macmillan into proposing a joint Anglo-American counterrevolution in the Middle East. Instead, the two Western powers joined in their separate interventions in Lebanon and Jordan, where the former was involved in civil war and the latter faced increasing dissent against the policies of a repressive regime. For the Eisenhower administration, deliberations on full-scale military intervention in the Lebanese civil war occurred against the background of discussions on nuclear test bans and controversies within the military, as the Republican Party worried about the impact of political scandals on the forthcoming elections.

U.S. military intervention in Lebanon proved to be fortuitous for President Eisenhower's domestic reputation. The events of Iraq and U.S. intervention in Lebanon's civil war combined to consolidate American hegemony in a region that more than a decade earlier had been the exclusive political bailiwick of the British. The collapse of the British-backed

Nuri Sa'id regime resulted in the consolidation of British military and political power in the area of the Gulf, and Washington's subsidization of Britain's role in Jordan further reinforced its economic and political decline in the region. U.S. full-scale intervention in Lebanon, as parts 4 and 5 of this volume indicate, did not constitute a fundamental break with U.S. policy so much as a realignment compatible with regional interests advanced by the events of 1951 to 1953 in Iran and those of 1956 in Egypt.

The image of the benign general, the antimilitarist in the White House, whose antipathy toward the military-industrial complex added to an internationally celebrated reputation, hardly does justice to the role of Eisenhower and his administration in the Middle East. Along with his declared sympathies for self-determination and his sensitivity to popular opposition to colonialism, which reached its peak in the Suez crisis, Eisenhower and his corporate establishment did not so much alter the legacy of the previous administration as pursue the logic of its policies.

Protection of U.S. oil interests and the exclusion of the USSR from the region remained the cardinal objectives of U.S. policy. They were among the prime concerns of Secretary of State Dulles when he included the Middle East on his inaugural trip to the region in May 1953. Designed to impress local regimes with the sincerity of American interest and to signal a break with the Truman administration and its identification with the creation of Israel, Dulles's elaborate trip was in practice an investigative journey intended to assess the status of U.S. oil interests in the light of the grand jury investigation, to review Anglo-American defense arrangements, to consider the status of Israeli-Arab relations, and to assess Communist and Soviet influence. These remained among the prime concerns of the administration in the area in the coming years.

From Saudi Arabia, where the former minister of the Legation in Beirut was now ambassador, George Wadsworth cautioned the State Department on February 14, 1954, that "operations of American oil companies in Near East in our opinion constitute national interest U.S., oil from Near East contributing vitally to both military and economic strength U.S. and other non-Commie countries. Thus follows that action rendering operations oil companies more difficult would be harmful U.S. interests."[19] Wadsworth warned against the adverse publicity that the case could be expected to generate and the risk that it would "lend color to recurring Soviet propaganda theme that under-developed countries Near East are 'enmeshed Wall Street tentacles.' " Added to the negative impact of U.S. Palestinian policy, Wadsworth argued, "we are apprehensive lest attack in U.S. courts on major U.S. economic interest in area would have similar effect in economic field." When Greek shipping tycoon Aristotle Onassis's agreement with the Saudi government to provide tanker service became known, it was readily disposed of, in accord with the fundamentals of cartel principles.[20]

Dulles had returned to Washington from his first trip to the Middle East in 1953 impressed not only by the admonitions of U.S. officials in the area but also by the futility of Anglo-American defense efforts. The continuing importance of Anglo-American cooperation barely masked the disadvantages of collaborating with an ally so clearly marked with the emblem of empire. Dulles lamented the inability of Middle Eastern regimes to understand the scope of Soviet danger to the area.[21] It was one of the leitmotivs of the secretary of state, manifested in U.S. political and defense policies that reflected his interpretation of the deficiencies of Arab politics.

With his unique access to the Dulles brothers, Wilbur Eveland remained confounded by the secretary of state's inability to understand why Arab regimes feared the USSR less than they did Israel. What the Dulles 1953 trip did succeed in doing, however, was to convince the Secretary of State of the failed status of Anglo-American defensive arrangements that relied on an Arab—specifically an Egyptian—connection. Egypt was temporarily demoted as a result, while Dulles, with Harold Stassen, director of the Mutual Security Program, concluded that MEDO was not feasible and, along with the Joint Chiefs of Staff, favored a largely non-Arab coalition under Anglo-American leadership. The case was thus made for the "Northern Tier" arrangements that reasserted the role of Iraq, Turkey, and Pakistan, leaving the Arab "interior" in a secondary position. It was a case that had no appeal to regimes in the region, save those that were locked into Anglo-American policy. The restructuring nonetheless led in 1955 to the Baghdad Pact system.

That the U.S. secretary of state found opposition to the ensuing bilateral accords that made the Baghdad Pact unacceptable was hardly surprising, but it was a revealing blind spot. Totally confident in the direction of U.S. policy and in the subordination of Middle East regimes, Dulles utterly failed to grasp its potential consequences. The connection between the Baghdad system and the steps leading to the Egyptians' purchase of arms from the East bloc came as a further affront. To Washington, Nasser's action had effectively broken the Western monopoly on arms deliveries to the Middle East.

The impact on Washington, combined with evidence of a sustained Soviet trade and aid policy throughout the third world, inspired Washington's economic defense policy, as well as a heightened campaign against the dangers of Soviet penetration in the region. Some U.S. intelligence officials and others involved in the covert efforts to broach a rapprochement between Egypt and Israel (code-named Alpha), took exception to this. Eveland observed that "the Alpha Group had no evidence of Russian success in lining up the Arabs against Israel or the West, and there were many reasons to conclude that the Soviet Union wished to avoid involvement in the Middle East, at least until it could quiet unrest developing within the satellite countries of the Soviet bloc."[22] Eveland did not discount the importance of the Egyptian move so much as he faulted U.S. policy for its outcome.

In Paris, independent initiatives involving a closer relationship with Israel occurred at about the same time, as France and Israel engaged in the highly secret negotiations leading to French support for the construction of an Israeli nuclear reactor.[23] The Israeli-French connection, reinforced by the emergence of Nasser, strengthened the hand of those within the Israeli political establishment who were skeptical of Project Alpha and concerned to distance the United States from Cairo (as in the Lavon Affair, which involved an Israeli espionage ring in Cairo whose exposure resulted in the resignation of the Israeli defense minister, Pinchas Lavon).

In early January, Dulles had considered applying economic pressure on the Egyptian regime, a recurring theme that was modulated at the time of the Suez crisis.[24] But the administration in Washington followed as Britain proposed that an international World Bank (i.e., U.S.-backed) loan be offered the Egyptian leader for the Aswan High Dam project. The World Bank estimate of $1 billion suggests the scope of the loan and the project.[25] Although U.S. policy was still "to leave Nasser a bridge back to good relations with the West if he so desires," the conditions set for such a political journey were not promising.[26] Dulles recommended that the United States and the United Kingdom combine efforts to deny Egypt export licenses for arms, whether their source was commercial or official; that both governments delay conclusion of the Aswan High Dam project; that the United States delay responding to Egyptian requests for grains and oil under Title 1 of PL 480; that the United States postpone approving a CARE project for Egypt; and that radio facilities be offered to Iraq to enable it to counter Egyptian programming.

The effort to court Nasser was more than matched by the reinforcement of allied positions, whether in Ethiopia, the Sudan, Libya, and Jordan, or in Saudi Arabia, where U.S. efforts to disengage the Saudis from their Egyptian sympathies focused on satisfying Saudi requests in exchange for new air base agreements, as well as pressing London for a settlement on the Buraimi issue. The regime in Beirut benefited from these moves as Washington recognized the need to "strengthen pro-Western elements in Lebanon by immediately offering economic aid in the form of grants or loans for projects designed to create the most favorable impact on public opinion."[27] Indeed, the Lebanese, who had long been frustrated by their failure to obtain U.S. military assistance, obtained arms from the French.

In spite of the conditions attached to the projected loans for the Aswan High Dam project, Nasser made known his decision to accept the Anglo-American proposal. Unfortunately, that decision coincided with the rejection of the loan by Secretary of State Dulles, who did so with the knowledge of British skepticism and anticipated U.S. congressional disapproval. Dulles's action was not uniformly supported among his own advisers, who appeared far more apprehensive about its impact than did Dulles himself. Withdrawal of the Aswan High Dam offer on July 19, although well within the logic of U.S. policies, was hardly an inevitable decision. Once that decision was made, however, the spiral of events led to Nasser's decision to nationalize the Suez Canal Company on July 26, 1956. In the political turmoil that followed, Western capitals were consumed with plans, proposals, and suspicions. The American position, repeatedly underscored, was that "nationalization of the Canal was not illegal—it was within Egypt's sovereign rights. Use of force could not be justified, legally or morally, as long as Nasser (1) was operating the Canal efficiently, and (2) was complying with the provisions of the 1888 Convention."[28] Subsequent efforts to establish a Suez Canal Users' Association (SCUA), designed to satisfy the Anglo-French positions while remaining acceptable to Egypt, did not achieve their purpose. At the end of September, Britain and France moved to bring the crisis to the Security Council of the United Nations, and the Egyptian foreign minister, the U.S. secretary of state, the UN secretary general, and British and French officials, appeared to be moving toward some form of accommodation on major issues, including transit rights and tolls. Franco-Israeli secret talks in Paris took place roughly one week later, followed by covert British collaboration within a month.

The meaning of Suez, for Britain, France, and Israel, revealed the intricate interweaving of political objectives and economic dependence. While the United States had financial interests in the Suez Canal Company, it was by no means dependent on it. As for Britain, "one-third of the total traffic through the canal was British registered," and one quarter of all British imports relied on the canal, as opposed to the 3.1 percent of ships using the canal under the U.S. flag.[29] Out of a total of 39.8 million tons of oil, Britain imported 23.3 million tons through the canal in 1956, and 3.5 million tons through IPC pipelines.[30] Kuwait alone shipped 44 million tons of crude oil through the Suez Canal.

In the case of France, the degree of its dependence was far less than that of its ally Britain. Of 26 million tons of oil imported, 13.8 million tons came via Suez. For Paris, however, Suez was Nasser, and Nasser was an ally of the FLN, which was leading the struggle against French control of Algeria. Hence, those who erroneously believed that cutting off the Egyptian source of support would undermine the Algerian struggle devoutly wished for his downfall.

On this, the French and Israeli views of Nasser met. Ben Gurion was not as concerned with Algeria as he was with Nasser's popularity that risked undermining status quo regimes less prone to respond to calls for action on the Palestinian question. In the case of the United States and ARAMCO, it was not the canal but the pipelines that were vital, since Saudi Arabia shipped 51 million tons of crude, of which only 8 million tons went through Suez. For Egypt and the Arab world, the assertion of national sovereignty over the canal—accompanied as it was by the commitment to its continued operation—was both a gesture of retribution for the past injustices of colonialism and an affirmation of sovereignty that transcended Suez.

At the end of July, Deputy Under Secretary Robert Murphy was sent to London to learn of British plans and to dissuade Anthony Eden's government from intervention.[31] The Joint Chiefs of Staff were grim as to the possible aftereffects of any such action.[32] Washington, then, opted for a negotiated solution calling for a conference of maritime powers to guarantee the operation of the canal, which was agreed to by France, Britain, and the United States, although with evident limited conviction. Harold Macmillan, who was at the time British chancellor of the exchequer, observed that "the experience with Mussadiq in Iran showed that these Middle East oil countries could not be relied on to be governed by commercial self-interest," while news from further East was that "the Governors of Aden, Somaliland, and Kenya had all warned that their Arabs were watching closely the outcome of the contest between Nasser and the West; if Nasser won, British influence in these colonies would be destroyed."[33]

At the end of October the action feared in Washington occurred. The invasion was planned in stages, with Israeli forces leading and Anglo-French forces following. On November 2, Israeli forces were in occupation of the Sinai and Gaza. Three days later, Anglo-French paratroopers were dropped at Port Sa'id and Fort Fu'ad, in Egypt. The reaction in Washington was electric, as the administration immediately distanced itself from its allies, condemning the invasion and calling for a cease-fire, the position endorsed by the UN that called for the formation of an emergency force. Against Britain, the administration used its most effective leverage, financial pressure. The result, in the words of Diane Kunz, was that "the position at the Suez Canal had been abandoned, but sterling had been saved, at least for the moment."[34]

U.S. action in Suez earned the administration praise in the Arab world, but the policies that accompanied it covertly and that soon followed overtly generated an altogether different response. Between Suez and the military coup in Baghdad and U.S. intervention in Lebanon, there was a continual train of ineffectual covert action in Damascus, which embarrassed even its U.S.–Middle East allies.[35]

On another level of operation, U.S. international oil companies in the Middle East profited from the post-Suez oil price increase, which was judged to cost consumers some $1 billion, including roughly $85 million for the U.S. military. Such developments led to a federal grand jury indictment of twenty-nine companies charged with violations of the Sherman Act in May 1958.[36]

Meanwhile, the U.S. president, reaffirming U.S. policy in the Middle East, offered the so-called Eisenhower Doctrine, which had been initiated in 1957. Promising U.S. assistance to regimes threatened by "international communism," it was modified in the Mansfield amendment that rendered it more practical as a tool for U.S. support to friendly regimes. Predictably, it dampened the support that the United States had won in the region during the crises over Suez and Sinai. The popularity of Nasser increased, as did Egypt's economic relations with the USSR. By 1958, "Egypt was sending nearly half of its exports to the Soviet Bloc (including China) and receiving almost a third of its imports from there. . . . At the same time, the Eastern Bloc was opening up as the most promising market for Egypt's expanding exports of manufactured goods."[37]

The full impact of 1956 emerged in the crises of 1958, at which time Eisenhower's restraint with respect to the invitation by Prime Minister Macmillan to intervene in Iraq was paralleled by U.S. military intervention in Beirut and a British cover over Jordan. The result, in conjunction with Anglo-American reassertion of power in oil-rich areas of Saudi Arabia, Kuwait, and the Gulf, led to the climax of American power in the region.

8

Lebanon: The "Bridgehead in the Orient"

We must utilize this good fortune wisely. Over-exercise our influence will embarrass Cabinet to our detriment. We can expect better cooperation in most fields as economic development possibly regional defense but must be prepared for difficulties re Palestine and pipeline concessions.
Harold Minor to John Foster Dulles,
May 4, 1953*

Oil and Politics: The Sacred and the Profane

When Kamil Sham'un became president of Lebanon, the State Department was reassured that the signs were favorable for the United States, as "[Sham'un] is definitely our friend."[1] It did not take long to realize that "our friend" was in difficulty. In the State Department, as in the U.S. Embassy in Beirut, there was no hesitation in identifying the problems plaguing Sham'un. Ten years after independence, Lebanon had yet to resolve the fundamental cleavages of class and caste that assumed the form of confessionalist clashes over questions of access and privilege. The reformist president had an insufficiently strong domestic base. Moreover, his foreign policy agenda pleased the United States and its regional allies more than it did the majority of Lebanon's political constituencies.

To the State Department, such problems were worrisome to the extent that they impinged on matters of direct concern. TAPLINE and the continuing demands for improved concessionary agreements were chief among them, with economic development projects associated with Point IV and agreement on Palestine as well. But the Sham'un era was also one in which U.S. political and strategic interests in Lebanon and the region increased, with direct consequences for Beirut. Nonetheless, the preoccupation to assure Lebanon's role as a transit state free of political challenge led to the direct intervention in Lebanon's domestic politics by U.S. oil company executives. Revealing of the nature of the relationship between the United States and Lebanon was the extent to which even pro-American Lebanese officials were castigated for daring to make demands of TAPLINE. With singular determination and with unconditional support from the U.S. Embassy, TAPLINE determined the rules of the game insofar as royalties were concerned. In spite of such clashes, however, there was no question as to the commitment of the United States to the regime. Indeed, Sham'un's collaboration with the United States, facilitated by what the State Department described as the most pro-American cabinet to emerge in Lebanon's experience, that of 1953, gave the Eisenhower administration virtually unlimited access to information and to consent in the pursuit of U.S. policy. Hence, the highly politicized clashes over confessionalism that racked the regime were instantly recognized as prejudicial to U.S. interests insofar as they risked regime survival, and its legitimacy. As Ambassador Raymond Hare concluded, Lebanon's role as "bridgehead in the Orient" was not to be jeopardized by changes in the confessional system.

Hare was no more flexible in terms of conflicts over TAPLINE or other signs of insubordination that surfaced in the most pro-American of Lebanese postwar cabinets, Sham'un's seminar of mostly American University of Beirut graduates. Ambassador Hare was impatient with those Lebanese "friends" of the United States who claimed the right to demand greater profits from TAPLINE. They suffered from an excess of the market mentality, elsewhere considered a highly reliable and desirable trait. Those with whom there was less friction constituted the more conservative wing of the Lebanese bourgeoisie, preoccupied with containing communism, whether in or out of the labor movement.

Within a month of his accession to power as Lebanon's second president, Sham'un conceded the right of U.S. oil companies to influence Lebanon's domestic politics, accepting the unveiled threats of U.S. international oil companies as though they came from heads of state. Judged by TAPLINE officials to bear an uncanny resemblance to Iranian prime minister Mossadeq, Kamal Junblat was ordered excommunicated from Lebanese domestic politics with the approval of Kamil Sham'un. The ban was temporary, and Junblat's Progressive Socialist Party (PSP) continued to grow for reasons comprehensible, if not acceptable, to Embassy officers. There was discontent in the land, and the regime did little to respond to it.

The Junblat case compels attention as a form of direct intervention in Lebanon's domestic politics, one to which the president does not appear to have taken exception. Collaborative intervention in this instance was facilitated by an unwritten political accord that overrode the "slight" to Lebanese sovereignty. For the oil company officials involved, Junblat was a political risk. That he was pro-American, a quixotic socialist committed to the path of reform that U.S. officials in the Legation regarded as the rational response to an irrational political system, did not matter. Nor did it matter that Junblat's program explicitly excluded the nationalization of oil companies, as his foreign policy adviser was to declare to the U.S. petroleum attaché, N. C. Ortiz.

Others in the Sham'un cabinet did not escape criticism on this score. Sa'eb Salam and George Hakim, neither socialists nor partisans of Junblat, were committed to obtaining additional profits from TAPLINE. Hakim was accused of supporting such demands and of obtaining information to validate his position. Indeed, three of the U.S. majors—the international oil companies Socony-Vacuum, Shell, and Esso—dominated the local Lebanese market, generating increasing profits as crude oil export from Lebanon increased along with tanker traffic to Europe and North America. Pressure from Lebanese politicians to share in the profits yielded little.

The timing of such demands, coming in the midst of the continuing Federal Trade Commission antitrust suit, was worrisome to officials in Washington. The State Department, along with Interior, Justice, Intelligence, Defense. and the White House, worried about the effects of the suit among opposition groups throughout the region. Developments in Cairo, where the Free Officers took power in 1952, raised other troubling prospects. What if Cairo were to block passage of the canal? The lessons of Iran, it seemed, had been lost, as the petroleum attachés in Beirut and the United Kingdom opined in early June 1952. The oil industry thought that Iran's situation had not had a sufficiently sobering effect on other states.

> The industry also doubts that Iran's predicament resulting from the extreme action taken by the government against AIOC has had any moderating influence on the other governments in the area. The consensus appears to be that the other governments are fully conscious of the adverse effects of the Iranian government's extreme action, have lit-

tle sympathy for that Government, but consistent with the behavior pattern of the "nouveau riche" will continue for some time to face the companies with ever-increasing demands short of nationalization.[2]

This is the background against which the Junblat case must be considered. Kamal Junblat himself was a man apart, and so recognized by the U.S. Embassy. His PSP party continued to win adherents in spite of his quixotic socialism. Junblat and his party had cooperated with Sham'un in the opposition to former president Besharah al-Khuri. As a result, Junblat anticipated obtaining a cabinet post. It was that possibility that resulted in the interference of U.S. oil companies. In spite of the lengthy interview by the PSP's foreign policy adviser with the Embassy's petroleum attaché, in which Clovis Maksoud emphatically denied accusations of would-be nationalization, Junblat was a marked man.

To grasp the extent of Sham'un's political pliability vis-à-vis the United States, it is sufficient to note the rapidity with which he acceded to the demands concerning the exclusion of Junblat. On October 2, the day on which Ortiz, the U.S. petroleum attaché, had had an interview with Maksoud, James Lobenstine, the U.S. chargé d'affaires, informed the State Department that "in hour's conversation with Pres [Sham'un] at Beit Ed-Eddine, we reviewed pending problems between two govts in atmosphere utmost cordiality. . . . Pres disarmed me immed by stating there are no problems between us that cannot be settled, not sometime in future but right now."[3] Lobenstine reviewed the subjects discussed: Point IV, Lebanon's tax laws, U.S. economic aid, arms. On the last, Sham'un was adamant and would remain so throughout the coming years. "We need arms, we need them badly, we need them now," he added. It was on this occasion that he underlined Lebanon's orientation toward the West, to which Lobenstine replied, "We had always known the sympathies most Lebs lay with West, but was glad to hear this from him." There was no mention of oil or Junblat. Instead, Lobenstine indicated a cautious optimism, tempered by concern as to whether the parliament would approve the Lebanese cabinet's request for "decree-law powers" to carry out Sham'un's program.

The news regarding Junblat appeared only a few days later. On October 7, the Embassy sent the State Department an alarmist message indicating that Junblat and his PSP were bent on "nationalization of concessionary companies, the distribution of public lands and the confiscation of ill-gotten wealth."[4] Clovis Maksoud, the party's foreign policy adviser, had laboriously set the record straight in an extensive interview with the Embassy on the preceding day, in which he had claimed the opposite. Describing the PSP as a democratic, anti-Communist party committed to a New Deal–type of social welfare program, Maksoud explained that the party leadership believed the Middle East to suffer from both exploitation by concessionary companies and Soviet "imperialistic conspiracy."

If reference to "concessionary companies" was sufficient to cause alarm, then probably the description of the PSP as not having "a capitalistic program . . . because Lebanon does not have capital" was not more reassuring. Maksoud's attempt to inscribe Junblati socialism in a historic framework, between the New Deal and the legacies of Karl Marx, Adam Smith, Saint-Simon, and John Locke, was an effort that doubtless similarly backfired, even if Maksoud pointed to information that the PSP had sought and obtained from the U.S. Department of Labor.

The Progressive Socialist Party platform included redistribution of large feudal estates, calculated to involve no more than some ten to twenty major landholders in Lebanon. Junblat volunteered to break up his own holdings as well. In addition, the PSP advocated social security regulations covering health insurance, unemployment, and workman's compensation. It supported free compulsory education, women's suffrage, and a bill of rights. Confessionalism as a form of political representation was to be abolished.

It was not the domestic program of reforms that compelled the Embassy's attention, however, but the discussion of the PSP's plans with respect to concessions. Here, Maksoud distinguished carefully between the French concessions that the PSP intended to nationalize—Electricité de Beyrouth, the Compagnie du Port, the Damas-Hama-Prolongements Railroad (DHP RR)—and those that were carefully excluded from such consideration—such as the banking system and TAPLINE, about which the Embassy specifically asked. Indeed, Maksoud was forthcoming with respect to TAPLINE, arguing that it was a transportation concession that passed through Lebanon without incurring any harm.

The content of the Maksoud interview cabled to the State Department was dated October 7. On October 8, N. C. Ortiz informed the State Department that Junblat intended to nationalize oil companies. The news arrived in Washington on the very day that Defense Secretary Robert Lovett, Treasury Secretary John Snyder, Attorney General J. P. McGranery, Joint Chiefs of Staff Chief Omar Bradley, and Secretary of State Dean Acheson were discussing possible approaches to resolving the Iranian crisis. Entirely compatible with their attitude toward Mossadeq, the State Department did not object to the interference by TAPLINE executives to assure Sham'un's exclusion of Junblat from office.

The information sent to the State Department from Beirut was designed to confirm the U.S. oil companies' worst fears. What was cabled to Washington was not the Maksoud interview but an earlier dialogue of September 28 between Junblat and Abdallah Yafi, at which Sham'un was reported to have been present. The text had been obtained by William Lenahan, president of MEDRECO, from an unidentified source. Its contents were already known to U.S. international oil companies. The substance of the exchange involved Junblat's response to Yafi's invitation that he join the government. Junblat's rejoinder was to demand support for his party's program, a program of the people and "the last revolution."[5] In this exchange, the PSP leader affirmed his intention to nationalize the cement company, the electricity company, and the oil industries. Yafi's response was that Lebanon had no oil, that the oil going through Lebanon belonged to Iraq and Saudi Arabia.

JUMBLATT: Well, these companies should pay more, and I suggest that they give us half the economy they realize by transporting their oil by pipelines and not by tankers.

YAFI: I know nothing about that, but what I know is that we are bound by contracts which we have to respect. We'll try to increase our profits; that is all.

JUMBLATT: No. I want to know, if you are ready to fight and to be the Mossadegh of Lebanon.

YAFI: No. I tell you very frankly that I am not and will never be such a man. I am not willing to create difficulties for my country with America and Great Britain. You are not reasonable.

JUMBLATT: I want also an exceptional levy on rich people.

YAFI: I don't understand you. Rich people, as all other people, are subject to the taxes provided for by the existing laws. Our tax system is based on progressive rates which reach the rich. And my duty will be to apply strictly these laws.

JUMBLATT: What are you speaking about? Laws? I am above laws. My conscience is the law and I am the man of the revolution which considers no laws and no constitution.

YAFI: It is useless to continue this discussion with a man who is losing his reason.

On the basis of this, Ortiz concluded that nationalization of oil was the PSP project, and TAPLINE executives concluded that Junblat had a strong resemblance to Mossadeq. Their fear was that with Junblat in the cabinet, the PSP could effectively press for an increase in Lebanese revenues from U.S. oil companies. In consequence, TAPLINE officials closely scrutinized PSP political options with respect to the new regime. Ortiz explained that "MEDRECO [Mediterranean Refining Company] is prepared to abandon plans for construction of the Sidon refinery if political developments result in Socialist Party attaining a determining role in formulating government policy. President [Sham'un] states the Lebanese Government will continue to honor its contractual obligations with foreign oil companies."

Sham'un's position was clarified in a visit that the U.S. oil company executives paid to him. Lenahan of MEDRECO (Caltex), Campbell of TAPLINE, Headley of Socony-Vacuum, and Coppach of Shell represented companies that accounted for 80 percent of total petroleum sales in Lebanon. Those who met with Sham'un on October 7 at Beit ed Dine, the president's summer residence, included William Lenahan, Floyd Bryant, senior director and vice president of Standard Oil (California), and Habib Abu Shahla, former member of the Lebanese Chamber and the key man in charge of TAPLINE matters in Beirut. Lenahan informed Ortiz of the president's positive reaction:

> After expressing to Mr Bryant his appreciation for their visit, President Chamoun had stated that the mutuality of interest between the Lebanese Government and the oil companies called for their working together in close harmony, and had promised that the companies could look forward to the Lebanese Government living up to its contractual obligations with the companies. . . . The President is also reported as having made statements of a strictly political nature relating to United States/Lebanese inter-governmental relations.[6]

What were the statements made? Did Sham'un go beyond what he had already committed himself to, in relation to the United States? The meeting ended with Lenahan indicating that MEDRECO would, for the time being, proceed with plans to acquire land and make preparations for the refinery that was to begin construction in January 1953. However, as Lenahan added, he would bear in mind "the instructions of the parent companies with respect to developments which might alter their present decision to go ahead with that construction." No laments for Junblat's exclusion were heard on this occasion, or reported.

In Washington, there were other considerations affecting State Department attitudes toward oil companies in the Middle East. It was not Junblat but the combination of the antitrust suit and the military coup in Egypt in 1952 coming after the crisis over AIOC in Iran in 1951 that explained the reaction of Acting Secretary of State David Bruce. It was Bruce who criticized U.S. international oil companies for a commitment to profit that put other interests at risk. Nationalization, Bruce pointed out, was the ultimate threat undermining U.S. policy in the Middle East, already weakened by its pro-Israeli position. Under the circumstances, Bruce warned that the State Department found the oil industry's position unsatisfactory, although it would not directly interfere in its policies.[7] Bruce explained that given the regional situation and the continuing U.S. "national interest as distinct from commercial interest, some accommodation to pressure for increased payments if necessary, coupled with play for time seems the only alternative feasible at this time. Do not believe present is time or case for diplomatic intervention."

The concerns of the acting secretary, the owner companies of ARAMCO, and Policy Planning Director Paul Nitze, among others, were focused on the U.S. grand jury investigation of the international oil cartel in the Middle East. And Bruce himself had conceded in communication with the U.S. Embassy in Beirut that the renegotiation of pipeline concessions was extremely problematic. Among the complicating factors in Beirut was that one of the cabinet ministers, George Hakim, "has made personal econ study worldwide pipeline conventions and reportedly was impressed by 1950 Oil Forum article suggesting yet uncompleted Tapline wld save company estimated sixty million dollars per year. Tapline officials indicate article highly speculative and inaccurate."[8]

In December, TAPLINE officials in Washington conceded that the company was in a particularly adverse situation with respect to Lebanon. When Paul Nitze inquired as to what TAPLINE was paying transit states, he was informed that Syria and Lebanon were each receiving roughly $1.3 million annually and Jordan somewhat less.[9] Among the reasons offered for difficulties in Lebanon were widespread anti-American sentiment and the timing of Lebanese demands. The latter referred to Lebanese insistence on renegotiating transit fees prior to the finalization of ARAMCO-TAPLINE- Saudi negotiations, on the basis of which TAPLINE profits and transit fees would be determined.

TAPLINE representatives in Beirut, including Colonel William Eddy, accused Sham'un of weakness in allowing his prime minister to exploit oil companies for domestic political purposes. Several months later,

Ortiz, the petroleum attaché, complained that the cabinet was unrelenting in its efforts to renegotiate concessions. First IPC, then TAPLINE, was targeted. Worse, the cabinet had authorized the relevant ministry to issue an "arrêter" that "would order IPC to distribute 20 percent of Lebanon's share in the IPC refinery output to various Lebanese national marketers."[10] Ortiz was outraged that Lebanon was violating its agreement to maintain an atmosphere favorable for "the investment of private foreign capital for development of its economy." Should the cabinet take such action, Ortiz indicated, the appropriate foreign embassies planned to take up the matter with the Lebanese government, "since the foreign marketers are determined to resist its implementation by every means, which would result in complications inimical to their overall interests."

The threats were meant to provide TAPLINE and IPC additional cover while they determined how to manipulate events in a manner favorable to their interests. In early June, the chief of the Petroleum Policy Staff in Washington, Robert Eakens, conceded, "It looks highly probable that the transit agreements of both companies with all these countries will have to be renegotiated in the not too distant future and the question is upon what basis of payments satisfactory and more stable agreements can be reached."[11] Both Syrian and Lebanese officials were insisting that TAPLINE's profits should be divided between transit states in a similar manner to the 50/50 profit-sharing accord devised by U.S.–Saudi Arabia–ARAMCO.[12]

When John Foster Dulles was preparing for his trip to the Middle East, the position paper given him by the State Department described Junblat as advocating a "Third Force, a socialist administration, and a program far removed from moderation and compromise; he is gaining considerable following."[13] What would hold the country together nonetheless, according to the State Department, was Lebanon's reliance on "religious equilibrium," as well as the country's "mercantile mentality, stemming from Lebanon's Phoenician ancestry, and a high literacy rate owing to well-developed educational institutions. There is not much danger that Lebanon will become fanatical like Iran or Egypt. There is some feudalism, but democratic government has a broader base in Lebanon than elsewhere in the Arab world."

Insofar as Lebanon's transit role was concerned, however, the "mercantile mentality" was not altogether reliable, since some of the high achievers in this area were judged as notorious precisely in response to their demands for greater compensation from U.S. oil companies. Petroleum attaché Ortiz complained that even the erstwhile friends of the United States were implicated in such activities. U.S. ambassador Raymond Hare concurred, with bitterness, that these friends of the United States were interested in profit maximization at the expense of TAPLINE, even though some had profited handsomely from the oil and Saudi connection. The problem extended beyond Sa'eb Salam, according to Hare; it affected other AUB alumni, who were particularly articulate "on the issues of oil and Israel."[14] When, at a later juncture, Salam was involved in the creation of the "Committee for the Renegotiation of Pipeline Concessions," Hare viewed it as nothing more than a political ploy designed to upstage the current prime minister, Abdallah Yafi. What Hare did not elaborate on, however, was the fact that Salam's Middle East Airlines had lost a lucrative TAPLINE contract to Air Liban, a loss that has to be situated in this context.

However recalcitrant TAPLINE was over renegotiation of its concessionary agreements, it was moved to reconsider its position in the light of cumulative evidence that local Arab governments were assuming a more independent stance—and surviving in the process. Furthermore, the impact of the ARAMCO-Saudi arrangement had undeniably spread to the transit states.[15] In Cairo, Embassy officials feared that Egypt, locked in frustrated negotiations with Britain over the Suez base, would be in a position to determine Suez Canal tolls, a prospect that "could present a serious matter for petroleum developments in the area if by coordination with the pipeline transit countries they should embark on a policy of seeking to increase national revenues by exploiting their location astride both Middle East crude oil transit routes."

With the stability of the existing oil pricing system placed in doubt, the Lebanon-based U.S. petroleum attaché, N. C. Ortiz, observed that transit agreements could no longer be made "solely on the moral argument of 'sanctity' of contracts, with the implied threat of the unfavorable influence exerted on foreign capital investments if they are not honored or lasting" (ibid.). In addition, Egyptian developments led to a reassessment of political and economic risks with respect to the future of the Suez Canal. Should canal tolls be in the hands of the Egyptian regime, the same source concluded that the

> relationship of the economics of pipeline vs tanker transport could be altered appreciably to the disadvantage of Aramco/Tapline and to Saudi Arabia (or other Persian Gulf countries) should the position of world market demand force a reduction in net sales realization for

crude oil at the producing source in order to remain competitive. Faced
with such a possibility, it would be advantageous for Aramco/Tapline
to involve the interests of Saudi Arabia in their pipeline transit agreements, hoping thereby to acquire a defendant in any Pan-Arab alignment which might seek to take advantage of a control over both transit routes as a means for increasing national revenues.   (Ibid.)

It is difficult to exaggerate the policy implications of the role assigned
Saudi Arabia as political and commercial "defendant" of ARAMCO-
TAPLINE and U.S. government interests—or, under the circumstances,
the significance of Lebanon's alignment with Saudi Arabia.

In Beirut, Sa'eb Salam and George Hakim had indeed suggested that
TAPLINE and the Lebanese government adopt a position similar to that
of ARAMCO in its 1950 arrangement with Saudi Arabia. Under pressure, TAPLINE favored a profit split to be divided equally between the
transit states Lebanon, Syria, and Jordan, with Saudi Arabia included as
a fourth partner only if necessary—hardly the kind of arrangement for
which the Lebanese had pressed.[16] When Abdallah Yafi replaced Salam
as prime minister, Hare found himself in the position of defending IPC
pricing, even though he privately conceded that the pricing methods were
not sacrosanct. The U.S. Embassy was not about to challenge IPC on
TAPLINE policies.

Such had been the meaning of the declaration of the U.S. chargé
d'affaires to Abdallah Yafi some months earlier, when he clearly reiterated
that it was not his role to contest U.S. oil policies but to represent them.
Bruins recalled in a letter to "Sandy" Campbell of TAPLINE that
Lebanese prime minister Abdallah Yafi had had the temerity to charge
that Lebanon was being exploited beyond reasonable measure by U.S. oil
companies and to request Bruins's intercession with TAPLINE in order to
be "more generous both in private contributions and in their financial
policies toward the Lebanese Government."[17] Yafi bolstered his argument
by referring to "a great friend of the United States," George Hakim, who
endorsed the same position, to which Bruins responded by denouncing
Hakim for his opposition to "what the Embassy considers to be the legitimate rights and operations of Tapline and the other American oil companies." Bruins's strongly worded recommendation was that Yafi abstain
from raising the issue of pipeline negotiations until U.S.-Saudi negotiations were completed. And Bruins further reminded Prime Minister Yafi
that the Saudis, in whose territory most of the TAPLINE pipes were set,
were to receive no payment for thirteen years from TAPLINE's inception.:

I concluded the conversation by saying rather jocularly but with all sincerity that Abdullah Bey had picked a very poor advocate for Lebanon vis-à-vis the American oil companies, whose interests it is my duty to protect, and ended by reminding him that this Embassy is in other ways carrying out matters of great assistance to the Lebanese, and consequently that they must not expect us to advocate their objectives against those of our own American business interests. The conversation ended in an amicable atmosphere.   (Ibid.)

Kamil Sham'un in Command

Sham'un's first cabinet of four, excluding the banned Kamal Junblat, consisted of Khalid Shihab as prime minister, Musa Mubarak as foreign minister, Salim Haidar as minister of defense and George Hakim as minister of finance. Reformist in purpose, it undermined the position of powerful landed interests such as Ahmad al-As'ad and Sabri Hamadeh, while attempting to modernize the bureaucracy. Women were given the vote, the total number of seats in the Chamber was cut to forty-four from seventy-seven, and electoral redistricting resulted in twenty-two districts' being represented by a single person and eleven districts by two people. Thirty-three positions were lost in the process and as many enemies created. Elections held in 1953 reflected the new look. Sham'un moved to nationalize the French concession that had been under attack—especially during the latter part of the Khuri regime. The president took action against Electricité de Beyrouth, seeking also to curtail the illegal profits claimed by those representing it. In appraising the results, Embassy reports noted that "although nearly 100 decree laws were promulgated the vast majority of them dealt with administrative reorganizations and had little public impact."[18] Among the exceptions was the electoral reform measures cited above and described as "spectacular."

In foreign policy, Sham'un maintained a posture of sympathetic support for Arab nationalists, praising the 1952 Egyptian revolution. But informally, the Lebanese president promoted Western defense arrangements, even when Lebanon was not directly involved. And, to the satisfaction of Washington, Sham'un moved closer to the Saudi monarch. On his return from Saudi Arabia, Sham'un informed U.S. officials that the Saudi king "proposed that [Sham'un] and himself work together more closely in full cooperation with 'the West' and that they together attempt to convince chiefs of nearby states to join them for definite actions to prevent inroads of communism."[19] The two leaders concluded that they preferred to implement "this idea primarily on high level rather than through Arab League channel."

As was to become increasingly clear in Beirut and in Washington, Sham'un's foreign policy generated more criticism than support. Nor were his critics only those who identified with Arab nationalist movements, and after 1954, with its Nasserist expression. There were members of the Lebanese ruling class who were skeptical with respect to Sham'un's policies. The State Department's Middle East experts chose to interpret such opposition as the disgruntlement of former allies who were politically frustrated "because a millennium has not issued forth, and by those who suffer from the general negative nature of Arab mentality."[20]

The contrast with the Embassy's celebration of the advent of Lebanon's most pro-American cabinet was striking. Sa'eb Salam became prime minister on April 30, in a cabinet that had been reshuffled, with new partners representing old alliances. For the U.S. Embassy it was a moment of elation. The Lebanese, it was argued in orientalist fashion, "can be expected to be less fanatical than other Arabs and more disposed to rational conduct. This is due chiefly to their better education, their commercial mentality and their agreement on the necessity for maintaining religious equilibrium."[21] If the president of the republic was similarly pleased, it was most likely for other reasons. The new alignment afforded him a greater measure of domestic political security in that it included National Bloc supporters such as Pierre Eddeh, George Hakim, and Albert Nsouli, and excluded Junblati and Khurist influence. In addition to representing a contingent of AUB graduates who were English-speaking, it was "known be extremely friendly to US."[22] So pleased were Embassy officials that the problem was one of restraint:

> We must utilize this good fortune wisely. Over-exercise our influence
> will embarrass Cabinet to our detriment. We can expect better cooper-
> ation in most fields as economic development possibly regional defense
> but must be prepared for difficulties re Palestine and pipeline conces-
> sions. Salaam has told me many times he favors MEDO but not to
> expect him secure Lebanese acceptance prior to progress Palestine
> Egypt issues.

The prime minister was interested in U.S. financing for various development projects, including the Litany River scheme begun under Besharah al-Khuri.[23] He was sympathetic to agricultural development reform, sought protective legislation on behalf of Lebanese industries, promoted the advantages of closer economic relations with Syria, and more generally favored Lebanon's playing a regional and international role, as in the Arab League and the United Nations. Salam, in short, was committed to advancing Lebanon's profile in regional as well as international affairs. This was the point at which U.S. Secretary of State Dulles arrived in Beirut, as part of his whirlwind Middle East tour. The timing could not have been more propitious.

In no more than two days, May 16 and 17, the Embassy arranged a series of conferences, dinners, and meetings with both U.S. officials and private citizens working in UN agencies and other institutions in Lebanon, as well as with prominent members of the Lebanese political elite. The Embassy judged the encounters a public relations success.

> Crowding 9 conferences, a presidential dinner, and an AUB luncheon into 10 hours, Secretary by his sympathetic listening and genuinely American friendliness charmed all those with whom he conversed. His statement to press and government officials that his presence evidenced new U.S. interest in Arab world tended to enkindle [sic] new hope for better treatment of Arabs by new U.S. administration. Voluminous editorializing which stressed Arab "demands" has subsided considerably. General reaction is one of "wait and see."[24]

On May 16, Dulles and Harold Stassen met with Ambassador Minor and Sham'un, who summarized his view of the regional situation, including discussion of both the Palestine question and Anglo-Egyptian negotiations. Dulles was informed of the risks of declining U.S. prestige in the area and of the concern that Arab states had with respect to U.S. policy on Palestine. He was asked to persuade his government to adopt a more forthcoming position with respect to Egypt and the situation in North Africa. The U.S. secretary listened but did not hear. He was disturbed by the greater concern generated by imperialism and Palestine, as opposed to the USSR and communism.[25] His response to descriptions of the situation facing Lebanon does not appear to have been any more positive. Salam's summary of Lebanese conditions was brief and blunt. "The first is misery. . . . The second is the Arabs' genuine fear of Israel. Communism is the third."[26] Salam ventured to proceed to another pressing matter, the regime's need for more favorable pipeline agreements. "In parting the Prime Minister asked the American visitors to do what they could indirectly to induce American oil companies to take a liberal view toward the upward revision of their pipeline agreements with Lebanon" (ibid. 71). On that score, Dulles was no more tolerant than were Embassy or TAPLINE representatives. Indeed, Salam's position on the subject very nearly eroded his good standing with U.S. officials.

Dulles had come prepared on the question of TAPLINE. He reiterated the ARAMCO subsidiary's position, which left no doubts as to the meeting of minds on that score. He was well informed with regard to Lebanon's transit role, and he had information at hand concerning previous requests for additional royalties made by Charles Malik (who had asked for $10 million annually) and George Hakim (who called for 50 percent of net profits). According to the May 5 position paper on Lebanon, as irritating as the Lebanese regime's demands were, they had not reached the point where political relations were at risk.

> The problem has not deteriorated to the point where the political aspects override the commercial, and consequently, the United States Government considers the matter one for direct discussion between the oil companies and the Lebanese Government. Respect for negotiated agreements on the part of the Lebanese Government should be the best inducement for further attraction of foreign capital into the Lebanon.[27]

In his third meeting of the day with Minister of Foreign Affairs Hakim, Director General of Foreign Affairs Fu'ad 'Ammun, participating along with Chief of Protocol 'Alem Abu-Izzuddin, Dulles was accompanied by Stassen, Minor, Assistant Secretary of State Byroade, State Department Counselor Douglas MacArthur II, Lieutenant Colonel Stephen Meade, U.S. Army (the "CIA political action specialist" involved in covert action in Syria), and Counselor of the Embassy John Bruins.[28] The menu of exchanges was substantially similar to that earlier reported. This time, Dulles attempted to inject a personal note, as though to indicate his human interest in Lebanon. Dulles thus reminded Salam that his sister had lived in Beirut for two years and "his brother was active in affairs which also were of considerable interest to Lebanon," a reference to Allen Dulles and the CIA.[29] In a fourth meeting on the same day, Dulles met with parliamentary deputies, including the former prime minister, the president of the Chamber, reporter on foreign affairs Ghassan Tuwayni, and others.

It was in his meetings with U.S. officials, those connected with the United Nations technical assistance programs and TAPLINE, that Dulles gave a better indication of his position on pressing Middle East issues. He made it clear that insofar as U.S. policy was concerned, it would remain in solidarity with that of Great Britain, which eliminated the option of taking a different stance in matters related to Egypt. And as for Israel, there was no change in the U.S. position.

Meeting with the acting director of UNRWA, Leslie Carver, and Acting U.S. Representative Donald C. Bergus, Dulles was given an overview of its operation in Lebanon. On May 17, Dulles and Stassen met with the country director of the Technical Cooperation Service in Lebanon, Hollis W. Peter, and his colleagues to talk of Point IV. There were about forty-eight technicians and fifteen staff persons working in Beirut in a program that was estimated to cost some $3.1 million over a two-year period. The U.S. delegation met with TAPLINE and ARAMCO consultant Colonel William Eddy, with the presidents of the Beirut College for Women and Aleppo College, and with the Presbyterian field representative, meetings during which they discussed U.S. policy toward Israel. Dulles explained that U.S. interests prohibited support for a pro-Arab policy, since that would mean an anti-British policy in Egypt, "and that meant turning over about the only strong point in the Near East to chaos."[30] As Dulles remarked, "it would be impossible, therefore, to have both a pro-UK and a pro-Arab policy. The Secretary indicated that there is a present British tendency to work out an alliance with Israel, basing their thinking on hard-headed military realities concerning the Suez and the Near East."

Such hardheadedness appealed to Washington as well, which meant that with the dissolution of tensions between Britain and Israel, the United States would not find itself divided between its British ally and Israel. These "strong points," said Dulles, referring to Suez and Israel, were not about to be undermined in Washington. Faced with the response of the ARAMCO consultant, Dulles sought to distance himself from British policy, indicating that that did not advocate "Churchillian theory," observing "that the British even had an occasional thought about occupying Cairo and Alexandria," a remark designed to demonstrate how far apart the United States and the UK were. Did Dulles think that the reoccupation of Egypt was ridiculous or that occupation per se was unacceptable? Most likely the former, since in 1958 the two powers discussed the possibilities of occupation of Saudi and Gulf regions to protect their oil interests. But insofar as U.S. policy toward Israel was concerned, Dulles countered his critics with the reflection that "perhaps the control of Israel's subsidy could be used to stop Israeli expansion and he noted that this tool has already had a salutary effect on Israeli immigration."

In Beirut, the Salam cabinet did not long survive. Its support in the Chamber was limited, which forced the call for its dissolution. Fall elections were promised, and then planned earlier, for summer. Sa'eb Salam was now out of office, not to the regret of U.S. ambassador Raymond Hare. Working out of the Embassy, USIS officers monitored the upcoming campaign with special interest, focusing on the parties involved and the role of the media. They identified important non-Communist newspapers and informed the State Department that USIS press service reports were accepted by Lebanese journalists.

That meant that some four thousand to five thousand "column inches of locally written stories, photographs, Wireless File items, and IPS features" were placed in the journalistic media every week, "partially offsetting what otherwise would be a thoroughly distorted picture of American policy and life."[31] Of parties to watch, a number attracted particular attention, including the traditional coalitions of the National Bloc that remained in opposition to the Constitutionalist bloc associated with the former president and his supporters. Then there were the sectarian paramilitary groups, such as the Kata'eb and the Muslim Najjadah. And the ideological parties, mostly illegal but operating either under tacit official protection or in spite of it, such as the PPS and the Communist Party, active in the urban centers of Beirut, Tripoli, and Sidon. The Arab Nationalist Movement (ANM) was regionally defined but locally based. The ANM supported Nasser and the Palestinian cause and generally challenged the pro-Western status quo regimes. Its impact was considerable, as some of its adherents joined parties of the Left, as well as Junblat's Progressive Socialist Party (PSP), one of the fastest-growing parties in Lebanon. In 1953, it had a reported membership of 18,000.[32] The Ba'thist Party, founded in 1952, appealed to the same constituency. Its major gains came after the crisis of 1956, when Junblat's party split on the question of support for Nasser.

U.S. Embassy officials, such as Armin Meyer, viewed the popularity of opposition parties such as the PSP as indicative of a generalized discontent. The rank and file, Meyer argued, "are not content with things as they are. They desire something better, politically, socially and economically. One could even suggest that this desire is also reflected in the vigor and success of the Communist movement in Lebanon."[33]

Far from supporting any of Lebanon's reformist parties, however, the Embassy was satisfied to report that as a result of the 1953 elections the Chamber had been emptied of the political opposition represented by

PSP members, supporters of the previous regime, as well as Communist Party supporters. Among other victories, according to Meyer, was the fact that women had voted for the first time, "assuming axiomatically that this is a mark of progress."[34] On the debit side of the ledger, the fact that the PPS had done poorly, and that its sole winner was Ghassan Tuwayni, were considered disappointing. Overall, the Embassy predicted chaos, claiming that the "new Parliament will be more or less a free-for-all, and the ego being what it is, the power scramble may see an unprecedented amount of flag-waving against 'peace with Israel,' MEDO, Tapline, Western 'imperialism,' Point Four, etc." By the end of 1953 Bruins was accusing Salam and his colleagues of a "public emotionalism" in select matters such as Palestine, that similarly inspired "excessive flag-waving."[35]

The regime also faced other problems, of a domestic nature, that compelled action. The cabinet of Abdallah Yafi, Pierre Eddeh, and Gabriel Murr confronted an explosive situation in the fall of 1953. It was one that reflected the bitter confessional grievances pitting those who felt excluded and alienated against the privileged of the political system. Confessional strife was about not issues of religion but those of political representation and its evident disparities. It was about access to power, such as the eligibility to hold offices traditionally withheld from Lebanese Muslims (for example, the ministries of Defense, Foreign Affairs, and Justice), and it was about access to the allocation of lucrative contracts, including those connected with Point IV projects.[36] Advocates of deconfessionalization were not in favor of secularizing Lebanese society so much as redrawing the relationship of church and state. But as both the opportunists and the committed knew, the subject generated instant revolt on the part of those who rejected any change in the existing arrangements. In practice, the Lebanese Muslim National Organization, headed by Mohammed Khalid, evoked immediate rejection on the part of the head of the Kata'eb, Pierre Jemayyel, who was unprepared to relinquish his constituency's privileged position. The pattern was to be repeated throughout the Sham'un regime and later. But Lebanon's second president came under increasing fire from domestic critics for failing to take remedial action. Sham'un had U.S. support in his rejectionist position, however, as the U.S. ambassador believed any change in confessionalism to be disadvantageous to U.S. interests. The position was hardly novel in 1953; it had been articulated by U.S. officials in Beirut in the late 1940s for the same reason.

U.S. officials in Beirut adopted a two-pronged response. On the one hand, they urged the State Department to be forthcoming with respect to economic assistance, while insisting that the Lebanese implement U.S. technical assistance projects. On the other, the U.S. ambassador maintained a steadfast opposition to any changes in the confessional system. Hare was an unconditional supporter of the status quo, explaining his position as a response to the risks of change, since "most Moslems who clamor for the abolition of confessionalism do so in the firm belief that the residency of political power in Lebanon would shift eventually from Christian to Moslem leadership."[37] Hare then urged that Western allies remain vigilant on the question of confessionalism, emphasizing that confessionalism was integral to the maintenance of the regime in the state. His communiqué to Dulles on the subject is worthy of citation because of its clarity with respect to the U.S. view of the risks of political change:

> Furthermore, the United States and other Western governments would do well to be thinking even now whether it is in their interest that Lebanon be preserved as a state and if so whether it might not have more capabilities than previously capitalized on for serving as a bridgehead in the Orient. In other words, because of its implications, the perennial problem of confessionalism in Lebanon, although it has by no means reached a critical stage, is not one which the United States and other Western powers should treat with complete indifference.

U.S. policy, from this perspective, rested on two conditions. The first was that the Lebanese ruling class continue to find its own interests to be entirely congruent with those of Sham'un. The second was that domestic discontent be contained to avoid the risks of civil strife and ensuing destabilization. In the absence of the first condition, the politics of U.S. collaborative intervention would be sorely tested and Washington would find itself isolated. With the inability to contain domestic discontent, on the other hand, opposition to the regime would force the United States to provide increased assistance for internal security and, eventually, military assistance. In the course of the next few years these very conditions led to an impasse in U.S. policies and to the near collapse of the regime. Such was the situation that developed between 1956 and 1958.

In the interim, the Lebanese cabinet did not remain quiescent. In the summer of 1954 it ordered a commission to consider "the just and equitable distribution of government posts 'so that all Lebanese may be truly represented in public offices.' "[38] Although not translated into meaningful practice, the move elicited sharp and menacing rebuttals from the Kata'eb. "Gemayel [Jemayyel] took the position that the activity of the National Organization threatens the existence of Christian communities and Lebanon and therefore of the Lebanese nation itself, and that it represents an attempt on the part of certain Moslem elements to create an Islamic state in Lebanon" (ibid.). The Kata'eb leader denounced the impact of "fanaticism" on the law of the land and promised "to counteract strikes by strikes, demonstrations by demonstrations, terrorism by terrorism and 'if the state remains powerless' to 'reconsider the form and structures of the state itself.' In thinly veiled words, he also mentioned the possibility of appealing to a foreign nation for protection" (ibid.). What did such references mean? Was Jemayyel threatening to have Maronite-led Christians secede to form a separate state? And to whom did he refer in what the Embassy described as "thinly veiled words"?

At the regime level, Prime Minister Abdallah Yafi requested assistance from Washington for internal security in October 1953. The request for grant aid for the Beirut police and plans for a gendarmerie were proposed to the Embassy, which passed the issue on to the State Department. At the time, the Eisenhower administration was contemplating agreement for the provision of military grant aid, but that did not formally apply to the gendarmerie, which was under the Lebanese president's supervision, as opposed to that of the military. As Ambassador Hare explained, "there might be some difficulty about supplying weapons from the United States to the Gendarmerie because it is not primarily a part of the Lebanese Military setup in peace time, although there is provision for it to operate with the military in war time."[39]

The advantages were obvious, if support of Sham'un was an American priority. Hare recommended its approval as an adjunct to internal security that was sufficiently modest not to be considered as "suitable for aggressive purposes. It would also appear that such assistance would not only augment Lebanese internal security, but would be in line with our overall objective of greater stability in this part of the Middle East, particularly in respect of repression of possible subversive activity." Yafi assisted Hare by justifying the request in the implausible terms of enabling the government to deal with "bandits and other lawless elements in the mountain districts," a task that evidently required assistance for the thousand-man police force and the approximately two thousand members of the gendarmerie. Hare's request was reinforced at the end of the year in a Joint FOA-State message sent to Dulles on December 30, in which the United States Operating Mission (USOM) underscored the necessity of providing further assistance in a difficult period. "Situation clearly indicates urgent need and timeliness expansion U.S. technical aid to include reasonable economic aid from special FY 1954 funds. Amount around $5 million is suggested for few selected impact and productive projects in water development and agriculture."[40] Reasons for such aid were plainly given:

> In conclusion it must be emphasized that granting economic aid to Lebanon at this juncture is essential to restore stability and create impact in favor US, which are of course our primary policy considerations. Without benefit such aid situation is likely deteriorate toward upheaval with increased negative reaction to present USOM program and U.S. policy in general.

Hare added that it was "important that ground gained in face of much difficulty in past should not (repeat not) be lost through failure to extend reasonable and relatively justifiable grant-economic aid." Thus, by the end of 1953, both the vulnerability of the regime and the commitment to maintaining it in power were evident.

9

Realities of Power in the "Rear Area"

Beirut Seeking Assistance

The advocacy of economic and technical assistance for Lebanon remained a constant feature of Embassy communiqués to Washington, one
on which U.S. ambassador Hare increasingly focused to offset domestic
tensions and regime weakness. On this, there were dissenting voices
among U.S. officers in Beirut. Parallel analyses of the state of the nation
after ten years of independence yielded a pessimistic appraisal that technical and even economic assistance programs could hardly remedy.
Reports on Lebanon's social and political divisions were scarcely novel,
nor was there any surprise that favorable indices of economic growth
were not translated into social policy. For the U.S. ambassador, the
assignment was not to promote reform but to assure continuity of power
without undue expenditure on Washington's part. Technical assistance,
in this context, was a program to be supported irrespective of the likelihood of its being implemented.

In Beirut, however, the Sham'un regime wanted other signs of U.S.
support. Military as well as economic assistance was requested, albeit
without success. For Charles Malik, the objective was to enroll Lebanon
into U.S. regional policy, in which military aid would be an adjunct to a
broader strategic design. The response from Washington was consistently negative, exposing the nature of the Lebanese-U.S. relationship

and the sharp limits of Beirut's power. But the same circumstances also exposed what the regime was prepared to accept in the illusory anticipation of a quid pro quo. In exchange for military intelligence and the penetration of the Lebanese military, to which the regime and its commander in chief agreed, Malik expected military assistance. The expectation was without foundation.

The vain attempts to obtain public ratification of U.S. support for the Lebanese government had little effect on political crises that assumed confessional form. But the latter aroused interest in Israel, where deliberation on the possibility of supporting a breakaway Maronite state had high-level support. The plan was abandoned in the absence of a credible Christian separatist bloc, while among U.S. officials the response to the domestic crises took the forms of an accelerated anti-Communist campaign and a renewed assessment of the regime's vulnerability.

Attempts to obtain U.S. military assistance began in earnest in 1952, although as previous discussion has shown, there were earlier indications of interest. It is worth reviewing this brief history in order to better situate the requests for internal security assistance that were made in 1953. The Sham'un government requested military assistance shortly after it was installed.

It was in the late fall of 1952, at the time of the pressure by U.S. international oil company executives on Sham'un to keep Kamal Junblat out of the cabinet, that he raised the subject. According to Sham'un's *Mémoires*, this was not the best of times in Lebanese-U.S. relations. Sham'un recalled learning of a coup against him that was allegedly fomented by a U.S. naval attaché in collusion with some Lebanese military officers.[1] In any case, in Washington, Sham'un's requests were heard. The State Department passed his requests for arms to the Defense Department. Henry Byroade, director of the Department of State's Near East and Africa Division, informed Secretary of Defense Robert A. Lovett that Lebanon "has expressed specific interest in securing limited arms from the United States and our Embassy in Beirut has recommended the provision of reimbursable assistance."[2] Byroade cited Sham'un's good political behavior in reminding Lovett that the Lebanese president had volunteered his nation's assets to the United States on his accession to power. Sham'un could "be expected to emulate the cordial relations which his predecessor's government maintained with the United States," Byroade pointed out. Furthermore, Sham'un had indicated that he would be " 'one hundred percent on the side of the West, with or without any treaty to that effect,' " in the event of an East-West confrontation and that he "would be willing to give military base privileges to the United States. Therefore, it is desirable to accord Lebanon treatment at least equal to that given Israel and most of the other Arab states."

The response on the part of Deputy Under Secretary H. Freeman Mathews, in his October 23 letter to Lovett, was positive. Lebanon met the eligibility requirements established in the amended 1949 Mutual Defense Assistance Act, its government was willing to pay for U.S. military equipment, and there were good reasons to provide it.[3] Among the supporting arguments marshaled in defense of the Lebanese request was the fact that Lebanon had "demonstrated consistent friendliness and cooperation with the West, an attitude which in all probability will be developed further under the new Presidency of [Kamil Sham'un]." The latter was written in October 1952, shortly after Sham'un had taken office.

The Lebanese government's offer to pay for the equipment it sought from the United States was an additional factor to consider. The requests were modest, especially in relation to anticipated rewards, as providing military assistance had an evident symbolic as well as practical value. In Freeman Mathews's terms, "It would enable Lebanon to build up the strength of the small Lebanese army, an army which was a large factor in the maintenance of public order and constitutionality during the recent political crisis." And finally, according to the same source, a positive response from the United States "would increase the likelihood of Lebanese participation in a Middle East Defense Organization, and create a favorable atmosphere in which to negotiate any air base rights which we might desire in the future." Both the Department of State and the Department of Defense jointly supported Lebanon's request to Harold Stassen, the director of the Mutual Security Program. The time was ripe, particularly since Saudi Arabia, Syria, Egypt, Iraq, and Israel had already qualified for similar status.

The Joint Chiefs of Staff extended their approval in a letter dated January 8, 1953.[4] The Lebanese government through its Legation in Washington duly submitted its requests for submarine parts as well as for telecommunication equipment. On February 5, Stassen approved Lebanon's eligibility, forwarding Ambassador Harold Minor a draft text, which he, in turn, was to submit to Lebanon's minister of foreign affairs, George Hakim. Among its conditions was that the material in question be used exclusively for the state's "internal security, its legitimate self-defense, or to permit it to participate in the defense of the area of which it is a part, or in United Nations collective security arrangements and measures, and that it will not undertake any act of aggression against any other state."[5] On April 2, Minor reported that Hakim had accepted the conditions of the reimbursable military assistance.

As a result of Dulles's trip to the Middle East in the spring of 1953, military assistance was offered a number of states, including Lebanon. In 1953 Lebanon obtained $2.5 million for economic and technical assistance, more than three times what it had received in the preceding year, with the biggest addition represented by technical assistance. In 1953, Egypt received $2.4 million for technical assistance, information, and educational exchange; Iraq, $1.3 million; and Jordan, $1.4 million. Saudi Arabia received $0.8 million; Syria, $0.5 million; and Israel, $59.9 million.[6]

One of the direct by-products of Dulles's trip was his recognition of the moribund status of MEDO (Middle East Defense Organization). This inspired the sequence of developments in U.S. strategic planning that culminated in the Baghdad Pact system. At this stage, however, Dulles recommended to the National Security Council that a new approach to regional security be attempted, one that bypassed Arab states of the interior in favor of the countries situated along the "Northern Tier." The plan, in short, built on the earlier practice of building up states on the Soviet border, which in this instance allowed the State Department to avoid Egypt, which had earlier rejected both MEC and MEDO. For a brief period, Dulles turned to Syria as the most promising focus for U.S. policy, but this lasted only until the fall of the Shishakly regime in 1954. Before this period, however, even though Lebanon was excluded from the Northern Tier arrangements, Sham'un was asked not only to support it but to obtain the support of other Arab states as well.

In early January 1954 Sham'un informed Embassy officials that he might be interested in the U.S. "equipping one entire division for them. However, it was pointed out that no provision for grant aid existed and that such equipment was not available since we were at that time still engaged in hostilities in Korea."[7] But matters did not end there. The Embassy had prepared a lengthy review of U.S. military aid to Lebanon, on the basis of which Bruins recalled that U.S. military aid had not been offered Lebanon since the end of World War II when "certain materials were furnished under the Surplus War Properties Agreement." Lebanon had paid off that account, and its requests were subsequently deferred to other countries, such as France and Great Britain.

Ambassador Raymond Hare repeatedly indicated his support for Sham'un's requests, passing on to the Department of State the list of radio, telephone, teletype machines, and other equipment requested. Above all, Hare stressed the importance of not turning away a state that offered the U.S. unconditional political support. To offer military aid to Syria while refusing it to Lebanon, Hare insisted, was courting political danger insofar as U.S.-Lebanese relations were concerned.[8] Dulles responded. The Defense Department, Hare was informed, had authorized a modest program for Lebanon, but its contingent character rendered it useless. The Defense Department preferred to consider assistance to Lebanon in conjunction with that to Syria, a project still under consideration. Furthermore, there were other priorities, such as Iraq, as Hare was reminded.[9]

For Beirut the outcome was humiliating, particularly since the regime was aware of the support offered Egypt, even after it had taken the lead in challenging Western defense policies. In responding to Sham'un's complaints, Hare directed his attention to the reorientation of U.S. strategic policy away from the Arab interior to non-Arab states of the Northern Tier.[10] Pressed for a more satisfactory explanation, Hare offered a ruder one. What, Hare wanted to know, did Lebanon offer to the United States? Would it be prepared to cooperate with Turkey or Pakistan? Did it envisage any form of Arab collective security in the aftermath of the Egyptian settlement with the British?

Sham'un reminded Hare that Lebanon had neither geographical nor significant political frontiers with the non-Arab states to which the United States was now turning its attention, i.e., Turkey and Pakistan. Sham'un pressed the Egyptian case, while the minister of defense, Majid Arslan, the commander of the Lebanese army, General Fu'ad Shihab, and the chief of staff of the Lebanese army, Colonel Salem, continued to insist on military assistance.[11] The effort failed. Even Charles Malik was moved to a supplicant's position, admitting to U.S. officials in November 1954 that he was under pressure to obtain some kind of economic or military agreement to provide tangible evidence of U.S. support.

Before the debacle of Lebanon's latest request for military assistance, the Embassy made the regime an offer it hoped would not be refused. The controversy it stirred might perhaps have been avoided had Washington acceded to Lebanon's previous requests for assistance. In Washington's view, however, there was no reason to do so. Lebanon, in fact, had little to offer in comparison to the major states of the region. What it did possess in terms of its strategic location, and the incomparable value of its transit and communication roles, required no further compensation. The political cost of Lebanon's client relationship with Washington was starkly revealed in the interlude that concerned the military geographic assignment in Lebanon endorsed by the United States.

In the summer of 1953 the Lebanese army was asked to consider a proposal that it eventually accepted. Cabinet approval was given for the U.S. Military Geographic Specialist assignment in Lebanon. To a nonspecialist, it was an exercise in military intelligence. All evidence of animate and inanimate objects on the Lebanese landscape was to be mapped, including the disposition of roads, bridges, rivers, telephone and telegraph lines, and other installations. As Colonel Robert C. Works, the U.S. Embassy army attaché, explained to General Shihab, military geographic specialist teams were attached to local army attaché offices in Iran, Iraq, Spain, Portugal, and Belgium, where they had been successful in obtaining comparable "terrain and transportation information."[12] Such teams were also at work in Norway, the Netherlands, France, Italy, Turkey, and Thailand. Pakistan was to be next.

> The Military Geographic Specialist Teams collect details of geographic information which are helpful in terrain evaluation. These cover routes, railroads, bridges, strategic avenues of approach, relief, drainage, vegetation, climate and the location and distribution of mines, buildings, ditches and other man-made objects. The teams also verify or correct existing maps; but they do not carry out new mapping projects.

On August 23, Works submitted a request to Fu'ad Shihab. Ambassador Hare was to take the matter up with the Foreign Office, assuming that Shihab's reply was positive. The subject was brought up at the initiative of the director of the Foreign Office more than one month later, when Fu'ad 'Ammun informed Hare that the matter had gone to the Foreign Office and the president. Foreign Minister Naqqash, who referred to the "delicate project," indicated that the Lebanese government was willing to approve it in exchange for U.S. military assistance.

> He said that while the provision of U.S. military assistance was not being attached as a "condition," the Lebanese government wished the United States to consider the approval of this delicate project, which in effect involved Lebanon's collaboration with the United States as an

ally, as the type of "advantages" that Lebanon can and will make available to the United States, even though a direct formal arrangement for defense is not effected. (Ibid.)

Hare rejected the offer and its implications, while seeking to persuade the Lebanese that they would benefit from such projects.

Colonel Works, in a separate letter addressed to General Shihab, repeated the same position, underlining the inaccessibility of U.S. military assistance, while setting forth the conditions of the U.S. offer. If Lebanon agreed to the U.S. request, Works explained, the United States would agree to assign Lebanese army personnel to work with the U.S. team; the U.S. officer in charge would be assigned to the Embassy's Office of the Military Attaché; and "he could be attached to the Lebanese Army if desired."

What did this mean in the absence of the quid pro quo that Sham'un sought? The answer was a level of military collaboration that assumed the subordination of Lebanese officers and the penetration of the Lebanese army by U.S. military. Colonel Works reminded Shihab that the project would offer Lebanon the opportunity to train its officers and that the Lebanese government would receive a copy of the results of the military team's study, which "would be held in strictest confidence by the United States Government and would not be released to other governments without the expressed approval of the Lebanese Government."

Works concluded by emphasizing that the implementation of the project depended entirely on Shihab's approval. Would he have offered it to Shihab if he had thought its rejection a possibility? And would Shihab and the Sham'un entourage have seriously considered rejecting the offer? Or was Malik's role in this a key, as the chief interlocutor with the United States who prided himself on his access to the Americans, in spite of their rebuff? The Sham'un regime persisted throughout this period in requesting military assistance, without success. Moreover, Malik continued to engage U.S. officials in discussions of Lebanon's role in regional U.S. defense.

In the fall of 1954, Malik met with the State Department's NEA officers, including Henry Byroade, who pointed out that Lebanon had been granted $6 million for fiscal year 1954, only six months earlier. Aid requests for 1955 were contingent on the demonstration of urgent need. Lebanon's situation was conditional on a more general clarification of regional defense planning, Byroade indicated. And regional differences effectively, if temporarily, blocked U.S. planning. Hence, Malik's question as to where Lebanon fit in the Northern Tier arrangement was to be determined, if at all, by decisions made in Washington as well as Teheran and Baghdad and Cairo, in addition to Tel Aviv.[13] As Byroade indicated:

> As far as Lebanon is concerned, if Iraq and Iran do go into a Northern Tier organization, and Arab-Israel relations improve, then military aid for Lebanon would be a real possibility. Perhaps Lebanon would support or join the organization itself, and military aid would be forthcoming due to the importance of communications, roads, ports, airports in Lebanon as a "rear area" behind the forward line of defense.
>
> (Ibid.)

Malik countered with a revised proposal that enhanced the status of the "rear area" states by recommending "a second defensive grouping behind the Northern Tier group (Turkey, Iraq, Pakistan, and Iran), the 'rear area' group to consist of Greece, Turkey, Lebanon, Syria, and Egypt, with Turkey as the connecting link between the two groups." Byroade admitted that no thought had been given to such a possibility, but it did not alter the conditions attached to military assistance. In 1955, these changed. The Sham'un regime's vulnerability had become more dangerous in Washington's view, calling forth internal security for the gendarmerie and eulogies for the president.

The frustrations in obtaining U.S. military assistance coincided with other developments, those rooted in national politics and party polemics. Confessional strife persisted through Sham'un's term in office, accelerating in accord with his domestic and foreign policies. By the spring of 1954, the advantages of exploiting Lebanon's domestic vulnerability on this score appealed to certain highly placed Israeli officials who viewed the Israeli-Lebanese connection as an instrument in fortifying Israel's Arab policies. Former prime minister David Ben-Gurion, Prime Minister Moshe Sharett, and Chief of Staff Moshe Dayan, thus assessed prospects for the emergence of a Lebanese Maronite state with Israeli support. The objective was the undermining of Arab nationalist forces, whether through arrangements with non-Arab regimes or anti-Arab elements in Arab states. In the context of Israeli policy, Iran and Ethiopia provide illustrations of the former, the Maronite separatists of Beirut, the latter.[14] Israeli policy, later justified in terms of protecting the Lebanese Christian minority, was otherwise motivated as the diaries of the then prime minister, Moshe Sharett, make clear. In practice, there was no Lebanese Christian bloc in Beirut favoring the Maronitist option, although there were Maronite clergy and Kata'eb politicians who preferred such a policy to the making of political concessions in Beirut. Christian Lebanese were by no means of one view on the question, however, as the core of the ruling class was committed to politics of the National Pact, provided that control remained in its hands. Electoral arrangements and the practices associated with the confessional system in politics assured such an outcome.

The diaries of Moshe Sharett for the period in question reveal that Ben-Gurion and his supporters in the Foreign Ministry had "contacts with certain circles in Lebanon" to explore the possibilities of creating a Maronite state.[15] Ben-Gurion's proposals were based on the assumptions "that Lebanon is the weakest link in the Arab League" and that its Christian population would be sympathetic to the idea of separate state, particularly in periods of sectarian tension.[16] Under existing circumstances, the "creation of a Christian State in our neighborhood" seemed plausible to Ben-Gurion, assuming Israel's role.

> Without our initiative and our vigorous aid this will not be done. It seems to me that this is the central duty, or at least one of the central duties, of our foreign policy. This means that time, energy and means ought to be invested in it and that we must act in all possible ways to bring about a radical change in Lebanon.   (Ibid.)

Sharett's reply of March 18, 1954, opposed the plan, arguing that there was inadequate support for it in Lebanon given that most Lebanese Maronites had "put all their cards on a Christian-Muslim coalition" (March 18, 1954, ibid. 26). The Ben-Gurion plan, insofar as Sharett was concerned, risked backfiring and alienating if not endangering the very element that it was designed to attract. Ben-Gurion had an ally in the chief of staff, while Sharett was in a minority. But his opposition was qualified. "I don't exclude the possibility of accomplishing this goal in the wake of a wave of shocks that will sweep the Middle East . . . will destroy the present constellations and will form others" (ibid.). Dayan, on the other hand, favored Ben-Gurion's proposal. From Sharett's diaries, May 16, 1954:

> According to him [Dayan], the only thing that's necessary is to find an officer, even just a major. We should either win his heart or buy him with money, to make him agree to declare himself the savior of the Maronite population. Then the Israeli army will enter Lebanon, will occupy the necessary territory, and will create a Christian regime

which will ally itself with Israel. The territory from the Litany south-
ward will be totally annexed to Israel and everything will be all right.
If we were to accept the advice of the Chief of Staff we would do it
tomorrow, without awaiting a signal from Baghdad, but under the circumstances the government of Iraq will do our will and will occupy
Syria.   (Ibid. 28)

What failed to be implemented in 1954 found acceptance under other
circumstances in the Israeli invasion of Lebanon in 1982. But in the 1954
case, Sharett insisted that the plan was "a crazy adventure," to be
rejected in favor of "prudent actions directed at encouraging Maronite
circles who reject Muslim pressures and agree to lean on us" (May 28,
1954, ibid. 29). Avi Shlaim reports that Sharett established a commission
in conjunction with Foreign Ministry officials and the Israeli military to
"deal with Lebanese affairs."[17]

Israeli-Lebanese matters did not end abruptly, however. In February
1955, "an adventurer and a visionary," the Lebanese Naguib Sfeir, whom
Sharett had known earlier, reportedly met the Israeli ambassador to Italy.
In a mission apparently approved by Sham'un, Lebanon was said to be
prepared "to sign a separate peace if we [Israel] accept the following
three conditions: a. guarantee Lebanon's borders; b. come to Lebanon's
aid if it is attacked by Syria; c. buy Lebanon's agricultural surplus. Sasson
[Israeli ambassador to Italy] . . . suggested a meeting between himself and
[Sham'un] during the latter's next visit to Rome."[18] There were further
contacts between Israelis and Lebanese recorded in Sharett's diaries, on
April 24, and references to the same several weeks later.[19]

What did U.S. officials know of these exchanges? What did they think
of the state of Lebanese politics at the time? As in the case of the late
1940s, the sharp critique of the obstructionist politics of Lebanon's leaders was not translated into policy. Nonetheless, U.S. officials, including
Donald Heath, who replaced Hare as ambassador and who remained
through the parliamentary elections of 1957 (which the United States, with
Heath's endorsement, fixed), were entirely lucid about the conditions they
observed. They repeatedly commented on the renewed tensions within and
between confessional-political groups; the conflicts between a disenfran-
chised Shi'i constituency and Sunni political leaders; and the chronic
expressions of political disdain for Lebanese Muslims among political
elites. Reports from the U.S. Embassy reveal the critical assessments and
complicit politics characteristic of U.S. policy and practice in Beirut.

In an August 23, 1954, dispatch sent by Ambassador Raymond Hare
to the State Department, Hare reported on an exchange in which Foreign

Minister Naqqash explained with barely concealed contempt that "he personally would have no objection to see more Moslems in Government offices, the simple truth was that there were very few Moslems who could qualify for civil service positions. In this connection, Naqqash referred to Prime Minister Yafi as a rabid Moslem who basically shared the views of the National Organization," a comment that situated Naqqash more accurately than it did Yafi.[20] When, in an effort to deflect bitter criticisms from the Shi'i constituency that complained of its lack of support, Sunni leaders endorsed the need for a more equitable distribution of offices, it aroused the man whom U.S. officials in Beirut described as the "self-appointed champion of Christian interests in Lebanon," Pierre Jemayyel. In one of his rejoinders that was reported in the same communiqué, Jemayyel reminded his Muslim brothers that Lebanese Christians "contribute 80 percent of the Lebanese budget." The Kata'eb leader's recommendation to his Muslim compatriots was that "the Moslems of Lebanon should be willing, if necessary, to give up all government positions in favor of the Christians."[21]

In mid-July of the following year, when the preceding exchange was reported to Washington, Embassy officer P. R. Graham concluded that the repeated clashes occurring in Beirut were symptomatic of the "awakening social and political consciousness of the Moslems of Lebanon and the increasingly militant and aggressive character of their [Muslim] organizations, coupled with the realization on the part of the Christians that they are fighting a losing battle as far as numerical strength is concerned." Donald Heath, Hare's successor in Beirut signed the report that Graham wrote, in which the Embassy officer offered a prophetic warning. Avoiding civil strife, according to this view, would be possible only if "the new generation of Lebanese can be imbued with such tolerance and patriotic sentiment that administrative skill and professional competence can replace confessionalism as the bases for the allocation of governmental positions" (ibid.). Whether or not Heath was in a position to press for an opening on this score is doubtful. His own tenure, as later discussion indicates, coincided with an intensification of support for Sham'un that he spearheaded.

Seeing Red

If the flaws of Lebanese ruling circles were so clearly exposed, why were the same U.S. officials who were masters at decoding Lebanese corruption consistently prepared to condone them? U.S. policy confirmed the benefits of retaining the status quo to assure the continuity of a Western-oriented, anti-communist ruling class and system advantageous to U.S. interests. Thus, Hare could be courteously abrasive to Sham'un in connection with his requests for military assistance, and Colonel Works no less pointed in making his case to General Shihab in connection with the military geographic team, while in another context, Hare could report favorably on plans initiated by a historic figure in Lebanon's political elite to "promote Western ideals" in Lebanon. The issuing of comprehensive dispatches that offered compelling analyses of Lebanon's political maldevelopment did little to alter the direction of such policies.

Anti-communist fervor in Washington was at its height in the mid-1950s, with evident effect on the Foreign Service. In the Middle East, reports of Communist advances and Soviet influence were commonplace. Lebanon figured prominently in such accounts. In 1954, there were reported to be an estimated "5,000 Communists in the official party in Israel; in the 'unofficial' Syrian party less than 10,000; 1,000 to 1,500 adherents to the (particularly active) Communist party of the Sudan, and 10,000 in the Lebanon, where the Communist party was somnolent."[22]

The Embassy, if aware of such figures, discounted the accompanying assessment. There was nothing somnolent, as far as it was concerned, about Lebanese Communists and fellow travelers. On the contrary, the Embassy argued that local Communists were more active than ever and that they had effectively infiltrated the press. Certain constituencies were considered to be particularly vulnerable, such as Palestinian refugees, followers of Greek and Armenian Orthodox churches, and Shi'i *ulema* in the Lebanese south. There were also certain social groups that were deemed particularly susceptible, such as urban intellectuals. In Beirut, the American University was viewed as a center of subversion, and the inability of police to contain demonstrations led directly to requests for U.S. assistance.

It was in the winter of 1954 that Hare conveyed a report of an encounter between Embassy officer John H. Bruins and the "Lebanese journalist and banker" Michel Chiha, whose "favorite editorial gambit is that the Islamic world from Tangier to Indonesia makes no sense ethnically nor politically and that the Arab world should be more identified with the Mediterranean civilization."[23] Bruins was aware of the past role of the man he described as a "well-known connoisseeur [*sic*] and collector of Middle Eastern antiquities . . . [who] lives in quiet luxury." Chiha, who was a brother-in-law and political intimate of the former president,

Besharah al-Khuri, as Bruins certainly knew, was one of the architects of the modern Lebanese state. Chiha's trajectory from Khuri to the U.S. Embassy is worth pondering, particularly since he does not appear to have been among the early lobbyists for a Lebanese-U.S. connection. Chiha appreciated the fervor of American anti-communism, however. In the winter of 1954, the banker, financier, and political thinker joined in conversation with U.S. Embassy officer Bruins to deliberate on a common anti-Communist project in Lebanon. To Chiha, Lebanon's most vulnerable target was its Muslim masses.

Chiha's approach appealed to Bruins. Recalling Gandhi's charismatic appeal, the Soviet Union's "battle for men's minds," and the claim that Lebanese Muslims were not materialists, Chiha recalled that "during the war when wheat and shoes were rationed, most of the Muslims in Lebanon disposed of their coupons because they did not really want those things." Chiha, like Malik, believed that Lebanon needed protection, and he had a proposal to offer the Embassy, which was "constantly looking for better means of bringing the ideals of the free world to the attention of those most susceptible to Communism. A positive approach coordinated with the desires and aspirations of the indigenous population is sought as possibly offering better results than to confine efforts to the negativistic theme of opposition to Communism" (ibid.). The plan was to be aimed at the "lower" classes, Bruins emphasized Chiha's usage. It was to underline the role of violence in Communist doctrine, and the contrasting "dignity of the individual" offered by the West. This message was to be promoted in the publication and distribution of Arabic pamphlets "serialized into six or a dozen parts, issued in thousands if not millions of copies, and 'fed' to the people through our usual USIS media with the cooperation of religious groups." Chiha recommended that Malik be the chosen author since he had "expert knowledge of the philosophical bases of both communism and freedom."

In the first week of April, Embassy officer Armin H. Meyer reported on the Lebanese regime's growing concern with communism, and the U.S. Embassy's recommendations to the State Department. In the dispatch of April 2, Meyer drew the State Department's attention to "the police-student clash at AUB on Mar 27 [that] may have had one salutary result in that it has awakened many Lebanese to the fact that subversive Communism is a real and serious threat."[24] Four days later, in another dispatch from the same source, Prime Minister Yafi was reported to have requested U.S. assistance.

Specifically, he would appreciate two forms of assistance, both to be provided without local publicity: an allotment of funds, possibly under the guise of economic assistance, which could be devoted to the purchase of equipment and materials for controlling street disturbances; and a specialist in anti-Communism who could work secretly and closely with the government radio broadcasting authorities to counter Communistic influence.[25]

Hare, who met with Yafi, conceded that the prime minister was not entirely certain of what the implementation of these plans entailed, but he himself had no doubts of what was to be done. Hare maintained that Lebanese security forces were lax or, worse, unprepared and ill-equipped, as he informed Sham'un. As evidence, Hare cited "Captain Joseph Haraki, promising new police captain in Beirut," who admitted that "he, the top policeman in Beirut, is totally unqualified to instruct his men in matters of this kind. He hoped earnestly that the United States might send someone to Lebanon who could recommend latest methods and equipment for combatting subversion and controlling street riots, most of the latter being at least in part of Communist inspiration" (ibid.). The British had been approached with a similar request for assistance, which the Foreign Office disdained. The matter was one of Lebanese responsibility, according to the British. For the U.S. Embassy in Beirut, the matter was of the greatest urgency—and doubtless opportunity. Hare's underlying premise was that the question at hand was too serious to be left to the Lebanese. They might not take the Communist "threat" seriously enough, particularly after individual crises and confrontations had waned.

> I am convinced, therefore, that the Department as well as the Embassy could profitably give thought to steps which the American Government might take, either overtly or covertly, to encourage and assist Lebanese anti-Communist initiative. The Department, I believe, may have had similar requests from elsewhere. If, from these experiences, the Department can indicate to the Embassy what avenues are open, the Embassy would carefully consider the various possibilities and in concert with the Department determine what assistance the United States Government might appropriately render to the Lebanese Government in this vital cause.   (Ibid.)

The Embassy continued to send reports to the State Department through the summer of 1954, providing ample details on the nature of Communist objectives, tactics, and agents, as well as "targets and tools."[26]

In addition to their increased emphasis on sports and cultural activities, Meyer was obviously wary of the ability of local Communists to work through effective political and electoral coalitions. Parliamentary elections demonstrated the risks of such arrangements.

> Prime Minister YAFI, for example, had Peace Partisan Habib Rubeiz on his executive committee. . . . It is reported that Economy Minister Rashid KARAMI was agreeable recently to withdrawing the permit for the sale of the two Swedish tankers to Poland, which he recognized was a mistake . . . but he was prevented from taking that appropriate course of action because of the pressure against it from the Communist segment of his constituency in Tripoli.   (Ibid.)

To the holding of meetings such as the "Congress for the Defense of the Peoples of the Near and Middle East," in Beirut in the winter of 1953, Meyer responded with the observation that such "public gatherings, if they are successfully staged, can have a tremendous effect on Near Eastern participants who as a rule are moved to action more by emotions than by reason" (ibid.) The reflexive orientalism served its rationalizing purpose. In Beirut, as in Guatemala during the same period, it was not reason or evidence that was called for in the identification of the "enemy" but a far lamer political method, namely, the so-called duck test, as it was described in the Guatemalan case. According to U.S. ambassador to Guatemala Patterson, "many times it is impossible to prove legally that a certain individual is a communist; but for cases of this sort I recommend a practical method of detection—the 'duck test,' i.e., if it looks and walks like a duck, it is safe to assume that it is one."[27] In Beirut in April 1954, Meyer maintained that "it is not necessary to establish either Mohammed X or Maroun Y as being card-carriers."[28]

Among those U.S. officials with whom Hare collaborated on the anti-Communist campaign was Paul Lunt, the commuting labor attaché, who divided his time between Beirut and Cairo. Lunt, however, was more skeptical than was Hare as to the extent of Communist expansion in Beirut. Among his informants on the situation in Lebanon was the director of the Communist Control section of the Egyptian security policy, Lieutenant Colonel Ahmad Hilmy. Hilmy considered Lebanese security policy to be incompetent. But as Lunt pointed out, Hilmy may not have been in a position to know, since he was also persuaded that information was being kept from him by the same incompetents.[29] Lunt, in fact, was not convinced of the dramatic advances of communism in Beirut or of the

competence of the anti-communist labor federation. Critical of its leadership, Lunt described those who "talk a strong anti-communist line but
at least some of them would probably sell out to the highest bidder." The
labor attaché admitted that there was a tacit competition between local
labor leaders to gain favors with both the U.S. and the British embassies,
which further undermined their credibility. Such observations did not fit
Hare's views on the matter. But then there were other unpleasant surprises in terms of Lebanese politics, insofar as the U.S. ambassador's
expectations were concerned. They confirmed his earlier criticisms of the
Lebanese bourgeoisie as inadequately sensitive politically. Hare was
aghast, in short, at the practice of a business class less concerned with the
color of money or its provenance than its value. Nevertheless, he concluded that when it comes to "such matters as Israel and oil, we all too
frequently find the Salaams, the Jamalis, the Hakims, the Boustanis and
other pro-Americans our greatest critics. A redeeming feature, on the
other hand, is that with respect to other issues, such as Communism, economic development, and personal friendships, these individuals usually
have an asset value."[30] But some months later, Emile Bustani, the millionaire contractor, was singled out as a virulent case of the violation of
the U.S. profit ethic. Interested in Lebanese–East bloc trade, Bustani was
accused of harassing Yafi to lift restrictions on the sale of strategic goods
to the East bloc. Tankers, however, were only part of the problem.

   In 1958 Hare was U.S. ambassador to Egypt and the UAR and Bustani
was one of the Lebanese businessmen committed to brokering a compromise with Sham'un and Egyptian/UAR President Nasser, about which
Hare was not enthusiastic.

National Development Versus
Profitable Developments

To U.S. and Lebanese business circles in Beirut, the Lebanon of the mid-
1950s was a thriving emporium. While the Embassy's political analyses of
the first decade of Lebanon's independence yielded incontrovertible evidence of a polarized society, those that focused on the regime's economic
achievements offered an altogether different vision. Embassy reports provided ample documentation of both conditions, as the State Department
contained the perils of political maldevelopment while catering to those
responsible for profitable accumulation. Ten years after independence,
Lebanon was in a precarious state. The regime was "not finding it easy to

walk or even stand on its own feet. Some observers believe the state is doomed unless rescued by a dictatorship or foreign intervention. More optimistic observers hope this vest-pocket experiment in democracy will somehow 'muddle through.' "[31] Cynicism about elections, parliamentary politics, and cabinet changes confirmed fears of unemployment. At the end of 1953, the Embassy cabled the State Department with the following message: "Dissatisfaction has been mounting again, involving potentially dangerous upheaval with threat to democratic form of government; most potent factor being frustrated socioeconomic development."[32] The response was to promote projects identified with Point IV, emphasizing their political and psychological impact (ibid.).

In the spring of 1954, the period that coincided with Hare's local anti-communist campaign, the State Department received a lengthy dispatch from Beirut titled "Political Stability in Lebanon Through Economic Development." Its content was apparently the cause of controversy, and its chief author (Joseph H. Cunningham) was transferred. The ensuing report was sent with the changes made by another Embassy officer (James C. Lobenstine).[33] At its core, the report contained a blunt and uncomplimentary depiction of Lebanese political society that was highly critical of the failure of economic development. To this was added a strong supportive statement on technical assistance projects, which appeared to be irrelevant to the conditions described, as were the pseudo-psychological evaluations offered as prerequisites of development and stability.

The Lebanon that emerged from this account was the site of an uneven development that was accompanied by increasing class differences and graphic signs of discontent. In this light, the remedies recommended were incongruous. They resembled those conformist modernization theorists who focused on the need for an increase in the confidence factor to stimulate development. According to this approach, what the Lebanese required was "confidence—in themselves, in their Government, and in their future. Population sectors most lacking in confidence and thus most likely to threaten stability include the urban workers and unemployed, the students and intellectuals, and the Palestine refugees."

Analysis of wealthy landowners and merchants offered in the same reworked text represented a concentration of power and influence that, according to this account, outweighed that of urban "bourgeois and professional classes and of the workers and farmers who make up the vast majority of the population." That majority was estimated to consist of approximately 700,000 people. Of this number, "over half own land, but fewer than 2,000 [out of some 700,000] own more than 10 acres." By comparison, there were about 370,000 people in commerce and the service sectors, with another 190,000 in industry and manufacturing. This population was concentrated in Beirut, Sidon, Zahle, and Tripoli. An estimated 40 percent of this number were classified as "artisans, clerks, shopkeepers, and their dependents," who were described as "more interested, informed, and articulate in political matters than the farming population," although they exercised no political influence in the legitimate political arena, a situation that could well change as they acquired power. The urban class made up of workers represented 60 percent of the total, with approximately 335,000 salaried workers and their families. Discontented, poorly paid, "the discontented city workers, having little to lose and not being subject to the conservative influences acting on the rural elements and the white-collar group, constitute a major potential threat to political stability in Lebanon and may become a political force of important dimensions."

Those who ruled or influenced the ruler were "at the opposite end of the scale, socially and economically, [and] are the few hundred wealthy landlords and businessmen who exercise political control in Lebanon." Citing the January 1952 report on Lebanon's political class, as "still generally valid," the author(s) emphasized the coherence of a group that was "essentially a force for stability in the short run, since all of them have at heart the preservation of the socio-economic *status quo*." No significant change could be expected from this class. The route to "political stability," according to this report, passed through the "spirit of trust, harmony and peaceful coexistence," which would have to be developed among Lebanon's diverse constituencies. Such recommendations had little to do with a vision of the existing leadership, which, to change, would have to evolve along the following lines. Imbued with a sense of social and civic responsibility, the leaders of the future

> would avoid, or at least be less addicted to, the time-honored Eastern practice of considering public office merely a God-given opportunity for private gain and advancement regardless of consequences to other people or to the nation; when in opposition to the Government, they would scorn the irresponsible obstructionism and destructive criticism which are standard political practice today. Most fundamentally, perhaps, they would have a capacity for compromise, an ability to combine, after mutual concessions, into groups large enough to exercise either positive leadership or significant opposition.

How such good wishes would translate the existing unemployment, which was frankly viewed as threatening to the state, remained unclear. Yet the author(s) of this review were unequivocal about the risks that it entailed. It would result in a "crisis of the first magnitude."

What did technical assistance offer in this situation? The centerpiece of the assistance projects was the development of the Litani River, a "TVA-type project [that] would provide low-cost electric power in quantities up to 750 million KWH per year, based on a potential of up to 200,000 KW, and could more than satisfy the water needs for irrigation and other purposes of the Litani and Bisri (Awali) River basins." It was expected that this would greatly enhance light industry as well as agriculture as a result of the availability of cheaper power sources and irrigation.

Related proposals of lesser scope, some of which were under private construction, included the Nahr Ibrahim, Nahr al-Bared, Yammouneh-Orontes hydroelectric projects. Irrigation projects with the capacity to affect more than 50,000 acres were either completed, under way, or under consideration throughout the country. Increased access to and availability of drinking water throughout the country was another favored project with obvious visibility. Various agricultural projects were envisaged, some focusing on production and improved wheat storage, others focusing on experimental farms, improved distribution, and marketing of products, and still others concerned with controlling soil erosion throughout Lebanon's terrace agriculture. The possibility of augmenting highway communication facilities, including a possible Mediterranean to Persian Gulf route and another of international dimension, were also under consideration. Technical assistance in coordination with UN advisers was under way in areas of public health and social welfare, policy-related education, aviation, and industry. The list of existing and planned projects was longer.

The authors conceded that these projects would not aid the poor or discontented, although they were inclined to accept the potential "trickle down" effect. On such matters as taxation, however, they conceded that more could be done by increasing tax revenue "through visible-property and income taxes, which now account for only 25 per cent of budgetary revenue as compared to 68 per cent for indirect taxes—largely customs revenues. The present dependence on customs revenues makes it almost axiomatic that Lebanon's hopes and plans will turn to ashes if a general economic decline strikes at the commercial basis of its prosperity."

What then was to be done? Who was to carry out these reforms? The answer, in practice, was to leave things as they were and to protect the status quo, particularly given its economic record. Throughout 1953–1954, as during the politically turbulent years that followed, the Lebanese economy showed few signs of difficulty. Between 1950 and 1956, the net national product increased at an annual rate of 6.5 percent. The budget for 1953–1954 included increases in spending on education, health, public works, among other factors. But the strongest sectors of the economy remained banking, trade, transit, and tourism. And these were immeasurably aided by the continued liberal gold and foreign exchange policy, the abolition of port taxes on transit goods (in agreement with Syria, Jordan, and Iraq), and the introduction of a policy of secret bank accounts, which appealed to those investing foreign capital in Beirut financial markets.

Tourists increased from 89,000 in 1951 to 233,000 in 1960, figures that omit those coming through Beirut in transit, or Syrian visitors, whose combined number exceeded 500,000.[34] Lebanon's import surplus continued with Syria, followed by the United States, its main suppliers. Syria remained its primary export market, followed by Saudi Arabia, France, Egypt, and the United States.[35] The growing transit trade was generated by petroleum from the Gulf, reflecting the impact of Gulf oil development on Beirut. The number of banks grew from seven in 1945 to more than forty-three in 1960.[36] And banking deposits increased from LL180.6 million in 1949 to LL392.2 million in 1954.[37] Most of these banks were to be found in the capital, which with Mount Lebanon represented the fastest-growing regions of a highly uneven economy, whose overall growth had limited impact on national development.

The well-known IRFED report on the state of the economy, prepared at the behest of the Shihab regime after the demise of Sham'un, provided the material evidence of growing economic disparities in this period, from the skewed patterns of regional development, which favored the capital and its environs in the Mount Lebanon area, to the most deprived areas of the north and south, with the intermediary region of the Biqa' offering a more diverse tableau of development.[38] Within these parameters, inadequate housing, sanitation, education, literacy, and rural indebtedness and underdevelopment were commonplace in the less privileged zones. National policies, according to the IRFED authors, promoted agriculture that grew at 1 percent, industry at 3.6 percent, services at 7 percent, administration at 5.8 percent, and transport at 10 percent (ibid. 1.145).

The sole source of loans for domestic development, the Banque de Crédit Agricole, Industriel et Foncier, established in 1955 and funded by the Banque de Syrie et du Liban, which still remained Lebanon's chief bank of issue and commerce, placed the bulk of its loans for the 1954–1958 period in industrial and real estate development. For the network of growing Beirut banks, the objective was what the IRFED authors dubbed, a policy of "hot money," in which the rapidly moving capital in search of profit eluded the wanting domestic sector (ibid. 1:294).

10

Our Man in Beirut

*Embassy considered judgment is that [Sham'un] is
best possible President for Lebanon at present state
in history and his continuation in office clearly in
U.S. interest.*
Embassy Beirut to Secretary of State, October 17, 1955*

*Throughout the [1957] elections I traveled regularly
to the presidential palace with a briefcase full of
Lebanese pounds.*
Wilbur Eveland, *Ropes of Sand**

"The Best Possible President"

The two quotations that appear above capture two moments in the turbulent politics of Lebanon and the complicitous policies of Washington in supporting the Sham'un regime through a period of unparalleled regional developments. Sham'un's successes in furthering Beirut's role as the financial and service center of the Middle East could not compensate for his political failures—hence his increasing dependence on external support. The more precarious Sham'un's predicament became, the more help he obtained from Washington. The best man in Lebanon needed regular injections of assistance to survive. By 1957 the political climate had become so charged that Charles Malik's earlier request for help from Washington for the forthcoming elections was supported by independent U.S. diplomatic and intelligence assessments in Beirut. It was not Sham'un who was facing an election but a Chamber whose members would then be in a position to select the next president. Hence, the above reference to Eveland's carrying a briefcase full of Lebanese currency.

In the rapid succession of events that transpired between 1955 and 1957, the regime obtained definitive indications of U.S. support. Not only was Sham'un the recipient of such expressions but the regime was finally able to win some recognition of its earlier demands for military assistance. These signs, welcomed in Beirut, were entirely inadequate to protect Sham'un as domestic opposition to his policies intensified, culminating in the coalition of the United National Front (UNF) in 1957. The effective organization of an opposition whose leadership consisted largely of the Lebanese bourgeoisie that U.S. officials had earlier identified as their chief collaborators presented the White House and the State Department with an uncommon quandary. Donald Heath, the ambassador who replaced Raymond Hare in this period, had a vivid eye for the absurd in Lebanese politics and was no stranger to its corruption. He was the man at the helm who requested covert U.S. funding to assure the right disposition in the forthcoming elections. And it was Heath who was in a position to recognize that the extent of American success in arranging the 1957 election was so extreme as to constitute another kind of risk. There were limits to what could pass, even in an environment as accustomed as was the Lebanese to political corruption.

The Sham'un regime was in such difficulty in 1955 that there was talk of the president being replaced. The question that worried the U.S. secretary of state concerned Lebanon's regional role. Sham'un had been so loyal a client that he was virtually isolated, save for his relations with Jordan and Iraq. But the Palestinian question and the Baghdad Pact were among the issues that dominated the attacks against the regime. By the fall of 1955, Sham'un's efforts to reshuffle his cabinet to better confront the opposition facing him in the Chamber had proved unsuccessful. Sami al-Sulh replaced Abdallah Yafi as prime minister, and then there was Rashid Karame, whose presence the president's allies and the U.S. Embassy regarded as undesirable but who was nonetheless named prime minister, only to be replaced in time by Yafi.

It was in this context that Sami al-Sulh informed the Embassy of Sham'un's hoped-for passage of an electoral law that would allow him to select a favorable cabinet. The news was not reassuring; neither was talk of alternative presidential candidates. The worst of possibilities, from the Embassy's perspective, was the return of the previous president, Besharah al-Khuri, who was one of the favored candidates of the opposition. His ties to Saudis and Syrians were cited in Embassy reports, but Khuri was also dismally remembered in connection with his neutralist outlook. There were others, but the Embassy came out staunchly for the existing duo, Sham'un and Sulh. Hence, "Embassy considered judgment is that [Sham'un] is best possible President for Lebanon at present state *in history* and his continuation in office clearly in U.S. interest."[1] The Embassy urged Secretary of State Dulles not to delay in responding, as "inaction in these circumstances would most probably have effect encouraging and promoting efforts of opposition. Consequently believe could appropriately express to President United States interest in stability this area and in Lebanon, particularly in present crisis, and assure him our confidence in him."

From Washington, Acting Secretary of State Hoover agreed with the thrust of the Embassy's cable and strongly endorsed the Sham'un-Sulh combination. Sham'un was accordingly informed that the United States supported him, his views of Lebanon, his conception of its interests, and their compatibility with U.S. policy. Sham'un, Hoover continued, was supported by the United States because of "his desire for independence progressive Lebanon," a pronouncement that exceeded the necessary limits of cynicism. Hoover praised Sham'un's support of the Johnston Plan for the Jordan Valley, with its proposed collaboration with Israel, Jordan, Syria, and Lebanon in the dispute over the Jordan River. Praise was offered Sham'un for his "efforts to maintain quiet on Israel border which shows importance he attaches to stability" and his recognition of the "insidious nature Communist threat and far reaching implications deals with Soviet bloc such as Egyptian arms arrangement."[2] Two weeks later, Eisenhower's right hand, General Andrew Goodpaster, recommended to presidential assistant Sherman Adams that Lebanon be offered arms.

Praise aside, things did not go as planned. In the fall of 1955, Sham'un faced a political roadblock. Foreign Minister Hamid Franjiyyah resigned in September; Prime Minister Sami al-Sulh proved unable to structure a viable coalition; and Rashid Karame, until then the nemesis of U.S. policymakers, became prime minister until he too was replaced by Abdallah Yafi in the same year. Karame's role as prime minister distressed the Embassy, which was unaccustomed to having to deal with a politician who welcomed the Egyptian purchase of Soviet arms and opposed the Johnston Plan, as well as a $5 million road-building project supported by the U.S. ICA (International Cooperation Administration).[3] Those whom the Embassy considered men of caliber, Charles Malik and Kamil Sham'un, were under attack.

In addition, although Hoover had lauded Sham'un for his position on Israel, visiting members of the House Foreign Affairs Committee who came to Beirut, representatives Judd, Adair, and Church, found no such consolation. On the twin issues of the Israeli-Palestinian-Arab conflict and Soviet-Communist advances in Lebanon and the Middle East, the U.S. representatives found the positions of their Lebanese hosts to be at odds with their own views.

Washington was unprepared to listen to, let alone to attempt to accommodate, Charles Malik's school of benign realism. Malik, in an effort to educate his guests as to the realities of the Israeli-Arab conflict, urged them to think in terms of long-range conflict resolution, compensation, and selective repatriation of Palestinian refugees, as well as border rectifications and the internationalization of Jerusalem. Although impressed by the stated willingness of the United States to come to Lebanon's aid, Lebanese officials, such as the president of the Chamber, 'Adel 'Usayran, were equally disconcerted by the exchange. Mutual expectations gave way to recriminations.

In the Embassy, the mood was no less grim and hostile. Thus, according to one Embassy officer, "the Arabs seem destitute of initiative, racked with emotionalism, and ready to do foolish things for spite." Yet Lebanon could not be abandoned. The increasing importance of Egypt and Syria, and their military accord, endowed Lebanon's "assets" with all the more value. Among them was its ruling class, depicted by an Embassy officer in a language that was close to that of the Lebanese elite. Thus the uncritical appraisal of the Christian elite and its views, described as diluting "Moslem fanaticism," and enhancing "the outward Western outlook of the country's people, and the strategic location of Lebanon. Furthermore, Lebanon is no threat to Israel; the Israelis look with tolerance and hope toward Lebanon. A more courageous Lebanon could have a useful influence on its Arab neighbors. Furthermore, there may be more opportunities now to do something about Lebanon than about Syria or Saudi Arabia" (ibid). To this was added the suggestion that "one should consider whether Lebanon does not offer possibilities for the exercise of influence which might then extend elsewhere."

On October 28, the State Department received a British memo suggesting that "we might try to find a few arms for him [Lebanese president] but some economic aid might be easier. Help of some kind might make wide difference in Middle East."[4]

The effort to assure Sham'un's tenure was accompanied by continuing discussions on the aggravated issue of military assistance. Once again, Malik had more ambitious projects to propose, a role for Lebanon in regional defense. In February 1955, the month that the Turkish-Iraqi accord, which constituted the cornerstone of the Baghdad Pact, was signed, Malik met with Dulles to discuss defense matters. Dulles took the opportunity to press Malik for an interpretation of Middle East politics, particularly Egypt's opposition to the pact. Malik explained Nasser's response in terms of Egyptian domestic politics, including the penchant for neutralism.[5]

It was actually not Egyptian politics that interested Malik, but the future of Lebanon. Among the proposals he made was one that involved Lebanon in a regional defense arrangement under Egyptian initiative. Another would exclude Turkey and Iraq but include other Arab states. Finally, Malik asked Dulles what the U.S. reaction would be to Lebanon's joining a regional defense scheme, "whether that organization was all-embracing or included only some Arab states together with the non-Arab states of the area excluding of course Israel." Dulles replied evasively, indicating general U.S. support for mutual defense projects without committing himself on the specifics of Malik's proposals. In exchange, Dulles turned to Malik for advice on the Israeli-Palestinian-Arab conflict, expressing his apprehensions about forthcoming elections in the United States:

> He wished to explain to the Ambassador on a personal basis, as he would not to anyone he did not know so well, that our coming elections in 1956 posed a most difficult problem. Both political parties during that year will be under strong pressure to favor Israel, and it is therefore most important to make as much progress as possible this year under our current policy of impartiality.   (Ibid.)

Malik's query to Dulles coincided with the inaugural of the Baghdad Pact system, which was set in place between February and October of 1955. It involved the coordination of bilateral agreements between Turkey and Iraq, Britain and Iraq, and Pakistan and Iran. By prior agreement, the United States remained formally outside the pact, but in practice, it was committed to and involved in its operations.[6] U.S. military arrangements in the region were inseparable from these accords, though U.S. defense interests were not limited to them.[7]

Lebanon was not a member of the Baghdad system but a sympathetic supporter. To his domestic opposition, such distinctions were irrelevant since Sham'un's solidarity with the politics of the pact was evident. In the spring, for example, Sham'un traveled to Turkey, with Prime Minister Sulh following, and both the Turkish president and the prime minister repaid the visits in June. In the interval, the impact of the Baghdad system was stark. It galvanized an opposition that materialized in the form of accords between Egypt, Syria, and Saudi Arabia. The latter constituted a warning to Washington that generated further antagonism, particularly in the light of Saudi participation. With Egypt's purchase of Soviet arms, the connection was disconcerting.[8]

U.S. military strategy in the period reaffirmed primary U.S. interests in the region, taking into consideration the need to expand the "logistic base complex" to support its implementation, including ports and communications lines. Lebanon had a place in this. In December a memorandum for the chairman of the Joint Chiefs of Staff, preliminary to his visit to the Middle East, was prepared by the deputy director for logistics for the Joint Chiefs, Alfred Johnson. It elaborated on atomic support forces and the "logistic base complex" underpinning U.S. strategy.[9] Securing "rail, road and air" routes was intimately tied to protecting Middle East oil, a process that engaged Arab states that were not part of the "Northern Tier." Assessing proven oil reserves of the Middle East to be between 100 billion and 150 billion barrels, roughly three to five times U.S. reserves, the document affirmed the importance of Middle East oil for Western European and NATO allies estimated to be 90 percent dependent on such supplies. "As there are already substantial communist elements in Syria, Iraq and Iran, any expansion of communist influence into Saudi Arabia could, if properly organized and with concentrated action in the other areas, disrupt the flow of oil to Western Europe through strikes, sabotage and political action, and create havoc with the supply and economy of Western Europe."

According to Alfred Johnson, U.S. military strategy had two requirements. The first involved "the provision of atomic support forces," the second, "the improvement and expansion of a logistic base complex to support the strategy." While the United States and the United Kingdom would be responsible for the defense of the Zagros mountains and other areas in the Northern Tier perimeter, the states of the Middle East would be responsible for the network of communications system. Lebanon's role was embedded in this function.

These lines of communication into and within the area will pass through several of the countries which are not now aligned effectively with the northern tier countries. These include Syria, Lebanon, Saudi Arabia, Kuwait and Egypt. The logistic base complex, including air bases, maintenance facilities, supply establishments and transfer points will extend into these same countries.

One week before the issuance of this memorandum, General Goodpaster recommended to presidential assistant Sherman Adams that the United States consider supporting the Embassy's recommendation with respect to Lebanon.

The Embassy believes Lebanon might play a constructive role in working toward relaxation of tensions in the Middle East if it is given encouragement and tangible support. To achieve the best effect, an offer of arms to Lebanon should be coupled with a simultaneous proposal that the Arab states and Israel meet separately with the United States and UK to discuss a solution of the Palestine issue.[10]

There was activity on a related level of U.S. policy at this time, involving U.S.-Israeli exchanges that can be considered in light of the previously cited Israeli planning regarding Lebanon. By the end of 1955, the Eisenhower administration was forced to concede that its overt and covert efforts in the Israeli-Palestinian-Arab conflict, failed. The Anderson mission, headed by the former deputy secretary of defense, as well as the covert Anglo-American ALPHA project, did not yield the anticipated results. Such efforts coincided with a U.S. policy that aimed to isolate Egypt and its allies through regional defense arrangements, clearly not the most propitious environment in which to press for Israeli-Egyptian accords. Indeed, the policy attracted considerable attention in Israel, where the possibility of a U.S.-Egyptian rapprochement was viewed as a major risk to be avoided. The exposé of the Israeli-run espionage ring in Cairo, involved in the so-called Lavon Affair, in July 1954, and the halting of the Israeli vessel *Bat Galim*, sent to test Nasser and the free passage of the Suez Canal, in September 1954, need to be situated in this context. Israeli approaches to the State Department during this period reflected the persistence of Tel Aviv's fears lest U.S.-Egyptian relations improve, at the expense of those with Israel.

On October 20, Israeli Foreign Office officials, including the Israeli ambassador to the United States, met with Dulles. Abba Eban and Reuven Shiloah emphasized that Israel desired closer relations with the United States.[11] Dulles, however, was unprepared to pursue ties with Israel at the time. In early December, Foreign Minister Moshe Sharett delivered the same message, additionally emphasizing Israel's desire to obtain U.S. guarantees of its boundaries with Egypt.[12] Dulles advised his guests on this occasion not to consider using U.S. Jewry in its lobbying for U.S. policy and not to block compromise in the region.

What kind of compromise did Mr. Dulles have in mind? Moshe Sharett's diaries of October 1 disclosed that the CIA's chief Middle East operative, Kermit Roosevelt, had informed Israel of the utter confusion that had befallen the State Department in the wake of the Egyptian decision to purchase Soviet arms. Furthermore, he indicated that "if, when the Soviet arms arrive, you will hit-Egypt-no one will protest."[13] To the Israeli security services, this meant U.S. approval for Israeli action, given that "the U.S. is interested in toppling Nasser's regime," but did not dare to repeat its Iranian or Guatemalan experiences in Cairo. The clandestine American view on the matter was reported by Mordechai Bar-On, who was "head of the Israeli Defense Force's Chief of Staff's Bureau" and General Dayan's secretary, as well as by Wilbur Eveland.[14]

It was in January 1956 that the Lebanese regime renewed its request for arms from the United States, with the Lebanese ambassador to Washington sarcastically remarking to the assistant secretary of state for NEA, George Allen, "What can we do with an army that is no more than a police force? . . . We simply want better equipment. There are no important political implications involved."[15] To the Defense and State Departments, the political rationale for such assistance was overridden by the absence of military considerations. Still, the requests from Beirut continued, accompanied by supportive cables from the Embassy. Lebanon, it reported, feared Syrian communist influence. Sham'un wanted a mutual security pact with the United States.[16] By March, the Lebanese president sought to exploit U.S. alarm over increasing Soviet trade to the area.

In May 1956 the Joint Strategic Plans Committee recommended to the Joint Chiefs that Lebanon be provided the arms and equipment it requested. Among the reasons offered was the considered opinion of the National Intelligence Advisory Committee that it would dissuade Lebanon from joining the Egyptian-Syrian-Saudi military agreements, particularly if Iraq continued to remain outside of it. Further, it would avoid the risk that Israel might exploit this "as a pretext for initiating hostilities." Hence, the recommendation that:

> If the United States were to sell Lebanon the arms requested, it would increase the ability of Lebanon to maintain its independence outside the ESS (Egypt-Syria-Saudi Arabia) Pact and reduce the possibility that

Lebanon will seek arms from the Soviet bloc. It would improve U.S.-Lebanese relations and facilitate the acquisition by the United States of base rights in Lebanon.[17]

Prior to the Suez and Sinai crises, then, Lebanon's rapprochement with the United States on the military level was attracting greater attention, though hardly what President Sham'un or his close advisers wished. That situation changed as a function of the regional crises that transpired.

Fatal Predicaments

There is little doubt that Sham'un's attempt to exploit the Eisenhower administration's reaction to increased Soviet activity in the region was well chosen. Whether or not it achieved its full objectives is another matter. Sham'un understood Dulles's political predilections and the advantages of structuring political dialogue in Dulles's language.[18] Sham'un, moreover, was as much a believer as was Dulles in the risks of Soviet advances in the region. The administration's 1955 "economic defense" policy reflected such an outlook, as the debate on imposing trade controls on strategic supplies indicated.[19] NATO allies were notably uninterested. But in Washington, it was not only the traffic of "strategic" supplies that was considered worrisome; it was also the increase in Soviet trade, technical assistance, and cultural exchanges.

Lebanon's situation figured in such calculations. As of 1955, estimates of imports from the East bloc (2.5 percent by value) and exports to the same area (2.1 percent by value) were modest, although an increase was anticipated in 1956 as a result of agreements negotiated between the USSR and Lebanese firms.[20] By 1956 signs of increasing commercial relations between Lebanon, the USSR, and the East bloc evoked alarm and consternation, as they were viewed as the prelude to full diplomatic relations. In January 1956, according to the Economic Intelligence Committee report, Lebanon opened trade relations with China, Poland, and Romania, and renewed those with the Soviet Union, East Germany, and Czechoslovakia.[21] The attraction of these agreements was that they held out the possibilities of new markets for Lebanon's citrus surplus. In the case of Czechoslovakia and Hungary, it was long-term credit arrangements that were appealing. Soviet Minister Kiklev visited Beirut after the Melnikov mission of February 1956, with offers in communication and road transport, hydroelectric dam projects, and nuclear reactors.[22]

Assessments of Sino-Soviet bloc trade with Lebanon since 1950 totaled about $5 million annually, equivalent to roughly 2 percent of Lebanon's total trade.[23] To the Eisenhower administration, this was 2 percent more than was acceptable, particularly as Soviet proposals for technical assistance coincided with the Lebanese cabinet's allocation of resources for infrastructural development. The cabinet allocated 75 percent of the $5.9 million Lebanese budget for public works, including highway construction and communication (ibid.). In addition, Washington was concerned over news of possible introduction of Soviet banking and credit facilities to those it recognized as "frequently at the mercy of money lenders"[24]

If Sham'un wished to exploit the visit of Soviet leaders to Beirut, he was no less eager to capitalize on the arrival of U.S. banker and adviser to U.S. presidents, John J. McCloy. McCloy, in fact, was passing through Beirut on his way to Saudi Arabia in his capacity as "head of the Rockefellers' Chase Bank, which was financing oil companies developing new fields in the Middle East and around the world."[25] McCloy was on assignment to offer King Sa'ud finance lessons, if not political warnings. His previous cooperation with UN Secretary General Dag Hammarskjöld in the aftermath of the Suez crisis enhanced his stature in the region.[26] But it remained to be seen whether such credentials would influence King Sa'ud and persuade him not to transfer his capital from Chase to Swiss banks.

In the three-day period in which he visited Beirut, February 8–11, McCloy was accompanied by the in-house petroleum consultants of Chase, John Pogue and Kenneth Hill, and by the chairman of the board of Empire Trust, Henry Brunie. Lebanese journalists covering the visit took note of the fact that this was the first time since the opening of Chase's Beirut branch in 1955 that McCloy had come to the Middle East. First National City Bank had opened its Beirut office in the same year, and Bank of America followed in the spring of 1956.[27] McCloy's visit, then, was savored by the pro-regime press as validation of Sham'un's financial policies, notably the practice that permitted the introduction of secret numbered bank accounts free of fiscal controls.[28]

In the months that followed, the combined effects of increased Soviet Middle East trade and the Egypt-Syrian-Saudi agreement contributed to a softening of U.S. policy on arms for Beirut. But the very same policies that created an ambience supportive of the regime's requests for military assistance intensified Dulles's visceral antagonism toward Nasser, leading him to make the decision not to support funding for the Aswan

High Dam project. The significance of the move, coming after extensive Anglo-American and Egyptian-U.S. deliberations on the subject, is difficult to exaggerate. In Cairo, Nasser responded with his own challenge, no less carefully planned—the nationalization of the Suez Canal Company. Nasser's move, however cautiously criticized and opposed within political circles, was recognized as a historic step whose electrifying effect on Egyptians and Arabs throughout the Middle East made it irresistible.[29]

On the international level, the effect of nationalization assumed an altogether different form, as the imperial powers in North Africa and the Middle East grasped its symbolic meaning, no less than its political and economic potential.[30] In London and Paris, the Egyptian leader was demonized, while in Washington the Eisenhower administration adopted a more cautious reaction. Nationalization was not categorically denounced; it was viewed as legal, provided that adequate compensation was offered, a condition that was juridically and politically satisfactory. The political implications of Nasser's actions were nevertheless immediately assessed as dangerous for U.S. policies. The report of the Special National Intelligence Estimate prepared with the aid of the CIA and the intelligence branches of the State and Defense Departments, was particularly instructive with respect to the implications of such action in Lebanon.

> The Lebanese government will probably adopt a noncommittal attitude until it ascertains the degree of Egypt's success in defying the West. While presently engaged in a dispute with the Iraq Petroleum Company concerning its share of the pipeline revenues, Lebanon would prefer to avoid drastic actions against Western interests because of its own economic self-interest as a trading and financial center in the area. Lebanon will, however, find it increasingly difficult to resist being swept along in any general wave of anti-Western sentiment and activities which may follow Nasser's action.[31]

U.S. Military Intelligence in Lebanon proceeded to collect data, including technical route information on areas of petroleum storage in the north. Approaches to highways, roads, and bridges were photographed from all directions. The resulting report was to be withheld "from all foreign nationals," including Lebanese and other Arabs, "because of Appendix VI and the references thereto in the table of contents. If Appendix VI is removed and the table of contents is appropriately changed, the reports can be released to authorized Lebanese Nationals."

Appendix VI contained an index of previous reports on the military geography of northern Lebanon communicated by the military attaché.[32]

In Beirut, as U.S. Intelligence estimates predicted, the impact of Suez on the Sham'un regime was thoroughly undermining, deepening existing political divisions and resulting in repeated cabinet changes. The year had begun with the threatened resignation of seven of Sham'un's cabinet ministers. At the top, Karame gave way to Abdallah Yafi and Sa'eb Salam, both of whom resigned at the time of the March earthquake in protest over the handling of that disaster. Salam had earlier been politically hurt by his failure to negotiate transit fees with IPC, a matter of particular concern to the Tripolitan population. Little did they know then that in the winter of the new year, IPC would dismiss five hundred workers in a display of its continued power.[33] The period between Suez and the Sinai campaign was marked by popular demonstrations in support of Nasser. Kamal Junblat's party, on the other hand, withheld support from Nasser, thereby precipitating defections from the ranks among "five old and close colleagues of this 'feudal Socialist' [which] was immediately welcomed by all the Arab Socialists who were tired of this 'progressive' party's deviations." Gebran Majdalany's comments referred to the defection of party supporters that included, in addition to his own withdrawal, that of Junblat's former foreign policy adviser, Clovis Maksoud.[34] The crisis was resolved only in 1958, when Junblat emerged as the leading radical figure in an otherwise conservatively led opposition to the regime.

In 1956, however, Sham'un attempted to project himself as an intermediary between Nasser and his regional as well as international opponents. On Nasser's request, Malik in August conveyed a message to Dulles through the Egyptian ambassador in Beirut. Nasser wanted Dulles to know that Egypt would not agree to international operation of the Canal but would be willing to offer guarantees and to cooperate with other states in its operation.[35] Malik conveyed the message with a subversive commentary:

> Although he personally liked Nasser and understood reasons for some of his actions and applauded some of his reforms, it was not in interest of peace or Western civilization that Nasser's government should remain in control of Egypt. This was his profound conviction and recommendation to the Secretary.   (Ibid. 184–85)

Malik was not alone in his sentiments, as the organization of the tripartite invasion of Egypt soon demonstrated. In September, however, U.S. officials in London reported to the State Department that the British assumed that the defeat of Nasser would restore Britain's prestige and position, and resolve its relations with the Arab world. They expressed confidence that certain states in North Africa and the Arab world, such as Tunisia, Libya, Saudi Arabia, Iraq, and Lebanon, would welcome such a defeat.[36]

Eager to be perceived as the regional mediator and not the lackey of the West, Sham'un called for a meeting of Arab leaders in October, at the time of the Anglo-French-Israeli invasion. As developments on the ground in Egypt changed, the objective of the conference was altered to demand compliance with UN resolutions on Anglo-French-Israeli withdrawal, as well as those bearing on the canal. Sham'un informed Eisenhower, whom he congratulated on U.S. policy, of his plans to hold a conference of Arab chiefs of state in Beirut in November. Jordan's King Husayn accepted and Nasser approved, though he did not plan to attend.[37] The conference met, urged compliance with UN resolutions, and proposed the idea of a joint military command. In purely domestic terms, the convening of the Arab meeting granted Sham'un a certain respite from those critical of his failure to break diplomatic relations with France and Britain. The cabinet had earlier fallen on this issue, with both Abdallah Yafi and Sa'eb Salam pressuring Sham'un at least to withdraw Lebanon's ambassadors from Paris and London.

There are conflicting reports on what transpired in Beirut at this period. Abdallah Yafi claimed that Arab participation at the conference had been premised on Sham'un's severing of diplomatic relations with Britain and France. The Lebanese president, on the other hand, indicated that he considered censure to be sufficient.[38] Only Damascus and Riyadh broke relations with France and Britain. Baghdad and Amman limited their actions to France for obvious reasons. According to Leila Meo's account, Yafi and Sa'eb Salam resigned when Sham'un rejected their request for the withdrawal of ambassadors. In an October 1960 interview, the former Lebanese president denied that he had ever intended to sever relations, arguing that to have done so would have undermined his utility as mediator. Sham'un recalled conferring with Nasser's emissary, Mustafa Amin, who had flown to Beirut to see him "bringing the salaams of Nasser and asking me to intervene with the British and the French for a quick cease-fire" (ibid. 99). According to Sham'un:

> I did what I could do and was able less than forty-eight hours later to give him good news about the cease-fire. Well, this is the proof that it

has never been either in Nasser's mind or my mind that diplomatic relations would be cut off. Otherwise, how could you cut off diplomatic relations and still intervene with these two nations?

Among witnesses to these developments was Emile Bustani, who had come with Amin to see Sham'un. Bustani claimed that "as the Arab conference was meeting in Beirut to discuss this matter, a messenger from President Abdul Nasser arrived to ask that Lebanon intervene (with the two aggressors). Consequently, Lebanon decided that it could not sever relations when it was being asked to act as a go-between" (ibid. 100).

Whatever the explanation, Sham'un did not fare well at home and was forced to reconstitute his cabinet, turning to Sami al-Sulh as prime minister, with Charles Malik as foreign minister, and Fu'ad Shihab as minister of defense.[39] That arrangement did not long survive. Shihab himself resigned about the time the Chamber prepared to discuss acceptance of the Eisenhower Doctrine. The controversy over the Eisenhower Doctrine in Beirut was soon eclipsed by praise from Beirut that brought Lebanon assistance, in the manner anticipated by the doctrine's authors. The tension in the Lebanese capital did not escape attention in Washington, but Under Secretary of State Hoover offered Eisenhower an interpretation that previewed the United States and Lebanese response to the civil war of 1958, i.e., the problem was entirely external. As Hoover informed Eisenhower, "Egypt has been caught instigating violence in Libya and Lebanon, and there was discussion of the possibility of inducing those countries to break off diplomatic relations with Egypt."[40]

The Opposition and the Election

There could have been no surprise that massive criticism from an angered opposition greeted news of Sham'un's acceptance of the Eisenhower Doctrine in 1957. The transparent purpose of the Middle East Resolution, coming after Suez and Sinai, not only clarified the Eisenhower administration's position in the Middle East, it reaffirmed its commitment to a politics of regional containment. In Beirut, the response led to the mobilization of the United National Front, the chief coalition of opposition forces. The events so unnerved U.S. officials in Beirut that they readily agreed to provide funding to assure parliamentary elections. The result constituted a further commitment to the regime. The elements that would prove troubling in the beginning of 1958 were fully apparent:

Sham'un's precarious political position; his rejectionist policy on domestic reform; the persistence of domestic discontent based on disparities of power; and the need to confront an opposition whose leaders were drawn from the circles of the ruling class on whom U.S. officials had relied in the past. It remained to predict when the Beirut political minefield would explode.

In January 1957 the Middle East Resolution, more commonly known as the Eisenhower Doctrine, was presented by the administration to a bipartisan congress. It was put to the House and Senate for approval, where it passed on January 30 and March 5, respectively. The delay reflected the lack of enthusiasm inspired by the resolution. Signed by Eisenhower on March 9, the commitment to "Promote Peace and Stability in the Middle East," was nonetheless incorporated into U.S. Middle East policy. Its defenders argued that it was designed as an alert to the American people regarding "the Soviet threat in the Middle East" and as a warning to the USSR.[41] The resolution warned that the United States was prepared to use military force to assist any "nation or group of such nations requesting assistance against armed aggression from any country controlled by international communism"—a problematic formula, given that no such regimes were to be found in the Middle East. The Mansfield amendment made the resolution more elastic, but not necessarily more popular in Congress, where its critics feared that it virtually offered a "blank check" to the administration. In the Middle East, the reception of the Eisenhower Doctrine was cool save among Western allies who feared publicizing their support. Lebanon, Israel, Iraq, and Jordan endorsed it. In mid-March 1957, James Richards, Eisenhower's special assistant, went to the Middle East to assess the situation. Richards's delegation included officials from the State and Defense Departments, the International Cooperation Administration (ICA), and the U.S. Information Agency. Its objective was to determine how to allocate the $200 million designated for economic and military assistance as part of the package identified with the Middle East resolution.

The response in Beirut was bitter. Sham'un's critics saw his adherence as further proof of his sycophantic reliance on the United States. Sham'un, on the other hand, anticipated the benefits that such adherence would bring. The U.S. Embassy, in solidarity with the regime, believed that all problems would be resolved once Charles Malik was named foreign minister. In that position, he would be well placed to control the domestic opposition. As to the reception of the Eisenhower Doctrine, the

Embassy reported that the press was favorable, with the exception of Communist, Socialist, and Muslim extremists. But U.S. ambassador Heath did not fail to point out that there was a general skepticism about the American guarantees that would "insure area against overt Communist aggression but fails provide against Zionist or colonialist aggress from non-Communist countries and does not go to heart of problems causing instability in area."[42] Either out of conformity or deference or conviction, Heath maintained that current policy would "strengthen hold present Government and moderate pro-Western elements in country facilitating policy of close cooperation with U.S. without compromising continued cooperation with Arab neighbors. It will tend to reduce susceptibility to Communist and Moslem extremist blandishments and help preserve generally favorable climate of relations with U.S. now prevailing." Within a matter of months, Heath was soliciting assistance for the election campaign, positive proof that his assumptions had backfired.

In the State Department, Assistant Secretary of State for Near Eastern, South Asian, and African Affairs William Rountree calculated that the time had come to compensate Lebanon for its support. In the overall context of the region, Iraq was the only state receiving grant aid, while Israel and Saudi Arabia had received reimbursable assistance. With the exception of Saudi Arabia, moreover, the other states were recipients of Western aid other than that offered by the United States.[43] In the post-Suez environment, Rountree recommended to Dulles that U.S. support to Lebanon be approved for such tangibles as equipment for road construction and communication, with special attention to the improvement of the Beirut airport. Dulles agreed, finally accepting Lebanon's persistent calls for military and economic assistance. In early February, he sought Eisenhower's approval for $2 million for the construction and communication equipment requested, while the Defense Department was deliberating on military assistance. In the interval, Heath threw his weight behind Sham'un, indicating that he and the assorted U.S. military attachés in Beirut were persuaded that assistance was "militarily necessary to Lebanon for internal and external security," to aid in its resistance of "Syrian and Egyptian pressure and subversion."[44]

The date of Heath's cable to Dulles was January 13. In compliance with the Eisenhower Doctrine and the anticipated visit of special assistant James Richards to the Middle East, the special assistant to the Joint Chiefs for Mutual Defense Assistance Affairs was advised by representatives of the Office of the Assistant Secretary of Defense (ISA) to include in its overview "military guidance that would be appropriate for Ambassador Richards."[45] It was in that context that Lebanon's strategic role was reaffirmed.

> Lebanon is important to the United States because of its lines of communication and bases which could be provided in the development of a forward defense in the Middle East. Lebanon possesses one of the best harbors and communication centers on the Eastern Mediterranean shore and potentially good air bases.
>
>   Most of the pipelines which transport oil from the Persian Gulf area and Iraq terminate in Lebanon ports on the Mediterranean. These consist of the pipeline which emanates from the Dhahran area on the Persian Gulf (capacity 33,000 barrels/day) and two of the five pipelines which emanate from the Kirkurk fields in Iraq (capacity of the three of the five normally in use: 560,000 barrels/day).

The U.S. military described Lebanon as a republic with a "European-type cabinet"; it was criticized for its excessively liberal attitude toward Communist activity. The same report, however, underlined the regime's vulnerability in the area of foreign policy, and specifically the pressures exerted by Egypt, Syria, and Saudi Arabia to "cool its pro-Western ardor." Further, U.S. officials recommended that the regime described as "the least intransigent of the Arab States regarding the state of Israel and [one that] is a pro-U.S. Arab State" be appropriately compensated. Defense support in the form of grant aid was deemed especially useful in the expansion of Beirut's petroleum storage capacity and the improvement of its port and airfield.

In a subsequent report by the Joint Strategic Plans Committee, the capacity of the Lebanese military to maintain internal security, "and thereby insure the continuation of a government in power which is friendly to the West," was underlined as justifying a response to Lebanese requests for military equipment.[46] The radar, aircraft, ammunition, communication, and engineering equipment requested was estimated at some $10 million.

On February 6 Malik met with Eisenhower to review Middle Eastern developments. Eisenhower's position reflected the themes of the doctrine that bears his name. With the Arab-Israeli problem identified as first in importance, the second was the "threat of international communism." Malik interpreted the roles of Syria and Egypt as conduits of Soviet influence in the Middle East. "Dr Malik thought Syria and Egypt were gradually falling under Communist domination. It was essential political change take place in Syria and Egypt."[47] Malik had made the same statement to Dulles on the previous day, emphasizing that "we should concentrate upon a radical defeat for Communists, not by word or by economic assistance, but by political change in Syria or Egypt."[48] The results would enhance the "prospects for all other Middle Eastern problems, including Israel."

Malik did not lose the opportunity to present Lebanon's case in this context, stressing that Lebanon wanted security from external aggression and, more precisely, "internal security through the development of a loyal army." Malik additionally raised the question of parliamentary elections in Lebanon, pointing to the dangers posed by Egypt, Syria, and Saudi Arabia, whose impact in the preelection period could be determining, Malik insisted. The implication was that the parliamentary majority might be lost and with it, support for an acceptable presidential candidate. Reference to Syria was particularly timely, given that U.S. covert action against the Syrian regime was under consideration in this very period.[49] Malik received profuse compliments on the occasion, but more practical assistance would be forthcoming. As Eisenhower explained, "relations between the United States and Lebanon were of special interest to us because of ties with that country and because our policies had similar objectives of opposition to Communism and of efforts to resolve Middle Eastern problems."[50]

The Richards Mission, come to implement the Eisenhower Doctrine, made its appearance in Beirut the following March. From the Lebanese capital, Richards informed Sham'un that the United States would provide $10 million in economic development aid and roughly $2.7 million for military purposes on a grant basis, and in addition would provide an undisclosed contribution for the forthcoming election. Reasons were clearly offered.

> During forthcoming elections pro-Western policies of present government will be very much on the block. Government must be in position to show tangible results from cooperation with West. Defeat of political grouping now in power would severely damage U.S. interests and could swing Lebanon into Syrian-Egyptian fold.[51]

At the end of April, Sham'un was pressing Eisenhower to come to the assistance of King Husayn of Jordan, who was confronting his own domestic critics. The alert aroused immediate response among U.S. allies in the area, with the U.S. Sixth Fleet making its show of strength, and Israel warned not to intervene.[52]

In Beirut, meanwhile, another alert had been issued, this time in the form of the creation of the United National Front. Formally established after the regime's acceptance of the Eisenhower Doctrine on March 16, the UNF represented a coalition of opposition forces mobilized by grievances against Sham'un's domestic and regional policies. While its organization represented a major step in Lebanese domestic politics, it was one contained by the nature of its leadership.

The UNF leadership was, with the exception of Kamal Junblat, a conservative ordering of those Lebanese politicians excluded by the outcome of the 1957 elections. Some twenty-three prominent political figures were involved, including Sa'eb Salam, who became its titular head, Husayn 'Uwayni, Philippe Taqla, Kamal Junblat, Nassim al-Majdalani, 'Ali al-Bazzi, and Ilyas al-Khuri. To these must be added the seven parliamentarians who had resigned from the Chamber immediately before its vote on the Eisenhower Doctrine: Hamid Franjiyyah, Sabri Hamadeh, Rashid Karame, Abdallah Yafi, Ahmad and Kamil al-As'ad, and 'Abdallah al-Hajj. On April 1, the UNF demanded that the regime cease making foreign accords in advance of the June elections and formation of a new cabinet; that a "neutral" cabinet be designated to oversee these elections; and that the size of the Chamber should not be contracted as the president called for, but expanded to eighty-eight as opposed to forty-four members. In addition, Sham'un was asked to annul the emergency measures that had been imposed on the country at the time of the Suez crisis.[53]

For Washington, the UNF represented a problem not because it constituted a radical challenge to Lebanese politics, which was hardly the case, but because its conservative leadership represented the foundation on which U.S. policy rested outside of the person of the president. That leadership vehemently objected to its marginalization in Lebanese domestic politics as a result of the 1957 elections, and it distanced itself from Sham'un's regional politics. The response of the Embassy was to focus on radical critics. "Commie and Leftist Press growing obviously more disenchanted with opposition, reportedly for failure to condemn American doctrine and refusal opposition accept communist candidate Antoine Tabet on election list."[54] In the midst of such developments, Eisenhower's cardiologist, Dr. Paul Dudley White, appeared on the scene, sent to administer greetings to Sham'un's prime minister, Sami al-Sulh, after Sulh suffered a heart attack in the wake of the Chamber's vote.[55]

The UNF, meanwhile, concentrated its demands on the formation of an interim cabinet to oversee the elections. There were ultimatums, regime rejection, and strikes and mass protests, as the regime claimed that Egyptian and Syrian officials interfered on behalf of the opposition. Confrontations between security forces and the opposition, followed by accusations that it was planning a coup d'état, led to the mass arrests of some three hundred to four hundred protestors and the wounding of Sa'eb Salam and Nassim al-Majdalani of the UNF, that transformed the nature of the conflict. Fahim Qubain reported that "instead of the reestablishment of order, terrorism and lawlessness spread," as the balance of power between the regime and the opposition began to tilt to the advantage of the latter.[56] With its threatened general strike ineffectual, Sa'eb Salam called off his hunger strike and Sham'un agreed to the introduction of two "neutral" figures in the cabinet, as well as the creation of a committee to investigate charges bearing on preelection activities. The compromise was the work of Commander in Chief Fu'ad Shihab.

On the eve of the election, in a report released to the State Department only the following spring, the U.S. military attaché, Robert C. Works, met with Shihab. Known to be critical of Sham'un, Shihab was viewed by U.S. officials with a mixture of disdain and partisan interest. His analysis of events was largely at odds with that of Malik, which is to say that it offered a marked contrast to what the Dulles brothers, John Foster and Allen, were hearing in Washington. Shihab blamed Sham'un's tactics for distancing an otherwise loyal Muslim constituency that was now in the ranks of the Opposition.

But Shihab went further. He conceded the validity of grievances against the state's preferential policies, and he denounced its absurd charges. "When the opposition is damned as being pro-Communist because it does not actively support our foreign policy, it is being driven into the hands of the communists. If Frangie [Franjiyyah] or Junblat are Communists then I am afraid you must consider me one also."[57] Shihab conceded that "there is no question that the Christians control politics in a manner disproportionate to their numbers. For this reason they must use their power wisely in order to prevent the Moslems from forming in the opposition." Instead, Sham'un "assumed dictatorial powers since Sinai and was acting like a dictator until yesterday morning." If there was to be a dictatorship in Lebanon, Shihab continued, it would be a military dictatorship, which he would not tolerate. Lebanon, he claimed, was not Jordan, where to maintain peace, the king imposed curfews and ruled with "rigid censorship, and all the other restrictions of a police state. Does the President wish Lebanon to be like Jordan," he asked.

While Robert Works was impressed with Shihab's exposition, the British ambassador, George Middleton, to whom he conveyed the exchange, was not totally convinced by Shihab's presentation. In Middleton's eyes, Shihab was obscuring the collaboration between the opposition and communist and anti-American activists. But for the attaché, the exchange demonstrated that "compromise at this time is still possible and that the United States should not find itself in Lebanon supporting the side of reaction, as they must in other countries."

The June elections were staggered so that they occurred at regular intervals at different locations throughout the month. The total victory for Sham'un was a step closer to his total defeat. Charges by the opposition of widespread bribery were countered by claims of Egyptian and Syrian intervention. The external ministers who had been appointed to oversee the elections resigned. The press went on strike, to which the regime responded by arresting journalists of opposition newspapers accused of libelous actions against the president. Middleton admitted that the elections had left something to be desired, even by Lebanese standards.[58] The remark said little of the violence and the "obvious use of foreign funds by the president and prime minister," as Wilbur Eveland recalled, having been one of the key conveyors of the same funds to the president.[59]

> Throughout the elections I traveled regularly to the presidential palace with a briefcase full of Lebanese pounds, then returned late at night to the embassy with an empty twin case I'd carried away for Harvey Armada's CIA finance-office people to replenish. Soon my gold DeSoto with its stark white top was a common sight outside the palace, and I proposed to Chamoun that he use an intermediary and a more remote spot. When the president insisted that he handle each transaction by himself, I reconciled myself to the probability that anybody in Lebanon who really cared would have no trouble guessing precisely what I was doing.   (Ibid. 252)

Before the elections, Heath was persuaded that U.S. funds would be necessary to assure the presidential selection in 1958, a conclusion with which local CIA officers in Beirut agreed. Eveland identified the "key operational members of his [Ghosn Zogby] station: Raymond Close, Eugene Trone, and James Barracks" [ibid. 164]. Zogby and Trone were identified as, respectively, political and economic officers of the Embassy in the Foreign Service listing for 1958. In Washington, an election specialist was brought in by "clandestine services," while the NSC's Operations Coordinating Board (OCB), which approved funding for covert actions, acted on Ambassador Heath's recommendations. In Beirut, Heath focused on the urgency of countering Egyptian and Syrian lobbying in Beirut. "To Close, the issues boiled down to the question of whether or not the benefits Lebanon might gain from adherence to the Eisenhower Doctrine could offset the emotional appeal to Lebanon's Moslems and young Palestinians of Nasser's brand of Arab nationalism" (ibid. 250). Eveland, replacing the absent head of the local CIA, was chosen to deal with Sham'un and to assure the efficient distribution of funds. In a planning meeting in the ambassador's office with Zogby, the Beirut CIA chief, it emerged that payments to Muslim candidates had already taken place, much to the disapproval of Sham'un, who was additionally opposed to Malik's candidacy. Eveland reports Sham'un's later asking him "to tell Washington that the U.S. government owed him 75,000 Lebanese pounds, the amount he'd paid out to reimburse Charles Malik's opponent for his campaign expenses" (ibid. 257). As Eveland explained, Malik had been paid the same amount that was "the price, then, of a relatively easy (and not very influential) Greek Orthodox seat in parliament."

U.S. officials were not nearly as intoxicated with the success of the elections as its winners were. The Embassy conceded to the State Department "that next parliament will be composed mainly of 'nonentities,' [Sham'un's] lacqueys etc. and is designed to re-elect President [Sham'un] in 1958."[60] Some weeks later, the Embassy sent a report of Junblat's prediction that the regime was jeopardizing the future of the nation and must be replaced, since "Christian-Moslem unity and cooperation with Arab States which are touch-stones future Lebanon not attainable under [Sham'un]-Malik team."[61]

In a period described as one of "terrorism and arms smuggling," Sham'un accused Syrian intelligence of working with Egypt to smuggle arms to the Lebanese Opposition.[62] The exposé of Anglo-American covert actions in Damascus offset such charges, particularly in the light of the Beirut CIA's involvement in the affair. Beirut, Eveland later pointed out, was where Operation WAPPEN was planned.[63] And in Damascus, a U.S. Embassy officer was revealed as having participated in the plot that involved Kermit Roosevelt and former Syrian president Shishakli. Eisenhower and Dulles were only temporarily distracted, and covert action only temporarily postponed. Loy Henderson was sent to the

Middle East to consult on Syrian matters with Jordanian king Husayn, Iraqi king Faysal, 'Abd al-Ilah, and Turkish prime minister Adnan Menderes on August 24, after which he met with Sham'un.[64]

Sham'un's expressions of solidarity with Syria notwithstanding, the Lebanese president faced increasing domestic hostility. Censorship of Egyptian and Syrian press and broadcast activities did not improve matters. Malik, who was visibly concerned, met with British ambassador George Middleton, and in September he ominously warned Dulles that Lebanon's days—like those of Jordan—were numbered. The problem, according to Malik, far outweighed the predicament of small Middle Eastern states. The attempt to internationalize the crisis of 1957 was repeated in 1958, with Malik offering the same arguments, to the effect that "this was a threat not merely to Lebanon but to the whole Middle East, in fact to the peace of the world."[65]

In Washington, the OCB and the NSC could not have been accused of neglect with respect to Lebanon, as the following excerpt from the "Operations Plan for the Lebanon" indicated.

> The U.S. should support the Lebanon in its efforts to preserve its independence, sovereignty and territorial integrity whether against aggression from without or subversion from within. U.S. programs and actions should be designed to strengthen the Lebanese Government's capacities for resisting aggression and subversion by increasing the strength, efficiency and loyalty of the Lebanese armed forces and internal security forces; to encourage the will to resist aggression and subversion on the part of those elements already so inclined by evidencing full and continuous support of Lebanese independence; and to stimulate in the minds of Lebanese in general an awareness that the maintenance of a free and independent Lebanon is the best possible guarantee for the eventual satisfaction of their political, social and economic aspirations.[66]

U.S. programs, the same report continued, were to target the Muslim population in particular, as the most vulnerable to "frequently irresponsible and emotional ideas emanating from within the Arab world [more] than to those originating in the West."

At the end of November, on Lebanon's Independence Day, Sham'un found himself upstaged in an unpleasant reminder of the opposition he faced. This time, it was the gesture of respect paid to the dissident Maronite patriarch, Paul Ma'oushi, by members of the Lebanese opposition as well as Syrian officials.[67] In an environment where domestic support for the regime was waning, Malik thought it imperative to offer tangible proof of American assistance. On November 27 he announced that "virtually unlimited U.S. aid to Lebanon including rocket missiles" was forthcoming.[68] Malik's claim was exaggerated, but it was not entirely false. U.S. arms had begun to flow into Beirut in accord with the Richards Mission in early June and mid-July. By then, Sham'un, with Shihab's support, was urging the U.S. Embassy to provide assistance for the gendarmerie. On July 6 Sham'un gave Heath a list of supplies that included small arms, radios, armored cars, two-and-a-half-ton trucks, pickup trucks, and sedans, collectively estimated to cost up to $1.3 million. Heath noted that "Gendarmerie also wants American tfc expert on permanent basis."[69] Shihab's recommendation that the gendarmerie could use "Staghounds for maintaining domestic tranquility and Army could more profitably use modern eqp." was added, along with Heath's comment that the "Gendarmerie needs strengthening." The July 30 "dynamitings of VOA and USIS installations" gave impetus to Heath's August call for emergency action "in a fluid and continually tense situation."[70]

Heath continued to call for assistance to Sham'un as the political environment worsened to the advantage of the opposition. In October, a new grouping of politicians emerged on the scene, acting as intermediaries between the regime and the UNF. Their defining characteristic was their endorsement of Sham'un's foreign policies, and specifically his policy vis-à-vis the United States. Where they differed with the president was on his domestic political ambitions.[71] The "Third Force" included Henri Far'oun in a circle of thirteen influential members of the Lebanese elite, who emerged in the civil war period as the U.S. Embassy's favorite opposition, as opposed to the UNF.

In spite of the domestic political troubles facing Sham'un, in 1957 as in 1954—which represented a far less threatening situation for the regime—the one area that appeared to be immune to such disturbance was the burgeoning service economy. The familiar anomaly was noted with evident satisfaction by the British ambassador to Lebanon, George Middleton, in his review of 1957. Lebanon had once again succeeded, in Middleton's view, in demonstrating that in spite of domestic and regional conditions, "her economy remained as resilient and flexible as ever."[72] The only sector that was cited as adversely affected was that of tourism. Otherwise, Lebanese civil aviation continued to expand, witness the success of MEA, Air Liban, and Lebanese International Airways. The Litany River project was under way, moreover, along with the "Lebanization" of French concessions (Compagnie du Port de Beyrouth and the DHP Railroad).

Middleton's review corresponded to the assessment of the IRFED report that identified 1957 as a peak year, albeit only for foreign trade.[73] There was other evidence supporting such a conclusion, in the form of increased Western business interests. In the spring of 1957, an international group of industrialists and bankers met to consider cooperative ventures that would ally Arab and Western capital. The International Study Group for the Near and Middle East was under the direction of Dr. Rykens, formerly chairman of Unilever.[74] In September, the group was invited to Washington, where it attended the Governor's meetings of the International Bank and the IMF, while establishing contacts in Lebanon, Jordan, Syria, Saudi Arabia, Iraq, Kuwait, Egypt, Sudan, and, later, Iran. Plans for investment in selected Arab—Western projects, which would facilitate coordination and a measure of control were under discussion.

At the beginning of 1958, precisely at the time when the U.S. Embassy in Beirut was pressing the State Department to clarify its position with respect to the presidential succession crisis in Beirut, U.S. participation in the group's activities increased. In contact with the IBRD, the Export-Import Bank, the State Department, and the U.S. Treasury, the group was in contact with Eugene Black, of the International Bank for Reconstruction and Development; U.S. Secretary of the Treasury Robert Anderson; Under Secretary of State Douglas Dillon; John J. McCloy and George Woods of First Boston Corporation, and others. Lebanon was on the agenda, along with other Arab states, as U.S. corporate interests considered the possibilities of investment in Lebanese petrochemicals, pharmaceuticals, food processing and refrigeration, motor car assembly, and U.S. aircraft repair. As the group's lawyer-rapporteur observed in reference to his contacts in Washington, "owing to increasing American political interest in the area it would be necessary henceforward for the authorities in Washington to be kept in close touch with developments." Those developments were becoming impossible to ignore, as the American business community and its diplomatic representatives in Beirut were discovering.

Habib Abu Shahla, TAPLINE attorney and parliamentarian, and
Fred Davies, chairman and CEO of ARAMCO, at the TAPLINE
Sidon Terminal, December 1950. (Photograph courtesy William R.
Chandler, former president, Trans-Arabian Pipeline Company.)

Habib Abu Shahla (left) and William "Sandy" Campbell of
TAPLINE (center), December 1950. (Photograph courtesy
William R. Chandler, former president, Trans-Arabian
Pipeline Company.)

President Kamil Sham'un
(center) and Amir
Abdallah ibn Musa, Amir
of the Northern Frontiers
of Saudi Arabia (right),
about 1956–1957.
(Photograph courtesy
William R. Chandler,
former president,
Trans-Arabian
Pipeline Company.)

William R. Chandler (left),
Prime Minister Rashid
Karame (center), and Amir
Abdul Aziz Shihab,
governor of South
Lebanon, about 1958.
(Photograph courtesy
William R. Chandler,
former president,
Trans-Arabian
Pipeline Company.)

Left to right: Colonel Tom
Lawlor, Defense attaché of
the U.S. Embassy; William
R. Chandler; Prime
Minister Rashid Karame,
the first post–civil war
prime minister; and
unidentified person. 1958.
(Photograph courtesy
William R. Chandler,
former president,
Trans-Arabian
Pipeline Company.)

William R. Chandler (second from left) and King Saʿud Ibn ʿAbdul Aziz (right). About 1958. (Photograph courtesy William R. Chandler, former president, Trans-Arabian Pipeline Company.)

Left to right: L. Bill Helmann, foreman; William Campbell, vice president, government relations, TAPLINE; Saleh al-Asʿad, TAPLINE public relations officer; William R. Chandler. Second from right: Colonel William Eddy. (Photograph courtesy William R. Chandler, former president, Trans-Arabian Pipeline Company.)

"A patrolling armored car passes government security troops behind sandbag barricades in the Basta area of Beirut, Lebanon." June 25, 1958. (Photograph courtesy AP/Wide World Photos.)

"Marines have situation well in hand." July 18, 1958. (Photograph courtesy AP/Wide World Photos.)

"Lebanese rebel leaders meet in conference at the residence of Saeb Salam" in Beirut. August 25, 1958. (Photograph courtesy AP/Wide World Photos.)

"Rebels in the Basta sector of Beirut, Lebanon, turned out for a parade in honor of visiting rebel leader." The occasion was Rashid Karame's visit on August 27, 1958. (Photograph courtesy AP/Wide World Photos.)

"An American Army M48 tank stands guard outside of the American University of Beirut." September 25, 1958. (Photograph courtesy AP/Wide World Photos.)

OPPOSITE PAGE:
"Sherman tanks of the Lebanese Army patrol the streets of Beirut." September 25, 1958. (Photograph courtesy AP/Wide World Photos.)

Phalangists [Kata'eb] in Beirut, "protesting against new government," of Rashid Karame, building roadblocks near Place des Canons. September 26, 1958. (Photograph courtesy AP/Wide World Photos.)

"U.S. Marines keep watch over a street in Beirut, Lebanon, from a rooftop machine gun emplacement." December 4, 1958. (Photograph courtesy AP/Wide World Photos.)

President Dwight D. Eisenhower and Secretary of State John Foster Dulles. August 14, 1958. With U.S. forces in Beirut. Dulles was on his way to London for the Suez Canal Conference. (Photograph courtesy AP/Wide World Photos.)

PART IV

Intervening Before Intervention

11
Civil War, May 1958

Provide Lebanon with political support, and with mili-
tary assistance for internal security purposes. . . . Stress
within and outside Lebanon the theme of Lebanon as
a highly successful experiment in which many peoples
of diverse religion and culture work together amicably
and effectively for the advancement of their country.
"Long Range U.S. Policy Toward the Near East,"
NSC 5801/1 January 24, 1958*

The Question of Presidential Succession

For those who followed the course of Lebanese domestic politics, 1958 confirmed the most pessimistic predictions. Civil war broke out in May, and two and a half months later the United States intervened, a decision to which the dominant coalition of opposition forces strongly objected. Considered in the light of the consistent pattern of support it afforded the Sham'un regime before July 15, full-scale U.S. intervention represented a significant expansion, though hardly an innovation in U.S. policy. The extent to which such a policy was resisted by U.S. officials—including the U.S. ambassador—is an aspect of this policy deserving of the closest attention. At the regional level, the response was the reverse among U.S. allies. But U.S. officials also maintained relations with the Egyptian/UAR president, who sought an open collaboration with Washington in Leba-non. The line with Cairo was maintained, in spite of the rebuffs to Nasser from Washington and the rejection that his proposals received in Beirut. In practice, Nasser's recommendations for Beirut were close to the polit-ical outcome of the 1958 crisis, and the candid dialogue between the UAR foreign minister and the U.S. secretary of state in the halls of the

United Nations, after U.S. intervention, was suggestive of wide areas of agreement. Yet, for all of its parochial character, the preoccupation of U.S. officials with the identity of the future Lebanese president was inseparable from regional developments that directly affected the aggravated course of Lebanese politics. These included the creation of the United Arab Republic (UAR) in February 1958, in which Egypt was joined by Syria as the first step in the realization of Arab unity. Another was the military coup in Baghdad in July 1958 that leveled British influence in Iraq, to the alarmist reactions of other Western allies, including Kamil Sham'un. The shock waves that reverberated through London and Washington led to Anglo-American deliberations that directly affected policy in Lebanon and Jordan, and in the Gulf, as well as Saudi Arabia.[1]

Insofar as the U.S. response to Lebanese developments in the months leading up to the outbreak of civil war in May 1958, is concerned, the focus appeared to be narrow in the extreme. Who would succeed Kamil Sham'un at the end of his term? And if the Lebanese president did indeed succeed himself in office, was that good for U.S. policy? Controversy over the presidential succession crisis preoccupied Lebanese politicians and opposition leaders, and U.S. officials. The narrow focus that U.S. communiqués on the subject reveal was not entirely parochial. Although the concentration on the succession issue did indeed reflect the belief—common to U.S. officials—that it was possible to separate the controversy at the apex of the Lebanese political system from its broader domestic crises, interpretations of the issue revealed a far deeper understanding of the stakes involved for Lebanon and the United States.

In addition to the by-now-familiar contrast between the views of U.S. officials in the field and those in Washington responsible for policy, the intense traffic between Beirut and Washington revealed the competitive and contrasting positions of two dominant figures, the U.S. ambassador and the CIA agent—Robert McClintock and Wilbur Eveland. With the former, the consistent demythification of Sham'unist claims revealed the skepticism of U.S. officials in the field. Eveland, on the other hand, offered an unusually loyalist view of Lebanese politics for a man identified with so obviously iconoclastic an interpretation of U.S. Middle East policy. The larger significance of the preoccupation with Lebanese presidential politics lies not merely in the obvious assumption that the presidency of Lebanon would directly affect U.S. interests in Beirut and the Middle East but also in the capacity of U.S. officials to influence the outcome of the political conflict. Eveland had the ear of both John Foster Dulles and

Allen Dulles; McClintock, more likely, that of his State Department colleagues. But it was McClintock's cables that exposed the extent of disillusionment with Sham'un before the end point of July 1958, the moment when he was given the full U.S. support that he requested. And it was in the course of exchanges between Beirut and Washington in these months, as earlier, that Embassy communiqués reveal the lucidity with which the long-term risks of U.S. policy and Lebanese politics were articulated.

In January 1958 the dominant question was what position the United States would adopt on the issue of the presidential succession in Beirut. By May, political turmoil had issued into civil war. And by the end of June, the Sham'un regime had lost control over much of the country. In the intervening months and, specifically, before the outbreak of civil war in May, the question of presidential succession became the new U.S. ambassador's introduction to Lebanese politics. Robert McClintock presented his credentials to President Sham'un as the new U.S. ambassador on January 15. McClintock had served briefly in Egypt (1952–1953), in Vietnam (1953–1954), and as ambassador to Cambodia (1954–1956). Experience in colonial settings does not appear to have predisposed him to opposition to imperialist politics. But it did give him a sense of the absurd in politics, including the propensity to pretentious posturing among those with power, which doubtless irked his superiors. The fictionalized account of the period by Edward R. F. Sheehan, *Kingdom of Illusion* (1964), may be the most useful guide to the genre of Embassy politics in the eastern Mediterranean at this time. McClintock was certainly in the Lebanese fray and not simply above it. Disdainful of the opposition, he rapidly lost whatever illusions he may have had concerning the Lebanese president or his close advisers. The choices he believed the United States confronted were nearly equally unpleasant as far as he was concerned. But McClintock was not blind to the effects of Sham'unist political rejectionism, even though he called for support for the regime, albeit without military assistance until that corner, too, was turned. The man whom McClintock viewed as the logical heir to the presidency was Shihab, the Lebanese commander in chief, who became Lebanon's third president in the fall of 1958. Toward Sham'un and Malik McClintock had a disdain that competed with the contempt he felt for the opposition.

Yet for all of his antipathy to uncritical backing of Sham'un and U.S. intervention, McClintock was no renegade in the ranks. His view of the presidential succession question was that it was possible to separate the leader from the regime, and thus to save U.S. interests identified with the latter.

To Wilbur Eveland, McClintock was a sign of U.S. diplomacy gone awry. In spite of his own critical evaluation of what he regarded as the unpardonable excesses of U.S. policy, its reflexive anticommunism, its attempts at destabilization, and its generous use of funding to achieve results, Eveland was a Sham'un and Malik loyalist. The CIA agent was alleged to have been sent to Beirut to " 'act as sort of balance to Ambassador McClintock,' " according to one of the informants cited by then former CIA agent Miles Copeland.[2] And as Copeland points out, the world and work of intelligence was not only in Eveland's hands. Nonetheless, Eveland's view of Beirut was hardly idiosyncratic. While McClintock feared the divisive impact of a second Sham'un presidency on Lebanon that would bode ill for the United States, Eveland argued that only Sham'un could safeguard U.S. interests, including the intelligence network operating out of Beirut, provided that the United States supported him.[3]

In spite of their differences, the U.S. ambassador and the CIA agent were linked in their complicity with the Lebanese politicians about whom they disagreed. McClintock was a de facto intermediary between Sham'un and Shihab, at the request of the Lebanese president. Eveland, on the other hand, was the confidant of the foreign minister and president. "Rapid Robert," as Eveland labeled McClintock, had influence by virtue of his position, but Eveland's arrangements, singular in other than covert circles, locked him into the Embassy and the Lebanese president's quarters. The CIA had installed a shortwave radio in Eveland's bedroom that allowed him to "communicate with sets installed in the sleeping quarters of the ambassador and [Sham'un], as well as with the embassy's command post and one of the navy destroyers positioned offshore" (p. 280).

In mid-January the State Department's officer in charge of Syrian and Lebanese affairs, Edward Waggoner, put the question of the Lebanese presidential succession crisis to the director of the Office of Near Eastern, South Asian, and African Affairs, Stuart Rockwell. Waggoner's memo suggested that Sham'un would not be the candidate of choice if a suitable alternative were found. The criteria for acceptance included the following: "1) could be counted on to maintain the Lebanon's present pro-West orientation, 2) is acceptable to important segments of the Moslem as well as the Christian community, and 3) for whom broad support can be generated."[4] Sham'un was not to be dropped entirely, according to this proposal; he was to be informed that the United States would consider supporting him for president in 1964. In the event that no alternative was found for 1958, Sham'un was to be actively assisted with advice "regarding the manner of conducting his campaign, particularly the desirability of effecting a rapprochement with important anti-Communist, pro-West political leaders who, for a variety of reasons are opposed to [Sham'un]'s reelection [six and a half lines of source text not declassified follow]" (ibid. 7). The reference to the opposition is instructive for its straightforward appreciation of the conservative, pro-American opposition leadership.

The U.S. ambassador in Beirut persisted along the same lines, persuaded that the crisis encapsulated the entire problem of Lebanese politics and that, once it was resolved, a semblance of normalcy would return. McClintock held firmly to this view, reducing the grievances that had confronted the regime over the past year to the question of presidential selection. Eveland, on the other hand, particularly after the declaration of the United Arab Republic on February 1, interpreted the Lebanese conflict in regional terms, as did Sham'un and Malik. Eveland argued that Sham'un was the only "candidate" who could assure U.S. interests and the continuity of U.S. intelligence operations in Syria and Egypt, and the only candidate who could confront his critics among co-religionists.[5] As Eveland maintained, "the probability that we'd not be able to use Lebanon for such purposes under a successor to [Sham'un]," made his reelection highly desirable (ibid. 268).

Throughout this period, Sham'un and Malik adopted a more aggressive stance with respect to demands for military assistance, arguing that Lebanon was on the verge of being overrun by an Egypto-Syrian conspiracy. Assistance for the Lebanese army as well as the gendarmerie was requested.[6] In addition, Malik stoked the anti-communist fires sure to alarm the U.S. secretary of state. At the end of January, Malik appealed to the Embassy for funds to launch an anti-communist campaign with the help of some thirty volunteers that he was prepared to recruit, "young men in the journalistic field who are desperately anxious to mobilize their combined strength to combat the noxious stuff which newspapers daily dole out. He estimates that with an annual budget of two million dollars communist exploitation of the local press could be neutralized."[7] This was followed by another, more ambitious proposal, which involved having the Sixth Fleet move into the eastern Mediterranean, without docking at Beirut harbor.

McClintock, meanwhile, undermined the Sham'un-Malik position by conveying persuasive information about the extent and breadth of domestic opposition. The Third Force, which kept the Embassy apprised of its views, made haste to inform McClintock that its anti-Sham'unist stance involved no anti-Western position. The "moderate" anti-Sham'unist forces, as Miles Copeland referred to them, were at least as hostile to the UNF leadership, and specifically to Salam, Mashnuq, Yafi, and Hakim, as to Sham'un's attempts to have himself reelected.[8] In the grand puzzle of Lebanese politics, efforts to tar the UNF leaders as unconditional Nasserists was somewhat mitigated as far as McClintock was concerned by two factors. The first was that Nasser was not interested in dividing Lebanon or in integrating it into the UAR; the second was evidence of the strained relations between the UAR ambassador to Beirut, Abdul Hamid Ghaleb, and the UNF leaders.[9]

Indicative of the relations between Sham'un, Malik, and McClintock was the request of the two former men that McClintock act as intermediary with Shihab and press him to be more accommodating to Sham'un's desire to have the army back the gendarmerie. Sham'un let it be known that if Shihab did not comply, the ambassador was to try to obtain shipment of armored vehicles from Cyprus, within a matter of hours. Shihab was described as "very pleased at intimation our possibility of assisting Lebanese armed forces in supply of aircraft and replacement of armored cars by light tanks, making former available to gendarmerie. We agreed army attaché would go into details on latter problem with general staff."[10] But McClintock's views on the matter were not to be put aside. The U.S. ambassador confided to the Lebanese commander in chief that he was annoyed at "being constantly importuned by government for U.S. or allied assistance to meet imagined threats to internal security."[11] The reference was to Shihab's "government." Ironically, McClintock complained to John Foster Dulles that the implementation of such a policy would lend credibility to the opposition's charges of U.S. intervention in Lebanon's domestic affairs.

The declaration of the UAR, prompted by internal Syrian political struggles between local Communists and Ba'thists, changed the dynamics of the region and quickened the U.S. response to Beirut. As a counter to the UAR, the administration promoted collaboration among Lebanon, Jordan, and Iraq, as well as Saudi Arabia. Proposed by Acting Secretary of State Christian Herter several days before the UAR merger, it was restated by Dulles several days later, and on February 14 the

Jordanian-Iraqi union was formally established. The union was a pallid effort from the outset, as the administration recognized, hoping that it might nevertheless prove useful in responding to the Lebanese situation. In Beirut, it was the excitement generated by the creation of the UAR that proved virtually impossible to contain, in spite of regime bans on demonstrations, foreign propaganda, and other expressions of support. Demonstrations were held in Beirut, Tripoli, Tyre, and Sidon. UNF delegations including Yafi, Hamadeh, 'Ammun, and Karame, paid homage to Syrian president Shukry al-Quwwatly in Damascus, while Lebanese businessmen attended a reception at which the Syrian president extended Lebanon an invitation to join the UAR. With the arrival of Nasser in Damascus on February 24, there came a veritable surge of Lebanese, including UNF leaders, pouring into the Syrian capital to pay their respects to the Egyptian leader, including Sa'eb Salam, Kamal Junblat, Ahmad and Kamil al-As'ad, Ma'ruf Sa'd, and Maronite patriarch Paul Ma'oushi.[12]

Assessing this as a point of no return, McClintock once again reminded Dulles that the Lebanese Chamber would move on the constitutional amendment question between mid-March and May and that presidential elections were scheduled for July.[13] Sham'un was still "top dog," according to the U.S. ambassador, albeit distrusted and disdained by Opposition circles. McClintock requested approval to approach the Lebanese president for clarification of his position, as well as to convey Washington's political mood. His own was pessimistic, as McClintock clearly regarded the prospect of Sham'un's staging a second presidential campaign nothing short of disastrous for the country, the guaranteed precursor of civil as well as confessional strife, since the opposition included Lebanese Christians as well as the more numerous Muslims.

> It is evident opposition to reelection of President [Sham'un] can cause a great deal of trouble and possibly disrupt delicate balance in this country which exists by elaborate feat of political and confessional equilibrium. If menaces of opposition can be taken at face value, upshot of attempt by [Sham'un] to succeed himself, even though crowned with immediate success, would result in Lebanon being divided not (repeat not) only on a Moslem versus Christian axis but on Maronite versus Maronite schism which would have effect of strengthening more fanatic Moslem factions in their anti-western bias and weakening elements friendly to US. Although external pressure of UAR may force Christian sects into closer step, it may draw Moslem ele-

ments toward greater magnetic field of Arab unity. Effect of a second
candidature by [Sham'un] will be divisive.   (Ibid.)

McClintock's cable is of interest in the light of U.S. policy, which followed the lines described above as constituting a major risk to Lebanese
domestic politics. In compliance with instructions, McClintock proceeded to question Sham'un concerning his political plans. He recommended that he postpone his presidential ambitions but said that if he
chose to pursue them, the United States would "not oppose that decision." McClintock understood that if Sham'un chose to succeed himself
in office, it was imperative to assure him a victory and then to minimize
the damage to U.S. policy. Acknowledging that U.S. support would not
be withheld, however, allowed the Lebanese president to assume the continuity of U.S. support. Kamal Junblat accurately characterized the U.S.
position as one that involved a conditional support of the president combined with an unconditional rejection of the opposition.[14]

In fact, the position that McClintock recommended was one premised
on a separation of the Lebanese president from his regime, an artificial
break that appeared to be both a convenient way of ignoring domestic
politics and a way of retaining the advantages of continuity of the system.
It was not only Sham'un that McClintock urged the secretary of state to
move aside but Charles Malik as well, for his pro-American politics were
too flagrant to be helpful. As the U.S. ambassador explained, the U.S. priority was "not (repeat not) allowing disappearance of [Sham'un] from
presidential scene to be interpreted as a disavowal of his foreign policies
including open support of U.S. and Eisenhower Doctrine."[15] McClintock,
in short, believed it desirable and possible to "divorce his identity with
policies we sponsor from his identity with domestic problems not of our
concern." Malik, in McClintock's view, was "the apostle of Americanism.
In my judgment, he should go fairly soon as he is focusing anti-American
opinion on himself and his eventual exit, unless expertly handled, might
be misinterpreted as a disavowal of Lebanon's pro-western policy. I recommend we go all out to secure Malik's selection as president of next
GA" (ibid.).

The reference was to the General Assembly, and this solution was
eventually implemented in the fall. As to alternative candidates for the
Lebanese presidency, McClintock operated as though he were a member
of the Lebanese establishment, sifting through political figures with an
eye to their acceptability. Included were Raymond and Pierre Eddeh, and

Salim Lahhud, although he was too closely identified with Sham'un. Shihab was considered apolitical, a definite drawback in this case, since he would support a neutralist foreign policy. To McClintock, who later became the general's political ally in Lebanese politics, Shihab was described as a "neutral legume who would require careful pruning to grow in the right direction. However, as was said of Louis XIV, 'All he has is common sense—but a great deal of that' " (ibid.). The response to McClintock's lengthy February 21 cable from the State Department's Near East Division was positive. William Eagleton, Edward Waggoner, and Stuart Rockwell of that division drafted the reply signed by the secretary of state that restated McClintock's basic position, while asking him to withhold such information from his British and French colleagues until U.S. policy had been made.[16]

In Beirut, political tensions showed no signs of abating in the months that followed. The president was rumored to be considering extending the parliamentary session to delay acting on the constitutional amendment. "Presidential election fever has mounted," an Embassy officer reported, as Sham'un was giving signs of continuing in office.[17] McClintock, meanwhile, continued to pressure Sham'un indirectly, meeting with Maronites who were known to be critical of the president, such as Maronite patriarch Paul Ma'oushi, who believed that Sham'un's reelection efforts would prove counterproductive for Lebanese Maronites and would eventually result in their loss of the highest office of the state in response to the anticipated Muslim counterattack. The patriarch recommended that Lebanese Christians take stock of the situation realistically and develop a means of coexisting with their Muslim brethren, or else convert or emigrate. Finally, to underscore a point he had earlier made to Dulles, McClintock insisted that the Lebanese crisis could not be defined in strictly sectarian terms. It was not simply a matter of Lebanese Christians versus Muslims, since there were differences within the Christian community. Indeed, according to the Embassy, more than half of the 30 percent of Lebanon's Christians were divided on the presidential question.

Sham'un was undeterred by the advice of either his American or his British supporters, in spite of the effort of both U.S. and U.K. ambassadors to persuade him to accept an extension—as opposed to a six-year renewal—of the presidency, which was proposed in February. On March 5, the Lebanese president was "already envisaging second term in office, said he was quite prepared to be clement to opposition and he would be willing early on to indicate readiness to bury hatchet."[18] McClintock made clear to Sham'un and Malik that they could not count on U.S. military intervention and that in the event of civil strife, it would be inadvisable to bring in the Marines.

> [Sham'un] replied he was in complete agreement. He said only time he had discussed possibility of deploying Sixth Fleet was when Jordan not Lebanon was in danger. I am sure he got point I desired to make; namely, that U.S. military strength in Mediterranean should not be used in forthcoming Lebanese political turmoil.   (Ibid. 16)

Sham'un insisted that the opposition was receiving arms smuggled into the country by agents of the UAR. The inability to document such claims embarrassed U.S. as well as U.K. officials in Beirut and in Washington and London, but it in no way altered the Lebanese president's position. Sham'un conceded that the guns allegedly smuggled in by Syro-Egyptian agents were actually sold. "This does not add up to a very convincing UAR inspired threat by Moslem element against Christian Lebanese," concluded McClintock.[19] Worse, "while denouncing smuggling of arms for Moslem element, president of a supposedly united country seeks to connive at smuggling arms for Christian elements," McClintock reported, warning of civil strife. Sham'un countered with the claim " 'I control most of Shiite Moslems and some of Sunnis in Beirut. Main danger is in Tripoli' " (ibid. 19). By contrast, the U.S. ambassador's view of the situation was that the policies Sham'un was pursuing risked transforming Lebanon into a garrison state, a "sort of Christian Israel beleaguered by its neighbors and incapable of sustaining itself except under guns of foreign warships."

In spite of his claims to be in full control, the Lebanese president was clearly aware of the spreading signs of dissidence. Demonstrations occurred in Tripoli and Tyre, and on the long-neglected peripheries of the Beirut center. Sham'unist forces consisted of Kata'eb and PPS (Syrian Social Nationalist Party) supporters, an unlikely combination that shared a common antagonism to the left-wing opposition. The president counted on a group of advisers and loyalists that included Na'im Mghabghab, Joseph Skaff, and Majid Arslan, representing Mount Lebanon and the Biqa'. For the Kata'eb, claiming a membership of some forty thousand, Lebanon's situation was symptomatic of the risks that opposition victory would entail for Lebanese of the Maronitist persuasion. The PPS, on the other hand, committed to a transnational state under an authoritarian leadership, offset the onus of collaborating with the Kata'eb by having presidential protection and the eventual lifting of its illegal status in Lebanon.[20]

By the spring of 1958, the dominant formations in the array of the opposition included the UNF, the Third Force, and the Progressive Socialist Party, with smaller parties of Ba'thists, Arab Nationalist Movement, and Communists. The array of groups, parties, and leaders was ideologically divided, yet cast in the historic role of collective opposition to the succession of the Lebanese president. In practice, the conservative leadership of the UNF, preoccupied with regaining the political positions its leaders had held before the 1957 elections, was forced to assume a more radical stance by virtue of a constituency that included urban poor and petty bourgeois supporters of an elemental Nasserism. Sham'un's identification with U.S. regional policies proved objectionable in this regard. Not only was it the long-term cause of the political alienation of a mass base, but it also aroused the concern of those dependent on unimpeded access to the Arab hinterland. In this context, disclosures of covert efforts to destabilize the Syrian regime that surfaced in March gave the opposition added momentum. Revelations that the Saudi king had been used to attempt to bribe Abdul Hamid Sarraj of Syria to accept an exchange in the form of separation from the UAR for U.S. support as Syrian president were greeted as shocking confirmations of U.S. policies that the Lebanese regime endorsed.[21] Among the responses in Beirut was the organization of a Congress with Henri Far'oun as president, Abdallah Yafi as vice president, and Kamal Junblat as secretary, that reaffirmed its commitment to the National Pact and to a unified Lebanese state, condemning the president for the deteriorating situation in the country. Sham'un was warned "that if he made any attempt to amend the Constitution to enable him to renew his term of office, this 'will justify the people in imposing their will by all means at their disposal.' "[22]

McClintock was not passive before these events, renewing his recommendations to the secretary of state that the U.S. support the candidacy of Raymond Eddeh, and that Shihab be reconsidered as well. In this context, McClintock forwarded an interview of Shihab by U.S. Army attaché Colonel Robert C. Works that had been conducted ten months earlier. McClintock underscored the fact that it provided "background on the thinking of a man who is running as a dark horse now and may later be riding a white one."[23] The possible candidacy of Shihab was described as "the balancing factor if election tensions precipitate civil strife." Shihab, McClintock pointedly noted, might well be the Opposition's candidate.

On April 10, clashes in Junblat's region of the Shuf attracted wide-spread attention and a spiral of charges against the regime. Rashid Karame, Husayn al-'Uwayni, Fu'ad 'Ammun, and Henri Far'oun blamed Sham'un and the aggravated issue of presidential succession, while urging Shihab to keep the army out.[24] The Third Force condemned the use of violence and accused the regime of fomenting the conditions that inspired it. The UNF attacked the president for promoting a dangerous sectarianism, while Junblat accused the regime and its supporters of attempting to assassinate him, as expressions of support were extended by Druze as well as opposition leaders, such as Ma'ruf Sa'd and Rashid Karame. The Islamic Council opposed reelection of the president as well. The succession of condemnations, warnings, and alarms affected the Embassy, simultaneously forcing its support of Sham'un while maintaining links to the opposition. McClintock was convinced that Sham'un had decided to try a run for the presidency, and Malik, on April 11, submitted a desperate plea for U.S. assistance in what McClintock referred to as " 'pistol-at-the-head tactics.' "[25] In coordination with British ambassador George Middleton, McClintock proposed a draft that both would submit to their French counterpart to summarize their view of the situation.

> Our (the West's) interests generally would probably be best served by [Sham'un's] reelection only if he commanded sufficient general support for his policies to be effectively implemented. They would probably be less well served by General in office (because his laziness and disinclination for the political game); and if he resigned in short time any likely successor (after perhaps a general election) would probably be less able to keep close bonds with West.[26]

Six days later, in response to the rumor that the Lebanese government might consider defecting from its adherence to the Eisenhower Doctrine, Dulles was moved to respond, clearly unnerved by Malik's action. He underscored the fact that according to the Eisenhower Doctrine, the U.S. had no obligations toward Lebanon.[27] Nonetheless, Sham'un was granted economic and military assistance on May 1, "to strengthen Lebanese security forces," as further aid was considered.[28] McClintock, in the interim, cabled Dulles of continuing tension and violence that "kept internal security pot boiling and political atmosphere surrounding presidential removal controversy charged over week-end."[29] But he also sent Dulles a description of the anticipated effects of the Sham'un-Malik effort to regionalize and internationalize the conflict. The United States,

McClintock's cable implied, would be in a difficult situation faced with Sham'un's redefinition of Lebanon—meaning himself—as the epicenter of anti-Nasserist forces struggling to survive.

> [Sham'un] is in our view almost certain to seek amendment of constitution and stand for re-election. We know he has solicited and been promised active sympathy and support of Iraq, Iran, Sudan and Turkey and possibly other countries such as Pakistan, Saudi Arabia, Greece, Italy, etc. His success or failure must therefore be judged in much wider context than mere internal Lebanese politics. Once he has announced his intentions western failure to support him will have repercussions among all most moderate and responsible friends and allies of west in ME area. [Sham'un] has come to symbolize to them forces of resistance to Nasser.[30]

The strategy was not resisted in Washington, as the Western ambassadors agreed to endorse Sham'un, thus accepting his role in the polarization of a regional politics that had become the centerpiece of Dulles's Middle East strategy. Sham'un was no longer seen primarily in the context of the Lebanese political conflict, which was now subordinated to regional policies whose international implications Sham'un and Malik did not fail to emphasize. It remained for McClintock to assure Sham'un of U.S. support, to manage the press, to distance the alternative candidates, and to arrange for assistance to the police and gendarmerie and such other security arrangements.[31]

With this decision, the marriage of U.S. policy and Lebanese regime politics was formalized. Its unraveling occurred in the aftermath of U.S. military intervention. In the light of U.S. policy, the report of the State Department's Bureau of Intelligence and Research, which was dated April 1, offered an assessment at odds with Dulles's support for Sham'un and, more generally, for his unconditional support of regime policies. "The Nature of Anti-Sham'un Disturbances in Lebanon" was formally prepared for Dulles and was practically ignored. Its recommendations for broadening the political base of Lebanese politics and for separating confessional from political arrangements through the adoption of a secular system were at odds with U.S. policy. Sham'un was not the only obstacle to such a transformation; the political system that his regime upheld had been consistently supported by U.S. policy.

> For the longer run, governmental stability will depend on (1) the development of means for the peaceful transformation of the country's

political system from a confessional to a secular structure, (2) adjust-
ments to cope with the increasing appeal of radical Arab nationalism
for Lebanese Moslems, and (3) reinforcements of Lebanon's traditional
neutral role as the commercial, educational, and recreational "Hong
Kong" of the Middle East.[32]

The United States Response to Civil War

On May 8, Secretary of State John Foster Dulles complained to the members of the National Security Council of the undue pressure being
applied to the United States by President Sham'un. There was nothing
apologetic in Dulles's position.[33] The U.S. secretary had not yet received
the news from Beirut. On the next day, in Copenhagen, Dulles met with
his British counterpart and agreed that it was imperative to reconsider
Anglo-American "measures to forestall or to counter an anti-Western
coup d'état in Jordan or the Lebanon."[34] What had happened in the
interim? The answer was the assassination of editor Nasib al-Matni. The
event ignited the powder keg that marked the onset of civil war. The date
was May 8. Five days later, Dulles cabled McClintock with a detailed list
of instructions for President Sham'un, to be followed in requesting U.S.
assistance. That event not only defined the terms on which the Lebanese
president would request intervention on July 14, it made a mockery of
subsequent claims that the United States was protecting the endangered
state of Lebanon, or that the Iraqi military coup in Baghdad was the
determining factor in initiating such action. It was not the military coup
in Baghdad that was on Sham'un's mind when he desperately sought U.S.
intervention. Nor was that a factor for Dulles when he issued his instructions. It was not Lebanese sovereignty or statehood that Dulles was protecting but a regime that Eisenhower was committed to upholding in the
midst of a civil war whose outcome both U.S. officials and the Lebanese
regime feared.

Nasib al-Matni, the Maronite editor of *at-Telegraf*, was a well-known
critic of the regime. He had exposed its corrupt electoral practices and
been rewarded with imprisonment, released and then arrested again on
charges of defaming the president. To Sham'un, Matni was "venomous
and communizing," a man killed by those who had been involved in a
plot against another journalist, who had escaped and fled to Syria.[35]
Sham'un's explanation paled before the electric response that the assassination provoked nationwide. Within a day of Matni's assassination, the

UNF called for a general strike, demanded Sham'un's resignation, and proposed an interim cabinet.

Demonstrations were organized throughout the country. On May 10, armed clashes between demonstrators and PPS partisans resulted in an American casualty in Tripoli—the USIS Library—which promptly led McClintock to call for a meeting with the opposition. Those invited to the Embassy were two representatives of the Third Force and the leader of the UNF—Henri Far'oun, Ghassan Tuwayni, and Sa'eb Salam. This triumvirate, characterized by its pro-American sympathies, was informed that the United States would not

> tolerate opposition to [Sham'un] becoming transformed into an anti-American movement. I likewise made it very clear that so far as U.S. public was concerned acts of violence against U.S. institutions in Lebanon by opposition would be most effective possible means of encouraging U.S. support for object of this enmity, namely [Sham'un].[36]

McClintock proceeded to meet with Malik to inform him that the United States government was taking measures to protect Americans in Tripoli, to which Shihab lent his assistance. The Lebanese president, in turn, assured McClintock that communist demonstrators were responsible. In the Embassy, the ambassador went into conference with members of the U.S. business community in Beirut, which was preparing its own security measures. TAPLINE, with its base outside of the capital, was among the U.S. firms "tied in by telephone to the command post so that they could be kept informed of what was going on in Beirut and could in turn inform the embassy of developments in the area."[37] The Embassy had become an American headquarters.

> In a normal month the code room handled between 100,000 and 150,000 words but after the rebellion broke out the traffic quintupled to 700,000 words. The eleven clerks in the section worked round the clock trying to keep up with the traffic. But operating coding machines is a meticulous job requiring a high degree of concentration. To relieve the pressure six additional code clerks were rushed to Beirut from neighboring posts.   (Ibid. 21)

U.S. military sources in Beirut estimated the casualty rate for the week that followed to be fifty to seventy deaths and some two hundred to three hundred wounded. McClintock requested emergency assistance: "Have determined there are certain urgent materiel requirements Beirut police which if met promptly would provide strong psychological support all local security forces additional to obvious operational benefits. Therefore propose following course action."[38] Thus, one thousand tear gas projectiles and grenades, a smaller number of tear gas guns, gas masks and submachine guns, one thousand rifles, and ammunition were requested. McClintock did not omit to instruct Washington to "eliminate shields or other ICA identifying devices from this and any subsequent shipment."

Keeping his lines of communication open to various elements in the opposition as well as to the office of the president and the commander in chief, McClintock sent Dulles a mix of signals that were mostly at odds with the direction of U.S. policy. He informed Dulles of the frantic efforts that were under way: first, to obtain final clarification of the president's political intentions while he finished his term; and second, to obtain his active support in allowing Shihab to temporarily lead a coalition government. Shihab's views of the situation could not have endeared him to his leader. For Shihab, what was occurring throughout Lebanon was an expression of "[Sham'un's] selfish determination to succeed himself in office. General explicitly disavowed any connection between foreign policies of [Sham'un] and his personal ambition again to be president. In other words, so far as Shehab is concerned issue is a straight personal one drawn between country and [Sham'un]" (ibid. no. 3772). Malik, predictably, maintained the opposite, insisting that there was no analogy between the events of 1958 and those of 1952, when Besharah al-Khuri had considered extending his own term. The contemporary crisis was a product of UAR infiltration, backed by the USSR. Malik was ready to ask for United States Marines, while Sham'un sent a note urging that twenty tanks be airlifted. Reverting to his earlier doubts, McClintock was adamant against U.S. military intervention, convinced that "nothing could be more harmful to [Sham'un] than that" (ibid. no. 3775).

The fear that violence would spread unless a compromise was reached was shared by the ideologically heterogeneous membership of the opposition. Raymond Eddeh spoke of civil war beginning in a matter of hours—an accurate prediction. In Tripoli, the number killed and wounded was high, with the city reported to have suffered heavy damage. In the Shuf, the area under Junblat's control, fighting was reported to be intense as PPS forces joined other Sham'un loyalists including pro-Sham'unist Druze to confront Junblati forces. Throughout the country, autonomous breakaway zones were emerging; in Beirut, Tripoli, Sidon, the Shuf, Ba'lbak, and the Hirmil.[39] In the Ba'lbak-Hirmil area that was not far from the Syrian border, the authority of the Beirut regime was reduced to some 18 kilometers. The incontrovertible nature of such evidence underscored the president's political weakness, but it was the growing strength of the Junblati forces in the opposition that came to worry the administration, and the UNF leaders. Within weeks, Junblat and his forces were within sight of the Beirut International Airport. That was at the end of June. The UNF leadership was not prepared to accept the political results of such developments. Neither was the United States.

Eisenhower's confidential secretary recalled May 13 as "another of the worst days of our lives. This was the day that Vice-President Nixon was attacked [by anti-American mobs] in Venezuela, that the two libraries in Lebanon were burned, that the French seemed to be in even greater trouble in Algeria than usual, for which we were being blamed, and that anti-American demonstrations were taking place in Bermuda."[40] It was the day that Eisenhower decided to send military assistance to the Lebanese president and that Dulles cabled McClintock the conditions that the Lebanese president would have to meet prior to U.S. military intervention. It was the same day on which British ambassador Middleton cabled the Foreign Office with this ominous declaration: "The struggle for the independence of Lebanon, which we had foreseen, is now engaged."[41] Here was the vindication of Middleton's view that "the Cabinet and most of the Christian politicians now seem conscious that the struggle is for the Lebanon, and not merely for reelection of [Sham'un]." Impatient with those who were still after a political solution, Middleton would have little use for McClintock's enduring Shihabist tendencies. Instead, the British ambassador was convinced that Sham'un must be supported by the United States and the United Kingdom, it being understood that the United States would play the major role. The news was transmitted to Washington via London and the Foreign Office (ibid.).

In Washington, agreement was reached to "supply internal security equipment air to arrive next two-three days. You will be informed re arrival time. Forward 18 tanks to arrive in approximately two weeks."[42] Such aid was decisive, according to U.S. military sources, in enabling the Lebanese government "to establish control over most of the country except for the northern part, along the Syrian border."[43] At the State Department, Dulles put his signature on the draft, prepared by William Rountree, that instructed Sham'un in requesting U.S. military intervention. The Lebanese president was told that the Eisenhower Doctrine was inapplicable. He was further informed that, given presidential authority under the United States Constitution, U.S. action would require no "further Congressional action but that the president is not authorized by Section 2 of the Joint Resolution to send armed forces to fight for Lebanon's independence since there has not occurred 'armed aggression from any country controlled by International Communism.' "[44] Dulles reiterated that the introduction of Western military forces in Lebanon was a step to be considered only under the most extreme circumstances.

1. The United States is prepared upon appropriate request from President and Rpt and GOL to send certain combat forces to Lebanon which would have the dual mission of (a) protecting American life and property and (b) assisting the GOL in its military program for the preservation of the independence and integrity of Lebanon which is vital to the national interests of the United States and to world peace. They would of course also be authorized to act in self-defense. FYI We believe these two courses are clearly within the President's constitutional authority without further Congressional action but that the President is not authorized by Section 2 of the Joint Resolution to send armed forces to fight for Lebanon's independence since there has not occurred "armed aggression from any country controlled by International Communism."

For these reasons the request should be couched in the terms indicated. Once the troops are there they would, in fact, serve to protect the independence of Lebanon. If for example they were stationed in Beirut and Tripoli to protect American life and property, that would presumably release Lebanese forces, and if the elements which were there to assist GOL in its military program became engaged in hostilities they would, acting in self-defense, counterattack.

You may use the foregoing on your own authority to explain the underlying rationale of point one. END FYI Steps are already being intiatied to put substantial combat forces into readiness to respond promptly, but the date of their arrival could not be counted on before two or three days after request received.

2. The U.S. would expect that at least concurrently with any public request to the U.S. the GOL would file a complaint with the United Nations Security Council, alleging the Interference from without in its internal affairs and the consequent threat to its integrity and independence.

3. The U.S. assumes that at least some Arab states will be prepared publicly to support Lebanon in its appeal to the U.S. and in its appeal to the Security Council.

4. The U.S. assumes that as stated in your 3826 President [Sham'un] recognizes that the crisis of Lebanon transcends the issue of Presidential election or the future of any particular person and that President [Sham'un] will not push his candidacy should this appear seriously to divide the support which should be counted upon to preserve the integrity and Western orientation of Lebanon.

The above four points are interdependent.   (Ibid.)

According to the U.S. Joint Chiefs of Staff, U.S. assistance materially altered the political as well as military balance of power. According to the JCS Report on 1958, the Lebanese regime's ability to remain in control was a function of such assistance, as "by emergency deliveries of arms and police equipment from the United States, government forces were able to establish control over most of the country except for the northern part, along the Syrian border."[45] The results were palpable in the U.S. ambassador's office, which, as Eveland described it, "resembled a command post" in which McClintock "seemed to enjoy communicating with the navy and U.S. military headquarters in Europe as much as he did sending crisis telegrams to Washington."[46]

The Eisenhower Doctrine presented more of a problem than a solution to the justification of U.S. policy. Its inapplicability was somewhat offset by the Mansfield Amendment, but in practice there was an evident reluctance to invoke it. Yet to publicly underscore its irrelevance was awkward. It was cited as legitimating U.S. intervention in U.S. military accounts, and Eisenhower himself was clearly ill at ease in his initial public pronouncements on the subject. James Reston of the *New York Times* quoted the president as recalling that

> there was an amendment passed that we had a very long study about around here, and we felt that as long as it was a friendly government, one with which we have associations like military assistance and so on, there were probably certain actions that we might be able to take that were beyond, or that were, yes, beyond just a mere overt Communist aggression, or I mean aggression from a Communist-controlled state.[47]

In the White House meeting of May 13, Christian Herter, Allen Dulles, Generals Twining, Gruenther, and Goodpaster, John Irwin of the Defense Department, and William Rountree of the NEA discussed whether to come to Sham'un's assistance. Not to do so seemed to the U.S. president impossible if the Lebanese regime's survival depended on U.S. support. But Eisenhower returned to the unlikely proposition that such assistance did not signify unqualified support for Sham'un and that he was to be so informed. As to the justification of such assistance, while the Eisenhower Doctrine clearly did not apply, the Mansfield Amendment, which defined U.S. national interests in the elastic terms of the preservation of the independence and integrity of Middle Eastern states, would be suitable, according to Eisenhower. Yet it was not the doctrine or the amendment that was ultimately the basis of the U.S. justification of policy. Finding the appropriate rationalization became an important issue, as the president recognized. Eisenhower "recalled our former so-called 'gun boat policy' and asked by what authority we had sent such missions to South American countries. The Secretary responded that this policy in the world today no longer represented an acceptable practice, unless the forces went in at the invitation of the host government."[48]

Intervention by invitation was to become the preferred formula to justify contemporary "gun boat policy," provided that the proper authorities could be found to issue the invitation. The Lebanese case posed no problem from this perspective. Nonetheless, both the State Department and the British Foreign Office, in spite of their differences, concurred that it would be more effective to "argue on the basis of an armed attack, especially if we were subsequently to justify military intervention to Lebanon. If we were not to stress the evidence of armed attack from outside, we might be vulnerable to the argument that it was our intervention which constituted a threat to peace rather than the situation which led up to it."[49]

What was the evidence? The question of the missing evidence, as the following chapter demonstrates, was a farce whose proportions embarrassed U.S. and U.K. officials and whose implications further undermined Sham'un's credibility in Washington. There was no dearth of claims. Charles Malik pointed to a succession of incidents, including the arrest of the Belgian consul general in Damascus who was caught and accused of smuggling arms into Lebanon; the five hundred persons crossing the Syrian border into Lebanon alleged to have been Syrian military involved in violent clashes in the same area in which the consul was arrested; and the two boatloads of eleven Palestinians from the Gaza Strip clandestinely traveling Lebanese coastal waters. UNF leaders discounted these charges as fabricated, rejecting claims of UNF links with the UAR and exposing the fraudulent charges against the Palestinians who were—it turned out—involved in a drug deal with a well-known figure.

The results of the May 13 deliberation eclipsed the problem of the missing evidence. The Joint Chiefs of Staff analysis of U.S. policy objectives in Lebanon identified the "dual mission of protecting U.S. nationals and property and of assisting Lebanon 'in its military program.' "[50] According to this interpretation, "while U.S. troops would not come with an avowed purpose of fighting for Lebanon's independence, their presence would free Lebanese forces from guard duties, and the exercise of the right of self-defense might engage U.S. forces in operations against the rebels" (ibid. 438–39). U.S. forces, on May 13, were on their way. Admiral James L. Holloway, Jr., commander in chief of Naval Forces, Eastern Atlantic and Mediterranean, later named CINCSPECOMME (commander in chief, U.S. Specified Command, Middle East), received orders on May 13 to proceed to the eastern Mediterranean. The Sixth Fleet, with two Marine battalions, moved toward Beirut. On May 14, Holloway was instructed "to proceed with the detailed U.S.-U.K. operational planning that had been contemplated in the combined contingency plan" (ibid. 435). The reference is to the joint Anglo-American plans devised in 1957 to deal with Syria and the possibility of intervention in Jordan and Lebanon. On May 16, the JCS sent a similar directive to the commander in chief, Europe, namely that "one Army battle group" be prepared for arrival in Beirut within twenty-four hours after receiving orders to so move. Additional arrangements were made to facilitate such a move by both U.S. and U.K. forces, although this preliminary "show of force" was reduced as the political situation of the regime appeared to improve.

Between Washington and London there was disagreement as to the limits of U.S. intervention that persisted through the summer, and that was a major factor affecting the Defense and State Departments' preference for redesigning the plan for a joint U.S.-U.K. intervention. In the interim, however, a joint U.S.-U.K. operation was in the planning, as Holloway's communications with Admiral Arleigh A. Burke, chief of naval operations, on May 16, indicated. Such plans had already been approved by the British military. Two scenarios were proposed, both premised on the central role of securing Beirut, whether by a U.S. Marine landing to be followed by the entry of British forces or, alternatively, by U.S. Air Force personnel coming from select European bases, to be followed by British advances on land.[51]

While these plans were under discussion, the situation on the ground in Beirut was changing to the advantage of the opposition and, more specifically, the Junblati forces. While Sham'un relied on anti-Junblati Druze under Majid Arslan to counter Junblat, Shihab continued to reject air attacks against such a target.[52] Shihab, moreover, continued to maintain that "revolution was a purely Lebanese affair with exception noted in the [Shuf], and this in General's opinion is much more grave and difficult to deal with. Other Syrian dispositions noted by G–2 were purely defensive in character and probably designed to meet what Damascus regards as threat of Allied intervention" (ibid.). McClintock was convinced of the validity of Shihab's analysis and persuaded that U.S. intervention would alienate those whose "antipathy" for Sham'un could not be denied or ignored, a position he conveyed to Dulles on May 13.[53] The mobilization of Anglo-American efforts and the course of the civil war did not alter his conclusion that "it would be a capital political mistake to support [Sham'un's] reelection if, in fact, we do forcefully intervene to maintain integrity and independence of Lebanon." With intervention accepted as an imminent event, McClintock reminded Dulles that the only Lebanese of stature who could restore a measure of Lebanon's "fraternity" was Shihab.[54] McClintock's support for Shihab was qualified by behavior that the U.S. ambassador found incomprehensible, namely, Shihab's social encounters with Lebanese "rebel" leaders. To U.S. officials this was as suspect as the commander in chief's systematic refusal to commit his troops to the destruction of the opposition.

What Shihab understood that U.S. officials in Washington failed to concede because it undermined their justification for intervention, was the character of the internal struggle that had penetrated the ranks of the army. In Beirut and in New York, at the United Nations, the UNF condemned U.S. military assistance and involvement in Lebanon's civil war (ibid.). As the same U.S. source continued from Beirut, "only Phalangist [Kata'eb] al-Amal reflected opposite view under headline 'Lebanon's International Friends Rush to Her Rescue' " (ibid. no. 3960).

The UNF charge was accurate, as was the Kata'eb statement. Dulles instructed the Embassy to define "the bases of our programs to assist Lebanon in maintaining its internal security, and actions taken over the past months to implement these programs." At the same time, there were evidently officers in the U.S. Embassy who remained skeptical of the Dulles approach. On May 18, for example, a dispatch provided a detailed account of a speech delivered by a prominent Sunni political leader. The address expressed the anger of a part of the country neglected by the Beirut regime, in spite of the economic decline it had suffered over the past years. The Funseth dispatch was sensitive to the social origins of political discontent, a dimension of the overall Lebanese crisis ignored in Washington. According to the document, its journey to the State Department took some six months. Routine for foreign dispatches perhaps, and indicative of the low-priority status of the subject. Was it ever read, let alone considered in Washington? Funseth's sense of urgency was evident.

> The declaration of Sheikh el-Jisr is one of the basic papers of the Lebanese revolution. In the six months since it was originally delivered, there has been no other statement to equal it in outlining and defining the grievances and aims of the Moslem Opposition. It is particularly useful in the language used which reflects accurately and gives an insight into the emotional feeling of the Moslems toward the entire crisis.[55]

The address on which Embassy officer Funseth commented was not an esoteric affair. Nadim al-Jisr's talk was a mix of history and politics, no doubt some part of it self-serving. But it offered a brief history of one of Lebanon's neglected regions, as well as an accusation of the state's political failure and its social cost. Reviewing Tripoli's fate under the Ottomans, French mandatory authorities, and Lebanese rulers, al-Jisr identified the causes of the region's impoverishment and political decline, emphasizing the deleterious impact of the Syro-Lebanese economic break and the havoc it had wreaked on the region.

> In discussing the point of view expressed by Sheikh Nadim el-Jisr with scores of Lebanese contacts, the reporting officer has found that most of these people agree that Sheikh el-Jisr's declaration represents closely the feelings of the Moslem masses. Even the most moderate Moslems accept generally what the sheikh said, though objecting to his choice of certain words and phrases.
>
> It is the emotional frame of mind that is evident in this paper, that the United States will find to be more and more in evidence in Lebanon in the immediate years ahead in Lebanese-American relations.

On May 18, the date of receipt of the above dispatch in the State Department, the opposition issued a nationwide appeal to the Lebanese, including the military and the gendarmerie, to "withdraw completely from Sham'un and the clique of plotting rulers, sympathize with the movement of your proud Lebanese people, remain in your barracks, and refuse to strike at the people. The noble attitude of your Commander, Fu'ad Shihab, places him above giving you orders of this sort."[56] To a critical Junblat, McClintock defended U.S. policy as acting in support of the legitimate government.[57] The limits of such legitimacy were the stuff of Shihab's exchanges with McClintock, however, as the general kept the

U.S. ambassador informed of the military situation in the Shuf, the massing of Shi'i partisans in Ba'lbak and the Hirmil areas, where the army's forces were limited. As Shihab explained:

> There were at all times some thousands of Syrian laborers in Lebanon and many of these were formerly conscripts who had done their military service in Syria. Their identity papers thus indicated a former military inscription; but it was too much to jump to conclusion that everyone thus picked up by a Lebanese police was a clandestine Syrian military agent.[58]

In spite of Shihab's disclaimers, the United States and its allies continued to send weapons. On May 19 an additional "five plane loads" of equipment arrived, which the commandant of the gendarmerie, Colonel Zuwayn, found gratifying.[59] British weapons for security forces were scheduled to arrive on May 20, in addition to the vampire jets requested by Sham'un, and the French promised to provide their own contribution to security forces. The latent tensions between British and American policymakers with respect to further intervention in Lebanon were the subject of discussion at a May 19 meeting in which John Foster Dulles, Allen Dulles, William Rountree (then assistant secretary of state dealing with the Near East, and other regions) participated. The British were described as eager to inform Sham'un of U.S.-U.K. plans to intervene militarily. British colonel Decker, of the JCS's Joint Middle East Planning Committee, informed Admiral Burke, U.S. chief of naval operations, of the U.K.'s desire to alert Sham'un to U.K.-U.S. willingness to intervene. In fact, neither the State nor the Defense Department was prepared to accede.[60] Rountree considered the situation in Lebanon prohibitive, and Dulles complained to British ambassador Caccia that "some of our people, not just in Washington but elsewhere, had the impression that we were being crowded by our British colleagues into intervention in Lebanon."[61] McClintock reported from Beirut that he and Middleton were in accord that "conditions for introduction of U.K.-U.S. forces in Lebanon are distinctly not propitious. There are no foreign forces engaged which can be easily identified and our troops would find themselves fighting Lebanese once they landed here."[62]

What emerges from such exchanges is at odds with the practical results of U.S. policy on the ground in Lebanon. Evidently Dulles did not regard U.S. intervention as definitive, yet the outward signs of such intervention daily increased. U.S. naval forces were on the way to the Mediterranean on May 17, with forces withdrawn from French and Spanish ports. Between May 19 and 24, one of the ships of the Sixth Fleet, which was scheduled to participate in NATO exercises in the Aegean, was put at the disposal of Admiral Holloway and his staff in Malta. On May 19 an alert at Camp Lejeune, North Carolina, warned Marines to be prepared to leave for the Mediterranean within four days. Keeping at a distance from the Lebanese coast in accord with the political situation, the Sixth Fleet was no more than twelve hours away on May 26 and was freely stopping merchant ships off the Lebanese coast until ordered to cease.[63]

Why should Sham'un have assumed that what he was receiving was anything other than a sign of U.S. support? Whatever reservations the U.S. administration had, of which he had to have been aware, U.S. statements were characteristically prefaced with a statement of the American commitment "to insure continuous existence of a genuinely independent Lebanon and the continuation of the pro-Western policies which he has done so much to establish and which we believe are in the true interests of Lebanon."[64] Yet on May 23, Dulles informed Sham'un "that he does not have blank check re sending of Western forces. He should be disabused of any confidence he may have that he can refrain from taking decisive action to dissolve continuing political problem because he can count upon foreign forces to back him against domestic opposition."[65] The combination of signals was echoed in Beirut, where McClintock alternately warned against supporting Sham'un to avert greater chaos, and informed the USIA in a memo of May 27, for public attribution, that he wished to be quoted as saying that were it not for threats of intimidation, the Lebanese president would have majority support in his land.[66] The ambassador's double-talk was not the problem. The real problem originated at higher levels, where the fiction was maintained that Sham'un was prepared to heed U.S. warnings against intervention, at the same time that he was benefiting from the U.S. assistance that buoyed his regime. While assistance and military intervention are by no means identical, the Lebanese president was shrewd enough to understand that assistance—under the present circumstances—was a form of intervention that assured his tenure.

Interests, Pressures, and Policies

In the interim, the Embassy in Beirut continued to send cables against support for Sham'un's succession, and Wilbur Eveland continued to echo

Malik's views. In Washington, Secretary of State Dulles was listening to other voices with contrary recommendations, even as he maintained contact with Egyptian/UAR president Nasser, who offered to collaborate with the United States in resolving the Lebanese crisis. Western allies in the Middle East, on the other hand, were uniformly in favor of maintaining the Lebanese president and his regime in power. Israeli-U.S. discussions, in fact, occurred in Washington in May. In the same period, former CIA agent Miles Copeland stayed in touch with the U.S. ambassador, Lebanese interlocutors for Sham'un and the acceptable opposition, Nasser, and U.S. oil and business interests in Beirut.

Sham'un and Malik's strategy was to identify the Lebanese crisis with U.S. regional interests, while maintaining that the civil war was a contemporary example of earlier historical tragedies in which aggressive states usurped the legitimate rights of sovereign nations while the world looked on. Israeli officials considered the argument useful insofar as it identified the United States as the only major power capable of protecting the Middle East against an expanding Nasserism, with its alleged threat of Sovietization. Dulles and Eisenhower were not indifferent to such claims, nor did they ignore Eveland's argument that Sham'un represented the only reliable guarantee of U.S. intelligence activities in the region. By comparison, support for Shihab was marred by suspicion of what Eisenhower and Dulles persisted in interpreting as weakness and lack of respect for the Lebanese commander in chief. Through the long month of May, as regional pressures were increasingly brought to bear on the administration in Washington, the situation of the regime in Beirut weakened. Four cabinet ministers, including the minister of defense and information, resigned. In Cairo, the U.S. ambassador and Nasser met and continued to exchange positions on the crisis through the coming months. Washington ultimately rejected Nasser's invitation to an open cooperation on Beirut, as did Sham'un, but his recommendations bear a striking resemblance to those endorsed in the postwar U.S. settlement.

Two years after Suez, Israel's relationship with the Eisenhower administration was vastly improved. Its collaboration with Britain and France caused temporary consternation in Washington, in response to its delayed withdrawal from Gaza. Crises in Jordan and Syria alerted the State Department and the CIA to the risks of Israeli intervention, but such risks were offset by other considerations, namely, a sense of Israeli potential. While the Eisenhower administration was unprepared to furnish Israel with military assistance or the guarantees it requested in 1957, in 1958 the relationship changed. The declaration of the United Arab Republic marked a turning point. Israeli contacts with Iran and Ethiopia, followed by the Iranian brokered meeting with Israeli officials in Ankara, opened possibilities for a "peripheral alliance" with non-Arab states of the region. Such arrangements involving Iran, Turkey, Ethiopia, and the Sudan, which was later invited to join, were appealing to Washington. The logic of the "peripheral alliance," after all, was comparable to that of the "Northern Tier" in its anti-Arab nationalist and anti-radical thrust. According to Hermann Eilts, then officer in charge of the State Department's Baghdad Pact–CENTO–SEATO Affairs, Israel proposed the peripheral alliance after the military coup in Iraq. While Washington rejected the Israeli suggestion that it join the Baghdad Pact, its relations with Turkey and Iran were encouraged.[67]

In 1958 Israeli officials emerged as strong advocates of U.S. support for the Sham'un regime. They argued, as did the Lebanese president and foreign minister, that the Lebanese case had to be defined in terms of the risks of the Sovietization of the Middle East. In the spring of 1958 the position of the Israeli government was that the Lebanon crisis was "perhaps last opportunity for United States to act in manner that will prevent all of ME from being engulfed by Soviets."[68] Prime Minister Ben-Gurion linked a Soviet advance with a Western retreat. As the U.S. ambassador in Tel Aviv reported to Washington, with the cable passed on to Beirut as well as to other capitals of the region, "if Lebanon falls, he said, it will mean not only to Arabs but all those governments in area which for one reason or another want west to win this global conflict, that United States cannot move effectively even to save its friends." Like the Shah of Iran, the Israeli prime minister insisted that only U.S. action could arrest such trends, and such action depended on the political will of the United States.

In meetings held on May 15, 22, and 26, Israeli officials in Washington, including Israeli ambassador to the United States Abba Eban, met with State Department officials. Although Eban conceded that the Lebanese civil war had domestic roots, he accepted the Lebanese president's explanation. Israeli-U.S. talks were designed to convince Dulles and Eisenhower that Israel had a privileged position as interpreter of Arab politics, including Egyptian/UAR intentions. If these were important to Washington, then it would follow that Israel's views and policies would be heard. The long-term objective was the integration of Israel into the orbit of U.S. policies in the Middle East, a move that would have the added benefit of persuading the State Department to adopt a more passive position on the Israeli-Palestinian-Arab conflict. Identifying itself with the ideological position of the administration, the Israeli delegation additionally reinforced the urgency of blocking the Sovietization of the region by containing Arab nationalist, and Nasserist, forces. On May 15, Eban and Ya'acov Herzog, minister at the Israeli Embassy, presented their views on the Lebanese situation at high-level meetings in Washington. Israel's fate was inseparable from that of Lebanon. "Israel believed that objectively the security of Lebanon and Israel were equivalent. If Lebanon fell, Jordan would be next, and the momentum of Nasserism would gather force."[69] Eban made it clear that the Israeli government considered Lebanon's request for assistance to be entirely legitimate, and "in determining the legal basis for such aid, one might work backward from the action one wished to take to find a legal justification." For Israel, Eban was reported to have said, "any alternative, however drastic, would be better than to allow Lebanon to go down. It believed that the Lebanese Army, if resolutely used, would be able to maintain control of the situation." In addition to proposals concerning troop withdrawals along the Israeli-Lebanese border, the Israeli government was prepared to consider "any proposals regarding ways in which Israel could be of assistance." The one cited by the under secretary was the question of overflight rights, which Eban approved.

The reference to troop withdrawal from the Israeli-Lebanese frontier led to a series of exchanges among Tel Aviv, Washington, and Beirut. As a result, Israel informed Shihab that Lebanon could withdraw its troops for redeployment in exchange for Israeli guarantees. Eban conveyed the proposal through the U.S. embassies in Tel Aviv and Beirut. McClintock on May 16 asked Shihab,

> since his forces were so thinly spread, if it would not be helpful if he could be relieved of present necessity of maintaining military guard on southern frontier. I asked General if by chance we could secure satisfactory guarantees from Israel he might consider using his southern forces for more urgent duty. General said instantly he would be happy to do so, adding he had one battalion on southern border. However, he said he would be reluctant to pull out this force unless he had absolute assurances there would be no sabotage on Israeli side.[70]

On the same occasion, McClintock reported that Shihab wanted the U.S. State Department to obtain "assurances from Israeli side and, in particular, detailed guarantees that Syrian-inspired sabotage, which he fears, will be forestalled." Shihab reduced his forces on May 17 as planned, and the director of the Israeli Foreign Ministry, General Eytan, transmitted the expression of assurances regarding Syrian activity. Further, Israel would inform Lebanon if changes occurred on its northern border. Malik, in turn, indirectly informed Israel of his worries about a possible Egyptian coup in Lebanon that "would possibly be staged under the pretense of bringing armed assistance to the Lebanese to meet an imaginary Israeli attack."[71] The news of this contact came through the Israeli Embassy to the British Foreign Office. On June 10, a report of Israel's capture and delivery of "fourteen Lebanese insurgents in chains to a Lebanese police unit" appeared in the *New York Times*. According to this source, "the men were captured during the week-end by Israeli patrols that broke up convoys of gun-runners bound from Syria to Lebanon."[72] Explaining that the Lebanese were "caught in a wedge of Israeli territory jutting into Lebanon," the newspaper noted that "two of the Lebanese captives remained in Israel. No explanation was available here tonight of why they had not been handed over."

Israel's views on the succession question, discussed at the May 26 meeting, overlapped with those of the United States. Eban made it clear that Israel favored Sham'un but in the event of necessity would support a Shihab candidacy. Advising Dulles to seize the opportunity for another victory for the Eisenhower Doctrine, Eban urged the United States to intervene without hesitation. As though to assure his Israeli guest that there were no differences in their views of Nasser, Dulles hastened to inform Eban that his own opinion of the Egyptian leader had not changed, that Nasser "was moved by a dream of pan-Arabism, something like Hitler's pan-Germanism," that Nasser remained a diabolical creature empowered by the absence of "recognized international practices for dealing with his type of intervention."[73] Dulles's description of Nasser would be reproduced and embellished in his talks with the Shah of Iran at the beginning of July. The political outlook was similar, and so was the U.S. response. Israeli officials were informed of the U.S.-UAR talks, including Nasser's denials of intervention in Lebanon. U.S. officials claim that the Egyptian president's offer on Lebanon was not discussed.[74]

In a different setting, one that involved U.S. business interests in Lebanon, the U.S. ambassador to Egypt, a former CIA agent in Cairo, Egyptian/UAR president Nasser, and Lebanese intermediaries, the possibilities of promoting a breakthrough in the Lebanese situation were under discussion. Ostensibly far removed from the tenor of Israeli-U.S.

talks, the conclusions reached were entirely compatible. "By the mid-1950s, Beirut had a large Western-oriented commercial community . . . builders, bankers, shipping companies, suppliers of building and oil-well equipment, field offices of companies selling consumer products, and a large number of consulting firms specialising in various aspects of the oil companies' (and other large companies') adjustment to the environment."[75] Miles Copeland, who was a former CIA agent when he penned this description, was also among those specializing in "adjusting" firms and interested parties to the local environment. Copeland was working in his "government-relations-consulting office" for airline, bank, and oil companies. According to him, major U.S. oil companies were doing the same thing, reinforcing existing government-relations offices that were already operating, such as those for TAPLINE under the direction of William Campbell and David Dodge. Confidential newsletters appeared at this time, circulating in the same circles. According to Copeland, there was confusion among U.S. officials as to what strategy to adopt in 1958. Copeland claimed that McClintock favored Sham'un at first and then "switched to the opposite view—leaving Bill Eveland, the CIA, and much of the business community with his original position" (ibid. 233).

Copeland claimed that one of the U.S. oil companies attempted to get an accord with non-UNF opposition leaders and Sham'un. He was referring to one of the TAPLINE owner companies, which suggests that from this venue a political compromise in Beirut that omitted Sham'un was not excluded. But what of the others? The Lebanese personalities with whom Copeland was in contact in Cairo, and who traveled to the Egyptian capital expressly to pursue the possibilities of brokering a political compromise in Beirut, were Emile Bustani and Fawzi al-Huss, millionaire contractors. Hare, it will be recalled, had been offended by the pragmatic market politics of Bustani years earlier in Beirut. The objective of the discussions held in May 1958 was to discover a means to bypass UNF leaders in Beirut while not eliminating select members of the opposition. The more "moderate" opposition elements, according to Copeland's account, would be encouraged to meet with Sham'un supporters. Was this a reference to the "Third Force"? In early June Copeland had confirmation from some of the parties with which he was engaged. "I had been in touch with both presidents before the Lebanese crisis came to the boil, and when, in early June one of the major oil companies endorsed the idea, I agreed to talk first to [Sham'un], then to Nasser, not to sell the idea but to test its chances of acceptance" (ibid. 235).

On May 21, Ambassador Hare conveyed Nasser's views on the Lebanese crisis in a lengthy cable to the State Department. Commenting on the pro-Western and elite character of the Lebanese opposition, Nasser told Hare he thought the "greatest mistake of USG in Middle East was that it failed understand that basic fact of life in area is that people are tired of being exploited. Why did we continue support leaders who were out of sympathy with people?"[76] Denying Egyptian intervention, arguing that his intelligence budget was too modest to permit such activities, Nasser indicated an interest in cooperating with the United States in Beirut. According to Hare, Nasser wanted some distance and leverage with respect to the Soviet Union. As evidence of his intentions, Nasser offered to intercede with the Lebanese opposition to obtain its agreement on a formula that included the following proposals:

(1) An amnesty for opposition. This is of first importance because greatest preoccupation of opposition leaders in that they will be court-martialed and, as long as there is prospect that [Sham'un] will take his revenge, they obviously will not talk of settlement.

(2) General Shehab to become Prime Minister since he is respected and enjoys confidence of both Christians and Moslems.

(3) [Sham'un] to disclaim intention to seek change constitution but to serve out term. Nasser said understood opposition insisting on his resigning now but this would obviously present complications and he saw no reason for insisting on this provided there was fully guaranteed amnesty.

(4) Possibly have new elections.   (Ibid.)

McClintock, in Beirut, refused to contact Sa'eb Salam directly, arguing that "as for Nasser's suggestion I get into 'discreet touch' with Saeb Salaam, no touch with that morally slimy rug merchant could ever be discreet enough to prevent him from putting in opposition newspapers that U.S. had now decided to treat only with loyal opposition as truly representative of Lebanese public opinion. I am, however, in constant contact with opposition through reliable intermediaries."[77] Who were those intermediaries? The Third Force and Shihab?

Justifying his reticence in terms of new developments in Beirut, McClintock claimed that Sham'un had agreed to renounce his presidential ambitions in favor of a Shihabist formula. The explanation proved fictitious, as Sham'un's conditions for supporting Shihab were guaranteed to be rejected. McClintock, in this period, seemed skeptical of Shihab, "politically a simple man," who was most likely to be susceptible to new elections. "If held they would almost certainly produce a larger parliament made up of deputies in favor of a line of strict neutrality, some of them of the 'positive' variety. Because of current pro-Western attitude of existing parliament, we would prefer if possible not to have new elections" (ibid.). Sham'un, however, chose to remain silent on the question of his own plans, claiming that to do otherwise was to demoralize his followers. And he maintained that he was prepared to pressure Shihab to adopt a policy of pacification.[78]

The response of the State Department was not to break off the talks with Nasser but to pursue them indirectly. Hare was instructed to approach Nasser in an unofficial capacity. If the approach was designed to move Nasser to reject further talks, it failed. Nasser insisted that the U.S. view of the Lebanese opposition was false, while Hare countered with the proposal that Nasser use his influence to persuade its leaders to drop their demand that Sham'un resign before his term expired. But Nasser was also told that although Washington and Beirut rejected his proposals concerning amnesty, they approved his position on Shihab. "As Nasser knows U.S. is pledged to assist Lebanon to defend its integrity, and we remain determined to do so."[79]

Some movement was evident in Beirut, nonetheless. The three Western ambassadors in Beirut had reached agreement on the need for a political settlement in which Shihab would become prime minister, provided that Sham'un clarified his intentions, which they believed would effectively terminate the civil war. The three understood that this involved a violation of the practice whereby the prime minister was a Lebanese Sunni, but they had separately agreed that the ends justified such a transgression. Although Sham'un claimed to support such a policy, the condition was that Shihab agree to let the army attack the Basta area. McClintock admitted the "test will come in my opinion on issue of whether [Sham'un] dares to dismiss Chehab and, if so, if General who said once more to me this afternoon, 'I have the rifles,' might then be tempted to take power. Fortunately, in Lebanon, everyone (except, of course, the three ambassadors) is decisively indecisive."[80]

In Cairo, Nasser continued to support an agreement that the United States "would underwrite any guarantee given to safeguard opposition."[81] In the absence of such, Nasser would not commit himself to any initiative in Beirut. Hare withdrew, insisting that Nasser's main flaw was that he wanted a joint agreement with the U.S. Nasser "remained obdurant (sic), maintaining that risk of unilateral action was too great; would only intervene in association with US." The frustrated talks stalled on the public level and continued through Copeland, as earlier indicated. Emile Bustani arrived from Beirut at the end of May in order to implore the U.S. ambassador to do what was necessary to avoid further escalation of the crisis by arriving at a common approach with Nasser. Bustani proposed that the United States and the UAR support an interim cabinet headed by Husayn 'Uwayni, which is precisely what occurred in the fall of 1958. He also proposed that the UAR and the United States use their influence in Beirut, as he would with other regime loyalists, to avert disaster.[82]

Nothing came of this venture, but as the Lebanese case was being debated before the United Nations, Hare informed Dulles that Nasser was prepared to work toward an improvement of the situation in Beirut and that he had no intentions of trying to absorb Lebanon into the UAR. Further, Nasser continued to propose cooperation in a joint approach with the United States or, barring that, a parallel but separate initiative. He was prepared to endorse Shihab as prime minister, much as the three Western ambassadors did and with the same apology to convention. In repeated cables, Hare indicated that there were no substantive differences separating the United States and the UAR.[83] In Washington, however, Dulles conveyed the Egyptian proposals to Sham'un, and on June 10 he informed McClintock that Nasser was prepared to support moves toward a solution of the crisis and that these were attracting attention in Washington and London. Sham'un was warned that "U.S. and U.K. Governments adhere scrupulously to prior commitments. As [Sham'un] knows we have foreseen grave difficulties surrounding the introduction of foreign forces in Lebanon, and continue to hope that Lebanese independence can be effectively preserved without this measure of last resort."[84]

Why was Nasser's offer rejected? Had it ever been taken seriously? What were the competing pressures affecting the decision of the U.S. secretary of state and the U.S. president? Dulles's relationship with Charles Malik was legendary in the State Department. Between them there was a commonality of spirit that informed their respective political outlooks. Joined by temperament, ideology, and theology, the two political figures were reported by contemporaries to have conferred together and prayed together. And one may assume that their collective views were passed on to State Department subordinates who met, at Dulles's call, for those urgent Sunday morning sessions when the Lebanese crisis was at its peak.[85] But this was not the only source of information or influence on

Dulles. Wilbur Eveland's views represented a different source, albeit one that reinforced the same position and personalities.

On June 20, according to Copeland, he and Fawzi al-Huss met with Sham'un in order to obtain his "authorization for me to quote him to President Nasser as agreeing to meet with Rashid Karami, Sabri Hamadi, and Kamal Jumblatt and to make an honest effort to obtain a truce with them in exchange for Nasser's agreeing to discontinue support of the Beirut Four."[86] Sham'un was not receptive. He was assuming that the Eisenhower Doctrine would provide him with the help he needed when he sought to request it. Sham'un's reference to the Eisenhower Doctrine is interesting in the light of the May 13 instructions from Dulles, which had clarified the conditions of the doctrine and their inapplicability to the Lebanese crisis. Was this Sham'un's rebuff to his visitors? Was it a ploy to remind them that the Lebanese president had his impeccable American connections on which he could rely? Copeland indicates that in spite of this turn of events, he met with Hare and subsequently with Nasser, who was bent on working out the Lebanese crisis with the United States. The U.S. secretary of state rejected such an offer. Hare informed Nasser instead that the United States would be pleased to facilitate a Lebanese-UAR meeting, not one involving the United States and the UAR. Nasser's formula, according to Copeland, did not differ from that previously described, in which the UNF leadership was to be excluded from the proposed solution. In meeting with Hare, Copeland expressed his disappointment at the American response, to which Hare replied that "from his exchanges with Washington he had received the impression that the business community in Lebanon would have objected strongly to a favorable reply" (ibid. 238). Did Hare reflect Dulles's reluctance to cooperate openly with Nasser? Did Hare contribute to the doubts afflicting Dulles and Eisenhower? What of U.S. oil interests? According to Copeland, Hare discussed the influential role of unidentified U.S. business interests in Lebanon. U.S. international oil companies in Lebanon were certainly included. But the reference is inadequate, given the highly competitive relations existing between some of those involved, notably, U.S. marketing companies that dealt with their Lebanese counterparts, for example. The U.S. marketers, by virtue of their function, were more closely attuned to local political trends than were other TAPLINE companies. According to the former TAPLINE president, the U.S. marketing companies were prone to be more Sham'unist in outlook. TAPLINE, well informed on Shihab through its own local sources, had little reason to be apprehensive concerning the possibility of a Shihab presidency.[87]

In light of the above developments, the June 1958 Council on Foreign Relations meetings on oil politics and the Lebanese crisis take on added interest insofar as they reinforced the rejectionist approach.[88] With Charles Malik as the exclusive spokesmen on the Lebanese civil war, the interpretation of that event was predictable. Prominent oil consultant Walter Levy addressed the topic "Western Security and International Oil," commenting on the predicament that oil companies faced with the advent of nationalist movements, as in 1956. Levy noted that the United States had an oil surplus at that time, which was to be a significant factor in interpreting the U.S. response to the coup in Baghdad. But on this occasion, Levy insisted on the need for collaboration between U.S. commercial and security interests in the region. He did not mention Lebanon in his remarks. Terry Duce of Texaco, the experienced ARAMCO and TAPLINE man in Washington, was one of the participants in the seminar. The record indicates that he urged that more attention be paid to Soviet economic as opposed to military interests in the Middle East, a position thoroughly compatible with that of Dulles and the Lebanese foreign minister. Malik's presentation, "The Middle Eastern Crisis Affecting Lebanon," subordinated the domestic roots of the Lebanese civil war to regional and international considerations. To the audience of the CFR, the combination of Levy and Malik yielded a straightforward conclusion. The alternative to Sham'un was Nasser and political chaos.

Maps of the United Nations Observation Group in Lebanon (UNOGIL), which accompanied reports from the Security Council on its findings in Lebanon. These maps indicate the location of UNOGIL forces as well as the political map of Lebanon during the civil war of 1958. These materials have been prepared with the cooperation of the Cartographic Section, LPD, Department of Public Information, United Nations.

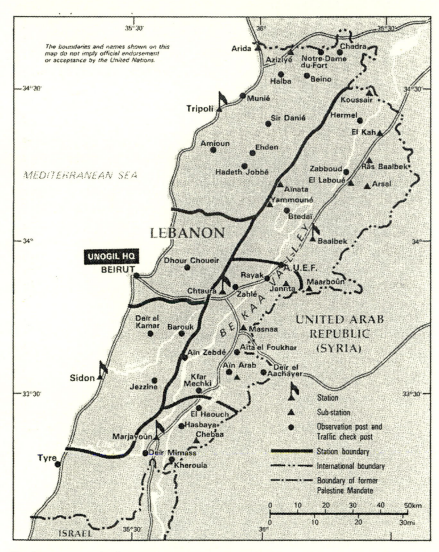

Deployment as of July 1958. Map no 3329 7 Rev 1

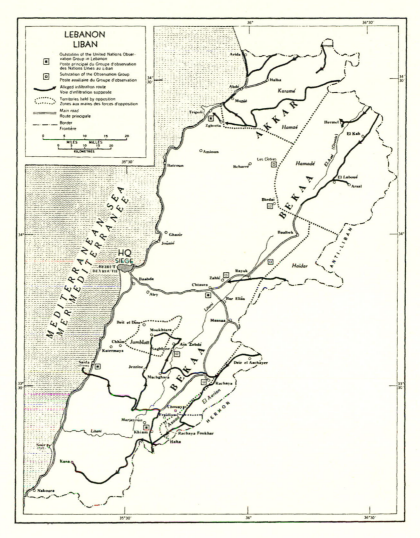

LEBANON
LIBAN

■ Outstation of the United Nations Observation Group in Lebanon
Poste principal du Groupe d'observation des Nations Unies au Liban

◙ Substation of the Observation Group
Poste auxiliaire du Groupe d'observation

Alleged infiltration route
Voie d'infiltration supposée

Territories held by opposition
Zones aux mains des forces d'opposition

Main road
Route principale

Border
Frontière

MILES   MILES
0   5   10   15   20
0   5   10   15   20
KILOMETRES

MEDITERRANEAN SEA
MEDITERRANEE

AKKAR
Karamé
Hamzé
Hamadé
BEKAA
ANTI-LIBAN
HQ
SIEGE
BEYROUTH
BEIRUT
Jumblatt
BEKAA
HERMON

Arida
Halba
Abdé
Munié
Tripoli
Zghorta
Hermel
El Kah
Amioun
Les Cèdres
Bcharré
El Laboué
Arsal
Batroun
Btedai
Baalbek
Ghazir
Jounié
Baabda
Haidar
Aley
Chtaura
Rayak
Zahlé
Bar Elias
Beit el Dine
Mreisté
Moukhtara
Chhim
Saghbine
Aïn Zebdé
Katermaya
Jezzine
Machghara
Deir el Aachāyer
Saida
(Sidon)
Rachaya
Chouaya
Fraidiss
El Aarian
Marjayoun
Aaiha
Rachaya Foukhar
Khiam
Libani
Haka
Nana
Sinir
(Syr)
Nakoura

Report of July 1, 1958. (S/4040.)

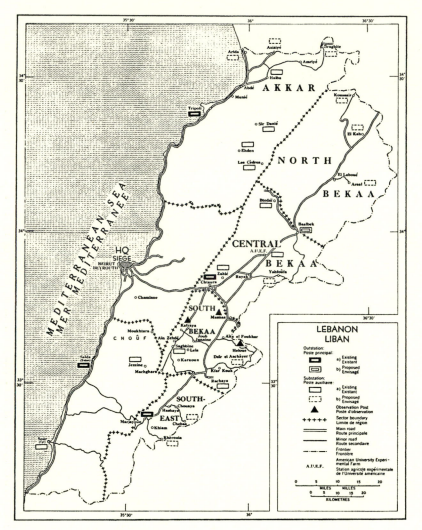

Report of July 25, 1958. (S/4069.)

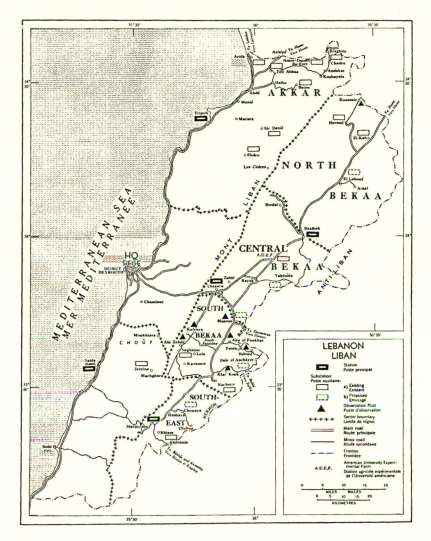

Report of August 12, 1958. (S/4085.)

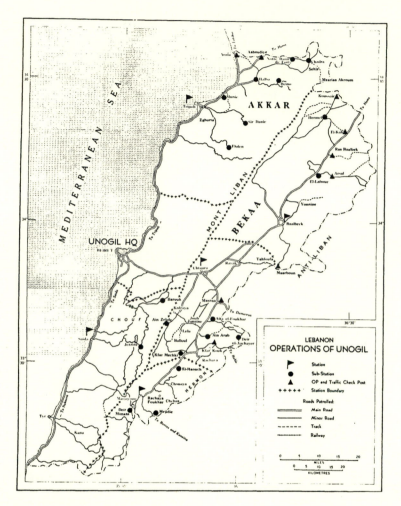

Report of September 21, 1958. (S/4100.)

Report of November 14, 1958. (S/4114.)

12
Doubt, Deliberation, and Preparation

While perhaps it would be better in some situations to request forces than not to, we do not repeat not consider that the introduction of Western forces into Lebanon would either solve the present crisis or enhance Lebanon's long term position in the area.
Dulles to McClintock, June 19, 1958[*]

With the exception of the port city of Tripoli, the areas to the north of Baalbak are largely under the control of the opposition, with pockets of resistance by pro-Government irregulars. The opposition controls the entire border area with Syria. The opposition forces under [Kamal Junblat] are in firm control of most of the Shuf area which in turn poses a serious threat to the environs of Beirut and its airport and to the Beirut Damascus road.
Department of State, June 25, 1958[*]

The Missing Evidence

Three aspects of the Lebanese crisis dominated the month of June 1958. The first was the presence of UNOGIL (United Nations Observation Group in Lebanon) forces; the second was the increasing control of the country won by the opposition in its military-political actions; and the third was the latest phase in the Eisenhower-Dulles ruminations on what was to be done, while continuing to send Sham'un support short of full-scale military intervention.

The case of the missing evidence illustrates the first phase of developments. The evidence that could not be located was that to which Sham'un pointed as proof of the massive intervention by the UAR in Lebanon. It proved an embarrassment to both the U.S. and the U.K. delegations. It perplexed the UNOGIL team, and it stalled but did not derail Western strategy devised in cooperation with Sham'un. That strategy entailed the internationalization of the Lebanese crisis, with Sham'un to request UN military intervention through the Security Council. Such a request would provoke a Soviet veto, according to Western sources, which would put the blame for the continued deterioration of the Lebanese situation on the USSR and free the United States to come to its assistance under Article 51 of the United Nations Charter.[1]

A previous chapter was also involved, since before going to the United Nations, the regime had agreed to have its case heard before the Arab League. The agreement reached there, however, was unacceptable to Sham'un, to the great embarrassment of the Lebanese delegation that accepted its recommendations. Malik's absence from Benghazi was revealing of the low priority in which Arab League recommendations were held. The important audience for Beirut and Washington, and London, was that of the United Nations. The position adopted at the Arab League session was unacceptable to Sham'un; it involved Lebanon's withdrawing its complaint before the United Nations and accepting a course of political conflict resolution at home. That the UAR and Lebanese delegations accepted such counsel made Sham'un's rejection all the more striking, but it did not alter the regime's course.

On the following day Malik was at the UN presenting his case to the Security Council. In a letter dated May 22, the president of the Security Council received formal notification of the complaint lodged by Lebanon regarding intervention by the UAR in Lebanon's domestic affairs. On May 25, the UNF cabled the UN with its denunciation of the regime's claims. In unambiguous terms, an assembly of prominent figures, including a former president and a prime minister, as well as cabinet ministers who had served since the nation's independence, challenged Sham'un's claims and condemned the submission of the conflict before the international organization.[2]

Notwithstanding such protests, or the embarrassment of having Lebanese ambassadors to the United States and Britain defect, Charles Malik presented his case to the Security Council on June 6. With characteristic eloquence and an unfailing confidence in his cause, Malik argued that Lebanon had no choice but to come before the United Nations, given the Arab League's unacceptable verdict. Malik's presentation assumed the legitimacy of historical analogy between Lebanon's regional crisis and the well-known cases of Munich and Manchuria. Beirut's trauma was offered as an opportunity for the international community to act in a manner that it had failed to do earlier. Here, Malik claimed in effect, was a domestic trial that could be understood only in regional and international terms. The structure of his argument began with the claim

> that arms are flowing into Lebanon from Syria; that Lebanese nationals are trained in subversion in Syria; that Syrian civilian nationals are also infiltrating into Lebanon and taking part in subversive activities; and, finally, that United Arab Republic governmental elements direct and, in some instances, take an active part in the subversive activity that is going on in Lebanon today.[3]

It continued with the extension of the undefined Lebanese case to other small states:

> What if the same thing one day happened to them? Are they sure that, if they do not now rally around this small nation, others will rally around them if at some future date they should God forbid, find themselves in the same predicament? The United Nations must above all protect the small nations, and the small nations themselves must co-operate with the United Nations in the protection of any one of them.[4]

What then, asked Foreign Minister Malik, did Lebanon want? The answer was fraternal relations with the UAR that could be achieved if "intervention in all its aspects stop. We want the press and radio campaigns to cease. We want the flow of arms to the insurgents to come to an end. We want the infiltration of subversives to terminate. We want to solve our internal problems in peace, between ourselves, and without external interference."[5]

The Iraqi representative, Fadhil Jamali, reinforced Malik's arguments, with full emphasis on the dangers of Nasserism to the peace of the Middle East and the world. What choice did Lebanon face under the circumstances? To capitulate "and accept being reduced to a satellite, or it will insist on its independence and be subjected to violent attacks and subversion from President Nasser's machinery."[6] Defending the Egyptian/UAR president and denying charges of UAR responsibility for Lebanon's continuing conflict, UAR foreign minister 'Umar Lutfi's rejoinder was as predictable as that of his adversaries. He denied intervention, disclaimed any aggressive intentions on the part of Nasser toward Lebanon, and insisted that the Lebanese civil war was a domestic affair.[7] The same position was echoed by the Soviet delegate, Arkady Sobolev, who insisted that outside intervention risked creating a "dangerous situation in the Near East and may have grave consequences not only for the future of the Lebanese State and its independence, but also for the future of peace in the Near and Middle East."[8]

Speaking for the United States, Henry Cabot Lodge, who had privately emphasized the risks of intervention to Secretary of State Dulles, publicly endorsed the Lebanese position. The purpose of UAR interference, according to Lodge, was to promote insurrection and to destabilize legitimate authority, and by so doing to prevent the restoration of "order and tranquility."[9] Lodge said nothing about the Nasser-Hare talks, although he acknowledged the expressed interests of the UAR in a peaceful resolution of the crisis. On June 11, Lodge moved to support the Swedish resolution before the Security Council, signaling the next phase of UN involvement. With its passage, adopted by all Security Council members save the abstaining USSR, the United Nations became directly involved in the Lebanese case. According to the UNSC resolution, the UN would dispatch an observation team to Lebanon to investigate charges of UAR infiltration.

Among the results of bringing the Lebanese case before the international organization was the decision by the UN to create an observation group that would investigate the charges made by the Beirut regime. Its findings were consistently contrary to those charges, much to the chagrin of the United States and Britain, as well as Lebanon. June 19 was set as the first date of the UNOGIL meeting in Beirut. The UN team, which included Galo Plaza, former president of Ecuador, Rajeshwar Dayal of India, and Major-General Odd Bull of Norway, along with their staffs and military observers, was subsequently increased in size. By June 15, observation groups had been dispatched to various parts of the country, including Tripoli, the Ba'lbak area, and Marjayoun. Beginning its assignment toward the end of June, the UNOGIL team continued to work through November. Rajeshwar Dayal arrived in Beirut on June 18. Within ten days the Security Council received a report from Secretary General Dag Hammarskjöld, describing the situation faced by UNOGIL in Lebanon. In the interim, Hammarskjöld traveled between Beirut, Cairo, and Jerusalem, raising hopes and eliciting skepticism. The UN team was in Lebanon during the entire period of U.S. military intervention, and in that time it produced five reports—two in July, one in August, and one each in September and November. As UN officials reported, their working conditions were hampered by the political divisions of the country, the waning authority of the state, and the limited access available to them—including areas under control of opposition forces. Nevertheless, the UNOGIL team prepared its reports as assigned. It was unable, however. to document the claim of "massive" UAR interference. Excluding border crossings as not constituting anti-regime activities in and of themselves, the team similarly eliminated the bearing of arms as an indelible sign of criminal behavior. As to weapons, the UNOGIL team reported that arms of British, French, and Italian origin were found, but these were in the possession of Lebanese citizens.

In Beirut, Shihab had remained skeptical of the regime's claims from the outset. He discounted the responsibility placed on foreign arms as the motor force of civil strife, and on June 15 he told McClintock:

> There are not more than 300 Syrians operating with insurgents plus perhaps 500 Druzes from across the border who are assisting Junblat not so much as Syrians but as Druze tribesmen. [Shihab] never heard of the 500 Palestinian-Egyptian commandos referred to by [Sham'un] (Deptel 4773). He fixes number of Syrian officers and non-coms who might be operating inside Lebanon as not more than a dozen.[10]

To McClintock, Shihab warned that the Lebanese army could be counted on to "cooperate in a lukewarm way," in the event of U.S. military intervention. In his 1967 account of the Lebanese crisis, McClintock confirmed that the extreme charges leveled at the opposition were vastly exaggerated. The situation on the ground was not what Sham'un or Malik claimed; indeed, McClintock estimated that "there probably were at maximum between five and seven thousand armed men on the insurgent side, with a small but significant cadre in Tripoli, Beirut, and, to a lesser degree, the [Shuf] made up of non-coms and a few officers from Syria."[11] Contrary to the regime's claim that the partisans as well as the equipment were of non-Lebanese origin, McClintock stated that "the bulk of the fighting forces on the rebel side were Lebanese."

In a series of interviews undertaken by Nawaf Salam several years after the outbreak of Lebanon's second civil war, when some of the same political figures were involved, UNF leaders confirmed that the UAR had funded newspapers, military aid, and reinforcement, although they continued to deny that such assistance explained civil war. Furthermore,

Syrian aid—estimated to have been on the order of £E 1.3 million—according to Abdallah al-Mashnuk and Sa'eb Salam, went primarily to the Tripoli region. Hamid Franjiyyah, according to these sources, was identified as the biggest recipient, with Kamal Junblat said to have received the bulk of Syrian arms. Junblat was also identified as having received support from approximately five hundred Syrian Druze, organized by Sultan Pasha al-Atrash.[12] Egyptian ambassador Ghaleb, known for his own charges and countercharges on the subject, was identified as the conduit for an estimated £E80 million, including approximately 12,000 to 14,000 light weapons designed for political, propaganda, and military purposes.[13]

In Beirut, Sham'un rejected the validity of UNOGIL's reports before they were even issued. He was not to be deterred, nor was Secretary of State Dulles. Before some of his NATO allies, Dulles remained adamant about charges of the UAR role, while maintaining the American abhorrence of military intervention, which, he conceded, might be unavoidable. In a June 25 meeting with the Italian ambassador, Dulles pointed to the "many weapons and much Syrian personnel [that] have been sent in across the Lebanese border."[14] The matter was contested.[15] How certain could Secretary Dulles have been if on the same day he cabled McClintock to make every effort to find usable evidence?

> DEPT agrees it would be useful if physical evidence of nature described REFTEL could be made available for possible use in UN. To spike likely rejoinder that evidence merely Egyptian equipment captured by Israelis in Sinai, important it include items bearing dates more recent than 1956 if possible. DEPT will want give thought to exact manner in which evidence might be used.
>
> Re use eye-witnesses in UN DEPT feels this not feasible and might have undesirable consequences. Believe affidavits supplied by GOL preferable. BEIRUT: Report soonest nature of evidence that could be made available.[16]

Sharing the Lebanese predicament with Dulles and the State Department was British ambassador Sir George Middleton, who had cabled the Foreign Office with a similar message. He also reported that an official of the Norwegian Legation in Cairo, who was assisting General Odd Bull of UNOGIL, had some bad news regarding the Lebanese regime's claims. In his Beirut press conference of June 25, Sham'un insisted that there were between 10,000 and 12,000 armed Opposition supporters in Lebanon, of which he estimated that 25 to 30 percent were Egyptians and Syrians.[17] UN observers put the figure closer to 5,000 to 12,000, among whom there were perhaps 300 to 1,000 Syrians. Middleton reported that UN officials could not understand the regime's inability to cope. "They are astonished that the Lebanese are unable, for example, to do a raid with tanks and armoured cars on a village in the north Bekaa [Biqa'] and round up a couple of dozen Syrians."[18] More information followed that constituted an indictment of Sham'un's position:

> 1. The Lebanese have so far produced no evidence before the observers of the infiltrations of men or arms, with the exception of two young men who are Syrians, and who have given to the observers stories which are different from those they told the Lebanese while in their custody. . . .
>
> 5. They believe that there has been a great deal of arming of Moslem villages in the Bekaa from across the Syrian border. Anyone, they believe, would be tempted by the offer of a free rifle and some money and would go over to collect this by night.
>
> 6. So far the observers themselves, including those in helicopters, have seen nothing to prove infiltration. They are debarred from the use of the interrogation reports which U.N.T.G.O. obtained from the Lebanese gangs captured by the Israelis. Not only were these reports obtained in a different context but they were also prior to the arrival in Lebanon of the observer group.   (Ibid.)

Middleton, who was a supporter of Sham'un, nevertheless reported that the impression derived from the Norwegian report was that the UN observers "were suspicions that the fairly heavy firing in Beirut on the night of June 26–27 was laid on by the Government authorities to bring pressure on the Secretary General after his return. Even the press had stated that there were no casualties." It was, as Middleton observed, reported to be a phony situation. In London, Foreign Secretary Selwyn Lloyd was prepared to blame the UN and Hammarskjöld for the problem, not the Lebanese.[19]

While U.S. and U.K. officials confronted the case of the missing evidence, Malik single-mindedly pursued his case before U.S. corporate and political leaders at the Council on Foreign Relations. On June 26, Malik spoke on "The Middle Eastern Crisis Affecting Lebanon." Whereas the UNOGIL team was reporting on the paucity of evidence to sustain Sham'un's charges, Malik asserted that his country was struggling to remain free and independent of the 10,000 UAR forces that were over-running Lebanon and providing the opposition with more than 80 percent of its arms. Lebanon was struggling on behalf of humanity, Malik argued, in a conflict that pitted Lebanon against the Nasserist-communist conspiracy of our time.[20]

Sham'un, on the other hand, was laying the groundwork for the next stage of foreign intervention in Lebanon. Warned by both Britain and the United States not to bypass the United Nations, Sham'un was to make a proposal that was guaranteed of rejection by the Soviet Union, thus leaving the way open for Lebanon to turn to the West for help. With his domestic base eroding and UNOGIL reports undermining his case, Sham'un was in an increasingly untenable position. Even before UNOGIL's July 3 report was issued, he had rejected its findings and continued to insist on the veracity of his arguments. Now relying on the strategy recommended by his supporters, Sham'un turned to Article 51 of the UN Charter, which assured members of the right of "individual or collective self-defense" in the event of armed attack. Requesting assistance under that aegis, then, would be entirely legitimate, provided that support for such assistance and intervention from the United States was forthcoming.[21]

The Lebanese government submitted its own response to the observation group's document.[22] At one and the same time, it sought to condemn the document as incomplete and misleading, yet as confirming, however poorly, the fact of illegal infiltration. It concluded that its original position was unblemished and that

> there has been and there still is massive, illegal, and unprovoked intervention in the affairs of Lebanon by the United Arab Republic; (2) That this intervention aims at undermining and does in fact threaten the independence of Lebanon; (3) That the situation created by this intervention is likely, if it continues, to endanger the maintenance of international peace and security.[23]

Contrary to the observation team's claim that there was no reliable evidence of massive infiltration, the Beirut regime countered with the reply that illegal infiltration had not been discontinued and that the number of armed infiltrators reached into the thousands, and that no less than 30,000 weapons were found to be in the hands of rebel forces who were trained in well-known camps in Syria. None of this was secret, it claimed. As proof, it pointed to the "independent sources of informa-

tion," which enabled the United States, Britain, and France "to corrobo-
rate" such claims, indifferent to the fact that these "independent"
sources were finding that task particularly difficult.[24]

In Beirut, Sham'un's position did not waver, while the UNF countered
claims of UAR intervention with pointed references to the supportive role
of Iraq via the PPS, not to mention Western military assistance. Dulles, in
turn, remained steady in his defense of the regime, irrespective of the fact
that he was among those privy to the precarious nature of Sham'un's
claims with respect to the external origins and determination of the course
of civil war. It was Dulles who categorically misinformed the special congressional meeting on the subject in the aftermath of U.S. intervention and
maintained the fictitious claims of the regime thereafter, referring to the
compilation of the "list of 125 direct acts of aggression by Syria and the
United Arab Republic from May 10 to the end of June," information
derived from U.S. and other intelligence sources in Lebanon.[25]

By the first week of July, Malik was at the State Department demanding U.S. assistance, Socony-Vacuum (Mobil) officials were similarly
pressing to learn of DOS's intentions, and Shah Mohammad Reza
Pahlevi of Iran was lacerating his hosts in the White House for their passivity before the Nasserist menace.

The June Days

While the debates at the United Nations continued, punctuated by
UNOGIL reports from the field, the civil war in Lebanon escalated.
White House, State Department and Defense Department reactions were
calibrated in accordance with the shifting fortunes of the regime on the
ground. Regime losses were reported from Beirut in blunt accounts by
U.S. military sources that left no doubts as to the utter weakness of the
regime, as well as its exaggerated claims. The question remained whether
or not to commit the United States to full-scale military intervention, and
to do so in alliance with Britain. There were doubts on both scores,
although the combination of incremental military assistance and full-
scale public political support for Sham'un consistently belied the efficacy
of such doubts. As to collaborating with Britain in Beirut, Defense and
State Department officials were in accord in opposing such a venue.

Within the first two weeks of June, Dulles and Eisenhower were faced
with renewed requests for military assistance from Sham'un to cope

with the situation. Eisenhower assured Sham'un of support: "the Pres said we should make sure [Sham'un] has what he needs and can use. The Sec thinks he is satisfied. We may want helicopters for the observers— he thinks we are taking steps for this. The Pres indicated definite approval."[26] Additional weapons were quickly sent, as the United States agreed to "make available to the Government of The Lebanon six Hawker-Hunter (Mark VI) military jet aircraft, together with spares and support equipment, not to exceed $2,857,700 in value."[27] On June 13 the British military attaché cabled the War Office from Tel Aviv that Israelis were more worried now by the direction of events in Lebanon than they had been earlier. Colonel Yehoshafat Harkabi, Israeli chief of military intelligence, indicated that "Israel would like to see interven- tion in Lebanon by the West."[28] On June 14, Dulles apologetically explained his interruption of Eisenhower's Gettysburg stay with the news that there was "just a little thing. It is the question of sending to Lebanon Three LCM's and 8,000 rounds of 75 millimeter ammuni- tion."[29] The president was between church and the golf course when Dulles again telephoned, this time to report on a conversation between Malik and Rountree. Malik had been assigned by Sham'un "to find out whether we would, if requested, send military forces into Lebanon," Dulles reported. Given the gravity of the appeal, Eisenhower decided to defer golf and to await further news, which duly arrived from the agi- tated Secretary Dulles.[30]

The staccato of demands for military assistance and commitments to intervene, set against the background of UNOGIL's reports, combined to pressure the administration to clarify its intentions. June 15 emerges as a significant though not a decisive day in this respect. It was a day, and doubtless not the only one, on which the U.S. president and his secretary of state parried back and forth as they expressed their relatively unguarded sentiments about the Lebanese situation. What made it note- worthy was, in fact, precisely this aspect of candor, of inside talk, in which doubts about the viability of a regime that the United States was committed to sustaining were coolly examined. At the same time, the *New York Times* was reporting that the administration was opposed to intervention. Thus, as Jack Raymond reassuringly affirmed, "there was virtually no chance that the United States would come to the support of the [Sham'un] Government with its Sixth Fleet, which patrols the Mediterranean Area."[31] Was it misinformation or disinformation? By the time this was written, the United States had already come to the support of the Lebanese regime, though not yet with the Sixth Fleet. That, however, was not far away on its routine rounds.

In their confidential discussions, Eisenhower and Dulles decided that Sham'un should be told that although the U.S. position on military intervention remained basically unchanged, there were "certain facts," that deserved attention. The facts in question explored the conditions of U.S. military intervention, identifying their purpose as it would be justified in Congress and before the public, though not before U.S. allies in Europe or the Middle East. In this context,

> the primary purpose would be to protect American life and property while at the same time assisting the GOL in its (rpt its) military program for the preservation of the independence and integrity of Lebanon. We believe that any request should be couched in terms of the inability of Lebanon to perform both the function of preserving its own independence and protecting American life and property and therefore the United States is requested to perform the latter function. . . . We went on to say that once the troops are there they would in fact serve to protect the independence of Lebanon.[32]

There was no reference to the Eisenhower Doctrine, already eliminated as inapplicable in the previous month's directives to Sham'un. How was the UN to be dealt with, however? The question was discussed with Sir William Hayter, deputy under secretary of the British Foreign Office. As Hayter acknowledged, it was not feasible to consider intervening in the presence of UN troops.[33] If those troops were to be regarded by the host government as inadequate to offer it protection, there might be other avenues open to Beirut to obtain help. Sham'un was thus to be advised to request an emergency meeting of the UN Security Council for the express purpose of requesting UN forces. The approach had the obvious merit of providing for Lebanese action within the framework of the UN and similarly offering the Anglo-American response an apparent semblance of legitimacy. The success of the strategy, however, was dependent on Soviet rejection of UN military intervention.

These were among the subjects on the agenda on June 15, at a meeting that included a review of the risks and consequences of intervening militarily in the face of UNOGIL's continued assignment, the political fate of Sham'un, and the opposition's successes in Beirut. Among those who participated were President Eisenhower and Secretary of State Dulles, Assistant Secretary Rountree, Department of State officials Macomber and Hanes, Deputy Defense Secretary Quarles, General Twining, Allen Dulles of the CIA, George Allen of the USIA, and Arthur Minnich of the White House. On the question of intervention and the UN, the embarrassment of having U.S. forces intervening while the UNOGIL team was investigating the regime's claims, Secretary Dulles was sanguine on the negative potential. Dulles, who would be faced with criticism on precisely this issue from U.S. allies after July 15, agreed on this occasion that there would be advantages to engaging Jordan and Iraq in some form of action instead. As he observed, "We probably ought not to make an immediate military response before exploring further with Iraq and Jordan what they were willing to do, and before taking certain further actions in the UN [deleted]."[34] William Rountree, assistant secretary for Near East, South Asian, and African Affairs, responded to questions on Sham'un's situation in Beirut, specifically how far the administration could pressure him to be more accommodating. Rountree thought "we would agree that he should not yield on any matter fundamental to the independence of Lebanon, but we would not agree that any reasonable compromise should be excluded."

What was a reasonable compromise, given that what Sham'un considered to be a "fundamental" matter was precisely the terrain of potentially significant compromise? Dulles, for one, did not hesitate to repeat these formulas in his meetings with foreign diplomats, basically leading astray those willing to believe him. The proposition that the United States favored compromise was a stock theme with no basis in practice. Rountree was sober about the probable impact of full-scale military intervention and cognizant of the widespread anti-interventionist sentiment in Lebanon. He warned that should the United States intervene, Sham'un would be in grave political danger and the United States would face the risk of being responsible for a regime incapable of surviving the withdrawal of U.S. troops. "This would mean in all probability a pro-Western dictatorship, since there is not sufficient popular support in Lebanon for western intervention." Eisenhower did not disagree, advising that if intervention proved necessary, the withdrawal of troops should be as rapid as possible. Other options were raised, including "massive military support, possibly accompanied by numbers of technicians, as the Soviets did in Syria, as an alternative to military intervention." Secretary Dulles inclined toward intervention, falling back on arguments of credibility and reminding those present that every pro-Western government would fall if the United States did not intervene. "This leaves us with little or no choice, even though every alternative is 'wrong.' " Eisenhower agreed both with the necessity and with its discontents.

What then was to be done with Sham'un? Eisenhower, Secretary John Foster Dulles, and CIA director Allen Dulles did not so much analyze the Lebanese domestic situation as assess the status of those they considered its three protagonists. Lebanon, for Eisenhower and the two Dulleses, was Sham'un, Malik, and Shihab. Law and order was defined as their uncontested control of state power. Those who challenged it were in the enemy camp. The problem with the Lebanese case, as Eisenhower and the Dulleses considered it, was that its leadership was seriously flawed. Sham'un was weak and Shihab was an incompetent in terms of following orders. Within this triumvirate, there was no choice but to support Sham'un.

What was necessary, Eisenhower opined at the same June 15 meeting, was "a strong leader whom we could back strongly. Otherwise we would be intervening to save a nation; and yet the nation is the people, and the people don't want our intervention." Eisenhower's assessment of the inexplicable failure of Sham'un to fire Shihab led him to pose "a rhetorical question: How can you save a country from its own leaders? [Sham'un], for example, has not yet fired [Shihab], despite more than ample cause."[35] In Beirut, Sham'un was reported as having come to the same conclusion—namely, that the time had come to replace Shihab. "Liquidate" was the graphic word that McClintock used.[36] Beyond the Sham'un-Shihab relationship, Eisenhower was reticent about becoming further involved in a situation in which the U.S. role seemed uncomfortably similar to that of Britain in relation to the Suez crisis, "with the entire population against them." Conceding that the Eisenhower Doctrine did not apply,

> the President considered therefore, what possible future there would be if we intervened except to remain indefinitely. He felt, in this regard, that the arguments which we had advanced to the British and French against their intervention in Suez might be pertinent also in this instance—particularly the question: "where would it lead; where would it end?"[37]

In another version of the same meeting, Eisenhower was reported to have made the analogy with Russia in Hungary. Under the circumstances, "the President wondered about the possibility of the UN requiring help, or of Iraq volunteering assistance—both of which would provide a basis for the United States to aid with arms and money."[38]

In the interim, there were rumors about a military coup that roused Secretary Dulles.[39] McClintock described Sham'un's mental state as grim. Sham'un, he cabled, was "in definite Gotterdammerung mood," as he put his wife's jewels in the safety of the U.S. Embassy and expressed concern for his family's security.[40] Rountree, meanwhile, was in consultation with Secretary Dulles about Anglo-American contingency plans developed by the Joint Chiefs of Staff in accord with Britain. To Rountree and others in the State and Defense Departments, they extended earlier plans in a manner considered unacceptable.[41] Admiral Holloway, commander in chief of U.S. Specified Command in the Middle East, who was to play a major role in Operation Blue Bat, reacted to the proposals negatively.[42]

These preparations aside, Sham'un was to be repeatedly warned of the disinclination of the United States to intervene. Dulles, in systematic style, reviewed the events of the month indicating the paths to be taken. At the United Nations, for example, Sham'un was reminded that Lebanon would have to call for an emergency session of the Security Council in order to be in a position to request "friendly military forces," which, as Dulles carefully observed, did not mean "that we would require the concurrence or recommendation of UNSYG prior to military assistance to GOL but some further reference to UN is necessary, and undoubtedly SYG's views would carry weight with other UN members."[43] Dulles did not fail to assure Sham'un of U.S. confidence in him, an approach designed to encourage Sham'un to assume that he had unconditional U.S. backing. "Tell him," he directed McClintock, "that we realize that he is the symbol of Lebanon's determination to defend its independence and integrity and the extensive support we have provided to the government over which he presides should convince him of our determination to stand by him in his efforts to resolve this crisis."

For all of these unmistakable signs of support, Dulles cautioned Sham'un about the self-perpetuating character of foreign intervention and the untold problems it might entail. In a series of straightforward warnings, Dulles clearly emphasized that the United States did not regard full-scale military intervention as a solution to Lebanon's political crisis; on the contrary, the Eisenhower administration feared that intervention would exacerbate the situation in a dangerous way. This was, perhaps, Dulles's most forthright statement on the subject. While it did not eliminate military intervention, it presented that as an option the U.S. preferred not to choose. As Dulles cabled Beirut for Sham'un: "we do not repeat not consider that the introduction of Western forces into Lebanon would either solve the present crisis or enhance Lebanon's long term position in the area."

The United States was prepared to provide assistance to make intervention unnecessary, as the Eisenhower administration feared the havoc—including confessional strife—that intervention might bring. Dulles's remarks suggested that he wished Sham'un to know that the United States was fully aware of intra-Christian differences on the question, which would prevent Sham'un from exploiting U.S. support for Lebanon's Christian population as though it were a monolithic bloc. Intervention, in Dulles's view, might

> set into train indigenous trends toward Lebanon's ultimate territorial partition or truncation. Lebanon's integrity would be assured only as long as foreign forces remained on Lebanese soil. Moreover, intervention could and probably would lead to solidification of opposition throughout Moslem world not only to Christians in Lebanon but to the West in general.   (Ibid.)

Finally, Dulles pointed to one of the administration's major concerns, namely, that U.S. intervention would directly promote Nasser's standing in the Arab world. Dulles considered this a virtual "certainty," insisting that it could generate "strong popular feeling which could well sweep away regimes or pro-Western Arab leaders in other countries. In this event the prospects of diminishing Western position in the Arab world, which is one of Nasser's prime objectives, would be greatly furthered" (ibid.). Dulles's warnings, and his repeated emphasis on the risks of U.S. intervention to Lebanon, had no noticeable influence on Sham'un's political demeanor. He remained politically intransigent, and the United States, in spite of the warnings issued, remained his chief backer. Washington's man in Beirut may have had clay feet, as far as Eisenhower and Secretary Dulles recognized, but they continued to hold him up.

While the administration deliberated on what was to be done in Beirut, matters came to a head in Amman. Jordanian prime minister Rifai alerted the United States about assassination plots against King Husayn, which confirmed U.S. ambassador Thomas K. Wright's opinion that "present HKJ pro-western government headed Prime Minister al-Rifa'i lacks popular support, is maintained in power only through imposition martial law carried out by army/security forces loyal to King [Husayn]."[44] The Jordanian crisis was a matter of British concern and Anglo-American planning. In London and Washington, evocations of Amman in turmoil immediately raised the possibility of Israeli incursion into the West Bank. That possibility, as Dulles explained to Mahmud Fawzi, when the two engaged in extensive talks on the Middle East in the fall of 1958 at the United Nations, was what conditioned Anglo-American policy vis-à-vis Israel, Jordan, and the Palestinians. In the early summer of 1958, the predicament of the Jordanian monarch appeared to be inseparable from that of the Lebanese president. The reason was not the parallels between the two states but the weaknesses of both regimes and the opposition they inspired in their respective—though highly diverse—populations.

The outbreak of civil war in Lebanon had forced the Eisenhower administration to confront the importance of maintaining a viable Lebanese regime in the broader context of U.S. policy in Lebanon and the Middle East. In the course of the following months, Eisenhower and Dulles pursued a policy that consisted of reinforcing Sham'un while insisting on its reluctance to intervene militarily. In the process, the administration in Washington adapted and adopted the Lebanese regime's rationalization of its own policies. That is, Washington echoed Sham'un's interpretation of civil war as a function of foreign meddling that simultaneously deflected attention from the domestic origins of the crisis and focused attention on its allegedly regional causes and their international implications. Dulles was to supplement this, with help from others, when the United States was on the point of intervening militarily. In the interim, he disseminated the administration's statement of the crisis to foreign visitors, to U.S. diplomats, and to NATO and other allies. The picture in Lebanon was confusing, he admitted, "but basic issue is that a civil war is going on in Lebanon which would not be prolonged and might not have started without foreign intervention."[45] Claiming historical parallels, Dulles referred to Munich, Manchuria, Abyssinia, and the Korean War.

In a manner reminiscent of Malik at the United Nations, Dulles supported the view that Lebanon was, in fact, a "test case for preservation of independence of small states and respect of their right to solve their internal problems by themselves." If the UN failed to act in time and so prevent this noxious interference, "it would be a terrible thing for conscience of world if small state like Lebanon, in danger of losing its independence as the result of indirect aggression, were to appeal for help and this help were refused." U.S. diplomats were warned to emphasize that this was not yet U.S. policy, and Dulles added, "we are frank to say that we do not clearly see end of this crisis although of course we hope for political solution by the Lebanese." Brief reference to doubts that colored inside talk among Eisenhower, Dulles, and administration officials and that were conveyed to Sham'un appeared in the following formulation but was overruled, albeit with some awkwardness:

> While we entirely agree that repercussions of Western military presence in Lebanon would be extremely grave we feel that insufficient attention and consideration has been devoted to the consequences of not responding to an appeal for help from Lebanon after UN has been tried and failed, permitting that nation to go under. It may be that Free World will be faced with eventual need to decide what course to follow in this dangerous crisis.   (Ibid.)

The closing refrain in this advisory to U.S. diplomats was revealing: "You should emphasize that extreme sensitivity of this question requires absolute secrecy be maintained re NAC discussions of it."

The United States Versus Lebanon

Contrary to the assumption implicit in U.S. and Lebanese rationalizations of civil war—that the motor force determining action in Beirut was the subversive interference of UAR agents—it was the progress of opposition forces on the ground that moved Washington closer to full-scale military intervention. The advance of the opposition explained the intensity of Sham'un's demands for assistance from Washington and the decision by Eisenhower and Dulles to respond to Sham'un. The above belied the highly suggestive claims that Dulles repeatedly made to the effect that the United States favored compromise above military commitment.

Embassy reports from Beirut reflected the tension in the city as Beirut awaited the visit of Secretary General Dag Hammarskjöld, while the opposition was described as maintaining a low profile to enhance its credibility. The Sham'un regime, on the other hand, was in a state of constant alert, beleaguered by embarrassing resignations and defections. The minister of justice, who had been at the Arab League Council meetings in Benghazi, submitted his resignation. There were even rumors that Commander in Chief Shihab himself had resigned and that the president had taken over his functions. Comparisons with 1956 were rife, as were fears that intervention might ignite a third world war. Trains from Beirut to Damascus were reported to be crowded. TAPLINE families had decided to leave, taking advantage of what air travel remained accessible. And other members of the international community in Lebanon appeared similarly inclined. Gasoline was running low in the capital, and military escorts were required to accompany gasoline trucks from Sidon. The sense of crisis affected the financial markets. Bankruptcies threatened, foreign investment was expected to decline, and expectations of price instability abounded. In addition, there was fear of increased shortages, layoffs, and work stoppages, as "distribution pattern national income is being greatly distorted from normal with many hardships anticipated groups with least savings."[46]

Evidence of the contraction of state power was everywhere, in autonomous zones that were scattered throughout the country. In Sidon, opposition deputy Mar'uf Sa'd reported that "plans being laid for establishment free Lebanese Government if crisis continues much longer."[47] In Beirut, the Basta functioned as a semiautonomous region, where "entry and exit strictly controlled by Basta elements and GOL forces unable to enter. Information not as extensive on Tripoli but Embassy has impression same process going on there."[48] Fighting was taking place in Tripoli and Ba'lbak, according to Lebanese intelligence. So intense was the conflict in the Tripoli area that the army and gendarmerie had been forced to withdraw. Intelligence reports confirmed that Lebanese security feared attacks on the presidential palace and the airport from Muslim quarters.[49] The reference was to the advance of Kamal Junblat's forces, whose Syrian Druze partisans were reported to be leaving. Sham'un had ordered Shihab to launch a new offensive on the morning of June 21.[50]

The Embassy received information from Lebanese intelligence, which, among other things, kept it informed of the progress of Junblati forces as well as other opposition developments, including activities of the Third Force. To Secretary Dulles, McClintock emphasized the extent to which U.S. intervention was opposed by a wide range of political groups, who had alternative political solutions to offer. Among the sources that McClintock cited were the Lebanese newspaper *Beirut al-Massa*, an "extreme opposition paper banned by GOL," which expressed the views of those who opposed intervention and who feared the outbreak of World War III.[51] There was nothing "extreme" in the support it offered to Junblat's position on parliamentary and presidential elections, electoral reform, and the urgency of a transitional government. Nor was there anything exceptional in its endorsement of a neutralist foreign policy and its criticism of Sham'un's attitude toward the work of UNOGIL. What was exceptional was McClintock's single-minded and futile effort to persuade the administration that opposition to intervention was too extensive to ignore, even in circles considered friendly to the United States.

In this context, McClintock offered the evidence of Raymond Eddeh, a member of the Third Force who opposed intervention, believing that it would encourage Sham'un's presidential ambitions. Eddeh had no illusions about the prospects of political compromise under Sham'un. The Third Force member, however, supported a compromise that called for a cease-fire and truce and a commitment to parliamentary and presidential elections, the latter to be set for July 24, with by-elections to follow. The opposition, by calling off its strike, would help bring about the cease-fire, and if the regime agreed not to pursue its leaders unless criminal action was involved, there was a chance that it would succeed. The army would assist by protecting the opposition, and a general amnesty would subsequently be granted, with compensation offered the innocent victims of war.[52]

The Council of Ministers did indeed meet to consider some compromise proposals, but to no avail. Sham'un responded to the opposition by issuing arrest warrants for fifteen of its members and by rejecting Eddeh's proposals, along with those of Junblat. In addition to this discouraging news, McClintock cabled Dulles that Fawzi al-Huss, Sunni deputy to the Lebanese Parliament, had resigned. While Lebanese critics were not much taken with a move that came too late in the course of the conflict to signal a meaningful political act, it was viewed otherwise by the Embassy. Here was another influential conservative who had given up on Sham'un—or calculated that it served his purposes better to exit at this stage.[53]

Hammarskjöld arrived in Beirut from Cairo, landing in the midst of this grim political environment. His visit did not alter the political landscape, although he met with various religious personalities, all of whom opposed intervention and so indicated. They included the Maronite patriarch, the Druze sheikh, the Grand Mufti, and a Shi'ite spiritual leader.[54] Against mounting signs of support for the Opposition and for a general condemnation of military intervention, the Sham'un regime responded that the Lebanese army, working with UN observers, was fully capable of sealing the state's borders and pacifying the country. In the interim, news that Secretary of Defense Neil McElroy had discussed the use of B-47s with atomic capability in the context of limited war, including possibly Lebanon, did little to dampen fears that military intervention was imminent. Efforts by the Defense Department to deny the relevance of McElroy's remarks to U.S. policy in Lebanon were ineffective. They may, in fact, have been central to the debate on "limited war" versus "massive retaliation" then ongoing in Washington, in which the Lebanese case served those who were partisans of "limited war."

By the end of June, U.S. military reconsideration of the Lebanese situation supported the view that the regime was on the point of collapse. In addition, there were rumors of possible coups within the military. In a June 25 U.S. Army analysis, Sham'un's control was defined as extending—although not firmly—from the central and southern Biqa' to south Lebanon. The forces of the opposition were in control of the area bordering Syria, Ba'lbak, and regions to the north. In the Basta area of Beirut, opposition leader Sa'eb Salam posed "an increasingly serious threat to the entire city of Beirut," while opposition forces of Kamal Junblat were depicted as threatening the capital itself. "The Opposition forces under Kamal Junblat are in firm control of most of the Shuf area, which in turn poses a serious threat to the environs of Beirut and its airport and to the Beirut—Damascus road."[55] Conceding Shihab's reluctance to assume a more aggressive role and recommending his dismissal, the U.S. military further confirmed the dissidence of army commanders, such as those in the south. UAR forces were described as prominent supporters of the opposition in the Basta and in the Shuf, while the regime was forced to rely on "irregulars and paramilitary groups," such as the PPS. Sham'un's situation was considered highly vulnerable, with two different military coups rumored, one involving pro-government supporters reputed to be unlikely candidates for success, the other involving senior officers said to be under Colonel 'Adel Shihab's direction and to be prepared to oust Shihab and Sham'un in order to restore order and support "the establishment of a provisional regime basically pro-Western but more moderately so than the present regime."

Under the circumstances, what could be expected of Sham'un? The same U.S. sources discounted the possibility of political compromise in the light of Sham'un's rejection of concessions and the "equally intransigent position of the extremist opposition elements." The Third Force was considered to be powerless. Sham'un could replace Shihab and order the army to get more actively involved, or he could request assistance from the UN in cordoning off the Syro-Lebanese border. While it was unclear that the UN would agree to such a role, Sham'un would still face internal challenges from the opposition. The third option, about which no more was said on this occasion, was the appeal for military intervention by the United States and Britain.

The alarm lest opposition forces effectively coordinate an attack on Beirut was probably the single most important factor preoccupying the U.S. military and White House advisers. And it was intensified at the end of the month when Junblat's forces attempted to occupy the capital in a battle lasting several days. Sham'un directly ordered the army to intervene, supported—according to opposition sources—by "gendarmes, PPS, Jordanians, and Iraqis," as well as some Bahrayni subjects and even a British officer posing as an Arab.[56] More important than the anecdotal information concerning stray foreigners was Junblat's assessment of the reasons for the failure of the opposition's military advance. It was an explanation that must have had particular appeal to Washington. According to Junblat, the failure of the opposition forces to take the capital was caused not by pro-government fighters but by the intentional defection of opposition leaders in Beirut.

At his June 25 press conference, Sham'un continued to argue that the majority of Lebanese stood with him and to insist that the civil war was inflamed by UAR forces.[57] Moreover, he repeatedly asserted that Lebanon would act only through the United Nations. In addition, he offered an estimate of the number of partisans in the opposition. The figure was 10,000 to 12,000, of which 25 to 30 percent were from the UAR, Sham'un claimed. Finally, to clarify his domestic plans, Sham'un made it clear that he intended no reforms, no changes in governing, and no departure from office until the end of his term, i.e., September 23. Until that time, there was no question of Shihab's becoming prime minister or of any other proposals being accepted. To Sham'un, his losses on the ground were the stuff of other people's fantasies.

In spite of this state of affairs, Dulles continued to present an image of U.S. intentions in Lebanon as both protective and conducive to compromise; his language was codified and opaque, though suggestive of America's commitments to a peaceful resolution of Lebanon's domestic crisis. Thus, in meetings with the Italian ambassador and counselor, as in his instructions to U.S. ambassadors meeting with NATO allies, Dulles maintained the same posture, repeating U.S. opposition to intervention and its imminent necessity, while reviewing the options facing President Sham'un.[58] To his Italian guests, Dulles argued that the United States was opposed to intervention but equally concerned about inaction on behalf of the regime that continued to rely on the UN. What Dulles omitted to mention were the Anglo-American recommendations to Sham'un on how to evade the UN while appearing to work within its guidelines. Instead, he indicated that "other possibilities will have to be looked into. There has been evidence that Iraq, Turkey, and Pakistan are all deeply concerned by the situation. The position of Iran is not known, although presumably they will be more cautious."[59] In fact, Iran was not at all cautious, as its Shah demonstrated in his passionate advocacy of intervention to President Eisenhower and Secretary of State Dulles several days later in Washington. As for Beirut, Dulles concluded that "it is, of course, possible that some internal compromise will be achieved which will remove the necessity for outside assistance to the Lebanese regime."

Anglo-American contingency plans that were issued on June 23 had been requested by Eisenhower on June 15. They revealed the political and military outlook as well as the internal differences of Anglo-American military planners. There was, for example, a common understanding in the memorandum by the Joint Middle East Planning Group for the Joints Chiefs of Staff that the Lebanese army, as well as the political elite, were politically unreliable. As to differences among the Anglo-American military officers, these were mirrored in the divergent positions on the nature and extent of the military undertaking involved. On the American side, the minimalist option was favored. Apprehensive about the viability of the Lebanese regime, the U.S. military appeared reluctant to introduce a long-term occupation, an undesirable option that "would materially reduce the U.S. ground forces available to meet requirements for general war." The objectives of military action were, in fact, defined as protecting U.S.-U.K. citizens and restoring "the friendly government." Regardless of the scope of the operation, it was assumed that "long-term military support of an independent Lebanese Government will be required."[60] Stripped of its political justification, the "Study of the Long Range Military Implications of U.S./U.K. Intervention in Lebanon" began by discounting the possibility of an attack led by the UAR, and jettisoned any talk of a Lebanese solution through political means.

The goal of the report was to estimate the "magnitude of U.S. military forces which may be required in Lebanon for an extended period of time as a result of U.S.-U.K. military intervention." If intervention extended beyond the mere protection of U.S. nationals, less than half of the Lebanese military could be expected to cooperate. The Lebanese army was of "doubtful reliability . . . which would preclude [its] use in the initial phase of operations in support of an independent Lebanese Government." The operation, identified as Blue Bat, was to involve air, naval, military, and amphibious forces "to assist the friendly government in the maintenance of order, to protect U.S.-U.K. nationals and interests, and in the event of the fall of the government, to reestablish the friendly government." Plans included "maintaining order and neutralizing opposition forces," to enable interventionary forces to reestablish order. Distinguishing between overall and limited objectives, the former projected an operation in the whole of Lebanon, while the latter concentrated on the Beirut region. U.S. Defense and State Department officials were in accord that such an operation was to be based on limited objectives only and that it was imperative not to encourage the more ambitious British planners.

The plan under consideration on June 23 included both a preliminary and an expanded set of objectives, however. The limited goal was defined as "containing the key airfield and Lebanese government installations . . . initial operations will be directed at establishing control of the air space over the area of operations, securing the Beirut airfield, the port and city of Beirut." After appropriate contacts had been established with Lebanese officials, this plan was to be augmented in the following manner:

> Expanded operations would be undertaken with a view toward securing control of interior key communications centers, main roads and railroads, and effectively sealing the Lebanese-Syrian border and Lebanese coastline. Since the reliability and effectiveness of indigenous Lebanese armed forces at the time these operations would be undertaken cannot be accurately predicted, it can only be assumed that they would be used to the maximum extent practicable. Should the forces committed under BLUE BAT prove to be incapable of accomplishing these operations, augmentation forces, probably from CONUS [the Continental United States], would be required.   (Ibid.)

British and U.S. officials maintained the formal position that military intervention was the "last resort" to save the Sham'un regime.[61] Once the decision to intervene had been made, however, it was understood that Sham'un would adopt the strategy vis-à-vis the UN that had been recommended earlier. Sham'un would eventually come before the UN General Assembly to appeal for emergency intervention under the articles of the Uniting for Peace Resolution. Anglo-American forces would intervene, possibly aided by those of the Arab Union. Sir William Hayter defined British objectives at this point as "limited," i.e.,

> to occupying and restoring order in Beirut and Tripoli, at the airfield at Rayak, and at any other places which it is necessary to hold for purely military purposes. Any attempt to extend beyond these centres to the frontiers, would mean committing Anglo/U.S. forces to the restoration of internal security throughout the country, which we think we should at all costs try to avoid.

The view from London was that the more comprehensive objective would nonetheless have to be considered, and that the U.S. State and Defense Departments were inclining in such a direction. But on the U.S. side, there was a distinct cooling that was interpreted in London as a temporary matter.[62]

Other sources were also pressuring the State Department during this period. Among regional allies and dependents, the Iranian Shah was second to none in the vehemence of his support for military intervention in defense of the Lebanese regime. And the Israeli government, with or without U.S. knowledge, undertook its own reconnaissance operation in Beirut harbor less than a week before Operation Blue Bat went into effect. On the other hand, the CIA opposed Secretary Dulles's view of Nasser and Arab nationalism as a necessary impediment to U.S. policy, while U.S. oil companies attempted to obtain clarification from the State Department as to the U.S. decision on Beirut. And Malik, ever impatient and demanding of State Department officials, was submitting itemized lists of arms and equipment for paramilitary groups operating in support of the Lebanese army and insisting that Lebanon be given no less aid than was given Greece a decade earlier.[63]

It was the Shah of Iran, however, with his anti-Arab and anti-Nasserist passion, who dismissed Eisenhower's and Dulles's hesitations as rank cowardice. The performance of the Iranian leader, whose dependence on American support and whose reliance on the network of pro-American allies in the Middle East was unmatched, was amazing in its arrogance and alarming in its implications for policy. It was outdone only by Dulles's mimicking of the Shah's anti-Nasserist denunciations. Intervention in Lebanon was an obligation, not a choice, according to the Iranian ruler. The inapplicability of the Eisenhower Doctrine was irrelevant, as was the search for a proper justification. When they met on July

1, Eisenhower, Dulles, and Rountree confronted the Shah with a series of questions on intervention and its risks. Eisenhower emphasized its negative aspects, including the fact that foreign troops would be viewed as supporting Sham'un rather than Lebanese independence. While Eisenhower and Dulles agreed that not to intervene would be worse, they sought the Shah's opinion on its consequences in the Middle East. Why?

Since the Shah's views on the subject were predictable, it is difficult not to question the value of the exercise. Was it confirmation that Dulles was looking for? If so, his guest was a perfect choice, as his identification of Nasserism with communism articulated a theme close to the secretary of state and some of his other Middle East informants, such as Charles Malik. Further, the Shah pointed to the issue of credibility and the domino effect that the fall of Sham'un might have in the region, i.e., if Sham'un fell, then Jordan and Iraq would go, and so on. More interesting was the Shah's view of the political roles of Israel and Saudi Arabia as countervailing forces. The existence of the Israeli state, he observed, "had an advantage in controlling somewhat Arab expansionism."[64] Eisenhower recalled on this occasion that the Shah had earlier advised him of the role he had recommended for the Saudi monarch, "namely, that the King's prestige should be built up as Keeper of the Holy Places and as a leader of the Arab people to counter Nasser. Dulles observed that King Saud had been making some progress in this direction but had virtually collapsed following the abortive plot with Sarraj."

The promotion of the Saudi monarch as favored antagonist of Nasserist forces was not a banal proposition. It had been previewed in the State Department's earlier recommendation (in 1952) in the aftermath of the Free Officers' seizure of state power. Then, the question raised was the possibility that the Free Officers might consider raising Suez Canal fees, which would directly affect the price of U.S. and Western oil. A Saudi role was envisioned to blunt the impact of such a risk and to represent U.S. oil interests indirectly. Six years later, Nasserism had become a major preoccupation in the Dulles State Department, and the promotion of the Saudi monarch had not been effective in containing its expansion. Nonetheless, the role that the Shah recommended for Saudi Arabia conformed entirely with what Dulles had hoped for. It coincided, moreover, with the early signs of an emerging "Petro Islam," as Aziz al-Azmeh has described it.[65] The marriage of oil and politics in the oil kingdoms was readily framed in the language of religion, a combination with political potential in the struggle against

Nasserism, Ba'thism, and other expressions of populist and radical Arab politics.

On the occasion of the Shah's July 1 visit, Eisenhower had countered the Shah's suggestion with the observation that some advocated a more conciliatory policy toward Nasser in order to win him to the West, referring to U.S. policymaking circles. With evident irritation, the Shah vented his view of Egypt as "nothing but a few million unhappy and impoverished beggars. Nasser's ambition was to gain control of large areas in the Middle East." Of course, if the price of cooperation was not excessive, it might be considered, the Shah conceded. Dulles, in an effort to reassure the Shah of his own hostility to Nasser, corrected an earlier reference to U.S. policy in 1956. That, Dulles explained, had been designed to save not Nasser but the United Nations. Far from being neutral on Nasser, Dulles made it clear that he viewed Nasser as consumed by the desire to control Western oil interests, to which the Shah added that those ambitions reflected Soviet efforts to promote nationalization schemes throughout the Arab world. Between them, the demonization of the Egyptian/UAR president was capped by the Shah's comparisons of Nasser to Hitler and Dulles's comparisons of pan-Arabism with "Hitler's pan-Germanism."

Eisenhower appeared to be restrained in this context, reminding the Shah that the USSR did not need Arab oil. He was doubtless gratified to hear how well the shah had learned the lessons of 1951–1953, as the Shah affirmed that it had taken the Iranians the years of the Mossadeq era to discover that there was no profit without cooperation with Western oil companies.

"Nasser obviously wanted to use the oil for blackmail," the Shah continued. "Even if, in the process of seizing oil in other Arab countries he found that he could not in fact export it, he would be losing nothing since Egypt itself now had no exportable oil resources." To these and other lessons, Eisenhower declared himself grateful, "very much impressed with the Shah's views on the Middle East situation." And as a parting thought, the Shah offered his own policy of "constructive nationalism" as an alternative to Nasserism, communism, and "positive neutrality." Here again, Eisenhower responded with the caveat that nationalism without liberalism and other "free world ideals" had its own dangers.

On the day after this meeting, Under Secretary of State Christian Herter met with Socony-Vacuum executives, who were probing the State Department about U.S. policy in Beirut. Herter was equivocal about intervention, suggesting that it was no more than one of a number of options facing the United States, although Herter emphasized that the victory of the Lebanese "rebels" would encourage Nasserist elements in Jordan and Iraq. He was quick to add that U.S. intervention might have the same effect.[66] On the very same day, according to Herter's papers, plans were being made to obtain "a waiver for the president's signature that allows us leeway and doesn't require new findings each time so that we could be in a position to supply small arms to Lebanon over the next three or so weeks."[67]

On July 7 Dulles met with Dag Hammarskjöld, at which time he calmly informed the UN secretary general that the United States was moved by moral obligations toward its allies in the region. Washington favored political compromise, Dulles explained, pointing to the desirability of finding a "third solution which would involve preserving the independence of Lebanon, while at the same time avoiding any victory for Nasser through a political compromise of [Sham'un] with the rebel elements."[68] Was this an allusion to the Cairo-Beirut connection? From Beirut, McClintock informed Dulles that Sham'un "had once and for all buried issue of his re-election in his statement to AP/Associated Press."[69]

While still denying intervention in Washington, in the second week of July the U.S. Embassy in Beirut was conducting surveys of the geopolitical condition of the Lebanese landscape. Through interviews and brief assessments of regional economies—including areas of deprivation, the functioning of IPC terminals, the conditions of roads, bridges, and wadis, radio and telephone connections with the capital—the Embassy collected data. For what purpose? Was this a routine exercise or a preliminary survey of the political lay of the land in anticipation of military intervention?

On July 9–10, the villages in the Batrun district were investigated, along with Tripoli, the IPC terminal, the district of Kura, and part of Zgharta. In Tripoli an IPC official reported on evidence of starvation and typhoid, leading U.S. Embassy officers to add that "Tripoli was always an economic hardship area. Now it is believed many people are in very serious economic difficulty."[70] IPC was shut down, apparently because its storage capacity was filled and the demand from Beirut was reduced.

Dispatch 46, of July 14, dealt with southern Lebanon, where local political conflict reflected the Sham'unist-Opposition struggles of the capital. Virtually everyone was described as supporting the opposition. Embassy reports underlined the miserable economic conditions of the south, noting that it suffered from "overdependence upon day labor and positions in Tyre, Sidon, and particularly Beirut, and lack of locally administered and staffed public works programs. Present harvests and the immediate agricultural outlook point to continued and increasing economic woes"—in sum, conditions long identified by labor leaders and political activists from these regions and ignored in the capital.

Dispatch 48, covering the route from Beirut, Sidon, Rum, Jezzine, Kfar Hunah, Beit ed-dine, and Bissur, was—with the exception of Sidon—pro-Sham'un in orientation. In this region, the report pointed out, there was widespread support for the regime and hostility toward the United Nations. Economic conditions were not adversely affected by the crisis, despite the fact that tourism had declined. Road conditions were good, "no telephone poles down" between Jezzine and Kfar Hunah, and between Beirut and Sidon, and more generally, "most important bridges are guarded by army and partially barricaded with a barbed wire fence on alternate sides at each end. There is a military check point at the entrance to the Sidon refinery compound." Concluding their survey, Leslie Polk and James Akins noted that there was often a general confusion surrounding the crisis but that they found the expression of hope for "the early solution of the crisis in the most peaceful manner possible."

Other significant preparations were under way as well, this time conducted by an Israeli "special forces intelligence-gathering operation" in Beirut harbor, one week before U.S. forces landed. "On July 9, 1958, a small force of IDF/navy commandos conducted a top-secret intelligence-gathering mission into Beirut harbor."[71] The action was carried out by a crew that approached the Beirut coast via an IDF/navy torpedo boat under the direction of a crew expert in sabotage and demolition. Classified as a success by the Israeli military in spite of the fact that it was uncovered by a Lebanese sentry whose alert brought Lebanese patrols that effectively terminated the effort, it was described as an effortless triumph in which "the underwater reconnaissance mission was attended to with routine ease. The divers, utilizing special and secret equipment, charted the harbor facility and made notations for future reference." The objective was "to lay the groundwork for a possible naval attack against Lebanese shipping should another full-scale conflagration erupt."[72] Sham'un was reputed to have "received some five hundred Thompson, Beretta, and Bren submachine guns from Israel."[73] And the then commander of Israel's Northern Command, Yitzhak Rabin, later recalled cooperating with Sham'un to prevent arms from Syria from reaching Lebanon.

In Washington, meanwhile, CIA analysts argued against the view that Nasserism and Arab nationalism were expressions of Soviet manipulation or that Arab nationalism was antithetical to U.S. interests. They proposed, on the contrary, that "the Arab objectives of maintaining independence and of utilizing the profits of Arab oil are compatible with two crucial U.S. interests—denial of the area to Soviet domination and maintenance of Western access to Middle East oil."[74]

> We do not believe that Nasser is a Communist or sympathetic to the Communist doctrine. He opposes Arab Communists because they are a challenge to his own authority. He regards the Soviet Union as a great power with interests and policies in the Middle East which happen at this stage to coincide with his own. He will continue to look to the USSR for support and to be responsive to Soviet allegations against the West. We believe that he continues to hope that the integrity of the Arab union he is trying to create will be protected by a balance of Soviet and Western influence in the Arab area, despite the events of the past three years which have certainly deepened Nasser's suspicions of the West and probably reduced his distrust of the Soviets.

This epitomized the position that Shah Mohammad Reza Pahlevi regarded as ignoble, that the Israeli government considered naive, that Lebanese foreign minister Malik fought to undermine, that U.S. oil companies rejected, and that U.S. secretary of state Dulles similarly set aside in his undeclared policies of going all the way in support of the Sham'un regime.

PART V

The Minefield Explodes:
U.S. Military Intervention

13

11,000 Sorties in Search of a Target

*Whatever happens in Iraq and other parts of the area,
we must, I think, not only try to bolster up both the
loyalties and the military and economic strength of
Lebanon and Jordan, we must also, and this seems to
me even more important, see that the Persian Gulf
area stays within the Western orbit. The Kuwait-
Dhahran-Abadan areas become extremely important
and Turkey and Iran have become more important.
We shall seek ways to help them be sturdy allies, first
in quality and second in quantity, insofar as that quantity can be usefully provided and maintained.*
Eisenhower to Macmillan, July 18, 1958*

Iraq, Lebanon, the United States, and Great Britain: Reflections on Connections

"At 2100 hours on the night of 13–14 July, the Twentieth Infantry Brigade, led by Staff Brigadier Ahmad Haqqi and consisting of three battalions of about a thousand men each, broke camp at Jalawla and, with Jordan as its ultimate destination, moved toward Baghdad, 140 kilometers to the southwest."[1] Some five hours later, Staff Colonel 'Abd al-Salam 'Arif, commander of the third battalion, altered the army's direction and with it, that of the state. The objective was no longer Jordan but Baghdad. The purpose, no longer securing the Jordanian monarchy but eliminating that in Iraq. Early on the morning of July 14 the nation was informed that the army had so acted, assuring it that power would be entrusted to a republic in the name of the people. By high noon, Staff Brigadier 'Abd al-Karim Qasim, commander of the 19th Infantry Brigade Third Division, arrived in Baghdad to assume the direction of the Defense Ministry.

The military coup that aspired to be a revolution set off seismic waves that reached well beyond the Euphrates and the eastern Mediterranean. No political figure, whether in Europe, the United States, or the Soviet Union, let alone the Middle East and North Africa, was indifferent to what transpired in Baghdad. None failed to grasp that a line had been crossed whose impact it was impossible to deny or to have foreseen. The events of Baghdad shocked by their brutality, but it was not only the violent end of the royal family that struck awe, it was also the sense of being witness to power of an altogether different kind. Hanna Batatu's description of Baghdad following the army's seizure of state power on the morning of the July 14, when the royal family had already been killed, captures the mood of the time. Supporters of the Free Officers who had organized the coup, including members of the Communist Party, whose role in Iraqi political mobilization had long preceded the events of July, now emerged in a crescendo of support.

> The movement increased from minute to minute until, about 8:00 A.M., the whole active following of the party was on the streets. Nationalists of all hues had also come out. Before very long the capital overflowed with people—shargawiyyas and others—many of them in a fighting mood and united by a single passion: "Death to the traitors and agents of imperialism!" It was like a tide coming in, and at first engulfed and with a vengeance Nuri's house and the royal palace, but soon extended to the British consulate and embassy and other places, and became so terrible and overwhelming in its sweep that the military revolutionaries, ill at ease, declared a curfew and later, in the afternoon, martial law. When in the end, after nightfall, the crowds ebbed back, the statue of Faisal, the symbol of the monarchy, lay shattered, and the figure of General Maude, the conqueror of Baghdad, rested in the dust outside the burning old British Chancellery.   (Ibid. 804–5)

To pro-Western governments—Jordan, Lebanon, Turkey, Iran, Saudi Arabia, and Israel—the impact of the coup was electric. The most vulnerable, Jordan and Lebanon, renewed their demands for Western military assistance. The most powerful redesigned their political-military strategies, and virtually all endured a heightening of domestic political tensions, some reaching deeply into ruling circles. In Western capitals, the response was no less profound, the sense of shock no less traumatic. Politicians in London and Washington expressed disbelief at the brutal demise of the Iraqi monarchy and decimation of the class on whom

British policy relied. Conspiracy, long attributed to the allegedly irrational instincts of the Middle Eastern mind, dominated speculation in Western capitals. Baghdad loomed as the distorted image of the invisible hand manipulating the Middle East. The first to be so indicted was Nasser, and behind him, the USSR. Resistance to the belief that the coup had domestic roots was a common political reaction. It had the virtue of attributing blame to external forces, a familiar disclaimer that provided a perverted consolation for the failures of British policy that the United States supported. Behind the coded language of diplomatic shock and disbelief, however, the fear of revolution and the loss of Western interests were palpable.

Central to interpretations of U.S. military intervention in Beirut has been the role of the July 14 military coup in Baghdad. British and American records strongly undermine conventional views of the Baghdad-to-Beirut connection, while revealing those that have been obscured. U.S. intelligence was a dismal failure in Iraq, a reflection of the transparently pro-British outlook of U.S. officials in Baghdad who were unaffected by the critical voices among local U.S. Embassy officers.[2] The pattern is familiar. It did not impede a response to the crisis provoked by the Iraqi officers coup. Between Washington and London the immediate questions were those affecting plans for joint intervention in Lebanon, the situation in Jordan, and the imperative of protecting Anglo-American oil interests. But Washington and London differed on strategy. In London, Prime Minister Macmillan urged the restoration of the Iraqi regime, while in Washington, Eisenhower and John Foster Dulles resisted. Intervention was not rejected, but its target was more restricted. Dual as opposed to joint interventions were approved with the United States in Lebanon, Britain in Jordan, and if necessary, intervention by Britain and the United States in Saudi Arabia, Kuwait, and the Gulf.

In Beirut, Sham'un later reported in his *Mémoires*, he had received the news of Baghdad on Radio London in its first Arab broadcast of the day shortly after he awakened at about 6:15 A.M. Within the hour, news of public reaction reached the presidency. In the words of the Lebanese president:

> In rebel neighborhoods, men and women had gone into the streets, filled cafes and public places, joyful, dancing with a frenetic joy, threatening legal authority with the fate that had been that of Baghdad leaders. On the other hand, a great fear had spread to those Lebanese com-

mitted to a peaceful and independent Lebanon. Their morale, long tested, suddenly reached the limits of the debacle.[3]

Sham'un claimed, disingenuously, that it had taken him just over two hours from the moment he awakened to the time he made his decision to ask for foreign intervention. He conveniently omitted reference to the assistance he had already received and to the instructions he had been given on how to make the penultimate request.

Sham'un's last call for intervention was not the only one that Eisenhower received. On July 14 and 15, a frenzied exchange with Prime Minister Macmillan involved another request, this one the invitation to intervene in Iraq. In the course of the exchanges between London and Washington on July 14 and 15, the differences between Eisenhower and Macmillan were clarified. On July 14, according to British records, Eisenhower informed Macmillan, "We have decided to implement the plan," the reference presumably to intervention in Lebanon.[4] Eisenhower made it clear to Macmillan that if he thought it appropriate to modify the plans, "you could do that unilaterally." Eisenhower envisioned a separation of roles.

> As I understand it, the contingent of your, [sic] is about 37,000 and it is apparently somewhere towards the rear of the procession. Now it is just possible that in view of the Iraq situation, which I understand has been put in your lap, that you may want to hold those people in reserve depending on Lebanon. If that involves modification in the military plan, you could do that unilaterally.

Lebanon, for Macmillan, was "part of a much larger operation because we shall be driven to take the thing as a whole." And, as he added, "I want to feel that we treat it as a whole. It looks like a showdown." In response to Eisenhower's objection, Macmillan insisted that things "are all tied up together now, and if this thing is done, which I think is very noble of you, in the Lebanon,—all the same it will set off a whole series of things throughout the whole area. The oil will be in jeopardy. Operation has got to be carried through to the end."

Eisenhower asked for clarification. "Let us make sure there is no misunderstanding. Are you of the belief that unless we have made up our minds to carry this thing on to the Persian Gulf, that we had better not start in the first place." Macmillan returned to the imperative of doing "the whole thing," to which Eisenhower responded with reference to congressional restraints, and his meetings with "Legislating leaders."

"We are at the beginning, to plan just the initiative of a big operation. It could run all the way through Syria and Iraq."

U.S. records for July 14 indicate that Eisenhower let Macmillan know that he was not in a position to contemplate action beyond Lebanon. From Washington, Eisenhower explained that while he understood Macmillan's position, "you must understand that so far as we are concerned, as of this moment we can't talk about anything happening elsewhere."[5] But then Eisenhower added, "I agree with you that the situation must contemplate more than that."

On July 15, Macmillan sent Eisenhower a written cable that reviewed the previous telephone exchange. The tone was more measured, the positions clearly delineated. On Lebanon, Macmillan assured Eisenhower support, indicating that "intervention in the Lebanon in response to [Sham'un's] request is certainly made much more necessary by what has happened in Iraq," adding that "no doubt" Eisenhower would justify U.S. action in terms of interference by the UAR.[6] But Macmillan proceeded to repeat his earlier fears regarding the possible effects of U.S. intervention in Beirut:

> What I was trying to say on the telephone was that the action you contemplate must necessarily have great repercussions. It will set off a lot of trouble. The installations at Tripoli cannot be immediately protected, and will probably be destroyed, and all the pipelines through Syria will be cut. There may also be attacks on other oil installations throughout the whole area, all of which will inflict great loss upon the international companies and particularly upon us who depend on sterling oil.   (Ibid.)

Macmillan followed this with a key qualification that echoed his earlier views. "We are prepared," he added, "to face these risks if it is part of a determination between us both to face the issues and be prepared to protect Jordan with the hope of restoring the situation in Iraq." In Macmillan's reformulation, then, protecting Jordan was prerequisite and instrument for a restoration in Iraq. And later in the same text, Macmillan returned to the theme of Lebanon as a secondary task, "not very important in itself" but a preface to the "wider issues" on which he hoped for a common Anglo-American front. In a concluding reference to Beirut, Macmillan reminded Eisenhower that the two had been cooperating in Lebanon before Iraqi events and would have continued to do so had these not intervened (ibid.).

In the hours and days that followed, Eisenhower and Dulles, along with Vice President Nixon and U.S. Defense officials, considered British proposals, the Iraqi coup, the mounting crisis in Jordan, and the prospects of an oil shortage in Britain. U.S. sources present Dulles as alternately endorsing a hard-line response and retreating to a more cautious position. On July 15 he argued that "we cannot give them a blank check. He said that if the British were worried about the oil situation, if the Iraq pipe line is destroyed, that we should of course help them meet their shortages. To intervene militarily would introduce problems that we have not even considered."[7] British sources show another Dulles, far more sympathetic than critical. Avoiding the question of joint Anglo-American intervention in Lebanon as something for the military to decide, Dulles suggested that even if a joint Anglo-American intervention in Lebanon took place, it would be advisable for Britain to maintain "adequate forces in reserve to deal with trouble elsewhere." Lord Hood, minister of the British Embassy in the United States, made a point of specifying where "elsewhere" was, i.e., Iraq and Kuwait.[8]

In the presence of Vice President Nixon, whose views on the U.S. response to the Iraqi military coup were uncompromising, Dulles seemed eager to indicate agreement. Nixon favored the Macmillan approach. Drop Lebanon, march on Iraq, and expel those U.S. ambassadors, such as McClintock, who opposed U.S. intervention in Beirut. Dulles responded positively to Nixon's view that the important thing "is to make it work all over that area and not to vacillate."[9] But Dulles recalled Suez and the flaws of British policy, and he reminded Nixon that the United States had "assets in Lebanon we don't have in other places." Hence, for Dulles, Macmillan's commitment to respond to the Iraqi situation in no way precluded the United States' maintaining its own interests in Lebanon. When he was before the special committee of congressional leaders called on July 14, Dulles was an unconditional advocate of U.S. intervention in Beirut, which he introduced as a joint Anglo-American plan, attributing the idea of reserving British forces for a possible move into Iraq to General Twining.[10]

After the initial exchange between Macmillan and Eisenhower, and the six-hour Cabinet meeting of July 14, the two leaders agreed that British "forces must be held ready for possible action in Iraq or Jordan rather than sent to follow the Americans into Lebanon, as the Blue Bat plan provided."[11] It was Dulles who, recognizing British discontent with the limits of U.S. assistance, conceded that it might be necessary to send a token force to Jordan to palliate British feelings. With the collapse of the anti-Nasserist, Iraqi-Jordanian Arab Union, Macmillan relayed the plaintive state of his royal client to Eisenhower (on July 14), the "chap" who survived the ordeal. Macmillan's sentimental contempt reflected the realities of dependent regimes in a language utterly free of the artifice of diplomatic talk and academic jargon. "We have had a request from two little chaps one has gone and other is there. The King! We do not really know the final reports. But the second one is going alone. We have a request, What are we going to do? His being deputy has a legal right over the whole."[12] The reference to "the second one" was to King Husayn; and the "request" in question concerned his taking action in Iraq. But whatever the plans might have been for Iraq, they were preempted by the situation in Amman, where Dulles informed Eisenhower of rumors of a coup and an oil shortage. On July 17, Husayn requested Western military assistance and took his case to the UN General Assembly, arguing much as did Sham'un about UAR interference.

Neither the U.S. Defense or State Department supported U.S. intervention in Amman, and Eisenhower agreed that there was no basis for U.S. action. The U.S. chief of naval operations, Admiral Burke, however, was prepared to evacuate the king, as he informed the commander of the Sixth Fleet.[13] The State Department indicated that flights over Jordan were being considered while the British planned to send troops from Cyprus to protect the king. Beyond that, as Dulles bluntly admitted, the United States was "hooked for 30–40 million a year to pay the budget deficit of Jordan," a sum that he would have preferred that Nasser or the USSR pay.[14] With U.S. forces in Lebanon and British forces in Jordan, Eisenhower reiterated his commitment to maintain control over the Gulf. We must see, Eisenhower explained in his July 18 cable to Macmillan, "that the Persian Gulf area stays within the Western orbit."[15] Kuwait, Dhahran, and Abadan were singled out, along with Turkey and Iran, the centerpieces of U.S. Middle East oil politics and its strategic protection.

British policy in Kuwait had been under discussion in London for months as the Foreign Office considered Kuwaiti requests for increased autonomy that had intensified in the period since 1956. The events of 1958 aborted any such moves, as securing Kuwait became Britain's avowed objective, with intervention the chosen means. On July 15 the Foreign Office cabled Kuwait with instructions that the Kuwaiti ruler was to be asked "to take all necessary precautions to protect oil installations and British buildings against demonstrations and sabotage."[16] The same text continued with the question as to whether or not the Kuwaiti ruler would, in fact, be in a position to accomplish this. "Can he handle this with his own forces, or would he like British military help which can come very quickly?" All necessary instructions, according to the same cable, were to be sent to Dubai and Muscat. The intentions of British forces in Kuwait were rapidly clarified.

The advantages of intervention were that Britain could directly control Kuwaiti oil; "we would get our hands firmly on the Kuwait oil," as Lord Hood explained to Macmillan.[17] The risks were evident—strikes in the oil fields leading to occupation and its integration as a Crown Colony (ibid.). The alternative, as Lord Hood recommended, was a "kind of Kuwaiti Switzerland," where even "mildly pro-Egyptian sentiments" would be tolerated as long as they did not issue into "an Iraqi type coup." Accepting such an alternative, Hood warned, "we must also accept the need, if things go wrong, ruthlessly to intervene, whoever it is has caused the trouble. The alternative course of immediate British occupation would bring a lot of political trouble in its wake and result in the permanent involvement of at least two brigades." The importance of securing a proper invitation to intervene in Kuwait as a prerequisite to intervention was underscored. As D. M. H. Riches put it, "I think that unless we can secure some kind of request for going into Kuwait we shall be in queer street not only with the Arab but also with the rest of the world. This is of course no reason for not going into Kuwait if we have to."[18]

Dulles found nothing to object to in British plans, particularly since the United States considered comparable action in Saudi Arabia. As the secretary informed his British counterparts, the United States was not averse to the British defending their oil interests any more than the secretary was averse to the United States using the means necessary to maintain the ARAMCO oil fields and Dhahran. In Lord Hood's turn of phrase, the United States "are disposed to act with similar resolution in relations to the Aramco oil fields in the area of Dhahran, although the logistics are not worked out. They assume that we will also hold Bahrain and Qatar, come what may. They agree that at all costs these oil fields must be kept in Western hands."[19] The operating assumption was that as "everything blows up at once and we are going into Kuwait when the Americans go into Hasa, presumably normal restraints on action from Bahrain will have to disappear."[20] In Washington, Dulles informed Eisenhower, Acting Under Secretary of State Herter, Assistant Secretary of State for Near Eastern, South Asian, and African Affairs Rountree,

Counselor of the State Department Frederick Reinhardt, Director of the U.S. Information Agency George Allen, Director of the CIA Allen Dulles, Secretary of Defense McElroy, Chairman of the Joint Chiefs of Staff Twining, Deputy Assistant Secretary of Defense for International Security Affairs Irwin II, Press Secretary of the President Hagerty, and White House Staff Secretary and Retired Brigadier General Goodpaster on July 20 about "certain decisions reached with Lloyd and approved by the President." [Paragraph deleted.][21] To George Allen, who was an advocate of greater flexibility in U.S. policy toward the Arab world, Eisenhower conceded that "it was clear we must win them to us, or adjust to them." It was winning rather than adjusting that dominated discussions, and deliberations on nuclear weapons in the event of an Iraqi move into Kuwait, according to William Quandt's review of the period.[22] Eisenhower ordered the redeployment of the Strategic Air Command (SAC), with a "Composite Air Strike Group" redirected from Europe to Turkey, and Marine combat missions ordered to the Gulf.[23]

Within a matter of days, then, the initial realization that the Iraqi military coup had totally annihilated Britain's political base in Baghdad led to the organization and projection of an Anglo-American response in the eastern Mediterranean, Kuwait, Saudi Arabia, and the Gulf. Macmillan's observation that Lebanon was dwarfed by the magnitude of events was accurate. But it failed to address U.S. interests in Lebanon or the false assumption that Eisenhower was prepared to collaborate with Britain in a rollback policy in Iraq. In practice, the Iraqi coup was followed by the decision to sever Anglo-American plans for joint intervention in Lebanon, to support a separate British intervention in Amman, and perhaps even to contemplate a British, but not a U.S., move in Baghdad, and above all to Washington, it provided legitimation for U.S. intervention in Lebanon. In Eisenhower's address to Congress in which he announced that he "received an urgent request from the President of the Republic of Lebanon that some United States forces be stationed in Lebanon," a phraseology whose avoidance of the term *intervention* is striking, he went on to refer to the coup in Iraq—in terms of its potentially deleterious effect on the regime in Beirut.[24]

There is another factor to consider, however, which may have further dampened U.S. support for intervention in Baghdad, namely, recognition that the new Iraqi regime intended to honor its contractual obligations to Western companies. In retrospect, the move to keep Iraqi (IPC) oil off the international markets worked in favor of U.S. international companies that stood to benefit by its exclusion.[25] Considered in conjunction with the political impact of the coup on Britain's position in the Middle East after 1956, the overall significance of these developments cannot be exaggerated. They contributed both to the drastic reduction of British power in the region and to the enhancement of that of the United States. Military intervention in Beirut, which was inevitably affected by developments in Baghdad, cannot be attributed to them. The impact of the fall of the Nuri Sa'id regime on the Lebanese president was predictably alarming, leading him to press ever more urgently for U.S. and Western intervention, to which Eisenhower responded. One may venture to suggest that the conservative opposition responded with no more enthusiasm to the coup, although it remained antagonistic to U.S. intervention in Lebanon. The nature of the U.S. response in Beirut was a function of prior planning that was rooted in U.S. policy in Lebanon before as well as during the civil war.

By early July, as earlier discussion has shown, military advances by opposition forces under the direction of Kamal Junblat, and the rumors of possible coups within the Lebanese army were sufficiently disquieting to make full-scale military intervention a serious option. In that context, the impact of the coup in Baghdad on the Lebanese regime, and fears of its potentially adverse effect on Anglo-American oil interests in Kuwait and Saudi Arabia, may be considered as the factors that precipitated U.S. intervention in Beirut.

Operation Blue Bat

> *"Armor," as Brigadier General Wade put it, "is an excellent weapon for a show of force. It really impresses the natives."*
> U.S. Marine Corps Historical Center, Washington, D.C.,
> July 1958

Within hours of the news of the assassination of Iraq's King Faysal II, the crown prince, and the prime minister, Washington policymakers were in a state of heightened alert. A comprehensive series of emergency meetings followed, involving the White House, the National Security Council, the Intelligence, Defense, and State Departments, and congressional leaders. John Foster Dulles and Allen Dulles, along with Deputy Under Secretary of State for Political Affairs Robert Murphy, Deputy Under

Secretary of State for Administration Loy Henderson, General of the USAF and Chairman of the Joint Chiefs of Staff Nathan F. Twining, and Deputy Secretary of Defense Donald Quarles, were among those immediately contacted, as Eisenhower and Dulles worked a nonstop schedule that included the top secret telephone communications with British prime minister Macmillan that have been previously discussed. At the same time, military contingency plans were put into operation. What followed on the ground in Beirut was a series of "undiplomatic encounters" involving awkward confrontations among the U.S. ambassador, U.S. military personnel, and Lebanese officials. In Washington, on the other hand, officials monitored international reactions.

Four aspects of this period are considered in the material that follows: the emergency session with congressional leaders; the military phase of Operation Blue Bat; the abrasive encounters between U.S. and Lebanese officials and opposition leaders; and the mobilization and monitoring of international reactions. There was nothing consensual about the process that unfolded. The Lebanese commander in chief, Fu'ad Shihab, was caught unawares, and the Lebanese army balked at being pushed aside. U.S. ambassador McClintock appeared to be overtaken by the actions of U.S. naval officers, and the Lebanese opposition was dealt with by Eisenhower's special emissary, Robert Murphy, in peremptory fashion. NATO allies were informed rather than consulted, and governments such as that of Japan were put under heavy pressure to align their positions with those of the U.S. administration. In Washington itself, the assemblage of U.S. congressmen called to consider the proceedings at the outset was offered formulaic pronouncements about the state of the Middle East as justification for U.S. intervention. For many present, there was considerable skepticism as to whether or not the decision they had allegedly been called to consider had, in fact, already been taken by President Eisenhower.[26]

At 8:30 A.M. on July 14, Secretary Dulles telephoned Eisenhower, already briefed by General Goodpaster.[27] Two minutes later, Dulles informed General Cutler that he should await further information from Iraq, adding that the United States and Britain had appeals from Sham'un for immediate intervention. A 10:30 meeting in the president's office was planned.[28] At 8:40, Dulles contacted Allen Dulles, then made similar calls to General Twining and Quarles, to attend the 10:30 session. Those participating included the major figures in Defense, Intelligence, and State (Henderson, Murphy, Macomber, Rockwell), in addition to

Secretary Dulles and Eisenhower. In the crescendo of meetings and the cascade of speculations that followed, the key question was what was to be done in Iraq? What of the possible reactions to the "effects of intervention and nonintervention in the Middle East, with particular reference to [Sham'un's] request"?[29] From the military angle, Twining had no doubts. There was no alternative but to intervene. He pointed out that "the Sixth Fleet is already moving east from the central Mediterranean and that the United States military can meet their planned schedule of landings which would get the first battalion landed twelve hours after the order is given." Quarles and Macomber urged that an appropriate UN cover be found that would give "adequate moral sanction" to the operation. The critical question of Soviet reaction was scrutinized.[30] Chairman of the Joint Chiefs of Staff General Nathan Twining recalled being questioned on the matter by Secretary Dulles: "Speaking for the Joint Chiefs of Staff, I assured him that the Soviets would do no more than wring their hands and deliver verbal protests. We knew this because U.S. military forces could have destroyed the USSR—and Russia knew it."[31]

U.S. Embassy reports from Moscow suggested that a Soviet political rather than military response should be anticipated. U.S. ambassador Thompson's reports indicated that the Soviet response would most likely consist of political denunciations as well as calls to action, of the following type. The USSR might call for a summit, send supplies to the UAR, and issue warnings to strategically situated states such as Turkey, as well as stage demonstrations against U.S. action. On the other hand, Thompson thought the Soviets would be "extremely cautious about committing themselves to any action from which it would be difficult for them to withdraw."[32] This was the message that Allen Dulles conveyed to the congressional meeting on the afternoon of July 14. The briefings were attended by Eisenhower, Nixon, the two Dulles brothers, Macomber, Anderson, Quarles, and Twining, among others. They elicited little by way of discussion, which appears to have been accepted as the preferred format. Thus, while Eisenhower insisted that no decision had been taken and that this consultation was of the essence in the decision-making process, the U.S. Navy was on its way.

What was striking about the special meeting was the brevity and banality of the analysis of U.S. policy that followed. While in their closed telephone exchange, Macmillan and Eisenhower left no doubt as to the centrality of protecting their Middle East oil interests; before the assorted congressional leaders, the question of U.S. economic interests was gingerly handled. Yet in discussion with Nixon on July 15, Eisenhower was emphatic about the importance of reaching "vitally needed petroleum supplies"—an American objective since 1945, he admitted.[33] But Eisenhower did not want this to be a public justification of policy. Allen Dulles, in turn, emphasized the role of oil in testimony before the Senate Foreign Relations Committee, albeit without explaining the connection with Lebanon.[34] For the most part, however, it was not oil but politics that dominated, and more particularly, a vision of Middle East politics as chaos.

Describing developments in Iraq as a catastrophic omen for Western interests in the Middle East, CIA director Dulles warned that the Iraqi coup constituted a risk to pro-Western regimes in the area. But he gave no indication of American support for rollback. On the contrary, the Iraqi situation was portrayed as ominous and murky. Its causes, leaders, and political direction remained unclear, which did not prevent Dulles from insinuating that Nasser was involved.[35] There was no doubt of the Saudi position, in Allen Dulles's description. King Sa'ud, facing domestic pressures, demanded U.S. action while threatening to defect to the UAR unless such action occurred. As Allen Dulles knew, it was not Sa'ud who was about to defect but another member of the royal family, Faysal, whose pro-Nasserist views were regarded by both British and American officials as influential in Kuwait.

The situation between Jordan and Israel was not more encouraging. Dulles offered an image of Jordanian-Israeli-Lebanese relations as inextricably linked. Hence, if the monarchy was to fall in Jordan, he informed his congressional audience, he anticipated an Israeli move that would extend into the West Bank and the Jordan River. "Israeli mobilization is probable," Dulles insisted in his July 14 briefing. Was this a threat or a promise? Eisenhower, according to other sources, "considered the merits of 'unleashing' Israel against Nasser, and General Twining seriously proposed that Israel should seize the West Bank of Jordan as part of an area-wide counteroffensive that would include British intervention in Iraq and Turkish intervention in Syria."[36]

For John Foster Dulles, the United States had no choice in Lebanon. Lebanon's survival, according to Dulles, was imperiled by UAR intervention (this was Sham'un's position, which went unquestioned). Since Lebanon could no longer count on Iraqi military aid, Dulles offered Sham'un's dire view of the situation. He "now says he is no longer able unaided to preserve Lebanese independence, and we agree, unless the Iraqi forces outside of Baghdad remain loyal to the former regime–this we consider unlikely."[37] The construction of the administration's case, which duplicated that of the Lebanese regime, assumed either the ignorance of Lebanese conditions on the part of the congressional audience or its conformity with official views. Dulles offered the formulaic model of the Lebanese case with what appears to have been, at this stage at least, little resistance. The existing record shows no one questioning what "holding Lebanon free" meant, particularly in the light of an ongoing civil war. The design of the Lebanese-U.S. justificatory argument was in full view, involving a construct of the following axioms: first, the Lebanon state at risk, i.e., imperiled Lebanon; then, the attendant consequence for U.S. life and property, now endangered; and, finally, the coup de grace, the Iraqi threat to Lebanon following the Iraqi coup. U.S. action appears as a response to this combination. Intervention thus functions as a means of "saving" Lebanon and as a "warning" to the Soviets, whose involvement in the Iraqi coup Dulles claimed as likely, even though he thought them unhappy with Nasser's role in Lebanon.

What was the basis of U.S. intervention in Lebanon, Senators Rayburn, McCormack, Mansfield, and Fulbright wanted to know. The single most persistent and frustrated question of this and later Senate Foreign Relations Committee hearings on the subject met with a steady series of evasive rejoinders. Dulles admitted the irrelevance of the Tripartite Accord of 1950 as well as the Middle East Resolution of 1957. The Eisenhower Doctrine, in whose name Lebanese and U.S. officials continued to explain U.S. action, did not apply. How, then, could the United States intervene in a civil war? This was the second most persistently asked question, and it was met with the same opaque responses as the above query on the basis of U.S. intervention. Dulles's reply was that the civil war was not a domestic affair only but one determined from the outside. To McCormack's question as to whether Eisenhower would act in accord with his powers as commander in chief or request congressional legislation before taking action, Eisenhower replied with evident unease. Debate, he thought, would expose U.S. policy to Soviet scrutiny. Aside from those representatives, such as Congressman Vorys, who was thoroughly satisfied with the analogy between Greece in 1947 and Lebanon in 1958, the general mood was one of palpable discontent. That restraint vanished in the course of the Senate hearings, before which many of the same administration officials appeared, with many of the same nonexplanations.

On July 15, the hastily summoned NSC members offered their support. Several days later, Secretary Dulles explained intervention as a necessary, though negative, response, one whose alternative was unacceptable. Not to intervene, he argued, relying on the credibility formula, "would have destroyed at one blow the faith and confidence of a score of nations."[38]

Operation Blue Bat was discussed among presidential advisers immediately after the congressional meeting, when a number of crucial decisions were made concerning the unilateral nature of intervention in Lebanon, the timing of U.S. intervention, and the manner in which the UN was to be informed. The United Nations was to be informed that the United States had taken action pursuant to the Lebanese initiative, taken under conditions of duress. With Eisenhower, Secretary Dulles, CIA director Dulles, General Twining, Defense Secretary Quarles, and Thomas Hagerty attending, "it was made clear that Defense should order the landing of the advance Marine contingent at 3PM, should order elements of the Sixth Fleet now in the Western Mediterranean to move at once to the Eastern Mediterranean."[39] In the late afternoon, Admiral Burke alerted U.S. forces in Europe and the Mediterranean. While U.S. Marines were landing in Lebanon, the presidential advisers assumed that British forces would prepare to intervene in Iraq or Jordan. The exchanges between Eisenhower and Macmillan occurred later in the day, and the cabled summary of Macmillan's position arrived on July 15. It was after his communication with Macmillan that Eisenhower contacted Canadian prime minister John Diefenbaker, who supported U.S. action in spite of the restraint recommended by his own cabinet. Diefenbaker, in short, was among the first to be informed of impending events.

> Two United States Marine landing battalions will land in Lebanon at 3:00 pm Lebanon time (9:00 am EDT) Tuesday, July 15. Soon thereafter our representative at the United Nations will report this action to a special session of the Security Council which Lebanon or we will have urgently asked be convened. Our representative will report that we have received an urgent appeal from President [Sham'un] for assistance in maintaining the independence and integrity of Lebanon and that, having concluded that the United Nations observers now in the Lebanon cannot suffice to preserve Lebanon's independence, under the circumstances now prevailing, we have affirmatively responded to [Sham'un's] request. We contemplate that these United States forces are in the Lebanon not [crossed out material] as combat troops but to assist in stabilizing the situation there. We hope that the United Nations will be able to organize a force quickly to take over this func-

tion and as soon as such a force arrives in the Lebanon United States forces will withdraw.[40]

Sometime in the course of the same day, Dulles received news that Radio Damascus had reported that the new Iraqi Republic had given Iraqi troops instructions to either report to airports or join "People's Forces" in Lebanon. McClintock volunteered that he had no evidence of such actions. On the morning of July 15, Dulles reported on his talks with the British. General Twining reported on the Beirut side of developments, recommending that SAC be placed on alert in addition to arrangements for other possible contingencies. In the interim, the question of how most effectively to present the U.S. landing to the American public was under consideration by Eisenhower, Nixon, and Dulles. At 6:30 P.M. Eisenhower addressed the nation, justifying U.S. intervention in terms of its stabilizing impact on Lebanon, its positive effect for the United States, and its international and historical significance, given the precedents of the 1930s. Referring to the appeal from the Lebanese government, Eisenhower explained: "After giving this plea earnest thought and after taking advice from leaders of both the Executive and Congressional branches of the government, I decided to comply with the plea of the Government of Lebanon. A few hours ago a battalion of United States Marines landed and took up stations in and about the city of Beirut."[41]

The U.S. landing was thus timed to take place no more than fifteen hours after Sham'un's plea for assistance. The Joint Chiefs instructed their commanders to maintain total discretion prior to the scheduled landing.

> After that deadline, USCINCEUR was to bring one Army battle group together with its airlift into readiness for a landing at the Beirut airport within 24 hours of the execution order, or within 36 hours if an airdrop proved necessary. [deleted]. . . .
> . . . would be supplied by the U.S. Tactical Air Command. On 15 July, two hours after the scheduled landing of the Marines, the Joint Chiefs of Staff directed CINCNELM and the other commanders involved to execute as soon as practicable the U.S. portion of BLUE BAT, as modified by the substitution of COMTAC aircraft.[42]

The arrangements that enabled the U.S. administration to land in Beirut had been set in place in 1957. The "unilateral U.S. limited war plan for operations in Lebanon" was recognized by the Joint Chiefs of Staff as having "materially facilitated the preparation of Commander American-British Forces OPLAN 1–58, 'Blue Bat,' the combined plan."[43]

The so-called limited war plan was a by-product of the Eisenhower Doctrine that had originally been prepared for military action in Syria. U.S. military and naval forces, including the Strategic Air Command, were mobilized in September and October 1957. At the time, Dulles, in advance of a meeting scheduled with Selwyn Lloyd in London on October 18, requested clarification from the U.S. Joint Chiefs of Staff in the event of a coup in either Jordan or Lebanon. "What could be made available in a) 24 hours, b) 48 hours, c) 72 hours?" Transit and overflight rights, Dulles assumed erroneously, would not be a problem. "The objective of U.S. intervention would be to reestablish the authority of the friendly local government and to help maintain order. The estimate should not take into account the possibility of armed intervention by hostile forces outside the country."[44] As pro-Western regimes complained of being under increasing pressure from Egypt and Syria, Dulles called for contingency plans involving joint Anglo-American intervention in Lebanon and/or Jordan. It was on the basis of this that subsequent plans for U.S. intervention in Lebanon were implemented or, in the language of the JCS, "OPLAN 215–58 superseded OPLAN 215–56, and it was to include the contingency plan for intervention in Lebanon or Jordan as a Tab" (ibid. 430).

Thus was "the first U.S. airborne-amphibious operation to occur in peacetime" planned.[45] While Eisenhower and his closest advisers deliberated on how most effectively to justify U.S. intervention, the Sixth Fleet was speedily moving eastward, arriving ten and a half hours after Sham'un's appeal to the United States and Britain. There were fifty ships off the Lebanese coast within the first three days of intervention.[46] Within a month of their arrival, U.S. military, naval, and air force troops from bases in Germany, Morocco, France, Malta, and Italy, and the U.S. reached 15,000, twice the size of the Lebanese army. But this figure does not include those involved in the transportation of some "4,000 tons of cargo plus Force ALPHA, Force CHARLIE, and other support personnel. Food, weapons, communications, bulldozers, jeeps, halftracks, and other logistical support material were flown from Germany, France, and the United States in 418 sorties without incident."[47] There were medical units and engineers specializing in water and sanitation. Three battalions, with some 5,000 troops, arrived as part of the initial forces, followed later by a fourth. In the first week alone, the Sixth Fleet disgorged the *Saratoga*, the *Essex*, and the *Wasp*, three attack carriers replete with atomic capacity, in addition to heavy cruisers, destroyers, and other accessory forces.

By the end of August, they were supplemented by the command ships *Taconic* and *Pocono*, as well as additional transport equipment.

Records and individual accounts of political insiders differ with respect to the total number of U.S. forces involved in this operation. Wilbur Eveland claimed that Holloway was in charge of a "seventy-six-ship, 35,000-man Sixth Fleet offshore."[48] The JCS Report on the Lebanese crisis estimated "peak strength of U.S. intervention" as roughly 14,357, divided between army and marines.[49] According to the Marine Corps Historical Center, the proportion of marines was less than that of the military.[50]

Numbers aside, the stated objective of Operation Blue Bat, as described by the military, was a

> "show of force" with psychological overtones achieved by demonstrations of combat capabilities, training assistance to the Lebanese Army, positioning of combat outposts, opposing sources of harassment, and operating numerous strong tank-infantry patrols in areas of civil disturbances. Included in U.S. actions were numerous shows of force by Air Force and Naval air units conducting low level fly-bys over Lebanon.[51]

The "demonstrations" were demonstrably political. The presence of U.S. forces in the midst of civil war did more than impress the natives, as General Wade suggested. Those forces were assigned to maintain "tactical dispositions designed to secure the city of Beirut against attack, whether initiated inside or outside the general perimeter of the beachhead. All forces maintained a fighting posture, conducted patrols, and demonstrated their readiness at all times to meet any contingencies with precision and power" (ibid.).

Official accounts of the Lebanon operation divided it into three phases: the landing, July 15–26; the "operations phase," July 26–September 15; and the withdrawal, September 15–October 25 (ibid. 16). U.S. Marines landed on the outskirts of Beirut shortly before 1 p.m., at Red and Yellow Beaches, the former near the airport, the latter north of the city. "Arriving at the same time was the 82nd Airborne Division based in Adana, that parachuted into Beirut airport," according to the then vice president of TAPLINE, whose family left for Rhodes on the same day. "A Marine landing team with full combat equipment, the 2d Battalion of the 2d Regiment (strength 1,771) went ashore over Red Beach at 1300Z, with air cover from the carriers and under the guns of the fleet. This force occupied

Beirut's international airport by 1600Z, three hours after the initial landing."[52] Three landing teams arrived with the Sixth Fleet, the third being a replacement for the British.

Contrary to British plans, no landing at Tripoli was intended by U.S. officials. Instead, on July 18, the battalion landed north of Beirut, and on the following day, U.S. Marines entered the capital, taking control of the harbor and principal routes into the city. They operated with full air force cover. Battle groups, such as Force ALPHA, numbering 1,755 infantry troops, arrived via the NATO air base at Adana, their number increased on July 19 with troops from Force CHARLIE. In less than seventy-two hours the United States had landed some 7,000 troops and within the first five days no less than 8,029 marines, reaching full capacity of combat troops by mid-August, at the same time that plans for withdrawal were under discussion.

Between July 15 and September 5, aircraft from the Sixth Fleet "flew some 11,000 sorties of every type in support of this operation. Every square foot of Lebanese territory was photographed by F8U 'Crusade' photo planes, so that the forces ashore would have the most complete intelligence should combat operations be necessary."[53] According to the historians of the Sixth Fleet in the Mediterranean,

> photographic coverage of key targets throughout the Middle East was available. Target intelligence for air strikes was generally adequate and current. Initially, coverage of interior areas of Lebanon was inadequate. To overcome this deficiency, extensive photo reconnaissance operations of all of Lebanon and portions of the Syrian interior and coastal areas were undertaken.[54]

In the November 1958 evaluation of the Lebanon operation, Admiral Holloway, commander in chief of the U.S. Specified Command Middle East headquarters, described the difficulties that the U.S. military faced in obtaining approval for such reconnaissance. Permission for aerial photography was granted by Sham'un, but even he, who had an acute understanding of his reliance on American power and support, was disconcerted by this request. Yet in the annals of the U.S. military, the 1958 U.S. military intervention in Lebanon stands out not only as an illustration of the military merits of "limited war" strategies but also in terms of the opportunities it offered in the area of aerial reconnaissance. The former was the subject of intense debate within defense circles between advocates of "limited war" and advocates of "massive retaliation." General

Twining considered Operation Blue Bat a negative example, which he opposed in consequence of the decision not to land U.S. nuclear weapons in Beirut. The politically motivated step was regarded by Twining as misplaced, considering that "we reinforced our nuclear-capable air garrisons in Turkey, and we also had en route all of the nuclear equipment that U.S. ground forces were authorized in their tables of organization and equipment. This equipment included Army short-range rockets with nuclear warheads."[55] With respect to aerial reconnaissance flights that Eisenhower regarded as inadequate, the Lebanese operation may have been particularly meaningful in the context of Eisenhower's recently established (1956) Photographic Intelligence Division, headed by two CIA appointees. In 1956, the Lockheed-built U-2 went into operation over the Soviet Union from its German base, with a second base planned for Turkey. Did Operation Blue Bat, with its 11,000 "sorties," contribute to this aerial reconnaissance project? If it did, the mystery implied in the title of this chapter, "11,000 Sorties in Search of a Target," is at least partially solved.[56]

In terms of the operation of Blue Bat a number of problems that arose dispel the myth of this undertaking. Some were logistical, others were bureaucratic, and still others were frankly political. There were overflight problems that affected both the United States in Lebanon and Britain in Jordan. With respect to the former, the only governments to give their approval to the United States were France, Italy, and Turkey. Libya and Greece requested that their actions be given a low public profile, while Austria and Switzerland, as neutral states, objected to U.S. action.

There were problems of a bureaucratic nature that had evident political overtones. Thus, the lack of coordination between the U.S. military and diplomatic corps in Beirut basically undermined McClintock's position, which may not have been an accident. As U.S. diplomat Charles Thayer recalled, there was "the failure of the Sixth Fleet to maintain its radio-telephone link with the embassy, the failure to keep the ambassador informed of the place of the landings, and finally the absurd spat about who was to call on whom," which compounded the difficulties.[57] This led to the White House's delayed efforts to clarify the proper chain of command. McClintock was pointedly told that he was the principal U.S. representative in relations with UNOGIL forces, but relations between Ambassador McClintock and U.S. naval forces commander Holloway remained tense. In principle, Admiral Holloway was subordinate to Ambassador McClintock. In practice, it was Holloway who was in charge during the landing, while Eisenhower's special envoy, Robert Murphy, intervened at every level. The transparent effect was lost on none of those involved, including Lebanese officials, eager to meet with the highest-ranking U.S. officials and not those known for their anti-interventionist disposition.

Among undiplomatic encounters, those between the U.S. military and civilian officers and the Lebanese army and officials were among the most awkward and politically revealing. The entire scenario of the U.S.-Lebanese relationship was played out in the hours following the landing. Lebanese aircraft sought to block the entry of U.S. Marines but turned back in the light of U.S. warnings, according to TAPLINE vice president Chandler.[58] On the ground there was McClintock, the ever-accessible intermediary for intra-Lebanese conflicts. There was Eisenhower's ever-ready special adviser, emissary, and confidant, Robert Murphy, prepared to threaten or cajole in the full knowledge of the power that he represented. And there were the Lebanese "rebels," not men in search of a cause but establishment leaders in search of their political power, subjected to the abrasive Americans.

This was the background to the awkward predicament that found McClintock, not Lebanese president Sham'un, informing Shihab of the imminent landing of U.S. forces. It was McClintock who found himself in the position of breaking the news and then attempting to broker an arrangement with Shihab, the Lebanese military, and U.S. forces to avoid confrontation between them. Fearful of the impact of intervention on the Lebanese army, Shihab attempted to persuade McClintock to halt the landing process. This, in turn, exposed the limits of McClintock's power, as his authority carried no weight with the task force commander. McClintock spent several hours attempting to make contact with Holloway after the landing had in fact begun. In the midst of this, McClintock received an alarm from Sham'un, demanding immediate protection against a rumored coup, to which McClintock responded by seeking the help of Shihab.[59] McClintock and Holloway, meanwhile, had arrived at a plan whereby U.S. Marines would enter Beirut with a Lebanese military escort.[60] To the Lebanese troops, who resented the orders given them by the U.S. forces—that they "pack up and go home"—this was hardly compensation.[61]

Shihab's combined opposition to U.S. intervention and to orders to attack the opposition leadership and its headquarters earned him the suspicion of most U.S. officials in Washington and Beirut.[62] Some who dissented, such as Marine Corps general Wade, praised the "excellent co-operation between the American and Lebanese Armies."[63] But the major complaint directed against him and his army by U.S. officers in Beirut and their superiors in Washington was that they resisted attacking so-called rebel centers, including that in Beirut. British officials in Beirut were critical of what they regarded as the passivity of the American troops. The particular incidents that aroused such reaction were those involving the disarming of U.S. Marines who had wandered into the Basta area and an incident involving a TAPLINE military guard in Sidon. TAPLINE officials claimed no protection had been requested, however, as assurances had been offered them by both the regime and the opposition leaders.[64]

U.S. sources do not confirm the British view. Robert Murphy, for one, was not notably reserved in his dealings with Lebanese officials. Eveland's account of the encounter between Shihab and Murphy, in which Shihab attempted to explain the reasons for his opposition to intervention, was met with threats. Pointing to the *Saratoga*, which was in Beirut harbor, Murphy

> quietly explained that just one of its aircraft, armed with nuclear weapons, could obliterate Beirut and its environs from the face of the earth. To this, Murphy quickly added that he'd been sent to be sure that it wouldn't be necessary for American troops to fire a shot. [Shihab], he was certain, would ensure that there were no provocations on the Lebanese side. That, Murphy told me, ended the conversation. It now seemed that the general had "regained control" of his troops.[65]

On another occasion, Murphy informed Sham'un that if U.S. troops were attacked from the Basta, there would be "very serious consequences. These would be good neither for Lebanese or ourselves. I therefore wanted to impress very firmly on President need for prompt and effective action by the Lebanese military."[66]

On July 19, when Murphy cabled this news to Washington, it appeared that he had reconsidered the position of Shihab. Was this the result of the encounters with Sham'un? Or was it a function of Shihab's being told that the United States was not committed to the occupation of Lebanon but would leave in favor of UN forces? Murphy was now describing Shihab as cooperative, explaining that he provided invaluable evidence of the link between Damascus and the Basta.[67] Given the paucity of evidence about which Dulles and the U.S. delegation to the UN had so bitterly complained, this was not a minor reward. Murphy corroborated Shihab's claim and found it valid, although his methods precluded the evidence's being used for public purposes.

What complicated matters for U.S. officials in Beirut was the response to intervention. On the surface, as McClintock drew the lines, it was simply a matter of enthusiastic Lebanese Christians versus "sullen" Muslims.[68] Admittedly, supporters of intervention were concentrated in Sham'un circles, including Prime Minister Sulh and regime loyalists, such as the Kata'eb. Opponents, on the other hand, predictably were to be found among opposition leaders. But Third Force figures were no less opposed—politicians, journalists, and even former presidents, such as Far'oun, Hilu, Tuwayni, and Besharah al-Khuri. 'Usayran, in the Lebanese Chamber, continued to argue as he had at the United Nations that Sham'un's action was taken illegally, i.e., without proper consultation. The problem, as McClintock, Murphy, Dulles, and Eisenhower soon realized, was not with the opponents of intervention but with those who thought that the United States had not gone far enough. Sham'un and Malik were in this category. Their insistence on a more comprehensive expedition reinforced the pervasive sense of unease with which U.S. officials contemplated continued support for Sham'un.

In the immediate aftermath of intervention, Sham'un's relief was palpable. He provided U.S. admiral Brown with intelligence concerning Syria, while promising that he intended to pacify rebellious areas in Tripoli, Ba'lbak, and Rashaya. His extended withdrawal into the safety of his palace, where he had remained since the beginning of the civil war, inspired some doubts about his condition among U.S. officials in Beirut.[69] These were aggravated by the kinds of political demands that he and Malik proceeded to make. Four days after U.S. Marines entered Beirut, the U.S. Embassy forwarded a preview of the response to the U.S. landings in the Biqa' valley. The sample was modest. as the U.S. officers reported, "the following impressions are based on conversations in the Bekaa with 12 civilians and 5 members of the Lebanese Security Forces, all Christian, and at least outwardly, all pro-Government."[70] Hardly a representative sample, but one guaranteed to be safe. What it confirmed was that "the landing of United States Marines in Lebanon was enthusiastically approved by most Christians in the Bekaa [Biqa']. Moslem attitudes, on the other hand, ranged from guarded acceptance through acquiescence to angry condemnation of the United States actions as an infringement of Lebanon's sovereignty." According to the same informants, not only were the Christian towns in the area exuberant but Lebanese Shi'ites were approving "to ensure their nonabsorption into a Sunni dominated UAR."

At the same time that this survey was undertaken, Sham'un staked out another claim that was to be reiterated in the coming days and weeks, namely, that U.S. intervention in Lebanon, like that of Britain in Jordan, was inadequate to stem "the combined onslaught of Nasserism and Communism" and that to stop at this point would further deplete "the moral energy of those who would like to see a general cleaning up in the Middle East."[71] Sham'un argued that if U.S. intentions were limited to handing responsibility for Lebanon to the " 'dubiously adequate' ability of the UN," then "it would be better if U.S. forces had not come in the first place." He wanted 20,000 U.S. troops in Jordan and Lebanon, consultation with Turkey about Iraq and Syria, and a "strong warning to Nasser."

Sham'un's response was unwelcome in Washington. Dulles insisted to Eisenhower that U.S. actions involved no "commitment to root out Nasserism and Communism" and that if that had been Sham'un's objective, "we would not have given an affirmative response." The "integrity and independence of Lebanon" was what U.S. policy was about, Dulles reflected, resisting Sham'un's attempts to "drag us into this thing in a bigger way."[72] There was no support for extending U.S. intervention from Murphy, Holloway, or Wade, and the dissenting voice of Admiral Brown was overruled. Eisenhower's reaction was indicative of his disenchantment with the Lebanese leadership. If they were incapable "of doing their business with us protecting their capital and their rear, then there is little more that we can do about it," he declared.[73]

Considerably more was, in fact, done, as plans were under way for the political stage of post–civil war intervention. Eveland's loyalty to Sham'un notwithstanding, the CIA agent was no match for Robert Murphy, who pressed for a political solution that excluded Sham'un and barred an extension of U.S. occupation. On July 25, Under Secretary of State Herter instructed John Irwin II, deputy assistant secretary of defense for international security affairs, to stop the landing of nuclear warheads on board ships coming from Bremerhaven. "It was proposed to disembark them but to keep what goes with them in its most violent form aboard ship."[74] Charges of U.S. forces' carrying nuclear weapons had been made by the opposition, and Herter conceded that their landing would be unnecessarily provocative "because it would be a big display and there would be much comment."

Mr. Irwin said he wanted to be sure he understood: the carrier is aboard the ship and they are loading aboard the next ship the actual weapons. State wants to keep both on board ship, and not have them landed. CAH [C. A. Herter] said that is right and referred to recent statement that we couldn't conceive of any situation which would require the use of nuclear warheads. Irwin said it is certainly possible to keep them aboard ship and he will look into it at once.   (Ibid.)

On the following day Irwin confirmed that instructions had been followed and that the military was now awaiting approval to bring the cargo to Adana, Turkey. As previous discussion has indicated, however, this was by no means the end of the operational phase of U.S. intervention, given Anglo-American preparations that were simultaneously made for the region of Saudi Arabia, Kuwait, and the Gulf.

The withdrawal of U.S. nuclear weapons avoided what Herter and others in Beirut viewed as a politically explosive situation, one that can be situated in the context of widespread international dissatisfaction with U.S. intervention. Press reports from major capitals brought unpleasant surprises, including critical reports of U.S., as opposed to UN, policy.

UN officials, of course, viewed U.S. intervention as interfering with their own work. Dismayed, they claimed that their achievements were largely nullified by the American move. Both critics and supporters of the unilateral U.S. action acknowledged the criticism.[75] Galo Plaza had been initially hostile to the idea of any collaboration between U.S. and UN forces. He was, in fact, persuaded that the UNOGIL report of July 17 to the United Nations would affect the outcome of the forthcoming UN debate and would lead to the dismantling of the UNOGIL operation. Such withdrawal would expose U.S. claims that intervention was compatible with UN principles, a position to which Lebanese delegates also subscribed in justifying their position.

Without reproducing the extensive debates in the UN on the Lebanese case, suffice it to recall that at the emergency session of the Security Council convened on July 15, the Lebanese representative to the UN, M. Azkoul, argued on the basis of UN Charter Article 51, while U.S. delegate Henry Cabot Lodge based the U.S. case on General Assembly resolutions pertinent to indirect aggression. From the outset, Lodge insisted that U.S. intervention was not intended to undermine UN efforts and that it would last only until the UN could effectively replace its forces. Not only was U.S. and Lebanese action legitimated in terms of the UN

Charter, but Lodge also maintained that the success of the UN would be determined by its support of such efforts. The relevant General Assembly resolution in this instance was that of 1950 (GA 380 v), which condemned intervention by one state in the affairs of another with the object of altering its legitimate government by force or its threatened use.[76]

As for the response of the USSR, it was as U.S. intelligence and diplomatic sources had predicted—of a political rather than a military nature. This was reflected on two levels, in Soviet-UAR relations, and in the Soviet-U.S. exchanges concerning proposed summits. In their relations with Egypt and the UAR, the Soviets had shown themselves to be cautious. Nasser confidant and editor of *al-Ahram* H. Haykal recalled that Khrushchev had told Nasser when he was in the Soviet Union in July that the USSR was unprepared for a confrontation with the West, although it would provide the UAR with political support, including military exercises. Khrushchev warned Nasser that he was not concerned that such actions would be misunderstood in the West. He was concerned, on the other hand, "that you yourself may believe there is more in it."[77] The Soviet response opened another venue altogether, as the USSR used Anglo-American intervention to denounce the risks of such unilateral action and to propose international guarantees in which it would participate.

The prospects were altogether inhibiting as far as Eisenhower was concerned. Khrushchev's correspondence with Eisenhower, which spanned the crisis, strongly underscored the Soviet leader's commitment to having the USSR play a role in the Middle East. To make matters worse, insofar as Eisenhower was concerned, Khrushchev offered a series of proposals that involved recognized Western oil interests while endorsing a more equitable commercial exchange between Middle Eastern oil producers and the West and while supporting the Middle East as a neutral zone.[78] Eisenhower was no less disconcerted by Khrushchev's proposals for an international conference and summit meeting with the United States, Britain, France, and India.[79] In the extensive and frustrating exchanges that followed on the subject, Eisenhower maintained that such meetings were inappropriate in the light of the existing UN forums and ongoing UN discussions of the international crises at issue.[80] Washington's objective was to find an acceptable exit while creating the impression that Soviet proposals had been taken under consideration. In Paris and London, Eisenhower was informed, however, that U.S. allies were not pleased with his response. To Eisenhower's relief, nothing came of the

USSR proposals, and the United States and the USSR were eventually able to agree on holding a special General Assembly session in early August. The date was important, as it prompted a hastening of U.S. troop withdrawal from Beirut.

Beyond the USSR's reaction, the response of various states to U.S. intervention elicited more discord than consensus. Those who cited the conflict between U.S. intervention and UNOGIL efforts included governments committed to the UN role, such as Ireland and Sweden, the latter out of solidarity with Secretary General Dag Hammarskjöld. There was talk in such circles of abolishing UNOGIL, which led Eisenhower to persuade Gunnar Jarring, newly appointed Swedish ambassador to the United States, to reconsider.[81]

The question of the UN was a factor in India, where Prime Minister Nehru opposed intervention and rejected both the Lebanese and the U.S. charges. U.S. officials regarded New Delhi press coverage as unfriendly. Criticism of U.S. intervention was interpreted as the product of a "highly emotional condemnation; all agree landings are in violation of UN charter; one paper even labelled 'armed intrusion' as 'no less crime than Soviet incursion into Hungary.' Embassy believes a statement from the Lebanese minister in defense of his government would be helpful; also strong detailed evidence of men, money and arms supplied to Lebanese rebels by UAR would greatly bolster U.S. case in India."[82]

The U.S. response to the Japanese reaction was far more revealing, given the nature of the Japanese relationship with the United States. The Japanese government faced widespread public criticism of the U.S. action, and specifically criticized it in the light of the UN presence and the absence of evidence backing U.S. and Lebanese charges with respect to claims of "massive intervention." Prime Minister Kishi explained his position to U.S. ambassador Douglas MacArthur II in such terms, emphasizing that "one of great difficulties with Lebanese situation was that Hammarskjöld Report had not RPT not established fact there was massive intervention in Lebanon from without, coupled with fact that Hammarskjöld had reported that present observation system was adequate and international UN force to seal off borders was not RPT not necessary."[83] MacArthur did not hesitate to recommend to Dulles that pressure be applied to Japan from allies such as Iran, Pakistan, Turkey, the Philippines, and Taiwan, along with South Vietnam, Thailand, and Malaya.[84] MacArthur further made Kishi understand the limits of his choice. If Nasser were allowed "to destroy independence of Lebanon, both Soviet Union and Communist China would probably feel free to intervene in other countries where there were domestic difficulties and end result would probably be World War III. Therefore it seemed imperative to support principle of Free World action to preserve independence of Lebanon." Kishi capitulated without delay, according to U.S. sources, explaining that he wanted Eisenhower to know that he "could be sure he (Kishi) placed paramount importance on maintenance and strengthening of U.S.-Japan relations."

In North Africa and the Middle East, pro-American regimes did not depart from the expected positions, even if they offered their support surreptitiously in deference to domestic opposition. Tunisia approved in this manner, as did Rabat, where the regime additionally requested that U.S. ships make an appearance in Morocco.[85] In Algeria, support for Egypt and the UAR was predictable. Further east, there were signs of division in the Saudi royal family. In Turkey and Iran, on the other hand, the response mimicked that in Beirut. In short, more, rather than less, intervention was demanded, although Selwyn Lloyd and John Foster Dulles opposed a Turkish proposal for intervention in Iraq.[86] Shah Mohammad Reza Pahlevi was irked by Western restraint, demanding clarification of U.S. intentions toward the Soviet Union and urging the United States to reduce its purchases of IPC oil in Iraq as a means of pressuring that regime, as well as Nasser and the USSR. In Israel, on the other hand, the events of 1958 led to a rapprochement with the United States.[87] In Cairo, Copeland found Nasser calm, unlike his Syrian partners.[88]

Deception and Self-Deception: Keeping Congress Uninformed

> *Although pledged to act only in behalf of nations*
> *threatened by Communist aggression, the United States*
> *undertook to interfere in Lebanon's internal political*
> *affairs to support a pro-Western government that was*
> *endangered by a crisis largely of its own creation.*
> Marine Corps Historical Center, Washington, D.C.
> July 1958

How was U.S. military intervention in Lebanon's civil war to be justified? The Marine Corps historian cited above had no hesitation in answering, but the answer was not fit for public consumption. The task of crafting a publicly acceptable formula required some engineering. Even before U.S. military intervention, the importance of arriving at a satisfactory justificatory formula was recognized by Eisenhower, Nixon, and Dulles, among others.

Dulles had mastered the art of evasion, coupled with that of deception, in innumerable exchanges on the subject. His approach to the Japanese, which used barely subtle threats to assure compliance, made it clear that he had no difficulty in distinguishing between public and private "discourse" on the subject. His instructions to U.S. diplomats, moreover, were replete with instructions about the importance of molding explanations to fit particular audiences. Thus, the anti-intervention theme was to be stressed before Latin American audiences adversely sensitized by U.S. policies. Another was to be found in the formulas for U.S. allies, which combined the anti-intervention theme with realpolitik, i.e., a warning that conditions might require the opposite. Private communications and deliberations with foreign officials, including Secretary General Dag Hammarskjöld, imposed one set of constraints, but confronting U.S. Senate committees was more difficult. Minimal support on the part of the U.S. public required a virtual blindness to U.S. Middle East policy and Lebanese politics and was achieved with considerable effort. The challenge to such an effort was reflected in the Senate hearings on the Middle East held in the summer of 1958, a political theater of the absurd that ended with a long whimper and a bang.

The consensus that was the practice in administration pronouncements on U.S. intervention relied on the intervention-by-invitation formula that was premised on Sham'un's justification for requesting assistance. In short, the rationalization adopted by U.S. administration officials mirrored that of Sham'un, whose commitment was to masking the domestic roots of civil war. Sham'un's formula, adopted by Eisenhower, Dulles, and Nixon, was disseminated throughout the bureaucracy and U.S. media. Its basic elements concerned the precarious state of Lebanon, whose regime was the target of a UAR-sponsored campaign of subversion. The problem, then, lay in UAR intervention. It was to protect Lebanon from such that the United States intervened.

The approach was designed to allow U.S. intervention to be perceived as anti-interventionist in character. No information relevant to the Egypt/UAR exchanges could be introduced, as it would have offset the prevailing assumptions with regard to Nasser's intransigence. U.S. intentions in Lebanon would thus appear to be morally sound and apolitical, a consideration as important to Eisenhower as avoiding the impression that U.S. interests in the Middle East had any economic basis. Nixon contributed to the assignment with suggestions of how to package U.S. intervention in conformity with support for self-determination and the rights of nations to their civil wars. First, then, was the problem of portraying U.S. intervention as a form of nonpartisan support for the principles of self-determination and nonintervention in the affairs of sovereign states. The assignment required that U.S. intervention be justified in anti-interventionary terms.

On July 15, Eisenhower offered what was to become a commonplace version of the events justifying U.S. intervention in Lebanon: "First of all we have acted at the urgent plea of the Government of Lebanon, a government which has been freely elected by the people only a little over a year ago. It is entitled, as are we, to join in measures of collective security for self-defense. Such action, the United Nations Charter recognizes, is an 'inherent right.' "[89]

U.S. troops, according to Eisenhower, "will protect American lives and by their presence help sustain Lebanese government in its defense of Lebanon's sovereignty and integrity. They do not go as combat forces and not in any act of war. They will be withdrawn as soon as possible."[90] Further, U.S. intervention was to be depicted as entirely apolitical. As Eisenhower continued, "You should make clear as appropriate that U.S. not sending forces to Lebanon because of interest in political fortune of any individual in that country but because of its conviction that what is at stake is continued existence of Lebanon as independent nation in face of indirect aggression."

Dulles was experienced in such exercises. In his directives to U.S. diplomats in Latin America, the latter were advised to "emphasize U.S. action Lebanon not rpt. not interference internal affairs another state but rather measure taken to sustain at its urgent request a freely-elected government clearly shown to be imperiled by armed uprising supported with men, arms, and money from outside sources."[91] The "basic issue," as Dulles had explained in late June, was that the Lebanese civil war was being perpetuated by outside forces, and indeed, that without them it might not have begun.[92] On July 14, on the eve of U.S. intervention, he instructed U.S. diplomats to inform their host governments of the American position in the following terms:

> USG has received from lawful government of Lebanon request that
> U.S. forces be dispatched temporarily to Lebanon in order by their

presence to assist to maintain integrity and independence their country. Lebanese government believes such action imperative if Lebanon's independence be preserved in face of continuing situation within Lebanon created by insurrection aided and abetted from outside, and of grave events which have occurred in Iraq where lawful government has been overthrown by those professing loyalty to alien elements. U.S. could not stand idly by when it received from small peace-loving state with which it has traditionally had most friendly relations an appeal for assistance to help that nation defend itself against aggression abetted from outside. U.S. accordingly responded affirmatively to Lebanese request and a contingent of U.S. forces is arriving in Lebanon July 15.[93]

Rebutting analogies with Suez was a major concern for Eisenhower and Dulles. The similarities did not escape them or the Joint Chiefs of Staff. In 1957 the JCS, considering the possibilities of joint U.S.-U.K. intervention in Lebanon and Jordan, confirmed that "this would be a military campaign with political overtones comparable in many respects to the United Kingdom-France-Israeli debacle of 1956 which dropped British-French prestige to an all time low and contributed greatly to advancing the position of the Soviet Union in the Middle East."[94] In June Eisenhower returned to the question, aware that earlier arguments against Anglo-French intervention in 1956 could now be redirected against the United States. On July 14 Dulles alerted U.S. diplomats specifically about the matter of 1956. "If question brought up of alleged similarity between U.S. actions and U.K.-French-Israeli action in Egypt, you should point out current move being made in response to request for help from lawfully constituted government of friendly state while former was act of hostility against legal government."[95]

Although there was disagreement between Eisenhower and Nixon as to how much to emphasize U.S. economic interests, Nasser's depiction as a pro-Soviet Arab nationalist bent on seizing Western oil interests was an important element in the Eisenhower administration's ideological offensive. Equally important was that total ignorance be maintained regarding the Hare-Nasser talks and the evidence of Nasser's initiatives with respect to Lebanon. Eisenhower's approach was to emphasize the punishing role of Nasser, contrasting his aggressive intentions with the otherwise benign policies of the United States. According to such a scenario. the United States had by amicable means sought access to Middle East oil "without hindrance on the part of anyone." The present political environment spoiled such harmonious relations, and Nasser was the personification of this transformation as he was committed to getting "control of these supplies—to get the income and the power to destroy the Western world."[96]

The vice president strongly believed that while U.S. audiences would not object to the linkage of oil and U.S. policy, "for world opinion you cannot allow it to appear that the Mid East countries are simply a pawn in the big power contest for their resources" (ibid.). Eisenhower disagreed, persuaded that for domestic as well as international audiences, it was imperative to couch American intervention in other than economic terms. According to a White House Memorandum, Eisenhower was reported to have said to Generals Twining and Goodpaster: "If, however, our only argument is economic—saying that the life of the western world depends upon access to oil in the Middle East—this would be quite different, and quite inferior to a purpose that rests on the right to govern by consent of the governed. The President said he is giving deep thought to finding a moral ground on which to stand if we have to go further."[97]

Vice President Nixon came to the rescue with a confusing package that Eisenhower thought satisfactory. Self-determination and the right of nations to civil war were at the heart of Nixon's recommendations. As he explained, "Any nation ought to have the right to revolution. We recognize the right of revolution. We also say every people has the right of self-determination—that right of self-determination is one that carries with it the right not to have outside interference that stimulates it."[98] The problem, then, was to explain the conditions under which a civil war was the aggravated result of external pressures. "What is required," Nixon said, is a "historical announcement of when a civil war becomes the type of action in which outside intervention by the United States is justified. When is a civil war not a civil war?" In the case of Lebanon, the answer is when the Lebanese president defines it thus to accommodate his interests and those of the United States.

> We go into Lebanon because we were invited in and because here is a man, [Sham'un], who was freely elected leader in his country who finds his country infiltered [sic] by corruption, subversion, and bribery. In the larger sense the President could say we have to find a way to deal with civil war—if we do not, we will loose [sic] the world. The Communists have developed the device of foreign-inspired revolution to create a civil war (a classic case was Czechoslovakia). What we are doing here is saying that finally the West has reached a conclusion. We will not stand by to allow civil war to deliver a country even to Nasser. (Ibid.)

The Eisenhower administration expounded on this and other forms of justification before selected congressional representatives on July 14. On that occasion, it was imperative to make the case for U.S. intervention rapidly and effectively. To judge by the response of some of those present, the success rate was far from 100 percent. It was a warning of things to come in the Senate forum, where some of the same U.S. representatives adopted a more aggressive brand of questioning. The Senate Foreign Relations Committee on the Middle East held hearings on U.S. policy in Lebanon and the Middle East throughout the spring and summer of 1958. Assigned the task of deliberating on U.S. policy, committee members consistently complained that they were systematically deprived of information. The complaint was not without validity. Committee members had no access to classified data, and they were offered little by way of coherent analysis of U.S. policy or Lebanese politics. What they were given was an opaque diet of nonexplanations, sometimes ludicrous, often insulting, with respect to the depiction of Lebanese politics as the outdoor parlor game of Mediterranean natives. The charade led one Senate member to conclude:

> The American public has really been misled . . . misled into believing that the Russian Communists were sending all kinds of arms and people across into Lebanon to knock down the duly constituted government, that that constituted an indirect threat of aggression under the Eisenhower doctrine which called for us to go in. But in point of fact, it seems to me from these briefings, the fair conclusion is that this was, perhaps, 90% . . .an internal disaffection for [Sham'un].[99]

Few among Senate committee members would have challenged Senator George D. Aiken's remark that "there are times when the State Department would just as soon this committee did not exist. [Laughter.]"[100]

In the days that followed the U.S. landing in Beirut, Eisenhower complained that the American public was not particularly interested in Lebanese developments: "gov't greatly concerned, people show no awareness."[101] The president ignored the fact that he himself had earlier discouraged debate on U.S. policy on the ground that it risked undermining U.S. initiatives.[102] In this he was supported by the JCS, who argued for a more effective conditioning of the American public, since "an apathetic if not opposition attitude on the part of the press and the general public to such positive action appeared prevalent."[103] In late June, the Senate committee had, in fact, attempted to gather information on administration policies in Lebanon. At the time, John F. Kennedy, then a committee member, asked Theodore Green, the committee chair, whether he had succeeded in so doing. Green replied that his meeting with Dulles had resulted in little news: "I don't think we got very much information."[104]

Dulles met with Senators Green, Fulbright, Sparkman, Wiley, and Hickenlooper, as well as Council on Foreign Relations chief of staff Carl Marcy, on June 23. This was the period during which U.S. and British officials in Washington and Beirut were embarrassed by the absence of evidence to substantiate Sham'un's claims that the UAR had engaged in "massive interference" in Lebanon's domestic affairs, and UNOGIL reports were underscoring the same point. Nonetheless, Dulles offered the usual arguments, emphasizing U.S. credibility, evidence of UAR interference in Lebanon's domestic affairs, and overall risk to those on the Soviet-Sino periphery, including Thailand, Viétnam, and China. The burden to resolve the crisis was on Nasser, according to Dulles, a pronouncement made at the very time of the unmentioned UAR-U.S. discussions in Cairo. Continuing along this line, Dulles argued that "if he does not discontinue UAR efforts to take over Lebanon, President [Sham'un] may cash the check which we gave him five weeks ago."[105] The reference was to the May 13 instructions that Dulles had conveyed to Sham'un on the proper language in which to couch his request for U.S. intervention.

As though to concede that there were internal problems in Lebanon not of the UAR's making, Dulles pointed to Sham'un's predicament in relation to his commander in chief, Shihab. The problem, according to Dulles, was that this compounded Sham'un's difficulties in getting "his own government forces to protect him because this man is thinking possibly of succeeding him. Now they are also having some difficulty in their armed forces in that the Moslems are beginning to defect. He [Sham'un] says there has just been a trickle."[106] Committee members responded with frustration. What was U.S. policy toward Nasser, if he was at the center of the problem? "Do they really want to get rid of Nasser or do they not want to get rid of him? Do they really think they can live with him or not? I just have no idea. Maybe I am wrong. Do you know, Senator Mansfield?" The questions were put by Fulbright (ibid. 483–84).

On July 15, John Kennedy asked his colleagues whether they intended taking any action in the light of U.S. intervention, recalling that earlier efforts to obtain information from the State Department had failed.

Wayne Morse declared that he would oppose U.S. policy, "the mixing of American blood with Arabian oil in the Middle East." Indignant, Morse insisted on the committee's right to know. "I do think that at least we should get our facts straight, that this committee is entitled to some report from the administration in regard to what is going on in the Middle East, because we are not of one mind in regard to what the proper policy in the Middle East is" (ibid. 506). Senate committee members repeatedly confronted administration officials with the question as to when the decision had been made to intervene. Was it on July 14? Russell Long asked Green whether he had been told of the plan to send troops. "No, I was not," answered Chairman Green. "The point I have in mind," Long explained, "is that the troops had to be on their way at that time. They could not have been there in Lebanon otherwise this morning" (ibid. 508). Hubert Humphrey called the decision to intervene "a mistake, a sad mistake, to send troops into Lebanon. I think that we will be hated, bitterly resented, for years to come. I think we are acting like the Metternich of the 20th Century. And I don't believe we are really dealing with the problems. We are dealing with symptoms" (ibid. 507). John Sparkman put the same question to Under Secretary of State Herter in the hearings of July 16. And Wayne Morse repeated it: "At the White House conference the other day did the President notify the Congressional leaders that were there that he had made his decision to move the troops toward Lebanon but had not made his final decision as to whether or not they should land?" (ibid, 539). Herter deferred to William Macomber Jr., special assistant to Dulles, since he had been present at the White House briefing. Macomber thought that the issue had not come up.

There were those present who criticized the critics. But the dissenting voices were loud and clear. Referring to Dulles, Wayne Morse insisted that "this man has a clear moral duty to the American people to get down here and inform their elected representatives, through the committee, what he is up to" (ibid. 513). On July 24, Fulbright returned to the question of the basis of U.S. action. "What was the nature of the commitment that we honored?" he asked (ibid. 600). William Macomber responded: "I was speaking of a commitment in the sense that a friendly small country called on us for help and we gave them help." Was the commitment written, did it come in the form of a treaty, Fulbright rejoined, to which Macomber replied that the Lebanese case was exceptional and that there had not been a written accord. Fulbright again: "What kind of agreement was there? What was the commitment that we fulfilled? You just said we fulfilled one and now we have great credit among everybody for fulfilling our commitments." At this point Macomber retracted the term, substituting the proposition that "we were under obligation—we were asked by a friendly small government to come to their aid when they thought that if we did not they would cease to be independent. Now that was the situation we were in. As far as any commitments are concerned, that is a different thing." Fulbright persisted, and Macomber complied by describing Sham'un's views in early May, his fear of Nasser as endangering the independence of Lebanon, and his concern regarding the response of the United States. When Fulbright returned to the question of why the United States had not intervened earlier, inquiring whether it was "because we weren't asked," Macomber replied in the affirmative. Fulbright again asked for clarification. "Under what authority did the President give this obligation, this commitment to [Sham'un] to come to his rescue with troops, under the Eisenhower doctrine or what?" Macomber explained: "We did not go in, the commitment was not given under the so-called Eisenhower Doctrine. That did not really apply here in this situation of indirect aggression" (ibid. 608). What did apply was Eisenhower's decision to "protect American life and property," a move, Macomber explained, that freed Lebanese troops "that were attempting to preserve the integrity of Lebanon. He did not go in to save [Sham'un]." Fulbright was not satisfied.

SENATOR FULBRIGHT: Mr Secretary, I get confused, but the commitment was given to save [Sham'un]. The commitment was not given to [Sham'un] to protect American lives and property, was it? That is certainly a non sequitur. I mean the commitment was given to protect [Sham'un], was it not? You do not go to [Sham'un] and say, "I will give you a commitment to protect American lives in Lebanon," do you? I mean that is ridiculous.

MR MACOMBER: We have several questions here.

SENATOR FULBRIGHT: I am asking about the commitment now. Under what authority was the commitment given? Was that given under his right to protect American lives? It couldn't be, could it?

MR MACOMBER: The President went into that country at the request of the country the way he can put troops or military officers into any country at their request. He was not going into a war.

SENATOR FULBRIGHT: Wait a minute, that is going pretty far. Can he put them in any country at their request? Is that understood to be his authority?

THE CHAIRMAN: I am sorry, we will have to end this meeting. (Ibid. 609)

Herter offered the classic U.S.-Lebanese formula. Responsibility for the crisis was in the hands of the UAR and its Lebanese agents. Of U.S. military assistance for Sham'un before July 15, nothing was said.

On July 22, Macomber turned to the Lebanese civil war, "Lebanese style," in which partisans without politics acted out a native drama largely incomprehensible to outsiders. Among the actors identified by name was Kamal Junblat, a man defined solely in terms of this response to the twin axes of U.S. policy. "He does not like Nasser at all, but he hates [Sham'un]."

> What happens is that an area, usually under a feudal leader, will go in revolt against the government for whatever reason, and when they go in revolt, what they do is they all put rifles on their shoulders and they wander around the area that they control but they do not do very much fighting. Now you take [Junblat], who is down in the South Central part of Lebanon, and is a Druse leader. He does not like Nasser at all, but he hates [Sham'un]. . . . He has his area in revolt. That revolt is a peculiar kind of thing. They wander around. They are left alone in their area. Occasionally they will come down and fire on the Damascus Road or fire onto the troops that are around it, mortar shots, maybe, a few rifle shots. The army fires back and then everything quiets down and they just look at each other, and you have a situation where they do not come out and really cause much trouble and the army does not come in and clean them up.
>
> They just stand each other off. Now that situation has prevailed almost all over Lebanon. In Beirut there is the Moslem sector there. Now they are in revolt in the same way, the people wandering around the street in the Moslem sector carrying rifles. Occasionally—they have some mortar in there—they lob a mortar up, occasional sniper fire, and when they go too far, troops open up and things quiet down again.
> (Ibid. 565–66)

To this Macomber hastened to add that it was the "Iraq thing" that had disrupted efforts at political settlement. At its origins, the Lebanese crisis exploded, he maintained, "because of the fact that it was time to get a new president and they suspected [Sham'un's] intentions, at the same time there was an assassination of a leftist editor which stirred the mobs up" (ibid. 566). More than forty years later, former high-level officials recalled the crisis in terms of Communists and mobs that had alarmed the administration.[107] Fulbright and Morse, confronted with

Macomber's description, concluded that in the light of such events it was "perfectly ridiculous that we sent the Marines in."[108]

The question of U.S. intervention in the midst of civil war was not to be brushed aside. Was Lebanon involved in civil war when the United States agreed to intervene, Morse asked Herter on July 16. Yes, but there was foreign influence, Herter replied. Morse, reminding Herter that such assistance was not unknown in American history, returned to the central issue. The United States had assumed a partisan role in a civil war, taking "sides in a revolution where a populace is split and is seeking to set up another form of government."

> I think the people of Lebanon have the right to determine what their form of government is. They may be getting some arms from other sources as some people in the Middle East have gotten arms from us. All I am asking you is whether or not we have not now gotten ourselves in a position, when we go in for a purpose over and beyond the protection of American lives and property, where we are not going to be charged around the world and those parts of the world particularly who support the Lebanese, in the next hundred years with having taken sides with the civil war in Lebanon.   (Ibid. 542)

The underlying principle of self-determination was violated, Morse insisted, reminding Herter that "there are some of us that feel that the principle of self-determination ought to prevail in Lebanon without American Marines in there doing more than protecting American lives" (ibid. 543).

What of the connection between Iraq and Lebanon? Critical of the administration's intelligence failure in Iraq, Senate members wanted to know the evidence linking the two events. Readily admitting that the United States did not entirely understand the Iraqi situation, Macomber argued that "we certainly understood potentialities that could flow into Lebanon regardless of any two or three different alternate explanations for which happened in Iraq" (ibid. 606). Humphrey reminded Macomber that that was conjecture: "I mean that is an assumption. I do not say that you can necessarily verify the assumption. It is an assumption." The explanation for U.S. action rested on the commitment to Sham'un, Humphrey conceded, a commitment whose clarity remained elusive. Would U.S. policy have differed if the administration had anticipated the action in Iraq, Lausche inquired, to which Macomber replied, "We would have warned our friends" (ibid. 607). The response evoked this rejoinder from Fulbright: "Do you think it is our duty if a country wishes to change its government—and I am told by some people there are good reasons to wish to change it. The fact that they are our friends, is that an adequate answer that we must protect our friends regardless of what the respective countries think of our friends?" The session of the committee was abruptly terminated.

Five days later, CIA director Allen Dulles appeared. Iraq was the principal issue on the agenda. Allen Dulles's testimony had much in common with that of Macomber, resting in the first instance on a view of Middle East politics as generically conspiratorial. Plots, Dulles explained, are commonplace to the peoples of the Middle East, just as military coups constitute "their form of elections," and every urban center has its "potential mob," which naturally leads to chronic instability (ibid. 647–48). The coup in Iraq was thus explained as a "result of uncontrolled mob action" (ibid. 644). Dulles maintained that the United States had known of difficulties facing its allies in Baghdad, that it miscalculated the strength of the Iraqi army and relied on an Iraqi leadership with an "exaggerated confidence in its own abilities" (ibid. 644).

Allen Dulles's presentation was challenged. Senator William Langer questioned the description of the "mob." "Do you mean the patriotic people of Iraq who were sick and tired of having those in control of Iraq bribed by the United States Government?"(ibid. 648). When Dulles indicated some confusion, Langer restated his question: "Do you mean the patriotic people of Iraq who were sick and tired of having 2 percent who were in control there, who were being bribed by the United States Government to run the country?" Allen Dulles replied with reference to the mob thesis. According to him, "There is a potential mob in each one of those cities, and it is not hard to get that moving if the military force is not there or the military force has been taken off." Conspiracy was at the heart of the matter, in addition to the peculiar politics of the region, the predilection for coups. "As some people have said, and quite true, this is in a sense their form of elections," Dulles continued. The Iraqi coup was the result of discontent with the Nuri Sa'id government, which was "not particularly corrupt, and had done something for the people, but they got tired of it. They did not think it was in tune with the wave of the future as they see it and the populace went along" (ibid. 647).

What did this mean for U.S. policy, if the Iraqi regime, the product of such turbulence, was prepared to do business with Washington? How dangerous was the new Iraqi regime to U.S. interests? And if it represented no such danger, what of the connection with Nasser and Lebanon? Further, how could one explain the rapid visit to Baghdad by Robert Murphy, given the role that Iraq was alleged to have played in the decision of Washington to intervene in Lebanon? Dulles conceded that the Iraqi military had not disturbed the flow of oil, and, furthermore, "the government as far as we know, has made every effort to protect American and British interests and other foreign interests there" (ibid. 657). How did this alter the view of the Nasser-Iraqi connection, Greene wanted to know. "Yes, yes. We cannot formally and directly tie it in, but we have what I would consider pretty conclusive evidence that Nasser knew about the plot, that the plotters had been in Egypt from time to time, and the circumstantial evidence is extremely strong and it follows the pattern of known activities [deleted] in the case of Jordan, and previously in the case of Syria, and to some extent in the case of Lebanon" (ibid. 646).

It was Lausche who was disturbed about U.S. recognition of the new regime in Iraq. "Has there been any talk anywhere that the speed with which we have recognized Iraq is indicative of an admission that we prematurely sent our troops into Lebanon?" (ibid. 710). This time it was Macomber who replied, providing information about Turkey's recognition of Iraq—which Lausche had also asked about—and the United States. "Now as far as our own position, we are certainly not going overly fast. We are getting sort of at the end of the pack here, an awful lot of people are ahead of us already. I know what you are saying is, 'Gosh, if we are going to move this quickly, maybe this wasn't the problem after all.' "

Senator Lausche was on the track, but neither he nor his colleagues were informed of the administration's calculations. In its review of the crisis, the JCS indicated that the United States had "avoided becoming the declared enemy of the new Iraqi regime," assuming that it would retain leverage by so doing. Macomber offered an interpretation of events that was of considerable interest, insofar as it effectively distinguished U.S. action in Lebanon from the events of Iraq:

> I can only say this: that regardless of how that government [Iraqi] turns out, the situation in Lebanon was a separate problem.
>
> Lebanon itself in the judgment of the Government of Lebanon and in our judgment was in grave danger of going down under the psychological impact of what had happened.
>
> Now that is separate from how the government turns out in Iraq. We do not rule as completely out of the question, the fact that this new government will turn out to be a genuinely neutralist government.

We think it unlikely. We think in all probability they will be a Nasser-type of operation, but as long as there is any possibility that that will not be the case, we do not want to slam the door in their face, providing they will make these other assurances.

Discussion of Western interests in Iraq led to the question of U.S. policy in the Gulf. Did the administration intend to use force in the event that Kuwait, Qatar, Bahrain, or Saudi Arabia supported Nasser? Would the U.S. support the British use of force? Herter replied with a studied vagueness: "I think we would be inclined to be sympathetic" (ibid. 591). When Allen Dulles appeared before the committee, Fulbright returned the discussion to Kuwait and the nature of Anglo-American oil policies. Kuwait, he declared, was owned by Anglo-American oil interests, and the anachronistic situation would have to change. This was not simply a matter of protecting private property, Fulbright argued, unless you were "teaching a course in classical economics at Harvard, but I think it is not a politically acceptable solution to that problem" (ibid. 671). Britain relied on Kuwaiti investment in London, as well on the benefits of oil company profits, Fulbright recognized, but the United States was not as dependent on such oil and profits as its British ally was. Under the circumstances, Fulbright continued: "I strongly recommend that we try to come up with some kind of a solution which would give the rest of the area some sense of participation in it, and whatever you call it, socialism or anything else. I think that is going to have to be done or you lose it all in some violent revolution" (ibid. 672). To this, Dulles noncommittally replied, "We are not blind to the arguments you raise." Fulbright and others present were blind, however, to the Anglo-American plans for Saudi Arabia, Kuwait, and the Gulf.

U.S. involvement in the postwar settlement was similarly met with denial. This was how Macomber explained the situation in Beirut, omitting to cite how and where U.S. officials in Beirut were maneuvering.

What you have now is like a political convention going on. They are out maneuvering in the corridors, trying to settle on somebody. They want to have it agreed on by the time that the Parliament convenes on the 31st to elect a new President, so that the actual meeting will be pretty pro forma and that the arrangements will all have been made ahead of time.   (Ibid. 617)

Senator Cooper wanted to know if this meant that Lebanon was no longer in a state of "revolution" and the United States was no longer interfering in the process of self-determination. Macomber's reply was a trilogy of confusion:

> Yes, we want that, the difficulty has been before that you not only had this indirect aggression going on, but you had the pro-government elements or the anti-indirect aggression people that would be against the indirect aggression badly split among themselves, because of the succession problem. Therefore they never really got on with the job of handling this rebellion.
>
> Now our feeling is that once you get it settled as to who is going to be President and that is generally accepted, that you will then cut down very much on the trouble. The trouble that will be left will be the trouble that is strictly originated from without. The country will then be unified and organized and ready to get on and do that job by itself.
>
> Now that is our long-range hope. You may have to keep the U.N. in there to be sure that this new group does not get additional support from without, but if you can isolate that support from without, we do feel that the Government of Lebanon has the capacity to get the situation back under control within the country.   (Ibid. 618)

When Assistant Secretary of State William Rountree appeared, Senator Aiken asked him about the possibilities of democratic reform in Lebanon and Jordan. This was not an option that the administration took seriously, claiming that conditions precluded such an outcome at present. The dismissal allowed Rountree to bypass the niceties of U.S. policy, let alone the nature of Jordanian and Lebanese domestic politics. Instead, emphasis was on the next stage in U.S. intervention in Beirut. With the end of the military phase of that intervention, and expectations that the political settlement the United States was helping to "broker" would yield a neutralist, albeit acceptable, regime, Senate critics remained resolute in their skepticism. Not only had the American people been misled by the Eisenhower administration with respect to the indirect role of the Soviet Union in Lebanon, Senator Clark concluded, but the argument about an "indirect threat of aggression," to which the United States had responded, was a farce. Administration briefings persuaded Clark that "this was, perhaps, 90 percent an internal disaffection for [Sham'un]" (ibid. 713). The civil war had been real to begin with, the senator concluded. It is "still primarily an internal Lebanese movement, isn't it?" he asked.

In a study of presidential power in the United States, Richard Neustadt observed that in 1958 Eisenhower's "approval fell to 49 percent in one month, April, and only once, in August, rose as high as 58 percent."[109] The explanation was, in part, "a contretemps in Lebanon, which led the President to send American troops," as another prominent interpreter of U.S. presidential politics and international relations explained.[110] The people of the United States had rallied to their president.

14

By Mutual Consent: July–October 1958

*The presence on their soil of American troops sobered
the Lebanese and evoked from them a spirit of responsibility. Thanks to this spirit, a workable political compromise was arranged.*
Marine Corps Historical Center, July 1958*

*Without firing a shot in anger, and in close and
friendly collaboration with the local authorities, our
forces have achieved what they were sent to Lebanon
and Jordan to do, at the request of the respective
Governments. They have preserved the independence
of these two small countries against aggressive subversive forces directed from outside.*
Eisenhower to Macmillan, November 3, 1958*

The Candidate

Arriving at an acceptable political solution was the primary objective of
the post–civil war phase of U.S. political-military intervention. Its implementation assumed a measure of intimidation that was implicit in the
American military presence and explicit in the veiled threats of U.S. officials vis-à-vis the opposition, which they alternately sought to undermine and co-opt. Such a politics was carried out with the collaboration
of major Lebanese political figures, hence the generally noncoercive
aspect of the achievement that Eisenhower celebrated in his November 3
message to Macmillan. No less self-congratulatory was the statement of
the Marine Corps historian who, contrary to President Eisenhower, was
not loathe to emphasize the role of military occupation in promoting
desired political objectives. Eisenhower's message to Macmillan had an
added dimension that must be included in any review of this phase of

U.S. policy, as it not only underscored the collaboration of the two Western powers in Lebanon and Jordan but also served as a reminder of the calibration of U.S. withdrawal plans from Beirut with those of the British from Amman. There is another necessary qualification to be made with respect to Eisenhower's statement, namely, that neither Lebanese nor Jordanian politicians dependent on U.S. and Anglo-American support aspired to independence, if such meant being cut off from their Western protectors.

The postwar phase of military-political intervention involved three interrelated facets of U.S. policy in Beirut. The first was assuring an acceptable presidential candidate, which meant assessing the real as opposed to the nominal risks of neutralist agendas common to Lebanese politicians of the period. The second was agreeing to a Cabinet that would be approved by a Sham'unist Chamber and that would meet the requirements of the postwar political situation, with respect both to Sham'unist partisans and to opposition leaders. The third was the matter of providing financial and internal security support for the new regime. And finally, the fourth dealt with the issue of withdrawal of U.S. troops.

Among U.S. figures who played a major role during the period was Robert Murphy, the peripatetic U.S. special envoy who was known for his close connections to the U.S. president. The tendency to glorify Murphy's role assumes a number of factors that are rarely credited, among them the American occupation of Beirut, which lent Murphy's pronouncements an immediacy that they might not otherwise have had. Murphy obviously overrode other U.S. officials present, in particular, McClintock. But there was little that Murphy learned and passed on to his Washington superiors that McClintock had not previously discovered, including the condition of Sham'un and the eclectic nature of the opposition that had little in common with its American caricature.

The most dramatic aspect of postwar U.S. policy, which appeared to discredit the stated objectives of U.S. intervention in Lebanon, was the decision to withdraw support from Sham'un. While Malik's exit from Lebanese politics had been considered earlier, it was now to be implemented in a demonstration of Anglo-American pressure tactics at the United Nations. Malik and Sham'un retained the support of the Dulles brothers through the initial period of Shihab's presidency. And the overall suspicion with which opposition figures were viewed in these circles was a tribute to the depth of their influence. The reversal with respect to Sham'un was not unforeseen. Doubts about his capacities, let alone his political judgment, were not unknown in Washington. But the logic of Secretary Dulles's policy rested on a loyalty to the man regarded as a uniquely reliable support for U.S. policy.

Within days after U.S. intervention, however, it became clear that America's man in Beirut had plans for the U.S. military that were unacceptable in Washington. Not only did Sham'un and Malik oppose U.S. withdrawal of troops, they asked for an expansion of U.S. occupation in Lebanon, a proposal that obviously undermined U.S. support for Shihab, Sham'un's successor. The implications of the former president's political views were not limited to such demands. Nor were they categorically rebuffed by Washington or U.S. officials in Beirut, as the intervention of McClintock in the Cabinet selection process indicated.

Less than a week after the arrival of U.S. forces, the atmosphere was marked by an exceptional cordiality between U.S. and Lebanese executives. On July 21, for example, Sham'un sent a letter of gratitude to Eisenhower for his incalculable aid in "responding to my call for help, based on a decision by the legitimate government of Lebanon, through the landing of United States forces in Lebanon to help us defend our independence and integrity in conformity with Article 51 of the United Nations Charter."[1] Eisenhower responded in kind, adding that "the purpose of our action was to help your country preserve its independence, in accord with the inherent right of nations to cooperate for self-defense." Eisenhower vowed, as did Sham'un, the continued friendship of both nations and their common support for the United Nations Charter. Even the artificiality of the statements rapidly became obsolete in the light of Sham'un's sense of betrayal by Washington, a feeling shared by his supporters. For his partisans he remained "the national hero, and [Shihab] a villain who had staked the sovereignty and independence of Lebanon at the most critical moment in the country's history to get the presidential chair."[2] This was not a group that would easily accept that "Americans had wider ranges in sight . . . and more important targets at which to aim."[3]

Malik's new role posed other problems, but they could scarcely be interpreted as betrayal. His interest in a UN position had been conveyed to U.S. officials earlier, but it was at this stage that Anglo-American delegates at the UN, including Dulles, made the necessary arrangements to assure his obtaining the presidency of the General Assembly. In the process, it became necessary to push aside the Sudanese foreign minister, who was also a candidate for the position. Dulles viewed his candidacy in these terms: "This Sudan fellow has a lot of support because he is a colored fellow."[4] U.S. delegate to the UN Henry Cabot Lodge discreetly suggested that Dulles attempt a more diplomatic approach in explaining why the United States did not support the "fellow" in question. Dulles was advised to express "something with the idea we would like to support him for something later—you think he is well qualified to hold high office and hope the time will come when we could support him. L[odge] thinks it would be a good thing to do. The colored angle is dangerous politically. The Sec said he would have to mention Malik too and L agreed."[5] And the double deed was done. Malik became General Assembly president in the fall of 1958.

Earlier, in Beirut, far from the scene of Malik's success, there were other manipulations at work in the designation of an acceptable presidential candidate. Nine days after a U.S. intervention advertised as a contribution to global peace and security, Eisenhower found the situation confusing: "Things are calm, but all uneasy. Can't see where going."[6] The observation was in stark contrast with the assessments offered by Deputy Under Secretary of State for Political Affairs Robert Murphy in Beirut. While Dulles instructed Murphy to leave Beirut during the elections in order to avoid the accurate impression that the United States was interfering in Lebanon's domestic politics, Murphy drew his own conclusions about what was to be done.[7] Sham'un had become a liability and his categoric treatment of the opposition had been in error. Sham'un, Murphy thought, was in a sorry state, a condition aggravated by a self-imposed two-month in-house exile. That Sham'un refused to tender his resignation only reinforced Murphy's view of the Lebanese president as hopelessly intransigent, a man unable to relinquish power and, ultimately, a victim of his own political excesses (ibid. 404). He had been mistaken in his treatment of the opposition leadership, whose pro-American outlook was inadequately appreciated by Washington. What, then, was to be done? The agenda was clear. First Sham'un would have to be replaced, and then the opposition would have to be scrutinized in terms of its political reliability.

In practice, Murphy and McClintock surveyed the Lebanese political field, moving between opposition and Sham'unist supporters, while Lebanese politicians plied their trade at the U.S. Embassy, keeping their hosts well informed as to political developments. The immediate task was the identification of presidential candidates that included, in addition to Fu'ad Shihab, Alfred Naqqash, Jawad Bulos, Besharah al-Khuri,

Salim Lahhud, Elie Abu Jawdeh, Raymond Eddeh, Charles Helu, Emile Tyan, and Badri al-Maʻoushi. Shihab was not the man of choice, as opposed to such figures as Naqqash and Bulos. Meeting with Eddeh, Karame, the Maronite patriarch, as well as Salam and Junblat, Murphy found his views of Shamʻun's political behavior reinforced. These were not men who should have been excluded from the political field in 1957. Referring to Junblat, Murphy maintained that it had been an error to exclude him and that this was nothing more than Shamʻun's self-interested maneuvering: "Conversation with Junblat indicated that he wanted a settlement, and he was pleased when I told him about the prospect of an early presidential election. He had thought the Marines had come to support [Shamʻun], and when he discovered this was not true, any opposition he might have had toward American intervention dissolved" (ibid. 406).

On July 25, McClintock cabled Dulles that information had reached him from a Lebanese editor to the effect that Junblat, Hamadeh, and Shiʻi supporters of Ahmad al-Asʻad were "prepared reach accommodation with U.S. and subsequently would not object to vigorous action against insurgent areas Beirut and Tripoli where Syrians control opposition movement through terror and intimidation."[8] The comment raises questions as to its origins, credibility, and political implications in the web of Lebanese politics. But evidently the "insurgent" leaders were a target of suspicion.

Relations with the core of the conservative political leadership of the opposition remained turbulent. Flattered by expressions of support that he received from the Greek Catholic and Greek Orthodox clergy, Murphy elicited no such sentiments from his encounters with Yafi, ʻUwayni, and Salam. Toward them, Murphy adopted a threatening posture, leaving no doubt as to the lengths to which the United States would go if it so chose. McClintock reported to Dulles that "Murphy very plainly indicated to opposition leader Abdallah Yafi that U.S. military are seriously concerned at security threat posed by insurrectionists in the Basta. Yafi was shaken when Murphy told him destruction of the Basta could be accomplished in a matter of seconds by forces now assembled in Beirut."[9] The reprehensible form of resistance to which Murphy alluded was "the 'boyscout' activity of irresponsible rebel elements headed on by Damascus Radio."[10] Murphy reminded the opposition that the Lebanese army was cooperating with U.S. forces, to reinforce their sense of vulnerability. When confronted by Sa'eb Salam's resistance, the

U.S. envoy concluded that "if UAR-supported revolution triumphed it might endanger U.S. security."[11] To Salam, American behavior was incomprehensible. Accepting Murphy's role as "working wisely and carefully to end crisis when USA sent occupation troops to Lebanon," he found Murphy's arrogance shocking. "Besides, who told him he has been appointed a judge of people in this country?" Salam asked.

In addition to the crude efforts to pacify the opposition, considerable attention was paid to the question of neutralism and its potential risks insofar as U.S. policy was concerned. The chief advocate of neutralism, whom U.S. officials categorically rejected, was Besharah al-Khuri. Yet it was precisely his efforts to resist U.S. co-optation that rendered him attractive to his supporters. McClintock wasted no time in cabling Secretary Dulles to the effect that "rebels reptd now shifting support Shihab to al-Khuri, former pres ousted 1952 for alleged corruptions. Al-Khuri election would not rep advantage for west."[12] Lebanese advocates of neutralism were not breaking new ground. Among the oft-repeated demands of opposition leaders and their supporters was that Lebanon reclaim its neutral stance in foreign policy in conformity with the National Pact. Those supporting a neutralist position included a wide array of political figures, such as former ministers Charles Helu and Philippe Taqla, who was currently chair of the Foreign Affairs Committee of Parliament and adviser to the UNF on foreign policy and a supporter of Besharah al-Khuri. Taqla, regarded as a friend of the United States in the early 1950s, thought that the Sham'un regime had erred in supporting the Eisenhower Doctrine and that Lebanon should have adopted a "policy of absolute neutrality in all of its foreign affairs—both between East and West and between other Arab States and blocs."[13] Rashid Karame, former prime minister and opposition leader, vowed support for a Nasserist "positive neutrality" and claimed that he would support only presidential aspirants who advocated a similar position. When he emerged as the prime minister in the postwar Cabinet of President Shihab, Karame's attitude toward the United States was entirely cordial. No threat to U.S. interests was involved. Indeed, the assessment of neutralism by the U.S. Embassy was that it posed few dangers.

> It is true that an absolutely neutral Lebanon would not mean Lebanon's severing its traditional ties with the West, but for Lebanon to adopt a policy which would mean its turning away from a previously committed foreign policy of close cooperation with the West and the United States would be interpreted by many as a serious tactical set-

back for the West in the Middle East. One example of what a permanent neutral Lebanon might mean tactically is that the present airlift to
Jordan, utilizing Beirut International Airport and Lebanese refineries,
probably would not have been possible.   (Ibid.)

Reference to the airlift was to the emergency shipment of diesel oil, gasoline, and kerosene, essential to Jordan, through Beirut via the auspices of
Socony, Esso, and Caltex.

Insofar as Lebanese political leaders were concerned, few were committed to severing their links with the United States or to forging closer
ties with Nasser. Moreover, some advocates of a neutral Lebanon
claimed that it offered Lebanese Christians a sounder basis for their protection than past policies had.[14] The critical question, as McClintock
realized, was, "Who defined neutralism?" According to Lebanese foreign
minister Taqla, for instance, the Helu proposal would make the United
States the sole guarantor of Lebanese neutrality, while reserving
Lebanon's right to determine its regional as well as international commitments, thus allowing it to avoid recognition of Israel while preserving
its Washington connections.

There were other proposals in circulation that offered additional
options. The French favored multilateral guarantees involving all major
powers, including the Soviet Union. There was a Ghanaian proposal at
the United Nations that recommended UN supervisors for elections, and
a Swiss or Austrian model for the state's foreign policy. And there was the
lame duck president, who considered the Austrian model unacceptable
since it risked Soviet interference. His own alternative was to transform
Lebanon into a base of UN police activity in the region (ibid. #731).

While McClintock deliberated on the ever-shifting political scene,
the opposition became more disenchanted with Shihab. Former president
Khuri was clearly their man, according to McClintock, who sought to
avoid such an outcome.[15] The opposition, at this stage, issued a "Revolutionary Manifesto."[16] The Embassy was fully informed regarding the
July 30 statement, which it had already seen in an earlier form. The fif-
teen-point list of domestic and foreign policy proposals included a
demand for the withdrawal of U.S. forces, along with Sham'un's immediate resignation. Members of the opposition wanted input into the selection of the new Cabinet, which it assumed would favor Lebanon's neutrality. On domestic issues, there was a call for a more democratically run
parliament, the amendment of elections laws, and greater decentraliza-

tion of government offices, as well as the protection of individual rights, the right of assembly, and freedom of the press. There was the formal commitment to a greater measure of equality and justice among different communities, as well as the "establishment of a fifty-fifty basis between Moslems and Christians in all government departments until agreement is reached concerning abolishment of confessionalism." The agenda was rejected. More than thirty years later, the formula was echoed in the Ta'if Accords that followed Lebanon's longest war, from 1975 through 1990. What would the course of Lebanon's political history have been if the earlier agenda had been implemented?

Sham'un and Malik, far from contemplating any such transformations of Lebanese politics, were considering a "military solution of rebellion with all possible means."[17] Indeed, earlier on the same day, July 30, Prime Minister Sulh had bluntly asked U.S. officials whether U.S. forces would "defend the present government by attacking the Lebanese army with our forces."[18] The request persuaded U.S. military and political officials Holloway, Murphy, and McClintock that Sham'un's tenure should be terminated in order to avoid the risks of further political destabilization. The possibility of a military coup was not ruled out. In the end, however, the position of U.S. officials was that "whatever safety there is for U.S. in this precarious situation lies with Shihab and his military establishment such as it is" (ibid.). On July 30, Shihab was meeting with Murphy and reviewing the date for the parliamentary election. The protection of opposition deputies against whom arrest warrants had been issued was assured. Murphy made plans to meet with Karame, who was to meet with Shihab, who, in turn, planned to meet with Junblat "and endeavor to work out a general agreement with moderate opposition leaders for elections on Friday."[19] The date was August 1, but it would be moved to July 31. Murphy exuded satisfaction:

> Shihab said explicitly in presence of Admiral Holloway that he would not request departure of American Forces until military aspect of rebellion had been reduced and contained. We feel that there will be no difficulty with Shihab with regard to an abrupt demand for removal of our forces. In fact, arrangements which have been slowly perfected for a cordial working relationship between American and Lebanese military will be an additional assurance against precipitate action of that nature.   (Ibid. 411)

Matters did not end there. In a last effort to prevent Shihab's presidency and the fall of Sham'un from power, Malik again met with Murphy, repeating President Sham'un's opposition to Shihab and claiming that only a military solution would do in the current crisis. At this point, the two Lebanese politicians who had been most closely identified with the United States confronted the undoing of the informal alliance that had defined their protected place in the American hierarchy. Murphy reminded Sham'un that he was powerless and that his regime depended on the man whose political future he was determined to subvert. Malik termed the proceedings a "coup d'état à la libanaise," referring to Shihab's emergence as the new leader.

Sham'un, meanwhile, attributed his situation to Shihab's policy of keeping the military out of politics (ibid. #242, p. 413). Elections were moved to July 31, at which point "on the first ballot General Shihab fell one vote short of winning the election. The results of the secret balloting were: 43 for Shihab, 10 for Eddeh, and three blanks. On the second ballot, he won. The results were 48 for Shihab, 7 for Eddeh, and one blank."[20] Shihab was not to take office until the end of September, which left Sham'un ample time to attempt to alter the political contours of the new regime.

The transition proved harrowing. Transferring their attention to Shihab, U.S. officials now sought to advise him on how to deal with the opposition, what opposition figures to deal with, and when pressure from Sham'un and Jemayyel increased, how to accede to their demands. Shihab himself turned to U.S. officials for help, relying on McClintock in a manner that made the political autonomy of the Lebanese presidency a mockery. Among the persistent questions affecting Anglo-American attitudes toward Shihab was his reluctance to attack the Basta, which remained a center of opposition. British officials, in particular, considered their U.S. counterparts unacceptably soft on this issue, and Shihab as highly unlikely to take action.[21] But on the matter of U.S. troop withdrawal, McClintock had every reason to find Shihab more than cooperative, and indeed, he was the man on whom U.S. officials relied to maneuver the troop withdrawal.

But the future president faced pressure from both opposition and Sham'unist quarters on this score. The former called for a rapid withdrawal commitment, while the latter exerted pressure to extend the U.S. presence in time and space. McClintock reported that Shihab was understanding:

Shihab is exceedingly friendly and willing to use his prestige to insure most practical arrangement of future relations with United States. However, he will, as he indicated to Holloway, Murphy and me yesterday, feel compelled by public opinion as well as by his own military estimate of situation to ask for our withdrawal once it is clear military aspects of insurrection have been dealt with. I believe his suggestion for a voluntary statement on our part is evidence of his desire to accomplish our eventual withdrawal by most tactful means.[22]

In mid-August, during a period of continued political tensions surrounding U.S. withdrawal, Shihab expressed his appreciation of the U.S. presence. He told McClintock that he was now convinced that "presence of U.S. forces in Lebanon had been of decisive beneficial effect. He said that had we not arrived with strength we deployed in Lebanon, it would have been difficult to see how country could have been saved from complete anarchy."[23] McClintock attributed Shihab's position to the pressures he faced from opposition leaders as well as Sham'unist supporters. The results were obviously welcomed. "Certainly insofar as his attitude toward our armed forces and CINCSPECOMME [Commander in Chief, U.S. Specified Command, Middle East] is concerned, it could not be more cooperative and sympathetic" (ibid. 479). Shihab offered the security that Washington required in a regime whose outward appearance would be less pro-American than that of its predecessor.

The question of U.S. withdrawal was obviously a sensitive issue politically in Beirut. To have U.S. forces continue to land in Beirut while plans were under discussion for their withdrawal was politically unacceptable and diplomatically awkward. Allen Dulles recommended that Holloway "put his tanks in an inconspicuous place . . . [so that] they are not roaming thru the streets. The ships are unloading in an orderly way and there is no congestion."[24] On August 7, the Department of Defense was duly informed by the State Department that there was to be a troop reduction in Lebanon. The moves that U.S. officials regarded as opportune were viewed as deplorable by Sham'un, who was now openly advocating international protection for Lebanon. It is an indication of the persistence of Sham'un's influence in the White House and with the U.S. secretary of state that they did not immediately reject such a proposal.[25] Dulles recommended obtaining commitments from the UAR, Israel, and Iraq "that they would keep their hands off Lebanon and Jordan and to make such countries realize that if they did not, they would be subject to serious condemnation."[26] The exercise was redundant, as Dulles must have known. Nothing was to be lost in endorsing such a request, but the focus of U.S. activity was now elsewhere.

Fixing the Cabinet

As crucial as was the presidential selection process given the power in the hands of Sham'un, the formation of Shihab's Cabinet proved no less vital or contentious. With the election of Shihab, the unresolved political struggle now focused on Cabinet selection. The first postwar Cabinet formed by the president became the immediate target of attack from Sham'unist and Kata'eb forces, whose internal differences did not prevent their cooperation. With the resumption of hostilities in the capital, the prospect of forming a military government, later revised in the form of a military-civilian government, was considered. In spite of the enthusiasm for such an option on the part of Sham'un and Jemayyel, political pressure to alter the size and composition of the Cabinet effectively aborted such an option. The arrangement arrived at altered the composition and size of the Cabinet in a manner acceptable to Sham'un and directly beneficial to Jemayyel, who was named Cabinet minister. Formally resolved, the Cabinet selection process signaled the perpetuation of the underlying conflicts at the core of Lebanese politics. It was a process in which the United States played a major role, thus strengthening the renewal of the status quo.

From McClintock to the Dulles brothers in Washington, the effort to appease Sham'un and to integrate Jemayyel into the Cabinet left no doubts as to the nature of U.S. policy in Lebanon. The evidence of contrary pressures notwithstanding, U.S. officials in Beirut were intimately involved in the construction of Shihab's Cabinet, even as Allen and John Foster Dulles remained suspicious of the former commander in chief and partisan to Malik's views. Thus, while Murphy, McClintock, and Holloway confronted Sham'un with the dimensions of his defeat, McClintock assured Pierre Jemayyel that he would not be denied political satisfaction in the new regime. For Secretary Dulles and the CIA chief, the scope of Sham'un's defeat did not undo anti-Shihabist sentiments. Yet much of the country remained outside of Sham'un's control, as it had been since the end of June.[27]

In the south, the regime retained partial control in the area between Sidon-Marjayoun and the Israeli border, but it was excluded from the autonomous zones in Sidon and Tyre. The region of the Biqa' close to the Syrian border and the northern region were beyond the reach of the regime. U.S. Embassy officials conceded that the area from Tripoli to the Israeli border extending inland to the Lebanon Mountains, was only nominally under control of the Lebanese state, while Junblat's region in the Shuf was entirely excluded, and the Mount Lebanon area that was in the heartland of Maronite control was not in Sham'unist hands, although it was loyal to the regime. That U.S. officials were able to override such overwhelming evidence of political defeat is indicative of the organizational and political limits of opposition forces. The U.S. Marine Corps history of the events that followed offered a simple interpretation:

> Shihab was elected. The new chief executive soothed the suspicious Moslems by agreeing to increase the number of representatives in the national parliament and by appointing certain prominent ex-rebels to his Cabinet. These reforms, however, would not have been carried out voluntarily. The implied threat that the United States would use its troops to enforce a dictated settlement was the goad that started the Lebanese along the path toward political stability.[28]

In the midst of the controversy over U.S. troop withdrawal, Eisenhower and Shihab exchanged vows of friendship, "in keeping with the traditional, cordial relations which so happily exist between Lebanon and the United States of America."[29] Not formally acknowledged were the other dimensions of relations between Washington and Beirut that were similarly renewed. To assure control over opposition demands, Shihab was advised to use the issue of troop withdrawal as a negotiating card. But neither U.S. officials in Beirut nor those in Washington were prepared for the resumption of hostilities on the ground in Beirut.

The strike, declared by the opposition UNF leaders at the time of the May assassination of Nasib al-Matni, was again enforced in a city marked by sporadic violence, cross fire, and kidnappings. In the light of the resumption of the conflict, the opposition renewed its demands, as U.S. officials renewed their pressure on Shihab to be more pliable. The role of the Basta area as headquarters of the UNF leadership once again came to the fore, and with it the question that had earlier dominated Eisenhower's and Dulles's deliberations in Washington. Why did Shihab, now president-to-be, resist moving against the Basta leaders? Shihab, in the interim, was advised to be selective in the opposition figures with whom he negotiated. McClintock's distaste for the UNF leaders, earlier identified as pro-Nasserist, including Sa'eb Salam, remained unchanged. It was the so-called moderate leaders that McClintock enjoined Shihab to consider. The rest, according to McClintock, were the "communists and lunatic fringe, possibly including Ba'athists" that could be dealt with subsequently.[30] McClintock further advised Shihab that the Lebanese army should play a more prominent role and that there should be more effective screening of those permitted to carry weapons. Parties of the Left were targeted, as opposed to the "PPS and Phalange not expected undertake campaign of terror or instigate widespread violence after Shihab's inauguration, although they will remain armed and watchful. Violence eventually expected to arrive at negligible level but not cease completely for indefinite future" (ibid. 541–42).

At the end of August, McClintock, Admiral Holloway, and Shihab were in closed meetings, reviewing the attempts at political pacification undertaken by Prime Minister Rashid Karame and Shihab's intermediaries vis-à-vis the Basta. The mediators were Taqiyuddin al-Sulh and Yusef Salam, the former an adviser to Shihab and the latter a prominent director of the commercial and industrial syndicate. McClintock phrased his advice in terms of "saving oriental face," with intimations of an amnesty after Shihab took office, and the promise of phased withdrawal.[31] With the lessening of tension in the city, McClintock recommended to Dulles that the funds planned for the new regime be provided. The reward, in the form of $1 million provided in coordination with the International Cooperation Administration (ICA), was to permit Shihab to buy back arms. In addition, the $5 million grant recommended on August 20 by the DOS Country Team, which was to be quadrupled in mid-October, was a sign of U.S. support.[32]

Five days before the appointment of Shihab's Cabinet, the uncertain political situation collapsed. On Sept 19, the assistant editor of the Kata'eb newspaper, al-'Amal, was abducted. With the disappearance of Fu'ad Haddad, conflict once again resumed, with the Kata'eb calling for a general strike to begin before Shihab's accession to the presidency. With the killing of Cesar Bustani, another Kata'eb member, the impact of the strike assumed more serious proportions. As McClintock recognized, "since the principal business and financial enterprises of Beirut were in Christian hands, the economic impact of this general strike was far more paralysing to Lebanon than the more protracted, but less effective general strike which had been imposed by the Moslem rebels since the outbreak of hostilities."[33] Shihab proceeded to name his first Cabinet on September 24. The response of the Kata'eb and Sham'unist forces left no doubt as to their continuing intransigence. The event accelerated the degeneration into civil strife that took a more openly confessional form.

Shihab's first Cabinet, which survived through October, consisted of Rashid Karame, prime minister; Philippe Taqla, foreign minister; Charles Helu, minister of economy and information; Muhammad Safiyuddin, minister of education and health; Yusef Sa'adeh, minister of justice and labor; Rafiq Najah, minister of finance; Farid Trad, minister of public works; and Fu'ad Najjar, minister of agriculture and post.

Sham'unist supporters objected, claiming the absence of representation. Malik, in Washington, encouraged Dulles to use his influence to discredit the Cabinet. Dulles did so, offering the spurious claim that Secretary General Dag Hammarskjöld supported accusations against Shihab for his persecution of former Sham'un allies.[34] The acting director of the CIA, Charles Cabell, similarly condemned the Shihab Cabinet as anti-American, identifying it as a victory for Nasser.[35] Allen Dulles was satisfied to describe the Lebanese situation as "tense," especially for the "Christian element in Lebanon."

What Christian element was Dulles referring to? Shihab's Cabinet had Christian politicians. The issue was not sect but politics. As McClintock knew and consistently conveyed to John Foster Dulles, there were intra-Christian differences among the political elite, and at this juncture in Lebanese politics, they were clearly and consistently articulated. Indeed, for some Lebanese politicians who were Christian, Jemayyel's tactics and political ambitions were rejected along with those of Sham'un.

Shihab, as McClintock informed Secretary Dulles, was persuaded that neither Sham'un nor Jemayyel was in control of his followers, whom McClintock accused of violence. McClintock's attitude toward Jemayyel was frankly opportunistic. The Kata'eb was undeniably a party with a strong following in the aftermath of the events of 1958, but the U.S. ambassador had no illusions as to its dominant outlook with respect to Lebanese politics. In July, McClintock had cabled Secretary Dulles to the effect that in spite of Jemayyel's claims to the contrary, his views on Lebanese Christian-Muslim relations were unchanged. "Jemayyel denied Christians enjoy privileged position in Lebanon and rejected any settlement with respect government positions, gratuities, et cetera."[36] In the fall, Shihab told McClintock that he felt that "there was an important political element in Lebanon which sought deliberately to continue state of conflict and in particular to destroy Lebanese army. Although Shihab did not say so straight out, it was clear he suspected Sham'un hoped by maintaining continuing turmoil to find an opportunity once more to step back into power."[37] Shihab went further, identifying the Kata'eb with a brand of extremism that was a legacy of Sham'un's supporters. The party "had been infiltrated with more extremist elements who took their orders from Moghabghab Sham'un's henchman and hatchetman. President said Jemayyel had been much more moderate and had sought in fact to restrain his more fanatic followers. (We have independent confirmation of this fact from other sources.)" According to McClintock, Shihab concluded "that now Christian fanatics had violated law and disturbed the peace he was in a position impartially to strike at any malefactors whether Moslem or Christian and this he intended to do." How much more evidence could McClintock have needed?

McClintock at this juncture, accompanied by Admiral Holloway, toured the Cabinet. What was their purpose? The U.S. ambassador and admiral, in meetings with Karame, among others, insisted that the United States was committed to Lebanese peace and unity, and, above all, to the integrity of the republic.[38] Karame replied in kind, vowing friendship and reiterating what he had previously told Robert Murphy, that "he hoped he could look for our assistance in helping him to achieve his policy of pacification, unification and preservation of the independence of Lebanon" (ibid. 587). As for Taqla, he bluntly asked McClintock to "use my influence particularly in the Christian community, in bringing people to a more moderate attitude of mind" (ibid. 586). Taqla accused Sham'un of fomenting disorder in order to reopen his own political chances, while the PPS and the Kata'eb were similarly described as opportunistic, and the latter as determined to get a Cabinet position in the new government. McClintock was to be a major contributor to this end.

The political tours of the U.S. officials continued, as Shihab was pursuing a frenetic course, meeting with Prime Minister Karame, Opposition figures, including Salam, Yafi, 'Uwayni and Junblat, Majdalany, and Mu'awwad, and shoring up support among powerful anti-Sham'unist forces, as well as Jemayyel. The latter had apparently agreed to the existing Cabinet with the provision that it be expanded in accord with his and former President Sham'un's specifications. The offer was rejected by the prime minister. At this point, with an invitation from Shihab, Taqla, and Jemayyel, McClintock agreed to act as intermediary. Aside from the obvious joy that such a taste of power brought him, McClintock cabled Dulles with the news that he had decided to mediate the crisis: since "political situation has shown little sign of improvement in recent days I have decided to move more energetically in taking up [Jemayyel's] request for my good offices," reported Embassy telegram 1724.[39]

McClintock invited the opposition to meet with him at his home. "I have asked Prime Minister Karame, Foreign Minister Taqla, Henri Far'oun, Maurice Zuwayn, Pierre Eddeh, Taqiyuddin al-Sulh, Ghassan Tuwayni, Joseph Skaff and 'Adel 'Usayran to meet at my house at six this evening to see if some formula cannot be found which will end general strike in Beirut and, in effect, terminate this civil war." Neither Junblat, Salam, Yafi, nor 'Uwayni accepted the U.S. ambassador's invitation. Not fazed by their rejection, McClintock pressed Shihab to satisfy the Sham'un-Jemayyel demands and proposed the following:

1. Vote of confidence for Karame Cabinet.
2. Widening of Karame Cabinet to grant 3 and possibly 4 portfolios to pro-[Sham'un] loyalists or Christian elements who now feel without representation in government.
3. Karame government and parliamentary deputies to agree on enlarging parliamentary representation from 66 to 88 seats.

McClintock offered the following as explanation of the situation:

Foregoing possible solution would satisfy practically everyone and at same time keep within strict constitutional bounds. [Shihab] has already told me he is willing to broaden Cabinet after vote of confidence; and he has indicated his personal preference for enlarging parliament to 88 seats. Moslem opposition, including Junblat's Druzes, should be pleased to have a chance to increase their presentation in parliament while, at the same time, so-called loyalists should have an equal opportunity to contend for these new seats. Loyalists and Christians should be appeased if they are given what they regard as a fair presentation in [Karame] government.

From Washington Dulles dispatched praise for "commendable influence which you exercising on Lebanese political scene," while repeatedly warning McClintock about the hazards of press leaks concerning his role in Lebanese politics.[40] Dulles warned that "reports of this nature provide communists and other anti-American elements material for charging U.S. meddling in GOL domestic politics. We should seek avoid creating public impression of U.S. interference in Lebanese internal affairs."

Privately, Dulles asked for no such arrest of his ambassador's activities, and McClintock proceeded to hold his rounds of meetings, including dissidents such as the Patriarch Ma'oushi, whose views he ultimately ignored.[41]

Contrary to McClintock's assumptions, Lebanese politics did not respond to his mediations in the anticipated manner. By the first week of October the situation appeared to be deteriorating, and Eisenhower was informed that Shihab was "finding extreme difficulty in reaching a Cabinet solution in Lebanon; Moslem and Christian split is growing."[42] What this cable omitted to convey was the continuing role played by Sham'un, whose disdain for Karame was well known. As far as he was concerned,

> Karame epitomized rebel from the barricades whom everyone knew had taken Syrian arms and money and who would follow a policy not only of going along with Nasser but of placing Muslims in places of preference in public administration. Other Cabinet members such as Taqla ("spineless"), Helu ("a Jesuit"), and Najjar ("a Druze chosen to please Junblat") could not under any stretch of imagination be regarded as representing half of Lebanon's population.[43]

McClintock, at this point, had reached the conclusion that Sham'un was prepared to fight. With the Chamber, elected under Sham'un's regime and with U.S. funds counted on to block approval of the Cabinet, McClintock expected another civil war or dictatorship. Shihab, in fact, was considering a military-civilian Cabinet under Karame, so he confided in McClintock, as the U.S. ambassador proudly cabled Dulles: "I saw [Shihab] last night at Junieh. He went over political crisis in great detail and seemed obviously happy to have a friend to confide in who had no personal interest in current intrigues."[44] The two reviewed the latest crises, including the possibility of introducing a combined civilian-military government:

> Shihab has in mind a "neutral" Cabinet made up largely of military officers with a leavening of experienced civilians. He said, for example, that the most important posts of Foreign and Economic Affairs and Finance would be entrusted to Taqla. Prime Minister would be either Nasim Akkari Sunni Moslem Chef de Cabinet at Prime Minister's office, an old wheelhorse in the Civil Service who once held Prime Ministership for three days in 1952, or Ahmed Da'ouk, long-time Ambassador in Paris, also a Sunni Moslem who has a good reputation and is regarded as completely non-partisan.   (Ibid.)

Shihab asked McClintock to act as intermediary with Sham'un, a situation that the two men must have appreciated, given the reversal of roles involved since the day of U.S. intervention—when it was Sham'un who had asked McClintock to break the news to Shihab. Now, it was not solely with regard to Sham'un that Shihab asked McClintock for his services; it was with Jemayyel as well. What did Shihab expect? In the negotiations that followed, McClintock's role became that of a facilitator to assure his client, Jemayyel, a satisfactory hearing. More than a hearing was desired, however, and McClintock proceeded to go all the way, until Jemayyel was in the Cabinet. He stood by as Jemayyel met with Karame. He patiently intervened as Shihab prepared to compromise by accepting a Sham'un-Jemayyel settlement, which meant the expansion of the Karame Cabinet "to include pro-[Sham'un] loyalist and perhaps representation from the Phalange [Kata'eb]." But opposition leaders were not passive through this period, and Sa'eb Salam informed McClintock that a twenty-five-man committee of Muslim leaders had met to consider the situation and that "leaders of a more moderate stripe" agreed to cooperate with the new Cabinet in formation.[45]

Jemayyel, McClintock reported, was "on the verge of desperation. He said a three-hour meeting with Karame had produced no result" (ibid.). Translated, this meant that the prime minister was unwilling to accept Jemayyel's proposals regarding the Cabinet. According to Jemayyel, Karame and his supporters "were only willing to take in a few face-saving personalities but would not honestly seek for an arrangement of 'no victor, no vanquished.'" As a result, Jemayyel threatened that the Kata'eb would not support the Karame Cabinet, and McClintock, now with Jemayyel, turned back to the idea of a military-civilian regime. Meeting with Jemayyel and his party secretary and former minister of finance Joseph Shader, McClintock found Jemayyel positive and Sham'un favorable to the idea. In fact, Jemayyel was persuaded that "this would have such a magical effect on country it would eliminate strike and restore order provided Shihab stood firm" (ibid., sec. 2).

McClintock persisted in his Lebanese role.

I thereupon resumed my weary journeying to Junieh and called on Shihab at 10 P.M. He was interested in negative result of [Jemayyel-] Karame interview and impossibility of resuscitating idea of a military Cabinet; but said his concern now was not to upset Moslem applecart in Tripoli and Saida. He speculated as to possibility of a military Cabinet presided over by Karame, but agreed when I pointed out

Christians would be up in arms at such an arrangement unless there were a balance of strongly pro-loyalist Christian ministers. President concluded a long day by saying he thought both sides were now so groggy with fatigue they would eventually stumble to some sort of live and let live solution.

U.S. officials determined that this was an auspicious moment to provide financial assistance that had been earlier planned. Under Secretary of State for Economic Affairs Douglas Dillon met with McClintock in Istanbul in mid-October to discuss the plans. Given the political situation in Beirut, the language in which the offer was packaged was striking. In response to Lebanon's success in "forming coalition government country team recommends total of $25 million budget support for period ending September 31, 1959. (This is $20 million in addition to $5 million already allotted.)"[46] No doubt mindful of the Point IV experience in Lebanon, McClintock recommended that technical assistance programs be discontinued.

In the interim, the regime's "success" consisted of agreeing to shrink the Cabinet of eight to four, in which half of the appointments were designed to satisfy the Sham'unist-Jemayyel opposition and its diverse constituencies. The first was Raymond Eddeh, whom McClintock described as "my closest friend in government"; the other was Pierre Jemayyel. The former became minister of the interior, in charge of posts and telegraph as well as social affairs; the latter, minister of education, health, public works, and agriculture. With Prime Minister Karame also acting as minister of economy, finance, defense, and information, and Husayn 'Uwayni, the foreign minister, accepting responsibility for the ministries of justice and planning, the Cabinet was approved. All together, the four ministers controlled a total of fifteen posts, a situation that survived nearly a year, at which point one of the four, Raymond Eddeh, resigned.[47]

Before this, McClintock indicated that arrangements had been made involving the cooperation of Raymond Eddeh, "for various elements of our official family to deal on a working level with opposite numbers in various ministries, in order to prevent clogging at top of such over-burdened ministers as Rashid Karame who has important portfolios of Defense, Finance and Economic Affairs in addition to Information."[48] McClintock's communiqué confirmed that existing problems were of bureaucratic rather than political origin. The Cabinet, in fact, offered the United States no resistance, but rather an unparalleled array of politically acceptable and cooperative figures.

Withdrawal and Compensation

The planning of U.S. troop withdrawal and internal security measures occurred at the final stages of U.S. occupation in Beirut. The former involved considerations external to Lebanon, though central to Anglo-American political interests in the region. In brief, U.S. troop withdrawal from Lebanon was made contingent on British withdrawal from Jordan. Lebanese domestic politics, in sum, were hostage to guarantees of Western interests in Jordan that involved Anglo-American calculations of Israeli intentions toward the West Bank.

Such considerations were implicit in tentative discussions of international guarantees for both Lebanon and Jordan that projected the replacement of U.S. forces with those of the UN. Dulles, Malik, and Shihab endorsed the position, although it was not formally implemented. Nonetheless, bilateral discussions sufficed to clarify the mutual interests of those directly involved. Those of greatest relevance had to do with exchanges among British, U.S., Israeli, and Egyptian officials on Israeli policy toward the West Bank and the future of Jordan.

Between the U.S. and U.K. delegations that met in the United Nations, it was not Lebanon but Israel that was the principal concern as the British were persuaded of Israeli intentions to occupy the West Bank in response to the precarious situation of King Husayn. According to Sir Pierson Dixon, Abba Eban thought in terms of a special status for the West Bank, since Prime Minister Ben-Gurion was loath to create "an Israeli Algeria."[49] Selwyn Lloyd, on the other hand, argued that Foreign Minister Golda Meir thought otherwise, and that, "if Jordan collapsed, Israel would march in," however much it was concerned about occupying an area with a population of some 850,000 Palestinians.[50] The figure was close to the number of those who had fled or been expelled ten years earlier. Meir wanted the British to remain, Lloyd added, since she thought "the present frontier between Israel and Jordan would be tolerable if there were some sort of international presence in Jordan." Unquestioned in such exchanges were both the potential of the Israel Labor government to exploit Anglo-American policies in the triangle of Israeli-Palestinian-Jordanian politics and the utilitarian role assigned the Jordanian regime. British accounts support the view that Nasser had no intention of moving into Jordan, a position that Dulles's highly enlightening talks with UAR foreign minister Mahmoud Fawzi confirmed. Dulles's unvarnished view of Jordan, as offered to the UAR delegate, additionally suggested a turning in U.S.-UAR relations in which emphasis was placed on the mutual commitment to the maintenance of the status quo. Dulles's dispassionate review of Jordanian history is worth citing:

> It was an artificial state which had been created by the U.K. as an alternate base, perhaps, in the Middle East. It had been subsidized first by the British, briefly by the three Arab states, and now by the U.S. It took a lot of money to keep it going. The reason for its existence was that its disappearance might reopen the Arab-Israeli war. We were paying tribute to hold Jordan so that war would not break out. Jordan had nothing of interest to us. It was of interest to all, however, that there be no chaos in the area. We did not know Israel's purposes, but there was a 50–50 chance that if Jordan collapsed, the Israelis would occupy the West Bank. This could start a lot of other things. There was a common interest to try to preserve peace so that Jordan's future could evolve peacefully. The Secretary admitted, however, that he was at a loss to know how such a peaceful evolution might take place.   (Ibid. #270, p. 471)

In subsequent talks, Dulles shared his sense of frustration as to the solution for Amman. Fawzi suggested that Iraq take over Jordan, a solution that Dulles thought acceptable, provided that it did not spark Israeli reprisal.[51] Jordanian foreign minister Samir al-Rifa'i did not reject the option, viewing such an alliance as a secular translation of the Arab Union favored by the late Iraqi monarch and King Husayn, the "two chaps" that British prime minister Macmillan had earlier referred to with derision. In the interval, U.S. ambassador to Jordan, Thomas K. Wright reported that more than external support was required:

> My opinion time has come USG must decide whether it wishes maintain "fortress Jordan" as a non-viable western satellite in the heartland Nasser hoped-for Middle East empire with clear understanding this can only be accomplished by force and against will majority Jordanian people or if in broader context our international relationships we should permit Arab nationalism of Nasser brand take over country leading to eventual incorporation within UAR, for I am convinced if Rifai government falls sooner or later that will happen.[52]

Within forty-eight hours, Dulles and Fawzi were meeting to discuss Jordan, in agreement that its collapse was better averted. Prepared to accept the idea of an Iraqi-Jordanian integration, Dulles was mainly concerned that the ensuing regime not be under UAR control. Politics now mixed with money, as Dulles warned that if that should occur, U.S. funding for Amman would be cut, putting the financial burden on the UAR, along with the Palestinians then under Jordanian control. Fawzi declined all such prospects as not in the interests of the UAR. The de facto accord meant that the United States would contribute something on the order of $50 million, to which the British would add another $6 million.[53]

In mid-September the Joint Chiefs of Staff and State Department officials confirmed that U.S. troop withdrawal from Lebanon was still delayed by the British position in Jordan. State Department official Stuart Rockwell conceded that "we have made clear to the British that we will not leave their forces in Jordan alone in the Middle East. The political problem in Jordan is more difficult and withdrawal might not be possible as early as in Lebanon."[54] Withdrawal was therefore delayed until the end of October. The announcement of plans for joint withdrawal of U.K. forces from Jordan on October 24, and U.S. forces from Lebanon by October 31, in fact, signaled the final stages of Anglo-American collaboration in Amman.

The withdrawal of the U.S. Air Force had begun on August 29, and by mid-September Admiral Holloway agreed to the withdrawal of military equipment and accompanying service units, as a preface to the departure of combat forces. Withdrawal was expected to be completed by November 10, although "the two U.S. Marine battalions will remain afloat in the Eastern Mediterranean."[55] Most troops were withdrawn by October 23. Holloway had moved to his London headquarters, after which the last vestiges of U.S. military presence were removed from Beirut. On November 2, British forces withdrew from Jordan.

The next step was disengagement of the Lebanese question from the United Nations. U.S. representative to the UN Henry Cabot Lodge, Lebanese foreign minister Husayn 'Uwayni, and Secretary General Dag Hammarskjöld, in turn, announced the withdrawal of troops, requested the deletion of the Lebanese government's complaint against the UAR, and declared the life of UNOGIL to have come to an end. Thus, on November 6, Lodge informed Hammarskjöld that U.S. troops had been withdrawn from Lebanon, being careful to emphasize that their departure was in compliance with the General Assembly Resolution of August 21, which by its language had vindicated Lebanese claims against the UAR, claims about to be deleted from the record. The UN now called on member states to respect each other's sovereignty and territorial integrity.

On November 16, Lebanese foreign minister Husayn 'Uwayni officially closed the Lebanese case in his letter to the Security Council. 'Uwayni formally requested that the Security Council delete the Lebanese government's complaint against the UAR, submitted on May 22.[56] This was followed by Hammarskjöld's announcement to the Security Council on November 17 that pursuant to the completion of UNOGIL's assignment in Lebanon, it was to be officially terminated. The UN phase of the Lebanese crisis was thereby ended, a seven-month trial in which the UN had been manipulated, its reports ignored by the major powers as well as by Lebanon. At its peak, "UNOGIL had 591 observers, 49 posts, 12 planes and six helicopters," which it subsequently withdrew between November 28 and December 9.[57] Rajeshwar Dayal, who had been in charge of UNOGIL, went on to another debacle, this time in what was then the Congo (Zaire), where he now found himself between the United States and Belgium, the target of their dealings to retain control of the area's mineral wealth.

In Washington, the issuance of NSC 5820/1 of November 4, 1958, addressed the new situation in Lebanon. The recommendations of the NSC underscored the advisability of changing the face of U.S. policy by maintaining a certain distance from Lebanese domestic politics. This involved no compromise with respect to U.S. interests or the nature of the U.S.-Lebanese connection. The latter was guaranteed through arrangements entered into with the new regime. The formal language of the NSC recommended the following:

> Support the continued independence and integrity of Lebanon, but avoid becoming too closely identified with individual factions in Lebanese politics and seek discreetly to disengage from relationships that may be disadvantageous to U.S. interests.
>   a. Provide Lebanon with political support and with military assistance for internal security purposes, stressing our support for the country as a whole rather than for a specific regime or faction.
>   b. Reduce grant economic assistance as feasible and emphasize Lebanon's capacity to borrow from international lending institutions for purposes of economic development.
>   c. Where appropriate seek to encourage the acceptance of Lebanon's unique status by its Arab neighbors, and, if desired by and acceptable to the people concerned, be prepared to subscribe to a United Nations guarantee of the continued independence and integrity of Lebanon.[58]

The fundamental premise of U.S. policy with respect to Lebanon's domestic situation was that the regime rested on an unstable base.

Intelligence sources in the military, as well as in the State Department and the CIA, maintained the fiction that U.S. intervention had arrested the emergence of a pro-Nasser regime. But they conceded that cleavages at the root of the Lebanese state remained intact. Shihab's future was regarded as uncertain, and Lebanon's Christian population was viewed as weakened, though most likely preparing for another confrontation with Lebanese Muslims.[59]

Steps to ensure the regime's first months had led to arrangements for financial assistance. In addition, a network designed to assure internal security was put in place under McClintock's direction, and with the advice of the U.S. army attaché, the State Department, the Country Team, and the OPS program of the ICA that had been established three years earlier.

U.S. officials recommended that non-American personnel be found to train Lebanese, "because of the differences in systems and public attitudes as between Lebanon and the United States in respect of police activity."[60] Further, according to the same source, "I /Edwin H. Arnold/ have dealt separately—/deleted/ on the possibility of providing technical advisers to the Lebanese Sûreté." The ICA was reluctant, in practice, to provide assistance to the Lebanese gendarmerie without prior agreement "to assignment of at least one *U.S.* Public Safety representative to screen civil police needs and provide technical advice and program control."

The Office of Public Safety specialized in the "modernization" of police forces and in counterinsurgency training. The candidate identified for the Lebanon position, Albert E. DuBois, had experience in the civil police and military, and was, at the time of his consideration, chief public safety director in a country where the United States had a major OPS operation in conjunction with its active support for the Thai military dictatorship.[61] Soliciting his presence in Beirut was evidence of how the United States intended to organize the containment of dissent in the new regime. McClintock further indicated that he planned to have DuBois on the Embassy staff, a move that posed no problems in Beirut since the Lebanese gendarmerie was then "under the command of a thoroughly capable and honest officer, one Colonel [deleted] who has had some military training in the United States and when the Minister of Interior is Raymond Eddeh, who is friendly to the U.S."[62] McClintock asked for "prompt word if ICA/W plans to so assign Mr DuBois so that maximum effect from his assignment could be achieved by discreet conversation with President Shihab."

In pursuit of the above, the army attaché prepared an itemized list of equipment and its probable cost, some $925,000, which was to cover three categories of materials.

> Priority one embraces rifles, ammunition, cots, trucks, batteries and trailers estimated to cost $350,000. Priority two embraces revolvers, bayonets, helmets, belts, blankets, Thompson sub-machine guns, jeeps, personal [sic] carriers and ammunition at an estimated cost of $350,000. Priority three embraces grenade launchers, hand grenades, machine guns, rifles, jeeps, trucks, ambulances, tents and ammunition at an estimated cost of $225,000.   (Ibid.)

Action on "priority three" was deferred until the public safety official was securely in place. Materials that plainly constituted military assistance were to be justified in terms of the "military internal security objectives" of the gendarmerie (ibid.). The U.S. European Command Report to the President's Committee to Study the U.S. M.A.P. for North Africa and the Middle East (the Draper Committee Reports of 1958–1959) confirmed such objectives as integral to U.S. military policy in Lebanon.[63] In 1958, the U.S. provided Lebanon with $3.6 million in military supplies, including engineering and communications supplies, and later, the assistance offered in connection with the Richards mission that had followed Lebanon's acceptance of the Eisenhower Doctrine. In the winter of 1958, under the M.A.P. and International Military Education and Training Program, a modest sum of grants and credits for the purchase of U.S. arms was offered, while military training for Lebanese students was provided, bringing the total personnel affected by such programs between 1950 and 1976 to 1,521. The number was comparable to that for Jordan and Saudi Arabia, though far below that for Iran (11,025) or Turkey (19,150).[64]

In 1954–1958 Lebanon received $7.5 million for military aid, of which only $3.4 million was delivered before July 1958. The figure offered for fiscal year 1959 was $0.5 million.

> With the exception of the $.5 million, no U.S. military aid is now programmed for Lebanon for FY 1959 or beyond. On the assumption that a certain amount of military aid will be necessary to maintain the independence of the government of Lebanon, $5.0 million a year for the period FY 1959–1961 has been projected as a probable program. The expenditures of $14.6 million for FY 1959–1961 reflect this illustrative program.[65]

In December 1958, $10 million in Development Loan Funds was also under consideration, in addition to the $2.5 million provided in September, and $5 million worth of wheat set aside for delivery to Beirut.[66] McClintock informed Shihab of these plans on December 1, 1958, indicating that such assistance was intended to assure the new regime the ability to deal with the postwar economic problems it faced. In the estimates of U.S. allocations through the Development Loan Fund for 1959, Lebanon's share was some $17.1 million out of a projected $114.5 million.

It remains to consider the political significance of U.S. policy.

Epilogue: 1958 in Retrospect

*Support the continued independence and integrity of
Lebanon, but avoid becoming too closely identified
with individual factions in Lebanese politics and seek
discreetly to disengage from relationships that may be
disadvantageous to U.S. interests.
Provide Lebanon with political support and with
military assistance for internal security purposes,
stressing our support for the country as a whole rather
than for a specific regime or faction.*
NSC 5820/1 "US Policy Toward the Near East."
November 4, 1958˙

*Secretary Dulles said we must regard Arab nationalism
as a flood which is running strongly. We cannot successfully oppose it, but we can put up sand bags
around positions we must protect—the first group
being Israel and Lebanon and the second being the oil
positions around the Persian Gulf.*
July 23, 1958˙

What is the meaning of 1958 in the context of U.S. Middle East policy?
Was the period that followed on the Iraqi military coup and the combined
Anglo-American interventions in Jordan and Lebanon the beginning of a
new era in Western diplomacy in the Middle East? Did the foundations
of U.S. policy in the region change? Or were the renewed emphases on
Turkey and Iran, the protected status of Lebanon, Israel, and the Saudi-
Gulf zone reaffirmations of fundamental U.S. objectives in the area? And
finally, what were the consequences of U.S. intervention in Lebanon? Did
the NSC recommendation that the United States adopt a more discreet

profile in Beirut and avoid entangling alliances while providing support to the new regime constitute a significant break with past policy?

While Eisenhower and Macmillan congratulated each other on their accomplishments in Beirut and Amman, observers in the Middle East might well have regarded those achievements as illusory. British attempts at counterrevolution had been squashed by American rejection. French influence had been virtually overshadowed by the catastrophe of Suez and its inability to defeat Nasser as a means of arresting the Algerian liberation struggle; while in Beirut, their role was effectively challenged by the United States. And on January 16, 1958, the NSC Staff Study "Long Range U.S. Policy Toward the Near East" (NSC 5801) conceded that in the Middle East, the United States was a status quo power:

> Our economic and cultural interests in the area have led, not unnaturally, to close U.S. relations with elements in the Arab world whose primary interest lies in the maintenance of relations with the West and the *status quo* in their countries . . . [deleted]. . . . These developments have contributed to a widespread belief in the area, particularly among the discontented elements mentioned above, that the United States desires to keep the Arab world disunited and is committed to work with "reactionary" Arab elements to that end.[1]

NSC analysts further confirmed the disadvantage of being identified with regimes that used "repressive measures in order to curb extremist elements and retain power" (no. 10, p. 4). The adverse effect of such association was not masked. "The impact of our efforts to bring home the facts concerning police state methods behind the Iron Curtain is blunted by the commonness of similar—if less efficient—methods in the Near East." The concern that the USSR was not identified with such states but exploited its support of Arab nationalism clearly aggravated U.S. officials who found added reason to amend U.S. policy. In the November 4, 1958, Statement of U.S. Policy Toward the Near East (NSC 5820/1), U.S. officials concluded that the principal challenge in the region was a function of the coincidence of Soviet objectives with those of Arab nationalism.[2] Arab nationalists could point to the viability of the UAR (until 1961) and the emergence of a new Iraqi regime with revolutionary ambitions. And in spite of the rift between the Iraqi and the UAR regimes, the appeal of Nasserism continued unabated, irrespective of the disenchantment of its democratic critics. The Saudi king could not contain the Nasserist sympathies of certain members of the royal family, and in the Gulf there were signs of revolt against the corrupt politics of oil.

Such a summary, however, is seriously incomplete. The year 1958 represented neither the demise of Western influence nor the apex of Arab nationalism. The United States emerged as the uncontested Western power in the region with the foundations of its policy objectives unchanged. Less than fifteen years after the end of World War II, and a long decade after the Truman Doctrine and the creation of the state of Israel, American power and presence in the region had entirely superseded that of its chief ally in the Middle East, Great Britain. U.S. policy goals, on the other hand, remained consistent, as the design of its strategy changed in accord with developments on the ground. Access to and control of Middle East oil resources and the denial of the area to the Soviet Union, as well as the containment of nationalist, populist, or radical regimes, remained cardinal elements of American policy, as did the containment of the Palestinians in a permanent low-intensity Israeli-Arab conflict that remained favorable to Israel. To this must be added the pursuit of preventive development policies through the agencies of acceptable political cadres.

Thus, 1958 proved to be a triple strategic victory for the United States. The calculations of Eisenhower, Dulles, intelligence, defense, and oil interests combined to exploit British weakness, Arab nationalist divisions, and the apprehensions as well as ambitions of regional allies. U.S. military action in Lebanon was not a surrogate intervention in response to Baghdad but a politico-military intervention designed to curb what the United States regarded as the potentially adverse outcome of civil war. America's special ally, Britain, was humbled if not humiliated by the elimination of the Nuri Sa'id regime in Baghdad.

But British power was not fatally undermined; it remained concentrated in the Gulf. With American interests in Kuwait and Saudi Arabia, the raison d'être of Anglo-American Middle East policy was to be protected at any cost. The Iraqi coup, it turned out, was not only a major factor in the further contraction of British power, it increased the political leverage of the Eisenhower administration in its relations with Arab nationalist regimes. Further, the collaboration of states of the former "Northern Tier" and the Baghdad Pact was strengthened by Israel's "peripheral alliance," which, with U.S. support, amplified the opportunities of political coordination and subversion. Hence, to the continued roles of Western allies such as Turkey, Iran, Lebanon, and Jordan was now added Israel, with its covert connections in the Arab and non-Arab parts of the Middle East. The consolidation of American power in 1958 was, then, a function of the political defeat of Britain in Iraq, the lessening of U.S.-UAR tensions, the rapprochement with Israel, and the realignment of U.S. policy in Beirut.

Within this framework, the November 4, 1958, National Security Council statement (NSC 5820/1) is an inadequate guide to U.S. policy or Lebanese developments. It does provide insight into the NSC's perception of Britain's situation in the aftermath of the Iraqi coup, as well as the reevaluation of Arab nationalist regimes. But the NSC statement was singularly misleading insofar as the situation of the United States in Lebanon was concerned. There was no mention of the arrangements that followed on Shihab's election, which belied the "discreet profile" of U.S.-Lebanese relations. Support for internal security and the provision of financial assistance to the Shihab regime were indicators of a continued commitment, albeit one that was not to be advertised as publicly as it had been under Sham'un and Malik.[3]

In retrospect, the evolution of the U.S.-Lebanese connection, which mirrored U.S. policy in the region, involved a progressively deeper level of engagement in Lebanese politics. In some fifteen years, from the inauguration of U.S.-Lebanese relations under Besharah al-Khuri to the redefinition of relations with the Shihab regime that followed U.S. intervention and occupation, the course of U.S. policy extended from the protection of TAPLINE and aviation to the increasing appreciation of the role and compatibility of U.S. interests with those of the influential Lebanese bourgeoisie, whose power remained central to U.S. policy. The political and military subsidization of the Sham'un regime, in return for its unconditional support of U.S. policies in Lebanon and the region between 1952 and 1958, represented the culmination and trials of such a policy.

Far from being the trivialized comic opera or the epic salvage operation of postwar American policy, U.S. military intervention in and occupation of Lebanon in July 1958 altered the outcome of civil war and contributed to shaping the postwar Cabinet while instituting the security and financial arrangements that defined U.S.-Lebanese relations. Such arrangements did not preclude a skepticism as to the long-term viability of the regime or, indeed, the state. The explosive potential of the Lebanese minefield was not dismantled in the arrangements negotiated in the fall of 1958. In fact, U.S. policy contributed then as in earlier years to assuring its perpetuation while lamenting its origins.

U.S. policy at the inception of the Shihab regime was marked by a cautious optimism, with the above qualifications. Nonetheless, Shihab's efforts to modernize and rationalize state power were welcomed, as was his appeal to a technocratic and bureaucratic elite. Talk of neutralism was no longer a matter of concern, with good reasons given for the existing arrangements.

But domestic politics was hardly free of tensions. Opposition to the regime's practices came from left- as well as right-wing critics. The Shihabist program antagonized those opposed to an increasing role for the state, as an unacceptable interference in the operations of the economy. At the same time, it frustrated and vexed those opposed to its reliance on the expansion of the security apparatus in the form of the Deuxième Bureau, its censorship of the press, and its failure to impose an effective system of taxation.

The mobilization of opposition under Pierre Jemayyel, who caricatured Shihab as an acolyte of Nasser, and Kamal Junblat, whose political support grew in proportion to internal dissent, was a reminder of the continuities and frustrations of Lebanese politics that U.S. officials could not ignore. It was also a reminder of the consequences of U.S. policies, as the cost of consistently undermining domestic reform starkly revealed. There was no question of where the weight of U.S. support had fallen in civil war. Junblat's sympathies for the U.S. notwithstanding, his reputation as a socialist critic of Lebanese politics rendered him permanently suspect in U.S. circles, a position reinforced by his internal critics.

Yet the endorsement of Jemayyel was not without its limits. Washington had no interest in a Lebanist politics. It had every reason to support Shihabist regional policies that were integral to the realignment of U.S. policy in Lebanon and that coincided with Washington's more flexible definition of U.S. relations with Arab nationalism. The continued expansion of Lebanon's service economy, and the further consolidation of the U.S. Saudi-Gulf connection, remained central to U.S. economic as well as political interests. If the Kata'eb was marginal to the operations of this regional political economy, it was central to the continued political struggles at the root of domestic politics, which were inseparable from the survival of the Lebanese system, to which the U.S. remained committed. From this perspective, Shihab's Cabinet of four, to which Mc-

Clintock contributed his unremitting efforts, represented a satisfactory realignment of U.S. interests. It not only secured the protection of U.S. economic and political interests, it reinforced the self-serving politics of confessionalism.

The setting of the realignment of U.S. policy in Beirut occurred against a triple background that included the post-Iraqi phase of U.S.-U.K. relations, the reconsideration of Arab nationalism, and the affirmation of Israel's role in regional policies. Britain's position, which was dramatically weakened in 1956, was further undermined by the loss of its Iraqi client. The cumulative impact sensitized British officials to what they perceived as the hostility of the State Department toward the obligations of empire. The department's lower echelons, excluding Dulles, were accused of being opposed to intervention by force in the Gulf. As Staff Study NSC 5801 of January 16, 1958 confirmed, Britain had not deviated from the view that its "predominance in the Persian Gulf is essential to guarantee the flow of oil necessary to maintain the British domestic economy and international position."[4] There was no disputing this position in Washington, which the NSC report classified among the "Principal Obstacles to U.S. Objectives." As U.S. officials recognized, the Gulf states and the Aden Colony and Protectorate were viewed by Arab nationalists "as *terra irridenta*," and the Saudis looked forward to the elimination of British influence in the area.

State Department officials who leaned toward a more flexible and open attitude vis-à-vis Arab regimes readily agreed on the disadvantages of the United States' being identified with British policies in the region. After the July 14 coup in Baghdad, discussion turned to the consequences of supporting the British use of force in Kuwait and the Gulf. U.S. sources do not reveal any references to the top secret Anglo-American exchanges on the subject between Eisenhower and Macmillan. Within the NSC, differences existed as to the merits of supporting existing agreements at any cost, as opposed to opting for an accommodation with pan-Arab nationalism as the basis of guaranteed access to Kuwaiti and Gulf oil.[5] Foreign Office records indicate that the question of protecting British interests in the Gulf as well as in Kuwait had been a subject of review earlier in the year.[6] Such reviews were accompanied by a scarcely veiled irritation with what was perceived as State Department hostility toward intervention. As D. M. H. Riches acidly observed: "We can all agree that force is to be deprecated and that it solves no problems permanently (perhaps because superior force is brought to bear on the other side). But theories of this kind are not a very helpful guide when the mob is battering at the gates."[7]

Dulles was absolved of such accusations. At the end of July, the British ambassador to the United States, Lord Hood, was eager to clarify Dulles's position, which left no doubts as to the nature of U.S. policy.

> I am sure that you are considering anxiously the problem of Kuwait. One of the most reassuring features of my talks here has been the complete United States solidarity with us over the Gulf. They are assuming that we will take firm action to maintain our position in Kuwait. They themselves are disposed to act with similar resolution in relations to the Aramco oilfields in the area of Dahran, although the logistics are not worked out. They assume that we will also hold Bahrein and Qatar, come what may. They agree that at all costs these oilfields must be kept in Western hands.[8]

Several days after Hood communicated Dulles's views to the Foreign Office, Dulles reiterated his adverse views of Arab nationalism. He did so with reminders of the critical roles assigned to Turkey and Iran in the face of Arab nationalism, which he compared to a flood that could not be opposed but had to be contained. Those directly identified as requiring protection included Israel and Lebanon and the second being the oil positions around the Persian Gulf . . . [deleted] lines."[9] The mood in the NSC was for accommodation, albeit without loss of interests or influence. Defense and Treasury officials in the NSC recommended that the United States deal with Nasser, but not as Arab leader, thus withholding recognition of his regional status while still reckoning with Arab nationalism. Among factors underlying such a position was that "in the long run Arab nationalism may prove to be the greatest counter-force to Soviet penetration of the area."[10]

To move in this direction, however, exposed the incompatibilities in U.S. objectives. In short, the accommodation with Arab nationalism required modifications—though not fundamental changes—in U.S. policy. The overriding commitment to the exclusion of the USSR from the region remained one of the two principal objectives of U.S. policy; the other was access to oil. To assure NATO allies the continued "availability of sufficient Near East oil to meet Western European requirements on reasonable terms as essential to their economic viability" required access to "at least one of the major Near East producing countries."[11] But, according to the same sources, such access "does not require retention of the present profit-sharing formula nor even of existing concessionary rights."

The importance of the qualification deserves emphasis, if only as a reminder of the differences that had long existed between the State Department and U.S. international oil companies over profit and practice, and more particularly over profit as opposed to U.S. interests, as David Bruce had argued years earlier. In 1958, a variety of factors were affecting the oil economy that contributed to such reevaluation. They included the increased Soviet oil output that had made it, in the 1955–1960 period, the second largest oil producer after the United States. Faced with an oil surplus, the Soviet Union began "selling low-cost oil to Europe," which intensified competition among the Western majors as well as the independents operating in the new fields in Libya and extended to the internal competition between U.S. allies, such as Iran and Saudi Arabia.[12] In this context, the French discovery of commercially profitable oil in Algeria and later in Gabon further altered the international parameters of the oil industry. The existence of "cheap oil" from the Middle East therefore constituted an unwelcome "glut on the market."[13]

The remarks of former CIA agent Wilbur Eveland on the subject of the Western majors and Iraq bear consideration. According to Eveland, the members of the international petroleum cartel were "relieved by the possibility of the Iraq oil production's being suspended," that is, excluded from the market, a move in keeping with the conditions described above.[14] With Iraq's oil thus neutralized, Eveland claimed that the CIA heard no "pleas to oust the Iraqi revolutionaries," a position possibly reinforced by the cautious and adverse international response to U.S. intervention in Lebanon and the fear that intervention in Baghdad risked confrontation with the USSR. Under the circumstances, the sabotaging of Iraqi oil wells to render them unavailable to the USSR was not considered. Instead, the decision was made to "keep Iraqi oil off the market for years" by protracted negotiations. The State Department subsequently sought to exclude foreign as well as independent U.S. oil companies operating outside of the cartel, from undermining the effectiveness of this policy. The implications of Eveland's comments as well as those of the Joint Chiefs of Staff cited earlier suggest a two-pronged approach to Iraq, one in which the Defense Department recognized the political advantages of not intervening, while U.S. oil companies and the CIA assessed the economic benefits of holding Iraqi oil at bay. It was against this background that the first Arab Oil Congress was convened by the newly formed Organization of Petroleum Exporting Countries (OPEC). The move was less an aggressive response of oil producers than the calculated design of Western oil interests that, in conjunction with their host regimes, sought to minimize the risks of shocks to the oil economy.

If U.S. sources suggest that Arab nationalism appeared to be a less ominous force in the Middle East, the protection of Western interests and military positions nonetheless remained of paramount concern. The importance attributed to technical assistance projects as direct contributions to reformist policies was unchanged, save in Lebanon, where Ambassador McClintock recommended that they be dropped. Elsewhere, they contributed to preventive development policies, in which attention was focused on the deterrent potential of such projects, provided that they were in the hands of reliable cadres. Neither the format nor the logic of such policies was new. Its origins can be traced to the post–World War II policies in which U.S. officials assessed the risks of widespread discontent and concluded that reform was preferable to revolution and that the manipulation of reform was the most satisfactory means of controlling the outcome.

In 1952, NSC recommendations were explicit in their endorsement of a system of elite controlled political change:

15. Support leadership groups which offer the best prospect of progress toward U.S. objectives in this area, but avoid becoming identified with specific internal issues or individuals. Seek to discredit groups which promote pro-Soviet thinking. Seek to increase the participation of urban "intellectuals" in Western-oriented activities. . . .

16b. Devote more effort to the development of local leaders, administrators and skilled personnel by strengthening educational institutions and by selectively expanding training programs in administrative and technical skills. . . .

16c. Provide selectively for emphasis on personnel exchange programs.[15]

The more flexible attitude adopted toward Arab nationalism in 1958 was facilitated by Washington's appreciation of Nasser's anti-Communist policies and by the increasing tensions between Egypt and the Soviet Union.[16] But it is useful to recall that Washington had offered to continue technical as well as military assistance to the new Iraqi regime. The NSC recommended that the United States "encourage elements within Iraq disposed to friendly relations with the West."[17] The Iraqi regime did not sever its ties with the Baghdad Pact until March 1959, although it had entered into an arms agreement with the Soviet Union some months earlier. As to the status of the Baghdad Pact in Iraq, its offices were closed and its assets frozen after the July 14 coup. In spite of the U.S. initiatives and Nasser's distance from the Iraqi regime, Nasser's position was insufficient to allay the political hostility of those who considered him a permanent and unchanging blight on U.S. policy.

The consideration of U.S.-Israeli relations has to be situated in this context. Israeli appeals to the United States before and after 1956 focused on the risks of Nasser to Western interests and, alternatively, the expert assistance that Israel could offer the United States in curbing its influence. In the aftermath of the events of 1958, the appeal was resumed, and it evoked more than a passing sympathy. The issue divided those persuaded of the need to pressure Israel to find an accommodation with Arab regimes by placing limits on immigration, promoting territorial settlement and the amelioration of the situation of Palestinian refugees, and those within the NSC who remained convinced that in the struggle with radical Arab nationalism, "a logical corollary would be to support Israel as the only strong pro-West power left in the Near East."[18]

The above position conformed to Israeli objectives, as Prime Minister Ben-Gurion sought to enlist Israel in U.S. regional policies. The attempt to synchronize Israeli policies with those of the United States was advanced by the crises of 1958, including the military coup in Baghdad and the Lebanese regime's invitation to U.S. intervention. Ben-Gurion was a firm advocate of U.S. intervention in both instances, making clear Israel's identification with the Lebanese regime's survival.[19] But the rapprochement with the United States was more than a function of Israeli endorsement of U.S. policy in Beirut. It represented coordination at another level, as the so-called peripheral alliance reinforced the organization of U.S. regional politics with its emphasis on support for antiradical and non-Arab regimes.

Did the initiative for such a policy originate in Washington or Tel Aviv? Those who argue that the Israelis were approached by the United States and Britain "to draw Israel into a secret pro-Western alliance" in 1958 maintain that "Washington and London advised Israel to participate in two cooperative groupings: the 'northern tier' of a peripheral alliance tying Israel to Turkey and Iran; and the 'southern tier' linking Israel with Ethiopia."[20] Hermann Eilts recalled that Israel had first inquired as to the U.S. response to its interest in joining the Baghdad Pact. When this was rejected, U.S. officials apparently encouraged "a more informal alliance between Israel and Turkey and Iran."[21] Ben-Gurion turned to both French president De Gaulle and Eisenhower after the events of 1958, offering the former assistance with the Algerian struggle and the latter similar support in exchange for political and financial aid, as well as the integration of Israel into U.S. regional policies. The appeal was to Arab allies, such as Jordan, Lebanon, Saudi Arabia, Libya, and the Sudan. But the project was to reinforce ties with non-Arab states, such as Iran, Turkey, and Ethiopia, to contain Arab nationalism and to confront Nasser and the Soviet Union.[22]

Did Dulles have this in mind when he referred to the flood tide of Arab nationalism and the need to protect Israel and Lebanon, along with "the oil positions around the Persian Gulf"? Eisenhower is reported to have endorsed Ben-Gurion's regional assessment, of which Dulles informed Iran, Turkey, and Ethiopia. Irrespective of who took the initiative in this case, there is no doubt that for Israel the move was propitious. It strengthened relations with the two states central to U.S. policy, Iran and Turkey, while affirming Israel's regional interests in containing Arab nationalist regimes. Following the coup in Baghdad, Ben-Gurion journeyed to Ankara on a secret mission on August 28, promoting "wide-ranging understandings about several joint activities aimed at blocking Nasser's influence in the Middle East" that lasted until the mid-1960s.[23] The Iraqi coup similarly provoked a further rapprochement between Iran and Israel, leading to contacts at the highest political and military levels, including the visit to Teheran by the chief of Israeli military intelligence, General Harkabi, and his subsequent meeting with Shah Reza Pahlevi (ibid. 37, 38).

Late in 1958, according to a CIA review of Israeli intelligence, the triangular relationship between Israel, Iran, and Turkey assumed a more formal structure among the intelligence services of the three states, as "the Trident Organization was established by Mossad with Turkey's National Security Service (TNSS) and Iran's National Organization for Intelligence and Security (SAVAK)."[24] Trident was part of an arrangement known as the KK Mountain, established by the CIA and Mossad to facilitate Israeli intelligence activities in the third world, subsidized by American intelligence and operated for mutual benefit in areas politically inaccessible to the United States. In the 1960s, according to a recent work, KK Mountain had a $10 million to $20 million budget, out of roughly $650 million (ibid. 100–101). Israel's activity in the "southern tier" involved the Sudan, where in 1954 a delegation of Sudanese 'Umma Party members in London met with Israeli diplomat Mordecai Gazit.[25] NSC policy recommendations in the fall of 1958 that were signed by Eisenhower included recognition of not only Britain's primacy in the Sudan but also "closer Sudanese relations with friendly African states, especially Ethiopia."[26] It was in November that the military coup bringing "outspokenly anti-communist" General Ibrahim 'Abbud to power occurred.

In February 1960, the NSC's Operations Coordinating Board reported that Israel and the United States continued their "generally close and friendly ties" and that Israel was seeking closer relations with Iran and Turkey.[27] In the early winter of 1960, the Operations Coordinating Board also reported on another facet of U.S. Middle East policy, its "support of the UAR's anti-communist propaganda offensive," with USIS assistance as well as "increased exchanges between the United States and UAR officials in the fields of finance and labor. Both the AFL/CIO and the International Confederation of Free Trade Unions have given indications of rapprochement with the Egyptian Federation of Labor" (ibid. no. 16, p. 6).

Little wonder that the OCB judged conditions in the Middle East to be "somewhat more favorable to the attainment of U.S. objectives than they previously had been."[28] Considered in the framework of a decade-long struggle in which Iranian and Arab nationalists sought to regain a measure of control over their resources, the United States response to the military coup in Baghdad and to the civil war in Beirut achieved its objectives. In Beirut, unlike Teheran or Cairo, U.S. officials did not confront a nationalist leadership in opposition, but the U.S. military was nonetheless directed to intervene to assure a political objective favorable to U.S. interests.

As U.S. military withdrawal from Lebanon was under way, the Eisenhower administration in Washington was considering its response to the crisis surrounding the two islands of Quemoy and Matsu. The Seventh Fleet moved in support of Chiang Kai-shek, as in Laos the right-wing government of Phoui Sananikone was installed. By late October, John Foster Dulles was discussing the demilitarization of the islands. In the case of the Middle East, the Joint Chiefs of Staff and the Defense Department changed the status of the Command forces responsible for the Middle East. Under the Middle East Emergency Defense Plan, approved in the spring of 1960, arrangements were made to "assist in the conduct of a strategic defense of the region in general war, holding the approaches to the Cairo-Suez-Aden area and the Persian Gulf 'as far forward as possible in the CENTO/Central Treaty Organization replacing the Baghdad Pact/area.' "[29] In the summer of 1960, responsibility for "planning for general war in the Middle East area" was assigned to the Commander in Chief, U.S. Naval Forces Eastern Atlantic and Mediterranean, and officially approved in the fall. CENTO forces, in which the U.S. role was indirect, though critical to military and other planning, were emphasized.[30] In that context, the JCS recommended that "primary reliance must be placed upon indigenous forces."[31] The advice applied not only to the identification of military proxies in the region but to their political counterparts, as in Beirut. There, such reliance contributed significantly to the perpetuation of the existing system at the cost of significant reform, a staple of U.S. policy in Lebanon and the Middle East during the postwar democratic era.

Notes

1. The Dynamic of Collaborative Intervention

1. Walter W. Rostow, *The United States in the World Arena*, pp. 362–63; Samuel F. Bemis, *A Diplomatic History of the United States*, pp. 982–83; Thomas A. Bailey, *A Diplomatic History of the American People*, p. 850. For more recent works, see Erika G. Allin, *The United States and the 1958 Lebanon Crisis*, and Agnes Korbany, *U.S. Intervention in Lebanon, 1958 and 1982*.

2. Blanche Wiesen Cook, *The Declassified Eisenhower*; Bruce Cumings, *The Origins of the Korean War*, vol. 11; Noam Chomsky, *Deterring Democracy*; Richard H. Immerman, *The CIA in Guatemala*; Audrey Kahin and George McT. Kahin, *Subversion as Foreign Policy*; Gabriel Kolko, *Confronting the Third World*; Walter LaFeber, *Inevitable Revolutions*; J. Dower, "Occupied Japan and the Cold War in Asia"; Robert McMahon, *Colonialism and Cold War*; McMahon, "The Cold War in Asia"; and McMahon, *Cold War in the Periphery*.

3. Works that raise issues relevant to such considerations, albeit in different settings, include: Cumings, *The Origins of the Korean War*, vol. 11, chs. 1, 2; Peter Gourevitch, "Second Image Reversed"; Clive Thomas, *The Rise of the Authoritarian State in Peripheral Societies*; Robert Vitalis, "Business Conflict, Collaboration, and Privilege in Interwar Egypt"; Vitalis, *When Capitalists Collide*; and David N. Gibbs, *The Political Economy of Third World Intervention*.

4. See the new edition of Irene L. Gendzier, *Development Against Democracy* (1995).

5. Mostafa Elm, *Oil, Power, and Principle*.

6. Chomsky, *Deterring Democracy*, pp. 393–94; Immerman, *The CIA in Guatemala*; "In Guatemala's Dark Heart, CIA Tied to Death and Aid," *New*

York Times, Apr. 2, 1995, p. 1; Alan Nairn, "CIA Death Squad," *The Nation*, Apr. 17, 1995.

7. Gibbs, *Political Economy*, p. 100.

8. Dulles to McClintock, May 13, 1958, box 16, chronological series, J. F. Dulles Papers, Eisenhower Library.

9. The following essays by Melvyn Leffler are particularly instructive in this context: "The American Conception of National Security and the Beginnings of the Cold War, 1945–1948" and "Strategy, Diplomacy, and the Cold War."

10. A. H. Meyer to DOS, Oct. 12, 1954, NA RG 59, 783A.5MSP/ 10–1254.

11. Miles Copeland, *The Game of Nations*, pp. 227–33.

12. Ibid., pp. 235–38.

13. PRO, FO to Washington, July 14, 1958, conversation between the president and the prime minister, FO 371/134154.

14. VP Nixon to Sec State Dulles, July 15, 1958, box 8, Telephone Call series, Dulles Papers, Eisenhower Library.

15. Eisenhower to Macmillan, London, July 18, 1958, DDQC 12, no. 3 (May–June 1986), 001416.

16. Washington to Foreign Office, July 19, 1958, FO 371/132779.

17. Ibid.

18. Senate Foreign Relations Committee, Hearings on the Middle East, 85th Cong., 2d sess., 10. Detailed discussion of the Senate hearings appears in Part V, chapter titled "Deception and Self-Deception: Keeping Congress Uninformed."

19. Michael Suleiman, *Political Parties in Lebanon*, chs. 1, 6, 7; Pierre Rondot, "The Political Institutions of Lebanese Democracy"; Ralph E. Crow, "Confessionalism, Public Administration, and Efficiency in Lebanon"; and Malcolm M. Kerr, "Political Decision Making in a Confessional Democracy."

20. Nubar Hovsepian, "The Lebanon Quagmire"; Roger Owen, ed., *Essays on the Crisis in Lebanon*; Michael Hudson, "The Lebanese Crisis and the Limits of Consociational Democracy," and Michael Hudson, "The Precarious Republic Revisited"; Halim Barakat, *Lebanon in Strife*; Salim Nasr, "The Crisis of Lebanese Capitalism."

21. "Long Range U.S. Policy Toward the Near East," Jan. 24, 1958, NSC 5801/1 Report, p. 16, NSC series, Eisenhower Library.

22. "The Political Control Exercised by the Commercial Class in Lebanon," Jan. 21, 1952, p. 109, RG 59, 783a.00/1–2152.

23. Avi Shlaim, "Israeli Interference in Internal Arab Politics"; Livia Rokach, *Israel's Sacred Terrorism*; and Laura Eisenberg, *My Enemy's Enemy*.

24. "Transmitting a Survey of the Economic Problems of Lebanon," American Legation to DOS, Beirut, July 3, 1946, RG 59, 890 E.50/7–346. Also, Policy Statement on Lebanon, Jan. 29, 1951, RG 59, 611.83a/1–2951.

25. I. F. Stone, *The Haunted Fifties*, p. 229.

26. Quincy Wright, "United States Intervention in Lebanon," pp. 112–25.

27. Although unconditionally supportive of Sham'un and Malik, *Ropes of Sand*, by Wilbur Eveland, is an unsparing account of U.S. policy in Lebanon dur-

ing this period. H. Symmes, who was stationed in Damascus and subsequently became assistant to Under Secretary of State W. Rountree, raises questions rarely heard in the conformist academic accounts of 1958, in his essay "Positive Deterrence in Local Conflicts"; and see also E. J. Hughes, *The Ordeal of Power*.

28. Rostow, *The United States in the World Arena*, p. 363.

29. Bemis, *A Diplomatic History of the United States*, p. 983.

30. Bailey, *A Diplomatic History of the American People*, p. 850.

31. Alan Dowty, *Middle East Crisis*; Stephen Genco, "The Eisenhower Doctrine."

32. Richard J. Barnet, *Intervention and Revolution*; Manfred Halpern, "The Mortality and Politics of Intervention"; Kolko, *Confronting the Third World*; Walter LaFeber, *The American Age*; William Quandt, "Lebanon, 1958, and Jordan, 1970"; William Stivers, "Eisenhower and the Middle East."

33. Joel Migdal, "Strong States, Weak States," p. 411; Dietrich Rueschemeyer and Peter Evans, "The State and Economic Transformation," p. 65.

34. Elie Kedourie, "Ethnicity, Majority, and Minority in the Middle East," p. 31; and the same author's "Constitutionalism in the Middle East."

35. The first citation is from E. Shils, who viewed these arrangements with far more skepticism, as in "Prospects for Lebanese Civility," p. 5, and the second is from Samir Khalaf, "Primordial Ties and Politics," in his *Lebanon's Predicament*, p. 103.

36. The citation is from Samuel P. Huntington, *The Third Wave*, p. 308.

37. Albert Hourani's review of Kamal Salibi's *Lebanon from Feudalism to Modern State*, p. 263.

38. Consider some of the following works: Ghassan Salame, " 'Strong' and 'Weak' States"; Halim Barakat, ed., *Toward a Viable Lebanon*; Ahmad Beydoun, *Identité Confessionelle et Temps Sociale Chez les Historiens Libanais Contemporains*; Claude Dubar and Salim Nasr, *Les Classes Sociales au Liban*; Georges Corm, "Myths and Realities of the Lebanese Conflict," p. 261; T. Hanf, "Homo Oeconomicus–Homo Communitaris," ch. 10; Hovsepian, "The Lebanese Quagmire" and "The Lebanese Opposition"; Salim Nasr, "Backdrop to Civil War," p. 73; Tabitha Petran, *The Struggle Over Lebanon*; Nawaf Salam, "L'Insurrection de 1958 au Liban"; Salam, *Mythes et Politiques au Liban*; Kamal Salibi, *A House of Many Mansions*; Fawaz N. Traboulsi, "Identités et Solidarités Croisées dans les Conflits du Liban Contemporain."

39. See note 20 for references that challenged such an approach, in addition to many cited in note 38.

40. Salim Nasr, "Lebanon," p. 13; see also "Lebanon Says 144,000 Died in Civil Strife," *New York Times*, Mar. 10, 1992; Dilip Hiro, *Lebanon*, p. 127.

41. Among the criticisms leveled at U.S. critics of Israeli policies in the media, see Ze'ev Chafets, *Double Vision*. For Israeli critics of Israeli policy, see *The Beirut Massacre: The Complete Kahan Commission Report*, Karz-Cohl, Publishing, Inc., New York City, New York, 1983; Amnon Kapeliuk, *Enquête sur un massacre*; Ze'ev Schiff, "The Green Light"; Ze'ev Schiff and Ehud Ya'ari,

Israel's Lebanon War. Critical analyses of U.S. policy are to be found in Avi Shlaim, "The Impact of U.S. Policy in the Middle East"; Jonathan Randall, *Going All the Way*; and Noam Chomsky, *The Fateful Triangle*.

42. The figure on U.S. casualties in 1958 is taken from Fahim Qubain, *Crisis in Lebanon*, pp. 120–21. Qubain writes that "casualties among American troops were minor. The total death toll came to less than eight persons. With the exception of one, all were due to accidents."

Among the works to analyze the roots of U.S. policy and its course in 1982, consider: George Ball, "America in the Middle East," and the same author's *Error and Betrayal in Lebanon*; Nasser Aruri, "The United States Intervention in Lebanon"; William Quandt, "Reagan's Lebanon Policy"; Michael Hudson, "The United States' Involvement in Lebanon"; Irene Gendzier, "The Declassified Lebanon, 1948–1958," and Gendzier, "No Forum for the Lebanese People"; Rashid Khalidi, "Problems of Foreign Intervention in Lebanon"; and Walid Khalidi, *Conflict and Violence in Lebanon*. The following issues of *Middle East Research and Information Project (MERIP)*, now named *Middle East Report*, are particularly useful for their analyses of the Lebanese situation: nos. 44, 51, 61, 66, 73. See also Edward Said, "Palestinians in the Aftermath of Beirut: A Preliminary Stocktaking," and Said, "Our Lebanon," reprinted in Said, *The Politics of Dispossession*; and I. Abu Lughod and E. Ahmad, eds., *Race and Class, The Invasion of Lebanon*, special issue.

2. U.S. Postwar Policy and the Middle East

1. Bruce Cumings, *The Origins of the Korean War*, vol. 11; Noam Chomsky, *Deterring Democracy*; Richard H. Immerman, *The CIA in Guatemala*; Gabriel Kolko, *Confronting the Third World*; Walter LaFeber, *Inevitable Revolutions*; J. Dower, "Occupied Japan and the Cold War in Asia," pp. 366–69; Audrey Kahin and George McT. Kahin, *Subversion as Foreign Policy*; Robert McMahon, *Colonialism and Cold War*; McMahon, "The Cold War in Asia"; and McMahon, *Cold War in the Periphery*; David Painter, "Oil and the Cold War."

2. Thomas Ferguson, "From Normalcy to New Deal"; Kim McQuaid, "Corporate Liberalism in the American Business Community."

3. David Painter, *Oil and the American Century*, p. 154.

4. Figure of $400 million appears in Melvyn Leffler, "Strategy, Diplomacy, and the Cold War," p. 807.

5. John Lewis Gaddis, *Strategies of Containment*, p. 100.

6. DOS, NSC 68, U.S. National Security Policy, Apr. 14, 1950, *FRUS 1950*, I (1977), p. 282.

7. Painter, *Oil and the American Century*, p. 156.

8. Mira Wilkins, *The Maturing of the Multinational Enterprise*, p. 301, table XII.1.

9. ARAMCO Handbook figures cited in Irvine H. Anderson, *ARAMCO*, p. 120.

10. Melvyn P. Leffler, "The American Conception of National Security and the Beginnings of the Cold War," p. 361.

11. Anderson, *ARAMCO*, p. 164.

12. See Melvyn P. Leffler, *A Preponderance of Power*, p. 222.

13. Cited in ibid., p. 353.

14. Cited in ibid., pp. 353–54; and see general discussion of the role of aviation in Lloyd Gardner, *Economic Aspects of New Deal Diplomacy*.

15. Gaddis, *Strategies of Containment*, p. 23.

16. William Roger Louis, *The British Empire in the Middle East*, p. 12.

17. "The Pentagon Talks of 1947," Between the United States and the United Kingdom Concerning the Middle East and the Eastern Mediterranean, *FRUS 1947*, V: *The Near East and Africa* (1971), p. 557.

18. Louis, *The British Empire in the Middle East*, p. 9.

19. "The Pentagon Talks," p. 557.

20. Report by the Coordinating Committee of the DOS, May 2, 1945, in *FRUS 1945*, VIII: *The Near East and Africa* (1969), p. 36.

21. Ibid., p. 35.

22. Thomas G. Patterson, "The Quest for Peace and Prosperity," p. 91.

23. Louis, *The British Empire in the Middle East*, p. 191; and James L. Gormly, "Keeping the Door Open in Saudi Arabia."

24. Gormly, "Keeping the Door Open in Saudi Arabia," p. 199.

25. Memorandum from the Assistant Chief of the Aviation Division (Walstrom) to the Director of the Office of Near East and African Affairs (Henderson), *FRUS 1945*, VIII, pp. 77–80.

26. "The Pentagon Talks," p. 524.

27. Louis, *The British Empire in the Middle East*, pp. 55, 65, 70; and consult the following works for discussion of the Iranian crisis: Aaron D. Miller, *Search for Security*; James A. Bill, *The Eagle and the Lion*; Ervand Abrahamian, *Iran Between Two Revolutions*; and Mostafa Elm, *Oil, Power, and Principle*.

28. Painter, *Oil and the American Century*, p. 115.

29. Ibid., p. 80.

30. Kennan's position appears in U.S. Chargé d'Affaires in Moscow to DOS, Nov. 7, 1944, *FRUS 1944*, V, pp. 470–71.

31. Painter, *Oil and the American Century*, p. 113, and "The Pentagon Talks," *FRUS 1947*, p. 530.

32. Leffler, "Strategy, Diplomacy, and the Cold War," p. 814; see also Bruce R. Kuniholm, *The Origins of the Cold War in the Near East*; Harry N. Howard, *Turkey, the Straits, and U.S. Policy*; J. Garry Clifford, "President Truman and Peter the Great's Will"; Louis, *The British Empire in the Middle East*, part 2.

33. Leffler, "Strategy, Diplomacy, and the Cold War," p. 818.

34. "The Pentagon Talks," *FRUS 1947*, p. 525.

35. Painter, *Oil and the American Century*, p. 52.

36. Miller, *Search for Security*, p. 55.

37. Painter, "Searching for Security in a Global Economy," p. 191.

38. Irvine H. Anderson, "Lend Lease for Saudi Arabia"; Painter, *Oil in the American Century*, p. 37.

39. Benjamin Schwadran, *The Middle East, Oil, and the Great Powers*, p. 312.

40. Douglas Little, "Pipeline Politics," pp. 255–85; in addition to discussions in Painter, *Oil and the American Century*, and Schwadran, *The Middle East, Oil, and the Great Powers*, ch. 12.

41. Schwadran, *The Middle East, Oil, and the Great Powers*, p. 324.

42. Draft memorandum to Truman, *FRUS 1945*, VIII (1969), p. 45.

43. John A. Loftus, "Middle East Oil and the Pattern of Control," p. 17.

44. Painter, "Searching for Security in a Global Economy," p. 192.

45. Daniel Yergin, *The Prize*, p. 416.

46. Joseph M. Jones, *The Fifteen Weeks*, pp. 46–47.

47. "The Pentagon Talks," *FRUS 1947*, p. 625. Hereafter cited in text by page numbers in parentheses.

48. DPS Comments on NSC 27, in *FRUS 1948*, V (1976), pp. 1360–61.

49. Anderson, *ARAMCO*, p. 165.

50. Telephone interview with William Chandler, Apr. 10, 1995. Chandler was chief engineer for TAPLINE in 1946–1947, assistant to the president of TAPLINE until 1955, and vice president and then president and CEO from 1963 to mid-1972. For further discussion of TAPLINE, see ch. 5.

51. Stephen Green, *Taking Sides*, ch. 3.

52. *Report by National Security Council on United States Policy Toward Israel and the Arab States*, Oct. 17, 1949, NSC 47/2, *FRUS 1949*, VI (1977), p. 1431.

53. Benny Morris, "The Causes and Character of the Arab Exodus from Palestine," p. 9.

54. Louis, *The British Empire in the Middle East*, p. 617; and see Memorandum from Pres Truman to Under Sec of State Lovett, Aug. 16, 1948. *FRUS 1948*, V (1976), p. 1313.

55. From *FRUS 1948*, V, p. 1136, cited by Louis, *The British Empire in the Middle East*, p. 543; analyses that rely on Israeli archival sources for this period include Tom Segev, *1949*; and by the same author, *The Seventh Million*; Benny Morris, *The Birth of the Palestinian Refugee Question*; and Simha Flapan, *The Birth of Israel*.

56. Jacob C. Hurewitz, *Diplomacy in the Near and Middle East*, 2:doc. 92; Avi Shlaim, *The Politics of Partition*, ch. 17, for developments on the ground; Louis, *The British Empire in the Middle East*, pp. 583–90.

57. Wilbur Eveland, *Ropes of Sand*, p. 142, note.

58. Anderson, *ARAMCO*, p. 194.

59. Elm, *Oil, Power, and Principle*, p. 108.

60. Ibid., p. 257.

61. See discussion of this exchange in ch. 12, specific reference to conversation between Eisenhower, Dulles, and the Shah is in note 64.

62. U.S. Senate, *The International Petroleum Cartel.* Memo by Dep Assistant Sec of State for Eco Affairs, July 28, 1952, cited in *FRUS 1952–1954*, IX, *The Near and Middle East*, part 1 (1986), pp. 605–6.

63. Yergin, *The Prize*, p. 503.

64. Senate, *The International Petroleum Cartel*, p. 23.

65. Ibid., p. 33.

66. Cited in John M. Blair, *The Control of Oil*, p. 73.

67. See the analysis of G. McGhee, *The U.S.-Turkish-NATO Middle East Connection.*

68. Presentation by Leo D. Welch, treasurer of Standard Oil of New Jersey, Nov. 12, 1946, on "Approach to the Problems in Maintaining and Expanding American Direct Investments Abroad," cited in Engler, *The Politics of Oil,* p. 267. Welch subsequently became chairman of Standard Oil in 1960.

3. *Learning Lebanon: A Primer*

1. G. Amin, *The Modernization of Poverty*, pp. 4–5.

2. Charles Issawi, "Economic Development and Political Liberalism in Lebanon," p. 73.

3. Dominique Chevalier, *La Société du Mont Liban à l'Epoque de la Révolution Industrielle en Europe*; and Claude Dubar and Salim Nasr, *Les Classes Sociales au Liban*, part 1, ch. 4; Boutros Labaki, "L'Economie Politique du Liban Indépendant," and Roger Owen, "The Economic History of Lebanon"; and see Owen's historical overview in *The Middle East in the World Economy.*

4. Carolyn Gates, "The Formation of the Political Economy of Modern Lebanon," p. 317. Gates's analysis is to be published by I. B. Tauris and the Centre for Lebanese Studies, Oxford, as *The Merchant Republic of Lebanon: Rise of an Open Economy* (1997).

5. Gates, "Formation of the Political Economy," p. 314.

6. American Legation Beirut to DOS, Beirut as a Gold Market, Mar. 6, 1953, RG 59, 883a.2531/3–653.

7. American Legation Beirut to DOS, Merchant Shipping and Shipbuilding, Lebanon, 1950, Apr. 2, 1951, RG 59, 983A.53/4–251.

8. See Hourani's description of Beirut as a mirror of changes in Lebanon in this period, as discussed in "Political Society in Lebanon."

9. Gates, "Formation of the Political Economy," p. 312.

10. The role of the Banque de Syrie et du Liban and René Busson is discussed in chapter 4.

11. Former ambassador of Lebanon Nadim Dimechkié argued this point in an exchange with Dr. Carolyn Gates and me on the occasion of the conference "Lebanon in the 1950s," at the University of Texas, Austin, Sept. 11–13, 1992.

12. Amin, *The Modernization of Poverty*, p. 78, n. 8.

13. Amiouni [Amyuni], "A Short Survey of Our Pre-War and Post-War Economic Problems," July 3, 1946, p. 6, cited in the American Legation survey of the same subject, RG 59, 890E.50/77–346 CS/JEC.

14. Ibid., p. 13.

15. Ibid.

16. Issawi, "Economic Development and Political Liberalism in Lebanon," p. 75.

17. Gates, "Formation of the Political Economy," p. 285.

18. Edmund Y. Asfour, "Industrial Development in Lebanon," p. 4.

19. Gates, "Formation of the Political Economy," p. 305.

20. Ibid., p. 306.

21. Amin, The Modernization of Poverty, p. 41.

22. Malcolm M. Kerr, "Political Decision Making in a Confessional Democracy," p. 211.

23. Gunnar Myrdal, The Challenge of World Poverty, pp. 208–10.

24. Michel Chiha, "Civisme et Devoir Social."

25. "Lebanon in the World," lecture presented at the Cénacle Libanais, Dec. 17, 1951, included in Michel Chiha, Lebanon at Home and Abroad, p. 117; and see also Nadim Shehadi, "The Idea of Lebanon."

26. Kerr, "Political Decision Making in a Confessional Democracy," p. 188.

27. Albert Hourani, "Visions of Lebanon." The following works provide additional information on this phase of Lebanon's development: Marwan Buheiry, "Beirut's Role in the Political Economy of the French Mandate," pp. 3–7; Pierre Rondot, "The Political Institutions of Lebanese Democracy," p. 128; Fawaz Traboulsi, "Le Système Chiha," in "Identités et Solidarités Croisées dans les Conflits du Liban Contemporain."
For informed analyses of the mandate and post-mandate periods in Lebanon and Syria, see Albert Hourani, Syria and Lebanon; Philip S. Khoury, Syria and the French Mandate; Michael Joseph, Class and Client in Beirut; Raghid Solh, "The Attitude of the Arab Nationalists Towards Greater Lebanon During the 1930s."

28. Figures cited in Suad Joseph, "Muslim-Christian Conflict in Lebanon," p. 64; and see Albert Hourani, Minorities in the Arab World and Syria and Lebanon; and Michael W. Suleiman, Political Parties in Lebanon.

29. In the early 1920s, "independent Syrian unionists" included the well-known political families of Karame, Salam, Beyhoum, 'Ammoun, and Istfan. On the other hand, the equally important names of Arslan, Sulh, Haidar, Tall, Daghir, al-Bisar and al-Manasfi, and Na'mani were among the members of Arab nationalist associations that looked to the possibility of "reconciling Syrian unionism and Lebanese particularism" (Solh, "The Attitude of the Arab Nationalists," p. 151).

30. Khoury, Syria and the French Mandate, p. 613; Fadia Kiwan, "La Perception Maronite du Grand-Liban," pp. 138–39; see also Meir Zamir, The Formation of Modern Lebanon.

31. Beirut to Washington, Aug. 12, 1942, #283, in Walter L. Browne, *Lebanon's Struggle for Independence*, part 1, p. 347.

32. "Lebanon Today, 1942," lecture given at the Catholic Youth Centre in Beirut, included in Chiha, *Lebanon at Home and Abroad*, pp. 43–44.

33. Ibid., pp. 44–45. Also see pp. 117–18.

34. Basam Abdel Qader Na'mani, "Confessionalism in Balance," p. 381.

35. Ibid., pp. 378–79.

36. In addition to Na'mani, see the interpretations by Michael Hudson, *The Precarious Republic*, p. 44; Suleiman, *Political Parties in Lebanon*, especially ch. 1; and the articles by Maksoud, Rondot, Kerr, and Crow in Leonard Binder, ed., *Politics in Lebanon*.

37. Michel al-Khoury, "Ebauche d'un Visage du Liban," Les Conférences du Cénacle, 1961, Beirut, p. 16.

38. Clovis Maksoud, "Lebanon and Arab Nationalism," p. 241.

39. Michael Joseph, *Class and Client in Beirut*, p. 122.

40. Amin, *The Modernization of Poverty*, p. 40.

41. R. Hrair Dekmejian, *Patterns of Political Leadership*, p. 38.

42. Michael Johnson, *Class and Client in Beirut*, pp. 120–22.

43. Hudson, *The Precarious Republic*, pp. 149–50; Samir Khalaf, *Lebanon's Predicament*, chs. 4–6.

44. Kerr, "Political Decision Making," p. 210.

45. Jacques Couland, *Le Mouvement Syndical au Liban*, part 3, ch. 3.

46. U.S. Rep. to UN (Austin) to Sec of State, #258, Mar. 2, 1949, *FRUS 1949*, VI (1977), p. 787; and see Ahmad Beydoun, "The South Lebanon Border Zone," p. 35.

47. Tom Segev, *1949*, p. 10.

48. Tabitha Petran, *The Struggle Over Lebanon*, p. 74 and pp. 73–76; Laurie Brand, "The Politics of Passports," pp. 29–35; Rosemary Sayegh, *Palestinians*, p. 67; and see Pinkerton to Sec of State, Nov. 26, 1948. RG 84, box 232, file 800.

49. Laura Zittrain Eisenberg, *My Enemy's Enemy*, p. 125–26.

50. Ibid., pp. 166–69.

51. Shlaim, "Israeli Interference in Internal Arab Politics," p. 236. See also Perkins to Sec. of State, Aug. 31, 1948, RG 59, 890E.00/8–3148.

52. Livia Rokach, *Israel's Sacred Terrorism*, pp. 24–30.

53. Citation appears in Simha Flapan, *The Birth of Israel*, p. 124.

54. Besharah al-Khuri, *Haqa'iq Lubnaniyyah*, vol. 3, chapter titled "1949."

55. Traboulsi, "Identités et Solidarités Croisées," p. 277.

56. Hudson, *The Precarious Republic*, p. 153.

4. Alternating Currents of Criticism and Conformity

*"The Political Control Exercised by the Commercial Class in Lebanon," Foreign Service Dispatch, Jan. 21, 1952, American Legation Beirut to DOS, RG 59, 783a.00/1–2152.

1. George Wadsworth to Loy Henderson, Beirut to Washington, July 11, 1945, RG 59, 890E.00/7–1145.

2. Gordon Merriam to author, personal communication, Sept. 8, 1992.

3. William Roger Louis, *The British Empire in the Middle East*, part 3, sec. 3, "Independence in Syria and Lebanon: The Significance of the Crisis of 1945"; E. E. Azar and K. Shnayerson, "United States-Lebanese Relations"; and A. B. Gaunson, *The Anglo-French Clash in Lebanon and Syria*.

4. Louis, *The British Empire in the Middle East*, p. 153.

5. Ibid., p. 168.

6. Phillip Baram, *The Department of State in the Middle East*, p. 124.

7. Ibid., p. 137.

8. For a discussion of U.S. policies with respect to Syria and Lebanon at this time, see *FRUS 1944*, V (1965); *FRUS 1945*, VIII (1969); and *FRUS 1946*, VII (1969).

9. Bruins to DOS, Sept. 24, 1953, RG 59, 883A.2553/9–2453.

10. Robert Engler, *The Politics of Oil*, p. 311.

11. James Byrnes to George Wadsworth, Mar. 20, 1946. DOS Central Files on Lebanon, 1945–1949, RG 59, 711.90E/3–2246.

12. Cited in Louis, *The British Empire in the Middle East*, pp. 159–60.

13. American Consulate, Beirut, to Sec of State, Washington, D.C. Subject: Lebanese Reactions to Treaty Proposals, June 28, 1936, cited in Walter L. Browne, *The Political History of Lebanon*, vol. 1, pp. 198–201.

14. Beirut Syria, William M. Gwynn, American Consul, to Sec of State, Washington, D.C., Oct. 1, 1942. In Browne, *The Political History of Lebanon*, vol. 11, pp. 366–68.

15. No. R-19–45, Military Intelligence Division, Military Attaché Report by Virgil A. Jackson, Jan. 17, 1945, RG 59, 890E.01/4–1845.

16. Wadsworth to Sec of State, Mar. 19, 1945, #702. Transmitting Study on French Historical Rights in Syria and Lebanon by Prof. Rustam, RG 59, 890E.01/3–1945.

17. Wadsworth to Acheson, Mar. 20, 1946, RG 59, 890E.00/3–2046.

18. Beirut to Washington, Apr. 14, 1947, RG 59, 890E.00/4–1447. Pinkerton to Acheson, May 14, 1947, RG 59, 890E.00/5–1447.

19. Cited in Oct. 31, 1946, American Legation cable, RG 59, 890E.00/10–3146.

20. For a Legation report on the existence of such feudal armies, see Report on the Government of Lebanon, May 29, 1950, RG 59, 783A.02/5–2950.

21. Incoming airgram from American Legation to DOS, Jan. 7, 1947, A-4, RG 59, 890E.00/1–747.

22. Pinkerton to Sec of State, Apr. 16, 1947. RG 59, 890.00/4–1647.

23. Pinkerton to Sec of State, May 28, 1947, RG 59, 890.E.00/5–2847.

24. Rev. Joseph E. Awad to G. Lewis Jones, director, Office of Near East Affairs, Apr. 9, 1951, RG 59, 783A.00/4–951.

25. Incoming airgram 1590, Aug. 28, 1947, RG 59, 890.00/8–2847.

26. Pinkerton to Sec of State, airgram A-432, Oct. 8, 1947, RG 59, 890E.415/10-847.

27. For CIA evaluations, see CIA Report for the President, Sept. 27, 1948. From the Papers of President H. S. Truman. In *CIA Research Reports: Middle East, 1946–1976*, edited by Paul Kesaris, compiled by Robert Lester (Frederick, Md.: University Publications of America, 1983). For State-War-Navy Coordinating Committee evaluation of Lebanon, see SWNCC Country Study on Long-Range Assistance to Lebanon, June 8, 1948, RG 59, 890E.00/6-848.

28. DOS Policy Statement on Lebanon, Jan. 29, 1951, RG 59, 611.83a/1-2951, p. 2.

29. USARMA Beirut to Deptar, Washington, D.C., Feb. 16, 1951, U.S. DOS Lebanon: Internal and Foreign Affairs, 1950–1954 (Frederick, Md.: University Publications of America, 1987).

30. DOS Policy Statement on Lebanon, Jan. 29, 1951, p. 3.

31. Memorandum of Interview with Prime Minister and Minister of National Economy of Lebanon, prepared by Commercial Attaché, Dec. 17, 1945, RG 59, 890E.50/12-1745.

32. Transmitting a Survey of the Economic Problems of Lebanon, American Legation, Beirut, July 3, 1946, RG 59, 890E.50/7-346.

33. Pinkerton to Acheson, June 4, 1947, DOS Central Files on Lebanon, 1945–1949, RG 59, 890E.002/6-447.

34. A-88 Wadsworth to Acheson, May 16, 1946, RG 59, 890E.5045/5-1646.

35. SWNCC Country Study on Long-Range Assistance to Lebanon, June 8, 1948, RG 59, 890E.00/6-848.

36. Samuel O. Ruff, the author of the report identified in note 38, was second secretary and both political and economic officer, as such he met informally with influential Lebanese figures, as did others in the Legation. Such meetings provided an invaluable entrée to Lebanese political society for U.S. officials and no less valuable contacts for the Lebanese. Interview with author, Aug. 6, 1992; confirmed in telephone interview, Mar. 7, 1995.

37. American Legation #3253 to DOS, Aug. 19, 1947, RG 59, 890E.50/8-1947.

38. "The Political Control Exercised by the Commercial Class in Lebanon," Foreign Service Dispatch, American Legation, Beirut to DOS, Jan. 21, 1952, RG 59, 783a.00/1-2152. Note that although Ambassador Harold Minor signed the dispatch, its author, as indicated on the text, was Samuel O. Ruff. Hereafter cited in text by page numbers in parentheses.

39. Francis A. Kittaneh was mentioned in the Dec. 17, 1945, Memorandum of Interview with Prime Minister and Minister of National Economy of Lebanon, prepared by commercial attaché. RG 59, 890E.50/12-1745. It is, however, in the naval attaché report of Sept. 8, 1949, "Background Information on Kettaneh Frères, Sami Shukair, and Salahheddine Baki," that the information cited here was presented. RG 84, Damascus 1949, box 681, file 350.3.

40. "The Political Control Exercised by the Commercial Class," p. 118.

41. Traboulsi, "Identités et Solidarités," p. 282.

42. "The Political Control Exercised by the Commercial Class," p. 124.

43. See the overall analysis offered by B. J. Odeh, *Lebanon*, chs. 4–5. For a contrasting interpretation of a distinctly different political economy that nonetheless offers relevant observations, see Robert Vitalis, "Business Conflict, Collaboration, and Privilege in Interwar Egypt."

44. Bruins to DOS, June 14, 1951, cited in *FRUS 1951*, V (1982), pp. 1003–4.

5. The Foundations of U.S. Policy, PACLIFT: Petroleum, Aviation, Commerce, Labor, Intelligence, and the Friendship Treaty

1. Beirut to DOS, Annual Petroleum Report: 1952, Apr. 23, 1953, RG 84, 84.883A.2553/4–2353.

2. Wadsworth to Sec of State, July 30, 1946, RG 59, 890E.6363/7–3046.

3. Acheson to Kuniholm, Aug. 22, 1946, RG 59, 711.90E/4–1646.

4. Proposed Refinery Construction Program Lebanon, Syria and Jordan, June 19, 1952, RG 84, 883A.3932/6–1952. See Charles Issawi and M. Yeganeh, *The Economics of Middle Eastern Oil*, p. 177. In addition, the discussion of this phase of IPC activity is to be found in two works of Stephen Hemsley Longrigg: *Oil in the Middle East* (1968) and *Syria and Lebanon Under French Mandate* (1958).

5. William Chandler was subsequently appointed assistant to TAPLINE president Clyde Swigart, remaining in that capacity until 1955, when he was elected vice president. During this period, he organized the Departments of Industrial Relations and (TAPLINE's) Government Relations in Saudi Arabia. He became executive vice president of TAPLINE in 1956 and president in 1963, a position he held until mid-1972. Information communicated to me by Mr. Chandler in a letter dated March 3, 1995. Where indicated in the text, Chandler's firsthand information is the primary source.

6. Wadsworth to Henderson, July 11, 1945, RG 59, 890E.00/7–1145.

7. Irvine H. Anderson, *ARAMCO*, p. 173, n. 46; Schwadran, *The Middle East, Oil, and the Great Powers*, p. 333; and see Minor to DOS, Proposed Refinery Construction Program—Lebanon, Syria, and Jordan, June 19, 1952, RG 84, 883A.3932/6–1952.

8. Chandler, letter, Mar. 3, 1995.

9. Ibid. The role of Habib Abu Shahla was confirmed by then Legation officer Samuel O. Ruff in interview, August 6, 1992, and by David Dodge, in telephone interviews of March 1 and April 22, 1995. Dodge was involved with the government relations department of ARAMCO (1949–1954) and with TAPLINE in the same capacity, beginning in 1954 and becoming manager of government relations with Syria, Jordan, and Lebanon through the 1960s and 1970s.

10. The citation in the text is taken from the Annual Petroleum Report: 1949, RG 84, 883A.2553/3–950. The position was confirmed in conversation with

David Dodge and Samuel O. Ruff in the respective interviews cited above. Dodge also acknowledged Sham'un's interest in TAPLINE affairs. The reference to Liquid Fuel Office that follows in the text is taken from G. Grassmuck and K. Salibi, *A Manual of Lebanese Administration*, p. 81.

11. The Legation source for the first citation is Pinkerton to Acheson, Legation to Sec of State, May 6, 1947, RG 59, 890E.504/4–2547. The reference to the Bahrein situation is cited in Joe Stork, *Middle East Oil and the Energy Crisis*, p. 70.

12. Annual Petroleum Report: 1949.

13. According to Chandler, when the future of the concession appeared uncertain in Damascus, construction continued in Saudi Arabia, "working westward toward Abu Hadriya, so that if a Syrian agreement was never obtained the line being built in Saudi Arabia would serve as part of the ARAMCO gathering system" (letter, Mar. 3, 1995). William Owen, attorney and later counsel for TAPLINE, reportedly had close relations with William Donovan of the OSS, according to William Chandler (telephone interview, Apr. 10, 1995).

14. Little, "Cold War and Covert Action," p. 55. In an interview with Wilbur Eveland in Boston, Oct. 27, 1988, the former CIA agent in the Middle East confirmed that the 1949 coup was carried out by Miles Copeland to obtain Syrian ratification of TAPLINE.

15. Little, "Cold War and Covert Action," p. 56. In a study on Bechtel by Laton McCartney, *Friends in High Places*, p. 115, the author cites unidentified State Department sources, as well as the U.S. minister to Saudi Arabia, J. Rives Childes, to the effect that a "multinational corporation" was involved in the Syrian coup. Suggestions that Bechtel may have played this role were denied by Bechtel officials, a position recently confirmed by William Chandler (telephone interview, Apr. 10 and Apr. 12, 1995) and by David Dodge (telephone interview, Apr. 22, 1995).

16. Daniel Yergin, *The Prize*, p. 427. The figure for the full length of the pipeline is taken from Chandler, letter, Mar. 3, 1995.

17. Proposed Refinery Construction Program—Lebanon, Syria, and Jordan, June 19, 1952, RG 59, 883A.3932/6–1952.

18. Beirut to DOS, Annual Petroleum Report: 1952, Apr. 23, 1953, RG 84, 883A.2553/4–2353.

19. Ibid.

20. The figures on payments by TAPLINE and IPC come from Issawi and Yeganeh, *The Economics of Middle Eastern Oil*, p. 138; information on security fee is from Chandler, telephone interview, Mar. 14, 1995.

21. Gates, "The Formation of the Political Economy of Modern Lebanon," p. 321.

22. Chandler, letter, Mar. 3, 1995.

23. Figures taken from Ministry of Finance and cited in Annual Petroleum Report: Lebanon 1949, RG 84, 883A.2553/950.

24. Issawi and Yeganeh, *The Economics of Middle Eastern Oil*, p. 147.

25. Stork, *Middle East Oil and the Energy Crisis*, pp. 69–70.

26. "Anglo-American Pentagon Talks," *FRUS 1947*, V, p. 556.

27. Legation Beirut to DOS, Annual Civil Aviation Report: Lebanon 1951, Feb. 19, 1952, RG 59, 983A.52/2–1952. Much of the material that follows is drawn from this rich source.

28. *Who's Who in Lebanon, 1963–1964* (Lebanon: Editions Publitec, Imprimé Chez L'Imprimérie Saint Paul Harissa, 1964), p. 219.

29. Annual Civil Aviation Report: Lebanon 1951, Feb. 19, 1952, RG 59, 983A.52/2–1952.

30. Wilbur Crane Eveland, *Ropes of Sand*, p. 128n.

31. Frances C. Mattison, ed., *A Survey of American Interests in the Middle East*, p. 27.

32. Annual Civil Aviation Report: Lebanon 1951, Feb. 19, 1952, RG 59, 983A.52/2–1952.

33. Halliday, *Arabia Without Sultans*, p. 412.

34. Annual Civil Aviation Report: Lebanon 1951, Feb. 19, 1952, RG 59, 983A.52/2–1952.

35. Mattison, *A Survey of American Interests in the Middle East*, p. xiv.

36. "Pentagon Talks," 1947, *FRUS 1947*, V, p. 557.

37. Mattison, p. xiv; and see for a later period, Issawi, *An Economic History of the Middle East and North Africa*, p. 221.

38. Gates, "The Formation of the Political Economy of Modern Iran," p. 227.

39. Ibid., p. 226. See also Mattison, *A Survey of American Interests*, pp. xiii–xv.

40. Damascus 1949, Sept. 8, 1949, RG 84, box 681, file 350.3.

41. For an instructive introduction to U.S. corporate elites, see Burch, *Elites in American History*, p. 146.

42. A wide-ranging analysis of the origins and domestic political significance of the affiliations of some of the corporate structures cited here is presented in Thomas Ferguson, "From Normalcy to New Deal"; see table 1, pp. 71–72 and 92.

43. Mattison, *A Survey of American Interests*, pp. 37–38.

44. U.S. Naval Attaché, Beirut, Individual Economic Personalities, Sept. 8, 1949, RG 84, Damascus 1949, box 681, file 350.3.

45. Mattison, *A Survey of American Interests*, p. 42.

46. Merchant Shipping and Shipbuilding—Lebanon 1950, Apr. 2, 1951, RG 59, 983A.53/4–251.

47. Mattison, *A Survey of American Interests*, p. 43.

48. Pinkerton to Acheson, Apr. 25, 1947, RG 59, 890E.504/4–2547. Samuel O. Ruff, Legation officer responsible for this report, identified Johnson Garrett as the recommended candidate. William Chandler, in the letter of Mar. 3, 1995, indicates that the party in question was Jean Seaholm.

49. Godfried, *Bridging the Gap Between Rich and Poor*, p. 79.

50. Gates, "The Formation of the Political Economy of Modern Lebanon," p. 181.

51. Maxfield and Nolt, "Protectionism and the Internationalization of Capital."

52. Acheson to Wadsworth, July 3, 1946, #662, RG 59, 711.90E 2/7–346.

53. Memo of Conversation, June 23, 1949, DOS Central Files, 1945–1949, RG 59, 890E.00/6–2349.

54. Gates, "The Formation of the Political Economy of Modern Lebanon," p. 315; and see Pending Treaty of Friendship, Commerce, and Navigation Between the United States of America and the Lebanese Republic, June 12, 1951, DOS Treaty Branch, RG 59, 611.83A4/6–1251.

6. Altered Circumstances and the Design of U.S. Political Strategy

1. Nov. 9, 1951, McGhee's discussion with Malik on the subject of U.S.-Lebanese relations, cited in editorial note, *FRUS 1951*, V (1982), pp. 1012–13.

2. Jacques Couland, *Le Mouvement Syndical du Liban*; Joel Beinin and Zachary Lockman, *Workers on the Nile*; Ervand Abrahamian, *Iran Between Two Revolutions*; H. Batatu, *The Old Social Classes and the Revolutionary Movement in Iraq*; and Marion Farouk-Sluglett and Peter Sluglett, "Labor and National Liberation"; Wilfrid Beling, "Political Trends in Arab Labor"; Eqbal Ahmad discusses labor in the North African context in a somewhat later period in his article "Trade Unionism."

3. Tenney to Sec of State, Aug. 17, 1949, RG 59, 890E.6363/8–1747.

4. DOS to Legation, May 16, 1946, RG 59, 890E.5045/5–1646.

5. Legation to Sec of State, Mar. 3, 1947, Foreign Service Despatch #1511, "The Anti-Communist Labor Movement in Lebanon," RG 59, 890E.504/3–347. Unless otherwise indicated, all citations that follow in the text are taken from this source.

6. Kuniholm to Acheson, Feb. 21, 1947, RG 59, 890E.5043/2–2147.

7. Peter Weiler, "The United States, International Labor, and the Cold War," p. 1; in addition, among informative sources on the subject, see Carolyn Eisenberg, "Working-Class Politics and the Cold War"; and Noam Chomsky, *Deterring Democracy*, pp. 338–42.

8. Beling, "Political Trends in Arab Labor," p. 31; Legation to DOS, "Communists Appear to Be Losing Numbers But Gaining Strength in Lebanon," June 21, 1951, RG 59, 783A.001/6–2151.

9. "The Pentagon Talks of 1947," *FRUS 1947*, V (1971), p. 532.

10. Minor to DOS, Dec. 21, 1951, RG 59, 883A.O6/12–2151.

11. Beinin and Lockman, *Workers on the Nile*, p. 414.

12. Labor Consultant for TCA Lebanon, Legation to DOS, Apr. 18, 1952, RG 59, 883A.00-TA/4–1852.

13. Communism in Lebanon, Bruins to DOS, Aug. 7, 1951, RG 59, 783A.001/8–751. The material that follows comes from this source.

14. Foreign Service Despatch, Beirut to DOS, Mar. 6, 1952. "Informal Assistance to Lebanese Government by Certain Diplomatic Missions to Combat Communism," RG 59, 783A.001/3–652. Citations that follow, unless otherwise

indicated, are from this source. See additional comments from the field on the subject of Turkey's participation in such projects in the Arab world, in George McGhee, *The U.S.-Turkish-NATO Middle East Connection*, appendix.

15. Foreign Service Despatch, AmLegation, Damascus to DOS, Dec. 6, 1951, RG 59, 783a.00/12–651.

16. Legation to DOS, June 17, 1952, RG 59, 783A.00/6–1752.

17. Foreign Service Despatch, AmLegation, Beirut to DOS, "Creation of New Internal Security Department," June 20, 1952, RG 59, 783A l/6–2052.

18. See the position of Michel Chiha, "Lebanon in the World," in Chiha, *Lebanon at Home and Abroad*, p. 129, and Fawaz Traboulsi, "Le Système Chiha," in "Identités et Solidarités Croisées dans les Conflits du Liban Contemporain."

19. SWNCC Country Study on Long-Range Assistance to Lebanon, June 8, 1948, RG 59, 890E.00/6–848.

20. Memo Submitted to the Government of the United States of America by the Jaffa and Districts Inhabitants Council, Beirut, Apr. 11, 1949, appears with I. Gendzier note, in *Journal of Palestine Studies* 18, no. 1 (Spring 1989).

21. Pinkerton to Sec of State, Jan. 11, 1949, RG 59, 890E.5045/1–1149.

22. Position paper, Jan. 29, 1951, RG 59, 611.83a/1–2951.

23. Beirut to Washington, Possible Point Four and Grant Aid Programs for Lebanon, Dec. 18, 1950, RG 59, 883A.00–TA/12–1850.

24. Legation to Sec of State, Mar. 5, 1952, RG 59, 883A.00-TA/3–552.

25. Harold Minor to Parker Hart, Director, ONEA, Aug. 19, 1952, RG 59, 883A.00-TA/8–1952.

26. Harold Minor to J. F. Dulles, Aug. 19, 1952, RG 59, 783A.00/8–1952.

27. Legation to Sec of State, Oct. 18, 1951, RG 59, 883A.00-TA/10–1751.

28. SWNCC Country Study on Long-Range Assistance to Lebanon, June 8, 1948, RG 59, 890E.00/6–848.

29. Pinkerton to Sec of State, Jan. 7, 1949, RG 59, 890E.00(W)1–749.

30. Policy Statement: Lebanon, DOS, Jan. 29, 1951, RG 59, 611.83A/1–2951.

31. Interview with Hon. Stuart Rockwell, Dec. 18, 1992.

32. DOS Memo, Mar. 4, 1949, RG 59, 890E.00/3–449.

33. Discussion Group on the Muslim World, chaired by James M. Landis, Dec. 20, 1948, CFR, Archives, vol. 28, 1948/9–1949/50.

34. DOS Memo of Conversation, Lebanese Proposals for Closer Relations with the United States, May 10, 1949, RG 59, 890E.00/5–1049.

35. Memo of Conversation, June 23, 1949, RG 59, 890E.00/6–2349.

36. ANE Cairo Conference, Country Summary, Lebanon, Feb. 23, 1950, RG 59, 783A.00/2–2350.

37. Memo of Conversation by Officer in Charge of Lebanon, Syria-Iraq Affairs (Clark), Aug. 1, 1950, *FRUS 1950*, V, The Near East, South Asia, and Africa, p. 1100.

38. McGhee to Maj. Gen. James Burns, Office of Sec of Defense, Nov. 15, 1950, RG 59, 783A.5/11–1550.

39. Policy Statement: Lebanon, DOS, Jan. 29, 1951, RG 59, 611.83A/1-2951.

40. George McGhee, *Envoy to the Middle World*, p. 352.

41. Legation to DOS, Communism in Lebanon, Aug. 7, 1951, RG 59, 783A.001/8-751.

42. Legislative Program of National Socialist Parliamentary Opposition Group, July 12, 1951, RG 59, 783A.2/7-1251. For discussion of earlier signs of opposition and dissent at home, including the crisis over the regime's handling of the capture and execution of PPS leader Antun Sa'adeh, see Besharah al-Khuri, ch. "1949," *Haqa'iq Lubnaniyyah*, vol. 3.

43. George Britt, "Lebanon's Popular Revolution," p. 11.

44. July 12, 1951, RG 59, 783A.2/7-1251.

45. Memo of Conversation, Asst Sec of State for Near East, South Asian, and African Affairs, Aug. 30, 1951, *FRUS 1951*, V, The Near East and Africa, p. 1009. On the Middle East Command, see Peter L. Hahn, "Containment and Egyptian Nationalism"; and the same author's *The United States, Great Britain, and Egypt, 1945-1956*, chs. 6 and 7; and Geoffrey Aronson, *From Sideshow to Center Stage*, pp. 29-35, 52-53.

46. Minor to DOS, Nov. 7, 1951, *FRUS 1951*, V, p. 1011.

47. Discussion Group on American Policy in the Middle East: The Oil Problem in Iran, Nov. 14, 1951, CFR, Archives, vol. 42.

48. Legation to DOS, Mar. 26, 1952, RG 59, 783A.00/3-2652; and see National Intelligence Estimate: Prospects for an Inclusive Middle East Defense Organization, Mar. 17, 1952, *FRUS 1952-1954*, IX, part 1, The Near and Middle East, p. 199.

49. Legation to DOS, "Religious Groups in Lebanon. Part II: Maronites," Nov. 20, 1951, RG 59, 883A.413/11-2051.

50. Acting Sec of State to the Legation in Lebanon, Aug. 6, 1952, *FRUS 1952-1954*, IX, part 1, no. 467, p. 977. Unless otherwise indicated, citations are taken from this source.

51. Memo of Conversation by First Sec of Embassy in UK, Nov. 19, 1951, *FRUS 1951*, V, p. 1013.

52. Embassy to DOS, Aug. 19, 1952, RG 59, 783A.00/8-1952.

53. "NSC Progress Report," Jan. 26, 1951, NSC 47/2, DDQC 8, no. 1 (Jan.-Mar. 1982), 00294.

54. Chargé in Lebanon (Lobenstine) to DOS, Sept. 19, 1952, *FRUS 1952-1954*, IX, part 1, p. 1001. Remaining citations are taken from this source, pp. 1001-1002.

7. *Pressure Points and Priorities*

1. Beirut to DOS, May 29, 1950, RG 59, 783A.02/5-2950.

2. Minor to DOS, Sept. 26, 1952, RG 59, 783.11/9-2692.

3. Chargé in Lebanon to DOS, Sept. 23, 1952, *FRUS 1952-1954*, IX, part 1, pp. 1008-9.

4. Memo by Asst Sec of State for Near Eastern, South Asian, and African Affairs, Byroade, to Sec of State, Jan. 26, 1953, *FRUS 1952–1954*, IX, part 1, p. 1105.

5. Chargé in Lebanon to DOS, Sept. 23, 1952, *FRUS 1952–1954*, IX, part 1, pp. 1008–9.

6. American Embassy to Sec of State, H. Freeman Mathews, Deputy Under Sec of Defense, to Robert A. Lovett, Sec of Defense, Oct. 23, 1952, RG 59, 783A.5-MSP 10–2352.

7. Cited in Wade Goria, *Sovereignty and Leadership in Lebanon*, p. 39.

8. Memo by Asst Legal Adviser for Eco Affairs, Dec. 19, 1952, *FRUS 1952–1954*, IX, part 1, p. 628.

9. Acting Sec of State to the Embassy in the United Kingdom, Dec. 12, 1952, *FRUS 1952–1954*, IX, part 1, p. 619.

10. U.S. Senate, *The International Petroleum Cartel*, p. 369.

11. Mostafa Elm, *Oil, Power, and Principle*, p. 293.

12. NSC 138/1, Report by Depts. of State, Defense, and Interior, Jan. 6, 1953, *FRUS 1952–1954*, IX, part 1, p. 637.

13. Kim McQuaid, "Corporate Liberalism in the American Business Community,"; see Ellis W. Hawley, "The Discovery and Study of a 'Corporate Liberalism,' " and Introduction to Michael J. Hogan, *The Marshall Plan*, for a more general analysis and bibliographic guide.

14. Robert Engler, *The Politics of Oil*, pp. 312–13; and see Philip H. Burch Jr., *Elites in American History*, p. 162.

15. Burch, *Elites in American History*, pp. 128–31, esp. p. 131.

16. Wilbur Crane Eveland, *Ropes of Sand*, p. 142n.

17. Audrey Kahin and George McT. Kahin, *Subversion as Foreign Policy*, p. 8.

18. For recent references to the role of the CIA in Guatemala, see *New York Times*, Apr. 2, 1995, pp. 1 and 12. On Iran, see Fred Halliday, *Iran: Dictatorship and Development*, esp. the discussion of the Army and SAVAK (ch. 4); James A. Bill, *The Eagle and the Lion*, ch. 3; and Mordechai Bar-On, *The Gates of Gaza*, p. 3.

19. Jidda, G. Wadsworth to DOS, Feb. 14, 1954, *FRUS 1952–1954*, IX, part 1, pp. 788–89.

20. Sec of Defense to Sec of State, enclosure dated Mar. 18, 1954, included in Apr. 16, 1954, *FRUS 1952–1954*, IX, part 1, p. 810.

21. Discussion at 147th NSC meeting, June 2, 1953, box 4, NSC Series, Eisenhower Library.

22. Eveland, *Ropes of Sand*, p. 156.

23. Seymour M. Hersh, *The Samson Option*, ch. 3, "The French Connection."

24. Memo of Conversation at White House, Jan. 11, 1956, DDQC 8, no. 1 (Jan.–Mar. 1982), 00316.

25. Diane Kunz, *The Economic Diplomacy of the Suez Crisis*, p. 51.

26. Memo for the President, White House, Mar. 28, 1956, DDQC 9, no. 2 (Apr.–June 1983), 001054.

27. Ibid.

28. Robert Bowie, "Eisenhower, Dulles, and the Suez Crisis," p. 201.

29. M. Abdel Wahab Sayed-Ahmad, *Nasser and American Foreign Policy*, pp. 123, 125.

30. Figures cited in Kunz, *The Economic Diplomacy of the Suez Crisis*, appendix C, p. 201.

31. Bowie, "Eisenhower, Dulles, and the Suez Crisis," p. 197.

32. Memo from Joint Chiefs of Staff to Sec of Defense, Aug. 3, 1956, *FRUS 1955–1957*, XVI, p. 155.

33. Keith Kyle, "Britain and the Crisis, 1955–1956," pp. 117–18; and Keith Kyle, *Suez*.

34. Kunz, *The Economic Diplomacy of the Suez Crisis*, p. 152.

35. See David W. Lesch, *Syria and the United States*; and Douglas Little, "Cold War and Covert Action."

36, Engler, *The Politics of Oil*, p. 244.

37. Owen, "Economic Consequences of Suez for Egypt," p. 373.

8. Lebanon: The "Bridgehead in the Orient"

*Minor to J. F. Dulles, May 4, 1953, RG 59, 783A.13/5–453.

1. Chargé in Lebanon to DOS, Sept. 23, 1952, *FRUS 1952–1954*, IX (1986), part 1, p. 1008.

2. Memo by David Longanecker of Office African Affairs to Deputy Director of Office of Near Eastern Affairs (Kopper), re Conference with Major Oil Companies in New York, June 6, 1952, *FRUS 1952–1954*, IX (1986), part 1, p. 597.

3. Chargé d'Affaires to DOS, Oct. 2, 1952, *FRUS, 1952–1954*, IX (1986), part 1, p. 1014.

4. Embassy, Beirut, to DOS, Programs and Organization of Jumblatt's Socialist Party, Oct. 7, 1952, RG 59, 783A.003/10–752.

5. Embassy, Beirut, to DOS, Concerned by Kamal Jumblatt's (Socialist Party): Statements Relating to Expropriation, Oct. 8, 1952, RG 59, 783A.003/10–852.

6. Ibid.

7. Bruce to U.S. Embassies in ME, Paris, and London, Dec. 12, 1952, NA/R-SM, RG 84, Beirut Petroleum Attaché, 1949–1953, box 5, Declassification Project 832852, Centre for Lebanese Studies, box 48.

8. Acting Sec of State to Embassy, Lebanon, Nov. 13, 1952, *FRUS 1952–1954*, IX (1986), part 1, p. 617.

9. Memo of Conversation by William McMaster of the Petroleum Policy Staff, Dec. 30, 1952, *FRUS 1952–1954*, IX, part 1, p. 636.

10. Embassy to DOS, *Annual Petroleum Report, 1952*, Apr. 23, 1953, RG 84, 883a.2553/4–2353.

11. Memo by the Chief of the Petroleum Policy Staff (Eakens), June 3, 1953, *FRUS 1952–1954*, IX, part 1, p. 669.

12. The transit states, according to the above source, argued that the TAPLINE savings "amounts to the differential between the posted price at Ras Tanura on the Persian Gulf ($1.75) and at Sidon on the Eastern Mediterranean coast ($2.41) or $O.66 as the value added to the crude oil by the pipeline transit. The Sidon price of crude has since been reduced to 2.29, thereby changing differential to O.54 per barrel in the interim" (p. 670).

13. DOS Position Paper, May 5, 1953, *FRUS 1952–1954*, IX, part 1, p. 1211.

14. Hare to DOS, Jan. 4, 1954, RG 59, 783A.00/1–454.

15. Beirut to DOS, Aug. 4, 1953, RG 84, 883A.2553/8–453.

16. Beirut to DOS, Petroleum Report—First Half of 1953, Sept. 15, 1953, RG 84, 883A.2553/9–1553.

17. Bruins to DOS, Problems of American Oil Companies in Lebanon, Sept. 24, 1953, RG 59, 883A.2553/9–2453.

18. Minor to DOS, Chemoun-Chehab Government in Retrospect, May 19, 1953, RG 59, 783A.0015–1953.

19. Bruins to Sec of State, Feb. 20, 1953, RG 59, 783A.11/2–2053.

20. DOS Position Paper on Lebanon, May 5, 1953, *FRUS 1952–1954*, IX, part 1, p. 1211.

21. Minor to DOS, Chamoun-Chehab Government in Retrospect, May 19, 1953, RG 59, 783A.00/5–1953.

22. Minor to Dulles, May 4, 1953, RG 59, 783A.13/5–453.

23. Minor to DOS, May 28, 1953, RG 59, 783A.13/5–2853.

24. From USARMA Beirut to Dept. Army, Washington DC for G2, Depts of State, Air Force, Navy, May 22, 1953, RG 59, 783.00(W)/5–2253.

25. Beirut, Memo Conversation Prepared in Embassy, May 16, 1953, *FRUS 1952–1954*, IX, part 1, no. 24, p. 65.

26. Memo of Conversation by 2d Sec of Embassy, May 16, 1953, *FRUS 1952–1954*, IX, part 1, no. 25, p. 68.

27. DOS Position Paper on Lebanon, May 5, 1953, *FRUS 1952–1954*, IX, part 1, p. 1214.

28. Meade is identified in Douglas Little's article "Cold War and Covert Action," p. 55.

29. Memo of Conversation by 2d Sec of Embassy, May 16, 1953, *FRUS 1952–1954*, IX, part 1, p. 73.

30. Memo of Conversation by 2d Sec of Embassy, May 17, 1953, *FRUS 1951–1954*, IX, part 1, p. 83.

31. Feb. 5, 1954, USIS, Beirut to USIA, Washington, RG 59, 983A.60/2–554. The Lebanese newspapers identified by U.S. officials included *al-Jarida*, *al-Hayat*, *an-Nahar*, *Bayrut*, and *ad-Diyar*.

32. Michael Hudson, *The Precarious Republic*, p. 187.

33. Minor to DOS, Chamoun-Chehab Government in Retrospect, May 19, 1953, RG 59, 783A.00/5–1953.

34. Bruins to DOS, Aug. 18, 1953, RG 59, 783A.00/8–1853.

35. Bruins to DOS, Aug. 19, 1953, RG 59, 783A.13/8–1953.

36. Hare to DOS, Nov. 27, 1953, RG 59, 883A.413/11–2753.

37. Hare to DOS, "Confessionalism in Lebanon," Nov. 13, 1953, RG 59, 883A.413/11–1353.

38. Embassy to DOS, Aug. 23, 1954, RG 59, 783.00/8–2354.

39. Hare to DOS, Lebanese Request for Arms for Internal Security, Oct. 13, 1953, RG 59, 783A.5 MSP/10–1353.

40. Beirut to Sec of State, Joint FOA-State Message, Dec. 31, 1953, RG 59, 783A.5 MSP/12–3153.

9. Realities of Power in the "Rear Area"

1. Camille Chamoun, *Crise au Moyen Orient*, p. 254.

2. Byroade to Sec of Defense Lovett, Oct. 16, 1952, RG 59, 783A.5-MSP/10–1652.

3. H. Freeman Mathews, Deputy Under Sec of State, to Robert A. Lovett, Sec of Defense, Oct. 23, 1952, RG 59, 783A.5-MSP/10–2352.

4. Deputy Sec of Defense to Sec of State, Jan. 8, 1953, RG 59, 783A.5-MSP/1–853.

5. Sec of State to U.S. Ambassador Minor, Feb. 16, 1953, RG 59, 783A.5-MSP/2–1653.

6. Financial Appendix for NSC 155/1, July 12, 1954, box 4, NSC series, Eisenhower Library.

7. Hare to DOS, American Military Aid for Lebanon, Jan. 7, 1954, RG 59, 783A.5-MSP/1–754.

8. Ibid., and see also Hare to DOS, Lebanese Request for American Military Grant Aid, Feb. 19, 1954, RG 59, 783A.5-MSP/2–1954.

9. Dulles to Embassy, Mar. 16, 1954, RG 59, 783A.5-MSP/3–1654.

10. Hare to DOS, President Chamoun Renews Request for Arms Aid, Aug. 10, 1954, RG 59, 783A.5-MSP/8–1954.

11. Hare to DOS, Bedlam on Arms Aid, Aug. 17, 1954, RG 59, 783A.5-MSP/8–1754.

12. A. H. Meyer to DOS, In Approving U.S. Military Geographic Specialist Team to Work in Lebanon, Lebanese Government Renews Request for Military Assistance, Oct. 12, 1954, RG 59, 783A.5-MSP/10–1254.

13. Memo of Conversation, U.S. Economic and Military Aid Programs for Lebanon, the "Northern Tier," Nov. 29, 1954, RG 59, 783A.5-MSP/11–2954.

14. Samuel Segev, *The Iranian Triangle*; Andrew Cockburn and Leslie Cockburn, *Dangerous Liaison*; Dan Raviv and Yossie Melman, *Every Spy a Prince*; Dan Connell, *Against All Odds*, p. 92.

15. Citations from Moshe Sharett's diary on the subject of a Maronite state in Lebanon are included in Livia Rokach, *Israel's Sacred Terrorism*, pp. 24–30, and see quote on p. 28. The subject is additionally discussed in the following sources:

Avi Shlaim, "Conflicting Approaches to Israel's Relations with the Arabs"; also by Shlaim, "Israeli Interference in Internal Arab Politics"; and Noam Chomsky, *The Fateful Triangle*, p. 303.

16. Ben-Gurion, cited in Sharett diaries, Feb. 27, 1954, in Rokach, *Israel's Sacred Terrorism*, p. 25.

17. Shlaim, "Israeli Interference in Internal Arab Politics," p. 242; see William Colby's testimony to the Senate Subcommittee on Refugees in July 1976 that referred to arms offered to Lebanese Christians, cited in Rokach, *Israel's Sacred Terrorism*, p. 56, n. 17.

18. Sharett diary of Feb. 12, 1955, cited in Rokach, *Israel's Sacred Terrorism*, p. 28.

19. Cited in Benjamin Beit-Hallahmi, *The Israeli Connection*, p. 20.

20. Raymond Hare to DOS, Aug. 23, 1954, RG 59, 783A.00/8–2354.

21. Donald Heath to DOS, July 18, 1955, RG 59, 783A.00/7–1855.

22. Hélène Carèrre d'Encausse, citing figures from Laqueur, in "The Background of Soviet Policy in the Middle East," p. 388.

23. Hare to DOS, A Suggestion for Promotion of Western Ideals, Feb. 23, 1954, RG 59, 783A.00/2–2354.

24. Hare to DOS, GOL Concern About Communism, Apr. 2, 1954, RG 59, 783A.001/4–254.

25. Hare to DOS, GOL Desire to Counter Communism, Apr. 6, 1954, RG 59, 783A.001/4–654.

26. Hare to DOS, New Emphasis in the Communist Approach to Lebanon, July 15, 1954, RG 59, 783A.00/7–1554.

27. Cited in Richard H. Immerman, *The CIA in Guatemala*, p. 102.

28. Meyer to DOS, Apr. 2, 1954, RG 59, 783A.001/4–254.

29. Beirut to DOS, Analysis of the Labor Movement in Lebanon, July 24, 1953, RG 59, 883A.06/7–2453.

30. Hare to DOS, Jan. 4, 1954, RG 59, 783A.00/1–454.

31. Hare to DOS, The Republic of Lebanon on Its Tenth Birthday, Dec. 7, 1953, RG 59, 883A.424/12–753.

32. Hare to Sec of State, Dec. 30, 1953, RG 59, 783A.5 MSP/12–3053.

33. Foreign Service Dispatch, Beirut to DOS, Mar. 15, 1954, RG 59, 783A.00/3–1554. The citations that follow are taken from this source, unless otherwise indicated.

34. Charles Issawi, "Economic Development and Political Liberalism," p. 75.

35. B. J. Odeh, *Lebanon*, p. 60.

36. IRFED, *Besoins et Possibilités de Développement du Liban*, 1:285, Beirut, 1960–1961.

37. Odeh, *Lebanon*, p. 61. See the analysis and figures offered in Issawi, "Economic Development and Political Liberalism," p. 75, according to which "deposits in Lebanese banks grew from LL232 million in 1952, to 307 million in 1956, and 792 million in 1961."

38. IRFED, *Besoins et Possibilités de Développement du Liban*, 2:96.

10. Our Man in Beirut

*Beirut to Sec of State, Oct. 17, 1955, RG 59, 783A.00/10–1755; Wilbur Eveland, *Ropes of Sand*, p. 252.

1. Beirut to Sec of State, Oct. 17, 1955, RG 59, 883A.00/10–1755.
2. DOS to Embassy, Beirut, Oct. 27, 1955, RG 59, 783A.00/10–2755.
3. Embassy to DOS, Oct. 25, 1955, RG 59, 783A.00/10–2555.
4. Telegram from delegate at FM meeting to DOS, Oct. 28, 1955, *FRUS 1955–1957*, XIII (1988), p. 178.
5. Memo of conversation, Feb. 9, 1955, DOS, DDQC 8, no. 1 (Jan.–Mar. 1982), 00309.
6. Joint Chiefs of Staff Decision on JCS 1887/117, A Report by the Joint Strategic Plans Committee on Arrangements Regarding Middle East Defense, Sept. 30, 1955, DDQC 4, no. 4 (Oct.–Dec. 1978), 367A.
7. Personal and Private, Israeli Relations, Oct. 18, 1955, Dulles Papers, 1951–57, box 10, DDQC 8, no. 1 (Jan.–Mar. 1982), 00312.
8. Jacob C. Hurewitz, *Middle East Politics*, p. 463.
9. Memo for the Chairman, JCS, Dec. 8, 1955, DDQC 4, no. 4 (Oct.–Dec. 1978), 367B.
10. Memo to Sherman Adams from Col. Andrew J. Goodpaster, Oct. 31, 1955, DDQC 8, no. 4 (Oct.–Dec. 1982), 002563.
11. Memo to Sec of State, Oct. 20, 1955, DDQC 12, no. 2 (Mar.–Apr. 1986), 00762.
12. Memo for Sec of State, Dec. 9, 1955, DDQC 12, no. 2 (Mar.–Apr. 1986), 00763.
13. Cited in Livia Rokach, *Israel's Sacred Terrorism*, p. 52.
14. Bar-On, *The Gates of Gaza*, pp. ix, 3–4; and Eveland, *Ropes of Sand*, p. 248.
15. Memo of conversation, Jan. 21, 1956, DOS, no. 122. *FRUS 1955–1957*, XIII, p. 181.
16. Memo from Ambassador Heath to Asst. Sec of State for NEA Affairs Rountree, Jan. 23, 1956, *FRUS 1955–1957*, XIII, p. 184, n. 2.
17. Report by the Joint Strategic Plans Committee, May 8, 1956, *FRUS 1955–1957*, XIII, p. 190.
18. Memo of discussion at the 266th meeting of the NSC, "United States Economic Defense Policy," Nov. 15, 1955, *FRUS 1955–1957*, X (1989), p. 28.
19. "United States Economic Defense Policy: United States Interest in Maintaining Multilateral Strategic Controls on Trade with the Soviet Union, the People's Republic of China, and Certain Other Nations," *FRUS 1955–1957*, X (1989), p. 28.
20. DOS, Intelligence Report, Sino-Soviet Activities in Lebanon, May 24, 1956, Office of Intelligence Research, #7260, DDQC 5, no. 4 (Oct.–Dec. 1979), 443A.
21. Bi-weekly report, Sino-Soviet Economic Activities in Underdeveloped Areas, Mar. 5, 1956, DDQC 3, no. 3 (July–Sept. 1977), 242C.

22. DOS, Intelligence Report, May 24, 1956, DDQC 5, no. 4 (Oct.–Dec. 1979), 443A.

23. Bi-weekly report, Sino-Soviet Economic Activities in Underdeveloped Areas, Mar. 5, 1956, DDQC 3, no. 3 (July–Sept. 1977), 242C.

24. DOS, Intelligence Report, Office of Intelligence Research no. 7260 on Sino-Soviet Bloc Activities in Lebanon, DDQC 5, no. 4 (Oct.–Dec. 1979), 443A.

25. Eveland, *Ropes of Sand*, p. 141.

26. Study Group for Near and Middle East, Note of Conversation with Dr. Paul Rykens and G. Nebolsine, Jan. 9, 1958, PRO, F0 371/133846.

27. Centre for Lebanese Studies (CLS), Heath to DOS, Apr. 30, 1956, RG 319, box 36, ACSI Message File in ACSI Project (Secretary of the Army, Asst. Chief of Intelligence) FOIA, box 37, 6-85-36.

28. "Mr. John McCloy in Beirut," *at-Telegraf*, Feb. 5, 1956; "Welcome," *as-Sahafa*, Feb. 8, 1956. I am grateful to Max Holland for bringing these articles to my attention.

29. Walid Khalidi, "Political Trends in the Fertile Crescent," p. 125.

30. See Keith Kyle, *Suez*, for a recent interpretation primarily of Britain's response.

31. Special National Intelligence Estimate, July 31, 1956, *FRUS 1955–1957*, XVI (1990), p. 90.

32. Report on N. Lebanon, RG 319, ID File (ACSI) (Military Intelligence) OARMA, Aug. 1956, Centre for Lebanese Studies, Oxford.

33. Annual Report on Lebanon for 1957, FO 371/1341/4.

34. G. Majdalany, "The Arab Socialist Movement," p. 347.

35. Telegram from Embassy in Lebanon to DOS, Aug. 10, 1956, *FRUS 1955–1957*, XVI, p. 184.

36. Telegram from U.S. Embassy in UK to DOS, Sept. 1, 1956, *FRUS 1955–1957*, XVI, p. 346.

37. Heath to Dulles, Nov. 5, 1956. DDQC 10, no. 3 (July–Sept. 1984), 001835. In another note of interest, William Chandler, then executive vice president of TAPLINE, made the decision not to allow British and French ships coming into Sidon to lift oil, on the assumption that such might risk aggravating existing tensions. Information communicated to the author in a telephone interview with William Chandler, May 22, 1995.

38. Leila M. T. Meo, *Lebanon, Improbable Nation*, p. 98.

39. American Embassy to DOS, Nov. 19, 1956, RG 59, box 3749, 783A.00/11–1956.

40. Memo of conference with Eisenhower, Nov. 23, 1956, box 19, DDE Series, Nov. 1956, Diary-Staff Memos, Eisenhower Library.

41. For the Middle East Resolution, see H. J. Res. 117, Mar. 9, 1957, U.S. Policy in the Middle East, Sept. 1956–June 1957, DOS #6505, Near and Middle East series 25 (Washington, D.C.: U.S. Government Printing Office, 1957). Among strong supporting statements, see that by John C. Campbell, "From 'Doctrine' to 'Policy' in the Middle East."

42. Telegram from Embassy, Lebanon, to DOS, Jan. 13, 1957. *FRUS 1955–1957*, XIII, p. 197.

43. Memo from Rountree to Dulles, Jan. 12, 1957, *FRUS 1955–1957*, XIII, p. 195.

44. Cited in n. 3 of Feb. 2, 1957, Telegram from DOS to Embassy, Lebanon, *FRUS 1955–1957*, XIII, p. 199.

45. US JCS decision on JCS 1887/340, a Report by the Joint Committee on Programs for Military Assistance on Military Aid for the Middle East, Feb. 3, 1957, Enclosure "B" in DDQC 6, no. 2 (Apr.–June 1980), 153B.

46. Joint Chiefs of Staff, Decision on JCS 1887/347, NA/C-WDC/RG 218, JCS 1950s.

47. Memorandum of conversation, Malik, Khoury (Khuri), Wilkins, President, Feb. 6, 1957, DDE papers as President of U.S., 1953–1961 (Ann Whitman File), box 34, international series, Lebanon (3), Eisenhower Library.

48. DOS, Memo of conversation, Feb. 3, 1957, *FRUS 1955–1957*, XIII, p. 207.

49. Douglas Little, "Cold War and Covert Action," p. 68.

50. Memo of conversation, Feb. 6, 1957, *FRUS 1955–1957*, XIII, p. 207.

51. Telegram from Embassy to Dulles, Mar. 16, 1957, *FRUS 1955–1957*, XIII, p. 211.

52. Memo for Mrs. Whitman, Apr. 24, 1957, White House Presidential Handling, DDE Papers as President of U.S., 1953–1961, Ann Whitman File, box 34, international series, Lebanon (3), Eisenhower Library.

53. Fahim Qubain, *Crisis in Lebanon*, p. 49.

54. Embassy to DOS, May 29, 1957, RG 59, 783A.00/5–2957; for Foreign Office reports of May disturbances in Beirut, FO 371/134114, Annual Report on Lebanon for 1957.

55. Memorandum for the president, from Dulles, May 10, 1957, DDE Diaries, [box 23], Apr. 1957, Misc (11), Rowley to Whitman, Apr. 28, 1957. The Chamber endorsed the president's action, voting 30–1 in his favor, Apr. 11, 1957. Embassy to DOS, dispatch, RG 59, 783A.00/4–1157, Eisenhower Library.

56. Qubain, *Crisis in Lebanon*, p. 55.

57. Foreign Service Dispatch, American Embassy to DOS, memo revealing personal political views of General Fu'ad Shihab, Apr. 2, 1958, RG 59, 783A.00/4–258.

58. Annual Report on Lebanon for 1957 from G. Middleton, Beirut, FO 371/134114,

59. Eveland, *Ropes of Sand*; see ch. 23 for Eveland's overall discussion of the period and his activities.

60. Centre for Lebanese Studies (CLS), Beirut to DOS, June 21, 1957, RG 319, box 34, ACSI Message File 1950s, Parts 1 and 2.

61. Centre for Lebanese Studies (CLS), Beirut to Sec of State, July 26, 1957. RG 319, box 34, ACSI Message File 1950s, Parts 1 and 2.

62. Qubain, *Crisis in Lebanon*, p. 59.

63. Eveland, *Ropes of Sand*, p. 245; and Little, "Cold War and Covert Action," p. 71.

64. David Lesch, *Syria and the United States*, p. 148; and FO 371/134114.

65. Memo of conversation between Malik and Dulles and Reinhardt, Sept. 18, 1957, *FRUS 1955–1957*, XIII, p. 712.

66. Operations Coordinating Board Report, Operations Plan for the Lebanon (NSC 5428), July 31, 1957, *FRUS 1955–1957*, XIII, p. 214.

67. Qubain, *Crisis in Lebanon*, pp. 59–60.

68. Annual Report on Lebanon for 1957, FO 371/134114.

69. Centre for Lebanese Studies (CLS), USARMA Beirut to DEPTAR Washington, July 12, 1957, RG 319, box 34, ACSI Message File, 1950s, Part 1 and Part 2.

70. Centre for Lebanese Studies (CLS), Heath to Dulles, Aug. 2, 1957, RG 319, box 34, ACSI Message File, 1950s, Part 1 and Part 2.

71. Qubain, in his *Crisis in Lebanon*, indirectly suggests that the Third Force was founded at about the same time as the UNF. In the interviews that Nawaf Salam conducted with contemporaries of these events, however, the October date is given. Nawaf Salam, "L'Insurrection de 1958 au Liban."

72. Annual Report on Lebanon for 1957, G. Middleton, Beirut to FO 371/134114.

73. IRFED, *Besoins et Possibilités de Développement du Liban*, 1:229

74. Study Group for Near and Middle East, FO 371/133846.

11. Civil War, May 1958

*"Long Range U.S. Policy Toward the Near East," NSC 5801/1, Jan. 24, 1958.

1. The question of Britain's role in U.S. policy formulation and, more generally, in determining the outcome of the Lebanon crisis of 1958 has elicited different responses. U.S. sources tend to treat British policies with the deference due an ally, but with little doubt as to their secondary nature in affecting Washington's decisions. Such a position was reinforced in interviews I conducted with General Andrew Goodpaster, Dec. 18, 1992, Washington, D.C., and with the Honorable Harrison Symmes, assistant to Under Secretary William Rountree in 1958, Dec. 20, 1992, Washington, D.C.

On the other hand, analyses that consider Anglo-American policy in Jordan, as well as Lebanon in the context of the broader crisis surrounding the military coup in Baghdad, place more importance on Britain's role, such as that by R. Ovendale, "Great Britain and the Anglo-American Invasion of Jordan and Lebanon in 1958." For a different interpretation see Wm. Roger Louis, "Britain and Lebanon in the 1950s" (paper presented at the Conference on Lebanon in the 1950s, University of Texas, Austin, Sept. 1991). The late Professor Albert Hourani was among those who maintained that this was Britain's last act in the Middle East (personal communication).

2. Miles Copeland, *The Game of Nations*, pp. 230–31.

3. Wilbur Crane Eveland, *Ropes of Sand*, p. 268.

4. Memorandum to director of Office of Near Eastern Affairs, Jan. 17, 1958, DOS 783A.OO/1–1758, in *FRUS 1958–1960*, XI, Lebanon and Jordan (1992), p. 6.

5. Eveland, *Ropes of Sand*, pp. 267–68.

6. Higgs to DOS, Jan. 9, 1958, cited in *FRUS 1958–1960*, XI, pp. 1–3; McClintock to DOS, Jan. 16, 1958, *FRUS 1958–1960*, XI, pp. 3–5.

7. Foreign Service dispatch, Beirut to Washington, Jan. 29, 1958, RG 59, box 3750, 783A.00/1–358 through 5/22/58.

8. Copeland, *The Game of Nations*, pp. 232, 238.

9. The first position emerges in a number of statements by Lebanese personalities as cited in Beirut to State Department, Jan. 29, 1958, RG 59, 783A.00/1–2958, and Mar. 24, 1958, RG 59, 783A.00/3–2458. Evidence of the second factor emerged at a later date, as relations between the UAR ambassador and the Beirut "four" became more strained.

10. McClintock to Dulles, Jan. 31, 1958, RG 59, box 3750, 783A.OO/1–3158.

11. Ibid.

12. Fahim Qubain, *Crisis in Lebanon*, pp. 62–63.

13. McClintock to Dulles, no. 2832, Feb. 21, 1958, RG 59, 783A.00/2–2158.

14. Cited in Nawaf Salam, *L'Insurrection de 1958 au Liban*, 5:105.

15. No. 2832, Feb. 21, 1958, RG 59, 783A.00/2–2158.

16. DOS to Embassy, Beirut, no. 3375. Feb. 27, 1958, RG 59, box 3750, 83A.00/2–2158.

17. Beirut to Washington, no. 474, Feb. 28, 1958, RG 59, 783A.00/2–2858.

18. McClintock to DOS, Mar. 5, 1958, cited in *FRUS 1958–1960*, XI, p. 15.

19. McClintock to DOS, Mar. 20, 1958, as cited in *FRUS 1958–1960*, XI, p. 18.

20. Labib Zuwiyya Yamak, *The Syrian Social Nationalist Party*, p. 72.

21. For the U.S. role, see Eveland, *Ropes of Sand*, p. 273.

22. Qubain, *Crisis in Lebanon*, p. 66.

23. Beirut to Washington, Memorandum Revealing Personal Political Views of General Fuad Chehab, Apr. 2, 1958, RG 59, 783A.00/4–258.

24. Qubain, *Crisis in Lebanon*, pp. 67–68.

25. Apr. 25, 1958, cited in *FRUS 1958–1960*, XI (1992), p. 22, n. 2.

26. McClintock to DOS, Apr. 23, 1958, cited in *FRUS 1958–1960*, XI, p. 25.

27. Dulles to Malik, Apr. 29, 1958, 783A.5-MSP/4–2958, cited in *FRUS 1958–1960*, XI, pp. 25–27.

28. DOS to Beirut, Baghdad, Tel Aviv, Amman, May 1, 1958, RG 59, box 3750, 783A.00/5–158.

29. McClintock to Dulles, May 5, 1958, DDQC 11, no. 1 (Jan.–Mar., Apr.–June 1976), 99B.

30. McClintock to DOS, May 4, 1958, RG 59, 783A.00/5–458, cited in *FRUS 1958–1960*, XI, p. 29.

31. McClintock to DOS, May 7, 1958, RG 59, 783A.00/5–758, cited in *FRUS 1958–1960*, XI, pp. 31–33.

32. Hugh S. Cuming, Jr., Bureau of Intelligence and Research, DOS, to Sec of State, Apr. 11, 1958, "Intelligence Note: The Nature of Anti-Sham'un Disturbances in Lebanon," RG 59, box 3750, 783a.00/4–1158.

33. Memorandum, Discussion at the 365th Meeting of the NSC. May 8, 1958, DDQC 6, no. 2 (Apr.–June 1980), 385A.

34. FO, May 9, 1958, 371/134156, E. M. Rose, Lebanon.

35. Camille Chamoun, *Crise au Moyen Orient*, p. 399.

36. McClintock to Dulles, no. 3766, May 10, 1958, DDQC 2, no. 1 (Jan.–Mar. 1976), and no. 2 (Apr.–June), DOS 99E.

37. Charles W. Thayer, *Diplomat*, p. 20.

38. McClintock to Dulles, no. 3770, May 11, 1958, RG 59, box 3750, 783A.00/5–1158.

39. Qubain, *Crisis in Lebanon*, pp. 79–80. I am grateful to Samir Khalaf for the opportunity to read his unpublished paper, "Civil Strife of 1958."

40. Robert J. Donovan, *Confidential Secretary*, p. 122.

41. Sir George Middleton to Foreign Office, no. 478, FO 371/134116.

42. Dulles to McClintock, May 13, 1958, RG 59, box 3750, 783A.00/5–1158; and see May 13, 1958, FO to Washington, FO 371/134116, no. 2644.

43. "Joint Chiefs of Staff and National Policy, 1956–1958," ch. 8, p. 435, US/NA/C-WDC, RG 218. JCS 1950s, JCS 1957 CCS 381 EMMEA (11–19–47), sec. 66, box 7RB. This chapter was obtained through FOIA from the office of the Organization of the Joint Chiefs of Staff. Since then, the following changes have occurred: According to Walter Poole of the Joint History Office, the JHO has now revised the entire volume and submitted it for declassification. The new declassified version, which is not yet available, includes changes of chapter title as well as the inclusive dates (1957–1960). (Information obtained Sept. 5, 1995.) All references in the present text are to the version previously declassified and located at the Centre for Lebanese Studies (box 46).

44. Dulles to McClintock, May 13, 1958, box 16, chronological series, May 1958, J. F. Dulles Papers, Eisenhower Library. Deleted comments at the end of Drafting Office Copy.

45. "Joint Chiefs of Staff," ch. 8, p. 435.

46. Eveland, *Ropes of Sand*, p. 274.

47. Article, May 29, 1958, by James Reston in the *New York Times* (p. 12), is cited in Mohammed S. Agwani, *The Lebanese Crisis, 1958*, p. 106.

48. The Lebanese Crisis, May 13, 1958, DDQC 9, no. 1 (Jan.–Mar. 1983), WH 001434.

49. The British position as described on May 16 in FO 371/134116, no. 938, may be contrasted with that of the U.S. DOS, as summarized in May 16/17,

1958, FO 371/134116, no. 1172.

50. "JCS and National Policy, 1956–1958," p. 438.

51. Editorial note cited in *FRUS 1958–1960*, XI, p. 60.

52. McClintock to Dulles, May 16, 1958, RG 59, 783A.00/5–1658.

53. McClintock to Dulles, no. 3832, May 13, 1958, RG 59, 783A.00/5–1358.

54. McClintock to Dulles, no. 3977, May 17, 1958, RG 59, box 1, Lebanon Crisis Files, 1952–1957, lot file no. 59, D-600.

55. Foreign Service dispatch, Beirut to DOS, no. 232, May 18, 1958, DDQC 3, 1 (Jan.–Mar. 1977), 65E.

56. Cited in Agwani, *The Lebanese Crisis, 1958*, p. 73.

57. Brooke to USIA, no. 326, May 19, 1958, RG 59, box 1, Lebanon Crisis Files, 1952–1957, lot file no. 59, D-600.

58. Beirut to Dulles, no. 4002, May 18, 1958, RG 59, 783A.00/5–1958.

59. McClintock to Dulles. May 19, 1958, RG 59, box 3750, 783A.00/5–1958.

60. Memorandum from Colonel D. J. Decker of the Joint Middle East Planning Committee of the Joint Chiefs of Staff to Chief of Naval Operations (Burke), May 19, 1958, cited in *FRUS 1958–1960*, XI, pp. 63–66.

61. Memorandum of conversation between Sec of State and British Ambassador Caccia, Washington, May 21, 1958, cited in *FRUS 1958–1960*, XI, p. 70.

62. McClintock to Dulles, May 22, 1958, cited in *FRUS 1958–1960*, XI, p. 72.

63. The following are the sources that I have found to be the most useful in reconstructing the military aspect of U.S. intervention:

a. Lebanon File, July 1958, no. 1, VE 23, 2, 58, Marine Corps Historical Center, Washington, D.C., p. IV-3. This version is at CLS, box 46.

b. "Joint Chiefs of Staff and National Policy, 1956–1958," ch. 8, pp. 435–36;

c. Memorandum for the Chief of Naval Operations. Department of the Navy, Office of Chief of Naval Operations, DDQC 9, no. 4 (Oct.–Dec. 1983), 002321, 002322;

d. "A Brief History of the U.S. Sixth Fleet in the Mediterranean Area, 1950–1958," Naval Historical Center, OPNAV Report 5750-5, Operational Archives Branch, post 1946 Command File, 1959, NA RG 59, box 5446, Lebanon 1950–1954, 883A.237/2–2952–883 A.2553/12–552.

e. May 17, 1958, RG 319, from: USARMA Beirut, Lebanon, to: ACSI DEPTAR WASH DC, etc., Department of the Army, Staff Communications Office.

64. Dulles to American Embassy, Beirut, London, Paris, May 19, 1958, RG 59, box 3750, 783A.00/5–1958.

65. DOS to Embassy, Beirut, May 23, 1958, cited in *FRUS 1958–1960*, XI, p. 74.

66. Brooke to USIA, May 27, 1958, #395, RG 59, box 1, Lebanon Crisis Files, 1952–1957, 783A.00/5–2758, lot file no. 59, D-600.

67. Hon. Ambassador Hermann Eilts, in a personal communication to author, dated Mar. 11, 1995. In 1958, H. Eilts was officer in charge of Baghdad Pact CENTO-SEATO Affairs, 1957–1959. For Israeli and U.S. sources on this period, see Samuel Segev, *The Iranian Triangle*, pp. 30–34; Douglas Little, "The Making of a Special Relationship,"pp. 563–85; Dan Raviv and Yossi Melman, *Every Spy a Prince,* pp. 83–84.

68. Lawson to Dulles, #1014, May 16, 1958, RG 59, box 3750, 783A.00/5-1658.

69. Mem of Conversation re: Situation in Lebanon, May 15, 1958, RG 59, box 3750, 783A.00/5-1558.

70. McClintock to Dulles, #3696, May 16, 1958, RG 59, box 3750, 783A.00/5-1658, sec. 2 of 2.

71. Tel Aviv to Sec of State, no. 1017, May 17, 1958, RG 59, 783.00/5-1758; and RM Hadow, FO Minute, FO 371/134155.

72. "14 Lebanese Rebels Returned by Israel," *New York Times,* June 10, 1958.

73. Memo of conversation re Situation in Lebanon, May 26, 1958, RG 59, box 3750, 783A.00/5-2658. For Eban's views of his changing relationship with Dulles in this period and through the end of the 1958 crisis, see the transcript of a recorded interview with the Hon. Abba Eban, Deputy Prime Minister of Israel, by Dr. Louis L. Gerson, interviewer, May 28, 1964, Rehovoth, Israel. Cited in the John Foster Dulles Oral History Project, Princeton University, Mudd Library.

74. Memorandum of Conversation, DOS, May 22, 1958, RG 59, box 3751, 783A.00/5-2258.

75. Copeland, *The Game of Nations*, pp. 229–30.

76. Hare to Dulles, no. 3029, May 20, 1958. RG 59, 783A/00/5-2058.

77. McClintock to Dulles, no. 4087, May 21, 1958, RG 59, box 3750, 783A.00/5-2158.

78. Beirut to London, no. 600, May 24, 1958, FO 371/134119.

79. Herter to American Embassy in Cairo, Beirut, London, Paris, no. 14927, May 27, 1958, RG 59, box 3750, 783A.00/5-2058.

80. McClintock to DOS, May 30, 1958, cited in *FRUS 1958–1960*, XI, p. 83.

81. Hare to Dulles, no. 3151, May 31, 1958, RG 59, box 3751, 783A.00/5-2358.

82. Hare to Dulles, no. 3140, May 30, 1958, RG 59, 783A.00/5-3058.

83. Dulles to Hare, June 9, 1958, cited in *FRUS 1958–1960*, XI, pp. 103–4; Dulles to Hare, June 12, 1958, cited in ibid., pp. 111–12.

84. Dulles to McClintock, Beirut and Cairo, June 10, 1958, DDQC 7, no. 3 (July–Sept. 1981), 371A; this source is dated June 11, in the *FRUS 1958–1960*, XI, doc. no. 67, which can be explained by the time of the cable, 12:26 A.M.

85. Interview with Stuart Rockwell, Washington, D.C., Dec. 18, 1992.

86. Copeland, *The Game of Nations*, p. 236.

87. Telephone interview with then vice president of TAPLINE, William Chandler, June 15, 1995; see, in addition, Copeland, *Game of Nations*, p. 238.

88. Walter J. Levy, "Western Security and International Oil," June 11, 1958, Archives of the Council on Foreign Relations, vol. 17, July 1957–June 1958 (J–Q).

12. Doubt, Deliberation, and Preparation

*Excerpt Dulles to McClintock, June 19, 1958, DDCQ 10, no. 2 (Apr.–June 1984), 001099. Second excerpt from June 25, 1958, political and military analyses of Lebanon situation (DDQC 2, 1 and 2) 1005.

1. The following are useful sources for the analysis of the UN phase of the Lebanese crisis: Michael G. Fry, "The Uses of Intelligence"; Mohammed S. Agwani, *The Lebanese Crisis, 1958*, ch. 4, "The Lebanese Question Before the Security Council"; and the Security Council Official Records, especially those of the 823d, 824th, and 825th meetings.

2. Those who protested included Abdallah al-Yafi, Husayn al-'Uwayni, Ilyas al-Khuri, Fu'ad 'Ammoun, Emile al-Khuri, 'Ali Bazzi, Anis Salih, Shafiq Murtada, Fu'ad al-Khuri, and Hasan al-Bahsali.

3. Speech by Charles Malik (Lebanon), June 6, 1958, Security Council Official Records (SCOR), 823d meeting, no. 24, pp. 13–14.

4. Ibid., no. 71, p. 22.

5. Ibid., no. 72, p. 22.

6. SCOR, June 10, 1958, F. Jamali of Iraq, no. 199, cited in Agwani, *The Lebanese Crisis*, p. 189.

7. SCOR, 'U. Lutfi, nos. 8–10, p. 36.

8. Ibid., A. Sobolev, no. 192, p. 35.

9. Ibid., no. 252, p. 47.

10. McClintock to DOS, June 15, 1958, cited in *FRUS 1958–1960*, XI, p. 125.

11. Robert McClintock, *The Meaning of Limited War*, p. 103.

12. Nawaf Salam, interviews with Abdullah al-Mashnuq, *L'Insurrection de 1958 au Liban*, 4:23–24; with Sa'eb Salam, pp. 53, 60, 99–102, and the author's assessment, 239. See also Fahim Qubain, *Crisis in Lebanon*, pp. 142–43.

13. N. Salam, *L'Insurrection de 1958 au Liban*.

14. Memorandum of conversation regarding the situation in Lebanon, June 25, 1958, DDQC 2, no. 1 (Jan.–Mar., Apr.–June 1976), 101A.

15. According to Jacques Derogy and Hesi Carmel's *The Untold History of Israel*, the Lebanese Ministry of the Interior revealed that some of the Egyptian arms captured by Israel (presumably in 1956) subsequently found their way to illegal arms markets, including those in Lebanon.

16. Dulles to McClintock, June 25, 1958, DDQC 3, no. 2 (Apr.–June 1977), 134E.

17. Press conference, June 25, 1958, cited in Agwani, *The Lebanese Crisis*, p. 207.

18. Sir George Middleton, from Beirut to Foreign Office, June 28, 1958, FO 371/134127.

19. Memorandum of a conversation between Minister of British Embassy and Asst Sec of State for NE, SA, and A Affairs, July 3, 1958, cited in *FRUS 1958–1960*, XI, pp. 198–99.

20. Council on Foreign Relations, Archives, Records of Meetings, vol. 27, July 1957–June 1958 (J-Q).

21. UN, *Everyman's United Nations*, p. 563.

22. UN Doc. S/4040, July 3, 1958.

23. Official comments of the government of Lebanon on the first report of the United Nations Observation Group in Lebanon, July 8, 1958, cited in Agwani, *The Lebanese Crisis*, p. 225.

24. Ibid., p. 226.

25. Dulles's remarks at Cabinet meeting, July 18, 1958, box 11, DDE Papers as President, Cabinet series, Eisenhower Library.

26. Telephone call to Eisenhower, June 12, 1958, 11:45 A.M., box 12, Dulles telephone call series, Memo telephone conversation, White House, Ap 1–July 31, 1958, Eisenhower Library.

27. Letter in June 20, 1958, dispatch 733, from McClintock to DOS, June 13, 1958, Lebanon Crisis Files, 1952–1957, RG 59, box 2, 783A. 00/6–1358, lot file no. 59, D-600.

28. Tel Aviv to War Office, June 13, 1958, FO 371/134123.

29. Dulles telephone call to Eisenhower, June 14, 1958, 5:36 P.M., box 12, Dulles telephone call series, memo tel conv., WH Ap 1–July 31, 1958, Eisenhower Library.

30. Dulles and Eisenhower, June 15, 1958, box 12, Dulles telephone call series, WH Ap 1—July 31, 1958, Eisenhower Library.

31. Jack Raymond, "Dulles Confers on Beirut Strife," *New York Times*, June 15, 1958.

32. Dulles and Eisenhower, June 15, 1958, box 12, Dulles telephone call series, memo tel conv., WH Ap 1–July 31, 1958, Eisenhower Library.

33. Sir William Hayter, June 12, 1958, FO Minute, FO 371/134124.

34. DOS Memo of Conversation, June 15, 1958, 5:30–6:45 P.M., DDQC 8, no. 3 (July–Sept. 1981), 371B.

35. This material appears in a somewhat different version in the June 16, 1958, memorandum of conference with the president on Lebanon situation, DDQC 8, no. 1 (Jan.–Mar. 1982), OOO337.

36. McClintock to DOS, June 15, 1958, cited in *FRUS 1958–1960*, XI, p. 139.

37. June 15, 1958, DDQC 7, no. 3 (July–Sept. 1981), 371B.

38. Memorandum of Conference with President on Lebanon Situation, June 16, 1958, DDQC 8, no. 1 (Jan.–Mar. 1982), 000337.

39. Dulles to McClintock, June 17, 1958, cited in *FRUS 1958–1960*, XI, p. 146.

40. McClintock to DOS, June 17, 1958, no. 88, cited in *FRUS 1958–1960*, XI, p. 143.

41. Memorandum from Rountree to Dulles, June 17, 1958, cited in *FRUS 1958–1960*, XI, p. 150.

42. DOS to American Embassy in U.K., July 3, 1958, no. 114, cited in *FRUS 1958–1960*, XI. Confirmation of these differences was provided by the Hon. Harrison M. Symmes, special assistant to William M. Rountree, in an interview on Aug. 27, 1992, Virginia.

43. Dulles to McClintock, June 19, 1958, DDQC 10, no. 2 (Apr.–June 1984), 001099.

44. Embassy in Jordan to DOS, June 28, 1958, cited in *FRUS 1958–1960*, XI, p. 292.

45. DOS to U.S. Embassies, Paris, Beirut, London, and to UN, June 24, 1958, DDQC 3, no. 1 (Jan.–Mar. 1977), 64C.

46. McClintock to Dulles, June 19, 1958, #4905, DDQC 2, nos. 1–2 (Jan.–Mar.; Apr.–June 1976), 100B.

47. McClintock to Dulles, #4873, June 18, 1958, DDQC 2, no. 1 (Jan.–Mar. 1976) and no. 2 (Apr.–June), 99J.

48. McClintock to Dulles, #4947, June 20, 1958, DDQC 3, no. 2 (Apr.–June 1977), 134D.

49. Current Intelligence Weekly Summary, Part 1: Lebanon, June 19, 1958, RG 59, DOS, Records of Bureau of Intelligence and Research, Lebanon Crisis Files, 1952–57; RG 59, box 4, Lebanon Crisis Files, 1958, 783A.00 (w)/6–1958.

50. McClintock to Dulles, #4947, June 20, 1958, DDQC 3, no. 2 (Apr.–June 1977), 134D.

51. McClintock to Dulles, #4942, June 20, 1958, DDQC 2, no. 4 (Oct.–Dec. 1976), 283E.

52. McClintock to Dulles, #4945, June 20, 1958, DDQC 2, no. 3 (July–Sept. 1976), 194E.

53. McClintock to Dulles, #5098, June 25, 1958, DDQC 2, no. 3 (July–Sept. 1976), 194G.

54. McClintock to Dulles, #5062, June 24, 1958, DDQC 2, nos. 1–2 (Jan.–Mar.; Apr.–June 1976) 100G.

55. Untitled political and military analysis of Lebanese situation as of June 25, 1958, FADRC, FOIA, Case No. 5. B. 88, as cited in DDQC 2, nos. 1–2 (Jan.–Mar.; Apr.–June 1976) 100J.

56. Qubain, *The Crisis in Lebanon*, pp. 78–79.

57. Sham'un press conference in *al-Hayat*, June 26, 1958, cited in Agwani, *The Lebanese Crisis*, p. 208.

58. DOS to U.S. Embassies, Paris, Beirut, London, UN, June 24, 1958, DDQC 3, no. 1 (Jan.–Mar. 1977), 64C.

59. Memorandum of conversation regarding the situation in Lebanon, June 25, 1958, DDQC 2, nos. 1–2 (Jan.–Mar.; Apr.–June 1976), 101A.

60. Memorandum for the Joint Chiefs of Staff, June 23, 1958, DDQC 7, no. 3 (July–Sept. 1981), 311A.

61. Sir William Hayter to Lord Hood, June 25, 1958, FO 371/134156.

62. Michael Weir to E. M. Rose, Levant Department, July 5, 1958, FO 371/134156.

63. Memorandum of conversations, DOS, July 2, 1958, cited in *FRUS 1958–1960*, XI, p. 195.

64. Memorandum of conversation, Lebanon and the Middle East, July 1, 1958, box 35, DDE Diaries, Eisenhower Library.

65. Aziz al-Azmeh, "Islamism and the Arabs," p. 32.

66. DOS Memorandum of conversation on the Lebanese situation, July 2, 1958, RG 59, 783A.00/7–258, Lebanon Crisis Files, 1958, in LCF 1952–1957, lot file no. 59, D-600.

67. C. A. Herter Papers, telephone calls, July 2, 1958, box 11, Eisenhower Library.

68. Memorandum of luncheon conversation, July 7, 1958, DDQC 9, no. 1 (Jan.–Mar. 1983), 001062.

69. McClintock to Dulles, July 10, 1958, cited in *FRUS 1958–1960*, no. 119, p. 204.

70. Beirut to DOS, Foreign Service Dispatch 49, July 13, 1958, RG 59, 783A.00/7–1358, Lebanon Crisis Files, 1952–1957.

71. Samuel M. Katz, *Soldier Spies*, p. 145.

72. Ibid., p. 146.

73. Jonathan C. Randal, *Going All the Way*, p. 200.

74. Arab Nationalism as a Factor in the Middle East Situation, July 12, 1958, DDQC 9, no. 2 (Apr.–June 1983), CIA 000772.

13. 11,000 Sorties in Search of a Target

*July 18, 1958, Outgoing telegram to American Embassy, London, Eisenhower to Macmillan, (signed Dulles), DDQC 12, no. 3 (May–June 1986), 001416.

1. H. Batatu, *The Old Social Classes and the Revolutionary Movements of Iraq*, p. 800.

2. See the discussion of U.S. policy in Iraq by Thacher and Axelgard in Robert A. Fernea and Wm. Roger Louis, eds., *The Iraqi Revolution of 1958*.

3. Camille Chamoun, *La Crise au Moyen Orient*, p. 423.

4. FO 134154, July 14, 1958. For an interpretation that emphasizes Britain's role in this period, see Ritchie Ovendale, "Great Britain and the Anglo-American Invasion of Jordan and Lebanon in 1958"; and for a critical assessment of U.S. policy toward Britain in the same period, see C. Watt, "Demythologizing the Eisenhower Era," in Wm. Roger Louis and Headley Bull, eds., *The "Special Relationship*," pp. 75, 83.

5. Chronology of telephone calls, July 14, 1958, DDQC 8, no. 2 (Apr.–June 1982), 00978.

6. FO telegram #4477 to Washington, July 15, 1958, FO 371/134130.

7. Telephone call, July 15, 1958, DDQC 7, no. 4 (Oct.–Dec. 1981), 627B.

8. Washington to FO, Viscount Hood, cable #1891, July 14, 1958, FO 371/134158.

9. Telephone call, Nixon to Dulles, July 15, 1958, box 8, telephone call series, J. F. Dulles Papers, Eisenhower Library.

10. Memorandum, July 16, 1958, of Conference with the President on July 14, 1958, box 35, DDE Diaries, Eisenhower Library.

11. "Joint Chiefs of Staff and National Policy, 1956–1958," ch. 8, p. 445. Dept. of Defense, Memorandum for the Record, July 14, 1958, DDQC 12, no. 2 (Mar.–Apr. 1986), 00759.

12. FO 371/134154.

13. Cited in *FRUS 1958–1960*, XI, p. 310, n. 3.

14. Dulles to Eisenhower, July 19, 1958, box 12, telephone call series, J. F. Dulles Papers, Eisenhower Library.

15. Eisenhower to Macmillan, outgoing cable to American Embassy, London, July 18, 1958, DDQC 12, no. 3 (May–June 1986), OO1416.

16. #427, July 15, 1958, FO 371/134158.

17. Washington to Foreign Office, July 19, 1958, FO 371/132779.

18. July 22, 1958, FO 371/133808.

19. Lord Hood to Macmillan, July 19, 1958, FO 371/132779.

20. D. M. H. Riches to W. Morris, July 23, 1958, FO 371/132779.

21. Memorandum, July 20, 1958, of Conference with the President, July 20, 1958, DDQC 10, no. 2 (Apr.–June 1984), 001394.

22. Quandt, "Lebanon, 1958, and Jordan, 1970," p. 256.

23. Alan Dowty, *Middle East Crisis*, p. 49.

24. "U.S. Dispatches Troops to Lebanon," *State Department Bulletin* 39, no. 997 (Aug. 4, 1958): 182.

25. Wilbur Eveland, *Ropes of Sand*, pp. 314–15.

26. Stephen E. Ambrose, *Eisenhower the President*, 2:470.

27. Chronology of telephone calls, July 14, 1958, DDQC 8, no. 2 (Apr.–June 1982), 00978; Eisenhower's recollections of the same period appear in his *Waging Peace, 1956–1961*, ch. 11; in *Middle East Crisis*, Alan Dowty provides a thorough survey of the events following the military coup in Baghdad, especially in ch. 3, "1958: 14 July–31 July."

28. Telephone call, Dulles to Gen. Cutler, July 14, 1958, box 12, telephone call series, J. F. Dulles Papers, Eisenhower Library.

29. Memorandum for the Record, Subject: Meeting Re: Iraq, July 14, 1958, box 16, chronological series, July 1958, J. F. Dulles Papers, Eisenhower Library.

30. "Joint Chiefs of Staff and National Policy, 1956–1958," ch. 8, p. 443.

31. Nathan F. Twining, *Neither Liberty Nor Safety*, p. 64; and Herbert K. Tillema, *Appeal to Force*, pp. 95–96.

32. Thompson to Dulles, July 15, 1958, DDQC 3, no. 2 (Apr.–June 1977), 135D; and see Allen Dulles, Briefing Notes, July 14, 1958, DDQC 5, no. 1 (Jan.–Mar. 1979), CIA, 12 D; and also John Foster Dulles's position, as on July 16, 1958, Memorandum of Conference with President of July 14, 1958, box 35, DDE Diaries, Eisenhower Library.

33. July 15, 1958, Staff Notes of discussion between the president and vice president, DDQC 7, no. 3 (July–Sept. 1981), WH 392B.

34. July 29, 1958, Executive Sessions of the Senate Foreign Relations Committee, 85th Cong., 2d sess., 1958, 10:649.

35. July 14, 1958, Allen Dulles, Briefing Notes, DDQC 5, no. 1 (Jan.–Mar. 1979), CIA 12 D.

36. Quandt, "Lebanon, 1958, and Jordan, 1970," p. 232.

37. July 16, 1958, Mem. of Conf. with President of July 14, 1958. DDE Diaries, Box 35.

38. J. F. Dulles's remarks at Cabinet. DDQC 7, no. 4 (Oct.–Dec. 1981), 628A. See also Minutes of Cabinet meeting, July 18, 1958, DDE Papers as president, box 11, Cabinet series, Eisenhower Library. References to attempts to gather NSC members in time appear in July 14, 1958, 8:32 A.M.; telephone call to President from John Foster Dulles, box 12, Telephone Call series, J. F. Dulles Papers, Eisenhower Library; and in "The JCS and National Policy, 1956–1958," ch. 8.

39. Memorandum, July 15, 1958, of conference with the president on July 14, 1958, Staff Memo, July 58 (2), box 35, DDE Diaries, Eisenhower Library.

40. Eisenhower to Diefenbaker, July 14, 1958, DDQC 10, no. 2 (Apr.–June 1984), 1100.

41. Statement by the president, July 15, 1958, box 36, international series, Eisenhower Library.

42. "Joint Chiefs of Staff and National Policy, 1956–1958," ch. 8, pp. 444–45.

43. "Lessons Learned from the Lebanon and Quemoy Operations," report by the J-3 to the Joint Chiefs of Staff on Dec. 31, 1958, JCS 2295/2, DDQC 7, no. 3 (July–Sept., 1981), 312A.

44. "Joint Chiefs of Staff and National Policy, 1956–1958," ch. 8, p. 424.

45. Dec. 31, 1958, JCS 2295/2, p. 16.

46. "A Brief History of the U.S. Sixth Fleet in the Mediterranean Area, 1950–1958," OPNAV Report 5750–55, Post-1946 Command File, 1959, Operational Archives Branch, Naval Historical Center, RG 59, 883A.237/2–2952–883A. 2553/12–552, box 5446, p. 14.

47. Dec. 31, 1958, JCS 2295/2, p. 18.

48. Eveland, *Ropes of Sand*, p. 294.

49. "Joint Chiefs of Staff and National Policy, 1956–1958," ch. 8, p. 452.

50. Marine Corps Historical Center, "Intervention in the Internal Affairs of a Foreign Country to Assure a Friendly Government," July 1958, Washington, D.C., Lebanon File #1, p. 4, CLS, box 46.

51. Dec. 31, 1958, JCS 2295/2, p. 20.

52. "Chronology of Operation 'Blue Bat,' " Nov. 26, 1958, Joint Chiefs of Staff, JCS 1735/347 DDQC 7, no. 3 (July–Sept. 1981), 311B, p. 5. TAPLINE information from W. Chandler, in June 15, 1995, telephone interview.

53. "A Brief History of the U.S. Sixth Fleet in the Mediterranean Area, 1950–58."

54. Project RECAP, U.S. Specified Command Middle East, Adm. James L. Holloway, Jr., USN Commander in Chief, Nov. 7, 1958, JCS 1887/516, DDQC 9, no. 4 (Oct.–Dec. 1983), DD2325.

55. Twining, *Neither Liberty Nor Safety*, p. 65. Stephen Ambrose was instrumental in bringing some of these issues to my attention (letter to author, July 29, 1992).

56. Seymour M. Hersh, *The Samson Option*, pp. 47–48.

57. Charles W. Thayer, *Diplomat*, pp. 32–33.

58. The information from TAPLINE vice president Chandler was obtained in interview of June 15, 1995. Previously cited information on chain of command is from memorandum to Paul D. Phillips, staff assistant to General Goodpaster, staff secretary to the president. Description of U.S. military operation in Lebanon, including chain of command and liaison with Lebanese and U.S. ambassadors, July 16, 1958, DDQC 5, no. 4 (Oct.–Dec. 1979), 377D.

59. British Embassy, Beirut, to FO, July 15, 1958, FO 371/134158.

60. Naval message. Navy Dept., July 15, 1958, RG 59, Lebanon Crisis Files, 1958, 783A.00/7–1958, lot file no. 59, D-600.

61. "Joint Chiefs of Staff and National Policy, 1956–1958," ch. 8, p. 448.

62. Murphy to Dulles, #496, July 18, 195, Lebanon Crisis Files, 1952–1957, RG 59, box 4, lot file no 59, D-600.

63. Marine Corps Historical Center, "Intervention in the Internal Affairs of a Foreign Country," p. 14.

64. Beirut to Foreign Office, July 17, 1958, FO 371/134154. The information from TAPLINE vice president Chandler was communicated to me on June 15, 1995.

65. R. Murphy, quoted in Eveland, *Ropes of Sand*, p. 296.

66. Murphy to Dulles, #530, July 19, 1958, RG 59, box 4, Lebanon Crisis Files, 1952–1957, lot file no. 59, D-600.

67. Murphy to Dulles, July 18, 1958, RG 59, 319/ACSI, Project Decimal File 1950s, FOIA, CLS.

68. McClintock to Dulles, #533, July 20, 1958, Lebanon Crisis Files, 1952–1957, RG 59, box 4, lot file no. 59, D-600.

69. American Embassy to DOS, July 19, 1958, cited in *FRUS 1958–1960*, XI, p. 333.

70. "Road Trip to the Bekaa [Biqa'] Valley, July 19, American Embassy, Beirut, to DOS, July 22, 1958, Foreign Service Dispatch, RG 59, 783A.00/7–2258, Lebanon Crisis Files, 1952–1957, lot file no. 59, D-600.

71. American Embassy to DOS, July 19, 1958, cited in *FRUS 1958–1960*, XI, p. 335.

72. White House, July 19, 1958, 4:57 p.m., box 12, Telephone Call series, Apr.–July 1958, Eisenhower Library.

73. Memorandum of conversation, White House, July 21, 1958, box 16, chronological series, July 1958, J. F. Dulles Papers, Eisenhower Library.

74. C. A. Herter, telephone call, July 25, 1958, 12:25 P.M., telephone log, box 11, C. A. Herter Papers, Eisenhower Library.

75. McClintock to Dulles, #442, July 17, 1958, RG 59, box 4, Lebanon Crisis Files, 1952–1957, lot file no. 59, D-600; and McClintock to Dulles, #466, July 17, 1958, box 4, Lebanon Crisis Files, 1952–1957, lot file no. 59, D-600.

76. For an instructive analysis of the UN and UNOGIL role, I am grateful to Michael G. Fry for allowing me to consult his paper on the subject, "The United Nations and the Lebanon Crisis, 1958," subsequently published under the title "The Uses of Intelligence."

77. For U.S. coverage of press reports, see Synopsis of Reports Relating to Mid-East Crisis Reported to the President, July 19, 1958, Covering 14–19 July, DDQC 7, no. 4 (Oct.–Dec. 1981), 00628B; Reaction to U.S. Landings, Selected from telegrams received by OCB, July 17, 1958, DDQC 11, no. 1 (Jan.–Mar. 1985), 00629; and H. Haykal, cited in Aryeh Yodfat and M. Abir, *In the Direction of the Persian Gulf*, p. 148, n. 18.

78. Synopsis of Reports, July 28, 1958, Office of the Secretary, box 14, Intelligence Briefing Notes (1), Eisenhower Library.

79. Thompson to Dulles, July 19, 1958, DOS, box 36, international series, Mid-East, July 1958, Eisenhower Library; see the exchange between Khrushchev and Eisenhower in Mohammed S. Agwani, *The Lebanese Crisis*, p. 8.

80. Letter from Eisenhower to Khrushchev, July 22, 1958, box 4, J. F. Dulles draft presidential correspondence, Eisenhower Library.

81. White House, presentation of credentials to the president by Swedish ambassador, July 17, 1958, Staff Memo, box 35. DDE Diaries, Eisenhower Library; and Synopsis, July 19, 1958, of July 14–19, DDQC 7, no. 4 (Oct.–Dec. 1981), 00628B.

82. Reactions to U.S. Landings, July 17, 1958, DDQC 11, no. 1 (Jan.–Mar. 1985), 00629.

83. American Embassy, Tokyo, to Dulles, DOS, July 18, 1958, DDQC 4, no. 1 (Jan.–Mar. 1978), 96B.

84. MacArthur to Dulles, #115, July 17, 1958, RG 59, box 4, Lebanon Crisis Files, 1952–1957, lot file no. 59, D-600. NA. Records of the Bureau of Research and Intelligence, lot file no. 59, D-600. Useful for this period is the recent article "CIA Spent Millions to Support Japanese Right in 50s and 60s," *New York Times*, Oct. 9, 1994.

85. White House Staff notes, #401, Aug. 4, 1958, DDQC 11, no. 4 (Oct.–Dec. 1985), OO2836.

86. Telegram from DOS to Embassy in UK, July 18, 1958, cited in *FRUS 1958–1960*, XI, p. 325.

87. For an analysis that reviews the period 1956–1958, with reference to Anglo-Israeli tensions in relation to overflight rights in 1958 and more general Israeli views of its relations with Britain and the United States, see Michael B. Oren, "The Test of Suez."

88. Reaction to U.S. Landings, July 17, 1958, OCB; see n. 76.

89. White House, Statement by the President, July 15, 1958, Statements by DDE, box 36, international series, Eisenhower Library.

90. White House, Statement by the President, July 14, 1958, DDQC 3, no. 2 (Apr.–June 1977), 134G.

91. Dulles to all ARA diplomatic missions, July 15, 1958, DDQC 3, no. 2 (Apr.–June 1977), DOS 135B.

92. DOS to U.S. Embassies, Paris, Beirut, London, UN, June 24, 1958, DDQC 3, no. 1 (Jan.–Mar. 1977), 64C.

93. Dulles to all American diplomatic posts, July 14, 1958, DDQC 3, no. 2 (Apr.–June 1977), 134G.

94. "Joint Chiefs of Staff and National Policy, 1956–1958," p. 432.

95. DOS to all American diplomatic posts, July 14, 1958, DDQC 3, no. 2 (Apr.–June 1977), 134G.

96. Staff Notes, July 15, 1958, box 36, international series, Mid-East July 1958, Eisenhower Library.

97. White House, Memorandum of Conference with the President, July 15, 1958, DDQC 7, no. 4 (Oct.–Dec. 1981), 627A.

98. Staff Notes of discussion between the president and vice president, July 15, 1958, DDQC 7, no. 3 (July–Sept. 1981), WH 392B.

99. Senator Clark, Aug. 4, 1958, Executive Sessions of the Senate Foreign Relations Committee, *Hearings*, 85th Cong., 2d sess., 1958, 10:713. Hereafter cited as *Hearings*.

100. *Hearings*, July 1, 1958, p. 483.

101. Office of Staff Secretary, July 18, 1958, handwritten notes of Cabinet meeting, box 5, Cabinet series, Eisenhower Library.

102. Legislative leadership meeting, May 19, 1958, box 32, DDE Diaries, May 1958, Staff Notes (1), Eisenhower Library.

103. Dec. 31, 1958, JCS 2295/2, p. 24.

104. *Hearings*, June 26, 1958, pp. 474–75.

105. DOS, Memorandum of a Conversation, June 23, 1958, cited in *FRUS 1958–1960*, p. 173.

106. *Hearings*, p. 475.

107. Interview with Gen. Goodpaster, Dec. 17, 1992, Washington, D.C.

108. *Hearings*, p. 580.

109. Richard E. Neustadt, *Presidential Power*, p. 96.

110. Kenneth N. Waltz, "Electoral Punishment and Foreign Policy Crises," in James N. Rosenau, ed., *The Domestic Sources of Foreign Policy*, p. 272.

14. By Mutual Consent: July–October 1958

1. DOS to Embassy, Beirut, 498, July 25, 1958, box 36, International series, Lebanon File, Eisenhower Library.

2. Kamal Salibi, "Recollections of the 1940s and 1950s" (paper presented at the Texas Conference on Lebanon in the Decade of the 1950s, Sept. 11, 1992).

3. Robert McClintock, *The Meaning of Limited War*, p. 118.

4. Telephone call to Herter from Dulles, Sept. 15, 1958, box 9, Telephone Call series, J. F. Dulles Papers, Eisenhower Library.

5. Telephone call from Ambassador Lodge to J. F. Dulles, Sept. 17. 1958, box 9, Telephone Call series, J. F. Dulles Papers, Eisenhower Library.

6. Legislative Leadership Meeting, Supplementary Notes, Staff memo, July 22, 1958, box 35, Eisenhower Library.

7. Robert Murphy, *Diplomat Among Warriors*, p. 408.

8. Cable #699, McClintock to Dulles, July 25, 1958, RG 59, box 4, Lebanon Crisis Files, 1952–1957, DOS, Records of the Bureau of Intelligence and Research, Lebanon Crisis Files, 1958, lot file no. 59, D-600, 783A.00/7–2558.

9. McClintock to Dulles, #649, July 24, 1958, RG 59, box 4, Lebanon Crisis Files, 1952–1957, DOS, Records of the Bureau of Intelligence and Research, Lebanon Crisis Files, 1958, lot file no. 59, D-600, 783A.00/7–2458.

10. McClintock to Dulles, #657, July 24, 1958, RG 319 /ACSI Message File; ACSI Project Decimal File, 1950s, FOIA, Centre for Lebanese Studies, Oxford.

11. McClintock to Dulles, July 26, 1958, #724, RG 59, box 4, Lebanon Crisis Files, 1952–1957, DOS, Records of the Bureau of Intelligence and Research, Lebanon Crisis Files 1958, lot file no. 59, D-600, 783A.00/7–2658.

12. Naval Message, #6259, July 26, 1958, RG 59, box 4, Lebanon Crisis Files, 1952–1957, DOS, Records of the Bureau of Intelligence and Research, Lebanon Crisis Files, 1958, lot file no. 59, D-600, 783A.OO/7–2658.

13. Foreign Service Despatch #67, American Embassy to DOS, July 28, 1958, RG 59, box 3, Lebanon Crisis Files, 1952–1957, DOS, Records of the Bureau of Intelligence and Research, Lebanon Crisis Files, 1958, lot file no. 59, D-600, 783A.00/7–2858.

14. McClintock to Dulles, #739, July 26, 1958, RG 59, box 4, Lebanon Crisis Files, 1952–1957, Gen Records of DOS, Records of Bureau of Intelligence and Research, Lebanon Crisis Files, 1958, lot file no. 59, D-600, 783A.00/7–2658.

15. McClintock to Dulles, #642, July 23, 1958, RG 59, box 3, Lebanon Crisis Files, 1952–1957, lot file no. 59, D-600, 783A. 00/7–2358.

16. McClintock to Dulles, #806, July 30, 1958, RG 59, box 3, Lebanon Crisis Files, 1952–1957, lot file no. 59, D-600, 783A.00/7–3058.

17. McClintock to DOS, #242, July 30, 1958, in *FRUS 1958–1960*, XI, p. 412.

18. Embassy to DOS, #240, July 30, 1958, in *FRUS 1958–1960*, XI, p. 409.

19. American Embassy in Lebanon to DOS, #241, July 30, 1958, cited in *FRUS 1958–1960*, XI, p. 410.

20. Fahim Qubain, *Crisis in Lebanon*, p. 156.

21. Sir George Middleton, Beirut to Foreign Office, #1163, Aug. 2, 1958, FO 371/134154.

22. Telephone call from American Embassy in Lebanon to DOS, #244, July 31, 1958, in *FRUS 1958–1960*, XI, p. 417.

23. Tel. from Embassy in Lebanon to DOS, #274, Aug. 15, 1958, *FRUS 1958–1960*, XI, p. 477.

24. Tel. call, Aug. 5, 1958, box 11, C. A. Herter Papers, Eisenhower Library.

25. Murphy to Herter, #275, Aug. 15, 1958, *FRUS 1958–1960*, XI, p. 480.

26. Memorandum of conversation, #276, Aug. 16, 1958, *FRUS 1958–1960*, XI, p. 482.

27. For the limits of regime control, see American Embassy to DOS, Aug. 29, 1958, in *FRUS 1958–1960*, XI, pp. 539–42.

28. "Intervention in the Internal Affairs of a Foreign Country to Assure a Friendly Government, " Marine Corps Historical Center, Washington, D.C., Lebanon File, July 1958, VE 23.2.58, Lebanon, IV-4.

29. General Shihab to Eisenhower, Aug. 5, 1958, Ann Whitman File, box 34, international series (Lebanon 1), DDE Papers as President of the United States, 1953–1961, Eisenhower Library.

30. *FRUS 1958–1960*, XI, p. 541.

31. Tel. Embassy to DOS, #307, Aug. 30, 1958, in *FRUS 1958–1960*, XI, p. 544.

32. Staff notes, #408, Aug. 20, 1958, box 35, DDE Diaries, Eisenhower Library.

33. McClintock, *The Meaning of Limited War*, p. 119.

34. Dulles, Memorandum of conversation with Mr. Malik, Sept. 26, 1958, box 1, correspondence and memoranda series, Memcon/Hammarskjöld. Eisenhower Library; and McClintock to Dulles, Sept. 29, 1958, DDQC 3, no. 1 (Jan.–Mar. 1977), p. 64E.

35. Editorial note on NSC meeting of Sept. 25, 1958, in *FRUS 1958–1960*, XI, pp. 579–80; for Allen Dulles's views, see pp. 590–91.

36. McClintock to Dulles, July 17, 1958, #453, RG 59. box 4, Lebanon Crisis Files, 1952–1957, DOS, Records of the Bureau of Intelligence and Research, Lebanon Files 1958, lot file no. 59, D-600, 783A.00/7–1758.

37. Tel. from Embassy, Lebanon, to DOS, #333, Sept. 25, 1958, in *FRUS 1958–1960*, XI, p. 581.

38. Tel. from Embassy in Lebanon to DOS, #336, Sept. 27, 1958, in *FRUS 1958–1960*, XI, p. 586.

39. McClintock to Dulles, #1757, Sept. 30, 1958, DDQC 3, no. 1 (Jan.–Mar. 1977), 64G. The material that follows is taken from this source.

40. Dulles to McClintock, Oct. 1, 1958, DDQC 3, no. 1 (Jan.–Mar. 1977), 65A.

41. Airgram from Embassy Beirut to DOS, Oct. 1, 1958, DDQC 3, no. 1 (Jan.–Mar. 1977), 65D.

42. Synopsis: State Department Items Reported to the President, Oct. 9, 1958, box 37, DDE Diaries, Eisenhower Library.

43. Tel. from Embassy to DOS, #342, Oct. 2, 1958, in *FRUS 1958–1960*, XI, p. 593.

44. McClintock to Dulles, #1895, Oct. 9, 1958, RG 319, ACSI Message File 1950s, Part 1 and 2, box 35, Centre for Lebanese Studies, Oxford.

45. McClintock to Dulles, #1931, Oct. 11, 1958, RG319/ACSI Message File 1950s, Part 1 and 2, box 35, Centre for Lebanese Studies, Oxford.

46. U.S. Consulate General, Geneva to DOS, #351, Oct. 14, 1958, cited in *FRUS, 1958–1960*, XI, p. 607.

47. Qubain, *Crisis in Lebanon*, p. 161.

48. Tel. from Embassy in Lebanon to DOS, #613, Oct. 16, 1958, in *FRUS 1958–1960*, XI, p. 614.

49. Sir Pierson. Dixon, New York to Foreign Office, #801, Aug. 8, 1958, FO 371/134271; and see the analysis of Israeli policy in Michael Oren, "The Test of Suez."

50. Memorandum of conversation, #267, Aug. 12, 1958, in *FRUS 1958–1960*, XI, p. 458.

51. Memorandum of conversation, #279, Aug. 18, 1958, in *FRUS 1958–1960*, XI, p. 493.

52. Tel. from Embassy in Amman to DOS, #281, Aug. 19, 1958, in *FRUS 1958–1960*, XI, p. 503.

53. Letter from Foreign Secretary Lloyd to Dulles, #295, Aug. 25, 1958, in *FRUS 1958–1960*, XI, p. 524.

54. Memorandum on the substance of discussion at the Department of State—Joint Chiefs of Staff Meeting, Pentagon, Washington, Sept. 12, 1958, cited in *FRUS 1958–1960*, XI, p. 564.

55. Memorandum of conference with the president, Oct. 15, 1958, Staff notes, Oct. 1958, box 36, DDE Diaries, Eisenhower Library.

56. 840th UN SCOR, Nov. 25, 1958, letter dated Nov. 16 from Leb Minister of Foreign Affairs to President of Security Council.

57. Michael G. Fry, "The Uses of Intelligence," p. 89, n. 36.

58. National Security Council, NSC 5820/1, Nov. 4, 1958, U.S. Policy Toward the Near East, DDQC 6, no. 4 (Oct.–Dec. 1980), 00386B.

59. Special National Intelligence Estimate, SNIE 30–6–58, Oct. 28, 1958, in *FRUS 1958–1960*, XI, p. 618.

60. Assistance to the gendarmerie of Lebanon: Status Report for the month of November 1958, in DDQC 7, no. 2 (Apr.–June 1981), 217B.

61. N. Chomsky and E. S. Herman, *The Washington Connection and Third World Fascism*, 1:219, but see pp. 218–30.

62. Status Report for Nov. 1958, DDQC 7, no. 2 (Apr.–June 1981), 217B.

63. The Draper Committee Reports, 1958–1959, U.S. European Command, Report to the President's Committee to Study the U.S. MAP, North Africa and the Middle East, Dec. 18, 1958, box 18, Eisenhower Library.

64. U.S. Defense Security Assistance Agency, Foreign Military Sales and Military Assistance Facts, Washington 1977, cited in Michael Klare and C. Arnson, *Supplying Repression*, p. 36.

65. NSC 5820/1, Financial Annex, p. 23.

66. McClintock to DOS, #2534, Dec. 2, 1958, RG 319, ACSI Message File 1950s, Part 1 and 2, box 34, Centre for Lebanese Studies, Oxford.

Epilogue: 1958 in Retrospect

*U.S. Policy Toward the Near East, DDQC 7, no. 3 (July–Sept. 1981), 337A;

Memorandum of Conference with the President on July 23, 1958, DDQC 8, no. 1 (Jan.–Mar. 1982), 000341.

1. NSC 5801, "Long Range U.S. Policy Toward the Near East," Jan. 16, 1958, no. 6, p. 3; for no. 10, see p. 4; NSC series, Eisenhower Library.

2. NSC 5820/1, Nov. 4, 1958, "U.S. Policy Toward the Near East," p. 1, NSC series, Eisenhower Library.

3. Fawaz Traboulsi, "Identités et Solidarités Croisées dans les Conflits du Liban Contemporain"; see especially pp. 370–72. On the more general subject of the nature of the nation-state promoted by the postwar development of global capitalism, which is evoked by some of the changes occurring in the Shihab period, see Cyrus Bina, "Farewell to the Pax Americana," p. 46.

4. NSC 5801, Jan. 16, 1958, p. 6.

5. "Factors Affecting U.S. Policy Toward the Near East," p. 7, box 23, NSC series, Policy Papers subseries, NSC5801/1—Policy Toward the Near East, White House Office, Office of the Special Assistant for National Security Affairs: Records, 1952–1961, Eisenhower Library.

6. "Future Policy in the Persian Gulf," FO 371/132778, Jan. 15, 1958; "Kuwait: The Possible Separation of British Representation from the Political Resident in Bahrain, and the Possible Change of Title," Jan. 17, 1958 (probable date), FO 371/132779.

7. Lord Hood's letter of Feb. 12, Minutes, "United States Government and the Gulf," Feb. 20, 1958, FO 371/132778.

8. Washington to Foreign Office, July 20, 1958, FO 371/132779.

9. Legislative Leadership Meeting, Supplementary Notes, July 22, 1958, DDE Staff Memo, box 35, Eisenhower Library; and Memorandum of July 23 Conference with the president, July 24, 1958, DDQC 8, no. 1 (Jan.–Mar. 1982), 00341.

10. "Factors Affecting U.S. Policy Toward the Near East," no. 21, p. 8, box 23, NSC series, NSC 5801/1, Policy Toward the Near East (1), Eisenhower Library. See also "Issues Arising Out of the Situation in the Near East," A., p. 3.

11. "Factors Affecting U.S. Policy," p. 3n.

12. Daniel Yergin, *The Prize*, pp. 525–26.

13. Wilbur Eveland, *Ropes of Sand*, p. 314; Yergin, *The Prize*, p. 515.

14. Eveland, *Ropes of Sand*, pp. 314–15.

15. Discussion of NSC 129/1 appears in Irene Gendzier, "The United States, the USSR, and the Arab World in NSC Reports of the 1950s." For an analysis of the postwar Labor government's position on preventive development, see Wm. Roger Louis, *The British Empire in the Middle East, 1945–1951*.

16. Fawaz A. Gerges, *The Superpowers and the Middle East*, p. 130.

17. NSC 5820/1, Nov. 4, 1958, p. 12.

18. "Should the United State Reconsider Its Policy Toward Israel," in "Issues," p. 6.

19. Samuel Segev, *The Iranian Triangle*, p. 35.

20. Dan Raviv and Yossie Melman, *Every Spy a Prince*, p. 83.

21. Ambassador Hermann Eilts, letter to author, Mar. 11, 1995.

22. Segev, *The Iranian Triangle*, p. 36; Michel Bar-Zohar, *Ben-Gourion, Le Prophète Armé*, pp. 346–47.

23. Segev, *The Iranian Triangle*, p. 36.

24. Andrew Cockburn and Leslie Cockburn, *Dangerous Liaison*, p. 100.

25. Raviv and Melman, *Every Spy a Prince*, p. 84.

26. NSC 5820/1, Nov. 4, 1958, NSC series, Eisenhower Library, p. 14.

27. Operations Coordinating Board, Feb. 3, 1960, NSC series, Eisenhower Library, no. 26, p. 8.

28. Opening statement of the Report on the Near East, NSC 5820/1, Eisenhower Library.

29. "Joint Chiefs of Staff and National Policy, 1956–1958," p. 484.

30. Ambassador H. Eilts, letter to author, Mar. 11, 1995.

31. "Joint Chiefs of Staff and National Policy, 1956–1958," p. 484.

Bibliography

Archival Sources

Records at the United States National Archives, Washington, D.C.:
General Records of the Department of State, Central Decimal Files:
>   Record Group 59: Lebanon,1945–1949; 1950–1954; 1955–1959; Lebanese Crisis Files, 1952–1957, 1958.
>   Record Group 84: Beirut Petroleum Attache, 1949–1954.
>   Record Group 165: Office of Strategic Services, Military Attache Reports, G-2 Intelligence files.
>   Record Group 218: Joint Chiefs of Staff, 1950–1960.
>   Record group 226: Records of the Office of Strategic Services. Research and Analysis.
>   Record Group 319: ACSI (Secretary of the Army, Assistant Chief of Staff of Intelligence) Message File and Project Decimal File, 1949–1960; Intelligence, Lebanese Military; Unclassified File, 1956–1958.
>   Miscellaneous other record groups.

Marine Corps Historical Center, Washington, D.C.
Naval Historical Division, Washington, D.C.
Dwight D. Eisenhower Library, Abilene, Kansas:
>   Papers of D. D. Eisenhower as President, Ann Whitman File.
>   D. D. Eisenhower Diaries.
>   Legislative Meetings series.
>   Cabinet series.
>   National Security Council series.
>   International series.

International Meetings series.

Speech series.

Records of the White House Office of Special Assistant for National Security Affairs.

Records of the White House Staff secretary.

White House Central Files.

J. F. Dulles Papers: telephone calls; chronological series.

C. A. Herter Papers.

C. D. Jackson Papers.

Lyndon Baines Johnson Library, Austin, Texas.

Papers of Lyndon B. Johnson, Prepresidential Papers.

The John Foster Dulles Oral History Collection, Mudd Library, Princeton University, Princeton.

British Public Record Office. London: Foreign Office Archives. FO 371, Lebanese, Syrian, and Middle East files.

Center for Lebanese Studies. Oxford: Archives from the Eisenhower Library, National Archives, Washington, D.C., and other U.S., Israeli, and Belgian sources.

Archives of the Council on Foreign Relations. New York: War and Peace Studies: Annual Reports, Records of Groups, Records Meetings through 1958. News clippings of 1958.

U.S. Congressional Hearings, Published Reports, and Other Sources

Declassified Documents Reference System, and *Declassified Documents Quarterly Catalogue* (DDQC). Washington, D.C.: Carrollton Press, 1975–1990.

Department of State Bulletin, 1958.

Documents on International Affairs, 1956 (1959) and *1957* (1960), edited, selected, and introduced by Noble Frankland assisted by Vera King.

Documents on International Affairs, 1958, edited and selected by Gillian King. New York: Oxford University Press, 1962.

Foreign Relations of the United States. Washington, D.C.: GPO, 1943–1960. Volumes bearing on Near East (Middle East), National Security Affairs; Foreign Economic Policy; General Economic and Political Matters; Foreign Information Program; Foreign Aid and Economic Defense Policy; and accompanying supplements.

Hoskins, Halford. "United States Interests and Policy Relative to the Middle East," Jan. 30, 1959. Legislative Reference Service, Library of Congress, Washington, D.C.

Interviews by the author with U.S. and Lebanese officials and personalities identified in Notes section.

United Nations: Security Council Original Records, The Lebanese Crisis. 1958.

United States Congress, Executive Sessions of the Senate Foreign Relations Committee, 85th Congress, 2nd session, 1958, Historical series, Vol. X, GPO, 1980.
___. Senate Special Committee Investigating Petroleum Resources. *American Petroleum Interests in Foreign Countries.*, 79th Congress, 1st session, 1946.
___. *The International Petroleum Cartel*: Staff Report to the Federal Trade Commission. Washington, D.C.: GPO, 1952.
___. *Multinational Oil Corporations and U.S. Foreign Policy.* Washington, D.C.: GPO, 1975.
University Publications of America. Frederick, Maryland, CIA Research Reports, 1946–1976.

> CIA Research Reports 1946–1976.
> Confidential U.S. State Department Central Files, Lebanon, 1955–1959, Internal Affairs and Foreign Affairs.
> National Security Council Documents, 1947–1977.
> O.S.S./State Department Intelligence and Research Reports, and supplement of the Middle East, 1950–1961.
> Records of the Joint Chiefs of Staff, Part 2: 1946–1953, the Middle East.

Books and Articles

Abrahamian, Ervand. *Iran Between Two Revolutions.* Princeton: Princeton University Press, 1982.
Abu Khalil, As'ad. "Druze, Sunni, and Shi'ite Political Leadership in Present-Day Lebanon." *Arab Studies Quarterly* 7, no. 4 (Fall 1985).
——. "The Palestinian-Shi'ite War in Lebanon: An Examination of Its Origins." *Third World Affairs* (1988).
——. "Shi'ites and Palestinians: Underlying Causes of the Amal-Palestinian Conflict." In Hagopian, ed., *Amal and the Palestinians: Understanding the Battle of the Camps.* Occasional Papers, Association of Arab-American University Graduates, Belmont, Mass., n.d.
Abu Lughod, I., and Eqbal Ahmad, eds. *Race and Class: The Invasion of Lebanon.* Beirut: MERIP reports, 1983.
Acheson, Dean. *Present at the Creation.* New York: Norton, 1969.
Agwani, Mohammed S. *The Lebanese Crisis, 1958: A Documentary Study.* Bombay: Asia Publishing House, 1965.
Ahmad, Eqbal. "Trade Unionism." In Brown, ed., *State and Society in Independent North Africa*, q.v.
Ahmad, Feroz. *The Turkish Experiment in Democracy, 1950–1975.* Boulder: Westview Press for the Royal Institute of International Affairs, 1977.
Alem, Jean-Pierre. "Troubles Insurrectionnels au Liban." *Orient* 6 (1958).
Allin, Erika G. *The United States and the 1958 Lebanon Crisis: American Intervention in the Middle East.* Lanham, Md.: University Press of America, 1994.

Alteras, Isaac. *Eisenhower and Israel*. Gainesville: University Press of Florida, 1993.

Ambrose, Stephen E. *Eisenhower the President*. Vol. 2. New York: Simon and Schuster, 1984.

Amery, H. A., and A. A. Kubursi. "The Litany River Basin: The Politics and Economics of Water." *Beirut Review*, no. 3 (Spring 1992).

Amin, G. *The Modernization of Poverty*. Leiden: Brill, 1980.

Anderson, Irvine H. *ARAMCO: The United States and Saudi Arabia*. Princeton: Princeton University Press, 1981.

———. "Lend Lease for Saudi Arabia: A Comment on Alternative Conceptualizations." *Diplomatic History* 3, no. 4 (Fall 1979).

Anonymous. "The Transitional Programs of the Lebanese National Movement," English language edition. Boston, 1977.

Aronson, Geoffrey. *From Sideshow to Center Stage: U.S. Policy Toward Egypt, 1946–1956*. Boulder: Lynne Rienner, 1986.

Aruri, Naseer. "The United States Intervention in Lebanon." *Arab Studies Quarterly* 7 (Fall 1985).

Asfour, Edmund Y. "Industrial Development in Lebanon." *Middle East Economic Papers, 1955*. Beirut: American University of Beirut, Economic Research Institute, 1955.

Atherton Jr., Alfred L. "The Soviet Role in the Middle East: An American View." *Middle East Journal* 39, no. 4 (Autumn 1985).

Azar, Edward E., P. A. Jureidini, R. D. McLaurin, A. A. Norton, R. J. Pranger, K. Shnayerson, E. N. Snider, J. Starr, eds. *The Emergence of a New Lebanon—Fantasy or Reality?* New York: Praeger, 1984.

Azar, Edward E., and K. Shnayerson. "United States–Lebanese Relations: A Pocketful of Paradoxes." In Azar et al., eds., *The Emergence of a New Lebanon*, q.v.

al-Azmeh, Aziz. "Islamism and the Arabs." In Aziz al-Azmeh, *Islam and Modernities*. London: Verso, 1993.

Badeau, John S. *The American Approach to the Arab World*. New York: Harper and Row, 1968.

Badre, Albert Y. "The Economy of the Contemporary Arab World." *Middle East Economic Papers, 1955*. Beirut: American University of Beirut, Economic Research Institute, 1955.

Bailey, Thomas A. *A Diplomatic History of the American People*. 8th ed. New York: Appleton-Century-Crofts, 1969.

Ball, George W. "America in the Middle East: A Breakdown in Foreign Policy." *Journal of Palestine Studies* 13, no. 3 (Spring 1984).

———. *Error and Betrayal in Lebanon: An Analysis of Israel's Invasion of Lebanon and the Implications for U.S.-Israeli Relations*. Washington, D.C.: Foundations for Middle East Peace, 1984.

Barakat, Halim. *The Arab World: Society, Culture, and State*. Berkeley and Los Angeles: University of California Press, 1993.

——. *Lebanon in Strife*. Austin: University of Texas Press, 1977.

Barakat, Halim, ed. *Toward a Viable Lebanon*. London and Sydney: Croom Helm, 1988.

Baram, Phillip J. *The Department of State in the Middle East, 1919–1945*. Philadelphia: University of Pennsylvania Press, 1978.

Barnet, Richard J. *Intervention and Revolution*. New York: New American Library and World Publishing Co., 1968.

——. *The Roots of War*. Baltimore: Penguin, 1973.

Bar-On, Mordechai. *The Gates of Gaza*. New York: St. Martin's, 1994.

Bar-Zohar, Michel. *Ben Gourion: Le Prophète Armé*. Paris: Fayard, 1966.

Batatu, Hanna. *The Old Social Classes and the Revolutionary Movements in Iraq*. Princeton: Princeton University Press, 1978.

Bavly, Dan, and Eliahu Salpeter. *Israel's War in Lebanon with the PLO*. New York: Stein and Day, 1984.

Beblawi, Hazem, and Giacomo Luciani. *The Rentier State*. London: Croom Helm, 1987.

Beinin, Joel. *Was the Red Flag Flying There?* Berkeley and Los Angeles: University of California Press, 1990.

Beinin, Joel, and Zachary Lockman. *Workers on the Nile*. Princeton: Princeton University Press, 1987.

Beit-Hallahmi, Benjamin. *The Israeli Connection*. New York: Pantheon, 1987.

Beling, Wilfrid. "Political Trends in Arab Labor." *Middle East Journal* 1, no. 1 (Winter 1961).

Bemis, Samuel Flagg. *A Diplomatic History of the United States* (1965). New York: Holt.

Bernstein, J. Barton, ed. *Politics and Policies of the Truman Administration*. Chicago: Quadrangle, 1970.

Beydoun, Ahmad. *Identité Confessionelle et Temps Sociale Chez les Historiens Libanais Contemporains*. Beirut: Publications de l'Université Libanaise, 1984.

——. "The South Lebanon Border Zone: A Local Perspective." *Journal of Palestine Studies* 21, no. 3 (Spring 1992).

Bialer, Uri. "The Iranian Connection in Israel's Foreign Policy 1948–1951." *Middle East Journal* 39, no. 2 (Spring 1985).

Bill, James A. *The Eagle and the Lion: The Tragedy of American-Iranian Relations*. New Haven: Yale University Press, 1988.

Bina, Cyrus. *The Economics of the Oil Crisis*. New York: St. Martin's, 1985.

——. "Farewell to the Pax Americana: Iran, Political Islam, and the Passing of the Old Order." In Hamid Zagane, ed., *Islam, Iran, and World Stability*. New York: St. Martin's, 1994.

——. "The Law of Economic Rent and Property Applied to the Oil Industry." *American Journal of Economics and Sociology* 50, no. 2 (April 1992).

——. "The Rhetoric of Oil and the Dilemma of War and American Hegemony." *Arab Studies Quarterly* 15, no. 3 (Summer 1993).

Binder, Leonard, ed. *Politics in Lebanon*. New York: Wiley, 1966.

Bird, Kai. *The Chairman. John J. McCLoy: The Making of the American Establishment.* New York: Simon and Schuster, 1992.

Bishku, Michael. "The 1958 American Intervention in Lebanon: A Historical Assessment." *Arab American Affairs* 31 (Winter 1989–90).

Blair, John. *The Control of Oil.* New York: Pantheon, 1976.

Blechman, B., and Stephen D. Kaplan. *Force Without War: U.S. Armed Forces as a Political Instrument.* Washington, D.C.: Brookings Institution, 1978.

Bourgey, André, ed. *Industrialization et Changements Sociaux Dans l'Orient Arabe.* Beirut: CERMOC, 1982.

Boutros, Fouad. "Les Fondements de Notre Vie Nationale." Beirut: Les Conférences du Cénacle, 1961.

Bowie, Robert. "Eisenhower, Dulles, and the Suez Crisis." In Owen and Louis, eds., *Suez, 1956,* q.v.

Brand, Henry W. *Cold Warriors: Eisenhower's Generation and American Foreign Policy.* New York: Columbia University Press, 1988.

——. "Decisions on American Armed Intervention: Lebanon, Dominican Republic, and Grenada." *Political Science Quarterly* 102 (Winter 1987–1988).

——. *Inside the Cold War.* New York: Oxford University Press, 1991.

Brand, Laurie. "The Politics of Passports: Palestinian Legal Status in Arab Host States, 1948–86." In Simon, ed., *The Middle East and North Africa,* q.v.

Britt, George. "Lebanon's Popular Revolution." *Middle East Journal* 7, no. 1 (Winter 1953).

Bromley, Simon A. *American Hegemony and World Oil: The Industry, the State System, and the World Economy.* University Park, Pa.: Pennsylvania State University Press, 1991.

Brown, L. Carl. *International Politics and the Middle East.* Princeton: Princeton University Press, 1984.

Brown, L. Carl, ed., *State and Society in Independent North Africa.* Washington, D.C.: Middle East Institute, 1966.

Browne, Walter L. *The Political History of Lebanon, 1920–1950.* 2 vols. Salisbury, N.C.: Documentary Publications, 1976.

——. *Lebanon's Struggle for Independence.* Salisbury, N.C.: Documentary Publications, 1980.

Buheiry, Marwan. "Beirut's Role in the Political Economy of the French Mandate, 1919–1939." *Papers on Lebanon,* no. 4. Oxford: Centre for Lebanese Studies.

Burch Jr., Philip H. *Elites in American History.* New York and London: Holmes and Meier, 1980.

Campbell, John C. "From 'Doctrine' to 'Policy' in the Middle East." *Foreign Affairs* (April 1957).

Carèrre d'Encausse, Hélène. "The Background of Soviet Policy in the Middle East." In Laqueur, ed., *The Middle East in Transition,* q.v.

CERMOC. *Etat et Perspectives de l'Industrie au Liban.* Beirut: Centre d'Etudes et de Recherches sur le Moyen Orient Contemporain, 1978.

Chamoun, Camille. *Crise au Moyen Orient*. Paris: Gallimard, 1963.

Chafets, Ze'ev. *Double Vision*. New York: William Morrow, 1985.

Chevalier, Dominique, ed. *Renouvellements du Monde Arabe, 1952–1982*. Paris: Armand Colin, 1987.

——. *La Societé du Mont Liban à l'Epoque de la Révolution Industrielle en Europe*. Paris: Librairie Orientaliste, Paul Geuthner, 1971.

Chiha, Michel. "Civisme et Devoir Social." *Politique Intérieure*. Beirut: Editions du Trident, 1964.

——. *Lebanon at Home and Abroad*. Translated by L. Arnold and J. Montegu. Beirut: Les Conférences du Cénacle, 1966.

——. "Lebanon in the World." *Cénacle Libanais*, December 17, 1951, p. 129.

Chomsky, Noam. *Deterring Democracy*. London: Verso, 1991.

——. *The Fateful Triangle*. Boston: South End Press, 1983.

——. *World Orders Old and New*. New York: Columbia University Press, 1994.

Chomsky, Noam, and E. S. Herman. *The Washington Connection and Third World Fascism*. Vol. 1. Boston: South End Press, 1979.

Clifford, J. Garry. "President Truman and Peter the Great's Will." *Diplomatic History* 4, no. 4 (Fall 1980).

Cobban, Helena. "The Growth of Shi'i Power in Lebanon and Its Implications for the Future." In Keddie and Cole, eds., *Shi'ism and Social Protest*, q.v.

——. *The Making of Modern Lebanon*. Boulder: Westview, 1985.

Cockburn, Andrew, and Leslie Cockburn. *Dangerous Liaison: The Inside Story of the U.S.-Israeli Covert Relationship*. New York: Harper Collins, 1991.

Cold War International History Project. *Bulletin* (Spring 1992, Fall 1992, Fall 1993). Washington, D.C.: Woodrow Wilson International Center for Scholars.

Connell, Dan. *Against All Odds*. Trenton, N.J.: Red Sea Press, 1993.

Copeland, Miles. *The Game of Nations*. New York: Simon and Schuster, 1969.

Corm, Georges. *Géopolitique du Conflit Libanais*. Paris: Editions la Découverte, 1987.

——. "Myths and Realities of the Lebanese Conflict." In Shehadi and Mills, eds., *Lebanon*, q.v.

——. *Le Proche-Orient Eclaté*. Paris: Editions la Découverte, 1983.

Couland, Jacques. *Le Mouvement Syndical au Liban, 1919–1946*. Paris: Editions Sociales, 1970.

Crow, Ralph E. "Confessionalism, Public Administration, and Efficiency in Lebanon." In Binder, ed., *Politics in Lebanon*, q.v.

Cumings, Bruce. *The Origins of the Korean War*. Vol. 1, *Liberation and the Emergence of Separate Regimes, 1945–1947*. Princeton: Princeton University Press, 1981. Vol. 2, *The Roaring of the Cataract, 1947–1950*. Princeton: Princeton University Press, 1990.

Dawisha, Adeed I. *Syria and the Lebanese Crisis*. New York: St. Martin's, 1980.

Dekmejian, Hrair. *Patterns of Political Leadership*. New York: State University of New York Press, 1975.

Derogy, Jacques, and Hesi Carmel. *The Untold History of Israel*. New York: Grove, 1979.

Divine, Robert A., ed. *American Foreign Policy Since 1945*. Chicago: Quadrangle, 1969.

Donovan, Robert J. *Confidential Secretary: Ann Whitman's 20 Years with Eisenhower and Rockefeller*. New York; Dutton, 1988.

Dower, John. "Occupied Japan and the Cold War in Asia." In M. Lacey, ed., *The Truman Presidency*. Washington, D.C.: Woodrow Wilson International Center for Scholars, 1989.

Dowty, Alan. *Middle East Crisis: U.S. Decision-Making in 1958, 1970, and 1973*. Berkeley and Los Angeles: University of California Press, 1984.

Dubar, Claude, and Salim Nasr. *Les Classes Sociales au Liban*. Paris: Presses de la Fondation Nationale des Sciences Politiques, 1976.

Eban, Abba. *An Autobiography*. New York: Random House, 1977.

Eden, Anthony. *Full Circle*. Boston: Houghton Mifflin, 1960.

Eisenberg, Carolyn. "Working-Class Politics and the Cold War: American Intervention in the German Labor Movement, 1945–1942." *Diplomatic History* 7, no. 4 (Fall 1983).

Eisenberg, Laura Zittrain. *My Enemy's Enemy*. Detroit: Wayne State University Press, 1995.

Eisenhower, Dwight D. *Waging Peace, 1956–1961*. Garden City, N.Y.: Doubleday, 1965.

Elm, Mostafa. *Oil, Power, and Principle*. Syracuse, N.Y.: Syracuse University Press, 1976.

Engler, Robert. *The Politics of Oil*. Chicago: University of Chicago Press, 1961.

Entelis, John. *Pluralism and Party Transformation in Lebanon*. Leiden: E. J. Brill, 1974.

Esman, Milton, and Itamar Rabinovich, eds. *Ethnicity, Pluralism, and the State in the Middle East*. Ithaca: Cornell University Press, 1988.

Evans, Peter, Dietrich Rueschemeyer, and T. Skocpol. *Bringing the State Back In*. Cambridge: Cambridge University Press, 1985.

Eveland, Wilbur Crane. *Ropes of Sand*. New York: Norton, 1980.

Falk, Richard, ed. *The International Law of Civil War*. Baltimore: Johns Hopkins University Press, 1971.

Farouk-Sluglett, Marion, and Peter Sluglett. "Labor and National Liberation: The Trade Union Movement in Iraq, 1920–1958." *Arab Studies Quarterly* 5, no. 2 (Spring 1983).

Fawaz, Leila Tarazy. *An Occasion for War: Civil Conflict in Lebanon and Damascus in 1860*. Berkeley and Los Angeles: University of California Press, 1995.

Ferguson, Thomas. "From Normalcy to New Deal: Industrial Structure, Party Competition, and American Public Policy in the Great Depression." *International Organization* 38, no. 1 (Winter 1984).

Fernea, Robert A., and Wm. Roger Louis, eds. *The Iraqi Revolution of 1958: The Old Social Classes Revisited*. New York: St. Martin's, 1991.

Flapan, Simha. *The Birth of Israel*. New York: Pantheon, 1987.

Fry, Michael G. "The Uses of Intelligence: The United Nations Confronts the United States in the Lebanon Crisis, 1958." *Intelligence and National Security* 10, no. 1 (January 1995).

Gaddis, John Lewis. "New Conceptual Approaches to the Study of American Foreign Relations: Interdisciplinary Perspectives." *Diplomatic History* 14, no. 3 (Summer 1990).

——. *Strategies of Containment*. New York: Oxford University Press, 1982.

——. *The United States and the Origins of the Cold War, 1941–1947*. New York: Columbia University Press, 1972.

Gardner, Lloyd C. *Architects of Illusion: Men and Ideas in American Foreign Policy, 1941–1949*. Chicago: Quadrangle, 1970.

——. *Economic Aspects of New Deal Diplomacy*. Madison: University of Wisconsin Press, 1964.

Gates, Carolyn. "The Formation of the Political Economy of Modern Lebanon." Sommerville College, Trinity, 1985.

——. "The Historical Role of Political Economy in the Development of Modern Lebanon." *Papers on Lebanon*, no. 10. Oxford: Centre for Lebanese Studies, 1989.

——. *Lebanon's Merchant Republic: The Rise of an Open Economy*. London: Centre for Lebanese Studies and I. B. Tauris, 1997.

Gaunson, A. B. *The Anglo-French Clash in Lebanon and Syria, 1940–1945*. New York: St. Martin's, 1987.

Gemayel, Pierre. *The Kataeb and the Current Events*. Beirut: Kataeb Party, 1969.

——. *Memorandum to the Presidency of the Council of Ministers on the Relations Between Lebanon and the Palestinian Resistance*. Beirut: Kataeb Party, 1970.

Genco, Stephen. "The Eisenhower Doctrine: Deterrence in the Middle East, 1957–1958." In George and Smoke, eds., *Deterrence in American Foreign Policy*, q.v.

Gendzier, Irene. "The Declassified Lebanon, 1948–1958: Elements of Continuity and Contrast in U.S. Policy Toward Lebanon." In Barakat, ed., *Toward a Viable Lebanon*, q.v.

——. *Development Against Democracy*. Hampton, Conn.: Tyrone, 1995. (New edition of previously titled *Managing Political Change: Social Scientists and the Third World*.)

——. "No Forum for the Lebanese People." *MERIP*, no. 162 (January/February 1990).

——. "Presidential Leadership in Foreign Policy: The Case of Lebanon, 1958." Paper presented at SHAFR (Society for the Historians of American Foreign Relations), June 1992.

——. "The United States, the USSR, and the Arab World in NSC Reports of the 1950s." *Arab American Affairs*, no. 28 (Spring 1988).

George, Alexander L., and Richard Smoke, eds. *Deterrence in American Foreign Policy: Theory and Practice*. New York: Columbia University Press, 1974.

Gerges, Fawaz A. *The Superpowers and the Middle East: Regional and International Politics, 1955–1967*. Boulder: Westview, 1994.

Gibbs, David N. *The Political Economy of Third World Intervention*. Chicago: University of Chicago Press, 1991.

Gilsenan, Michael. *Recognizing Islam*. New York: Pantheon, 1982.

Godfried, Nathan. *Bridging the Gap Between Rich and Poor*. New York: Greenwood, 1987.

Gordon, David. *Lebanon: The Fragmented Nation*. London: Croom Helm, 1980.

Goria, Wade R. *Sovereignty and Leadership in Lebanon, 1943–1976*. London: Ithaca, 1985.

Gormly, James L. "Keeping the Door Open in Saudi Arabia: The United States and the Dhahran Airfield, 1945–1946." *Diplomatic History* 4, no. 2 (Spring 1980).

Gourevitch, Peter. "Second Image Reversed: The International Sources of Domestic Politics." *International Organization* 32, no. 4 (Autumn 1978).

Grassmuck, George, and Kamal Salibi. *A Manual of Lebanese Administration*. Beirut: American University of Beirut, 1955.

Green, Stephen. *Taking Sides*. New York: Morrow, 1984.

Haddad, George. *Fifty Years of Modern Syria and Lebanon*. Beirut: Dar al-Hayat, 1950.

Hahn, Peter L. "Containment and Egyptian Nationalism: The Unsuccessful Effort to Establish the Middle East Command, 1950–1953." *Diplomatic History* 2, no. 1 (Winter 1987).

———. *The United States, Great Britain, and Egypt, 1945–1956*. Chapel Hill: University of North Carolina Press, 1991.

Hakim, George. "Industry." In Himadeh, ed., *Economic Organization of Syria*, q.v.

———. "Land Tenure Reform." *Middle East Economic Papers*. Beirut, 1954.

Halliday, Fred. *Arabia Without Sultans*. New York: Vintage, 1975.

———. *Iran: Dictatorship and Development*. New York: Penguin, 1979.

Halpern, Manfred. "The Morality and Politics of Intervention." In J. N. Rosenau, ed., *International Aspects of Civil Strife*. Princeton: Princeton University Press, 1964.

Hanf, Theodor. "Homo Oeconomicus–Homo Communitaris: Crosscutting Loyalties in a Deeply Divided Society: The Case of Trade Unions in Lebanon." In Esman and Rabinovich, eds., *Ethnicity, Pluralism, and the State in the Middle East*, q.v.

Harik, Iliya. *Lebanon: Anatomy of Conflict*. Hanover, N.H.: American Universities Field Staff, 1981.

Hawley, Ellis W. "The Discovery and Study of a 'Corporate Liberalism.' " *Business History Review* 52 (Autumn 1978).

Hayley, P. Edward, and L. W. Snider, eds. *Lebanon in Crisis*. Syracuse: Syracuse University Press, 1979.

Hersh, Seymour M. *The Samson Option*. New York: Vintage, 1993.

Himadeh, S., ed. *Economic Organization of Syria*. Beirut, 1936.

Hiro, Dilip. *Lebanon: Fire and Embers*. New York: St. Martin's, 1992.

Hof, Frederick F. *Galilee Divided*. Boulder: Westview, 1984.

Hoffman, Stanley. *Gulliver's Troubles, or the Setting of American Foreign Policy*. New York: McGraw Hill, 1968.

Hogan, Michael J. *The Marshall Plan*. Cambridge: Cambridge University Press, 1987.

——. "Revival and Reform: America's Twentieth-Century Search for a New Economic Order Abroad." *Diplomatic History* 8, no. 4 (1984).

Hogan, Michael J., and Thomas G. Paterson. *Explaining the History of American Foreign Relations*. Cambridge: Cambridge University Press, 1991.

Horowitz, David, ed. *Corporations and the Cold War*. New York: Monthly Review Press, 1969.

Hourani, Albert. "Lebanon from Feudalism to Modern State." *Middle Eastern Studies* 2, no. 3 (April 1966).

——. *Minorities in the Arab World*. London: Oxford University Press, 1947.

——. "Political Society in Lebanon: A Historical Introduction." *Papers on Lebanon*, no. 1. Oxford: Centre for Lebanese Studies, 1986.

——. Review of K. Salibi's *Lebanon from Feudalism to Modern State*. *Middle Eastern Studies* 2, no. 3 (April 1966).

——. *Syria and Lebanon: A Political Essay*. London: Oxford University Press, 1946.

——. "Visions of Lebanon." In Barakat, ed., *Toward a Viable Lebanon*, q.v.

Hovsepian, Nubar. "The Lebanese Opposition: Who's Against Gemayel and Why?" *The Nation*, March 17, 1984.

——. "The Lebanese Quagmire." *The Nation*, June 6, 1981.

Howard, Harry N. *Turkey, the Straits, and U.S. Policy*. Baltimore: Johns Hopkins University Press, 1974.

Hudson, Michael. "The Electoral Process and Political Development in Lebanon." *Middle East Journal* 20, no. 8 (Spring 1966).

——. "The Lebanese Crisis and the Limits of Consociational Democracy." *Journal of Palestine Studies* 5, no. 3/4 (1976).

——. *The Precarious Republic*. New York: Random House, 1968.

——. "The Precarious Republic Revisited: Reflections on the Collapse of Pluralist Politics in Lebanon." Institute of Arab Development, Center for Contemporary Arab Studies, no. 2, Georgetown University, 1977.

——. "The United States Involvement in Lebanon." In Barakat, ed., *Toward a Viable Lebanon*, q.v.

Hughes, E. J. *The Ordeal of Power: A Political Memoir of the Eisenhower Years*. New York: Atheneum, 1963.

Huntington, Samuel P. *The Third Wave: Democratization in the Late Twentieth Century.* Norman: University of Oklahoma Press, 1991.

Hurewitz, Jacob C. *Diplomacy in the Near and Middle East: A Documentary Record, 1914–1956.* Vol. 2. Princeton: D. Van Nostrand, 1956.

———. "Lebanese Democracy in Its International Setting." *Middle East Journal* 17, no. 5 (Autumn 1963).

———. *Middle East Politics: The Military Dimension.* New York: Praeger, 1969.

Immerman, Richard H. *The CIA in Guatemala.* Austin: University of Texas Press, 1982.

———. "Confessions of an Eisenhower Revisionist: An Agonizing Reappraisal." *Diplomatic History* 14, no. 3 (Summer 1990).

Issawi, Charles. "Economic Development and Liberalism in Lebanon." *Middle East Journal* 18, no. 3 (Summer 1964).

———. "Economic Development and Political Liberalism in Lebanon." In Binder, ed., *Politics in Lebanon,* q.v.

———. *An Economic History of the Middle East and North Africa.* New York: Columbia University Press, 1982.

———. "Social Structure and Ideology in Iraq, Lebanon, Syria, and the United Arab Republic." *Journal of International Affairs* 19, no. 1 (1965).

Issawi, Charles, and Mohammed Yeganeh. *The Economics of Middle Eastern Oil.* New York: Praeger, 1966.

Jabber, Paul. *Not by War Alone: Security and Arms Control in the Middle East.* Berkeley and Los Angeles: University of California Press, 1981.

Jargy, Simon. "Réalités Libanaise." *Orient* 9 (1959).

Johnson, Michael. *Class and Client in Beirut. The Sunni Muslim Community and the Lebanese State, 1840–1985.* London: Ithaca, 1986.

Jones, Joseph M. *The Fifteen Weeks, February 21–June 5, 1947.* New York: Harcourt Brace and World, 1955.

Joseph, Suad. "Muslim-Christian Conflict in Lebanon: A Perspective on the Evolution of Sectarianism." In Joseph and Pillsbury, eds., *Muslim-Christian Conflicts,* q.v.

Joseph, Suad, and Barbara Pillsbury, eds. *Muslim-Christian Conflicts: Economic, Political, and Social Origins.* Boulder: Westview, 1978.

Joumblatt (Junblat), Kamal. *Pour le Liban.* Paris: Stock, 1978.

Junblat, Kamal. *Haqiqat al-Thawra al-Lubnaniyya.* Beirut: Dar al Nashr al-'Arabiyyah, 1959.

Kahin, Audrey, and George McT. Kahin. *Subversion as Foreign Policy.* New York: New Press, 1995.

Kapeliuk, Amnon. *Sabra et Chatila: Enquête sur un Massacre.* Paris: Seuil, 1982.

Kapetanakis-Sifakis, Catherine. "L'Internationalisation du capital en Grèce: Le Cas du raffinage du petrol." Doctoral thesis, Université des Sciences Sociales, Grenoble, 1978.

Karame, Nawaf, and Nariya Karame. *Waqa'i Thawra al-Lubnaniyya* [Facts of the Lebanese revolution]. Beirut, 1959.

Kassir, Samir, and Farouk Mardam-Bey. *Itinéraires de Paris à Jérusalem: La France et le Conflit Israélo-Arabe*. Vol. 1, *1917–1958*. Washington, D.C.: Institut des Etudes Palestiniennes, 1992.

Katz, Samuel M. *Soldier Spies: Israeli Military Intelligence*. Novato, Calif.: Presidio, 1992.

Kaufman, Burton I. *Trade and Aid: Eisenhower's Foreign Economic Policy, 1953–1961*. Baltimore: Johns Hopkins University Press, 1982.

Keddie, Nikki, and Juan Cole, eds. *Shi'ism and Social Protest*. New Haven: Yale University Press, 1986.

Kedourie, Elie. "Constitutionalism in the Middle East." In Elie Kedourie, *Arabic Political Memoirs and Other Studies*. London: Frank Cass, 1974.

——. "Ethnicity, Majority, and Minority in the Middle East." In Esman and Rabinovich, eds., *Ethnicity, Pluralism, and the State*, q.v.

Kennan, George F. *Memoirs, 1925–1950*. Boston: Little Brown, 1967.

Kerr, Malcolm M. "The Lebanese Civil War." In Luard, ed., *The International Regulation of Civil Wars*, q.v.

——. "Lebanese Views on the 1958 Crisis." *Middle East Journal* 15, no. 2 (Spring 1961).

——. "Political Decision Making in a Confessional Democracy." In Binder, ed., *Politics in Lebanon*, q.v.

Khalaf, Samir. *Lebanon's Predicament*. New York: Columbia University Press, 1987.

Khalidi, Rashid. "Problems of Foreign Intervention in Lebanon." *Arab American Affairs* 7 (Winter 1983–1984).

Khalidi, Walid. *Conflict and Violence in Lebanon: Confrontation in the Middle East*. Cambridge: Harvard University Center for International Affairs, 1979.

——. "Political Trends in the Fertile Crescent." In Laqueur, ed., *The Middle East in Transition*, q.v.

al-Khazen, Farid. "The Lebanese Economy After a Decade of Turmoil, 1975–1985." *Arab American Affairs*, no. 12 (1985).

al-Khoury, Michel. "Ebauche d'un Visage du Liban." Les Conférences du Cénacle, 1961, Beirut.

Khoury, Philip S. *Syria and the French Mandate: The Politics of Arab Nationalism, 1920–1945*. Princeton: Princeton University Press, 1987.

al-Khuri, Besharah K. *Haqa'iq Lubnaniyyah* [Lebanese realities]. Lebanon: Manshurat Awraq Lubnaniyyah, 1960.

Khuri, Fuad I. "The Changing Class Structure in Lebanon." *Middle East Journal* 23, no. 1 (Winter 1969).

——. *From Village to Suburb: Order and Change in Greater Beirut*. Chicago: University of Chicago Press, 1975.

King, Gillian, ed. *Documents on International Affairs*. New York: Oxford University Press, 1962.

Kiwan, Fadia. "La Perception Maronite du Grand-Liban chez les Maronites dans la Période du Mandat." In Shehadi and Mills, eds., *Lebanon*, q.v.

Klare, Michael, and C. Arnson. *Supplying Repression: U.S. Support for Authoritarian Regimes Abroad.* Washington, D.C.: Institute for Policy Studies, 1977.

Kolko, Gabriel. *Confronting the Third World, 1945–1980.* New York: Pantheon, 1988.

———. *The Politics of War.* New York: Pantheon, 1968.

Kolko, Joyce, and Gabriel Kolko. *The Limits of Power.* New York: Harper and Row, 1972.

Korany, Bahgat, and Ali E. Hillal Dessouki. *The Foreign Policies of Arab States.* Boulder: Westview, 1991.

Korbany, Agnes G. *U.S. Intervention in Lebanon, 1958 and 1982.* New York: Praeger, 1991.

Koury, Enver M. *The Crisis in the Lebanese System.* Washington, D.C.: American Enterprise Institute for Public Policy, 1978.

Krasner, Stephen. *Defending the National Interest.* Princeton: Princeton University Press, 1978.

———. "Oil Is the Exception." *Foreign Policy* 13 (Spring 1974).

Kuniholm, Bruce R. *The Origins of the Cold War in the Near East.* Princeton: Princeton University Press, 1980.

Kunz, Diane. *The Economic Diplomacy of the Suez Crisis.* Chapel Hill: University of North Carolina Press, 1991.

Kyle, Keith. "Britain and the Crisis." In Owen and Louis, eds., *Suez, 1956,* q.v.

———. *Suez.* New York: St. Martin's, 1991.

Labaki, Boutros. "L'Economie Politique du Liban Indépendant, 1943–1975." In Shehadi and Mills, eds., *Lebanon,* q.v.

———. "Structurations Communautaires: Rapports de Force Entre Minorités et Guerres au Liban." *Guerres Mondiales et Conflits Contemporains. Revue Trimestrielle d'Histoire* 151 (July 1988).

LaFeber, Walter. *America, Russia, and the Cold War, 1945–1966.* Ithaca: Cornell University Press, 1967.

———. *The American Age: U.S. Foreign Policy at Home and Abroad from 1790 to the Present.* New York: Norton, 1989.

———. *Inevitable Revolutions: The United States in Central America.* New York: Norton, 1983.

Laqueur, Walter Z. *Communism and Nationalism in the Middle East.* New York, Praeger, 1957.

———. *The Soviet Union and the Middle East.* London: Routledge and Kegan Paul, 1959.

———. ed. *The Middle East in Transition.* New York: Praeger, 1958.

Leffler, Melvyn P. "The American Conception of National Security and the Beginnings of the Cold War, 1945–1948." *American Historical Review* 89, no. 2 (April 1984).

———. *A Preponderance of Power.* Palo Alto, Calif.: Stanford University Press, 1992.

——. "Strategy, Diplomacy, and the Cold War: The United States, Turkey, and NATO, 1945–1952." *Journal of American History* 71, no. 4 (March 1985).

Lesch, David W. *Syria and the United States*. Boulder: Westview, 1992.

Levy, Walter. "Oil and the Decline of the West." *Foreign Affairs* 58 (Summer 1980).

——. *Oil, Strategy, and Politics, 1941–1981*. Boulder: Westview, 1982.

Little, Douglas. "Cold War and Covert Action: The United States and Syria, 1945–1958." *Middle East Journal* 44, no. 1 (Winter 1990).

——. "The Making of a Special Relationship: The United States and Israel, 1957–1968." *International Journal of Middle East Studies* 25, no. 4 (November 1993).

——. "The New Frontier on the Nile: J.F.K., Nasser, and Arab Nationalism." *Journal of American History* 75, no. 2 (September 1988).

——. "Pipeline Politics: America, TAPLINE, and the Arabs." *Business History Review* 64 (Summer 1990).

Loftus, John A. "Middle East Oil and the Pattern of Control." *Middle East Journal* 2, no. 1 (January 1948).

Longrigg, Stephen H. *Oil in the Middle East*. 3d ed. London: Oxford University Press, 1968.

——. *Syria and Lebanon Under French Mandate*. London: Oxford University Press, 1958.

Lord, Carnes. *The Presidency and the Management of National Security*. New York: Free Press, 1988.

Louis, Wm. Roger. "Britain and Lebanon in the 1950s." Paper presented at the Conference on Lebanon in the Decade of the 1950s, University of Texas, Austin, September 10–13, 1992.

——. *The British Empire in the Middle East, 1945–1951*. Oxford: Clarendon, 1984.

——. *Imperialism at Bay*. New York: Oxford University Press, 1978.

Louis, Wm. Roger, and Headley Bull, eds. *The "Special Relationship": Anglo-American Relations Since 1945*. Oxford: Clarendon, 1986.

Louis, Wm. Roger, and Robert W. Stookey, eds. *The End of the Palestine Mandate*. Austin: University of Texas Press, 1986.

Luard, Evan, ed. *The International Regulation of Civil Wars*. New York: New York University Press, 1972.

Luciani, Giacomo, ed. *The Arab State*. Berkeley and Los Angeles: University of California Press, 1990.

Luciani, Giacomo, and Ghassan Salamé, eds. *The Politics of Arab Integration*. London: Croom Helm, 1988.

Majdalany, G. "The Arab Socialist Movement." In Laqueur, ed., *The Middle East in Transition*, q.v.

Maksoud, Clovis. "Lebanon and Arab Nationalism." In Binder, ed., *Politics in Lebanon*, q.v.

——. "The Revolution in Lebanon." *Foreign Affairs Reports* (New Delhi) 7, no. 7 (July 1958).

Malik, Charles. *The Problem of the West.* Washington, D.C.: Lebanese Information and Research Center, 1979.

Mallat, Chibli. "Shi'i Thought from the South of Lebanon." *Papers on Lebanon,* no. 7. Oxford: Centre for Lebanese Studies, April 1988.

Mattison, Frances C., ed. *A Survey of American Interests in the Middle East.* Washington, D.C.: Middle East Institute, 1953.

Maxfield, Sylvia, and James Nolt. "Protectionism and the Internationalization of Capital." *International Studies Quarterly* 34, no. 1 (March 1990).

McCartney, Laton. *Friends in High Places: The Bechtel Story.* New York: Simon and Schuster, 1988.

McClintock, Robert. "The American Landing in Lebanon." *U.S. Naval Institute Proceedings* 88 (October 1962).

———. *The Meaning of Limited War.* Boston: Houghton Mifflin, 1967.

McGhee, George. *The U.S.-Turkish-NATO Middle East Connection.* New York: St. Martin's, 1990.

———. *Envoy to the Middle World.* New York: Harper and Row, 1983.

McLaurin, R. D., ed. *The Political Role of Minority Groups in the Middle East.* New York: Praeger, 1979.

McLellan, David S. *Dean Acheson: The State Department Years.* New York: Dodd, Mead, 1976.

McMahon, Robert. "The Cold War in Asia: Toward a New Synthesis?" *Diplomatic History* 12, no. 3 (Summer 1988).

———. *Cold War in the Periphery.* New York: Columbia University Press, 1994.

———. *Colonialism and Cold War: The United States and the Indonesian Struggle for Independence, 1945–1949.* Ithaca: Cornell University Press, 1981.

McQuaid, Kim. "Corporate Liberalism in the American Business Community, 1920–1940." *Business History Review* 52, no. 3 (Autumn 1978).

Melanson, Richard, and David Mayers, eds. *Reevaluating Eisenhower.* Urbana and Chicago: University of Illinois Press, 1989.

Meo, Leila M. T. *Lebanon, Improbable Nation: A Study in Political Development.* Bloomington: Indiana University Press, 1965.

Migdal, Joel. "Strong States, Weak States: Power and Accommodation." In Weiner and Huntington, eds., *Understanding Political Development,* q.v.

Migdal, J., A. Khli, and V. Shue, eds. *State Power and Social Forces.* Cambridge: Cambridge University Press, 1994.

Miller, Aaron D. *Search for Security.* Chapel Hill: University of North Carolina Press, 1980.

Miller, Richard I. *Dag Hammarskjold and Crisis Diplomacy.* New York: Oceana Publications, 1961.

Millis, Walter, ed. *The Forrestal Diaries.* New York: Viking Press, 1951.

Ministère du Plan et Mission IRFED, 1960–1961. *Besoins et Possibilités de Développement du Liban.* 2 vols. Beirut.

Morris, Benny. *The Birth of the Palestinian Refugee Problem, 1947–1949.* Cambridge: Cambridge University Press, 1987.

——. "The Causes and Character of the Arab Exodus from Palestine: The Israel Defence Forces Intelligence Branch Analysis of June 1948." *Middle Eastern Studies* 22, no. 1 (January 1986).

——. "Israel, the Lebanese Phalange: The Birth of a Relationship, 1948–1951." *Studies in Zionism* 5, no. 1 (Spring 1984).

Murphy, Robert. *Diplomat Among Warriors*. London: Collins, 1964.

Myrdal, Gunnar. *The Challenge of World Poverty*. New York: Vintage, 1970.

Naccache, Georges. "Un Nouveau Style: Le Chéhabisme." Beirut: Les Conférences du Cénacle, 1961.

Na'mani, Basam Abdel Qader. "Confessionalism in Balance: The 1943 National Pact." In Simon, ed., *The Middle East and North Africa*, q.v.

Nasr, Nafhat, and Monte Palmer. "Alienation and Political Participation in Lebanon." *International Journal of Middle East Studies* 8, no. 4 (October 1977).

Nasr, Salim. "Backdrop to Civil War: The Crisis of Lebanese Capitalism." *Middle East Research and Information Project* 8, no. 10 (December 1978).

——. "Lebanon: New Social Realities and Issues of Reconstruction." In *Précis 3*, no. 1 (Winter 1991). Massachusetts Institute of Technology, Center for International Studies.

Nasrallah, Fida. "The Questions of South Lebanon." *Papers on Lebanon*, no. 5. Oxford: Centre for Lebanese Studies, May 1992.

Neustadt, Richard E. *Presidential Power*. New York: Wiley, 1960.

Nolte, Richard H., and William R. Polk. "Toward a Policy for the Middle East." *Foreign Affairs* 36, no. 4 (July 1958).

Norton, Augustus Richard. "Israel and South Lebanon." *Arab American Affairs*, no. 4 (Spring 1983).

——. "Shi'ism and Social Protest in Lebanon." In Keddie and Cole, eds., *Shi'ism and Social Protest*, q.v.

Nour, Francis. "Particularisme Libanais et Nationalisme Arabe." *Orient*, no. 7 (1958).

Odeh, B. J. *Lebanon: Dynamics of Conflict*. London: Zed, 1985.

Odell, Peter R. *Oil and World Power*. Middlesex, Eng.: Penguin, 1979.

Oren, Michael B. "The Test of Suez: Israel and the Middle East Crisis of 1958." *Studies in Zionism* 12, no. 1 (1991).

Ovendale, Ritchie. "Great Britain and the Anglo-American Invasion of Jordan and Lebanon in 1958." *International History Review* 16, no. 2 (May 1994).

Owen, Roger. "Economic Consequences of Suez for Egypt," in R. Owen and William Roger Lovis, eds., *Suez, 1956: The Crisis and Its Consequences*. Oxford: Clarendon, 1989.

——. "The Economic History of Lebanon, 1943–1974: Its Salient Features." In Barakat, ed., *Toward a Viable Lebanon*, q.v.

——. *The Middle East in the World Economy, 1800–1914*. London and New York: Methuen, 1981.

——. ed. *Essays on the Crisis in Lebanon*. London: Ithaca, 1976.

Owen, Roger, and Wm. Roger Louis, eds. *Suez, 1956: The Crisis and Its Consequences*. Oxford: Clarendon, 1989.

Painter, David. *Oil and the American Century*. Baltimore: Johns Hopkins University Press, 1986.

——. "Oil and World Power." *Diplomatic History* 17, no. 1 (Winter 1993).

——. "Searching for Security in a Global Economy." *Daedalus* 120, no. 4 (Fall 1991).

Patterson, Thomas G. "The Quest for Peace and Prosperity: International Trade, Communism, and the Marshall Plan." In Bernstein, ed., *Politics and Policies of the Truman Administration*, q.v.

Person, William. "Lebanese Economic Development Since 1950." *Middle East Journal* 12, no. 3 (Summer 1958).

Petran, Tabitha. *The Struggle Over Lebanon*. New York: Monthly Review Press, 1987.

Picard, Elizabeth. *Liban, Etat de Discorde*. Paris: Flammarion, 1988.

Pogue, Forrest C. *George C. Marshall: Statesman*. New York: Viking, 1987.

Quandt, William. "Lebanon, 1958, and Jordan, 1970." In Blechman and Kaplan, eds., *Force Without War*, q.v.

——. "Reagan's Lebanon Policy: Trial and Error." *Middle East Journal* 38 (Spring 1984).

Qubain, Fahim. *Crisis in Lebanon*. Washington, D.C.: Middle East Institute, 1961.

Ramazani, R. K. "Iran and the Arab-Israeli Conflict." *Middle East Journal* 32, no. 4 (Autumn 1978).

Randal, Jonathan C. *Going All the Way: Christian Warlords, Israeli Adventurers, and the War in Lebanon*. New York: Viking, 1983.

Ranelagh, John. *The Agency: The Rise and Decline of the CIA*. New York; Simon and Schuster, 1986.

Raviv, Dan, and Yossie Melman. *Every Spy a Prince*. Boston: Houghton Mifflin, 1990.

Rokach, Livia. *Israel's Sacred Terrorism*. Belmont, Mass.: AAUG, 1980.

Rondot, Pierre. *The Changing Patterns of the Middle East*. New York: Praeger, 1962.

——. *Les Institutions Politiques du Liban: Des Communautés Traditionnelles à l'Etat Moderne*. Paris: Institut d'Etude de l'Orient Contemporain, 1947.

——. "Quelques Reflexions sur les Structures du Liban." *Orient*, no. 6 (1958).

——. *L'Expérience du Mandat Français en Syrie et au Liban, 1918–1945*. Paris: PUB 1948.

——. "The Political Institutions of Lebanese Democracy." In Binder, ed., *Politics in Lebanon*, q.v.

——. "Les Structures Socio-politiques de la Nation Libanaise." *Revue Française de Science Politique* 4, no. 1 (1954).

Roosevelt, Archie. *For Lust of Knowing*. Boston: Little, Brown, 1988.

Rosenau, James N., ed. *The Domestic Sources of Foreign Policy*. New York: Free Press, 1967.

Rostow, Walt W. *The United States in the World Arena*. New York: Harper, 1960.

Rueschemeyer, Dietrich, and Peter Evans. "The State and Economic Transformation." In Evans, Rueschemeyer, and Skocpol, *Bringing the State Back In*, q.v.

Sadaka, Linda, and Nawaf Salam, eds. *The Civil War in Lebanon, 1975–1976: A Bibliographical Guide*. Beirut: Center for Arab and Middle East Studies and American University of Beirut, 1982.

Said, Edward. *Culture and Imperialism*. New York: Knopf, 1995.

———. *The Politics of Dispossession*. New York: Pantheon, 1994.

Salam, Nawaf. "Les Communautés Religieuses au Liban." *Social Compass* 25, no. 4 (1988).

———. "*L'Insurrection de 1958 au Liban*." 5 vols. University of Paris-Sorbonne, 1979.

———. *Mythes et Politiques au Liban*. Paris: Editions FMA.

Salamé, Ghassan. *Lebanon's Injured Identities: Who Represents Whom During a Civil War?* No. 2. Oxford: Centre for Lebanese Studies, 1986.

———. " 'Strong' and 'Weak' States: A Qualified Return to the Muqaddimah." In Luciani, ed., *The Arab State*, q.v.

Salem, Eli. "Cabinet Politics in Lebanon." *Middle East Journal* 31, no. 4 (Autumn 1967).

———. *Crossroads to Civil War: Lebanon, 1958–1976*. London: Ithaca, 1976.

———. "Lebanon's Political Maze: The Search for Peace in a Troubled Land." *Middle East Journal* 33, no. 4 (Autumn 1979).

———. *Modernization Without Revolution: Lebanon's Experience*. Bloomington: Indiana University Press, 1973.

Salibi, Kamal. *A House of Many Mansions*. Berkeley and Los Angeles: University of California Press, 1988.

———. "Lebanon Under Fuad Chehab, 1958–1964." *Middle Eastern Studies* 2, no. 3 (April 1966).

———. *The Modern History of Lebanon*. London: Weidenfeld and Nicolson, 1965.

———. *A Manual of Lebanese Administration*. Beirut: American University of Beirut, 1955.

———. "Recollections of the 1940s and 1950s." Paper presented at the Conference on Lebanon in the Decade of the 1950s, University of Texas, Austin, September 10–13, 1992.

Sampson, Anthony. *The Seven Sisters*. New York: Bantam, 1975.

Sayed-Ahmad, M. Abdel Wahab. *Nasser and American Foreign Policy, 1952–1956*. Cairo: American University in Cairo Press, 1991.

Sayegh, Rosemary. *Palestinians: From Peasants to Revolutionaries*. London: Zed, 1979.

Sayigh, Yusif A. *Entrepreneurs of Lebanon*. Cambridge: Harvard University Press, 1962.

Schiff, Ze'ev. "The Green Light." *Foreign Policy* 50 (Spring 1983).

Schiff, Ze'ev, and Ehud Ya'ari. *Israel's Lebanon War*. New York: Simon and Schuster, 1984.

Schurmann, Franz. *The Logic of World Power: An Inquiry into the Origins, Currents, and Contradictions of World Politics*. New York: Pantheon, 1974.

Schwadran, Benjamin. *The Middle East, Oil, and the Great Powers*. New York: Praeger, 1955.

Seale, Patrick. *Asad of Syria: The Struggle for the Middle East*. Berkeley and Los Angeles: University of California Press, 1988.

——. *The Struggle for Syria: A Study of Post-War Politics, 1945–1958*. London: Oxford University Press, 1965.

Segev, Samuel. *The Iranian Triangle*. New York: Free Press, 1988.

Segev, Tom. *1949: The First Israelis*. New York: Free Press, 1986.

——. *The Seventh Million*. New York: Hill and Wang, 1993.

Shehadi, Nadim. "The Idea of Lebanon: Economy and State in the Cénacle Libanais, 1946–1954." *Papers on Lebanon*, no. 5. Oxford: Centre for Lebanese Studies, 1987.

Shehadi, Nadim, and Dana Haffar Mills, eds. *Lebanon: A History of Conflict and Consensus*. Oxford: Centre for Lebanese Studies and I. B. Tauris, 1988.

Shils, E. "Prospects for Lebanese Civility." In Binder, ed., *Politics in Lebanon*, q.v.

Shlaim, Avi. "Conflicting Approaches to Israel's Relations with the Arabs: Ben Gurion and Sharett, 1953–1956." *Middle East Journal* 37, no. 2.

——. "The Impact of U.S. Policy in the Middle East." *Journal of Palestine Studies* 17, no. 2 (Winter 1988).

——. "Israeli Interference in Internal Arab Politics: The Case of Lebanon." In Luciani and Salamé, eds., *The Politics of Arab Integration*, q.v.

——. *The Politics of Partition*. New York: Columbia University Press, 1988.

Simon, Reeva S., ed. *The Middle East and North Africa: Essays in Honor of J. C. Hurewitz*. New York: Columbia University Press, 1989.

Snider, Lewis W. "The Lebanese Forces: Their Origins and Role in Lebanon's Politics." *Middle East Journal* 38, no. 1 (Winter 1984).

Solh, Raghid. "The Attitude of the Arab Nationalists Towards Greater Lebanon During the 1930s." In Shehadi and Mills, eds., *Lebanon*, q.v.

Spagnolo, John P. "International Intervention in Lebanon." *International History Review* 16, no. 2 (May 1994).

Spiegel, Steven L. *The Other Arab-Israeli Conflict: Making America's Middle East Policy, from Truman to Reagan*. Chicago: University of Chicago Press, 1985.

Stevens, Georgiana S., ed. *The United States and the Middle East*. Englewood Cliffs, N.J.: Prentice Hall, 1964.

Stewart, Desmond. *Turmoil in Beirut*. London: Allen Wingate, 1959.

Stivers, William. "Eisenhower and the Middle East." In Melanson and Mayers, eds., *Reevaluating Eisenhower*, q.v.

Stoakes, Frank. "The Supervigilantes: The Lebanese Kataeb Party as Builder, Surrogate, and Defender of the State." *Middle Eastern Studies* 11, no. 3 (October 1975).

Stoff, Michael B. *Oil, War, and American Security*. New Haven: Yale University Press, 1980.

Stone, I. F. *The Haunted Fifties, 1953–1963*. Boston: Little, Brown, 1963.

Stork, Joe. *Middle East Oil and the Energy Crisis*. New York: Monthly Review Press, 1975.

Suleiman, Michael W. "Crisis and Revolution in Lebanon." *Middle East Journal* 26, no. 1 (Winter 1972).

——. *Political Parties in Lebanon: The Challenge of a Fragmented Political Culture*. Ithaca: Cornell University Press, 1965.

Symmes, Harrison M. "Positive Deterrence in Local Conflicts." Unpublished paper prepared for the Center for International Affairs, Harvard University, 1963.

Tanzer, Michael. *The Political Economy of International Oil and the Underdeveloped Countries*. Boston: Beacon, 1969.

Taylor, Maxwell D. *The Uncertain Trumpet*. New York: Harper's, 1960.

Thayer, Charles W. *Diplomat*. New York: Harper's, 1959.

Thomas, Clive. *The Rise of the Authoritarian State in Peripheral Societies*. New York: Monthly Review Press, 1984.

Tillema, Herbert K. *Appeal to Force: American Military Intervention in the Era of Containment*. New York: Crowell, 1973.

Traboulsi, Fawaz. "Identités et Solidarités Croisées dans les Conflits du Liban Contemporain." 2 vols. University of Paris VIII, 1993.

Tueni, *Une Guerre pour les Autres*. Paris: Editions Jean-Claude Lattès, 1985.

Tuwayni (Tueni), Ghassan. *Al-Ayyam al-'Asibah*. Beirut: Dar al Nakhar, 1958.

Twining, Nathan F. *Neither Liberty Nor Safety*. New York: Holt, Rinehart, and Winston, 1966.

Vitalis, Robert. "Business Conflict, Collaboration, and Privilege in Interwar Egypt." In Migdal, Khli, and Shue, eds., *State Power and Social Forces*, q.v.

——. *When Capitalists Collide: Business Conflict and the End of Empire in Egypt*. Berkeley and Los Angeles: University of California Press, 1995.

Weiler, Peter. "The United States, International Labor, and the Cold War: The Breakup of the World Federation of Trade Unions." *Diplomatic History* 5, no. 1 (Winter 1981).

Weiner, Myron, and Samuel P. Huntington, eds. *Understanding Political Development*. Boston: Little, Brown, 1987.

Wiesen Cook, Blanche. *The Declassified Eisenhower*. Garden City, N.Y.: Doubleday, 1981.

Wilkins, Mira. *The Maturing of the Multinational Enterprise: American Business Abroad, 1914–1970*. Cambridge: Harvard University Press, 1974.

Wright, Quincy. "U.S. Intervention in Lebanon." *American Journal of International Law* 53, no. 1 (January 1959).

Yamak, Labib Zuwiyya. *The Syrian Social Nationalist Party: An Ideological Analysis.* Cambridge: Harvard University Press, 1966.

Yergin, Daniel. *The Prize: The Epic Quest for Oil, Money, and Power.* New York: Simon and Schuster, 1992.

Yodfat, Aryeh, and M. Abir. *In the Direction of the Persian Gulf.* London: Frank Cass, 1977.

Zamir, Meir. *The Formation of Modern Lebanon.* Ithaca: Cornell University Press, 1985.

Index

454   Index

Printed in the United States
28653LVS00003B/30